Secure Data Management in Decentralized Systems

Advances in Information Security

Sushil Jajodia
Consulting Editor
Center for Secure Information Systems
George Mason University
Fairfax, VA 22030-4444
email: jajodia@gmu.edu

The goals of the Springer International Series on ADVANCES IN INFORMATION SECURITY are, one, to establish the state of the art of, and set the course for future research in information security and, two, to serve as a central reference source for advanced and timely topics in information security research and development. The scope of this series includes all aspects of computer and network security and related areas such as fault tolerance and software assurance.

ADVANCES IN INFORMATION SECURITY aims to publish thorough and cohesive overviews of specific topics in information security, as well as works that are larger in scope or that contain more detailed background information than can be accommodated in shorter survey articles. The series also serves as a forum for topics that may not have reached a level of maturity to warrant a comprehensive textbook treatment.

Researchers, as well as developers, are encouraged to contact Professor Sushil Jajodia with ideas for books under this series.

Additional titles in the series:

NETWORK SECURITY POLICIES AND PROCEDURES by Douglas W. Frye; ISBN: 0-387-30937-3
DATA WAREHOUSING AND DATA MINING TECHNIQUES FOR CYBER SECURITY by Anoop Singhal; ISBN: 978-0-387-26409-7
SECURE LOCALIZATION AND TIME SYNCHRONIZATION FOR WIRELESS SENSOR AND AD HOC NETWORKS edited by Radha Poovendran, Cliff Wang, and Sumit Roy; ISBN: 0-387-32721-5
PRESERVING PRIVACY IN ON-LINE ANALYTICAL PROCESSING (OLAP) by Lingyu Wang, Sushil Jajodia and Duminda Wijesekera; ISBN: 978-0-387-46273-8
SECURITY FOR WIRELESS SENSOR NETWORKS by Donggang Liu and Peng Ning; ISBN: 978-0-387-32723-5
MALWARE DETECTION edited by Somesh Jha, Cliff Wang, Mihai Christodorescu, Dawn Song, and Douglas Maughan; ISBN: 978-0-387-32720-4
ELECTRONIC POSTAGE SYSTEMS: Technology, Security, Economics by Gerrit Bleumer; ISBN: 978-0-387-29313-2
MULTIVARIATE PUBLIC KEY CRYPTOSYSTEMS by Jintai Ding, Jason E. Gower and Dieter Schmidt; ISBN-13: 978-0-378-32229-2
UNDERSTANDING INTRUSION DETECTION THROUGH VISUALIZATION by Stefan Axelsson; ISBN-10: 0-387-27634-3
QUALITY OF PROTECTION: Security Measurements and Metrics by Dieter Gollmann, Fabio Massacci and Artsiom Yautsiukhin; ISBN-10: 0-387-29016-8
COMPUTER VIRUSES AND MALWARE by John Aycock; ISBN-10: 0-387-30236-0

Additional information about this series can be obtained from
http://www.springer.com

Secure Data Management in Decentralized Systems

edited by

Ting Yu
North Carolina State University
USA

Sushil Jajodia
George Mason University
USA

Ting Yu
North Carolina State University
Dept. Computer Science
3254 EB II
Raleigh NC 27695
yu@csc.ncsu.edu

Sushil Jajodia
George Mason University
Center for Secure Information Systems
4400 University Drive
Fairfax VA 22030-4444
jajodia@gmu.edu

SECURE DATA MANAGEMENT IN DECENTRALIZED SYSTEMS
edited by Ting Yu and Sushil Jajodia

ISBN-13: 978-1-4899-9670-1
ISBN-10: 1-4899-9670-2
ISBN-13: 978-0-387-27696-0 (eBook)
ISBN-13: 0-387-27696-3 (eBook)

Printed on acid-free paper.

9 8 7 6 5 4 3 2 1

springer.com

Contents

Preface

Database security is one of the classical topics in the research of information system security. Ever since the early years of database management systems, a great deal of research activity has been conducted. Fruitful results have been produced, many of which are widely adopted in commercial and military database management systems.

In recent years, the research scope of database security has been greatly expanded due to the rapid development of the global internetworked infrastructure. Databases are no longer stand-alone systems that are only accessible to internal users of organizations. Instead, allowing selective access from different security domains has become a must for many business practices. Many of the assumptions and problems in traditional databases need to be revisited and readdressed in decentralized environments. Further, the Internet and the Web offer means for collecting and sharing data with unprecedented flexibility and convenience. New data services are emerging every day, which also bring new challenges to protect of data security. We have witnessed many exciting research works toward identifying and addressing such new challenges. We feel it is necessary to summarize and systematically present works in these new areas to researchers.

This book presents a collection of essays, covering a wide range of today's active areas closely related to database security organized as follows. In Part I, We review classical work in database security, and report their recent advances and necessary extensions. In Part II, We shift our focus to security of the Extensible Markup Language (XML) and other new data models. The need for cross-domain resource and information sharing dramatically changes the approaches to access control. In Part III, we present the active work in distributed trust management, including rule-based policies, trust negotiation and security in peer-to-peer systems. Privacy has increasingly become a big concern to Internet users, especially when information may be collected online through all kinds of channels. In Part IV, privacy protection efforts from the database community are presented. Topics include micro data release and k-anonymity. In Part V, we include two essays, which are about challenges in the database-as-a-service model and database watermarking.

The audience of this book includes graduate students and researchers in secure data management, especially in the context of the Internet. This book serves as helpful supplementary reading material for graduate-level information system security courses.

We would like to express our sincere thanks to Li Wu Chang (Naval Research Laboratory), Rohit Gupta (Iowa State University), Yingjiu Li (Singapore Management University), Gerome Miklau (University of Massachusetts, Amherst), Clifford B. Neuman (University of Southern California), Tatyana Ryutov (Information Sciences Institute), and Yuqing Wu (Indiana University) for their valuable and insightful comments on the chapters of this book.

Ting Yu
Sushil Jajodia

Part I

Foundation

Basic Security Concepts

Sushil Jajodia[1] and Ting Yu[2]

[1] Center of Secure Information Systems
George Mason Unversity
jajodia@gmu.edu
[2] North Carolina State University
yu@csc.ncsu.edu

1 Introduction

The computer security problem is an adversary problem: there is an adversary who seeks to misuse the storage, processing, or transmittal of data to gain advantage. The misuse is classified as either *unauthorized observation* of data, *unauthorized or improper modification* of data, or *denial of service*. In denial of service misuse, the adversary seeks to prevent someone from using features of the computer system by monopolizing or tying up the necessary resources.

Thus, a complete solution to the computer security problem must meet the following three requirements:

- *Secrecy or confidentiality:* Protection of information against unauthorized disclosure
- *Integrity:* Prevention of unauthorized or improper modification of information
- *Availability:* Prevention of denial of authorized access to information or services

These three requirements arise in practically all systems. Consider a payroll database in a corporation. It is important that salaries of individual employees are not disclosed to arbitrary users of the database, salaries are modified by only those individuals that are properly authorized, and paychecks are printed on time at the end of each pay period. Similarly, in a military environment, it is important that the target of a missile is not given to an unauthorized user, the target is not arbitrarily modified, and the missile is launched when it is fired.

The computer security problem is solved by maintaining a separation between the users on one hand and the various data and computing resources on the other, thus frustrating misuse. This separation is achieved by decomposing the computer security problem into three subproblems: *security policy*, *mechanism*, and *assurance*. Thus, a complete solution consists of first defining a security policy, then by choosing some mechanism to enforce the policy and, finally, by assuring the soundness of both the policy and the mechanism. Not only each subproblem must be solved, it is important that each solution fit the solutions of the other two subproblems. For example, it does not make sense to have a security policy that cannot be implemented, nor does it make sense to have a mechanism that is easily bypassed.

2 Security Policy

The security policy elaborates on each of the three generic objectives of security—secrecy, integrity, and availability—in the context of a particular system. Thus, computer security policies are used like requirements; they are the starting point in the development of any system that has security features. The security policy of a system is the basis for the choice of its protection mechanisms and the techniques used to assure its enforcement of the security policy.

Existing security policies tend to focus only on the secrecy requirement of security. Thus, these policies deal with defining what is authorized or, more simply, arriving at a satisfactory definition of the secrecy component.

The choice of a security policy with reasonable consequences is nontrivial and a separate topic in its own right. In fact, security policies are investigated through formal mathematical models. These models have shown, among other things, that the consequences of arbitrary but relatively simple security policies are undecidable and that avoiding this undecidability is nontrivial [5, 7, 8]. To read more about the formal security models, see [3].

All security policies are stated in terms of *objects* and *subjects*. This is because in reasoning about security policies, we must be careful about the distinction between users and the processes that act on behalf of the users. Users are human beings that are recognized by the system as users with an unique identity. This is achieved via identification and authentication mechanisms; the familiar example is a user identifier and password.

All system resources are abstractly lumped together as objects and, thus, all activities within a system can be viewed as sequences of operations on objects. In the relational database context, an object may be a relation, a tuple within a relation, or an attribute value within a tuple. More generally, anything that holds data may be an object, such as memory, directories, interprocess messages, network packets, I/O devices, or physical media.

A subject is an abstraction of the active entities that perform computation in the system. Thus, only subjects can access or manipulate objects. In most cases, within the system a subject is usually a process, job, or task, operating on behalf of some user, although at a higher level of abstraction users may be viewed as subjects. A user can have several subjects running in the system on his or her behalf at the same time, but each subject is associated with only a single user. This requirement is important to ensure the accountability of actions in a system.

Although the subject–object paradigm makes a clear distinction between subjects and objects (subjects are active entities, while objects are passive entities), an entity could be both a subject and an object. The only requirement is that if an entity behaves like a subject (respectively, object), it must abide by rules of the model that apply to subjects (respectively, objects).

The reason a distinction must be made between users and subjects is that while users are trusted not to deliberately leak information (they do not require a computer system to do so), subjects initiated by the users cannot be trusted to always abide by the security policy. Example 1 given below in section 2.2 illustrates just such a situation.

2.1 Identification and Authentication

Any system must be able to identify its users (*identification*) and confirm their identity (*authentication*). The system assigns each legitimate user (i.e., user that is allowed to use the system) a unique identification (userid), which is kept in an identification (id) file. A user must present the userid at login, which is matched against the id file. The usual means of performing authentication is by associating a reusable password with each userid. (A password is *reusable* if the same password is used over and over for authentication.) The password files are typically protected through encryption.

Reusable passwords are inherently risky since often users choose weak passwords (such as their own name, their own name spelled backward, or some word that also appears in a dictionary) which can be guessed by password cracker programs. A more elaborate method of defeating reusable passwords is called *spoofing*. Spoofing is a term borrowed from electronic warfare, where it refers to a platform transmitting deceptive electronic signals that closely resemble those of another kind of platform. In the computer system context, spoofing is a penetration attempt made by writing a false user interface, say, for the operating system or the DBMS. The spoofing program mimics the portion of the user interface that requests user identification and password, but records the user's password for use by the writer of the spoofing program. If it is properly done, the spoof will be undetected.

One does not have to rely on password cracker or spoofing programs to capture reusable passwords in today's networked environment. Unless special measures are taken (which is rarely the case), computer systems exchange information over the network in clear text (i.e., in unencrypted form). It is a trivial matter to capture the host name, userid, and password information using either Trojan network programs (e.g., telnet or rlogin) or network packet sniffing programs.

To overcome this vulnerability, systems have been developed that provide *one-time* passwords (i.e., passwords that are used only once). These systems include smart cards, randomized tokens, and challenge-response systems. Some methods of authentication are based on biometrics (e.g., fingerprint matching, retina scan, voice recognition, or key stroke patterns). However, there are problems associated with each of these methods. For example, tamper resistance of smart cards is problematic [1] and biometrics are not always reliable.

One way to prevent spoofing attacks is to provide a special mechanism to counter it. One such mechanism, called *trusted path*, will be discussed below. Untrusted DBMSs and their operating systems provide no such special mechanism and are vulnerable to spoofing and other attacks.

2.2 Access Control Policies

Access control policies define what is authorized by means of security attributes associated with each storage, processing or communication resource of the computer system. The attributes take the form of modes of access: `read`, `write`, `search`, `execute`, `own`, etc., and security is defined in terms of allowable access modes.

The accesses are held by subjects. A subject has privileges, i.e., the accesses it is potentially allowed to have to the objects. The privileges of the subjects and the accesses they currently hold make up the *protection* or *security state* of the computer system.

As mentioned above, access control policies usually assume that mechanisms are present for uniquely associating responsible human users with subjects (typically via an identification and authentication mechanism).

Discretionary Access Control

The most familiar kind of access control is discretionary access control. With discretionary access control, users (usually the *owners* of the objects) at their discretion can specify to the system who can access their objects. In this type of access control, a user or any of the user's programs or processes can choose to share objects with other users.

Since discretionary access control allows users to specify the security attributes of objects, the discretionary access control attributes of an object can change during the life of the system. For example, the UNIX operating system has a discretionary access control under which a user can specify if `read`, `write`, or `execute` access is to be allowed for himself or herself, for other users in the same group, and for all others. Unix uses access model bits to implement these controls; these bits can be set and changed for files owned by the user by means of the `chmod` command.

A more advanced model of discretionary access control is the *access matrix model* in which access rights are conceptually represented as an access matrix (see figure 1). The access matrix has one row for each subject and one column for each object. The (i, j)-entry of the access matrix specifies the access rights of the subject corresponding to the ith row to the object corresponding to the jth column.

Since the access matrix is often sparse, the access matrix is implemented using one of the following methods:

- *Access control lists*: Each object has a list of subjects that are allowed access to that object. Entries in the list also give the possible modes of access that a particular subject may have. In terms of the access matrix, each column of the access matrix is stored with the object corresponding to that column.
- *Capabilities*: Each subject has a list of objects that the subject is allowed to access, together with the allowed modes of access. In terms of the access matrix, each row of the access matrix is stored with the subject corresponding to that row.

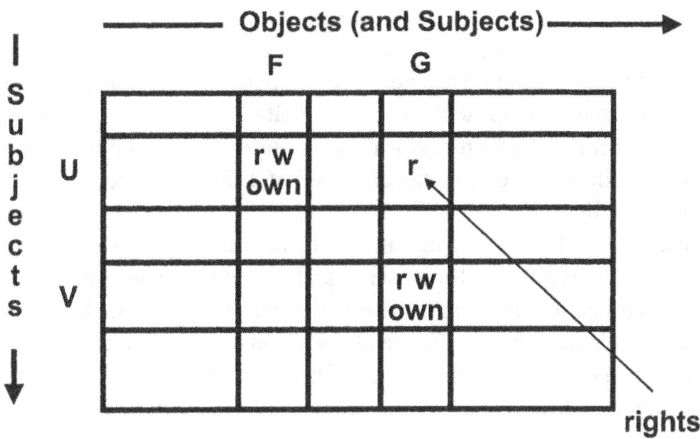

Fig. 1. Example of an access matrix

The Trojan Horse Problem

The essential purpose of discretionary access control is to prevent human users from directly accessing other user's objects. It cannot prevent indirect access via malicious software acting on behalf of the user. A user can have indirect access to another user's objects via a malicious program called a *Trojan horse*. A Trojan horse is a malicious computer program that performs some apparently useful function, but contains additional hidden functions that surreptitiously leak information by exploiting the legitimate authorizations of the invoking process.

Inability to defend against security violations due to Trojan horses is a fundamental problem for discretionary access control. An effective Trojan Horse has no obvious effect on the program's expected output and, therefore, its damage may never be detected. A simple Trojan horse in a text editor might discreetly make a copy of all files that the user asks to edit, and store the copies in a location where the penetrator, the person who wrote or implanted the program can later access them. As long as the unsuspecting user can voluntarily and legitimately give away the file, there is no way the system is able to tell the difference between a Trojan horse and a legitimate program. Any file accessible to the user via the text editor is accessible to the Trojan horse since a program executing on behalf of a user inherits the same unique ID, privileges and access rights as the user. The Trojan horse, therefore, does its dirty work without violating any of the security rules of the system. A clever Trojan horse might even be programmed to delete itself if the user tries to do something that might reveal its presence. Thus, a Trojan horse can either copy a file, set up access modes so that the information can be read directly from the files at a later time, or delete, modify or damage information.

To understand how a Trojan horse can leak information to unauthorized users in spite of the discretionary access control, we give a specific example.

Example 1 [Trojan Horse] Suppose that user A creates file f_1 and writes some information in it. Suppose now user B creates file f_2. As the owner of the file, user B is allowed to execute any operation on the file f_2. In particular, B can grant other users authorization on the file. Suppose then that B grants A the write privilege on file f_2, and converts a program P which performs some utility function into a Trojan horse by embedding a hidden piece of code composed of a read operation on file f_1 and a write operation on file f_2.

Suppose now that A invokes program P. The process which executes program P runs with the privileges of the calling user A and, therefore, all access requests made in P are checked against the authorizations of user A. Consider, in particular, the execution of the hidden code. First the read operation on file f_1 is requested. Since P is executing on behalf of A who the owner of the file, the operation is granted. Next, the write operation on file f_2 is requested. Since A has been given the write privilege on f_2, the write operation is also granted. As a consequence, during execution of program P contents have been read from file f_1, on which user B does not have read authorization, and written into file f_2, on which user B does have read authorization (see Figure2). In this way, an illegal transmission of information to unauthorized user A has occurred in spite of the discretionary access control.

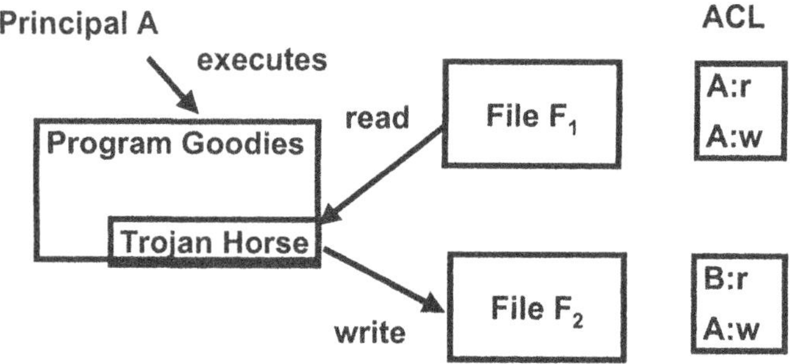

Fig. 2. Example of a Trojan horse

This simple example illustrates how easily the restrictions stated by discretionary authorizations can be bypassed and, therefore, the lack of assurance on the satisfaction of authorizations imposed by the discretionary policy. To overcome this weakness, further restrictions, beside the simple presence of the authorization for the required operations, must be imposed on discretionary access control to provide assurance that the accesses which are not authorized will not be executable indirectly (by employing a Trojan horse).

Rather than severely restricting user capabilities, as required by these solutions, another approach is to use mandatory access control rather than discretionary access control. We define mandatory access control next.

Mandatory Access Control

Mandatory access control contains security restrictions that are applied to all users. Under mandatory access control, subjects and objects have *fixed* security attributes that are used by the system to determine whether a subject can access an object or not. The mandatory security attributes are assigned either administratively or automatically by the operating system. These attributes cannot be modified by either the users or their programs on request.

To explain mandatory access control fully, we need to introduce lattice-based policies since almost all models of mandatory security use lattice-based policies.

Lattice-based policies Lattice-based policies partition all the objects in the system into a finite set SC of security classes. The set SC is partially ordered with order $\preceq$. That is, for any security classes A, B, and C, in SC, the following three properties hold:

(1) Reflexive: $A \preceq A$
(2) Antisymmetric: If $A \preceq B$ and $B \preceq A$, then $A = B$
(3) Transitive: If $A \preceq B$ and $B \preceq C$, then $A \preceq C$

The partial order $\preceq$ defines the *domination* relationship between security classes. Given two security classes L_1 and L_2, L_1 is said to be *dominated by* L_2 (and, equivalently, L_2 *dominates* L_1) if $L_1 \preceq L_2$.

We use $\prec$ to denote strict domination. Thus, L_1 is *strictly dominated* by L_2 (and, equivalently, L_2 *strictly dominates* L_1), written $L_1 \prec L_2$, if $L_1 \preceq L_2$, but $L_1 \neq L_2$.

Since $\preceq$ is a partial order, it is possible to have two security classes L_1 and L_2 such that neither L_1 dominates L_2 nor L_2 dominates L_1, in which case L_1 and L_2 are said to be *incomparable*.

Throughout this chapter, we use the terms *High* and *Low* to refer to two security classes such that they are comparable and the latter is strictly dominated by the former. Also, we sometimes use the notation $L_2 \succeq L_1$ as another way of expressing $L_1 \preceq L_2$.

SC with partial order $\preceq$ is in fact a *lattice* (hence the term lattice-based policy). In a lattice, every pair of elements possesses a unique *least upper bound* and a unique *greatest lower bound*. That is, for any pair of security classes A and B in SC,

(1) There is a unique security class C in SC such that
  (a) $A \preceq C$ and $B \preceq C$, and
  (b) If $A \preceq D$ and $B \preceq D$, then $C \preceq D$ for all D in SC.
  Security class C is the least upper bound of A and B.
(2) There is a unique security class E in SC such that
  (a) $E \preceq A$ and $E \preceq B$, and
  (b) If $D \preceq A$ and $D \preceq B$, then $D \preceq E$ for all D in SC.
  Security class E is the greatest lower bound of A and B.

Since SC is a lattice, there is a lowest security class, denoted by *system-low*, and a highest security class, denoted by *system-high*. Thus, by definition, *system-low* $\preceq$ A and $A \preceq$ *system-high* for all A in SC.

Explicit and Implicit Information Flows In a lattice-based model, the goal is to regulate the flow of information among objects. As a simple example of information flow, consider the program fragment given below:

```
if (A = 1)
        D := B
    else
        D := C;
```

Obviously, there is an explicit information flow from B and C into D since the information in B and C is transferred into D. However, there is another implicit information flow from A into D because the future value of D depends on the value of A. Access control only determines that the program has read access to A, B, and C, while it has write access to D. Thus, access control is only capable of detecting explicit information flows; however, they can easily permit implicit information flows.

In a lattice-based model, the partial order $\preceq$ determines if the information in object A can flow into object B. Information in A can flow into B only if $A \preceq B$. As a result, information can either flow upward along the security lattice or stay at the same security class.

Although there are security models based on information flow, determining information flow is much more complex than determining accesses. Thus, its use in computer security is restricted to special cases where only static analysis is needed to determine information flow, for example, in covert channel analysis, discussed later in this chapter.

Example 2 [Military Security Lattice] A security class (or level) in the military security lattice is an ordered pair consisting of a *sensitivity level* as the first component and a set of *categories* (or *compartments*) as the second component. The set of categories could be empty, in which case we write only the sensitivity level as the security class.

The usual sensitivity levels are *Unclassified, Confidential, Secret*, and *Top Secret*, which are hierarchically ordered as follows:

$$\textit{Unclassified} < \textit{Confidential} < \textit{Secret} < \textit{Top Secret}$$

There is an unordered list $\mathcal{C}$ of categories consisting of labels such as *Conventional, Nuclear, Crypto*, and *NATO* (North Atlantic Treaty Organization). The set of categories is a subset of this list. Different categories are partially ordered using the set inclusion as follows: Given categories C_1 and $C_2 \subseteq \mathcal{C}$, $C_1 \leq C_2$ if $C_1 \subseteq C_2$.

The partial orders defined on sensitivity levels and compartments are used to define a partial order on the set SC consisting of all security classes as follows:

> Given two security classes (A_1, C_1) and (A_2, C_2) in SC, $(A_1, C_1) \preceq (A_2, C_2)$ if $A_1 \leq A_2$ and $C_1 \leq C_2$.

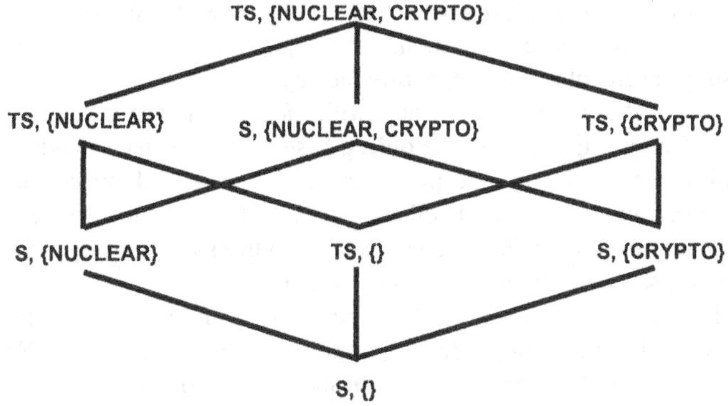

Fig. 3. A portion of the military security lattice

It is easy to see that military security classes form a lattice. For any pair of security classes (A_1, C_1) and (A_2, C_2) with $A_1 < A_2$, $(A_1, C_1 \cap C_2)$ is their greatest lower bound and $(A_2, C_1 \cup C_2)$ is their least upper bound. In fact, the *system-high* and *system-low* elements are given by (*Unclassified*, $\emptyset$) and (*Top Secret*, $\mathcal{C}$), respectively.

A security lattice can be naturally viewed as a directed acyclic graph where the security classes in $\mathcal{SC}$ are its nodes and there is a directed edge $A \rightarrow B$ whenever $A \preceq B$. The arrows in the graph indicate the allowable information flow.

A portion of the military security lattice is shown in Figure 3.

The Bell-LaPadula Security Model

The Bell-LaPadula security model is a widely used formal model of mandatory access control. It is an automata-theoretic model that describes lattice-based policies [2].

The model contains a lattice $(\mathcal{SC}, \preceq)$ of security classes, a set $\mathcal{S}$ of subjects, and a set $\mathcal{O}$ of objects with a function $\mathcal{L}$ that assigns security classes to both subjects and objects: $\mathcal{L}$: $\mathcal{S} \cup \mathcal{O} \rightarrow \mathcal{SC}$. Subjects also have a maximum security level, defined as a function $\mathcal{L}_{max}$: $\mathcal{S} \rightarrow$SC, but objects have a constant security level. By definition, $\mathcal{L}(S) \preceq \mathcal{L}_{max}(S)$.

There is a set $\mathcal{R}$ of access privileges (or rights) consisting of following access modes:

`read:` subject has read access to the object
`append:` subject can append to an existing object
`execute:` subject can invoke the object
`read-write:`subject has both the read and write access to the object

With only a `read` access, a subject cannot modify (i.e., append or write) the object in any way. With only an `append` access, a subject can neither read nor make a destructive modification (by overwriting) to the object. With only an `execute` access, a subject can neither read nor modify the object. Finally, with a `read-write` access, a subject can both read and modify the object.

There is a *control* attribute associated with each object. The control attribute is granted to the subject that created the object. A subject can extend to other subjects some or all of the access modes it possesses for the controlled object. The control attribute itself cannot be extended to other objects. (Thus, a control attribute is similar to the ownership flag in the discretionary access control since it governs the right to grant other subjects discretionary access to the object.)

The privileges of the subjects can be represented by an $m \times n$ access matrix $\mathcal{M}$. The entry $\mathcal{M}[i, j]$ is the set of privileges that subject $\mathcal{S}_i$ has to object $\mathcal{O}_j$. Note that a right is not an access. Accesses in the current state are described by an $m \times n$ current access matrix $\mathcal{B}$.

The protection state of the model is the combination of $\mathcal{M}$ and $\mathcal{B}$. The model reads in a sequence of *requests* to change the protection state; transitions to new states either satisfy or reject the request. Specific access control policies are modeled by a set of rules that define satisfiable requests (i.e., allowable transitions to new states) in a given security state. An important characteristic of the model is the open-ended nature of the rules. This can lead to problems, but we will simply present the two most widely used rules which have been found to be reasonable for practical implementation, assuming objects have a constant security class. The two rules are usually presented as invariants:

THE SIMPLE SECURITY PROPERTY. The access mode `read` is in $\mathcal{B}[i, j]$ only if `read` is in $\mathcal{M}[i, j]$ and $\mathcal{L}(\mathcal{O}_j) \preceq \mathcal{L}(\mathcal{S}_i)$.

THE $\star$-PROPERTY (read "the star property"). The access mode `append` is in $\mathcal{B}[i, j]$ only if `append` is in $\mathcal{M}[i, j]$ and $\mathcal{L}(\mathcal{S}_i) \preceq \mathcal{L}(\mathcal{O}_j)$, and the access mode `read-write` is in $\mathcal{B}[i, j]$ only if `read-write` is in $\mathcal{M}[i, j]$ and $\mathcal{L}(\mathcal{S}_i) = \mathcal{L}(\mathcal{O}_j)$.

Thus, the simple security property puts restrictions on read operations ("no read up"), while the $\star$-property restricts append operations ("no append down") and read-write operations ("read-write at the same level").

As an example, a file with security class (*Secret*, {*Nato, Nuclear*}) can be read by a subject with security class (*Top Secret*, {*Nato, Nuclear, Crypto*}), but not by a subject with security class (*Top Secret*, {*Nato, Crypto*}). Also, a subject with (*Secret*, {*Nato*}) security class cannot gain either read or read-write access to a file at (*Secret*, {*Crypto*}) security class since these two classes are incomparable. Note that these restrictions are consistent with the information flow shown in Figure 3.

There are several different versions of the $\star$-property. The two most popular versions of the $\star$-property do not make any distinction between append and read-write operations. Thus, there is a single `write` access mode that gives a subject the right to read as well as modify (append and write) the object.

THE REVISED $\star$-PROPERTY. The access mode `write` is in $\mathcal{B}[i, j]$ only if write is in $\mathcal{M}[i, j]$ and $\mathcal{L}(\mathcal{S}_i) \preceq \mathcal{L}(\mathcal{O}_j)$.

With simple security property and the revised $\star$-property, a subject is not allowed to either read up or write down.

RESTRICTED $\star$-PROPERTY. The access mode `write` is in $\mathcal{B}[i,j]$ only if `write` is in $\mathcal{M}[i,j]$ and $\mathcal{L}(\mathcal{S}_i) = \mathcal{L}(\mathcal{O}_j)$.

With simple security property and the restricted $\star$-Property, a subject can read objects at its session level and below, but can write objects at its session level only.

The Bell-LaPadula Model and the Military Security Policy

The Bell-LaPadula model was designed to mirror the military security policy that existed in the paper world. To see how well it meets this goal, we review the military security policy for handling paper documents.

Each defense document is stamped with a security label giving the security level of the document. Any document that is *Confidential* or above is considered classified. Any user that requires access to classified documents needs an appropriate clearance. The clearance is assigned by some process which is external to the system, usually by the system security officer.

A user is trusted to handle documents up to his clearance. Accordingly, it is permissible for a user to read a document if the clearance level of the user dominates the security label of the document. A user may be authorized to reclassify documents, down or up (but not above his clearance level).

Suppose now that a user logs into a system that controls accesses in accordance with the Bell-LaPadula model. At the time of the login, he must specify a security level for the session. The system requires that this session level is dominated by the clearance level of the user, and any process running on behalf of the user during this session is assigned this session level. In terms of the Bell-LaPadula model, the function $\mathcal{L}_{max}$ corresponds to the clearance levels of the users. When a user reads an object O, $\mathcal{L}(O) \leq \mathcal{L}(S)$ by the simple security property, and since $\mathcal{L}(S) \leq \mathcal{L}_{max}(S)$, clearance level of the user dominates the security label of the object, which is consistent with the military security policy.

When a user creates a file f, the security label for the file f dominates the session level (because of the $\star$-property which prevents any write downs). This means that during a *Secret* session, any files created by the user will have a *Secret* or higher security label. If this user wishes to create a file which is labeled only *Confidential*, he must first initiate another session at the *Confidential* level and then create the *Confidential* file.

Thus, the $\star$-property is more restrictive than the military security policy. However, there is a very good reason why this is so, illustrated by the following example. *Example 3 [Trojan Horse Revisited]* Consider once again the Trojan horse example given earlier with following modification. Suppose now that the file f_1 is a *Top Secret* file and that B is a malicious user that wants to access f_1 even though he is cleared only up to the *Confidential* level. To accomplish this, B knows that the user A has a *Top Secret* clearance and often uses the program P. As before, B creates a

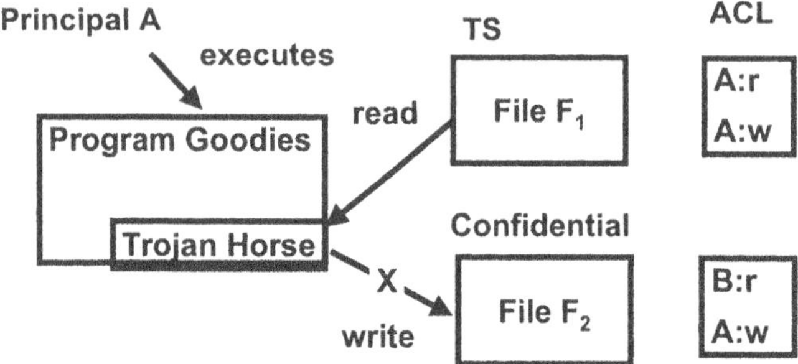

Fig. 4. Example of a Trojan horse that fails

Confidential file f_2 and gives A the write access to f_2 and hides the malicious code inside P that copies the contents of f_1 into f_2.

Without the $\star$-property restrictions, were A to invoke P, the contents of f_1 will be copied in f_2. Thus, the Trojan horse in effect downgrades a file which is *Top Secret* to a file which is merely *Confidential*. (Note that the user A is not aware that this downgrading has taken place.) The purpose of the $\star$-property is to foil just such attacks.

To see this, suppose now that the system has a mechanism, called the *reference monitor*, that enforces the two Bell-LaPadula restrictions faithfully. Given this, suppose the user A invokes the program P while logged in at a *Top Secret* session. As before, program P runs with the same privileges as those of user A. Although the read operation on file f_1 will succeed (by the simple security property), the write operation on file f_2 will fail (since this operation will violate the $\star$-property). See figure 4.

Note that although the $\star$-property plays an important role in foiling the Trojan horse attack in Example 4, there is another hidden assumption that is equally important. This hidden assumption is the mandatory access control requirement that security levels of subjects and objects are fixed; they cannot be modified by the users or the processes running on their behalf. Since the Trojan horse cannot change the security attributes of an object, the Trojan horse cannot make it available to a subject that is not privileged to access it. Since the static assignment of security classes is an essential assumption, we make it explicit as a principle, as follows.

The Tranquility Principle A key assumption that has been made so far is that the security attributes of an object are fixed. The security attributes are assigned when the object is created and are derived from the privileges of the creating subjects. A simple example of this is the security class. Each object is assigned a security class at creation time which cannot change. This assumption has been formalized by the following axiom.

THE TRANQUILITY PRINCIPLE. A subject cannot change the security class of an object.

Trusted Subjects In the model described thus far, we have assumed that security attributes of objects and subjects are fixed. However, this assumption is too restrictive in a real situation since there are legitimate tasks which cannot be performed under the Bell-LaPadula model (due to "no write down" restrictions of the ⋆-property). The legitimate tasks include system maintenance tasks such as specification of clearance levels of users and tasks such as, reclassification, sanitization, and downgrading of objects, all of which entail lowering the security classes of these objects. The concept of a *trusted subject* was added to overcome the restrictions.

TRUSTED SUBJECT. A subject is said to be *trusted* it is exempt from one or more security policy restrictions, yet it will not violate these restrictions.

Thus, even if a trusted subject has the power to violate our security policy, we trust it not to do so. For reclassification, sanitization, and downgrading tasks, a subject only needs exemption from the "no write down" restriction of the ⋆-property.

2.3 Illegal Information Flow Channels

Even if we have a lattice-based mandatory access control policy implemented by a reference monitor, an adversary can still launch attacks against our system's security. As we observed earlier, access controls only protect direct revelation of data, but not against violations that produce illegal information flow through indirect means. A program that accesses some classified data on behalf of a process may leak those data to other processes and thus to other users. A secure system must guard against implicit leakage of information occurring via these channels.

Covert Channels

In terms we have established so far, a *covert channel* is any component or feature of a system that is misused to encode or represent information for unauthorized transmission, without violating our access control policy. Potential unauthorized use of components or features can be surprising; the system clock, operating system interprocess communication primitives, error messages, the existence of particular file names, and many other features can be used to encode information for transmission contrary to our intentions.

Two types of covert channels have been identified thus far. A *covert storage channel* is any communication path that results when one process causes an object to be written and another process observes the effect. This channel utilizes system storage such as temporary files or shared variables to pass information to another process. A *covert timing channel* is any communication path that results when a process produces some effect on system performance that is observable by another process and is measurable with a timing base such as a real-time clock. Covert timing channels are much more difficult to identify and to prevent than covert storage channels. A system with B2 rating or higher must be free of these channels. The most important parameter of a covert channel is its bandwidth, i.e. the rate (in bits per second) at which information can be communicated. Surprisingly, the higher the speed of the system the larger the bandwidth of these covert channels. According to the Orange Book standards, a channel that exceeds the rate of 100 bits per second is considered as having a *high* bandwidth.

The covert channel problem is of special interest for us because many database system concurrency control mechanisms are potential covert channels. We will distinguish between covert channels that are implementation invariant and covert channels that are found only in some implementations. The former are called *signaling channels*. Thus, a signaling channel is a means of information flow inherent in the basic algorithm or protocol, and hence appears in every implementation. A covert channel that is not a signaling channel is a property of a specific implementation, and not of the general algorithm or protocol. Thus a covert channel may be present in a given implementation even if the basic algorithm is free of signaling channels. It is critical to exclude signaling channels from our algorithms as much as possible. The absence of signaling channels in an algorithm does not guarantee the absence of other implementation-specific covert channels in a particular implementation.

3 Mechanism

Once the security policy is defined, we need to design and implement a sound protection mechanism. The efficiency and power of the available protection mechanisms limits the kinds of policies that can be enforced. Mechanisms should have the following qualities:

(1) Every user and every system operation affected by the mechanism should have the *least privilege* necessary.
(2) It should be simple.
(3) It should completely mediate all operations defined for it (i.e., it cannot be bypassed).
(4) It should be tamper resistant.
(5) Its effectiveness should not depend on keeping the details of its design secret.

This last requirement is used in cryptography, where the strength of an encryption algorithm does not depend on concealment of the algorithm itself.

3.1 *Reference Monitor*

The Bell-LaPadula model is associated with an enforcement mechanism called a *reference monitor*. The reference monitor is defined to be at the lowest levels of implementation, that is, any access to data or metadata will be subject to checks made by the reference monitor and will be prevented if the access violates the security policy (see Figure 5). The term "any" includes arbitrary use of individual machine

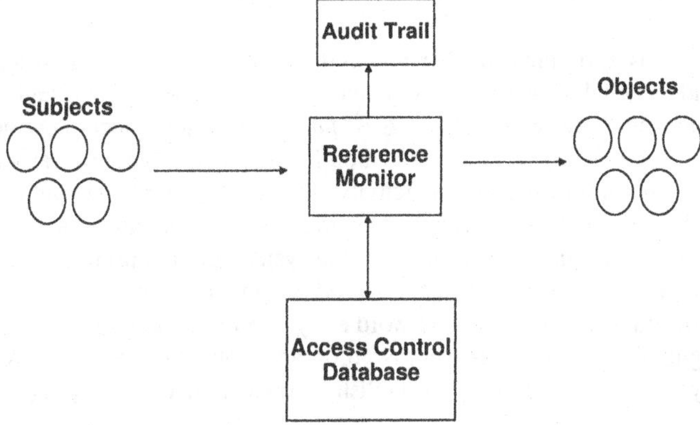

Fig. 5. Reference monitor abstraction

instructions or of system utilities such as debuggers. By definition, the reference monitor is correct, tamper resistant, and unbypassable. Thus we assume all accesses are forced to be in accordance with our security policy unless they are made by trusted subjects.

3.2 *Trusted Software and Trusted Components*

One of the key features of the trusted systems is trusted software. Generally, a trusted software is a program that is correct with respect to its specification. In the context of security, a software is said to be *trusted* if it has the power to violate our security policy, but we trust it not to do so.

A trusted component is a system component containing only the trusted software. By definition, trusted components cannot be exploited by a subject to violate the security policy of the system.

In practice, trusted components are generally undesirable because they must be verified and validated at extra expense to show they deserve the trust. According to DOD's Trusted Computer System Evaluation Criteria (the Orange Book) [4], trusted components require that they be formally verified and certified as correct by a formal evaluation process.

3.3 *Trusted Computing Base*

The reference monitor itself must unavoidably be trusted. Additional trusted components are needed to support the reference monitor, for example identification and authentication mechanisms such as logins and passwords. We use the term *trusted computing base* to refer to the reference monitor plus all of its supporting trusted components.

3.4 *Trusted Path*

To protect against spoofing and other attacks that capture passwords, a trusted system must provide a reliable two way communication path between itself and its users. This path is often referred to as a *trusted path*, but is more accurately described as a *secure attention key*. A secure attention key is a dedicated key that will cause the reference monitor to suspend all activity at the user interface and put the user in direct, reliable communication with the identification and authentication mechanisms of the system. With this mechanism, both the system and the user can be sure that they are communicating with the other instead of a malicious program.

If the trusted path is used for password entry, it provides good protection against password guessing programs as well. No program is able to simulate the secure attention key and, therefore, cannot establish a connection with the password entry software.

4 Assurance

Assurance provides the glue that binds the security policy and the mechanism that purportedly implements the security policy. Assurance is needed in order to trust the reference monitor or any other components used for security policy enforcement. Assurance is justified confidence that a trusted computing base enforces its security policy in an unbypassable fashion.

Assurance is obtained through careful design and implementation, accompanied by explicit justification (present technology does not permit the more desirable full formal verification of all trusted components) and comes in varying degrees, depending on the degree of care and rigor that are applied. Trusted components are expected to be made up of simple parts that are related in simple ways, without exception. For higher degrees of assurance, the components must be increasingly modular, object-oriented in design, and layered according to a uses hierarchy [6]. Finally, the components must only perform functions related to security. Trusted components are expensive to implement and their use is to be avoided if possible.

5 Basic Architecture for Trusted Operating Systems

There are many commercial (untrusted) operating systems, e.g., MS-DOS and the original Unix operating system, that do not have a well-defined structure. In MS-DOS, application programs can access the basic I/O routines to write directly to the disk drives. This leaves MS-DOS vulnerable to malicious programs that can cause system crashes, for example.

Currently it is possible to build general-purpose operating systems that enforce access control policies with high assurance. All trusted operating systems are carefully engineered as a collection of layers such that each layer is implemented using only those operations that are provided by lower layers.

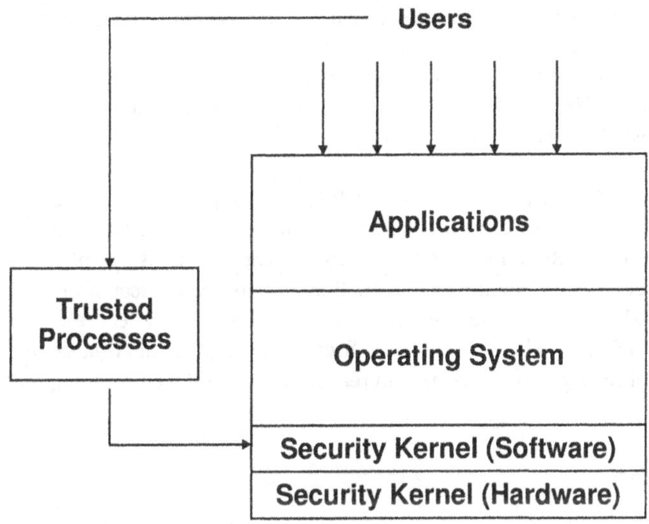

Fig. 6. Basic architecture for trusted operating systems

A basic trusted operating system architecture is shown in Figure 6. The two lowest layers, consisting of the hardware and software security kernels, constitute the TCB of the system. As such, they satisfy all the properties of a TCB. In particular, they are responsible for enforcing the system security policy on every access to an object by a subject.

The operating system software is partitioned into two layers. The lower layer is the software security kernel that provides a small subset of the operating system functions. The upper layer, called the *supervisor*, uses the kernel primitives to provide the remainder of the operating system functions. The supervisor primitives define the application interface to the trusted operating system.

How functionalities are divided between the kernel and the supervisor depends on the security policy. Obviously all security relevant functions must be inside the kernel. An example of such a function is memory and disk management. Since these parts are shared by multiple users, the way they are managed must be inside the kernel.

Since trusted subjects are essential for performing certain legitimate tasks, they are implemented as extensions of the security kernel. Clearly, trusted subjects must be carefully engineered since it is critical that they work properly.

6 Conclusion

In this chapter, we introduced the basic concepts and terminologies in information system security. To build a secure system requires careful integration of security policies, mechanisms and assurance. In particular, a system's security is always constrained by available resources, e.g., funding and time. It is often not practical to have the most stringent security requirements and adopt the strongest security mechanism and assurance. There is always a cost and benefit tradeoff. Therefore, risk analysis is indispensable when deciding appropriate security policies and mechanisms for a system.

A system's security relies not only on the adopted specific techniques, but also on the security practices of users in the system. Many systems' security is compromised due to attackers' exploitment of human users' negligence instead of the failure of security mechanisms. Human factors are thus an important aspect of information security. Besides educating users about good security practices, a secure system should also be designed to be intuitive and user-friendly. Though the importance of this principle is well recognized, realizing it in real systems is still a challenging problem.

References

1. Ross Aderson and Markus Kuhn. Tampter Resistance - A Cautionary Note. In *Proceedings of the 2nd Workshop on Electronic Commerce*, Oakland, California, November 1996.
2. D. Elliot Bell and Leonard J. LaPadula. Secure Computer Systems: A Mathematical Model, Volume II. *Journal of Computer Security*, 4(2/3):229–263, 1996.
3. Matt Bishop. *Computer Security: Art and Science*. Addison-Wesley, 2003.
4. Trusted Computer System Evaluation Criteria, 1985.
5. Michael A. Harrison, Walter L. Ruzzo, and Jeffrey D. Ullman. Protection in Operating Systems. *Communications of the ACM*, 19(8):461–471, August 1976.
6. David Lorge Parnas. Designing Software for Ease of Extension and Contraction. *IEEE Trans. Software Eng.*, 5(2):128–138, 1979.
7. Ravi S. Sandhu. The Schematic Protection Model: Its definition and analysis for acyclic attenuating systems. *Journal of ACM*, 35(2):404–432, 1988.
8. Ravi S. Sandhu. The typed access matrix model. In *Proceedings of the 1992 IEEE Symposium on Security and Privacy*, pages 122–136, Los Alamitos, California, May 1992. IEEE Computer Society Press.

Access Control Policies and Languages in Open Environments

S. De Capitani di Vimercati[1], S. Foresti[1], S. Jajodia[2], and P. Samarati[1]

[1] Università degli Studi di Milano
{decapita, foresti, samarati}@dti.unimi.it
[2] Center of Secure Information Systems
George Mason University
jajodia@gmu.edu

1 Introduction

Access control is the process of mediating every request to resources and data maintained by a system and determining whether the request should be granted or denied. Access control plays an important role in overall system security. The development of an access control system requires the definition of the regulations (*policies*) according to which access is to be controlled and their implementation as functions executable by a computer system. The access control policies are usually formalized through a security *model*, stated through an appropriate specification *language*, and then enforced by the access control *mechanism* enforcing the access control service. The separation between policies and mechanisms introduces an independence between protection requirements to be enforced on the one side, and mechanisms enforcing them on the other. It is then possible to: *i)* discuss protection requirements independently of their implementation, *ii)* compare different access control policies as well as different mechanisms that enforce the same policy, and *iii)* design mechanisms able to enforce multiple policies. This latter aspect is particularly important: if a mechanism is tied to a specific policy, a change in the policy would require changing the whole access control system; mechanisms able to enforce multiple policies avoid this drawback. The formalization phase between the policy definition and its implementation as a mechanism allows the definition of a formal model representing the policy and its working, making it possible to define and prove security properties that systems enforcing the model will enjoy [30]. Therefore, by proving that the model is "secure" and that the mechanism *correctly implements* the model, we can argue that the system is "secure" (*with respect to the definition of security considered* [37]).

The definition of access control policies (and their corresponding models) is far from being a trivial process. One of the major difficulty lies in the interpretation of, often complex and sometimes ambiguous, real world security policies and in their translation in well defined and unambiguous rules enforceable by a computer system. Many real world situations have complex policies, where access decisions depend on the application of different rules coming, for example, from laws, practices, and organizational regulations. A security policy must capture all the different regulations to be enforced and, in addition, must also consider possible additional threats due to the use of a computer system. Given the complexity of the scenario, there is a need for flexible, powerful, and expressive access control services to accommodate all the different requirements that may need to be expressed, while at the same time be simple both in terms of use (so that specifications can be kept under control) and implementation (so to allow for its verification).

An access control system should include support for the following concepts/features.

- *Expressibility.* An access control service should be expressive enough so that the policy can suit all the data owner's needs. To this purpose, several of the most recent language designs rely on concepts and techniques from logic, specifically from logic programming [16,28,32–34,48]. Logic languages are particularly attractive as policy specification languages (see Sect. 3). One obvious advantage lies in their clean and unambiguous semantics, suitable for implementation validation, as well as formal policy verification. Second, logic languages can be expressive enough to formulate all the policies introduced in the literature. The declarative nature of logic languages yields a good compromise between expressiveness and simplicity. Their high level of abstraction, very close to the natural language formulation of the policies, makes them simpler to use than imperative programming languages. However, security managers are not experts in formal logics, either, so generality is sometimes traded for simplicity.
- *Efficiency.* Access control efficiency is always a critical issue. Therefore, simple and efficient mechanisms to allow or deny an access are key aspects (see Sect. 3).
- *Simplicity.* One of the major challenges in the definition of a policy language is to provide expressiveness and flexibility while at the same time ensuring easiness of use and therefore applicability. An access control language should therefore be based on a high level formulation of the access control rules, possibly close to natural language formulation (see Sect. 4).
- *Anonymity support.* In open environments, not all access control decisions are identity-based. Resource/service requesters depend upon their *attributes* (usually substantiated by certificates) to gain accesses to resources (see Sect. 5).
- *Policy combination and conflict-resolution.* If multiple modules (e.g., for different authorities or different domains) exist for the specification of access control rules, the access control system should provide a means for users to specify how the different modules should interact, for example, if their union (maximum privilege) or their intersection (minimum privilege) should be considered (see Sect. 6). Also, when both permissions and denials can be specified, the problem naturally arises of how to deal with *incompleteness* (accesses for which no rule is specified) and *inconsistency* (accesses for which both a denial and a permission are specified). Dealing with incompleteness (requiring the authorizations to be complete would be very impractical) requires support of a default policy either

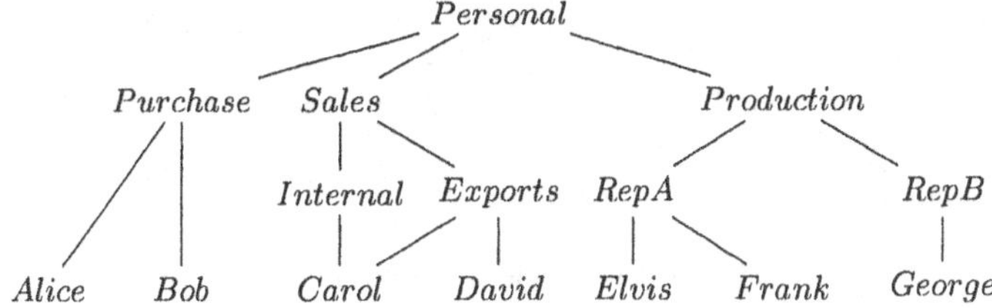

Fig. 1. An example of user-group hierarchy

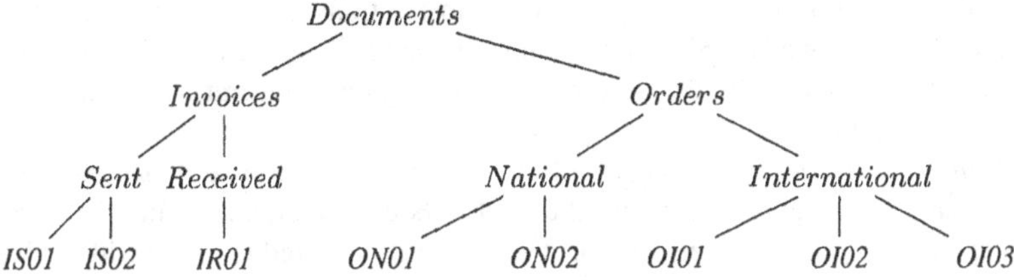

Fig. 2. An example of object hierarchy

supported by the system or specified by the users. Dealing with inconsistencies require support for conflict resolution policies.

In this chapter, after a brief overview of the basic concepts on which access control systems are based, we illustrate recent proposals and ongoing work addressing access control in emerging applications and new scenarios. The remainder of this chapter is structured as follows. Section 2 introduces the basic concepts of access control. Section 3 presents a logic-based framework for representing access control policies. Section 4 briefly describes some XML-based access control languages and illustrates the XACML policy model and language. XACML is a OASIS standard that provides a means for expressing and interchanging access control policies in XML. Section 5 introduces recent solutions basing the access control decisions on the evaluation of users' attributes rather than on their explicit identity. Section 6 addresses the problem of combining authorization specifications that may be independently stated. We describe the characteristics that a policy composition framework should have and illustrate some current approaches. Finally, Sect. 7 concludes the chapter.

2 Basic Concepts

A first step in the development of an access control system is the identification of the *objects* to be protected, the *subjects* that execute activities and request access to objects, and the *actions* that can be executed on the objects, and that must be controlled. More precisely, an access control system should support the following concepts.

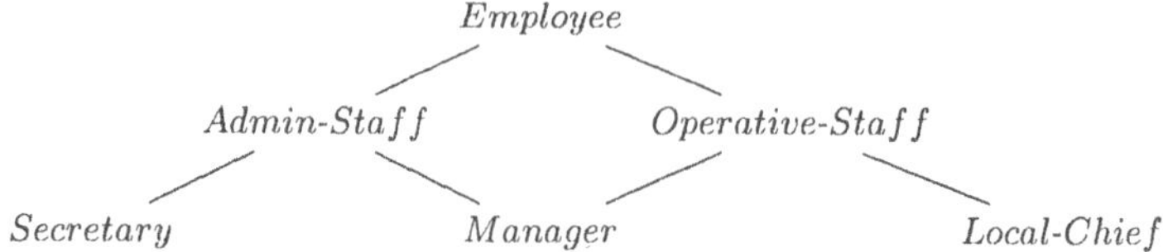

Fig. 3. An example of role hierarchy

- *Users* (U) are entities requesting access to objects. Abstractions can be defined within the domain of users. Intuitively, abstractions allow to define group of users. Users together with their groups, denoted G, define a partial order that introduces a hierarchy on the user domain. Figure 1 illustrates an example of user-group hierarchy.
- *Data Items* (Obj) are the objects of the system that have to be protected and on which access rights can be specified. Objects can be organized in a hierarchical structure, defining sets of objects that can be referred together with a given name. The definition of groups of objects (*object types*), denoted T, introduces a *hierarchy* of objects and groups thereof. For instance, a file system can be seen as an object hierarchy, where files are single objects and directories are groups thereof. Figure 2 illustrates an example of object hierarchy.
- *Access Types* (A) are the actions that can be executed on an object. The actions may vary depending on the kind of objects considered.
- *Roles* (R) are sets of privileges. A user playing a role has the ability to execute the privileges associated with the role. Roles can be organized hierarchically. Figure 3 illustrates an example of role hierarchy.
- *Administrative policies* regulate who can grant and revoke authorizations in the system.

Note that groups and roles are different concepts with two main differences:

- a group is a named collection of users and possibly other groups, and a role is a named collection of privileges, and possibly other roles;
- while role can sometimes be activated and deactivated directly by users at their discretion, the membership in a group cannot be deactivated.

These two concepts are not exclusive but complementary to each other. The hierarchical structure of data items, users/groups, and roles can be formally represented through a mathematical structure called *hierarchy*.

Definition 1 (Hierarchy). *A* hierarchy *is a triple* $(X, Y, \leq)$ *where:*

- *X and Y are disjoint sets;*
- $\leq$ *is a partial order on* $(X \cup Y)$ *such that each* $x \in X$ *is a minimal element of* $(X \cup Y)$*; an element* $x \in X$ *is said to be* minimal *iff there are no elements below it in the hierarchy, that is, iff* $\forall y \in (X \cup Y)$: $y \leq x \Rightarrow y = x$.

According to this definition, X represents primitive elements (e.g., a user or a file), and Y represents aggregate entities (e.g., a set of users or objects).

Given a system composed of the elements listed above, an *authorization* specifies which *authorization subjects* can execute which actions on which *authorization objects*. An authorization can then be represented as a triple (s, o, a), indicating that authorization subject s can execute action a over authorization object o.

In addition to positive authorizations, recent access control languages support also *negative authorizations*, that is, authorizations indicating that an authorization subject cannot execute a stated action on the specified authorization object. The combined use of positive and negative authorizations has the great advantage of allowing an easy management of *exceptions* in policy definition. For instance, if all users in the system but *Alice* can access a resource and we use only positive authorizations, it is necessary to specify for each subject but *Alice* a triple indicating that user u can access resource r. By contrast, with negative authorizations, we can simply state that *Alice* cannot access r, supposing, as a default policy, that everybody can access r.

To represent both positive and negative access rights, authorization triples become of the form $(s, o, \pm a)$, where $+a$ indicates a positive authorization and $-a$ indicates a negative authorization.

Given a set of authorizations explicitly specified over the elements in the system, it is possible to obtain a set of derived authorizations obtained according to a hierarchy-based derivation. Some of the most common propagation policies (which include also some resolution policies for possible conflicts) are described below [26].

- *No propagation.* Authorizations are not propagated. For instance, a triple specified for a node is not propagated to its descendants. No propagation is applicable when non-leaf nodes can appear in an access request and therefore authorizations that apply to them as subject/object must be considered (as it is, for example, the case of roles).
- *No overriding.* Authorizations of a node are propagated to its descendants.
- *Most specific overrides.* Authorizations of a node are propagated to its descendants if not overridden. An authorization associated with a node n overrides a contradicting authorization[3] associated with any supernode of n for all the subnodes of n.
- *Path overrides.* Authorizations of a node are propagated to its descendants if not overridden. An authorization associated with a node n overrides a contradicting authorization associated with a supernode n' for all the subnodes of n only for the paths passing from n. The overriding has no effect on other paths.

The combined use of positive and negative authorizations brings now to the problem of how the two specifications should be treated when conflict authorizations are associated with the same node in a hierarchy. In these cases, different decision criteria could be adopted, each applicable in specific situations, corresponding to different *conflict resolution policies* that can be implemented. Examples of conflict resolution policies are the following.

[3] Authorizations $(s, o, +a)$ and $(s', o', -a')$ are contradictory if $s = s'$, $o = o'$, and $a = a'$.

- *No conflict.* The presence of a conflict is considered an error.
- *Denials take precedence.* Negative authorizations take precedence.
- *Permissions take precedence.* Positive authorizations take precedence.
- *Nothing takes precedence.* Neither positive nor negative authorizations take precedence.

It may be possible that after the application of a propagation policy and a conflict resolution policy, some accesses are neither authorized nor denied (i.e., no authorization exists for them). A *decision policy* guarantees that for each subject there exists a permission or a prohibition to execute a given access. Two well known decision policies are the *closed policy* and the *open policy*. The closed policy allows an access if there exists a positive authorization for it, and denies it otherwise. The open policy denies an access if there exists a negative authorization for it, and allows it otherwise.

3 Logic-Based Access Control Languages

Several authorization models and access control mechanisms have been implemented. However, each model, and its corresponding enforcement mechanism, implements a single specified policy, which is built into the mechanism. As a consequence, although different policy choices are possible in theory, each access control system is in practice bound to a specific policy. The major drawback of this approach is that a single policy simply cannot capture all the protection requirements that may arise over time. Recent proposals have worked towards languages and models able to express, in a single framework, different access control policies, to the goal of providing a single mechanism able to enforce multiple policies. Logic-based languages, for their expressive power and formal foundations, represent a good candidate. The main advantages of using a logic-based language can be summarized as follows:

- the semantic of a logic language is clear and unambiguous;
- logic languages are very expressive and can be used to represent any kind of policy;
- logic languages are declarative and offer a better abstraction level than imperative programming languages.

The first work investigating logic languages for the specification of authorizations is the work by Woo and Lam [48]. Their proposal makes the point for the need of flexibility and extensibility in access specifications and illustrates how these advantages can be achieved by abstracting from the low level authorization triples and adopting a high level authorization language. Their language is essentially a many-sorted first-order language with a rule construct, useful to express authorization derivations and therefore model authorization implications and default decisions (e.g., closed or open policy).

In [5] the authors propose a temporal authorization model that supports periodic access authorizations and periodic rules. More precisely, deductive temporal rules with periodicity and order constraints are provided to derive new authorizations based on the presence or absence of other authorizations in specific periods of time. Another approach based on *active rules*, called *role triggers*, has been presented in [6]. The authors extend the RBAC model by adding temporal constraints on the enabling/disabling of roles.

Other logic-based access control languages support inheritance mechanisms and conflict resolution policies. The *Hierarchical Temporal Authorization Model* adopts the denials-take-precedence principle and does not distinguish between original and derived authorizations: an authorization can override another one independently from the category to which they belong. The main problem of this logic language is that it is not stratifiable. However, it supports a dynamic form of stratification that guarantees a polynomial computation time. A framework based on the C-Datalog language has also been presented. The framework is general enough to model a variety of access control models.

Although these proposals allow the expression of different kinds of authorization implications, constraints on authorizations, and access control policies, the authorization specifications may result difficult to understand and manage. Also, the trade-off between expressiveness and efficiency seems to be strongly unbalanced: the lack of restrictions on the language results in the specification of models that may not even be decidable and implementable in practice.

Starting from these observations, Jajodia et al. [26] worked on a proposal for a logic-based language that attempted to balance flexibility and expressiveness on the one side, and easy management and performance on the other. The language allows the representation of different policies and protection requirements, while at the same time providing understandable specifications, clear semantics (guaranteeing therefore the behavior of the specifications), and bearable data complexity. In the remainder of this section, we will describe this proposal in more details.

3.1 Flexible Authorization Framework

The *Flexible Authorization Framework* (FAF) [26] is a powerful and elegant logic-based framework where authorizations are specified in terms of a locally stratified rule base logic. FAF is based on an access control model that does not depend on any policy but is capable of representing any policy through the syntax of the model. In FAF, a data system to which protection must be ensured is formally defined as follows.

Definition 2 (Data System). *A data system (DS) is a 5-tuple* $(\mathsf{OTH}, \mathsf{UGH}, \mathsf{RH}, \mathsf{A}, \mathsf{Rel})$ *where:*

- $\mathsf{OTH} = (\mathsf{Obj}, \mathsf{T}, \leq_{\mathsf{OT}})$ *is an object hierarchy;*
- $\mathsf{UGH} = (\mathsf{U}, \mathsf{G}, \leq_{\mathsf{UG}})$ *is a user-group hierarchy;*
- $\mathsf{RH} = (\emptyset, \mathsf{R}, \leq_{\mathsf{R}})$ *is a role hierarchy;*
- A *is a set of actions;*
- Rel *is a set of relationships that can be defined on the different elements of DS;*

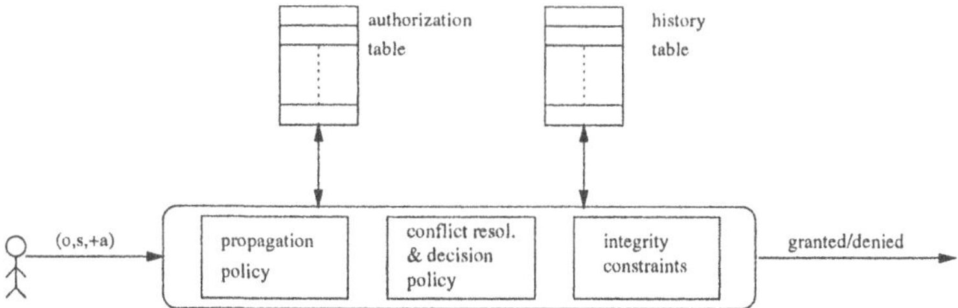

Fig. 4. Functional authorization architecture [26]

- OTH, UGH, *and* RH *are disjoint.*

Note that this definition of data system is very general as it may be used to represent any system by appropriately instantiating the five components listed above. Also, a system with no user-group, object, or role hierarchy can be represented by this definition. For instance, a data system with no role hierarchy is represented by a data system where $x \leq_{\mathsf{R}} y$ iff $x = y$.

Given an authorization triple $(s, o, \pm a)$, the authorization subject s can be a user, a group, or a role and the corresponding hierarchy, called *authorization subject hierarchy* (ASH), is intuitively obtained placing the two hierarchies UGH and RH side by side. The authorization object o can be an object, a type, or a role and the corresponding hierarchy, called *authorization object hierarchy* (AOH), is obtained placing the OTH and the inverse of RH side by side. The reason why the RH hierarchy is inverted, is to simplify the propagation rule for authorization objects: an authorization over a set of objects propagates down in the object hierarchy, while an authorization over a role propagates up in the role hierarchy. By inverting the RH hierarchy, we can simply propagate authorizations down in the authorization object hierarchy.

As depicted in Fig. 4, FAF includes the following components.

- A *history table* whose rows describe the accesses executed.
- An *authorization table* whose rows are authorizations composed of the triples (s, o, $\langle sign \rangle a$), where s is the subject, o the data item, a the action and $\langle sign \rangle$ may be '+' if the action is allowed and '−' if it is denied. This is the set of explicitly specified authorizations.
- The *propagation policy* specifies how to obtain new derived authorizations from those explicitly stored in the authorization table. Typically, derived authorizations are obtained according to hierarchy-based derivation policies. However, derivation policies are not restricted to this particular form of derivation. It is important to note that different propagation policies can be adopted in different hierarchies (ASH, AOH) and that, in the same structure, different sub-hierarchies may follow different policies.
- The *conflict resolution policy* describes how possible conflicts between the (explicit and/or derived) authorizations should be solved.

- A *decision policy* defines the response that should be returned to each access request. In case of conflicts or gaps (i.e., when an access is neither authorized nor denied), the decision policy determines the answer. In many systems, decisions assume either the open or the closed policy, where, by default, access is granted or denied, respectively.
- A set of *integrity constraints* that may impose restrictions on the content and output of the other components. Integrity rules can be used to individuate errors in the hierarchies or in the explicitly specified authorizations, or for implementing duty separation.

When a subject s requires the execution of action a on object o, the system needs to verify whether the authorization $(s, o, +a)$ or $(s, o, -a)$ can be derived using the authorization table, propagation policy, history table, conflict resolution policy, and decision policy that have been defined in the system. If a positive authorization is derived, then the access is allowed. Otherwise, if a negative authorization is derived, the access is denied.

As previously discussed, FAF allows the representation of different propagation policies, conflict resolution policies, and decision policies that a security system officer (SSO) might want to use. However, these policies represent only some of the possibilities and FAF is flexible enough to allow a SSO to express what she needs for her applications. To address this issue, the functional authorization architecture can be realized through the following approach:

- the authorization table is viewed as a database;
- policies are expressed by a restricted class of logic programs, called *authorization specification*, which have certain properties;
- the semantics of authorization specifications is given through the well known stable model semantics and well founded model semantics of logic programs, ensuring thus the existence of exactly one stable model;
- accesses will be allowed or denied on the basis of the truth value of an atom associated with the access in the unique stable model.

Accordingly, the *authorization specification logic* language (ASL) is a logic language used to encode the system security needs. ASL is created from the following alphabet.

- *Constant symbols* are members of the sets of users U, groups of users G, objects Obj, types of objects T, roles R, and actions A.
- *Variable symbols* are variables ranging over the sets U, G, Obj, T, R, and A.
- *Predicate symbols* are partitioned into three categories. The first category contains predicates needed to express the *access control policy*:
  - `cando`$(o, s, \pm a)$ explicitly represents the authorizations defined by the SSO: it allows (or denies, depending on the sign) subject s to execute action a on object o;
  - `dercando`$(o, s, \pm a)$ represents authorizations derived by the system;

- do(o, s, $\pm a$) represents the accesses that must be allowed or denied, and are obtained after the application of the conflict resolution and decision policies;
- done(o, s, r, a, t) keeps the history of the accesses executed. A fact of the form done(o, s, r, a, t) indicates that s operating in role r executed action a on object o at time t.
- over represents overriding policies in the authorization subject and/or authorization object hierarchies;
- error signals errors in the specification or use of authorizations; it can be used to enforce static and dynamic constraints on the specifications.

The second category of predicate symbols is the hie-predicates for the evaluation of hierarchical relationships between the elements of the data system (e.g., user's membership in groups, inclusion relationships between objects). There are two predicates:

- in(x, y, H) evaluates to true only if $x \leq y$ in the structure represented by hierarchy H, where H is ASH or AOH;
- dirin(x, y, H) evaluates to true only if x is a direct descendant of y in the hierarchy H, where H is ASH or AOH.

The third category of predicates is the rel-predicates that are used to express different relationships between elements in the data system. These predicates are not fixed by the model and are application specific. Examples of such predicates are the following:

- owner(o, s) specifies that subject s is the owner of object o in the system;
- isuser(s), isgroup(g), and isrole(r) evaluate to true only if their argument is a user, a group, or a role, respectively.

If p is one of the above-mentioned predicate symbols with arity n and $t_1, \ldots, t_n$ are terms appropriate for p, then $p(t_1, \ldots, t_n)$ is an *atom*. A *literal* is an atom or its negation. All these predicates, atoms and literals can be exploited to express a policy. We now illustrate how each component in Fig. 4 is represented by a set of rules.

History table. It contains only done predicates to keep track of the past accesses performed by the users. The instances of the done predicate are stored in a relation table with schema (Object, User, Role, Action, Time). For instance, done(*IS01, David, Admin, read, 15/05/2005 15:30*) denotes a *read* on object *IS01* executed by *David* playing role *Admin* at time *15/05/2005 15:30*.

Authorization table. It contains a finite set of *authorization rules* of the form:

$$\texttt{cando}(o,\ s,\ \langle sign\rangle a) \leftarrow L_1 \& \ldots \& L_n$$

where o is an object or an object type, s is a user or a group, $\langle sign\rangle$ is either '+' or '−', a is an action, and $L_1, \ldots, L_n$ are either done, hie- or rel- literals. If these literals are evaluated to true, the authorization on the left of the rule is granted. For instance, rule cando(*IS02*, s, $+r$) ← in(s, *Sales*, ASH) & ¬done(*IS02*,s, w, t) states that members of group *Sales* can read object *IS02* if they have not already modified object *IS02* at time t.

Propagation Policy	*Rules*		
No propagation	dercando(o, s, $+a$)	$\leftarrow$	cando(o, s, $+a$).
	dercando(o, s, $-a$)	$\leftarrow$	cando(o, s, $-a$).
No overriding	dercando(o, s, $+a$)	$\leftarrow$	cando(o, s', $+a$) & in(s, s', ASH).
	dercando(o, s, $-a$)	$\leftarrow$	cando(o, s', $-a$) & in(s, s', ASH).
Most specific overrides	dercando(o, s, $+a$)	$\leftarrow$	cando(o, s', $+a$) & $\neg$over$_{AS}$(s, o, s', $+a$) & in(s, s', ASH).
	dercando(o, s, $-a$)	$\leftarrow$	cando(o, s', $-a$) & $\neg$over$_{AS}$(s, o, s', $-a$) & in(s, s', ASH).
	over$_{AS}$(s, o, s', $+a$)	$\leftarrow$	cando(o, s'', $-a$) & in(s, s'', ASH)& in(s'', s', ASH)& $s'' \neq s'$.
	over$_{AS}$(s, o, s', $-a$)	$\leftarrow$	cando(o, s'', $+a$) & in(s, s'', ASH)& in(s'', s', ASH)& $s'' \neq s'$.
Path overrides	dercando(o, s, $+a$)	$\leftarrow$	cando(o, s, $+a$).
	dercando(o, s, $-a$)	$\leftarrow$	cando(o, s, $-a$).
	dercando(o, s, $+a$)	$\leftarrow$	dercando(o, s', $+a$) & $\neg$cando(o, s, $-a$) & dirin(s, s').
	dercando(o, s, $-a$)	$\leftarrow$	dercando(o, s', $-a$) & $\neg$cando(o, s, $+a$) & dirin(s, s').

Fig. 5. Rules enforcing different propagation policies on ASH

Propagation policies. The propagation policy is composed of two sets of rules: *overriding rules*, stating when an authorization can override another one; and *derivation rules*, representing the set of authorizations that can be derived by the authorizations explicitly defined. Overriding rules can be defined on the authorization subject hierarchy (over$_{AS}$) or on the authorization object hierarchy (over$_{AO}$) and are rules of the form:

$$\texttt{over}_{AS}(s, o, s', \langle sign\rangle a) \leftarrow L_1\& \ldots \& L_n$$
$$\texttt{over}_{AO}(o, o', s, \langle sign\rangle a) \leftarrow L_1\& \ldots \& L_n$$

where o and o' are objects or object types, s and s' are users or groups, $\langle sign\rangle$ is either '+' or '−', a is an action, and $L_1, \ldots, L_n$ are either cando, done, hie-, or rel- literals. If these literals evaluate to true, the overriding rule is applied. The derivation rules are of the form:

$$\texttt{dercando}(o, s, \langle sign\rangle a) \leftarrow L_1\& \ldots \& L_n$$

where o is an object or an object type, s is a user or a group, $\langle sign\rangle$ is either '+' or '−', a is an action, and $L_1, \ldots, L_n$ are either cando, over, dercando, done, hie-, or rel- literals. If these literals evaluate to true, the derivation rule is applied. For instance, rule dercando(*Received*, s, $+r$) $\leftarrow$ dercando(*Orders*, s, $+r$) derives a permission for a subject to read object type *Received* if there exists an (explicit or implicit) authorization for the subject to read object type *Orders*.

The set of dercando rules in the system is composed of all the authorizations that can be derived through the propagation policy defined by the SSO. Figure 5 illustrates the set of rules enforcing the most common propagation policies on the ASH hierarchy.

Conflict resolution and decision policies. The conflict resolution and decision policies allow the SSO to specify how conflicts are to be solved. A *decision rule* is a rule of the form:

$$\texttt{do}(o, s, +a) \leftarrow L_1 \& \ldots \& L_n$$

where o is an object or an object type, s is a user or a group, a is an action, and $L_1, \ldots, L_n$ are either cando, dercando, done, hie- or rel- literals. In addition to these positive decision rules, there is also the rule: $\texttt{do}(o, s, -a) \leftarrow \neg\texttt{do}(o, s, +a)$. This rule guarantees the completeness of the policy, that is, for each triple (o, s, a), one of the two $\texttt{do}(o, s, +a)$ or $\texttt{do}(o, s, -a)$ holds. Intuitively, the set of atoms $\texttt{do}(o, s, +a)$ specifies the set of all authorized accesses. For instance, rule $\texttt{do}(o, s, +r) \leftarrow \neg\texttt{dercando}(o, s, +r)\ \&\ \neg\texttt{dercando}(o, s, -r)\ \&\ \texttt{in}(o, \textit{Invoices}, \textsf{AOH})$ states that a subject s can read an object o if no authorization has been derived for s on an object of type *Invoices*. Figure 6 illustrates possible rules enforcing the most common conflict resolution and decision policies.

Integrity rules. Since there is a great potential for errors in the authorization specifications, it is possible to specify integrity rules defining constraints that must hold on the authorization specifications. An *integrity rule* is a rule of the form:

$$\texttt{error} \leftarrow L_1 \& \ldots \& L_n$$

where $L_1, \ldots, L_n$ are either cando, dercando, done, do, hie- or rel- literals. If these literals evaluate to true, an error occurs. Restrictions imposed through integrity constraints can be both general or specific to an application. For instance, rule $\texttt{error} \leftarrow \texttt{cando}(o, s, +a)\ \&\ \texttt{cando}(o, s, -a)$ states that an error occurs if there are two contradictory explicit cando predicates.

The integrity rules are evaluated after the access decision has been taken and can block its execution if an error is derived. They are also checked whenever a change occurs in some table used by the authorization framework: if the change implies an error, the corresponding operation is denied.

Authorization specifications are stated as logic rules defined on the predicates of the language. To ensure clean semantics and implementability, the format of the rules is restricted to guarantee (local) stratification of the resulting program (see Fig. 7).[4] The stratification also reflects the different semantics given to the predicates: cando will be used to specify basic authorizations, dercando will be used to enforce implication relationships and produce derived authorizations, and do to take the final access decision. Stratification ensures that the logic program corresponding to the rules has a unique stable model, which coincides with the well founded semantics [22]. Also, this model can be effectively computed in polynomial time. The authors of FAF also present a materialization technique for producing and storing the model corresponding to a set of logical rules. The model is computed on the initial specifications and updated with incremental maintenance strategies.

[4] A program is locally stratified if there is no recursion among predicates going through negation.

Conflict	*Decision*	*Rules*		
No conflict	**open**	error	$\leftarrow$	dercando(o, s, $+a$)& dercando(o, s, $-a$).
		do(o, s, $+a$)	$\leftarrow$	$\neg$dercando(o, s, $-a$).
No conflict	**closed**	error	$\leftarrow$	dercando(o, s, $+a$)& dercando(o, s, $-a$).
		do(o, s, $+a$)	$\leftarrow$	dercando(o, s, $+a$)& $\neg$dercando(o, s, $-a$).
Denials take p.	**open**	do(o, s, $+a$)	$\leftarrow$	$\neg$dercando(o, s, $-a$).
Denials take p.	**closed**	do(o, s, $+a$)	$\leftarrow$	dercando(o, s, $+a$)& $\neg$dercando(o, s, $-a$).
Permissions take p.	**open**	do(o, s, $+a$)	$\leftarrow$	dercando(o, s, $+a$).
		do(o, s, $+a$)	$\leftarrow$	$\neg$dercando(o, s, $-a$).
Permissions take p.	**closed**	do(o, s, $+a$)	$\leftarrow$	dercando(o, s, $+a$).
Nothing takes p.	**open**	do(o, s, $+a$)	$\leftarrow$	$\neg$dercando(o, s, $-a$).
Nothing takes p.	**closed**	do(o, s, $+a$)	$\leftarrow$	dercando(o, s, $+a$)& $\neg$dercando(o, s, $-a$).
Additional closure rule		do(o, s, $-a$)	$\leftarrow$	$\neg$do(o, s, $+a$).

Fig. 6. Conflict resolution and decision policies rules

Stratum	*Predicate*	*Rules defining predicates*
0	hie-predicates	Base relations.
	rel-predicates	Base relations.
	done	Base relation.
1	cando	Body may contain done, hie-, and rel- literals.
2	dercando	Body may contain cando, dercando, done, hie-, and rel- literals. Occurrences of dercando literals must be positive.
3	do	When head is of the form do(_, _, $+a$), body may contain cando, dercando, done, hie-, and rel- literals.
4	do	When head is of the form do(o, s, $-a$), body contains just one literal $\neg$do(o, s, $+a$).
5	error	Body may contain do, cando, dercando, done, hie-, and rel- literals.

Fig. 7. Rule composition and stratification of FAF

An Example of FAF Application

A simplified scenario is constructed to describe the application of the FAF model and language. Consider an online computer store where objects are organized according to the hierarchy in Fig. 2, and users are grouped as illustrated in Fig. 1. Suppose also that the system does not use roles.

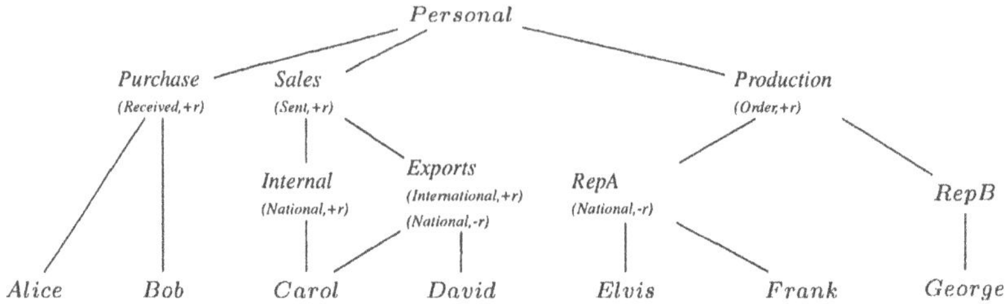

Fig. 8. An example of labeled user-group hierarchy

The SSO defines the set of initial `done`, `hie`-, and `rel`- literals. For simplicity, we assume that the system has no `done` predicates. The `dirin`-literals necessary for the definition of the subject and object hierarchies follow the arcs in the graphs in Fig. 1 and in Fig. 2, respectively.

From the `dirin` literals explicitly specified by the SSO, it is possible to verify the validity of the `in` literals. The following are examples of protection requirements, where r is used to denote the read action.

- Members of the *Purchase* group can read *Received Invoices*.
  `cando`(o, s, $+r$) ← `in`(s, *Purchase*, ASH) & `in`(o, *Received*, AOH)
- Members of the *Sales* group can read *Sent Invoices*.
  `cando`(o, s, $+r$) ← `in`(s, *Sales*, ASH) & `in`(o, *Sent*, AOH).
- Members of the *Internal* group can read *National Orders*.
  `cando`(o, s, $+r$) ← `in`(s, *Internal*, ASH) & `in`(o, *National*, AOH).
- Members of the *Exports* group can read *International Orders*.
  `cando`(o, s, $+r$) ← `in`(s, *Exports*, ASH) & `in`(o, *International*, AOH).
- Members of the *Production* group can read any kind of *Orders*.
  `cando`(o, s, $+r$) ← `in`(s, *Production*, ASH) & `in`(o, *Orders*, AOH).
- Members of the *RepA* group cannot read *National Orders*.
  `cando`(o, s, $-r$) ← `in`(s, *RepA*, ASH) & `in`(o, *National*, AOH).
- Members of the *Exports* group cannot read *National Orders*.
  `cando`(o, s, $-r$) ← `in`(s, *Exports*, ASH) & `in`(o, *National*, AOH).

After the definition of these explicit authorizations, the SSO needs to choose a propagation policy. Suppose that the *most specific overrides* principle has been chosen and that the propagation is performed on the authorization subject hierarchy ASH. First, for each explicit authorization (s, o, $\pm a$), the propagation process associates with subject s in the hierarchy a pair of the form $\langle obj, \pm a \rangle$. Figure 8 illustrates the resulting labeled hierarchy.

The authorizations are then propagated along the hierarchy thus obtaining the following set of `dercando` literals.

- `dercando`(*Received*, *Purchase*, $+r$)
- `dercando`(*Received*, *Alice*, $+r$)
- `dercando`(*Received*, *Bob*, $+r$)
- `dercando`(*Sent*, *Sales*, $+r$)

- dercando(*Sent*, *Internal*, $+r$); dercando(*National*, *Internal*, $+r$)
- dercando(*Sent*, *Exports*, $+r$); dercando(*International*, *Exports*, $+r$); dercando(*National*, *Exports*, $-r$)
- dercando(*Sent*, *David*, $+r$); dercando(*International*, *David*, $+r$); dercando(*National*, *David*, $-r$)
- dercando(*Sent*, *Carol*, $+r$); dercando(*International*, *Carol*, $+r$); dercando(*National*, *Carol*, $+r$); dercando(*National*, *Carol*, $-r$)[5]
- dercando(*Orders*, *Production*, $+r$)
- dercando(*International*, *RepA*, $+r$); dercando(*National*, *RepA*, $-r$)
- dercando(*International*, *Elvis*, $+r$); dercando(*National*, *Elvis*, $-r$)
- dercando(*International*, *Frank*, $+r$); dercando(*National*, *Frank*, $-r$)
- dercando(*Orders*, *RepB*, $+r$)
- dercando(*Orders*, *George*, $+r$)

It is easy to see that there are some conflicts. The first conflict arises because members of the *RepA* group can read the objects in *Orders* and cannot read objects in the subset *National*. However, according to the *most specific overrides* principle, members of the group *RepA* can read *Orders* that do not belong to the *National* category and cannot read objects in the *National* category.

The second conflict involves user *Carol* who is a member of the group *Internal* and group *Exports* and for which there is a positive and negative authorization on *National*, respectively. In this case, the conflict can be solved by applying, for example, the *denials take precedence principle* together with the *closed* policy. The result of this last step is a set of do literals representing all the triples (s, o, $\pm a$) derivable in the structure.

We now examine some examples of access requests and analyze whether these requests will be granted or denied.

Request 1. *Alice* requests to read object *IS02*.
Access denied. There is neither an explicit authorization nor an implicit authorization and therefore, according to the default closed policy, the access is denied.

Request 2. *Carol* requests to read object *ON01*.
Access denied. Object *ON01* is a member of class *National* and according to the denials take precedence principle *Carol* cannot read national orders.

Request 3. *Frank* requests to read object *ON01*.
Access denied. *Frank* is a member of group *RepA*, object *ON01* is a member of class *National* and, according to the most specific overrides principle, the *RepA* group cannot read national orders.

Request 4. *Frank* requests to read object *OI01*.
Access allowed. *Frank* is a member of group *RepA* and object *OI01* is a member of class *Orders* and is not a member of class *National*.

[5] There is a conflict that cannot be solved at this point of the policy evaluation process.

4 XML-Based Access Control Languages

Although logic-based access control models and languages are powerful and expressive, they are not immediately suited to the Internet context, where simplicity and easy integration with existing technology must be ensured. Therefore, an interesting aspect to be addressed concerns the definition of a language for expressing and exchanging policies based on a high level formulation that, while powerful, can be easily interchangeable and both human and machine readable. Insights in this respect can be taken from recent proposals expressing access control policies as XML documents. Indeed, the *eXtensible Markup Language* (XML) [49], a markup metalanguage standardized by the World Wide Web Consortium (W3C), is the standard language for information exchange on the Internet and many XML-based access control languages have been proposed. The first advantage of this class of access control languages is their simplicity in policy definition. Another important advantage of XML-based access control languages is the *interoperability*, that consists in the possibility of exchanging policies through different systems using the same access control language. This feature is particularly interesting in an open environment like the Internet, where a single system, which has to be protected as a single entity, may be distributed over the Net.

Initially, XML-based access control languages were thought only for the protection of resources that were themselves XML files [14, 15, 20, 21]. In [14, 15] authorizations can be positive and negative and can be defined both at the document-level or at the Document Type Definition (DTD) level (in this case authorizations propagate to all instances of the DTD). Authorizations are characterized by a type field defining how the authorizations must be treated with respect to propagation at finer granules and overriding (exception support). The model in [29] supports read and write privileges. The authors define three types of propagation policies: no propagation, propagation up (an authorization referring to an element is propagated to all its parent elements) or propagation down (an authorization referring to an element is propagated to all its sub-elements). The conflict resolution policy is either "denials take precedence" or "permissions take precedence". The main contribution of this paper is the definition of *provisional authorizations* that specify actions that a user has to perform before obtaining a given privilege. The model in [21] supports the read privilege only. The authors do not define any propagation policy. The conflict resolution policy is based on the priority of the different rules. More recently, in [20] has been proposed an approach that tries to address the `write` privilege based on the non-standard XML update language `XUpdate`. The author separates the existence of an XML value and its content adding a new position privilege that allows to know the existence of a node but not its content. Nodes tagged with a position privilege are shown with a `restricted` label.

These proposals have the common characteristic that they present a model for securing XML documents. Recent proposals instead use XML to define languages for expressing protection requirements on any kind of data/resources [2, 13, 17, 39]. Two relevant XML-based access control languages are WS-Policy [13] and the *eXtensible Access Control Markup Language* (XACML) [17]. Based on the WS-

Security [3], WS-Policy provides a grammar for expressing Web service policies. The WS-Policy includes a set of general messaging related assertions defined in WS-PolicyAssertions [11] and a set of security policy assertions related to supporting the WS-Security specification defined in WS-SecurityPolicy [44]. In addition, WS-PolicyAttachment [12] defines how to attach these policies to Web services or other subjects such as service locators. XACML is the result of a recent OASIS standardization effort proposing an XML-based language to express and interchange access control policies. XACML is designed to express authorization policies in XML against objects that can themselves be identified in XML. The XACML language has the great advantage that it can be used to express a variety of different policies and has the basic functionalities of most policy representation mechanisms. Moreover, XACML has standard *extension points* for defining new functions, data types, combining logic, and so on. While XACML and WS-Policy share some common characteristics, XACML has the advantage of enjoying an underlying policy model as a basis, resulting in a clean and unambiguous semantics of the language [2]. For this reason, XACML is the most common XML-based access control language used. In the remainder of this Section, we illustrate XACML as our choice of language.

4.1 XACML Policy Definition

XACML relies on a model that provides a *formal* representation of the access control security policy and its working. This modeling phase is essential to ensure a clear and unambiguous language which could otherwise be subject to different interpretations and uses. The main concepts of interest in the XACML policy language model are *rule*, *policy*, and *policy set*.

An XACML policy has, as root element, either a `Policy` or a `PolicySet`. A `PolicySet` is a collection of `Policy` or `PolicySet`. An XACML policy consists of a set of *rules*, a *target*, an optional set of *obligations*, and a *rule combining algorithm*. A `Rule` specifies a permission (`permit`) or a denial (`deny`) for a subject to perform an action on an object. A `Target` basically consists of a simplified set of conditions for the subject, resource, and action that must be satisfied for a policy to apply to a given request. If all the conditions of a `Target` are satisfied, then its associated `Policy` (or `PolicySet`) applies to the request. An `Obligation` is an operation that has to be performed in conjunction with the enforcement of an authorization decision. Each `Policy` also defines a rule combining algorithm used for reconciling the decisions each rule makes. The final decision value, called *authorization decision*, is the value of the policy as defined by the rule combining algorithm. An authorization decision can be `permit`, `deny`, `not applicable` (when no applicable policies or rules could be found), or `indeterminate` (when some errors occurred during the access control process). XACML defines different combining algorithms such as *deny overrides* (i.e., denials take precedence), *permit overrides* (i.e., permissions take precedence), *first applicable* (i.e., the first applicable rule is considered), and *only-one-applicable* (i.e., a deny or permit result is obtained only if exactly one rule is applicable).

The `PolicySet` element is similar to the `Policy` element and consists of a set of *policies* (instead of *rules*), a *target*, an optional set of *obligations*, and a *policy combining algorithm* (instead of a rule combining algorithm).

The `Rule` element specifies the actual conditions under which access is to be allowed or denied. The components of a rule are an optional *target*, an *effect*, and a *condition*. The target defines the set of resources, subjects, and actions to which the rule is intended to apply. The effect of the rule can be `permit` or `deny`. The condition represents a boolean expression that may further refine the applicability of the rule.

An important feature of XACML is that a rule is based on the definition and evaluation of attributes corresponding to specific characteristics of a subject, resource, action, or environment. Any request is mainly composed of attributes that will be compared to attribute values in a policy to make an access decision. Attributes are identified by the `SubjectAttributeDesignator`, `ResourceAttributeDesignator`, `ActionAttributeDesignator`, and `EnvironmentAttributeDesignator` elements. These elements use the `AttributeValue` element to define the value of a particular attribute. Alternatively, the `AttributeSelector` element can be used to specify where to retrieve a particular attribute. Note that both the attribute designator and attribute selector elements can return multiple values. To this reason, XACML provides an attribute type, called *bag*, that is an unordered collection and can contain duplicate values for a particular attribute. To correctly handle the data type bag, XACML has a powerful set of functions that can work on arbitrary collections of values and return any kind of attribute value supported in the system. Functions can also be nested, that is, the output of a function is the input of another. The XACML defines a set of basic functions that can be enriched by adding application-specific functions. Since often resources are represented in a hierarchical structure (e.g., file system), XACML v. 2.0 introduces a method for handling hierarchical resources (see Sect. 2). More precisely, XACML v. 2.0 provides a mechanism for:

- representing the identity of a node;
- requesting access to a node;
- stating policies that apply to one or more nodes.

The hierarchy can be both a tree or a forest and cannot have cycles. It is important to note that there are two different ways for representing a resource in a hierarchy [42]. In the first one, the hierarchy to which the node belongs is represented as a XML document and the resource is represented as a node in the XML document. In the second case, the hierarchy is not represented as a XML document and has no representation. Analogously, subjects can be hierarchically represented (see Sect. 2) but XACML does not offer any functionality for managing groups of subjects. This is mainly due to the fact that XACML is used in distributed systems, consequently the resource handler cannot know the whole user-group hierarchy. However, XACML provides a way for checking at any time if a user belongs to a specific group: when a request for a resource is submitted, the resource handler checks the requester's properties, as these are automatically inserted in the same request. Among these properties, there is the set of groups to which the user belongs. XACML also supports the role-based access control [19].

As a simple example of policy, consider the example introduced in Sect. 3.1. Suppose that the online computer store defines the following high level policy: "Members of the *Sales* group can read invoice *IS02*".

Figure 9 shows the XACML policy corresponding to this high level policy. The policy applies to requests on the `http://www.example.com/documents/invoices/sent/IS02.xml` resource. It has one rule with a target that requires a read action and a condition that evaluates to true only if the subject is a member of the group *Sales*.

4.2 XACML Request and Response

XACML defines also a standard format for expressing requests and responses. Each request contains attributes for the subject, resource, action, and, optionally, for the environment. More precisely, each request includes exactly one set of attributes for the resource and action and at most one set of environment attributes. There may be multiple sets of subject attributes each of which is identified by a category URI.

A response element contains one or more results each of which corresponds to the result of an evaluation. Each result contains three elements, namely `Decision`, `Status`, and `Obligations`. The `Decision` element specifies the authorization decision, the `Status` element indicates if some error occurred during the evaluation process, and the optional `Obligations` element states the obligations to fulfill.

As an example, suppose that *Carol* wants to read the `http://www.example.com/documents/invoices/sent/IS02.xml` resource. Figure 10 illustrates the corresponding XACML request. This request is compared with the XACML policy in Fig. 9. The result is that the user is allowed to access the requested resource.

```
<Policy PolicyId="SentInvoice" RuleCombiningAlgId="urn:oasis:names:tc:
xacml:1.0:rule-combining-algorithm:deny-overrides">
  <Target>
    <Subjects>
      <AnySubject/>
    </Subjects>
    <Resources>
      <Resource>
        <ResourceMatch MatchId="urn:oasis:names:tc:xacml:1.0:
        function:anyURI-equal">
          <AttributeValue
          DataType="http://www.w3.org/2001/XMLSchema#anyURI">
            http://www.example.com/documents/invoices/sent/IS02.xml
          </AttributeValue>
          <ResourceAttributeDesignator
          DataType="http://www.w3.org/2001/XMLSchema#anyURI"
          AttributeId="urn:oasis:names:tc:xacml:1.0:resource:resource-id"/>
        </ResourceMatch>
      </Resource>
    </Resources>
    <Actions>
      <AnyAction/>
    </Actions>
  </Target>
  <Rule RuleId="ReadRule" Effect="Permit">
    <Target>
      <Subjects>
        <AnySubject/>
      </Subjects>
      <Resources>
        <AnyResource/>
      </Resources>
      <Actions>
        <Action>
          <ActionMatch MatchId="urn:oasis:names:tc:xacml:1.0:
          function:string-equal">
            <AttributeValue
            DataType="http://www.w3.org/2001/XMLSchema#string">
              read
            </AttributeValue>
            <ActionAttributeDesignator
            DataType="http://www.w3.org/2001/XMLSchema#string"
            AttributeId="urn:oasis:names:tc:xacml:1.0:action:action-id"/>
          </ActionMatch>
        </Action>
      </Actions>
    </Target>
    <Condition FunctionId="urn:oasis:names:tc:xacml:1.0:
    function:string-equal">
      <Apply FunctionId="urn:oasis:names:tc:xacml:1.0:
      function:string-one-and-only">
        <SubjectAttributeDesignator
        DataType="http://www.w3.org/2001/XMLSchema#string"
        AttributeId="group"/>
      </Apply>
      <AttributeValue DataType="http://www.w3.org/2001/XMLSchema#string">
        Sales
      </AttributeValue>
    </Condition>
  </Rule>
</Policy>
```

Fig. 9. An example of XACML policy

```
<Request>
  <Subject>
    <Attribute AttributeId="urn:oasis:names:tc:xacml:1.0:subject:subject-id"
      DataType="urn:oasis:names:tc:xacml:1.0:data-type:rfc822Name">
        <AttributeValue>Carol@example.com</AttributeValue>
    </Attribute>
    <Attribute AttributeId="group"
      DataType="http://www.w3.org/2001/XMLSchema#string"
      Issuer="administrator@example.com">
        <AttributeValue>Sales</AttributeValue>
    </Attribute>
  </Subject>
  <Resource>
    <Attribute AttributeId="urn:oasis:names:tc:xacml:1.0:resource:resource-id"
      DataType="http://www.w3.org/2001/XMLSchema#anyURI">
      <AttributeValue>http://www.example.com/documents/invoices/sent/IS02.xml
      </AttributeValue>
    </Attribute>
  </Resource>
  <Action>
    <Attribute AttributeId="urn:oasis:names:tc:xacml:1.0:action:action-id"
      DataType="http://www.w3.org/2001/XMLSchema#string">
        <AttributeValue>read</AttributeValue>
    </Attribute>
  </Action>
</Request>
```

Fig. 10. An example of XACML request

4.3 XACML Architecture

Figure 11 illustrates the main entities involved in the XACML domain. The standard gives a definition of these concepts that we summarize as follows.

- The *Policy Evaluation Point* (PEP) module receives initially the access request in a naive format and passes it to the Context Handler. Similarly, when a decision has been taken by the decision point, PEP enforces the access decision that it receives from the Context Handler.
- The *Policy Decision Point* (PDP) module receives an access request and interacts with the PAP that encapsulates the information needed to identify the applicable policies. It then evaluates the request against the applicable policies and returns the authorization decision to the Context Handler module.
- The *Policy Administration Point* (PAP) module is an interface for searching policies. It retrieves the policies applicable to a given access request and returns them to the PDP module.
- The *Policy Information Point* (PIP) module provides attribute values about the subject, resource, and action. It interacts directly with the Context Handler.
- The *Context Handler* translates the access requests in a native format into a canonical format. Basically, it acts as a bridge between PDP and PEP modules and it is in charge for retrieving attribute values needed for policy evaluation.
- The *Environment* provides a set of attributes that are relevant to take an authorization decision and are independent from a particular subject, resource, and action.

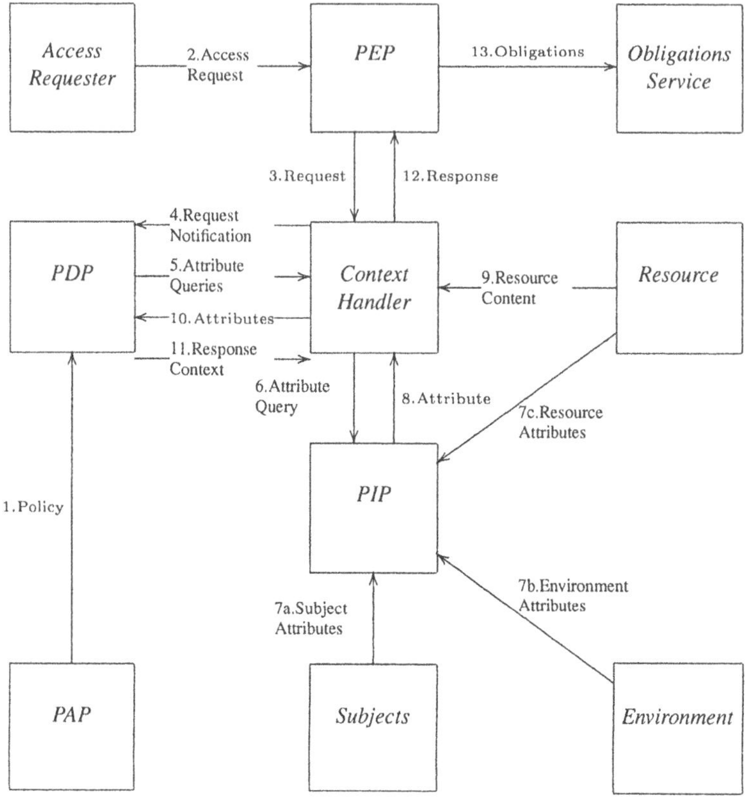

Fig. 11. XACML overview [17]

- The *Obligations Service* module manages obligations, which are the operations that should be performed by the PEP when enforcing the final authorization decision.
- The *Access Requester* module makes requests to the system in a naive form.
- A *Resource* is a service or a data collection available for requests.
- The *Subjects* are the actors of the system; they usually have attributes that can be used in predicates.

The XACML data-flow (Fig. 11) is not limited to the phase of evaluating an access request but involves also an initialization phase. More precisely, the data-flow consists of the following steps.

1. The policies are made available by the PAP to the PDP to fulfill the resource owner needs.
2. The access requester communicates her request to the PEP module in a naive format.

3. The PEP transmits the original request to the Context Handler, possibly together with attributes of the subject, resource, action and environment involved in the request.
4. The Context Handler builds *XACML request context*, with the information provided by the PEP and sends it to the PDP.
5. In case of additional attributes of the subject, resource, action, or environment are needed, the PDP asks for them to the Context Handler.
6. The Context Handler sends the attribute request coming from the PDP to the PIP module.
7. The PIP module retrieves the attributes interacting directly with Subject, Resource, and Environment.
8. The PIP sends the attributes just obtained to the Context Handler.
9. The Context Handler inserts the resource in the context created at step 4.
10. The attributes obtained from the PIP and eventually the resource involved in the access request are sent by the Context Handler to the PDP. The PDP can now evaluate the policies and take a decision.
11. The PDP sends to the Context Handler the *XACML response context* that includes the final decision.
12. The Context Handler translates the *XACML response context* in the naive format used by the PEP module and sends the final response to the PEP.
13. The PEP fulfills the obligations included in the response and, if the access is permitted, the PEP grants access to the resource. Otherwise, the access is denied.

Although XACML is suitable for a variety of different applications, the PDP module needs to receive standardized input and returns standardized output. Therefore, any implementation of XACML has to be able to translate the attribute representation in the application environment (e.g., SAML or CORBA) in the corresponding XACML context.

5 Credential-Based Access Control Languages

Open environments are characterized by a number of systems offering different services. In such a scenario, interoperability is a very important issue and traditional assumptions for establishing and enforcing access control regulations do not hold anymore. A server may receive requests not just from the local community of users, but also from remote, previously unknown users. The server may not be able to authenticate these users or to specify authorizations for them (with respect to their identity). The traditional separation between *authentication* and *access control* cannot be applied in this context, and alternative access control solutions should be devised. A possible solution to this problem is represented by the use of *digital certificates* (or *credentials*), representing statements certified by given entities (e.g., certification authorities), which can be used to establish properties of their holder (such as identity, accreditation, or authorizations) [18, 23].

The development of access control systems based on credentials is not a simple task and the following issues need to be investigated [10].

- *Ontologies.* Due to the openness of the scenario and the richness and variety of security requirements and attributes that may need to be considered, it is important to provide parties with a means to understand each other with respect to the properties they enjoy (or request the counterpart to enjoy). Therefore, common languages, dictionaries, and ontologies must be developed.
- *Client-side and server-side restrictions.* In an open scenario, *mutual access control* is an important security feature in which a client should be able to prove its eligibility for a service, and the server communicates to the client the requirements it needs to satisfy to get access.
- *Credential-based access control rules.* It is necessary to develop languages supporting access control rules based on credentials and these languages have to be flexible and expressive enough for users. The most important challenge in defining a language is the trade off between expressiveness and simplicity: the language should be expressive enough for defining different kinds of policies and simple enough for the final user.
- *Access control evaluation and outcome.* Users may be occasional and they may not know under what conditions a service can be accessed. Therefore, to make a service "usable", access control mechanisms cannot simply return "yes" or "no" answers. It may be necessary to explain why accesses are denied, or - better - how to obtain the desired permissions. Therefore, the system can return an *undefined response* meaning that current information is insufficient to determine whether the request can be granted or denied. For instance, suppose that a user can access a service if she is at least eighteen and can provide a credit card number. Two cases can occur: *i)* the system knows that the user is not yet eighteen and therefore returns a negative response; *ii)* the user has proved that she is eighteen and the system returns an undefined response together with the request to provide the number of a credit card.
- *Privacy-enhanced policy communication.* Since the server does not return a simple yes/no answer to access requests, but returns the set of credentials that clients have to submit for obtaining access, there is a need for correctly and concisely representing them. The naive way to formulate a credential request, that is, giving the client a list with all the possible sets of credentials that would enable the service, is not feasible, due to the large number of possible alternatives. Also, the communication process should not disclose "too much" of the underlying security policy, which might also be regarded as sensitive information. Analogously, the client should be able to select in private a minimal set of credentials whose submission will authorize the desired service.

Blaze et al. [8] presented an approach for accessing services on the Web. This work is therefore limited to the Web scenario and is based on identity certificates only. The first proposals investigating the application of credential-based access control regulating access to a server were made by Winslett et al. [38, 47]. Here, access control rules are expressed in a logic language and rules applicable to an access can be communicated by the server to clients. In [46, 50] the authors investigate trust negotiation issues and strategies that a party can apply to select credentials to submit to the opponent party in a negotiation. More recently, in [50] the *PRUdent NEgotiation Strategy* (PRUNES) has been presented. This strategy ensures that the client communicates its credentials to the server only if the access will be granted and the set of certificates communicated to the server is the minimal necessary for granting it. Each party defines a set of *credential policies* that regulates how and under what conditions the party releases its credentials. The negotiation consists of a series of requests for credentials and counter-requests on the basis of the parties' credential policies. The credential policies established can be graphically represented through a tree, called *negotiation search tree*, composed of two kinds of nodes: *credential nodes*, representing the need for a specific credential, and *disjunctive nodes*, representing the logic operators connecting the conditions for credential release. The root of a tree node is a service (i.e., the resource the client wants to access). The negotiation can therefore be seen as a backtracking operation on the tree. The backtracking can be executed according to different strategies. For instance, a *brute-force* backtracking is complete and correct, but is too expensive to be used in a real scenario. The authors therefore propose the PRUNES method that prunes the search tree without compromising completeness or correctness of the negotiation process. The basic idea is that if a credential C has just been evaluated and the state of the system is not changed too much, than it is useless to evaluate again the same credential, as the result will be exactly as the result previously computed.

It has been demonstrated that the PRUNES method is correct and that the communication time is $O(n^2)$ and the computational time is $O(n \cdot m)$, where n is the number of credentials involved in the trust establishment process, and m is the total size of the credential disclosure policies related to the same credentials.

The same research group proposed also a method for allowing parties adopting different negotiation strategies to interoperate through the definition of a *Disclosure Tree Strategy* (DTS) family [52]. The authors show that if two parties use different strategies from the DST family, they are able to establish a negotiation process. The DTS family is a closed set, that is, if a negotiation strategy can interoperate with any DST strategy, it must also be a member of the DST family.

In [51] a *Unified Schema for Resource Protection* (UniPro) has been proposed. This mechanism is used to protect the information in policies. UniPro gives (opaque) names to policies and allows any named policy P_1 to has its own policy P_2 meaning that the contents of P_1 can only be disclosed to parties who have shown that they satisfy P_2. Another approach for implementing access control based on credentials is the *Adaptive Trust Negotiation and Access Control* (ATNAC) [36]. This method grants or denies access to a resource on the basis of a *suspicion level* associated with subjects. The suspicion level is not fixed but may vary on the basis of the probability that the user has malicious intents. In [43] the authors propose to apply the automated trust negotiation technology for enabling secure transactions between portable devices that have no pre-existing relationship.

In [53] the same research group proposed a negotiation architecture, called *TrustBuilder*, that is independent from the language used for policy definition and from the strategies adopted by the two parties for policy enforcement.

Other logic-based access control languages based on credentials have been introduced. For instance, D1LP and RT [32–34], the SD3 language [28], and Binder [16]. In [27, 48] logic languages are adopted to specify access restrictions in a certificate-based access control model.

5.1 A Credential-Based Access Control Language

A first attempt to provide a uniform framework for attribute-based access control specification and enforcement was presented by Bonatti and Samarati in [10]. Like in previous proposals, access regulations are specified as logical rules, where some predicates are explicitly identified. Each party has a *portfolio*, that is, a collection of credentials and declarations (unsigned statements), and has associated a set of services that can provide. Credentials are essentially digital certificates, and must be unforgeable and verifiable through the issuing certificate authority's public key; declarations are instead statements made by the user herself, that autonomously issues a declaration. Abstractions can be defined on services, grouping them in sets, called *classes*. The main advantage of this proposal is that it allows to exchange the minimal set of certificates, that is, client communicates the minimal set of certificates to the server, and the server releases the minimal set of conditions required for granting access. To this purpose, the server defines a set of *service accessibility rules*, expressing the necessary and sufficient conditions for granting access to a resource. On the other hand, both clients and severs can specify a set of *portfolio disclosure rules*, used to establish the conditions under which credentials and declarations may be released.

The rules both in the service accessibility and portfolio disclosure sets are defined through a logic language. The language includes a set of predicates whose meaning is expressed on the basis of the current *state*. The state indicates the parties' characteristics and the status of the current negotiation process, that is, the certificates already exchanged, the requests made by the two parties, and so on. The basic predicates of the language are the following.

- `credential(c, K)` evaluates to true if the current state contains certificate `c` verifiable using key `K`.
- `declaration(d)` evaluates to true if the current state contains declaration `d`, where `d` is of the form *attribute-name=value-term*.
- `cert-authority(CA, K`$_{CA}$`)` evaluates to true if the party using it in her policy trusts certificates issued by certificate authority `CA`, whose public key is K_{CA}.
- A set of non predefined predicates necessary for evaluating the current *state* values; these predicates can evaluate both the *persistent* and the *negotiation state*. The persistent state contains information that is stored on the site and is not related to a single negotiation but to the party itself. The negotiation state is related to the information on a single negotiation and is removed at the end of the same.

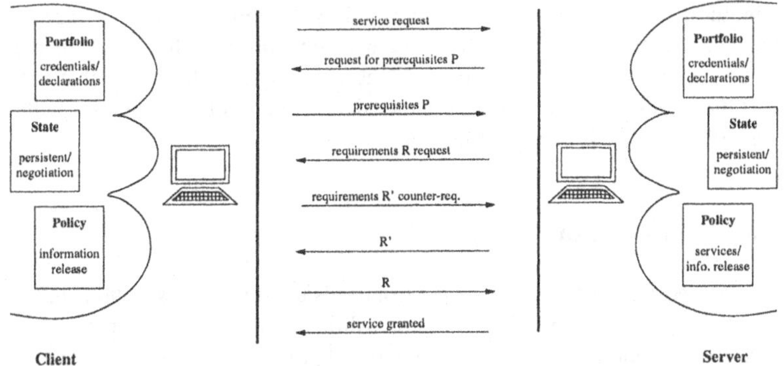

Fig. 12. Client-server negotiation

- A set of non predefined *abbreviation* predicates that are used to abbreviate requirements in the negotiation phase.
- A standard set of mathematical built-in predicates, such as $=$, $\neq$, and $\leq$.

The rules for service accessibility and portfolio disclosure have, in their body, a composition of the above-mentioned predicates, and in their head the specification of the services accessible or the certificates releasable according to the same rule. Figure 12 illustrates the client/server interaction that can be summarized as follows.

1. The client sends a request for a service to the server.
2. The server asks to the client a set of prerequisites, that is, a set of necessary conditions for granting access.
3. The client sends back the required prerequisites.
4. If the prerequisites are sufficient, than the server individuates the credentials and declarations needed to grant access to the resource.
5. The client evaluates the requests against its portfolio release rules and makes, eventually, some counter-requests.
6. The server sends back to the client the required certificates and declarations.
7. The client fulfills the server's requests.
8. The service is then granted to the client.

Since there may exist different policy combinations that may bring the access request to satisfaction, the communication of credentials and/or declarations could be an expensive task. To overcome this issue, the *abbreviation* predicates are used to abbreviate requests. Besides the necessity of abbreviations, it is also necessary for the server, before releasing rules to the client, to evaluate state predicates that involve private information. For instance, the client is not expected to be asked many times the same information during the same session and if the server has to evaluate if the client is considered or not trusted, it cannot communicate this request to the client itself.

Communication of requisites to be satisfied by the requester is then based on a filtering and renaming process applied on the server's policy, which exploits partial evaluation techniques in logic programs. The authors formally prove that the set of requirements that enable a service under the original policy coincides with the requirements specified by the filtering rules.

6 Policy Composition

In many real world situations, access control needs to combine restrictions independently stated that should be enforced as one, while retaining their independence and administrative autonomy. For instance, the global policy of a large organization can be the combination of the policies of its different departments and divisions as well as of externally imposed constraints (e.g., privacy regulations); each of these policies should be taken into account while remaining independent and autonomously managed. Policy composition is an orthogonal aspect with respect to the ones described in the previous sections, as policy composition should be independent from the languages adopted by each single entity.

In [9], the authors presented the following criteria that a composition framework for access control policies should satisfy.

- *Heterogeneous policy support.* The framework should support policies expressed in different languages and enforced by different mechanisms.
- *Support of unknown policies.* The framework should support policies that are not known a priori or that are only partially defined. Policies are therefore treated as black-boxes that can be queried at access control time and return a correct and complete response.
- *Controlled interference.* Policies cannot simply be merged as this may cause interferences and side effects. For instance, the accesses granted/denied might not correctly reflect the specifications anymore.
- *Expressiveness.* The language should support different methods for combining policies, without changing the input specifications and without ad-hoc extensions to authorizations.
- *Support of different abstraction levels.* The composition should highlight the different components and their interplay at different levels of abstraction.
- *Formal semantics.* The composition language should be declarative, implementation independent, and based on a solid framework to avoid ambiguity.

Various models have been proposed to reason about security policies [1, 24, 25, 35]. In [1, 25] the authors focused on the secure behavior of program modules. McLean [35] proposed a formal approach including combination operators: he introduced *the algebra of security*, that is a Boolean algebra that enables to reason about the problem of policy conflict, arising when different policies are combined. However, even though this approach permits to detect conflicts between policies, it did not propose a method to resolve the conflicts and to construct a security policy from inconsistent sub-policies. Hosmer [24] introduced the notion of meta-policies (i.e., policies about policies), an informal framework for combining security policies. Subsequently, Bell [4] formalized the combination of two policies with a function, called *policy combiner*, and introduced the notion of *policy attenuation* to allow the composition of conflicting security policies. Other approaches are targeted to the development of a uniform framework to express possibly heterogeneous policies [7, 26, 27, 31, 48]. A different approach has been illustrated in [9] where the authors proposed an algebra for combining security policies together with its formal semantics. Following this work, Jajodia et al. [45] presented a propositional algebra for policies with a syntax consisting of abstract symbols for atomic policy expressions and composition operators. This framework has two classes of operators: *internal* and *external*. In the following, we will explain more in details the algebra for policy composition presented in [9].

6.1 An Algebra for Composing Access Control Policies

The need for a policy composition framework by which different component policies can be integrated while retaining their independence was first identified in [9]. Here, the authors propose an algebra of security policies together with its formal semantics and illustrate how complex policies can be formulated as expressions of the algebra. A policy is defined as a set of triples of the form (s,o,a), where s is a constant in (or a variable over) the set of subjects S, o is a constant in (or a variable over) the set of objects Obj, and a is a constant in (or a variable over) the set of actions A. Here, complex policies can then be obtained by combining policy identifiers, denoted P_i, through the *algebra operators*. The proposed algebra is parametric with respect to two languages: the *authorization constraint language*, used to specify the conditions under which a ground authorization is valid; and the *rule language*, used to state how a set of ground authorizations can be closed by deriving new authorizations from the ground set.

Algebra Syntax and Semantics

We are now ready to define the syntax and semantics of the algebra. Formally, the syntax is given by the following BNF grammar:

$$E ::= \mathbf{id} | E + E | E \& E | E - E | E \hat{} C | o(E,E,E) | E * R | T(E) | (E)$$
$$T ::= \tau \mathbf{id}.E$$

where **id** is a unique policy identifier, E is a policy expression, T is a construct, called *template*, C is a construct describing constraints, and R is a construct describing rules. The order of evaluation of operators is determined by the precedence which is (from higher to lower) τ, ., + and & and -, * and ^.

The semantics is a function mapping each policy expression in a set of ground authorizations and each template is a function over policies. Each policy identifier is mapped to sets of triples by *environments*.

Definition 3 (Environment). *An* environment *e is a partial mapping from policy identifiers to sets of authorization triples. By* e$[X/S]$ *we denote a modification of environment* e *such that*

$$e[X/S](Y) = \begin{cases} S & \textit{if } Y = X \\ e(Y) & \textit{otherwise} \end{cases}$$

The semantic of an identifier X in the environment e can be denoted as $[\![X]\!]_e = e(X)$. The operators of the algebra are defined as follows.

- *Addition* (+). It merges two policies by returning their union.

  $$[\![P_1 + P_2]\!]_e = [\![P_1]\!]_e \cup [\![P_2]\!]_e$$

  Intuitively, additions can be applied in any situation where accesses can be authorized if allowed by any of the component policies (maximum privilege strategy).
- *Conjunction* (&). It merges two policies by returning their intersection.

  $$[\![P_1 \& P_2]\!]_e = [\![P_1]\!]_e \cap [\![P_2]\!]_e$$

  This operator enforces the minimum privilege strategy.
- *Subtraction* (−). It deletes from a policy all the accesses in a second policy.

  $$[\![P_1 - P_2]\!]_e = [\![P_1]\!]_e \setminus [\![P_2]\!]_e$$

  Intuitively, subtraction specifies exceptions to statements made by a policy, and has the same functionalities of negative authorizations in existing approaches without introducing conflicts.
- *Closure* (∗). It closes a policy under a set of derivation rules.

  $$[\![P * R]\!]_e = \mathbf{closure}(R, [\![P]\!]_e)$$

  The closure of policy P under derivation rules R produces a new policy that contains all the authorizations in P and those that can be derived evaluating R on P, according to a given semantics. The derivation rules in R can enforce, for example, an authorization propagation along a predefined subject or object hierarchy.
- *Scoping Restriction* (^). It restricts the applicability of a policy to a given subset of subjects, objects, and actions of the system.

  $$[\![P_1^\wedge c]\!]_e = \{t \in [\![P]\!]_e \mid t \text{ satisfy c}\}$$

  where c is a condition. It is useful to enforce authority confinement (e.g., authorizations specified in a given component can be referred only to specific subjects and objects).
- *Overriding* (o). It overrides a portion of policy P_1 with the specifications in policy P_2 and the fragment that is to be substituted is specified by a third policy P_3.

  $$[\![o(P_1, P_2, P_3)]\!]_e = [\![(P_1 - P_3) + (P_2 \& P_3)]\!]_e$$

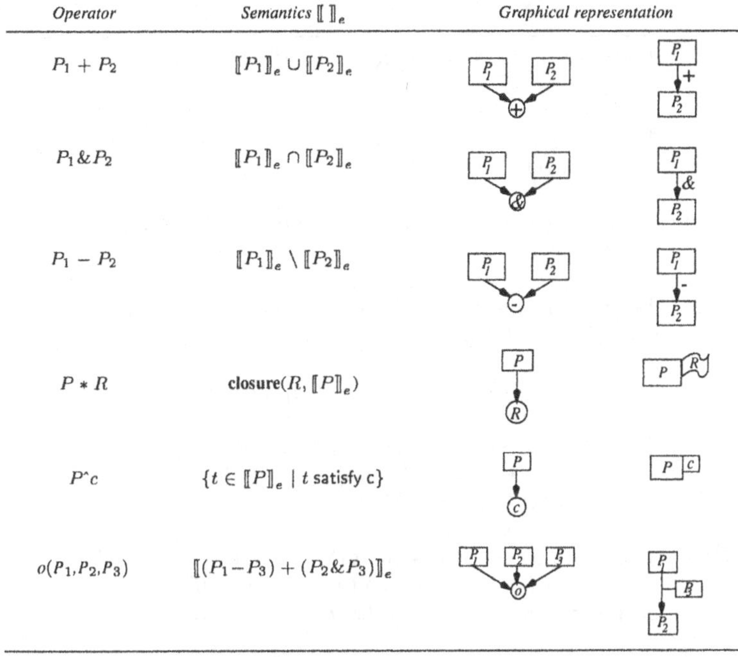

Operator	*Semantics* $[\![\ ]\!]_e$	*Graphical representation*
$P_1 + P_2$	$[\![P_1]\!]_e \cup [\![P_2]\!]_e$	
$P_1 \& P_2$	$[\![P_1]\!]_e \cap [\![P_2]\!]_e$	
$P_1 - P_2$	$[\![P_1]\!]_e \setminus [\![P_2]\!]_e$	
$P * R$	closure$(R, [\![P]\!]_e)$	
$P\hat{\ }c$	$\{t \in [\![P]\!]_e \mid t \text{ satisfy c}\}$	
$o(P_1,P_2,P_3)$	$[\![(P_1 - P_3) + (P_2 \& P_3)]\!]_e$	

Fig. 13. Operators of the algebra and their graphical representation

- *Template*(τ). It defines a partially specified (i.e., parametric) policy that can be completed by supplying the parameters.

$$[\![\tau X.P]\!]_e(S) = [\![P]\!]_{e[S/X]}$$

  where S is the set of all policies, and X is a parameter. Templates are useful for representing policies where some components are to be specified at a later stage. For instance, the components might be the result of further policy refinement, or might be specified by a different authority.

The algebraic operators just described have also a graphical representation summarized in Fig. 13.

The formal semantics on which the algebra is based allows us to reason about policy specifications and proves properties on them.

Evaluating Policy Expressions

Enforcement of compound policies is based on a translation from policy expressions into logic programs, which provide executable specifications compatible with different evaluation strategies. In particular, the following strategies can be applied:

E	TR(E,e)
P	$\{\mathtt{auth}_P(s,o,a) \mid (s,o,a) \in e(P)\}$ if $e(P)$ is defined, $\emptyset$ otherwise.
$F +_i G$	$\{\mathtt{auth}_i(x,y,z) \leftarrow mainp_F(x,y,z), \mathtt{auth}_i(x,y,z) \leftarrow mainp_G(x,y,z)\}$ $\cup \mathsf{TR}(F,e) \cup \mathsf{TR}(G,e)$.
$F \&_i G$	$\{\mathtt{auth}_i(x,y,z) \leftarrow mainp_F(x,y,z) \land mainp_G(x,y,z)\}$ $\cup \mathsf{TR}(F,e) \cup \mathsf{TR}(G,e)$.
$F -_i G$	$\{\mathtt{auth}_i(x,y,z) \leftarrow mainp_F(x,y,z) \land \neg mainp_G(x,y,z)\}$ $\cup \mathsf{TR}(F,e) \cup \mathsf{TR}(G,e)$.
$F\hat{}_i c$	$\{\mathtt{auth}_i(x,y,z) \leftarrow mainp_F(x,y,z) \land c\} \cup \mathsf{TR}(F,e)$.
$o_i(F,G,R)$	$\{\mathtt{auth}_i(x,y,z) \leftarrow mainp_F(x,y,z) \land \neg mainp_R(x,y,z),$ $\mathtt{auth}_i(x,y,z) \leftarrow mainp_G(x,y,z) \land mainp_R(x,y,z)\}$ $\cup \mathsf{TR}(F,e) \cup \mathsf{TR}(G,e) \cup \mathsf{TR}(R,e)$.
$F *_i R$	$\{\mathtt{auth}_i(s,o,a) \leftarrow \mathtt{auth}_i(s_1,o_1,a_1) \land .. \land \mathtt{auth}_i(s_n,o_n,a_n) \mid$ $((s,o,a) \leftarrow (s_1,o_1,a_1) \land \ldots \land (s_n,o_n,a_n)) \in R\}$ $\cup \{\mathtt{auth}_i(x,y,z) \leftarrow mainp_F(x,y,z)\} \cup \mathsf{TR}(F,e)$.
$(\tau_i X.F)(G)$	$\{\mathtt{auth}_X(x,y,z) \leftarrow mainp_G(x,y,z)\} \cup \mathsf{TR}(F,e) \cup \mathsf{TR}(G,e)$.

Fig. 14. Translation TR: from policy expressions to logic programs

- *Materialization.* The policy expressions are evaluated thus determining the set of ground authorization terms corresponding to the accesses allowed by the policy. This strategy can be applied when all the individual policies are known and reasonably static.
- *Partial materialization.* Partial materialization can be considered mainly for two reasons. First, some of the component policies may be unknown at materialization time (black-box policies); clearly, such policies cannot be materialized. Second, some policies may be too dynamic to be materialized (as the cost of updating the materialization may exceed that of run-time evaluation).
- *Run-time evaluation.* This strategy enforces a run-time evaluation of each request (access triple) against the policy expression to determine whether the triple belongs to the result.

The authors propose a strategy, called *pe2lp*, for translating algebraic expressions into an equivalent logic program that is compatible with the different evaluation strategies above-mentioned. The logic program is then used for access control enforcement. Basically, the translation process creates a distinct predicate symbol for each policy identifier and for each algebraic operator in the expression. Since operators are not distinguishable, each of them is associated with a label, that is, an integer number associated from left to right and starting form 0. The result of this labeling process is a *canonical labeling* of the initial policy expression. Note that the *main label* of an expression is the integer associated with the outermost operator of the expression. Translation *pe2lp* takes a labeled policy expression and an environment as input and produces a logic program equivalent to the given expression. The translation process defines a predicate $\texttt{auth}_P$, for each policy identifier P, and a predicate $\texttt{auth}_i$, for each operator op_i. These predicates have three arguments: a subject, a resource, and an action. Figure 14 shows the translation of each operator. The *pe2lp* translation is semantic preserving, provided that the resulting program is interpreted according to the stable model semantics [22] or any other semantics equivalent to the stable model semantics on stratified programs. The logic programming formulation of algebra expressions can be used to enforce access control. First, for each *foreign policy* (i.e., policies expressed in different languages or stored at another site) a wrapper is needed that should be queried by the logic program [41]. The access control enforcement is then obtained by applying a materialization strategy, a partial materialization strategy, or a run-time strategy. In particular, partial materialization is obtained by applying standard partial evaluation techniques [40] to the logic program obtained by the translation process. It is important to highlight that partial evaluation preserves the meaning of the original logic program.

An interesting feature of the proposed algebra is that it can also be used to specify different elementary policies, such as the open or closed policies, or propagation rules along a hierarchy. To evaluate the expressiveness of the algebra, it can be useful a comparison with the *First Order Logic* (FOL). The composition algebra captures only a strict subset of the FOL because policy expressions refer to a well known fixed relation schema, corresponding to the authorization triple. In this way, the *containment* decision problem (P_1 is contained in P_2) and the *checking strong equivalence* (P_1 and P_2 are exactly equivalent) are decidable for policy expressions. As a result of the comparison between FOL and the algebra we have that:

- closure-free policy expressions capture exactly the quantifier-free 0-1 fragment[6] of monadic first-order logic;
- quantifiers can be captured with the closure operator and one simple rule.

The first-order language is induced by predicates $\{P_{all}, P_1, P_2 \ldots\}$, representing policy identifiers (P_{all} denotes the set of all authorization triples), and $\{C_1, C_2 \ldots\}$, representing constraints.

It is important to note that, from the basic domains S, Obj, and A, from the interpretation of constraint predicates, satisfy, and from an environment e, the interpretation structures for the monadic first-order logic just introduced are of the form: (S × Obj × A, e, **satisfy**), denoting that triple (s, o, a) is or not an authorization for environment e.

As an example of policy composition, consider the scenario introduced in Sect. 3.1 and suppose that the computer on-line store is composed of three depart-

[6] A *0-1 formula* F is a formula where each sub-formula of F has at most one free variable.

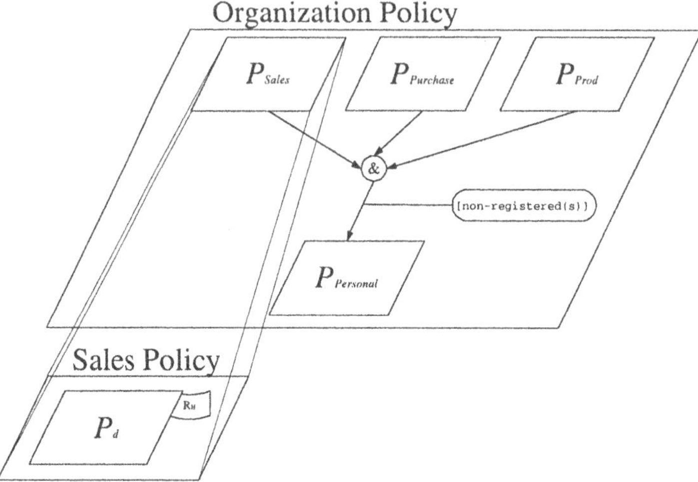

Fig. 15. An example of policy composition

ments, named *Purchase*, *Sales*, and *Production*. The manager of each department is responsible for granting access to data under his responsibility. Let $P_{Purchase}$, P_{Sales} and P_{Prod} be the policies of the three departments. Suppose now that an access is authorized if any of the department policies state so and that authorizations in policy P_{Sales} are propagated to individual users and documents by classical hierarchy-based derivation rules, denoted R_H. Also, suppose that to access the on-line store, non-registered users need also the *Personal* manager consent, stated by policy $P_{Personal}$. In terms of the algebra, the computer store policy can be represented as:

$$o(P_{Purchase} \& P_{Sales} * R_H \& P_{Prod}, P_{Personal}, (P_{Purchase} \& P_{Sales} * R_H \& P_{Prod})^\wedge (non-registered(s)))$$

Figure 15 reports the graphical representation of the computer on-line store policy.

While this algebra is expressive and powerful, it leaves space for further work. Future work to be carried out includes investigation of administration policies for regulating the specification of the different component policies by different authorities; the analysis of incremental approaches to enforce changes to component policies; the analysis of mobile policies, that is, policies associated with objects and that follow the objects when they are passed to another site. Because different and possibly independent authorities can define different parts of the mobile policy in different time instants, the policy can be expressed as a policy expression. In such a context, there is the problem on how to ensure the obedience of policies when the associated objects move around.

7 Conclusions

An important requirement of any system is to protect its data and resources against unauthorized disclosure and/or improper modifications, while at the same time ensuring their availability to legitimate users. A fundamental component in enforcing protection is represented by the access control service whose task is to control every access to a system and its resources and ensure that all and only authorized accesses can take place. Throughout the chapter we presented the basic concepts of access control and investigated different issues concerning the development of an access control system, discussing recent proposals in the area of access control models and languages.

8 Acknowledgments

This work was supported in part by the European Union within the PRIME Project in the FP6/IST Programme under contract IST-2002-507591 and by the Italian MIUR within the KIWI and MAPS projects.

References

1. Abadi M, Lamport L (1992). Composing specifications. ACM Transactions on Programming Languages, 14(4):1–60.
2. Ardagna CA, Damiani E, De Capitani di Vimercati S, Samarati P (2004). XML-based access control languages. Information Security Technical Report.
3. Atkinson B, Della Libera GD, et al. (2002). Web services security (WS-Security). http://msdn.microsoft.com/library/en-us/dnglobspec/html/ws-security.asp.
4. Bell D (1994). Modeling the multipolicy machine. In Proc. of the New Security Paradigm Workshop, Little Compton, Rhode Island, USA.
5. Bertino E, Bettini C, Ferrari E, Samarati P (1998). An access control model supporting periodicity constraints and temporal reasoning. ACM Transactions on Database Systems, 23(3):231–285.
6. Bertino E, Bonatti P, Ferrari E (2001). TRBAC: a temporal role-based access control method. ACM Transactions on Information and System Security, 4(3):191–223.
7. Bertino E, Jajodia S, Samarati P (1999). A flexible authorization mechanism for relational data management systems. ACM Transactions on Information Systems, 17(2):101–140.
8. Blaze M, Feigenbaum J, Lacy J (1996). Decentralized trust management. In Proc. of the 1996 IEEE Symposiumon Security and Privacy, Oakland, CA, USA.
9. Bonatti P, De Capitani di Vimercati S, Samarati P (2002). An algebra for composing access control policies. ACM Transactions on Information and System Security, 5(1):1–35.
10. Bonatti P, Samarati P (2002). A unified framework for regulating access and information release on the web. Journal of Computer Security, 10(3):241–272.
11. Box D, et al. (2003). Web services policy assertions language (WS-PolicyAssertions) version 1.1. http://msdn.microsoft.com/library/en-us/dnglobspec/html/ws-policyassertions.asp.

12. Box D, et al. (2003). Web Services Policy Attachment (WS-PolicyAttachment) version 1.1. http://msdn.microsoft.com/library/en-us/dnglobspec/html/ws-policyattachment.asp.
13. Box D, et al. (2003). Web services policy framework (WS-Policy) version 1.1. http://msdn.microsoft.com/library/en-us/dnglobspec/html/ws-policy.asp.
14. Damiani E, De Capitani di Vimercati S, Paraboschi S, Samarati P (2000). Securing XML documents. In Proc. of the 2000 International Conference on Extending Database Technology (EDBT2000), Konstanz, Germany.
15. Damiani E, De Capitani di Vimercati S, Paraboschi S, Samarati P (2002). A fine-grained access control system for XML documents. ACM Transactions on Information and System Security, 5(2):169–202.
16. DeTreville J (2002). Binder, a logic-based security language. In Proc. of the 2001 IEEE Symposium on Security and Privacy, Oakland, CA, USA.
17. eXtensible Access Control Markup Language (XACML) Version 2.0 (2004). eXtensible Access Control Markup Language (XACML) Version 2.0. OASIS. http://www.oasis-open.org/committees/xacml.
18. Farrell S, Housley R (2002). An internet attribute certificate profile for authorization. RFC 3281.
19. Ferraiolo D, Kuhn R (1992). Role-based access controls. In Proc. of the 15th NIST-NSA National Computer Security Conference, Baltimore, Maryland.
20. Gabillon A (2004). An authorization model for XML databases. In Proc. of the ACM Workshop Secure Web Services, George Mason University, Fairfax, VA, USA.
21. Gabillon A, Bruno E (2001). Regulating access to XML documents. In Proc. of the Fifteenth Annual IFIP WG 11.3 Working Conference on Database Security, Niagara on the Lake, Ontario, Canada.
22. Gelfond M, Lifschitz V (1988). The stable model semantics for logic programming. In Proc. of the 5th International Conference and Symposium on Logic Programming, Cambridge, Massachusetts.
23. Gladman B, Ellison C, Bohm N (1999). Digital signatures, certificates and electronic commerce. http://jya.com/bg/digsig.pdf.
24. Hosmer H (1992). Metapolicies II. In Proc. of the 15th National Computer Security Conference, Baltimore, MD.
25. Jaeger T (2001). Access control in configurable systems. Lecture Notes in Computer Science, 1603:289–316.
26. Jajodia S, Samarati P, Sapino ML, Subrahmanian VS (2001). Flexible support for multiple access control policies. ACM Transactions on Database Systems, 26(2):214–260.
27. Jajodia S, Samarati P, Subrahmanian VS, Bertino E (1997). A unified framework for enforcing multiple access control policies. In Proc. of the 1997 ACM International SIGMOD Conference on Management of Data, Tucson, AZ.
28. Jim T (2001). Sd3: A trust management system with certified evaluation. In Proc. of the 2001 IEEE Symposium on Security and Privacy, Oakland, CA, USA.
29. Kudoh M, Hirayama Y, Hada S, Vollschwitz A (2000). Access control specification based on policy evaluation and enforcement model and specification language. In Symposium on Cryptograpy and Information Security (SCIS'2000), Japan.
30. Landwehr CF (1981). Formal models for computer security. ACM Computing Surveys, 13(3):247–278.
31. Li N, Feigenbaum J, Grosof B (1999). A logic-based knowledge representation for authorization with delegation. In Proc. of the 12th IEEE Computer Security Foundations Workshop, Washington, DC, USA.

32. Li N, Grosof B, Feigenbaum J (2003). Delegation logic: A logic-based approach to distributed authorization. ACM Transactions on Information and System Security, 6(1):128–171.
33. Li N, Mitchell JC (2003). Datalog with constraints: A foundation for trust-management languages. In Proc. of the Fifth International Symposium on Practical Aspects of Declarative Languages (PADL 2003), New Orleans, LA, USA.
34. Li N, Mitchell JC, Winsborough WH (2002). Design of a role-based trust-management framework. In Proc. of the IEEE Symposium on Security and Privacy, Oakland, CA, USA.
35. McLean J (1988). The algebra of security. In Proc. of the 1988 IEEE Computer Society Symposium on Security and Privacy, Oakland, CA, USA.
36. Ryutov T, Zhou L, Neuman C, Leithead T, Seamons KE (2005). Adaptive trust negotiation and access control. In Proc. of the 10th ACM Symposium on Access Control Models and Technologies, Stockholm, Sweden.
37. Samarati P, De Capitani di Vimercati S (2001). Access control: Policies, models, and mechanisms. In Focardi R, Gorrieri R, editors, Foundations of Security Analysis and Design, LNCS 2171. Springer-Verlag.
38. Seamons KE, Winsborough W, Winslett M (1997). Internet credential acceptance policies. In Proc. of the Workshop on Logic Programming for Internet Applications, Leuven, Belgium.
39. Security Assertion Markup Language (SAML) V1.1 (2003). Security Assertion Markup Language (SAML) V1.1. OASIS. http://www.oasis-open.org/committees/security/.
40. Sterling L, Shapiro E (1997). The art of Prolog. MIT Press, Cambridge, MA.
41. Subrahmanian V, Adali S, Brink A, Lu J, Rajput A, Rogers T, Ross R, Ward C. Hermes: heterogeneous reasoning and mediator system. http://www.cs.umd.edu/projects/hermes.
42. The XACML Profile for Hierarchical Resources (2004). The XACML Profile for Hierarchical Resources. OASIS. http://www.oasis-3893open.org/committees/xacml.
43. van der Horst TW, Sundelin T, Seamons KE, Knutson CD (2004). Mobile trust negotiation: Authentication and authorization in dynamic mobile networks. In Proc. of the Eighth IFIP Conference on Communications and Multimedia Security, Lake Windermere, England.
44. Web services security policy (WS-SecurityPolicy) (2002). Web services security policy (WS-SecurityPolicy). http://www-106.ibm.com/developerworks/library/ws-secpol/.
45. Wijesekera D, Jajodia S (2003). A propositional policy algebra for access control. ACM Transactions on Information and System Security, 6(2):286–325.
46. Winsborough W, Seamons KE, Jones V (2000). Automated trust negotiation. In Proc. of the DARPA Information Survivability Conf. & Exposition, Hilton Head Island, SC, USA.
47. Winslett M, Ching N, Jones V, Slepchin I (1997). Assuring security and privacy for digital library transactions on the web: Client and server security policies. In Proc. of the ADL '97 — Forum on Research and Tech. Advances in Digital Libraries, Washington, DC.
48. Woo TYC, Lam SS (1993). Authorizations in distributed systems: A new approach. Journal of Computer Security, 2(2,3):107–136.
49. World Wide Web Consortium (W3C) (2004). eXtensible Markup Language (XML) 1.0 (Third Edition). World Wide Web Consortium (W3C). http://www.w3.org/TR/REC-xml.
50. Yu T, Ma X, Winslett M (2000). An efficient complete strategy for automated trust negotiation over the Internet. In Proc. of the 7th ACM Computer and Communication Security, Athens, Greece.

51. Yu T, Winslett M (2003). A unified scheme for resource protection in automated trust negotiation. In Proc. of the IEEE Symposium on Security and Privacy, Berkeley, California.
52. Yu T, Winslett M, Seamons KE (2001). Interoperable strategies in automated trust negotiation. In Proc. of the 8th ACM Conference on Computer and Communications Security, Philadelphia, Pennsylvania.
53. Yu T, Winslett M, Seamons KE (2003). Supporting structured credentials and sensitive policies trough interoperable strategies for automated trust. ACM Transactions on Information and System Security, 6(1):1–42.

Trusted Recovery

Meng Yu[1], Peng Liu[2], Wanyu Zang[2], and Sushil Jajodia[3]

[1] Department of Computer Science
Monmouth University
myu@monmouth.edu

[2] School of Information Sciences and Technology
The Pennsylvania State University
{pliu,wyzang}@ist.psu.edu

[3] Center for Secure Information Systems
George Mason University
jajodia@gmu.edu

1 Introduction

Database security concerns the confidentiality, integrity, and availability of data stored in a database. A broad span of research from access control [16, 20, 48], to inference control [1], to multilevel secure databases [50, 56], and to multilevel secure transaction processing [4], addresses primarily how to protect the security of a database, especially its confidentiality. However, very limited research has been done on how to survive successful database attacks, which can seriously impair the integrity and availability of a database. Experience with data-intensive applications such as credit card billing, banking, air traffic control, logistics management, inventory tracking, and online stock trading, has shown that a variety of attacks do succeed to fool traditional database protection mechanisms. In fact, we must recognize that not all attacks – even obvious ones – can be averted at their outset. Attacks that succeed, to some degree at least, are unavoidable. With cyber attacks on data-intensive Internet applications, i.e., e-commerce systems, becoming an ever more serious threat to our economy, society, and everyday lives, attack resilient database systems that can survive malicious attacks are a significant concern.

One critical step towards attack resilient database systems is intrusion detection, which has attracted many researchers [10, 39, 45]. Intrusion detection systems monitor system or network activity to discover attempts to disrupt or gain illicit access to systems. The methodology of intrusion detection can be roughly classified as being either based on *statistical profiles* [21] or on known patterns of attacks, called *signatures* [18, 51]. Intrusion detection can supplement protection of database systems by rejecting the future access of detected attackers and by providing useful hints on how to strengthen the defense. However, intrusion detection makes the system attack-aware but not attack resilient, that is, intrusion detection itself cannot maintain the integrity and availability of the database in face of attacks.

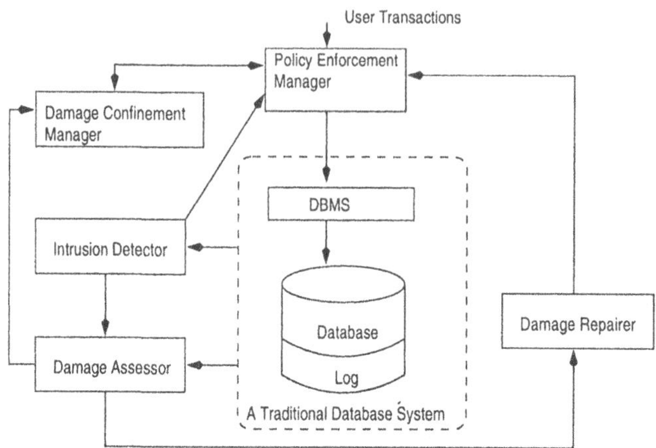

Fig. 1. An Intrusion Tolerant Database System Architecture

To overcome the inherent limitation of intrusion detection, a broader perspective is introduced, saying that in addition to detecting attacks, countermeasures to these successful attacks should be planned and deployed in advance. In the literature, this is referred to as *survivability* or *intrusion tolerance*. In this article, we will study a critical database intrusion tolerance problem beyond intrusion detection, namely *attack recovery*, and present a set of innovative algorithms to solve the problem.

The attack recovery problem can be better explained in the context of an intrusion tolerant database system. Database intrusion tolerance can typically be enforced at two levels: *operating system (OS) level* and *transaction level*. Although transaction level methods cannot handle OS level attacks, it is shown that in many applications where attacks are enforced mainly through malicious transactions, transaction level methods can tolerate intrusions in a much more effective and efficient way. Moreover, it is shown that OS level intrusion tolerance techniques such as those proposed in [6,38,39,41,42], can be directly integrated into a transaction level intrusion tolerance framework to complement it with the ability to tolerate OS level attacks. This article will focus on transaction level intrusion tolerance, and our presentation will be based on the intrusion tolerant database system architecture shown in Figure 1.

The architecture is built on top of a traditional "off-the-shelf" Database Management System (DBMS). Within the framework, the *Intrusion Detector* identifies malicious transactions based on the history kept (mainly) in the log. The *Damage Assessor* locates the damage caused by the detected transactions. The *Damage Repairer* repairs the located damage using some specific cleaning operations. The *Damage Confinement Manager* restricts the access to the data items that have been identified by the Damage Assessor as damaged, and unconfines a data item after it is cleaned. The *Policy Enforcement Manager* (PEM) (a) functions as a proxy for normal user transactions and those cleaning operations, and (b) is responsible for enforcing system-wide intrusion tolerant policies. For example, a policy may require the PEM to reject every new transaction submitted by a user as soon as the Intrusion Detector finds that a malicious transaction is submitted by the user.

We need this architecture because current database systems are relatively easy to attack (especially for malicious insiders) and very limited in surviving attacks, although access controls, integrity constraints, concurrency control, replication, active databases, and recovery mechanisms deal well with many kinds of mistakes and errors. For example, access controls can be subverted by the inside attacker or the outside attacker who has assumed an insider's identity. Integrity constraints are weak at prohibiting plausible but incorrect data; classic examples are changes to dollar amounts in billing records or salary figures. To a concurrency control mechanism, an attacker's transaction is indistinguishable from any other transaction. Automatic replication facilities and active database triggers can serve to spread the damage introduced by an attacker at one site to many sites. Recovery mechanisms ensure that committed transactions appear in stable storage and provide means of rolling back a database, but no attention is given to distinguishing legitimate activity from malicious activity.

The attack recovery problem has two aspects: *damage assessment* and *damage repair*. The complexity of attack recovery is mainly caused by a phenomenon denoted *damage spreading*. In a database, the results of one transaction can affect the execution of some other transactions. Informally, when a transaction T_i reads a data item x updated by another transaction T_j (We say T_i *reads x from* T_j), T_i is directly *affected* by T_j. If a third transaction T_k is affected by T_i, but not directly affected by T_j, T_k is indirectly affected by T_j. It is easy to see that when a (relatively old) transaction B_i that updates x is identified malicious, the damage on x can spread to every data item updated by a transaction that is affected by B_i, directly or indirectly. The goal of attack recovery is to locate each affected transaction and recover the database from the damage caused on the data items updated by every malicious or affected transaction.

In some cases, the attacker's goal may be to reduce availability by attacking integrity. In these cases the attacker's goal not only introduces damage to certain data items and uncertainty about which good transactions can be trusted, but also achieves the goal of bringing the system down while repair efforts are being made. 'Coldstart' semantics for recovery mean that system activity is brought to a halt while damage is being repaired. To address the availability threat, recovery mechanisms with 'warmstart' or 'hotstart' semantics are needed. Warmstart semantics for recovery allow continuous, but degraded, use of the database while the damage is being repaired. Hotstart semantics make recovery transparent to the users. It is clear that the job of attack recovery gets even more difficult as use of the database continues because the damage can spread to new transactions and cleaned objects can be re-damaged by new transactions.

2 Basic Concepts in Attack Recovery

2.1 Dependency Relations

Dependency relations are important because not only data items are calculated through dependency relations, but also executing orders of concurrent transactions are determined by dependency relations. Furthermore, we need the dependency relations to determine proper defensive executions.

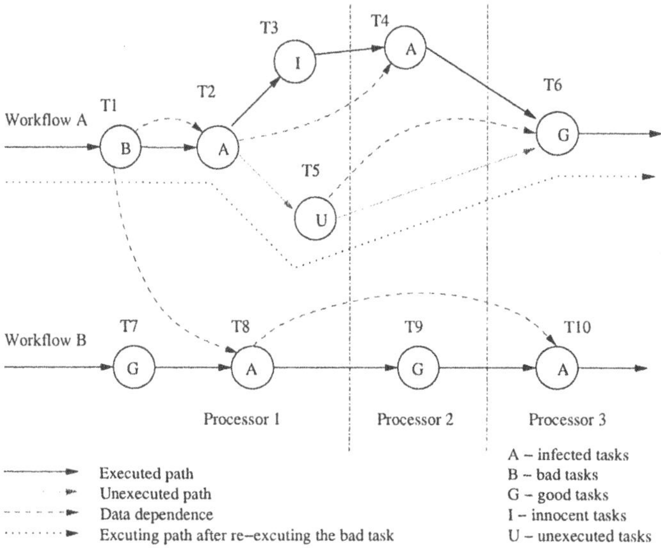

Fig. 2. A group of related transactions

During the execution of normal transactions and recovery transactions, there are some specific partial orders that need to be satisfied. In this section, we introduce some set and partial order relations related to our theories.

Preceding relations

Given two transactions T_i and T_j, if transaction T_i is executed before T_j, then T_i *precedes* T_j *by definition*, which is denoted by $T_i \prec T_j$.

In the example shown in Figure 2, a solid directed edge indicates a preceding relation. For example, $T_1 \prec T_2$, $T_2 \prec T_3$, $T_7 \prec T_8$ and $T_8 \prec T_9$. Relation $\prec$ is transitive. We can get $T_1 \prec T_3$ from $T_1 \prec T_2$ and $T_2 \prec T_3$. The relation $\prec$ is a partial order because some transactions have no preceding relations among them, such as T_4 and T_5 in the example.

When transactions of are executed in the system, they have preceding relations that are determined by the transaction scheduler. We use $T_i \prec_s T_j$ to denote that transaction T_i runs before T_j by scheduling, which we say transaction T_i *precedes* transaction T_j *by scheduling*.

Given any two transactions in the same transactional process, if $T_i \prec T_j$ then T_i should be scheduled before T_j, namely $T_i \prec_s T_j$, and T_i will occur earlier than T_j in the system log. For two transactions within two different processes and without a $\prec$ relation, or at least one of these two transactions is a recovery transaction, they will ultimately be scheduled by the scheduler and they will have $\prec_s$ relations. Before they are done and committed, they have only $\prec_s$ relation, which is the difference between $\prec$ and $\prec_s$ relation.

Assuming that $\prec$ is a relation on set $\mathcal{S}$ then we define minimal$(\mathcal{S}, \prec) = x$ where $x \in \mathcal{S} \wedge \nexists x' \in \mathcal{S}, x' \prec x$. If $\mathcal{S}$ is a set including all transactions in Figure 2 then minimal$(\mathcal{S}, \prec) = T_1$. Note that there may be more than one result qualified to the definition of minimal$(\mathcal{S}, \prec)$. For example, if $\mathcal{S} = \{T_i, T_j, T_k\}$, $T_i \prec T_k$ and $T_j \prec T_k$, then both T_i and T_j are qualified results for minimal$(\mathcal{S}, \prec)$. In cases like these, we randomly select one qualified result as the value for minimal$(\mathcal{S}, \prec)$.

Data dependency and multi-version data objects

We use $R(T)$ and $W(T)$ to denote the reading set and the writing set of transaction T. For example, given a transaction $T_x : x = a + b$, $R(T_x) = \{a, b\}$ and $W(T_x) = \{x\}$.

We introduce some concepts that are usually discussed in the field of parallel computing. Given two transactions $t_i \prec t_j$,

- If $(W(t_i) - \bigcup_{t_i \prec t_k \prec t_j} W(t_k)) \cap R(t_j) \neq \phi$, then t_j is *flow dependent* on t_i, which is denoted by $t_i \rightarrow_f t_j$.
- If $R(t_i) \cap (W(t_j) - \bigcup_{t_i \prec t_k \prec t_j} W(t_k)) \neq \phi$, then t_j is *anti-flow dependent* on t_i, which is denoted by $t_i \rightarrow_a t_j$.
- If $(W(t_i) - \bigcup_{t_i \prec t_k \prec t_j} W(t_k)) \cap W(t_j) \neq \phi$, then t_j is *output dependent* on t_i, which is denoted by $t_i \rightarrow_o t_j$.

Intuitively, if $t_i \rightarrow_f t_j$, then t_j reads some data objects written by t_i. If $t_i \rightarrow_a t_j$, then t_j modifies some date objects after t_i reads them. If $t_i \rightarrow_o t_j$, then t_i and t_j have some common data objects that they modify.

Consider another transaction $T_b : b = x - 1$, where $T_x \prec T_b$, $R(T_b) = \{x\}$ and $W(T_b) = \{b\}$, we have $T_x \rightarrow_f T_b$ and $T_x \rightarrow_a T_b$. All the relations $\rightarrow_f$, $\rightarrow_a$ and $\rightarrow_o$ are data dependency relations and are not transitive. From the well known results of parallel computing, if a transaction T_j is data dependent on another transaction T_i then they cannot run in parallel and T_j should be executed after executing T_i, otherwise we will get wrong results.

With a single version of each data object, T_x must be executed before T_b to get the correct result. The order can be changed by introducing multiple versions of data objects. Suppose b^1 is one version of b with revision number 1, and b^2 is another version of b with revision number 2, and so on. The anti-flow dependency among T_x and T_b can be broken by revising $T_x : x = a + b^1$ and $T_b : b^2 = x - 1$. Even if T_b is executed before T_x, T_x still gets correct results by reading b^1. Multi-version data objects also can be used to break output dependencies.

By introducing multi-version data objects, restrictions caused by anti-flow and output dependencies are removed. Note that executing orders determined by flow dependencies are not changed by multiple-version data objects.

Control Dependency

Given two transactions $T_i \prec T_j$ within the same transactional process, if the execution of transaction T_j is decided by transaction T_i, then we say T_j is *control dependent* on T_i, which is denoted by $T_i \rightarrow_c T_j$. A control dependency relation is transitive. If $T_i \rightarrow_c T_j$ and $T_j \rightarrow_c T_k$ then $T_i \rightarrow_c T_k$. In the example shown in Figure 2, $T_2 \rightarrow_c T_3$, $T_2 \rightarrow_c T_4$ and $T_2 \rightarrow_c T_5$.

We use $\rightarrow$ to denote data or control dependency when the concrete type of dependency does not matter to our discussion. If there exist such transactions $T_1, T_2, \ldots, T_n, n \geq 2$ that $T_1 \rightarrow T_2 \rightarrow, \ldots, \rightarrow T_n$, then $T_1 \rightarrow^* T_n$.

If $T_i \rightarrow_c T_j$ then there are two possibilities about the execution of T_j: T_j should be executed or should not. We define two sets to describe these possibilities.

$\mathcal{S}_T(T_i)$ is a set of x, where $T_i \rightarrow_c^* x$ and x should be executed according to the executing result of T_i.

$\mathcal{S}_F(T_i)$ is a set of x, where $T_i \rightarrow_c^* x$ and x should not be executed according to the executing result of T_i.

$\mathcal{S}_T(T_i)$ is the set of transaction T_i's *true successors* and $\mathcal{S}_F(T_i)$ is the set of transaction T_i's *false successors*.

Note that the definition of these two sets are specific to concrete executions. For the same transaction, these two sets may have different contents in different executions. If $T_j \in \mathcal{S}_T(T_i)$, then T_j is on the executing path according to the current execution. Otherwise T_j is not on the executing path according to the current execution. So, if there are more than two possible branches going out of transaction T_i, only transactions on one branch belong to $\mathcal{S}_T(T_i)$ in a specific execution. Others belong to $\mathcal{S}_F(T_i)$. Consider the example in Figure 2, in the attacked execution $\mathcal{S}_T(T_2) = \{T_3, T_4\}$ and $\mathcal{S}_F(T_2) = \{T_5\}$. After we carry out the undo transactions and redo(T_2), it is another story. That is, $\mathcal{S}_T(\text{redo}(T_2)) = \{T_5\}$ should be in the recovered execution. Therefore, $\mathcal{S}_T(T_i)$ may be different from $\mathcal{S}_T(\text{redo}(T_i))$, which indicates that the recovered transactional process may go through a different path from the previous path executed.

2.2 Unrecoverable Transactions

In a distributed system, we need to consider both inside operations and interactions with the outside world. The formal models in previous work, such as [60, 61] were unable to formalize interactions with the outside world. Since interactions with the outside world are not recoverable, we use an OWS (outside world site) to model the outside world. All transactions happened on an OWS are *unrecoverable*. We consider all inputs obtained from users and all outputs to the users happen on a user site S_u which is a OWS. All user's transactions are called OWTs (outside world transactions). For example, a transaction that a user withdraws money from a ATM cannot be recovered. It is an OWT and the ATM is an OWS.

2.3 Transactional Processes

With above notations, transactional processes can be modeled as $(T, S, \prec, \rightarrow_f, \rightarrow_a, \rightarrow_o, \rightarrow_c)$, where T is a set of transactions, S is a set of sites that are corresponding to a host or a processor in the distributed system, $S_u \in S$ is an OWS, and all dependency relations among transactions.

2.4 Concurrency Restrictions and Domino-Effects

We use a simple example to explain that there do exist such restrictions on executing orders of transactions in dependency relation based recovery.

Consider transactions $t_1 : a = 1, t_2 : b = 2$, and $t_3 : y = a + b$, which are executed in the sequence of $t_1 \prec t_2 \prec t_3$. We have $t_1 \rightarrow_f t_3 \wedge t_2 \rightarrow_f t_3$. Assume that t_2 has been identified as compromised by an IDS (Intrusion Detection System), so the value of b is corrupted. Therefore, t_3 is also corrupted since it reads a incorrect b. During the concurrency restrictions, the rolling back and redoing damaged transactions have to strictly follow specific orders [60, 61]. The effects that a compromised transaction affects all legitimate transactions depending on it are called *Domino-effects*.

To recover, t_2 needs to be undone followed by redone. t_3 needs to be redone. We must satisfy the sequence of undo(t_2) $\prec$ redo(t_2) $\prec$ redo(t_3) in the recovery. Any other execution will get wrong results. The precedence relations introduced by dependency relations is called *concurrency restrictions*.

The concurrency restriction is also caused by dependency relations. However, we can break anti-flow dependency relations by introducing multi-version data, as described in Section 6.

3 Transaction Models for Attack Recovery

At first glance, attack recovery, which aims to efficiently remove the effects of malicious or affected, committed transactions by exploiting traditional database recovery facilities as much as possible, seems to violate durability which implies that committed transactions should not be undone. This suggests that we need to bridge the theoretical gap between classical database recovery theory and attack recovery practice before addressing concrete recovery algorithms.

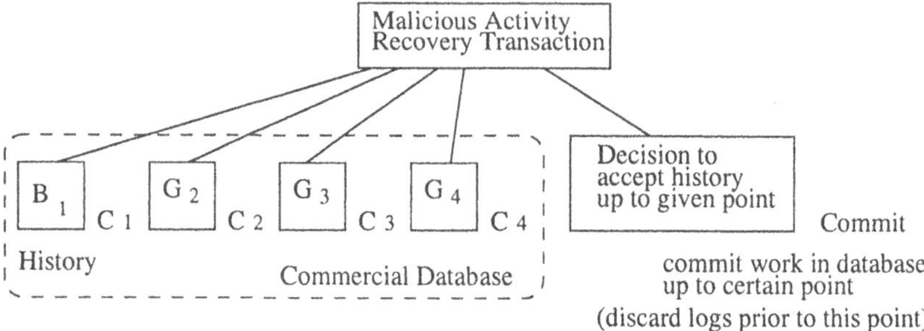

Fig. 3. Using Nested Transactions to Model Attack Recovery

A straightforward approach to bridge the gap is using a *flat-transaction* recovery model where transactions are *flat* without containing any subtransactions, and committed transactions are 'undone' by building and executing a specific type of transactions, denoted *undo* transactions. Undo transactions *semantically* revoke the effect of a committed transaction without really undoing it, so this model keeps durability. In particular, to 'undo' a committed transaction T_i, the corresponding undo transaction U_i is built as follows: for each update (write) operation of T_i, a write operation is appended to the program of U_i (in reverse order) which writes the before value of the item updated. Undo transactions comprise only write operations. It should be noticed that using this model to 'undo' a committed transaction can be quite different from a traditional undo operation. Undoing a committed transaction T_i can only remove its direct effects, but cannot remove the indirect effects (if there are any) of T_i which are caused by the transactions affected by T_i. In contrast, undoing an active transaction T_j can remove all the effects of T_j because the isolation property ensures that T_j can be backed out without affecting other transactions.

Although undo transactions are easy to build, the flat transaction recovery model cannot exploit traditional undo mechanisms. It is desirable that we can directly use existing undo facilities (to do attack recovery) without sacrificing performance objectives. This goal can be achieved by a *nested-transaction* recovery model shown in Figure 3, where B_1 is a bad transaction, G_2, G_3 and G_4 are good transactions, and C means a commit operation of a transaction.

Consider a commercial database system where a history is composed of a set of (committed) flat transactions [4], for a history to repair, we build the model by introducing a specific virtual transaction, called *malicious activity recovery transaction* (MART), on top of the history, and letting the MART be the parent of all the flat transactions in the history. As a result, the history is evolved into a nested structure where the MART is the top-level transaction and each flat transaction turns out to be a subtransaction whose execution is controlled by the MART. Since subtransactions can theoretically be undone or compensated at any time before the corresponding

[4] Note that the recovery model can be easily extended to incorporate histories of multilevel or nested transactions.

top-level transaction commits [15, 40, 44], the model inherently supports undoing flat (commercial) transactions. This is also one of the reasons why we use the word 'undo' to denote one of our basic repair operations.

One interesting question about the model is 'Can a MART commit or abort?'. It is clear that aborting the MART is equivalent to rolling back the history to its initial state. However, how to commit the MART is tricky. In fact, the MART should be able to commit, because as the system keeps on executing new transactions the history can get tremendously long and the MART needs to maintain too much information for the purpose of attack recovery if the MART never commits. In practice, such information may no longer be available for a transaction T_i after T_i is committed for a long period of time. However, if we commit a MART at the end of the current history and start another new MART, then the work of some malicious transactions in the history supervised by the old MART could be committed before they are recovered. Hence we need to commit the work of good transactions while keeping the ability to recover from bad transactions. This goal is achieved by the following MART splitting protocol which is motivated by [47].

- When the history is recovered to a specific point p_i, that is, it is believed that the effects of every bad transaction prior to p_i are removed, we can commit the work of all the transactions prior to p_i by splitting the MART into two MARTs: one supervising all the transactions prior to p_i, the other supervising the latter part of the history. Interested readers can refer to [47] for a concrete process of transaction splitting, which is omitted here.
- We commit the MART which supervises the part of the history prior to p_i. From the perspective of attack recovery, the corresponding log records prior to p_i can be discarded to alleviate the system's resource consumption.
- We keep the other MART active so it can still be repaired.

The advantage of the nested transaction recovery model is that it fits in current commercial database systems very well thus attack recovery need not be designed from scratch. First, flat transactions can be undone by directly applying traditional undo operations. In fact, in this model a savepoint is generated after each subtransaction commits so that the MART can rollback its execution to the beginning of any flat transaction. Second, this model causes very little performance penalty. The drawback of this model is that after a MART commits there is no automatic ways to undo a flat transaction supervised by the MART even if the transaction is later on identified malicious. Therefore, decisions to commit a MART should be made carefully.

4 Damage Assessment and Repair

4.1 Correctness Criteria

When attackers inject malicious transactions into the transactional processing system, the malicious transactions generate or corrupt some data objects directly. In addition, the data dependency relations and the control dependency relations among transactions can further spread the damage to other data objects.

Therefore, a data object is dirty or corrupted if it was generated in any of the following ways

1. Generated directly by a malicious transaction or corrupted directly by attackers
2. Calculated based on dirty data
3. Generated by a transaction that should not have been executed
4. Generated by a transaction that references data that is created by transactions that should have been executed, but were not

Above four items describes all possible patterns of damage spreading. In this article we use the term *bad transaction* to represent a transaction that generates dirty data. Bad transactions consist of malicious transactions and affected transactions. We classify corrupted data objects, *dirty data objects*, into two categories based on their generation. One is *Generated Dirty Data Object* corresponding to item 1 and 3. The other is *Spread Dirty Data Object* corresponding to item 2 and 4.

In Figure 2, transaction T_1 marked with 'B' was corrupted directly by attackers. So data that T_1 generates are dirty, which is indicated by item 1.

According to our definition of flow dependency, if T_j reads data that transaction T_i writes then $T_i \rightarrow_f T_j$. In Figure 2, transaction T_2 marked with 'A' is data dependent on transaction T_1. T_2 is affected by bad transaction T_1 because it reads dirty data from T_1 then creates wrong results which are also dirty. So does transaction T_4, which reads dirty data from T_2. T_8 and T_{10} fall in the same case, which is described by item 2.

The third situation described in item 3 is shown by transaction T_3 marked by 'I' in Figure 2, which is 'innocent'. In Figure 2 the execution of transaction T_3 is based on the executing result of transaction T_2. Since transaction T_2 is affected by T_1, it is possible that the selection of executing path is wrong. We need to redo transaction T_2 and then check whether T_3 is still a true successor of redo(T_2) in the recovered execution. If it is a false successor of redo(T_2) in the recovered execution, then the data T_3 generated before are dirty and T_3 needs to be undone, although the calculating results of T_3 are correct.

For the last case, refer to the execution of transaction T_6 marked by 'G' in Figure 2. T_6 is flow dependent on transaction T_5 which was not executed in the attacked execution. When we redo transaction T_2, the transactional process may be executed along a new path that continues with T_5. Then T_5 may generate different data from what T_6 has read in the attacked execution. Thus T_6 will get different results in the recovered execution. Therefore transaction T_6 produced a wrong result in the attacked execution and the data it generated are dirty.

The following definition describes the correctness criteria for our attack recovery scheme.

Definition 1. *Given normal transactions and recovery transactions, the recovery is* strictly safe *if and only if the following conditions hold.*

1. (Completeness of recovery) *No incorrect data exists after the recovery.*

2. (Safety of recovery) *No incorrect data is generated while executing recovery transactions.*
3. (Safety of normal services) *No incorrect data is generated while executing normal transactions.*
4. (Consistency to the specification) *The execution of normal transactions and recovery transactions does not violate the specification of transactional process.*

A safe recovery scheme is not isolated from the transactional processing system. When we are carrying out the recovery, there definitely exist some scheduled preceding relations between the recovery transactions and the normal transactions. Condition 3 describes that execution of normal transactions should be clean. In other words, if a new transaction tries to read corrupted data from some unrecovered transactions, it should be suspended for future execution until the data is clean.

Note that Condition 1 does not imply Condition 2 and Condition 3. Condition 1 requires that the recovery should be complete while it implies nothing about the procedure of the recovery.

In this article, we assume that if a transaction t_i is corrupted, we can remove its effects in the system by executing a transaction $undo(t_i)$, which can be implemented by reading the last version of the data objects before the attack from the log of the system. To recover affected transactions, we need to re-execute them. We denote the re-execution of transaction t_i by $redo(t_i)$. t_i and $redo(t_i)$ are different executions of the same transaction. $redo(t_i)$ refers to the execution when carrying out the attack recovery.

4.2 Recovery Transactions

The recovery transactions include the undo and redo transactions. In this section, we describe how to find the undo and redo transactions.

Undo transactions

Assume that $\mathcal{B}$ is the set of malicious transactions already known. Transaction t_j generates incorrect data and needs to be undone if and only if, any of the following conditions are satisfied.

1. $t_j \in \mathcal{B}$
2. $\exists t_i \in \mathcal{B}, t_j \in \mathcal{L}, t_i \rightarrow_c^* t_j$, and $t_j \notin succ(redo(t_i))$
3. $\exists t_i \in \mathcal{B}, t_i \rightarrow_f^* t_j$
4. $\exists t_i \in \mathcal{B}, \exists t_k \notin \mathcal{L}, t_i \rightarrow_c^* t_k, t_k \rightarrow_f^* t_j$, and $t_k \in succ(redo(t_i))$

We explain the rules by Figure 2. Transaction t_1 marked with 'B' was corrupted directly by attackers and is reported by the IDS, $\mathcal{B} = \{t_1\}$. The data that t_1 generates is corrupted, and t_1 needs to be undone, as indicated by condition 1.

In the figure, transaction $t_1 \rightarrow_f t_2$, where $t_1 \in \mathcal{B}$. t_2 is infected by transaction t_1 because it reads corrupted data from t_1 and then creates wrong results that are also corrupted. Transactions t_4, t_8, and t_{10}, as described by condition 3 also create wrong results. Now, $\mathcal{B} = \{t_1, t_2, t_4, t_8, t_{10}\}$.

The situation described in condition 2 is shown by transaction t_3. The execution of transaction t_3 is based on the executing result of transaction t_2, where $t_2 \in \mathcal{B}$. Since transaction t_2 is affected by t_1, it is possible that the choice of execution path is wrong. We must redo transaction t_2 and then check whether t_3 is still on the execution path: check if $t_3 \in succ(redo(t_2))$ in the recovery. If $t_3 \notin succ(redo(t_2))$ is in the recovery, then the data t_3 generated before is corrupted, and t_3 needs to be undone, although the computing of t_3 is correct.

For the last condition, refer to the execution of transaction t_6. t_6 is flow dependent on transaction t_5 which was not executed in the attacked execution. When we redo transaction t_2, the process is executed along a new execution path that continues with t_5. Then t_5 may generate different data from what t_6 has read in the attacked execution. Thus t_6 will get different results in the recovery execution. Therefore, t_6 got a wrong result in the attacked execution, and the data that it generated was corrupted.

We call the transactions described by condition 2 and condition 4 as *candidate undo transactions* because we do not know if they really should be undone until $redo(t_i)$ is executed. If they need to be undone, then they are added to $\mathcal{B}$.

The transactions that have already been undone and are still on the re-executing path should be redone.

Redo transactions

Assume that $\mathcal{B}$ is the set of bad transactions already known and $t_i \in \mathcal{B}$, then t_i should be redone if and only if any of the following conditions are satisfied.

1. $\nexists t_j \in \mathcal{B}, t_j \rightarrow_c^* t_i$
2. $\exists t_j \in \mathcal{B}, t_j \rightarrow_c^* t_i, t_i \in succ(redo(t_j))$

We call the transactions described by condition 2 *candidate redo transactions* because we do not know if they really should be redone until $redo(t_j)$ is executed.

In Figure 2, transaction t_1, t_2, t_6, t_8, and t_{10} need be undone. Since they are not control dependent on any bad transaction, they need be redone, as stated in case 1. Since neither transaction t_3 nor transaction t_4 is on the re-executing path of the transactional process, they do not need to be redone. Redoing them does not meet the specification of the transactional process because redoing them will generate corrupted data.

4.3 Partial Orders Caused by Dependency Relations

Since undo and redo transactions are not defined by the original process, we must create partial orders among these transactions and normal transactions to guarantee that our recovery is strictly safe.

Partial orders among recovery transactions

Given any two transactions t_i and t_j and the system log $\mathcal{L}$, the recovery is strictly safe only if the partial orders of the recovery transactions are derived by the following rules.

1. $t_i \prec t_j \Rightarrow redo(t_i) \prec redo(t_j)$
2. $\forall t_i, undo(t_i) \prec redo(t_i)$
3. $t_i \rightarrow_a t_j \Rightarrow undo(t_j) \prec redo(t_i)$
4. $t_i \rightarrow_o t_j \Rightarrow undo(t_j) \prec undo(t_i)$
5. $t_i \rightarrow_c t_j, t_j \in succ(t_i) \Rightarrow redo(t_i) \rightarrow_c redo(t_j) \wedge redo(t_j) \in succ(redo(t_i))$
6. $t_i \in \mathcal{B}, \exists t_k \notin \mathcal{L}, t_i \rightarrow_c^* t_k, t_k \rightarrow_f^* t_j$ and $t_k \in succ(redo(t_i)) \Rightarrow redo(t_i) \rightarrow_c undo(t_j) \wedge undo(t_j) \in succ(redo(t_i))$

Rule 1 to rule 5 are easy to understand. We explain rule 6 by Figure 2. Task t_2 is an affected task ($t_2 \in \mathcal{B}$), $t_5 \notin \mathcal{L}$, $t_2 \rightarrow_c t_5$, and $t_5 \rightarrow_f t_6$. Task t_5 should have been executed if there is no intrusion ($t_5 \in succ(redo(t_2))$). Then the execution of $undo(t_6)$ depends on the results of $redo(t_2)$.

Partial orders among recovery transactions and normal transactions

In order to run both the recovery transactions and normal transactions concurrently, we introduce partial orders among recovery transactions and normal transactions.

Given normal transactions $\mathcal{N}$ and the system log $\mathcal{L}$, if every data object has only one copy, say, the value of a data object will be lost after writing, the recovery is strictly safe only if the precedence relations are derived by the following rules.

1. $(t_i \rightarrow_f t_j) \vee (t_i \rightarrow_a t_j) \vee (t_i \rightarrow_o t_j) \vee (t_i \rightarrow_c t_j), t_j \in \mathcal{N} \Rightarrow undo(t_i) \prec redo(t_i) \prec t_j$
2. $t_i \rightarrow_c^* t_k, t_k \rightarrow_f^* t_j, t_k \notin \mathcal{L} \cup \mathcal{N}, t_j \in \mathcal{N} \Rightarrow undo(t_i) \prec redo(t_i) \prec t_j$

The above two rules are pretty reasonable. For example, we cannot expect a transaction that refers to the corrupted x to get correct results before x is repaired. If there exists such transaction, it should wait until x is recovered. Similarly, if a recovery transaction $redo(t_i)$ needs to read from y to repair x, then a normal transaction that writes to y is supposed to wait until $redo(t_i)$ is done. Otherwise, the recovery transaction $redo(t_i)$ will be corrupted.

To guarantee the strictly safety of recovery, a normal transaction cannot be executed before all recovery transactions are figured out. Unfortunately, we do not know the set of recovery transactions until the analysis of recovery transactions is complete. In other words, we cannot run any normal transaction until all malicious transactions reported by the IDS have been processed, which may cause temporary delay to process normal transactions when the attacking rate is high and the system is busy analyzing damages.

If no partial order is defined between two transactions, they can be run in any sequence without comprising the safety of the execution results.

The proofs of all above rules can be found in [61].

4.4 Recovery Strategies

The above theories described concurrency restrictions among recovery transactions and normal transactions. If we ignore specific restrictions, we may corrupt either the recovery procedure, or the execution of normal transactions. Depending on what concurrency restrictions we are interested in, we may have three different recovery strategies for the attack recovery.

Strictly safe strategy. This strategy guarantees the correctness of executing both the recovery and normal transactions. We may delay normal transactions while damages are analyzed. This strategy will be introduced in Section 5.

Conservative strategy. This strategy guarantees the correctness of recovery but not the execution of normal transactions. Theorem 4.3 is derived from the assumption that every data object has one copy. Multiple versions of data objects can break anti-flow and output dependence relations. If every data object has multiple versions, normal transactions can be executed without blocking while we guarantee the correctness of recovery. However, since the recovery is not complete, we cannot guarantee the correctness of executing normal transactions. Furthermore, multiple versions for each data object also introduce extra storage costs. We will discuss this strategy in Section 6.

Aggressive strategy. In this strategy, the system executes a transaction before knowing all dependency relations. However, as we mentioned before, both recovery transactions and normal transactions may be corrupted and we need to repair them again. This strategy in fact introduces more recovery transactions and costs, because the more transactions are executed, the more transactions may be corrupted. Even worse, we cannot guarantee the system will be repaired, since we cannot guarantee the recovery is correct and terminable.

Our work [2] takes the the aggressive strategy. First, our technique in [2] can guarantee that when the recovery terminates, the recovery is correct. Second, our technique in [2] can slow down the execution of new transactions so that the recovery will terminate. Once the recovery terminates, the termination can be detected. The aggressive strategy also needs to address the concurrency control issues. Due to the space limit, refer to [2] for more technical details.

5 Single-Version based Recovery

In this chapter, we introduce single-version based recovery based on theories discussed in Chapter 4.

5.1 Recovery System and State Transition Model

The structure of the recovery system is shown in Figure 4. Our recovery system consists of an independent IDS to identify attacks, a recovery analyzer to evaluate damages of the system, and a scheduler to schedule both recovery transactions and normal transactions.

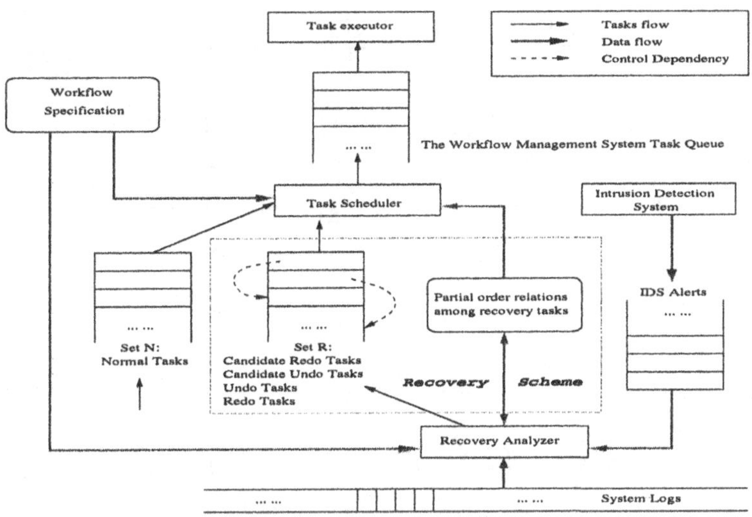

Fig. 4. Processing Structure of an Attack Recovery System

In the system, the IDS periodically reports intrusions to the system by putting 'IDS Alerts' in a queue. Based on our theory in Chapter 4, the recovery analyzer generates recovery transactions works out related partial orders, and puts them in the queue of recovery transactions. The transaction scheduler schedules both recovery transactions and normal transactions according to the partial orders among them. Since the algorithms of the recovery analyzer and the scheduler can be designed in a straightforward way according to the related theorems, we will not provide further details due to the space limit.

5.2 State Transition of the System

The state transition graph (STG) of the system is shown in Figure 5. In the figure, we denote by 'N' the NORMAL state. 'S:n' represents the SCAN state with n IDS alerts in the queue, and 'R:n' represents the RECOVERY state with n units of recovery transactions in the queue, where 1 unit of recovery transactions corresponds to a set of transactions for repairing damages caused by 1 attack.

There are three categories of states of the attack recovery system: 'NORMAL', 'SCAN', and 'RECOVERY'.

In the NORMAL state, there is no intrusions reported in the system. The recovery analyzer does nothing and the scheduler executes normal transactions.

In the SCAN states, intrusions are reported, and the queue of IDS Alerts is not empty. The recovery analyzer analyzes damages to the system, and generates recovery transactions and partial orders among them. As we mentioned before, recovery may redo some transactions to repair damaged data objects. The redo transactions

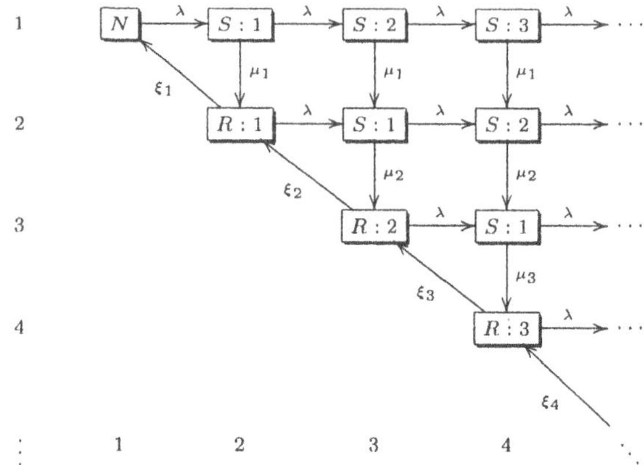

Fig. 5. State Transition Graph of the Recovery System

may read some data objects that new IDS alerts try to mark as damaged data objects, which in turn will corrupt recovery transactions. Therefore, in the SCAN state, recovery transactions may not be executed.

In the RECOVERY states, the queue of IDS alerts is empty. All damages of the system are identified. The scheduler schedules recovery transactions and new transactions according to their partial orders.

Although the structure in Figure 4 looks like a queuing network, according to the restrictions that the system does not execute recovery transactions in the SCAN state, which leads to that the scan and the recovery cannot run in parallel, the system cannot be modeled by a queuing network.

The recovery system starts form the state NORMAL. It transits to the SCAN states whenever there are IDS alerts arrived. After all IDS alerts have been processed, the system goes to the RECOVERY states. The system returns to the NORMAL state when all recovery transactions have been executed.

If there are no further intrusions, the recovery will definitely be terminated because the system will transit to the RECOVERY states after all damages are analyzed, then transit to the NORMAL state after all recovery transactions are executed.

5.3 Parameters of the System

It is well known that intrusions occur sporadically, with long time periods where there are no successful attacks, interspersed with short bursts of multiple attacks. However, there is still no agreement about what probability distribution best describes the intrusions.

To obtain reasonable analytical results, we consider the continuous rate of intrusions to learn the response of our system when intrusions happen.

In our model, we assume that the arriving of IDS alerts is a Poisson distribution. The probability of n IDS alerts arrived in $[0, t)$ is $P_n(t) = \frac{(\lambda t)^n}{n!} e^{-\lambda t}$. In other words, any S:$n$ state transits to S:$n+1$ with transition rate λ. The distribution function of IDS alerts is $F(t) = 1 - e^{-\lambda t}$. Thus, the probability density function of inter-arrival times of the IDS alerts is given by $f(t) = \lambda e^{-\lambda t}$, which is exponential distribution with parameter λ. Since an IDS alert causes one unit of recovery transactions, the transition direction always directs to the right side. We assume the processing time of IDS alerts and recovery transactions are exponential distribution with parameter μ_k and $\xi_k, 1 \leq k \leq \infty$, respectively, where $\mu_k = f(\mu_1, k)$ and $\xi_k = g(\xi_1, k)$. μ_k and ξ_k can also be considered as transition rates among states.

Since both the analyzer and scheduler need to check dependence relations to all items in queues, the more items in the queues, the more time will be spent. Say, $\mu_1 \geq \mu_2 \geq \cdots \geq \mu_k \cdots$, and $\xi_1 \geq \xi_2 \geq \cdots \geq \xi_k \cdots$, where $1 \leq k \leq \infty$. We use function f and g to simulate the degradation of performance when the number of items in queues increases. Given λ, μ_1, ξ_1, f and g, a model is solely determined.

Although the recovery system can find more damages than the IDS, the recovery still depends on the accuracy of the IDS. However, we assume that all corrupted transactions will ultimately be identified by the administrator of the system, even if they are not identified by the IDS. Since our system does not depend on timely reporting from the IDS, the delay of identifying a malicious transaction is not a problem.

5.4 Fit Infinite States to a Real System

Our model has infinite states, which is not practical in the real world. A real system has limited resources so its buffer size for queues is limited. Therefore, the number of states of a real attack recovery system is limited. In fact, when a queue is full, no further state transition about the queue can be made. Hence, the number of total states is restricted.

Based on the assumptions about parameters and the above discussion, the state transition of our model becomes a finite states Continuous-Time Markov Chain (CTMC) [49, 55] that can be characterized by a *generator matrix* $\mathbb{Q} = (q_{i,j})$ and initial state probability vector $\underline{\pi}(0)$, where $q_{i,j}$ is the transition rate from i to j and $q_{i,i} = -\sum_{j \neq i} q_{i,j}$.

There are two important queues in the system: the queue of recovery transactions, and the queue of IDS alerts. The queue size of recovery transactions is critical to the performance of the system. Once the buffer of recovery transactions is full, no new IDS alerts can be processed because there is no space to store new recovery transactions. For example, let the buffer size of recovery transactions be 4. The STG for the system will look like the STG in Figure 5 except all parts beyond row 4 would be eliminated. When the buffer of recovery transactions is full (number of IDS alerts is 4), any new arrival IDS alerts cannot be processed. The recovery analyzer is simply blocked. As long as the recovery analyzer keeps on blocking, the queue of IDS alerts will fill up. After the queue of IDS alerts is full, it will lose IDS alerts. Therefore, all parts beyond column 4 are not helpful for improving the overall performance of the system. However, a larger buffer for IDS alerts can help to cache peak traffic.

As long as the mean rate of the IDS alerts remains stable, the system can handle the situation of some peak traffics with a larger buffer of IDS alerts.

According to our discussion, the buffer size of recovery transactions determines the overall performance of a system. In this article, an n size buffer of recovery transactions is modeled by a n rows by n columns STG.

As long as the queue of recovery transactions is full, the system will be at states at the right edge of STG, indicating that the system has limits, beyond which IDS alerts are lost by the recovery system. When and how long a system stays at the right edge of STG describes how many IDS alerts could be lost by the system. Given a probability distribution among all states of a STG, we define *loss probability* as follows.

Definition 2. *Given an n states STG, a vector of probability distribution $\pi = (p_1, p_2, \cdots, p_n)$, and a set $\mathcal{E}$ of states at the right edge of STG, the loss probability of the STG with respect to π is $lp_\pi = \sum_{i \in \mathcal{E}} p_i$.*

Loss probability describes whether a system reaches its limits under given condition π. If lp_π is very small, the system is prone to working very well. Otherwise, the system is prone to losing IDS alerts and failing to work efficiently.

Definition 3. *If a system exists a steady state whose probability distribution is given by π, where $lp_\pi = \epsilon$, we say the system is ϵ-convergence.*

ϵ-convergence describes how many IDS alerts could be lost at the steady state of a system. It is more practical for introducing features of a real system. A 1-convergence system is the worst system in theory and is useless in practice. The goal of designing a system is to let the ϵ as small as possible.

5.5 Steady-State Behaviors

The steady state of a system is the state that all features of the system do not change any more after running a long period of time. It may not exist at all for a specific CTMC. Fortunately, most real systems do have their steady states. Once a n by n generator matrix $\mathbb{Q}$ is given, the steady-state probability vector $\underline{\pi}$ is determined by Equation 1.

$$\underline{\pi}\mathbb{Q} = \underline{0}, \sum_{1 \le i \le n} \pi_i = 1. \tag{1}$$

Impacts on the loss probability with different buffer size, f and g

Case 1. $\lambda = 1, \mu_1 = 15$, and $\xi_1 = 20$, buffer size changes from 2 to 30. The results are shown in Figure 6 with different f and g.

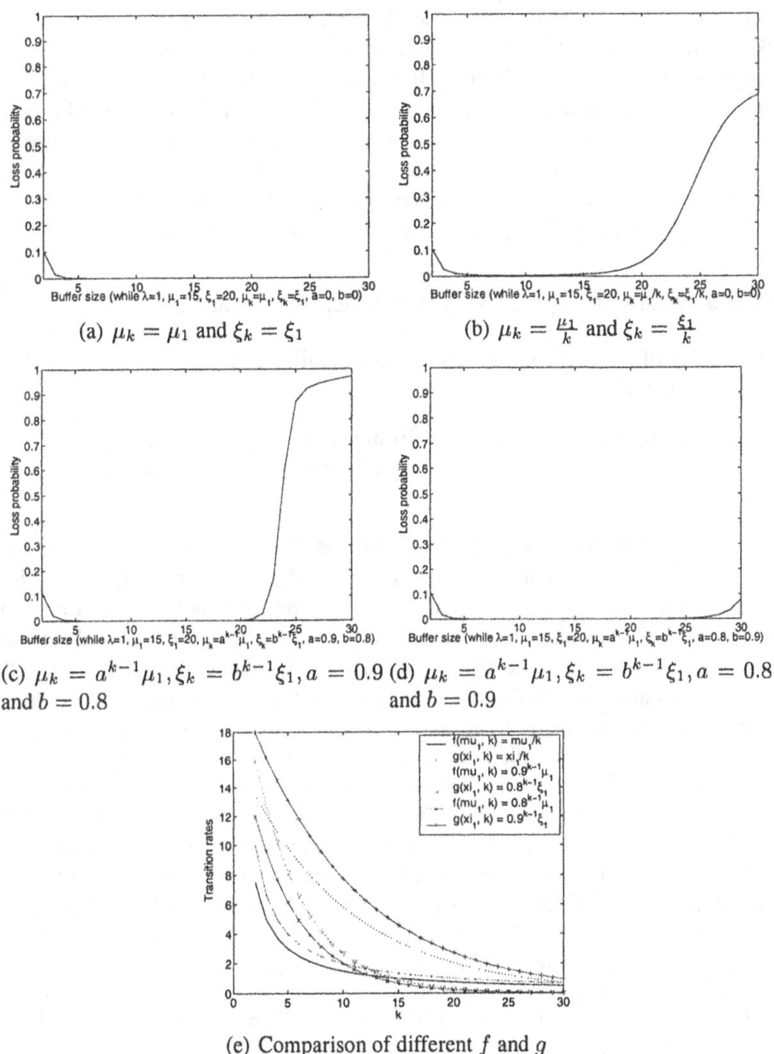

(a) $\mu_k = \mu_1$ and $\xi_k = \xi_1$

(b) $\mu_k = \frac{\mu_1}{k}$ and $\xi_k = \frac{\xi_1}{k}$

(c) $\mu_k = a^{k-1}\mu_1, \xi_k = b^{k-1}\xi_1, a = 0.9$ and $b = 0.8$

(d) $\mu_k = a^{k-1}\mu_1, \xi_k = b^{k-1}\xi_1, a = 0.8$ and $b = 0.9$

(e) Comparison of different f and g

Fig. 6. Impacts on the loss probability with different buffer size of IDS alerts, f and g

Remark: If the speed of degradation of μ_k and ξ_k is very slow while k increases, loss probability can be reduced significantly by increasing the buffer size of IDS alerts, as shown in Figure 6(a). The condition does not hold in most real systems. The analyzer needs to check all dependence relations among existing recovery transactions to generate a correct recovery scheme after new IDS alert arrives. The checking time will be a function of the number of existing recovery transactions. It is more realistic that μ_k and ξ_k decrease while k increases. When the attenuation of μ_k and ξ_k is very quick and there are too much items in queues to process, the steady state of the system is prone to higher loss probability. Intuitively, when the buffer size increases not too much and the attenuation of μ_k and ξ_k is not too much, the loss probability decreases. If we allow the queues to be too large, the loss probability will increase due to significant degradation of processing speed, which can be found in Figure 6(b) and Figure 6(c). When μ_k decreases faster than ξ_k, the results are better than the contrary case, which can be found in Figure 6(d) comparing with Figure 6(c).

Impacts on steady-state probability with different λ, μ and ξ

For simplicity of comparison, we stick to the condition of $\mu_k = \mu_1/k, \xi_k = \xi_1/k$ and buffer size is 15 in this section.

Case 2. $\mu_1 = 15, \xi_1 = 20$, λ changes from 0 to 4. The probability distribution is shown in Figure 7(a). The expected values of number of items in queues are shown in Figure 7(b)[5].

Remark: When the arrival rate of IDS alerts λ is less than 1, the system has high probability (> 0.8) to stay at the NORMAL state. The loss probability is very low. The expected values are also less than 1. The system can handle the situation very well. When λ is larger than 1, especially larger than 1.5, the loss probability and the probability of staying at the SCAN state increase very quickly, indicating that the system cannot handle all intrusions, and consequently, the performance of processing normal transactions degrades almost 100%. We can also observe that the queue of recovery transactions is full even though the expected number of IDS alerts is 1. The system cannot accept new IDS alerts to generate more recovery transactions although the buffer of IDS alerts is almost empty. Therefore, the buffer size of recovery transactions is a critical parameter for system performance. By checking the expected number of IDS alerts in the queue, we can reduce the buffer size for IDS alerts without compromising the loss probability of the system. In fact, we observed that the probability distribution on states that are near the right up corner of the STG usually are zeros if the system has low loss probability ($< 1\%$).

Case 3. $\lambda = 1, \xi_1 = 20$, μ_1 changes from 0 to 20. The probability distribution is shown in Figure 7(c). The expected number of items in queues are shown in Figure 7(d).

Case 4. $\lambda = 1, \mu_1 = 15$, ξ_1 changes from 0 to 20. The probability distribution is shown in Figure 7(e). The expected number of items in queues are shown in Figure 7(f).

[5] In Figure 7(b), Figure 7(d) and Figure 7(f) the loss probability is also drawn in the figures for reference. Note that the value of loss probability is between 0 and 1, and it is not an expected value as read from label of y axis.

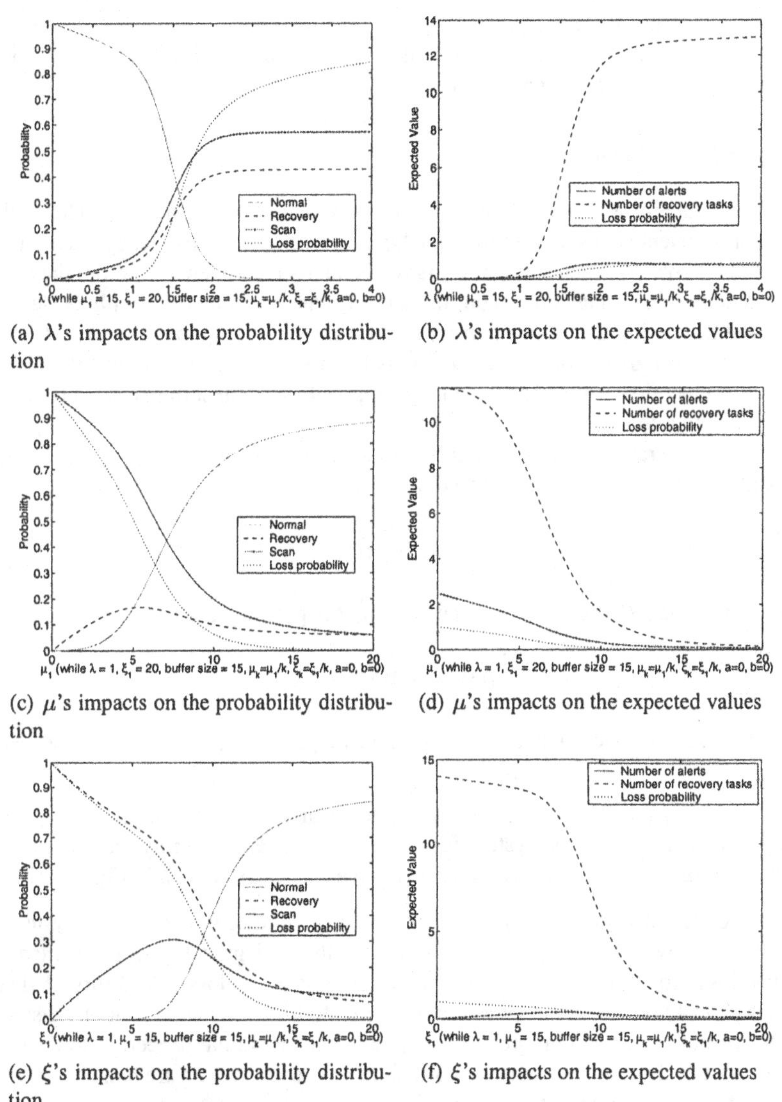

(a) λ's impacts on the probability distribution

(b) λ's impacts on the expected values

(c) μ's impacts on the probability distribution

(d) μ's impacts on the expected values

(e) ξ's impacts on the probability distribution

(f) ξ's impacts on the expected values

Fig. 7. Impacts on steady-state probability with different λ, μ and ξ

Remark: Case 3 and Case 4 show that μ_1 and ξ_1 have similar effects on the system behaviors. When they are large enough, *e.g.* > 15, the system has high probability (> 0.8) to stay at the NORMAL state, which indicates that the degradation of performance for new arrival transactions is less than 20%. After exceeding a specific value, e.g. 15, μ_1 and ξ_1 has no significant impacts on improving the steady probability of the NORMAL. There exists a cost effective range of μ_1 and ξ_1, which can be observed in Case 3 and Case 4. Given a value of λ, the μ_1 and ξ_1 are supposed to be in the cost effective range for designing a new system.

5.6 Transient Behaviors

A transient state of a system is the state of the system at a specific time. The evaluation of transient states shows how quickly a system goes to its steady state, how much time is spent on each state, how many IDS alerts have been lost before the system enters its steady state, and so on. In fact, a system may satisfy us with its steady states, but disappoint us with its transient behaviors, e.g. taking too long to go to the steady states or loosing too many IDS alerts before it can effectively handle them. Transient behaviors also tells us what may happen if a system suffers a short term of high attacking rate.

Given a generator matrix $\mathbb{Q}$ and initial state probability vector $\underline{\pi}(0)$, transit state probability $\underline{\pi}(t)$ at time t is determined by Equation 2.

$$\frac{d}{dt}\underline{\pi}(t) = \underline{\pi}(t)\mathbb{Q} \tag{2}$$

Cumulative time $\underline{l}(t)$ spent on each state at time t is given by Equation 3.

$$\frac{d}{dt}\underline{l}(t) = \underline{l}(t)\mathbb{Q} + \underline{\pi}(0) \tag{3}$$

In this section, we stick to the condition of $\mu_k = \mu_1/k$, $\xi_k = \xi_1/k$, and buffer size $= 15$.

Case 5. $\lambda = 1, \mu_1 = 15, \xi_1 = 20$ and the system starts from the NORMAL state. We observe the behaviors of the system for 4 time-units. The probability distribution is shown in Figure 8(a). Cumulative time spent on each state is shown in Figure 8(b).

Remark: Case 5 shows what a good system looks like after it starts. Such systems enter their steady state very quickly and remain both low degradation of performance and low loss probability of IDS alerts in its steady state. Its loss probability of IDS alerts is almost not noticeable, given its proximity to the x axis and cannot be distinguished from the x axis in Figure 8(a). A system that has similar properties to Case 5 spends most of its time on executing normal transactions. Attacks are handled effectively and cost little time of the system. A real system is supposed to be designed in this style.

Case 6. $\lambda = 1, \mu_1 = 2, \xi_1 = 3$ and the system starts from the NORMAL state. We observe the behaviors of the system for 100 time-units. The probability distribution is shown in Figure 8(c). cumulative time spent on each state is shown in Figure 8(d).

Remark: Case 6 demonstrates what a system will be a given times during a period of rush hour attacks, or when the attacking rate is much higher than the value that a system is designed for. Under such conditions, the degradation of performance will

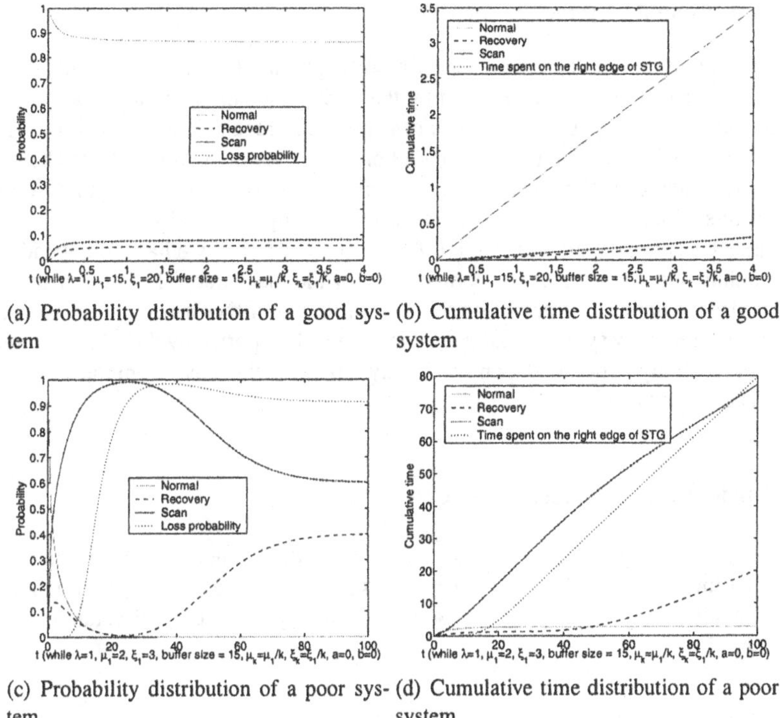

(a) Probability distribution of a good system

(b) Cumulative time distribution of a good system

(c) Probability distribution of a poor system

(d) Cumulative time distribution of a poor system

Fig. 8. Transient state probability

be almost 100%, and there is no chance to serve new arrival transactions. The loss probability goes up very quickly (< 30 time-units) and remains at the range from 0.9 to 1. Moreover, such systems spend most of their time on analysis and recovery. By observing time spent on the right edge of STG in Figure 8(d), the system spent about 80% time on the right edge of STG, indicating that the queue of recovery transactions is full.

An interesting fact is that $\mu_1 = 2$ and $\xi_1 = 3$ is already good enough for a small λ, such as $\lambda = 0.1$. If the system is designed for $\lambda = 0.1$ we cannot say the system shown in Figure 8(c) is a poor system simply based on results in Case 6, since the attacking rate to the system is 9 times larger than the goal of its design. But we can learn transient behaviors of the system from Case 6 when attacking rate is much higher than what it is designed for. In the case, the system can resist such high attacking rate about 5 time-units if it is at the NORMAL state when the attacks start. After 5 time-units, the loss probability goes up. The results show how long the system can resist to a specific high attacking rate without compromising its loss probability.

5.7 Impacts on the System by the IDS

Our techniques do not depend on timely reporting by the IDS. As long as the damage is reported, whether it is reported by the IDS or the administrator of a system, our techniques work out all affected transactions and repair them. However, if the reporting delay is significant, more transactions in the system will be affected before recovery, which leads to more time being spent on recovery. Any system that has an IDS suffers with this problem, except intrusion masking systems [59].

Since we cannot guarantee that an IDS is 100% accurate, we have to depend on the administrator of a system to compensate for the inaccuracy. The administrator may revise the damaged-transaction set $\mathcal{B}$ according to further investigation. Consequently, the recovery system repairs the damage newly reported by the administrator. Since our techniques do not depend on timely reporting, the delay from the administrator is acceptable.

6 Multi-Version based Recovery

In this section, we introduce a multi-version based data structure to break the partial order limitations between the normal transactions and the recovery transactions. Note that all other rules discussed in Section 4 still apply to the multi-version based recovery.

6.1 Revision History

In the system, any data object x has multiple versions. x has its first version x^{v_1} when it is created. When x is written again, the system adds a new version x^{v_2}. If x has been written n times, it has n versions, which we call the revision history of x. The revision history of x is formed as $\langle x^{v_1}, x^{v_2}, \cdots, x^{v_n}\rangle$, where each $v_i, 1 \leq i \leq n$ is a revision number of x and v_j is later than v_i if $j > i$. If we know that x^{v_k} is corrupted by the attacker then any transaction that reads x^{v_k} gets wrong results.

Note that it is possible that in x's revision history, there is only a specific version that is corrupted. For example, x is generated periodically by a trustable transaction T and an attacker only corrupts a specific version of x, e.g., x^{v_k}. Therefore, we cannot conclude if x^{v_j}, where $j > k$, is dirty without further analysis.

For a specific version x^{v_k}, when it has a value that it is not supposed to have, it is *dirty*. For example, when x^{v_k} is created by an attacker or computed based on dirty data objects, it is dirty. Otherwise, it is *clean*.

A revision history can be built at the system level or application level. In fact, it does exist in the system log or application level. For example, some system logs record different versions of data objects written at different times. A history of a bank account is also a revision history.

Besides the revision history, the system needs to record which versions a specific transaction reads and which versions the transaction writes, recording this information is also implemented in modern database systems.

6.2 Operations on the Revision History

A normal transaction reads data objects with the highest revision number, and it writes data objects with the highest revision number in their revision histories. So, a revision history does not change dependency relations among normal transactions. It operates just as if multiple versions did not exist.

A recovery transaction, whether it is an undo or redo transaction, operates on data objects with the same revision numbers as it used the first time it executed. For example, a undo(T_i) is implemented by removing all specific versions from revision histories of data objects written by T_i. A redo(T_i) will generate data objects with the same revision number as it executed first time. A revision history does not change dependency relations among recovery transactions either. We can consider that recovery transactions are for revising part of the history of the system.

When we find a dirty version x^{v_k}, there are two possible ways that the dirty version was generated. One possibility is that x^{v_k} should not exist at all, e.g, it was created by the attacker. Any transaction that reads x^{v_k} is supposed to read $x^{v_{k-1}}$ instead of x^{v_k}. Another possibility is that x^{v_k} has a dirty value and needs to be recomputed by a redo transaction. Any transaction that reads x^{v_k} needs to wait until the redo transaction has completed to get a correct value of x^{v_k}. In this case, we mark x^{v_k} as $x_b^{v_k}$ to block possible reading until the redo transaction is complete.

Multi-version data objects break dependency relations among recovery transactions and normal transactions, which enable us to run the recovery transactions and normal transactions concurrently. According to the structure of the revision history, operations on old versions happen as "in the past." Therefore, execution of normal transactions does not corrupt recovery transactions.

Note that flow dependencies cannot be broken, which guarantees that the semantics of execution are correct. From the point of view of recovery transactions (or normal transactions), there is only a single version for each data object to ensure correct semantics.

There is no special order that needs to be satisfied while scheduling normal and recovery transactions. After a recovery transaction T_b is done, release transactions that are blocking on it and provide them data objects with revision number t_m if the number exists, otherwise with revision number t_{m-1}.

6.3 Architecture

The architecture of a multi-version based recovery system can be simplified as the structure in Figure 9.

In this architecture, there are two independent processing parts, the recovery analyzer and the transaction scheduler. An independent Intrusion Detection System (IDS) reports malicious transactions to the system by periodically putting IDS alerts in a queue. The recovery analyzer processes IDS alerts one by one. It determines the amount of damage and generates recovery transactions. The recovery transactions are sorted and put into another queue. The scheduler schedules recovery transactions and normal transactions concurrently.

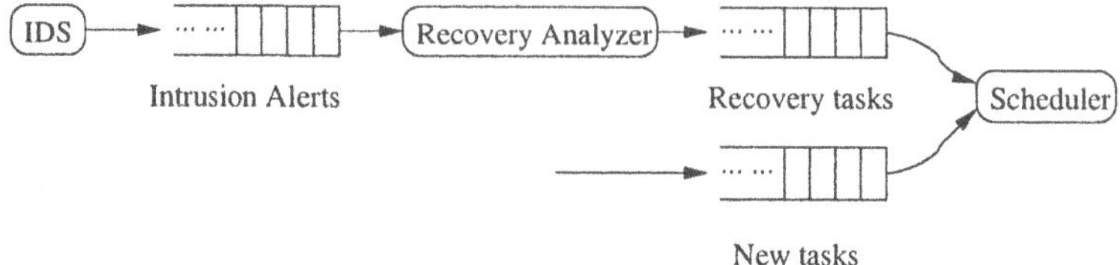

Fig. 9. Processing Structure of an Attack Recovery System

6.4 Algorithms

The recovery analyzer runs the following algorithm.

1. Wait until the queue of IDS alerts is not empty. Get one IDS alert and continue.
2. Determine all damage caused by the attack that the IDS reported and generate undo transactions. Abort and block all running transactions that are dependent on damaged transactions.
3. Generate redo transactions. For all $T_i : undo(T_i) \in \mathcal{R}$, if $redo(T_i) \notin \mathcal{R}$, mark $undo(T_i)$ as $undo(T_i)_b$. Otherwise, mark $redo(T_i)$ as $redo(T_i)_b$.
4. Set up precedence orders among recovery transactions.
5. Sort recovery transactions and put them into the queue of recovery transactions.
6. Goto step 1.

6.5 Performance

There are two queues in the system. The analyzer and the scheduler work independently if both queues are not full. Suppose the arrival of IDS alerts has a Poisson distribution with rate λ_1, the time distribution of processing IDS alerts is exponentially distributed with parameter μ_1, and the time distribution of executing recovery transactions is also exponentially distributed with parameter μ_2. The system behaves like a tandem Jackson network.

We are interested in relationships among λ_1, μ_1 and μ_2 while considering the loss probability of IDS alerts.

While $\mu_2 \leq \mu 1$, the queue of recovery transactions becomes the bottleneck of the system. The queue of recovery transactions will be full and no further recovery transactions could be generated. Therefore, no further IDS alerts could be processed. This situation should be avoided.

While $\mu_1 < \mu_2$, the queue of IDS alerts becomes the bottleneck of the system. The loss probability of IDS alerts is determined by the processing rate μ_1. Consider the buffer size of the queue is K. According to our assumptions the queue becomes a $M/M/1/K$-queue [49, 55]. The steady state probability for such a queue is given by:

$$p_0 = \frac{1-\rho}{1-\rho^{K+1}} \tag{4}$$

$$p_k = p_0 \rho^k \tag{5}$$

where $1 \leq k \leq K$, $\rho = \frac{\lambda_1}{\mu_1}$, and p_k indicates that there are k IDS alerts in the queue. Let us assume $\lambda_1 < \mu_1 < \mu_2$, $\rho < 1$. We have

$$E[N] = \sum_{k=0}^{K} k p_k = \frac{\rho}{1-\rho} - \frac{K+1}{1-\rho^{K+1}} \rho^{K+1} \tag{6}$$

Thus,

$$E[T] = \frac{E[N]}{\lambda_1} = \frac{1}{\mu_1 - \lambda_1} - \frac{K+1}{\mu_1 - \lambda_1 \rho^k} \rho^k \tag{7}$$

6.6 Integrity Level

Suppose the expected delay time of IDS reports is $E[T']$, the total time an IDS alert exists in the system is $E[T'] + E[T]$. During that time, $l = \mu_3(E[T'] + E[T])$ transactions have been executed, where μ_3 is the executing rate of normal transactions. In fact, l is the number of transactions that the analyzer is supposed to scan in the system log. The larger l is, the more unidentified bad transactions there are, and the longer time the analyzer takes to scan the log.

l describes the integrity level of the system. In other words, how many transactions exist where it is unknown whether they are infected or not. Although reducing μ_3 improves integrity, it will enlarge the degradation of performance simultaneously. An extreme situation is where $\mu_3 = 0$, in other words, stop service to normal transactions. Then no further damage occurs. We can also reduce the delay time of IDS reports and increase the processing speed of IDS alerts to improve the integrity level of the system without sacrificing the performance μ_3, which is what we usually do.

Another parameter affecting the integrity level of the system is *loss probability* of IDS alerts. The loss probability is given by:

$$p_{loss} = p_K = \frac{\rho^K - \rho^{K+1}}{1-\rho^{K+1}} \tag{8}$$

The higher p_{loss} is, the more unidentified malicious transactions there are in the system.

The queue of recovery transactions is the second queue of the tandem Jackson network. We assume that the probability of its overflow [24] is relative small compared with the loss probability of the first queue since $\mu_1 < \mu_2$.

6.7 A Case Study

A case study is more intuitive than equations. We set up a case, where $E[T'] = 10, K = 20, \mu_1 = 5, \lambda_1 = 2, \mu_3 = 4$, to investigate the integrity level of the system. When parameters change, the results are shown in Figure 10.

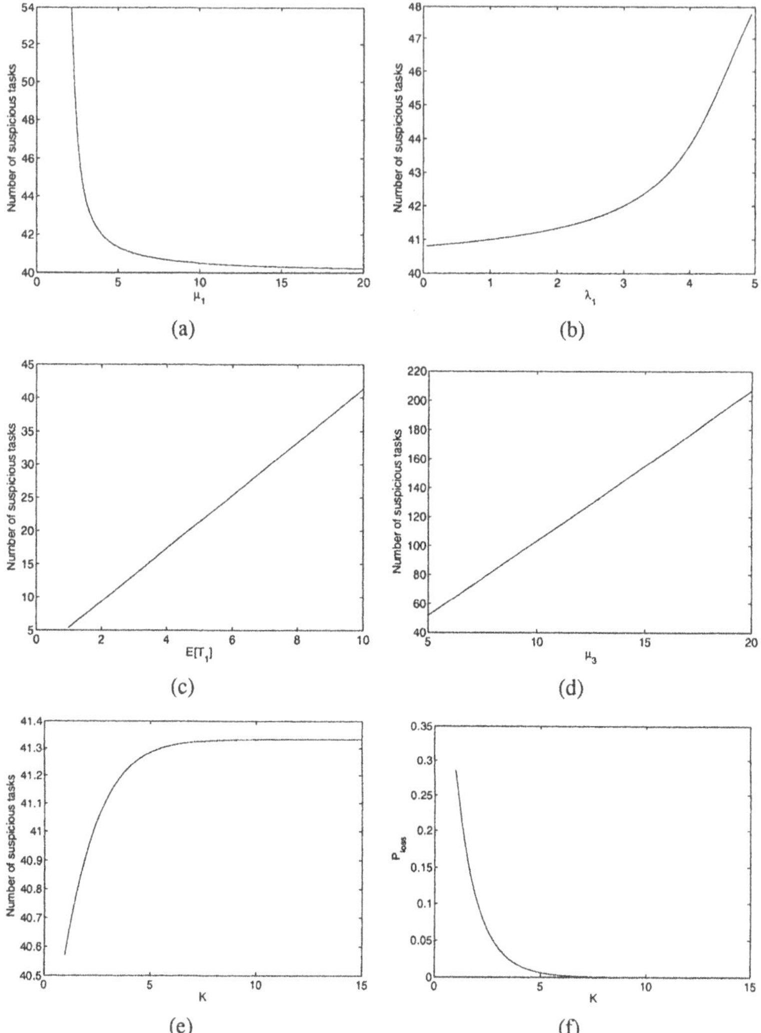

Fig. 10. Impacts on the system with different parameters

In this case, K has little effect on l after it is large enough, e.g., > 5 in the figure. Both $E[T']$ and μ_3 have linear impacts on l while μ_3 has relatively more significant impact on l. As for μ_1 and λ_1, as soon as $\rho = \frac{\lambda_1}{\mu_1}$ is small enough, their changes have little effect on l.

7 Related Work

7.1 Intrusion Detection

One critical step towards intrusion-tolerant systems is intrusion detection (ID), which has attracted much attention over the past years [10, 17, 19, 25, 26, 37–39, 45]. An Intrusion Detection System (IDS) [27] can detect some intrusions. But, in a distributed computing system, the damage directly caused by the attacker may be spread by executing normal transactions without being detected by the IDS. The IDS is unable to trace damage spreading and cannot locate all damage to the system.

7.2 Survivability and Intrusion Tolerance

The need for intrusion tolerance, or survivability, has been recognized by many researchers in such contexts as information warfare [14]. Recently, extensive research has been done in general principles of survivability [23], survivable software architectures [52], survivability of networks [43], survivable storage systems [13, 53, 57, 58], etc. Although the proposed techniques are helpful for database survivability, they cannot be directly applied to build intrusion tolerant database systems.

Some research has been done in database survivability. For instance, in [3], a fault tolerant approach is taken to survive database attacks where (a) several phases are suggested to be useful, such as attack detection, damage assessment and repair, and fault treatment, but no concrete mechanisms are proposed for these phases; (b) a color scheme for marking damage (and repair) and a notion of integrity suitable for partially damaged databases are used to develop a mechanism by which databases under attack could still be safely used. This scheme can be viewed as a special damage containment mechanism. However, it assumes that each data object has an (accurate) initial damage mark, our approach does not. In fact, our approach focuses on how to automatically mark (and contain) the damage, and how to deal with the negative impact of inaccurate damage marks. There is also some work on OS-level database survivability. In [42] a technique is proposed to detect storage jamming, malicious modification of data, using a set of special detect objects which are indistinguishable to the jammer from normal objects. Modification on detect objects indicates a storage jamming attack. In [6], checksums are smartly used to detect data corruption. Similar to trusted database system technologies, both detect objects and checksums can be used to make our techniques more resistant to OS level attacks.

7.3 Fault Tolerance

The failure handling of workflow has been discussed in recent work [8, 11, 54]. Failure handling is different from attack recovery in two aspects. On one hand, they have different goals. Failure handling tries to guarantee the atomic of workflows. When failure happens, their work finds out which transactions should be aborted. If all transactions are successfully executed, failure handling does nothing for the workflow. Attack recovery has different goals, which need to do nothing for failure transactions even if they are malicious because malicious failure transactions have no effects on the workflow system. Attack recovery focuses on malicious transactions that are successfully executed. It tries to remove all effects of such transactions. On the other hand, these two systems are active at different times. Failure handling occurs when the workflows are in progress. When the IDS reports attacks, the malicious transactions usually have been successfully executed. Failure handling can do nothing because no failure occurred. Attack recovery is supposed to remove the effects of malicious transactions after they are committed.

The checkpoint techniques [28,29] also do not work for efficient attack recovery. A checkpoint rolls back the whole system to a specific time. All work, including both malicious transactions and normal transactions, after the specific time will be lost, especially when the delay of the IDS is very long. In addition, checkpoints introduce extra storage cost.

7.4 Distributed Computing Systems

Decentralized distributed computing is becoming more and more popular. In distributed computing models, transactions specifications cannot be accessed in a central node. They are carried by workflow itself or stored in a distributed style. In either case, our theories are still practical. We need to process the specifications of distributed transactional processes in a distributed style.

In some work such as [5], security and privacy is important, and the whole specification of workflows avoids being exposed to all processing nodes to protect privacy. Our theories are based on the dependence relations among transactions. The specification can be best protected by exposing only dependent relations to the recovery system.

7.5 Rollback Recovery

Rollback recovery (e.g. [7,22]) is surveyed in [12]. Rollback recovery focuses on the relationship of message passing and considers temporal sequences based on message passing. In contrast, we focus on data and control dependence relations inside transactions. In fact, message passing is a kind of data dependence relation but not vice versa (e.g., a data dependence relation caused by more than one message passing steps or by sharing data). We also observed that in attack recovery an execution path may change due to control dependence, causing different patterns of message passing. In addition, our methods exploit more detail in dependence relations than the methods that are message passing based; therefore our method is more effective and efficient for attack recovery. Our method also better matches the workflow model.

In our work, we deal with transactional processes. Although rollback recovery is a good analogy to transactional processes, it is simply not a dual of the latter and its results cannot be simply applied to transactional processes. A comparison between transactional processes and the message passing model is shown in Figure 11, Figure 12, and Table 1.

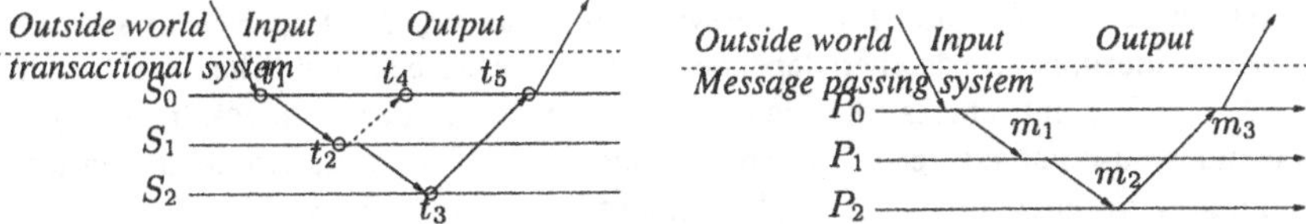

Fig. 11. A transactional process moving through sites

Fig. 12. Message passing system

Table 1. A Comparison between the Dependency Relation based Model and the Message passing Model

	Dependency Relation based Model	Message Passing Model
Where to execute a process	on multiple sites	on a single site
Where failures happen	in the middle of a transactional process	at the end of a computing process
Domino effects	forwards	backward
Recovery	through compensate transactions	through check pointing
Damage caused	is not strictly time related while strictly dependence related	is strictly time related while not strictly dependence related
Consequences	orphan transactions and orphan processes	orphan messages and orphan processes

7.6 Repairable Database Systems

Work [9,46,62,63] is obviously the most similar work to ours, and also takes dependency relation based approaches. Our work presented in this article is more comprehensive in the discussion of dependency-relation based theories. Our work discussed more types of dependency relations and more detailed concurrency restrictions than theirs. We also created different performance models for different recovery systems that use different recovery strategies.

7.7 Our Previous Work

In [2,31], when intrusions have been detected by the IDS, the database system isolates and confines the impaired data. Then, the system carries out recovery for malicious transactions. We have proposed a set of transaction-level trusted recovery algorithms. ITDB has actually implemented the on-the-fly damage assessment and repair algorithm proposed in [2]. In [33], we have proposed a general isolation algorithm. However, this algorithm cannot be directly implemented on top of an off-the-shelf DBMS. ITDB has developed a novel SQL rewriting approach to implement the algorithm. Finally, the design and implementation of almost every key ITDB component have been described in detail in our previous publications [2, 30, 32, 34–36], Recent work considering more detailed dependency relations has been published in [60, 61].

Work [31] introduces the concept of "semantics-based attack recovery". Semantics-based attack recovery can save the work of more transactions than the techniques presented in this article, but semantics-based attack recovery is primarily a 'coldstart' recovery technology and not easy to be extended to do 'warmstart' or 'hotstart' attack recovery.

This article provides a comprehensive view on both theoretical issues and practical issues of self-healing distributed transactional processes.

8 Conclusion

Attack recovery techniques provide an option to improve the availability under attacks. In this article, we introduced important concepts and techniques for attack recovery. While an independent IDS reports malicious tasks periodically, attack recovery techniques identify all damage caused by the malicious tasks and repair them automatically. We also presented an architecture of the recovery system and analyzed its performance when intrusions happen. Both the steady states and transient states are analyzed with a CTMC model. To solve concurrency conflicts caused by on-line recovery, we have to do multi-version based recovery since multi-version data items can remove anti-flow and output dependencies. More details of such techniques should be worked out in future work. We believe that attack recovery is not only the last efforts while all defensive mechanism are broken, but also a necessary component for all critical infrastructures.

9 Acknowledgment

Peng Liu is partially supported by NSF grant CCR-TC-0233324. Sushil Jajodia is partially supported by NSF grants IIS-0242237 and IIS-0430402.

References

1. M. R. Adam. Security-Control Methods for Statistical Database: A Comparative Study. *ACM Computing Surveys*, 21(4), 1989.
2. P. Ammann, S. Jajodia, and P. Liu. Recovery from malicious transactions. *IEEE Transaction on Knowledge and Data Engineering*, 14(5):1167–1185, 2002.
3. P. Ammann, S. Jajodia, C.D. McCollum, and B.T. Blaustein. Surviving information warfare attacks on databases. In *Proceedings of the IEEE Symposium on Security and Privacy*, pages 164–174, Oakland, CA, May 1997.
4. V. Atluri, S. Jajodia, and B. George. *Multilevel Secure Transaction Processing*. Kluwer Academic Publishers, 1999.

5. Vijayalakshmi Atluri, Soon Ae Chun, and Pietro Mazzoleni. A chinese wall security model for decentralized workflow systems. In *Proceedings of the 8th ACM conference on Computer and Communications Security*, pages 48–57. ACM Press, 2001.
6. D. Barbara, R. Goel, and S. Jajodia. Using checksums to detect data corruption. In *Proceedings of the 2000 International Conference on Extending Data Base Technology*, Mar 2000.
7. Yi bing Lin and Edward D. Lazowska. A study of time warp rollback machanisms. *ACM Transactions on Modeling and Computer Simulations*, 1(1):51–72, January 1991.
8. Qiming Chen and Umeshwar Dayal. Failure handling for transaction hierarchies. In Alex Gray and Per-RAke Larson, editors, *Proceedings of the Thirteenth International Conference on Data Engineering, April 7-11, 1997 Birmingham U.K*, pages 245–254. IEEE Computer Society, 1997.
9. Tzi cker Chiueh and Dhruv Pilania. Design, implementation, and evaluation of a repairable database management system. In *International Conference on Data Engineering*, pages 1024–1035, 2005.
10. D. E. Denning. An intrusion-detection model. *IEEE Trans. on Software Engineering*, SE-13:222–232, February 1987.
11. Johann Eder and Walter Liebhart. Workflow recovery. In *Conference on Cooperative Information Systems*, pages 124–134, 1996.
12. E. N. (Mootaz) Elnozahy, Lorenzo Alvisi, Yi min Wang, and David B. Johnson. A survey of rollback-recovery protocols in message-passing systems. *ACM Computing Surveys*, 34(3):375–408, September 2002.
13. Gregory R. Ganger, Pradeep K. Khosla, Mehmet Bakkaloglu, Michael W. Bigrigg, Garth R. Goodson, Semih Oguz, Vijay Pandurangan, Craig A. N. Soules, John D. Strunk, and Jay J. Wylie. Survivable storage systems. In *DARPA Information Survivability Conference and Exposition*, volume 2, pages 184–195, Anaheim, CA, 12-14 June 2001. IEEE.
14. R. Graubart, L. Schlipper, and C. McCollum. Defending database management systems against information warfare attacks. Technical report, The MITRE Corporation, 1996.
15. J. Gray and A. Reuter. *Transaction Processing: Concepts and Techniques*. Morgan Kaufmann Publishers, Inc., 1993.
16. P. P. Griffiths and B. W. Wade. An Authorization Mechanism for a Relational Database System. *ACM Transactions on Database Systems*, 1(3):242–255, September 1976.
17. P. Helman and G. Liepins. Statistical foundations of audit trail analysis for the detection of computer misuse. *IEEE Transactions on Software Engineering*, 19(9):886–901, 1993.
18. K. Ilgun, R.A. Kemmerer, and P.A. Porras. State transition analysis: A rule-based intrusion detection approach. *IEEE Transactions on Software Engineering*, 21(3):181–199, 1995.
19. R. Jagannathan and T. Lunt. System design document: Next generation intrusion detection expert system (nides). Technical report, SRI International, Menlo Park, California, 1993.
20. S. Jajodia, P. Samarati, M. L. Sapino, and V. S. Subrahmanian. Flexible support for multiple access control policies. *ACM Trans. Database Syst.*, 26(2):214–260, 2001.
21. H. S. Javitz and A. Valdes. The sri ides statistical anomaly detector. In *Proceedings IEEE Computer Society Symposium on Security and Privacy*, Oakland, CA, May 1991.
22. David R. Jefferson. Virtual time. *ACM Transaction on Programming Languages and Systems*, 7(3):404–425, July 1985.
23. J. Knight, K. Sullivan, M. Elder, and C. Wang. Survivability architectures: Issues and approaches. In *Proceedings of the 2000 DARPA Information Survivability Conference & Exposition*, pages 157–171, CA, June 2000.
24. Dirk P. Kroese and Victor F. Nicola. Efficient simulation of a tandem jackson network. *ACM Transactions on Modeling and Computer Simulation*, 12(2):119–141, April 2002.

25. T. Lane and C.E. Brodley. Temporal sequence learning and data reduction for anomaly detection. In *Proc. 5th ACM Conference on Computer and Communications Security*, San Francisco, CA, Nov 1998.
26. Wenke Lee, Sal Stolfo, and Kui Mok. A data mining framework for building intrusion detection models. In *Proc. 1999 IEEE Symposium on Security and Privacy*, Oakland, CA, May 1999.
27. Wenke Lee and Salvatore J. Stolfo. A framework for constructing features and models for intrusion detection systems. *ACM Transactions on Information and System Security*, 3(4):227–261, 2000.
28. Jun-Lin Lin and Margaret H. Dunham. A survey of distributed database checkpointing. *Distributed and Parallel Databases*, 5(3):289–319, 1997.
29. Jun-Lin Lin and Margaret H. Dunham. A low-cost checkpointing technique for distributed databases. *Distributed and Parallel Databases*, 10(3):241–268, 2001.
30. P. Liu. Dais: A real-time data attack isolation system for commercial database applications. In *Proceedings of the 17th Annual Computer Security Applications Conference*, 2001.
31. P. Liu, P. Ammann, and S. Jajodia. Rewriting histories: Recovery from malicious transactions. *Distributed and Parallel Databases*, 8(1):7–40, 2000.
32. P. Liu and S. Jajodia. Multi-phase damage confinement in database systems for intrusion tolerance. In *Proc. 14th IEEE Computer Security Foundations Workshop*, Nova Scotia, Canada, June 2001.
33. P. Liu, S. Jajodia, and C.D. McCollum. Intrusion confinement by isolation in information systems. *Journal of Computer Security*, 8(4):243–279, 2000.
34. P. Liu and Y. Wang. The design and implementation of a multiphase database damage confinement system. In *Proceedings of the 2002 IFIP WG 11.3 Working Conference on Data and Application Security*, 2002.
35. P. Luenam and P. Liu. Odar: An on-the-fly damage assessment and repair system for commercial database applications. In *Proceedings of the 2001 IFIP WG 11.3 Working Conference on Database and Application Security*, 2001.
36. P. Luenam and P. Liu. The design of an adaptive intrusion tolerant database system. In *Proc. IEEE Workshop on Intrusion Tolerant Systems*, 2002.
37. T. Lunt, A. Tamaru, F. Gilham, R. Jagannathan, C. Jalali, H. S. Javitz, A. Valdes, P. G. Neumann, and T. D. Garvey. A real time intrusion detection expert system (ides). Technical report, SRI International, Menlo Park, California, 1992.
38. Teresa Lunt and Catherine McCollum. Intrusion detection and response research at DARPA. Technical report, The MITRE Corporation, McLean, VA, 1998.
39. T.F. Lunt. A Survey of Intrusion Detection Techniques. *Computers & Security*, 12(4):405–418, June 1993.
40. N. Lynch, M. Merritt, W. Weihl, and A. Fekete. *Atomic Transactions*. Morgan Kaufmann, 1994.
41. J. McDermott and D. Goldschlag. Storage jamming. In D.L. Spooner, S.A. Demurjian, and J.E. Dobson, editors, *Database Security IX: Status and Prospects*, pages 365–381. Chapman & Hall, London, 1996.
42. J. McDermott and D. Goldschlag. Towards a model of storage jamming. In *Proceedings of the IEEE Computer Security Foundations Workshop*, pages 176–185, Kenmare, Ireland, June 1996.
43. D. Medhi and D. Tipper. Multi-layered network survivability - models, analysis, architecture, framework and implementation: An overview. In *Proceedings of the 2000 DARPA Information Survivability Conference & Exposition*, pages 173–186, CA, June 2000.

44. J. Eliot B. Moss. *Nested Transactions: An Approach to Reliable Distributed Computing*. The MIT Press, 1985.
45. B. Mukherjee, L. T. Heberlein, and K.N. Levitt. Network intrusion detection. *IEEE Network*, pages 26–41, June 1994.
46. Brajendra Panda and Kazi Asharful Haque. Extended data dependency approach: a robust way of rebuilding database. In *SAC '02: Proceedings of the 2002 ACM symposium on Applied computing*, pages 446–452, New York, NY, USA, 2002. ACM Press.
47. C. Pu, G. Kaiser, and N. Hutchinson. Split transactions for open-ended activities. In *Proceedings of the International Conference on Very Large Databases*, August 1988.
48. F. Rabitti, E. Bertino, W. Kim, and D. Woelk. A model of authorization for next-generation database systems. *ACM Transactions on Database Systems*, 16(1):88–131, 1994.
49. Robin A. Sahner, Kishor S. Trivedi, and Antonio Puliafito. *Performance and Reliability Analysis of Computer Systems*. Kluwer Academic Publishers, Norwell, Massachusetts, USA, 1996.
50. R. Sandhu and F. Chen. The multilevel relational (mlr) data model. *ACM Transactions on Information and Systems Security*, 1(1), 1998.
51. S.-P. Shieh and V.D. Gligor. On a pattern-oriented model for intrusion detection. *IEEE Transactions on Knowledge and Data Engineering*, 9(4):661–667, 1997.
52. V. Stavridou. Intrusion tolerant software architectures. In *Proceedings of the 2001 DARPA Information Survivability Conference & Exposition*, CA, June 2001.
53. John D. Strunk, Garth R. Goodson, Michael L. Scheinholtz, Craig A. N. Soules, and Gregory R. Ganger. Self-securing storage: Protecting data in compromised systems. In *Operating Systems Design and Implementation*, pages 165–180, San Diego, CA, 23-25 October 2000. USENIX Association.
54. Jian Tang and San-Yih Hwang. A scheme to specify and implement ad-hoc recovery in workflow systems. *Lecture Notes in Computer Science*, 1377:484–498, 1998.
55. Henk C. Tijms. *Stochastic Models*. Wiley series in probability and mathematical statistics. John Wiley & Son, New York, NY, USA, 1994.
56. M. Winslett, K. Smith, and X. Qian. Formal query languages for secure relational databases. *ACM Transactions on Database Systems*, 19(4):626–662, 1994.
57. Jay J. Wylie, Mehmet Bakkaloglu, Vijay Pandurangan, Michael W. Bigrigg, Semih Oguz, Ken Tew, Cory Williams, Gregory R. Ganger, and Pradeep K. Khosla. Selecting the right data distribution scheme for a survivable storage system. Technical Report CMU-CS-01-120, Carnegie Mellon University, 2001.
58. Jay J. Wylie, Michael W. Bigrigg, John D. Strunk, Gregory R. Ganger, Han Kiliccote, and Pradeep K. Khosla. Survivable information storage systems. *IEEE Computer*, 33(8):61–68, August 2000.
59. Meng Yu, Peng Liu, and Wanyu Zang. Intrusion masking for distributed atomic operations. In *The 18th IFIP International Information Security Conference*, pages 229–240, Athens Chamber of Commerce and Industry, Greece, 26-28 May 2003. IFIP Technical Committee 11, Kluwer Academic Publishers.
60. Meng Yu, Peng Liu, and Wanyu Zang. Self-healing workflow systems under attacks. In *The 24th International Conference on Distributed Computing Systems(ICDCS'04)*, pages 418–425, 2004.
61. Meng Yu, Peng Liu, and Wanyu Zang. Multi-version based attack recovery of workflow. In *The 19th Annual Computer Security Applications Conference*, pages 142–151, Dec. 2003.

62. Jing Zhou, Brajendra Panda, and Yi Hu. Succinct and fast accessible data structures for database damage assessment. In *Distributed Computing and Internet Technology*, pages 420–429, 2004.
63. Yanjun Zuo and Brajendra Panda. Damage discovery in distributed database systems. In *Database Security*, pages 111–123, 2004.

Part II

Access Control for Semi-Structured Data

Access Control Policy Models for XML

Michiharu Kudo and Naizhen Qi

IBM Tokyo Research Laboratory
{kudo,naishin}@jp.ibm.com

1 Introduction

Security concerns have been rapidly increasing because of repeated security incidents such as unexpected personal information leakage. Since XML [38] has been playing an important role in IT systems and applications, a big surge of requirements for legislative compliance is driving enterprises to protect their XML data for secure data management as well as privacy protection, and the access control mechanism is a central control point. In this chapter, we are concerned with fine-grained (element- and attribute-level) access control for XML database systems, rather than with document-level access control. We use the term *XML access control* to address such fine-grained access control. The *XML access control* deals with XML data and access control policies as well as schema definitions, e.g. XML Schema [40], and queries, e.g. XQuery [36]. The scope of *XML access control* is not limited to a specific application but covers broader areas that involve XML-based transactional systems such as e-commerce applications (Commerce XML [7] etc.), medical and health record applications (HL7 [16] etc.), and newspaper article distribution and applications (NewsML [17] etc.).

Figure 1 shows a generic XML access control architecture based on standardized authorization framework [18] with some modifications. An access requester, a human user or an application program, submits a query to the `PEP` (Policy Enforcement Point) which manages the XML data, optionally with the schema definition. Then the `PEP` asks the `PDP` (Policy Decision Point) for the access decision and the `PDP` retrieves the applicable access control policies from the policy repository. In some cases, the `PDP` retrieves actual values from the target XML data. The `PDP`'s decision is returned back to the `PEP` which grants or denies the access according to the decision's semantics. Note that this figure represents the logical relationships among the functional units, so the actual `PEP`, `PDP`, and the store may be built as one software module.

In the following sections, we explain how these components work together with a concrete example. The rest of this chapter is organized as follows. After introducing a sample access control policy in Section 1, we describe the access control policy

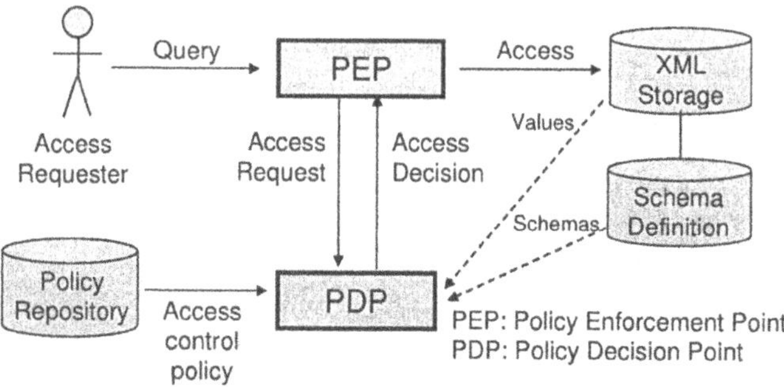

Fig. 1. Architecture of XML Access Control

model in Section 2. Then two XML access control policy languages are introduced in Section 3. In Section 4, we describe three kinds of runtime optimization techniques for *XML access control*. In Section 5, we summarize our conclusions.

1.1 Related Work

Fine-grained access control for XML documents has been studied by many researchers [3,8,13,23]. They all provide flexible and rich access control policy models that need runtime checking of access control policies. Their algorithms for run-time checking all assume that the XML documents are in the main memory or easily available and can be examined repeatedly.

DOM-based approaches [13,23] can support full XPath [37] expressions to provide expressiveness with naive implementations by creating the projection of the access control policy on a DOM tree. However, these approaches incur massive runtime costs when handling a large access control policy or a deeply layered XML document.

A different approach with document-level optimizations was proposed by Yu et al. [41]. Their scheme enforces efficient access control with an accessibility map generated by compressing neighboring accessibility rules to improve cost efficiency. However, since the maps are generated at the document level, document or policy updates may trigger expensive re-computations especially for large XML databases.

Stack-based access control [5] focuses on a streaming evaluator for encrypted documents. The stack allows the system to process XML access control requests in a streaming fashion, and a streaming index structure allowing skipping the irrelevant parts of the document. This approach performs access control on client side, and therefore once the document is sent out with the compiled access control rules, any updates on the document or the rules are not possible.

Automata-based models were proposed by Murata et al. [25,26] to optimize the pre-processing steps by minimizing the number of runtime checks for determining the accessibility of nodes in a query with automata. The proposed mechanism works very efficiently, in particular when the query is modifiable according to a static analysis, though there are more limitations when the dynamic nature of the policy needs to be taken into account.

Tree-based document filtering systems [2, 10] also provide value-based access control enforcement and independence of the XML data through a pre-computed data structure. The ideas introduced in [2, 10] share the same tree-based data structure with our proposed PMT model in that a tree is used to depict the policy and to perform the data matching. However, these approaches focus more on data filtering rather than on data selection. For example, they do not specify access denial on document fragments in a grant sub-tree. Therefore, they are unable to completely satisfy the needs of real XML access control applications.

In addition, the approaches of [1, 2, 4, 5, 10, 15, 24, 25, 32, 41] cannot support real-time updates on the access control rules. In many applications, such as digital libraries or net banking, the access control rules may be added, removed, or edited in real time. Besides that, the approaches of [1, 4, 5, 15, 32, 41] cannot support XML data update owing to their data-based optimization. These approaches are not applicable for applications with frequent updates such as business transaction systems. Therefore, both real-time policy-update and real-time document-update support are important system requirements.

Optimizations were also the focus of a number of research efforts on XML query languages (e.g., XPath and XQuery). The methods include query optimization based on (i) the tree pattern of queries [6, 9, 27] (ii) XML data and XML schema [12, 20, 21, 24]; and (iii) the consistency between integrity constraints and schemas [11]. However, these usually perform efficient data selection at the level of documents and require indices. Therefore, in a large XML database, for instance, a database with 10,000 document collections and 10,000 documents for each document collection, such optimization mechanisms may consume a prohibitive amount of space. In addition, these technologies are designed for XQuery and they cannot handle other query languages and primitive APIs such as the DOM.

2 Example XML Document and Policy

In this Section, we use a sample XML document and the associated policy to illustrate how an *XML access control* system works. The example here is a Web-based application that simulates a typical anonymous paper-reviewing process [1] which is described as follows.

- Authors submit their papers and a chairperson assigns one or more reviewers to each submitted paper.
- The reviewers read and evaluate the paper assigned to them. The system must not reveal the identities of authors to the reviewers.

[1] Since both the author's name and the reveiwer's name are anonymous, this anonymous review is often called as double-blinded review.

```
<review_summary>
  <notification>7/31/06 0:0 AM</notification>
  <entry>
    <paper id="0120">XML Security</paper>
    <contents encoding="Base64">Im9XWw...</contents>
    <author>Alice</author>
    <review>
      <reviewer>Robert</reviewer>
      <rating>4.5</rating>
    </review>
    <result status="final">Accept</result>
  </entry>
</review_summary>
```

Fig. 2. An XML document example

- The program committee members read the reviewers' evaluations and decide on which papers should be accepted.
- The chairperson decides on the final list of accepted papers.
- The authors receive notifications of acceptance or rejection.

We assume there is one XML document that stores all of the information and the states regarding the reviewing process, such as the author information and the evaluation results. The Web-based application allows the authors, the reviewers, and the chairperson to access the review summary XML document and appropriate fine-grained access control policy preserves anonymity, confidentiality, and integrity of the process. Figure 2 shows such an XML document which includes one paper submission from Alice with a final decision to accept[2] it as reviewed by the reviewer Robert with a rating 4.5. This XML document is stored in the XML Storage in Figure 1. All operations regarding the paper review process can be represented as accesses to the XML document, such as a read access to the paper `id` attribute or an update access to the `result` element.

Figure 3 shows an example access control policy associated with the review XML document. The `R1` is the default policy for the chairperson. The `R2` gives write permission on the `result` field to the chairperson. The `R3` allows the reviewers to read any node below an `entry` element except for the `author` element. The `R4` allows the reviewers to update a `rating` element. The `R5` allows author's access to their paper submissions. The `R6` defines the temporal policy with regards to the notification date.

For instance, when the chairperson issues a read access request for the `author`'s name element, the access should be permitted according to `R1`. On the other hand, when a reviewer tries to read the `author`'s name element, the access should be denied according to `R3`. When an author tries to read the `result` element, the access should be permitted only after the notification time has passed according to `R6`. Therefore, a query like "retrieve all of the XML nodes below an `entry` element" must reflect all of the access control policies at the time of the access and applying to the requesting subject.

[2] This sample XML data is small to make the description concise

R1 : The chairperson can read any elements, attributes and text nodes of the review documents.
R2 : The chairperson can write the `review` results (accept or reject) in the result fields.
R3 : The reviewers can read `entry` element (and any subordinates nodes) assigned to them except for the `author`'s name.
R4 : The reviewers can fill in the `rating` elements assigned to them.
R5 : The authors can read their own submission `entry`s except for the `review` elements.
R6 : The authors can read the `result` of their submissions after the date of notification.

Fig. 3. An access control policy example

3 Access Control Policy Model

In this section, we describe broad variations of an *XML Access Control* model which help readers look into their application-specific security requirements. It is usually true that the requirements for an access control policy model are different between applications. For example, Example 3 requires both element- and attribute-level access control in a dynamic context-dependent manner but another application may not require that level of the fine-grainness nor have any temporal features. This aspect of the requirements obviously bring the complexity into the system which affects the runtime performance.

The semantics of the XML data are another important aspect. For example, some applications may assume that every XML document in the data storage should be validated against a pre-defined XML Schema. In some cases, the XML documents are frequently updated, so a certain performance optimization technique would not be effective. Therefore, it is important to make the application requirements and functional features explicit. We describe broad requirements in the following sections.

3.1 Semantics of Access Control Policies

In general, the access control policy consists of a set of access control rules and each rule consists of an *object* (e.g. a target resource), a *subject* (e.g. a human user), an *action* (e.g. a read action), and a *permission* (grant or denial) meaning that the *subject* is (or is not) allowed to perform the *action* on the *object*. In the case of *XML access control*, a typical *object* is each node, such as an element and an attribute consisting of an XML document. *Action* is either *read*, *write*, *create*, or *delete* but is not limited to those.

The access control policy is associated with the pre-defined semantics of how to interpret a set of access control rules that may conflict with each other. Such semantics should satisfy the following requirements: *succinctness*, *least privilege*, and *soundness*. *Succinctness* means that the policy semantics should provide ways to specify a minimal number of rules. *Least privilege* means that the policy should grant the minimum privilege to the requesting subject. *Soundness* means that the policy evaluation must always generate either a grant or a denial decision in response to any access request.

3.2 Authorization Objects

In *XML access control*, a typical authorization object (or object reference) is either an XML instance document, a sub-document unit, such as an element and an attribute, or an XML schema definition. When the authorization object is an XML instance document, it means that the access control policy is applied only to a specific XML document. A typical way to identify an XML document is to use either a file name, URI, or object ID (for a database). When the authorization objects are XML sub-document units, then it means that the access control policy is applied to all of the specified node(s) of any applicable XML documents. XPath expressions [37] are often used to specify target elements, attributes, text nodes, etc. Using XPath expression, the `notification` element, the `status` attribute, and the text node of a `paper` element in Figure 2 are specified as *"/review_summary/notification"* , *"/review_summary/entry/result/@status"*, and *"/review_ summary/entry /paper/text()"*, respectively.

On the other hand, when the authorization object is a schema definition, it means that the access control policy is applied to all of the XML documents that comply with the specified schema. In other words, specifying the schema definition as an authorization object is identical to listing all of the XML documents that comply with the specified schema definition. Either DTD [38] or XML Schema [40] are often used to specify the schema definitions but other systems can be used.

3.3 Combination of Authorization Objects

When two or more object references are specified in an access control rule, then the two references are usually combined in a conjunctive way. For example, if both the file name and the XPath expression are specified, then the authorization object is any XML node that is selected by the XPath expression against the XML document which also has the specific file name. These object references can be expressed as a logical combination of each expression. Suppose that an authorization object in which the location of the XML instance is *"http://www.abc.com/a.xml"* and the target element is *"/review_summary/notification"*. An expression like $\$url = \text{“}http : //www.ibm.com/a.xml\text{”}\ and\ \$xpath = \text{“}/review\_\ summary/notification\text{”}$ represents the target nodes that exist below *"/review_summary/notification"* of the *a.xml* located at *"http://www.ibm.com"*. XLink [34] and the XPointer [35] specification provides other ways to specify the same semantics in a single format such as *xlink:href="http: //www.ibm.com/a.xml#xpointer(/review_summary/notification)"*

When the name of the schema definition is specified, then the system interprets it as specifying a set of XML data that all complies to that schema definition. It is important to note that a schema-level access control policy is not necessarily exclusive of an instance-level access control policy. Conflicts between two policies can be resolved by assuming some resolution schemes such as instance-level policy overrides schema-level policies, while the schema-level policy is applied if no instance-level policy is specified. For details, please refer to the description in the section about Combining Access Control Rules.

3.4 Access authorizations

Access authorizations can be either positive (permissions) or negative (denials). Supporting both positive and negative authorizations in an access control model is a concise way to specify authorization rules. For example, it is easy to exclude a certain node (e.g. `author` elements) from a sub-document unit (e.g. `entry` elements) by specifying both positive and negative access control policies. In this chapter, we use "+" and "-" marks to represent positive and negative authorizations, respectively.

When the authorization rules consists of only positive permissions, then the combining semantics is called a *closed world policy*, meaning that the access should be denied unless a positive permission is explicitly specified. On the other hand, when the authorization rules consists of only negative permissions, then the combining semantics is called the *open world policy*, meaning the opposite of the *closed* one. Generally, the *closed world policy* is considered as more secure because the access is denied by default, which follows the *least privilege* principle of the security policy.

3.5 Authorization action

There are four typical actions performed on an XML object, which are `read`, `update`, `create`, and `delete` for any node. Table 1 summarizes the semantics typical of the authorization action for three important authorization objects. An XML node such as `Comment` or `PI` (Processing Instructions) is also controlled by element-level policies. Please note that each action has its own semantics and has a different effect e.g. on an element, an attribute or a text node. For example, it does not make sense to independently allow the update action on each attribute, because one has to have update access to the parent element in order to have update access to the attribute. Therefore, it implies that the semantics of an update action on an attribute is dependent on the update action on the parent element.

3.6 Combining Access Control Rules

Access control policy consists of one or more access control rules. It is often the case that two or more access control rules generate conflicting decision results when positive and negative permissions are specified in the access control policy. For example, in Rule `R3` in Example 3, the first half of the rule permits access to `author` elements while the last half denies the access to `author` element. Another example would be to have a positive rule at the XML instance level while having a negative rule at the XML schema definition level. One way to resolve such conflicts is to apply a *more-specific-takes-precedence* resolution policy. For example, the document-level access control rule has priority since the document-level is more specific than the schema-level. Another resolution policy is a *denial-takes-precendence* policy, where a denial decision always overrides a positive decision.

Associating priority with each rule (instance-level or schema-level) is another way of resolving this problem. For example, Ernesto et al. [8] proposes using precedence criteria, *strong* or *weak*, where a *weak* rule is over-

Table 1. Typical semantics of authorization actions

Action	Effect	Node	Semantics
`Read`	+	Element	The element's name, comment nodes, PI nodes can be read
		Attribute	The particular attribute (the name and the value) can be read
		Text	All of the text nodes can be read
	-	Element	The element, including any text nodes, attributes, comment nodes and PI nodes are invisible (as if they don't exist).
		Attribute	The attribute (the name and the value) is invisible (as if it doesn't exist)
		Text	All of the text nodes under the element are invisible (as if they don't exist).
`Update`	+	Element	The element's existing text nodes can be updated and all of the existing attribute values can be updated. Note that the update action on an element does not mean that the element's name and the attribute's name are updateable.
		Attribute	N.A.
		Text	N.A.
	-	Element	The element's text nodes and attributes, are not updateable
		Attribute	The attribute is not updateable.
		Text	All of the text nodes under the element are not updateable.
`Create`	+	Element	An element with that name and path can be inserted.
		Attribute	An attribute with that name and path can be inserted.
		Text	A text node with that path can be inserted.
	-	Element	An element with that name and path cannot be inserted.
		Attribute	An attribute with that name and path cannot be inserted.
		Text	A text node with that path cannot be inserted.
`Delete`	+	Element	An element with that name and path can be deleted.
		Attribute	An attribute with that name and path can be deleted.
		Text	A text node with that path can be deleted.
	-	Element	An element with that name and path cannot be deleted.
		Attribute	An attribute with that name and path cannot be deleted.
		Text	A text node with that path cannot be deleted.

ridden by a *strong* rule. The XACML policy language standardized in OASIS also supports that notion using a more flexible scheme. Each policy specifies a rule-combining algorithm that indicates how to combine subordinate access control rules. The rule-combining algorithm is referred to by a specific URI, e.g. `urn:oasis:xacml:1.0:rule-combining- algorihtm :deny-overrides`. Application developers may specify their own combining algorithm if their application needs unique priority semantics such as *high*, *medium*, and *low* for the rules.

3.7 Denial Downward Consistency

We consider another interesting feature called *denial downward consistency*, which is specific to XML access control [25]. It requires that whenever a policy denies

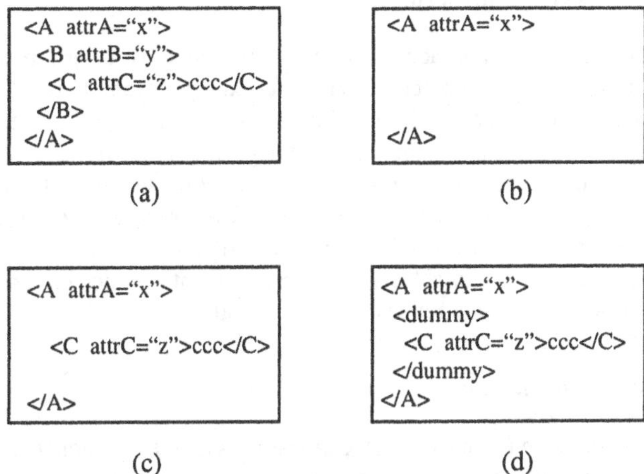

Fig. 4. Access controlled XML document regarding Denial Downward Consistency

access to an element, it must also deny access to its subordinate elements and attributes. In other words, whenever access to a node is allowed, access to all the ancestor elements must be allowed as well. We impose this requirement since we think that elements or attributes isolated from their ancestor elements are sometimes meaningless. For example, if an element or attribute specifies a relative URI, its interpretation depends on the attribute `xml:base` [38] specified at the ancestor elements, which implies that the *denial downward consistency* requirement is necessary if XML-consistent semantics are to be accurately preserved. Another advantage of the *denial downward consistency* is that it makes implementation of runtime policy evaluation easier.

Actually, there are several access control models that do not comform to *denial downward consistency*. We compares several solutions using the sample XML document in Figure 4 (a). Suppose that the policy allows read access to elements `A` and `C` but denies access to element `B` without following *denial downward consistency*. The access to the element `C` must be denied if *denial downward consistency* is supported. Therefore, the resultant XML document should contain only element `A` as shown in Figure 4 (b).

Now we consider two other solutions that do not support *denial downward consistency*, which are often regarded as normal access control policy models. The first solution is to just remove element `B` while the element `C` remains. The resultant XML document appears in Figure 4 (c). Another solution is to replace element `B` with some dummy element like `dummy` and to remove the attribute values and text nodes from element `B` as depicted in Figure 4 (d).

3.8 Value-based access control rule

It is often the case that the access to a certain node is determined by the value in the target XML document. Using the example from Figure 2, a person who plays a reviewer's role is allowed access if the requesting individual's name is equivalent to the value stored in the XML reviewing document. We use the term *value-based access control* to refer to this type of rule. It is possible to express the *value-based access control* rule using an XPath expression, `/review_summary/entry[review/reviewer/text() = $userid`[3]`]`. This selects an `entry` element in which the `reviewer` name element is identical to the requesting subject's id.

3.9 Provisional authorization

Provisional authorization is a new notion contrasting with the traditional access control framework, which usually consists of an authorization subject, object, and action. The provisional access control adds one extra argument called an *obligation* or *provisional action* to tell the user that the request will be authorized (or perhaps denied) provided the system takes certain action(s) such as signing the statement prior to the authorization of the request. The following are examples:

- Employees are allowed to access confidential information, *provided that the access is first logged*
- Consultants are allowed to read sensitive information, *provided that the consultant signs a terms and conditions statement*
- Unauthorized access should be denied and *a warning message must be sent to an administrator*

The sentences above in italics represent the *obligations*. Table 2 shows some typical obligations. Refer to the papers [19, 22, 23] for more concrete policy examples.

Table 2. List of Possible Obligations

Type	Obligations
Transformation	anonymize, decrypt, encrypt, fingerprint, sign, ssl, verifysign
Synchronous Transaction	antivirus, basicauth, charge, confirm, count, create, delete, expire, locate, log, notify, payupfront, pkiauth, securetoken, warning, write
Asynchronous Transaction	delete, expire, investigate, notify

[3] We use a variable $userid to refer to the identity of the requesting user in the access control policies.

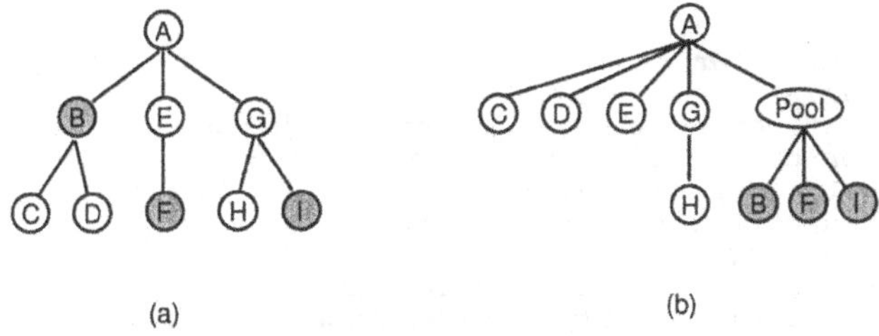

Fig. 5. XML Pool Encryption

3.10 XML Access Control and XML Encryption

A method called "XML Pool Encryption" [14] provides fine-grained XML access control using XML encryption [39]. Figure 5 (a) shows the original XML document. Suppose that elements `B`, `F`, and `I` are not readable while the other elements are readable according to the current policies. Then XML Pool Encryption removes the access-denied nodes from the original XML document and adds them in encrypted format using XML Encryption below a "Pool" element. Figure 5 (b) shows the modified XML document. The XML document preserves information about the original location of the encrypted elements and conditions who can read those elements. This scheme allows secure XML transmission over networks and guarantees appropriate *XML Access Control* policy at a remote server by combining encryption and access control.

4 Access Control Policy Languages

4.1 XACL

The XACL (XML Access Control Language) is a fine-grained access control policy specification language for XML data [23, 33]. It allows application programmers to specify policies at element and attribute levels with various conditional expressions. The XACL uses XPath expressions to specify the targets of a policy with either positive or negative permissions. The XACL provides several ways to resolve conflicts between the decisions, either by the *permit-takes-precedence* or the *denial-takes-precedence* resolution policies. The XACL also defines how the access effects propagate on the XML tree structure. By default, a read permission specified on a certain element automatically propagates upward to the root node as well as propagating downward to its descendants.

Policy Syntax and Semantics

The XACL policies are specified using `xacl` elements and one or more `rule` elements that specifies permit or deny authorization conditions. Two or more rules

```
<policy xmlns="http://www.trl.ibm.com/projects/xml/xacl">
<xacl id="R3-1">
   <object href="/review_summary/entry"/>
   <rule><acl>
     <subject><group>reviewer</group></subject>
     <action name="read" permission="grant"/>
     <condition operation="and">
       <predicate name="compareStr">
         <parameter value="eq"/>
         <parameter><function name="getValue">
           <parameter value="./review/reviewer/text()"/></function>
           </parameter>
         <parameter><function name="getUid"/></parameter>
       </predicate>
     </condition>
   </acl></rule>
 </xacl>
 <xacl id="R3-2">
   <object href="/review_summary/entry/author"/>
   <rule><acl>
     <subject><group>reviewer</group></subject>
     <action name="read" permission="deny"/>
   </rule></acl>
 </xacl>
```

Fig. 6. XACL Policy

are disjunctively combined according to the pre-defined combining algorithms. The authorization subject is specified using one or more subject descriptors of `group`, `role`, or `userid` under a `subject` element. As regards the authorization objects, the XACL only supports XPath expressions as a `href` attribute of the `object` element. There are four types of authorization actions in XACL, `read`, `write`, `create`, and `delete`. Arbitrary conditional expressions can be specified using the `operation` attributes, the `predicate` elements, or the `parameter` elements below the `condition` elements. Figure 6 expresses a Rule `R3` of Figure 3.

Rule `R3-1` specifies a permissive rule on a `/review_summary/entry` element for the reviewer group with the condition that only the reviewer in charge can access the paper content and the submission information. Since the XACL supports the downward propagation from the target node by default, any subordinate nodes below the `entry` element, e.g. the `author` and `reviewer` elements, are also the target authorization objects of this rule.

On the other hand, Rule `R3-2` specifies a denial rule on the */review_summary/entry/author* element for all reviewers. While this rule contradicts the permissive `R3-1` rule, the conflict resolution `denial-takes-precedence` policy, which is supposed to be specified for the `property` element below the `policy` element, finally denies access to the `author` element.

Binding Scheme

How to bind a set of policies written in XACL with target documents is out of the scope of the XACL. There are two fundamental approaches. One is association at the schema definition (e.g. DTD) level and the other is an association at the level of each specific document. In the schema-definition approach, a set of policies is bound to all documents that are valid according to the specified DTD. Therefore one needs to maintain a mapping between a particular DTD and the associated policy. In the specific approach, a policy is bound to each specific document. In this case, an associated policy, which is encoded as a `policy` element, may be an element contained within the target document.

Decision Algorithm

We provide a policy evaluation algorithm that takes as input an authorization request and outputs an authorization decision including *provisional actions*. The algorithm consists of the basic matching algorithm and the policy evaluation algorithm.

`Input:` An authorization request
`Output:` A decision list, which may contain multiple decisions

- `Step 1. Object-Check:` Search the associated policy for `xacl` element such that a set of elements expressed by its `object` element contains the object specified in the authorization request.
- `Step 2. Subject-Check:` For each `xacl` element, check if the subject of the requester and the requested action is semantically equal to a corresponding requester and action as specified in the `xacl` element.
- `Step 3. Condition-Check:` For each of the remaining `xacl` elements, check if the specified condition holds.
- `Step 4. Decision-Record:` Make a decision for each of the remaining `xacl` elements, where a decision includes the requested object, the subject of the requester and the action specified in the `xacl` element, and append all the decisions to the authorization decision list.

The policy evaluation algorithm deals with the propagation and the conflict-resolution. We note that this algorithm outputs exactly one authorization decision.

`Input:` An authorization request
`Output:` A decision list with only one decision

- `Step 1. Propagation Processing:` Call the Matching algorithm for the input authorization request and perform propagation operations.
- `Step 2. Conflict Resolution:` If there is no authorization decision in the list, make a decision according to the default policy for the requested action and append it to the list. If there is a conflict, resolve it according to the resolution policy for the requested action.
- `Step 3. Select only one decision:` The list contains at least one decision (obtained via propagation) or contains more than one decision (eliminate any decision that was obtained via propagation)

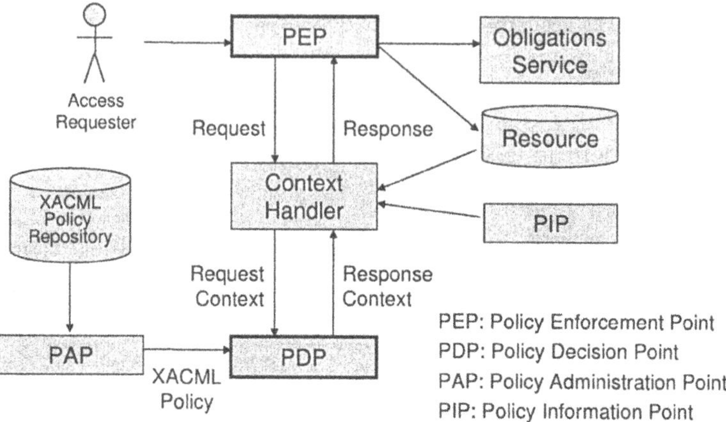

Fig. 7. XACML Architecture

4.2 XACML

The XACML [28] is an access control policy specification language that has been standardized in the OASIS[4]. The scope of this language is to cover access control systems as broadly as possible. Therefore, the XACML core schema is extensible for as yet unknown features. The XACML addresses the effect of characteristics of the access requestor, the protocol over which the request is made, authorization based on classes of activities, and content introspection. One of the purpose of the XACML is the interoperability of the access control policy among heterogeneous computing platform. The biggest difference from the XACL language is that the XACL focuses on the access control policy only for XML data[5] while the XACML policy supports any resources including XML data.

XACML Architecture

The XACML policy model assumes the underlying architecture that is similar to the generic access control framework shown in Figure 1. Figure 7 shows XACML data-flow diagram. The XACML adds one additional component called a `Context Handler` between the `PEP` and the `PDP`, which supplies sufficient information for any access request using the `Policy Information Point (PIP)`. The interface from the `PIP` to the `PDP` is defined in XACML specification as a `Request Context`. The `PDP` retrieves applicable access control policies from the `Policy Administration Point (PAP)` and makes the decision using these policies and the request context. The decision is returned back to the `PEP` via the `Context Handler`.

[4] Organization for Advanced Semistructured Information Systems

[5] Many portions of XACML policy model is originated from the XACL language

Policy Syntax and Semantics

The XACML policy is specified using a `Policy` element which consists of a `Target` element that specifies the conditions when the policy is applicable, and one or more `Rule` elements that specifies permit or deny authorization conditions. The XACML also provides a flexible way to extend the semantics in order to support application-specific access control policies by an extensible Rule (or Policy) combining algorithm. The following XACML policy (Figure 8) corresponds to the third rule *R3* of Figure 3[6].

The `Target` element specifies the applicability of `R3` by saying that the role of the requesting subject should be *Reviewer* and the requested action should be *read*. The policy `R3` consists of three `Rules`, `R3-1`, `R3-2`, and `R3-3`. `R3-1` signifies that an access to the `review_summary` element is permitted. Note that this rule does not indicate anything about subordinate nodes, since the `xpath-node-equal` matching function checks the access only for the specified node, which is a `review_summary` element. `R3-2` signifies that a read access to an `entry` element and its subordinate nodes is permitted when the name of the requesting subject is identical to the value specified in the `reviewer` element. The semantics of the propagation to subordinate nodes is handled by the `xpath-node-match` matching function. `R3-3` states that a read access to the `author` element is denied. These three rules are combined by the combining algorithm called `denial-overrides`, which basically means that if any rule evaluates to "Deny", then the result of the rule combination shall be "Deny". For example, `R3-2` permits read access to the `author` element while `R3-3` explicitly denies the access. Then the `denial-overrides` algorithm concludes that the access to the `entry` element should be denied. There are several other rule combining algorithms in the XACML specification, such as `first applicable` and `only one applicable`.

Access Request

The XACML specification also defines how the access request in Figure 7 should appear. Figure 9 shows a sample `XACML Request Context` format where Robert asks for a read access to the first `entry` element of the review summary XML document. The request context consisting of three sub structures, `Subject` information, `Resource` information, and `Action` information, each consists of one or more attribute type-value pairs. In this example, `subject-id` and `role` are attribute types and `Robert` and `reviewer` are attribute values, respectively. It is assumed that those attributes are given by a separate authentication mechanism that is out of the scope of the XACML specification.

As regards resource information, the `XACML request context` can contain the target XML data as relevant information about the target resource.

[6] The syntax used in Figure 8 has some abbreviation due to the space limitation. The exact URI specification of the rule combining algorithm is "urn:oasis:names:tc:xacml:1.0:rule-combining-algorithm:*deny-overrides*".

```
<Policy xmlns:rs="reviewpaper.xsd" PolicyId="R3"
        RuleCombiningAlgId="deny-overrides">
 <PolicyDefaults><XPathVersion>Rec-xpath-19991116</XPathVersion>
 </PolicyDefaults>
 <Target>
  <Subjects><Subject>
   <SubjectMatch MatchId="string-equal">
    <AttributeValue DataType="string">Reviewer</AttributeValue>
    <SubjectAttributeDesignator AttributeId="role" DataType="string"/>
   </SubjectMatch>
  </Subject></Subjects>
  <Actions><Action>
   <ActionMatch MatchId="string-equal">
    <AttributeValue DataType="string">read</AttributeValue>
    <ActionAttributeDesignator AttributeId="action-id" DataType="string"/>
   </ActionMatch>
  </Action></Actions>
 </Target>
 <Rule RuleId="R3-1" Effect="Permit">
  <Target><Resources><Resource>
   <ResourceMatch MatchId="xpath-node-equal">
    <AttributeValue DataType="xpath-exp">//rs:review_summary</>
    <ResourceAttributeDesignator AttributeId="resource-id" DataType="xpath-exp"/>
   </ResourceMatch>
  </Resource></Resources></Target>
 </Rule>
 <Rule RuleId="R3-2" Effect="Permit">
  <Target><Resources><Resource>
   <ResourceMatch MatchId="xpath-node-match">
    <AttributeValue DataType="xpath-exp">//rs:review_summary/rs:entry</>
    <ResourceAttributeDesignator AttributeId="resource-id" DataType="xpath-exp"/>
   </ResourceMatch>
  </Resource></Resources></Target>
  <Condition><Apply FunctionId="string-equel">
   <AttributeSelector DataType="xpath-exp"
    RequestContextPath="//rs:review_summary/rs:entry/rs:review/rs:reviewer/rs:text()"/>
   <SubjectAttributeDesignator AttributeId="subject-id" DataType="xpath-exp"/>
  </Apply></Condition>
 </Rule>
 <Rule RuleId="R3-3" Effect="Deny">
  <Target><Resources><Resource>
   <ResourceMatch MatchId="xpath-node-match">
    <AttributeValue DataType="xpath-exp">//rs:review_summary/rs:entry/rs:author</>
    <ResourceAttributeDesignator AttributeId="resource-id" DataType="xpath-exp"/>
   </ResourceMatch>
  </Resource></Resources></Target>
 </Rule>
</Policy>
```

Fig. 8. XACML access control policy corresponding to R3

The `ResourceContent` element contains the `review_summary` XML data with the namespace prefixed by `rs:`. The target XML document is referred to from the access control policy using the `AttributeSelector` function. For example, `R3-2` of Figure 8 specifies `//rs:review_summary /rs:entry/rs:review/rs:reviewer/text()`, which refers to `Robert`. This is one of the advantages of the XACML policy model that allows the policy to refer to any of the values of the target XML data embedded in the `Request Context` and to compare them against constant value(s).

```
<Request>
  <Subject>
    <Attribute AttributeId="subject-id" DataType="string">
      <AttributeValue>Robert</AttributeValue>
    </Attribute>
    <Attribute AttributeId="role" DataType="string">
      <AttributeValue>Reviewer</AttributeValue>
    </Attribute>
  </Subject>
  <Resource scope="EntireHierarchy">
    <ResourceContent>
      <rs:review_summary xmlns:rs="urn:review_summary:schema">
          <rs:notification>7/31/06</rs:notification>
          <rs:entry>
            <rs:paper id="0120">XML Security</rs:paper>
            <rs:author>Alice</rs:author>
            <rs:review>
              <rs:reviewer>Robert</rs:reviewer>
              <rs:rating>4.5</rs:rating>
            </rs:review>
            <rs:result status="final">Accept</rs:result>
          </rs:entry>
      </rs:review_summary>
    </ResourceContent>
    <Attribute AttributeId="resource-id"
          DataType="xpath-expression">
      <AttributeValue>//rs:review_summary/rs:entry[position()=1]
      </AttributeValue>
    </Attribute>
  </Resource>
  <Action>
    <Attribute AttributeId="action-id" DataType="string">
      <AttributeValue>read</AttributeValue>
    </Attribute>
  </Action>
</Request>
```

Fig. 9. XACML sample request context

Access Decision

The XACML specification also defines how the access decision in Figure 7 should appear. Figure 10 shows the resultant `XACML Response Context`. The decision is `Deny` since the requested `entry` element contains an `Author` element that should not be accessible to the Reviewer. The `EntireHierarchy` scope parameter specified in the `Resource` of the `XACML Request Context` defines the semantics of the response context such that if any of the descendants nodes of the requested node have one or more access-denial nodes, then the resultant decision should be denial[7].

[7] There are other scope parameters, `Child` and `Descendants`, which forces to return repetitive access decisions for each descendant nodes instead of returning only one decision.

```
<Response>
  <Result>
    <Decision>Deny</Decision>
  </Result>
</Response>
```

Fig. 10. XACML sample response context

Other Features

XACML supports the notion of provisional action as described in Section 3 as an `Obligation` which is defined as *an operation specified in a policy or policy set that should be performed by the PEP in conjunction with the enforcement of an authorization decision*. Since XACML only provides a framework to specify obligations, there is no standardized set of obligations. The application developers are permitted to support any obligations as long as they comply with the semantics specified in the XACML specification. The XACML specification says that "a *policy* or *policy set* may contain one or more *obligations*. When such a *policy* or *policy set* is evaluated, an *obligation* shall be passed up to the next level of evaluation (the enclosing or referencing *policy*, *policy set* or authorization decision) only if the effect of the *policy* or *policy set* being evaluated matches the value of the *FulfillOn* attribute of the *obligation*".

5 Efficient Policy Enforcement Mechanisms

In this section, we present access control system that is built on the access control model described in the previous sections. We show our access control system structure, which supports both of our implementation-specific policy models. Then we present three implementation-specific policy models which provide efficient access control decision and enforcement on the basis of access control policy.

5.1 Access Control System Structure

The proposed access control system is structured through Policy Conversion and Model Deployment as shown in Figure 11 . The key point of our access control system is that it separates the access control enforcement mechanism from the database engine so that security-related support is not required from the underlying database. This enables any XML DBMS, even off-the-shelf products, to provide efficient, flexible and scalable access control.

Policy Conversion can be considered as a pre-processing stage. In Policy Conversion, the access control policy is converted to an internal data structure(s), which can be an access condition table (ACT), a policy matching tree (PMT), or a set of rule functions. Concisely, the ACT-based approach shifts some of the runtime processes

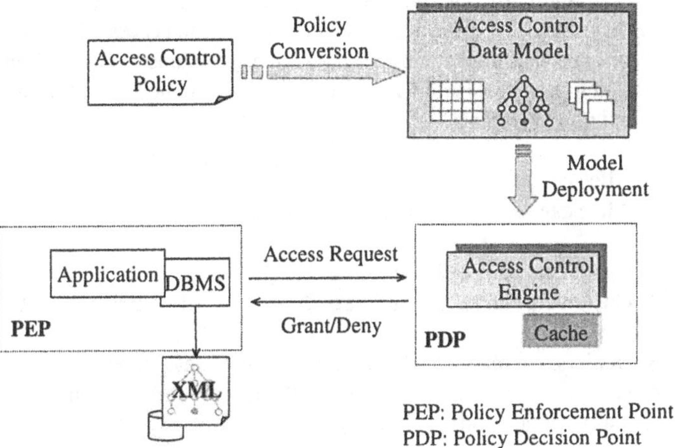

Fig. 11. Access control system structure

to the pre-process phase to gain efficiency, the PMT-based approach is highly expressive since complicated XPath expressions are supported, and the rule-function-based approach is a scalable approach to support large-scale access control policies.

A separate process, Model Deployment, initially loads the essential system-global data structures into main memory. At runtime, given an access request containing at least five attributes: a userID, role, group, action, and path, the access control engine runs the accessibility check mechanism to get the decision result. If accessibility check returns deny, the access-denied response will be sent back to the DBMS without data retrieval from the XML database. Otherwise, the output is generated after data retrieval and returned back to the user. Moveover, caching can be employed inside the access control system to achieve significant gains in runtime performance.

One of the characteristics of these approaches is that the policy conversion process does not need to examine the XML data as part of performance optimization. Since the data structures are built in isolation from the DTDs and XML instances, they remain static as long as the access control policy itself is not updated.

5.2 Access Control Data Models

In this section, we introduce three access control data models, the ACT model, the PMT model, and the rule function model, individually. In addition, the efficiency and expressiveness of the three models are analyzed and compared.

Access Control Policy Examples

In this section, we use two access control policies, *P1* and *P2*. *P1* says that user Alice can access `/a` and the subtree of `/a/b`, which means `/a/c`, a descendant of `/a` but not `/a/b`, is implicitly not allowed to be accessed. *P2* says that a customer can access his or her own order information, while a dealer can access all of the information except for classified information. The XPath expressions in *P2* are complicated since they contain predicates and use `//` to select specific nodes on the basis of the data values and node locations.

P1:

(1) Alice can read `/a`
(2) Alice can read `/a/b` and its subordinate nodes

P2:

(1) Customers can read `/Orders`
(2) Customers can read `/Orders/Order[CustKey=$custID]` and its subordinate nodes.
(3) Dealers can read `/Orders` and its subordinate nodes.
(4) Dealers cannot read `/Orders//ClassifiedInfo` and its subordinate nodes.

ACT Model

An ACT is a table storing access conditions for a specific subject. The ACT is directly generated from an access control policy with target paths as keys, and Boolean expressions describing the access conditions to the corresponding paths as their values. The significance of this approach is that i) any path can be used to look up the conditions for the accessibility check from the ACT without consideration of conflict resolution or propagation enforcement; and ii) access conditions are not required to be prepared for each possible path.

Each entry in an ACT has two access conditions, an Access Condition (AC) and a Subtree Access Condition (SAC), as values. ACs and SACs can be true, false or any XQuery expressions. The AC is for the accessibility check when the user accesses the corresponding path, while the SAC is for the paths not existing in the ACT when looking up the SAC of the closest ancestral path for accessibility checks. The idea of a SAC allows access to an arbitrary descendant in the subtree to be checked with an identical expression, so that we do not need to list up the access conditions for each possible descendant.

ACT Generation

The key of the ACT is that it shifts some of the computation from run time to a pre-processing step. The computations include propagation enforcement, conflict resolution, and result combination. In addition, when a subtree structure appears multiple times in an XML document, identical propagation and conflict resolution is repeated for every duplicate. Since such computations are visible in during pre-processing on the basis of the relative relationship of the paths with the access effects, we can gain efficiency by eliminating them from run time when the ACT is built.

Each rule in an access control policy is converted to an entry in the ACT such that the AC is generated from the object and the action permission, while the SAC is generated from the object, and the access effect. Since in some cases multiple rules may result in one entry, the size of an ACT is limited by the number of rules of the subject. Generally, the ACT for a subject is generated with the following five steps (see [29] for details).

- Step 1: Generate the target paths
  - If the object contains predicates, take the path removing the predicates as the target path. (i.e. `/a/c` is the target path for `/a/c[g>1]`.)
  - If the object has a `//`(or `*`), take the path previous to `//`(or `*`) as the target path. (i.e. `/a/b` is the target path for `/a/b//e`.)
  - Otherwise, the object itself is taken as the target path.
- Step 2: Generate the local ACs
  - True, false, or the expression generated from the predicate and the relationships with the node where the predicate is imposed.
- Step 3: Generate the local SACs
  - `True`, `false` generated from the propagation permission, or the expression containing ancestor-or-self axis generated based on `//`. When predicates are involved, Ref(path) is used to indicate the accessibility should refer to the result of the AC of that path.
- Step 4: Perform access propagation
  - Propagate the access effect down from the ancestor target paths to the descendant target paths.
- Step 5: Perform conflict resolution and expression combination of the AC and the SAC on each target path.

As an example, the ACT of $P1$ and $P2$ is shown in Table 3.

Table 3. The ACT of $P1$ and $P2$

	Target Path	AC	SAC
P1	`/a`	`true`	`false`
	`/a/b`	`true`	`true`
P2 : customer	`/Orders`	`true`	`false`
	`/Orders/Order`	`CustKey=$custID`	`Ref(/Orders/Order)`
P2 : dealer	`/Orders`	`true`	`not(ancestor-or-self::ClassifiedInfo)`

PMT Model

A PMT is a tree structure providing a fast matching mechanism. The PMT searches for matched rules by matching the request against a tree that is the internal data structure of the access control policy. The PMT outputs matched targets upon which the accessibility, grant or deny, can be decided. Due to the rich expressiveness of the

PMT model, the significance of this approach is that it supports complicated access control rules which involve predicates, *s, and //s.

The PMT model consists of four components: a node, edge, match target, and link. The node represents a property name of the access request. The edge represents a matching condition on the property name. The matching condition consists of an operator and the associated value. The edge ends at another node for further refinement or a match target which is the leaf node representing the matching result. As occasion demands, the match target may also contain an attribute list, and a link for further matching.

With nodes and edges, each rule, including action permission, propagation permission, subject, object and predicates, can be represented with the five basic elements shown in Figure 12. P_n represents the property name at depth n and P_{n++} appearing in //x and //* automatically increases the depth counter variable for each loop.

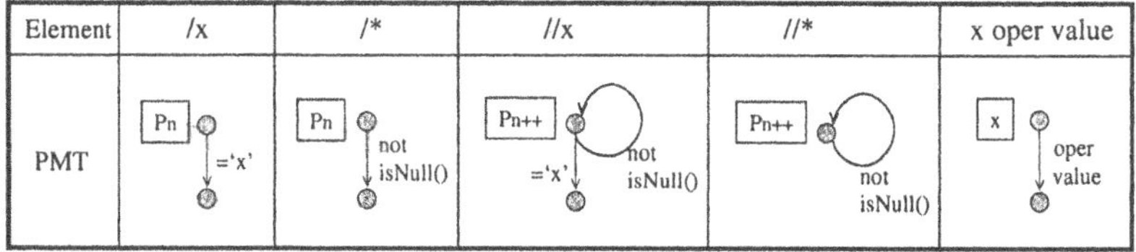

Fig. 12. Five basic elements to represent XPath expressions

PMT Generation

Each access control rule is individually converted into three matchings, or four when a predicate(s) is involved, with a corresponding match target. It is important that a match target represents not only the access permission, but also represents the link to any further refinement performed by predicates. The idea of the link in a match target enables the rules to share the part built for the same predicate. A PMT is constructed by adding or sharing nodes, edges, and match targets in the following four steps (see [30] for details).

- Step 1: Generate Action Matching
  - Start a new PMT with `action` as the property name and the action type of the rule on the edge.
- Step 2: Generate Subject Matching
  - Add to the PMT with the subject type as the property name and the subject value on the edge.
- Step 3: Generate Object Matching
  - If the object contains predicates, the path after removing the predicates is added to the PMT. Also, link information is stored in the match target to indicate the corresponding predicates.

- Otherwise, each step of the XPath expression is added to the PMT using the basic components in Figure 12.
- If the downward propagation is not needed, a test on whether the requested path is the object is performed by adding an extended edge labelled with `isNull()` leading to the match target.

• Step 4: Generate Predicate Matching
- Predicates can be shared by multiple rules.

As examples, the PMTs of $P1$ and $P2$ are shown in Figure 13.

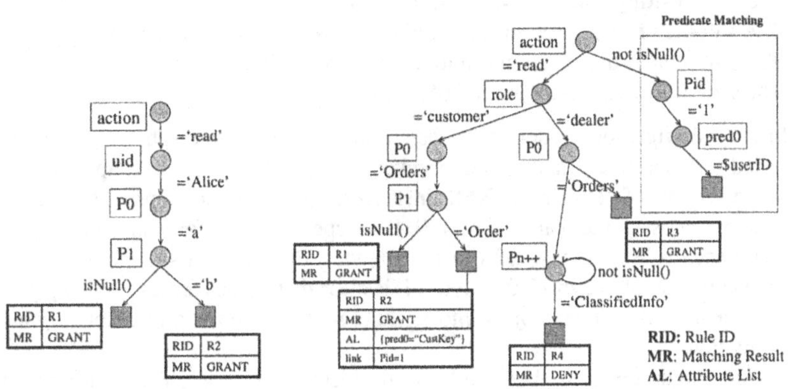

Fig. 13. The PMTs of $P1$ and $P2$

Rule Function Model

A rule function is a code fragment that performs access control on a specific subject. The key idea is to encode the access control policy as a set of rule functions that separately perform the actual accessibility checks for a subject, and therefore only necessary rule functions are required to reside in the main memory for access control.

Each rule function encapsulates a group of access control rules sharing the same subject. The input is the accessed path, and the output is `true`, `false`, or `undecided` if no rules are explicitly or implicitly specified for the access request. However, to maximize data security, the default action of denying permission is applied for `undecided`.

Since this is a Java-based implementation, each rule function is actually a Java method. The rule functions are grouped into Java classes and further organized into Java packages to benefit from the memory and update management support of the Java Virtual Machine. Therefore, besides the rule function, the mapping table is another key component that connects an access request to the appropriate rule function for the accessibility check. The mapping table uses the subject as a key and the 3-tuple of *package name*, *class name*, and *function name* as its value.

Rule Functions and Mapping Table Generation

Owing to Java-based implementation, it is necessary to generate rule functions and classes with considering the size limitations. In the Java Virtual Machine, the total numbers of heap and stack cannot exceed 65,536. Therefore during the generation, we must monitor the size so that:

- The total length of field and rule function names, and the number of characters in constant string values stays below 65,536.
- The number of rule functions declared by a class cannot exceed 65,536.
- The size of any rule function cannot exceed 65,536 bytes.
- The size of a class cannot exceed 65,536 bytes.

In our rule function model, the rules specified for the same subject are finally converted into one rule function. We checked 22 types of XML-based applications to see the number of paths in the XML instances, and found the number is no more than 300 and most of them are below 100. If we specify a rule for a subject on each path, and each rule costs uses less than 100 bytes, then we can say that each rule function is mostly less than 10,000 bytes. It is clear that in most cases we can group the rules sharing the same subject into a single rule function without violating the size limitation.

A more important factor that should be considered in generation is the number of files in a Java package, since this affects the runtime performance. In the Windows operating system, looking up a specific file becomes quite slow when the number of files in the directory exceeds 1,024. Therefore, we group at most 1,024 Java classes in each Java package.

Rule functions and the corresponding mapping table are generated as follows (see [31] for details).

- Step 1: Sort the access control rules by subjects.
- Step 2: Sort each access control rule group by access effects.
  - Sort in the order of a negative rule with downward propagation, a positive rule with downward propagation, and a positive rule without downward propagation. This order satisfies the requirements of the accessibility dependency and conflict resolution.
- Step 3: Convert each access control rule group into a rule function.
  - In the rule function, rules are distinguished by the object, so that the corresponding evaluation result is coded as the return value when the accessed path satisfies the object condition.
- Step 4: Add a new entry to the mapping table using the subject as the key, and the triple of *package name*, *class name*, and the *rule function name* as the value.

During the rule function generation, the predicate(s) and the path of a value-based object are coded separately. Since the evaluation requires XML data, the data referenced in the predicate needs to be retrieved before the evaluation. Therefore, an API, *retrieve*, is provided to retrieve the data from the DBMS. The system variable *custID* is automatically set when a customer logs in. If the value of *custID* is obtained by *obtainSystemData*, then the Java program fragment for $P1$ and $P2$ is as shown in Figure 14. In addition, when // or * is involved in access control, we use java.util.regex to represent the matching expressions.

```
static public Integer rf_Alice(String path) {
    if (path.startsWith("/a/b"))                  // for (2)
        return GRANT;
    else if (path.equals("/a"))                   // for (1)
        return GRANT;
    else return UNDECIDED;
}
```

```
static public Integer rf_customer(String path) {
    String value0 = Data.retrieve("CustKey", "/Orders/Order");
    String value1 = Data.obtainSystemData("custID");
    if (path.startsWith("/Orders/Order") && value0.equals(value1))  // for (2)
        return GRANT;
    else if (path.equals("/Orders")) return GRANT                   // for (1)
    else return UNDECIDED;
}

static Pattern p1 = Pattern.compile("/Orders/.*/ClassifiedInfo|
                                      /Orders/.*/ClassifiedInfo/.*");
static public Integer rf_dealer(String path) {
    Matcher m1 = p1.matcher(path);
    if (m1.match()) return DENY;                                    // for (4)
    else if (path.startsWith("/Orders")) return GRANT;              // for (3)
    else return UNDECIDED;
}
```

Fig. 14. The rule functions of $P1$ and $P2$

Limitations and Requirements of Data Models

The three access control data models with different data structures each have limitations on XPath expressions and impose some requirements to achieve efficiency. The limitations on XPath expressions come from the capability for using //, *, and predicates, and especially from the data required for predicate evaluation. As for efficiency, whether or not the evaluation mechanism is embedded in the data structure influences the efficiency of runtime performance.

Table 4 shows how the limitations and requirements of the various data models impinge upon their expressiveness and the runtime efficiency. The PMT model has the weakest limitations and that it is most expressive in access control enforcement. On the other hand, both the PMT model and the rule function model provide efficient evaluation mechanisms for predicates and //, but the ACT model calls for specific functions from the underlying XML database.

Table 4. Limitations and Requirements of Data Models

	XPath Expressiveness
ACT	1. // is limited to appearing once. 2. A wildcard * should always be accompanied with a // in the form of //*. (i.e. `/a//b/*/@d` is not allowed.) 3. // and * never appear in predicates. (i.e. `/a[*>1]/b` is not allowed.) 4. Only one node can be identified after //. (i.e. `/a//c/d` is not allowed.)
PMT	1. // and * never appear in predicates. (i.e. `/a[*>1]/b` is not allowed.) 2. Predicates are never followed by //.
Rule function	1. // and * never appear in predicates. (i.e. `/a[*>1]/b` is not allowed.) 2. Predicates are limited to expressions connected with the operators: $=$, $<$, $>$, $\neq$, $\leq$ and $\geq$.
	XPath Evaluation Requirements
ACT	1. The evaluation of `ancestor-or-self` should be supported by the XML database. 2. Evaluations for predicates should be supported.
PMT	No requirements. Evaluation mechanism is built in the PMT.
Rule function	No requirements. Evaluation mechanism is encoded in the rule functions, and compiled before runtime.

5.3 Real-time Policy Update

The access control policy is updated when any rules are added, removed, or updated. In some real applications, access control policy may be updated at runtime. For instance, if a new subject is introduced into a net banking system, then the corresponding access control rules should be added as well. However, it is inconvenient for a net bank to stop the server to rebuild the related data structures at every time when the policy is updated. In this section, we analyze the update mechanism and performance of each approach.

ACT-based Real-time Update

The entries of the ACT are generated by combining related access effects, both explicitly and implicitly, imposed on the target paths. Therefore when a rule is added, removed, or updated, it is impossible to update the only some related part of the ACT. It is obvious that XML databases with frequent policy updates may incur unacceptable costs since the entire ACT has to be rebuilt at every time the policy is updated. Therefore, the ACT-based access control system does not reasonably support real time policy updates.

PMT-based Real-time Update

In the PMT model, it is possible to perform real-time updates on the PMT, since each rule built in PMT has a corresponding match target. RID in the match target plays a crucial role in runtime rule removal. The match target, nodes and edges are removed bottom-up if the components are not shared by other rules. When a rule is updated, the PMT reacts by removing and adding the corresponding components without changing the RID in the match target. It costs $O(m)$ time to add, remove, or update the rules, where m is the number of concerned rules.

Ruel-function-based Real-time Update

The Java-based implementation allows the access control engine to load the required classes into memory, but any updates to classes on disk will not automatically change those residing in memory. However the class reload mechanism provided by Java can be used when we wish to update memory-resident classes.

When a policy is updated at runtime, generally we update the system in four steps:

1. . Generate a new Java class or multiple new Java classes for the updated rules,
2. . Compile the generated Java classes,
3. . Update the mapping table, and
4. . Remove the corresponding entry from cache data if the Java class for the updated subject resides in memory.

In Step 3, if the corresponding entry exists in the mapping table, the system updates the entry with a new package name, a new class name, and a new method name. In addition, if rules for new subjects are added to the policy, new entries are inserted into the mapping table.

Comparison

Table 5 shows a brief comparison of the three access control data models. From Table 5, it is clear when the access control policy for an application is rarely updated, and the policy itself is simple enough without value-based access control involved, the ACT-based access control system can perform efficiently with low memory consumption. If the policy is updated frequently, both the PMT-based and the rule-function-based access control system can handle the system well but the rule-function-based access control system is more scalable and efficient. However, when access control is specified with complicated rules using //, *, and predicates, the PMT-based access control is powerful and capable of coping with the policy updates.

Table 5. Comparison of Access Control Data Models

	ACT	PMT	Rule Function
Expressiveness	-	Better	Good
Runtime Efficiency	Good	-	Better
Memory Consumption	Better	-	Good
Real-time Update	-	Supported	Supported

6 Summary

In this chapter, we described a fine-grained (element- and attribute-level) access control for XML data. The architecture of the access control system consists of `PEP`, `PDP`, and an XML data store. As a working example, we used a Web application for a double-blind paper submission and refereeing process which shows how the fine-grained access control policy can satisfy the application-specific security requirements. We also described an access control policy model using various model components proposed to date. This model also covers new notions such as provisional authorization and XML Pool Encryption. Then two access control policy languages, XACL and XACML were introduced. In the later sections, we introduced a novel access control system structure which can implement these access control policy models. Three implementation schemes were described, the ACT scheme, the PMT scheme, and the Rule Function scheme, each of which has unique advantages compared to the other schemes. We compared the expressiveness of the data models and the efficiency of their policy updates.

References

1. R. J. Lipton A. K. Jones and L. Snyder. A linear time algorithm for deciding security. In *Proc. 17th Symposium on Foundations of Computer Science*, pages 33–41, 1976.
2. M. Altinel and M. Franklin. Efficient filtering of xml documents for selective dissemination of information. pages 53–64, 2000.
3. E. Bertino, S. Castano, E. Ferrari, and M. Mesiti. Controlled access and dissemination of xml documents. pages 22–27, 1999.
4. M. Bishop and L. Snyder. The transfer of information and authority in a protection system. 1979.
5. L. Bouganim, F. D. Ngoc, and P. Pucheral. Client-based access control management for xml documents. In *Proc. of VLDB*, pages 84–95, 2004.
6. S. Cho, S. Amer-Yahia, L. V. S. Lakshmanan, and D. Srivastava. Optimizing the secure evaluation of twig queries. In *Proc of VLDB*, pages 490–501, 2000.
7. cXML. *cXML Version 1.2.014*, Jun 2005. http://www.cxml.org/.
8. Ernesto Damiani, S. De Capitani di Vimercati, S. Paraboschi, and Pierangela Samarati. Securing xml documents. In *Advances in Database Technology - EDBT 2000, 7th International Conference on Extending Database Technology Konstanz, 2000 Proceedings, Springer Verlag LNCS 1777*, pages 121–135. VLDB, Mar. 2000.

9. A. Deutsch and V. Tannen. Containment of regular path expressions under integrity constraints. In *Proc. of KRDB*, 2001.
10. Y. Diao, P. Fischer, M. Franklin, and R. To. Efficient and scalable filtering of xml documents. In *Demo at ICDE*, page 341, 2002.
11. W. Fan and L. Libkin. On xml integrity constraints in the presence of dtds. In *Proceedings of Symposium on Principles of Database Systems*, pages 114–125, 2001.
12. M. F. Fernandez and D. Suciu. Optimizing regular path expressions using graph schemas. In *Proc. of ICDE*, pages 14–23, 1998.
13. A. Gabillon and E. Bruno. Regulating access to xml documents. In *Proc of Working Conference on Database and Application Security*, pages 219–314, 2001.
14. Christian Geuer-Pollmann. Xml pool encryption. In *Proceedings of Workshop on XML Security 2002*, 2002.
15. L. Gong. A secure identity-based capability system. In *Proc. IEEE Symposium on Security and Privacy*, pages 56–65. IEEE, 1989.
16. HL7. *Health Level 7 Ver 2.5*, Jun 2003. http://www.hl7.org/.
17. International Press Telecommunications Council. *NewsML 1.2*, Oct 2003. http://www.newsml.org/.
18. ISO/IEC. *Information technology - Open Systems Interconnection - Security frameworks for open systems: Access Control Framework, International Standard, ISO/IEC 10181-3*, Sep. 1996.
19. Sushil Jajodia, Michiharu Kudo, and V. S. Subrahmanian. *Provisional Authorizations*, volume E-Commerce Security and Privacy, pages 133–159. Anup Ghosh, ed., Kluwer Academic Publishers, Boston, 2000.
20. R. Kaushik, P. Bohannon, J. F. Naughton, and H. F. Korth. Covering indexes for branching path queries. In *Proc. SIGMOD*, pages 133–144. ACM, 2002.
21. D. D. Kha, M. Yoshikawa, and S. Uemura. An xml indexing structure with relative region coordinate. In *Proc. ICDE*, pages 313–320, 2001.
22. Michiharu Kudo. Pbac: Provision-based access control model. *International Journal of Information Security*, 1(2):116–130, Feb 2002.
23. Michiharu Kudo and Satoshi Hada. Xml document security based on provisional authorization. In *7th ACM Conference on Computer and Communications Security*, pages 87–96. ACM, Nov 2000.
24. Q. Li and B. Moon. Indexing and querying xml data for regular path expressions. In *Proc. VLDB*, pages 361–370, 2001.
25. M. Murata, A. Tozawa, M. Kudo, and S. Hada. Xml access control using static analysis. In *10th ACM Conference on Computer and Communication Security*, pages 73–84. ACM, Oct 2003.
26. M. Murata, A. Tozawa, M. Kudo, and S. Hada. Xml access control using static analysis. *ACM Transactions on Information and System Security*, 2006.
27. F. Neven and T. Schwentick. Xpath containment in the presence of disjunction, dtds, and variables. In *Proc. ICDT*, pages 315–329, 2003.
28. OASIS. *OASIS eXtensible Access Control Markup Language (XACML)*, Apr. 2002.
29. N. Qi and M. Kudo. Access-condition-table-driven access control for xml databases. In *9th European Symposium on Research in Computer Security*, pages 17–31. ESORICS, 2004.
30. N. Qi and M. Kudo. Xml access control with policy matching tree. In *Proc. ESORICS*, pages 3–23, 2005.
31. N. Qi, M. Kudo, J. Myllymaki, and H. Pirahesh. A function-based access control model for xml databases. In *Proc. CIKM*, pages 115–122. ACM, 2005.

32. R. S. Sandhu, E. J. Coyne, H. L. Feinstein, and C. E. Youman. Role-based access control models. *IEEE Computer*, 29(2):38–47, Feb 1996.
33. Satoshi Hada and Michiharu Kudo. *XML Access Control Language: Provisional Authorization for XML Documents*, Apr 2002. http://www.trl.ibm.com/projects/xml/xss4j/docs/xacl-spec.html.
34. W3C. *XML Linking Language (XLink) Version 1.0, W3C Recommendation 27 June 2001*, Jun 2001. http://www.w3.org/TR/xlink/#N781.
35. W3C. *XPointer Framework, W3C Recommendation 25 March 2003*, Mar 2003. http://www.w3.org/TR/xptr-framework/.
36. W3C. *XQuery 1.0: An XML Query Language, W3C Candidate Recommendation 3 November 2005*, Nov 2005. http://www.w3.org/TR/2005/CR-xquery-20051103/.
37. World Wide Web Consortium. *XML Path Language (XPath) Version 1.0*, Nov. 1999.
38. World Wide Web Consortium (W3C). *Extensible Markup Language (XML) 1.0, Second Edition*, Aug. 2000.
39. World Wide Web Consortium (W3C). *XML Encryption Syntax and Processing, W3C Candidate Recommendation 04 March 2002*, Mar. 2002.
40. World Wide Web Consortium (W3C). *XML Schema Part 1: Structures Second Edition*, Oct. 2004.
41. T. Yu, D. Srivastava, L. V. S. Lakshmanan, and H. V. Jagadish. Compressed accessibility map: Efficient access control for xml. In *Proc. VLDB*, pages 478–489, 2002.

Optimizing Tree Pattern Queries over Secure XML Databases

Hui Wang[1], Divesh Srivastava[2], Laks V.S. Lakshmanan[1], SungRan Cho[3], and Sihem Amer-Yahia[2]

[1] Department of Computer Science
University of British Columbia
hwang, laks@cs.ubc.ca

[2] AT&T Labs–Research
{divesh, sihem}@research.att.com

[3] L3S Research Center
University of Hannover
scho@l3s.de

1 Introduction

The rapid emergence of XML as a standard for data representation and exchange over the Web has sparked considerable interest in models and efficient mechanisms for controlled access, especially using queries, to information represented in XML (see, e.g., [3, 5–7, 11–13, 31]).

A naive approach to secure XML query evaluation is: (i) compute the query result without consideration of any security policy, and (ii) filter the query result using the access control policies in a post-processing step. While this approach may appear attractive, it's not secure. For example, consider the XML database with its DTD illustrated in Figure 1, which has information about items and customer accounts. Assume that a specific user is allowed access to the item (`book` and `software`) information but not to any account information. If *only* query results are filtered for accessibility, then the following XQuery path expression:

```
/OnlineSeller[.//Account/ID='00190']//Book
```

would allow the user to check the existence of account `00190`, which is clearly not the desired intent of the access control policy. In the above example, since the user is not allowed to access account information, the query result returned to that user should be empty, whether or not there is a customer with that ID. This example shows that we have to ensure that every data element that is accessed by the query is authorized to be accessible by the user. In general, secure query evaluation requires the evaluation engine to ensure that user queries *only* be permitted to check conditions on, and return, XML data that the user is allowed to access.

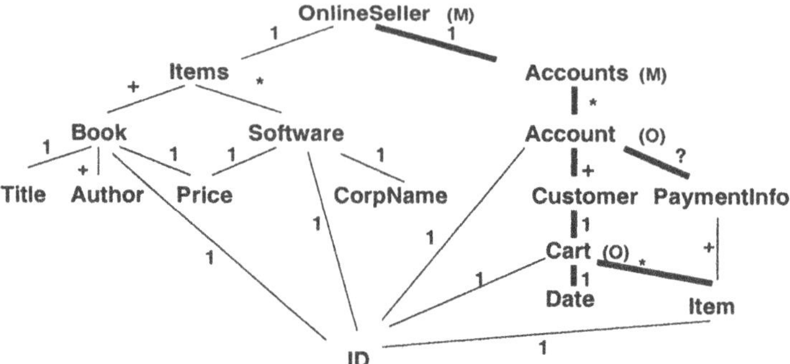

Fig. 1. Example XMark-based DAG DTD: nodes not marked M (mandatory) or O (optional) don't have their security explicitly defined.

However, such security checks can cause a considerable overhead for query evaluation. Thus it is important to optimize the evaluation of queries over secure databases by minimizing the number of such security checks. We focus on tree pattern queries that are the basis of many XML query languages. We show the following in this chapter:

- First, we introduce a simple but elegant multi-level security model for XML data where the security level of each element is specified locally or inherited from its parent. The DTD specifies which elements must, may, or cannot specify a value for their security level attribute. This model supports inheritance of security levels (down the XML tree) with overriding. We also study how to implement the security check operation on this security model (Section 3).
- Checking the security level associated with an element for this security model would, in general, require (recursively) traversing through the chain of ancestors of an element to find the nearest ancestor with an explicitly defined security level. Second, to eliminate as many such expensive recursive checks as possible, we study how to optimize the security check operations for tree pattern queries when a tree-structured schema is present. We show the intricacy and subtlety of this problem by a set of examples (Section 5).
- A straightforward extension from tree-structured schema to DAG schema by reasoning over sets of schema paths would lead to an *exponential-time* algorithm. Third, to address this problem, we study the problem of efficiently (in polynomial-time) optimizing security checks over tree pattern queries against DAG (i.e., acyclic) schemas without choice nodes. We propose a sound and complete set of rules for optimizing security checks on tree pattern query nodes against DAG DTDs and develop efficient, polynomial-time algorithms for this task (Section 6).
- There is an additional source of complexity of this problem when the schema contains choice nodes, since a schema with choice nodes is logically equivalent to the disjunction of potentially exponentially many "candidate" DAG DTDs

without choice. The optimization we perform needs to be correct with regard to all database instances that are valid with regard to any one of these candidate DTDs. Fourth, we identify how the rules for the schema without choice nodes can be enhanced to deal with the schema with choice nodes, and then develop efficient, *polynomial-time* algorithms for the task of security check optimization based on an elegant strategy for dealing with the combinatorial explosion (Section 7).

- Finally, we ran an extensive set of experiments to measure the utility and effectiveness of security check optimization, using the XALAN evaluation engine on various benchmark data sets and DTDs. Our experiments complement our analytical results, and demonstrate that security check minimization can make an order of magnitude difference in query evaluation performance, while incurring negligible overhead for optimization.

Next, we introduce the related work in Section 2. In Section 3, we present the relevant background and formally state the problem we address in this chapter. The definitions and conventions we use in this chapter are given in Section 4. We study how to optimize the security check operations for tree pattern queries for the case that a tree-structured schema is present in Section 5, for case of a DAG schema without choice nodes in Section 6, and a DAG schema with choice nodes in Section 7. Some experimental results are shown in Section 8. We summarize our results and discuss future work in Section 9.

2 Related Work

Recent research on XML security has focused considerable attention on the complementary problems of: (i) development of sophisticated access control models, and (ii) efficient mechanisms to enforce policies in these models. We describe the recent work on these two problems in this section.

2.1 XML Access Control Models

A number of security models have been proposed for XML (see [16] for a recent survey). Bertino et al. [6–8] defined an access control model that is capable of describing a set of access control policies ranging from multiple documents to specific elements within a document. The access control policies are based on the notion of subject credentials and on policy specifications at different granularity levels, with different propagation options. A credential is a set of attributes concerning a subject that are relevant for security purposes. Credentials of similar structure are grouped into the same credential type. The credentials and credential types are encoded by an XML-based language (more details of the language can be found in Bertino et al. [4]). Access control policies are specified both at the DTD and at the document level. Policies can be specified on the granularity of whole DTDs (respectively, documents) or on selected elements and/or attributes within DTDs (respectively, documents). Elements/attributes can be either explicitly specified, or can be selected on the basis of their content. The access control language used to specify authorization policies is a variant of XPath and is based on the composition of element names and attribute names. The semantics of access control to a user is a particular view of the documents determined by the relevant access control rules. An idea similar to this access control model is used in the implementation of the Author-X prototype [3, 5].

Damiani et al. [13, 14] proposed an access control model for XML documents and schema, which is an extension of their earlier work on object-oriented database, that defines positive and negative authorizations and authorization propagation. Authorizations specified on an element can be defined as applicable to the element's attributes only, or, in a recursive approach, to its sub-elements and their attributes. They developed an approach for expressing access control policies using XML syntax. The semantics of access control has the same flavor of the view idea in [5]. In the same framework, Kudo et al. [19] stressed richer authorization decisions by incorporating the notion of provisional authorization into traditional authorization semantics, where the users' requests for data will be authorized provided he takes certain security actions such as signing his statement prior to authorization of his request. It enables the client not only to browse XML documents securely but also to update each document element securely. This provisional model provides an XML access control language named XACL that integrates several security features such as authorization and audit trail in an unified manner.

Anutariya et al. [2] explored a rule-based XML access control model. They used an XML-based rule language, namely XML Declarative Description (XDD), for authorization and policy definitions. XDD extends ordinary XML elements by incorporation of variables so that the expressiveness and representation of implicit information are enhanced. By means of XDD the model permits one to describe declaratively fine-grained access control and to define multiple, different policies to be enforced on different authorization definitions. In addition, they defined a special type of query, named access evaluation query, which returns a access decision (grant or deny) by retrieving the matching specified authorization rules from the authorization database and applying an appropriate policy to resolve conflicts or to yield a default permission.

Wang et al. [27] presented a role-based approach to access control by using the role graph model and the object-oriented database authorization model as the basis. In this model the users are grouped by roles. In particular, based on the role graph model, the access control model supports that when a privilege is added to a role, all implied privileges are added as well. The privileges on the roles can be associated with any part of an XML document, a single attribute or element value, or a set of documents. By combining with the ideas of object-oriented database authorization model, the XML schema would be used to construct the authorization object schema, and the XML documents would be used for the authorization object graph construction. With the aid of role graph model and the object-oriented database authorization model, a complex authorization model can be built and enforced.

Recently, Cho et al. [11] proposed a simple multi-level security (MLS) model for XML data, where individual XML elements may each have an explicitly associated security level (represented as an attribute of that element), as do all users. If an element does not have a security level explicitly associated with it, it inherits the security level associated with the closest ancestor where it is explicitly defined. To identify which elements must, may or cannot have security levels explicitly associated with them, the model of [11] allowed the DTD (schema) to be labeled with this information.

Our contributions are complementary to this body of work since our techniques are applicable for a wide variety of access control models (including the ones mentioned above) that support inheritance of security levels (down the XML tree) with overriding.

2.2 Efficient Enforcement Mechanisms

Most of the existing mechanisms for authorization policy enforcement can be categorized as: (1) authorization views, (2) access control index, (3) static analysis of the queries, and (4) query rewriting.

Authorization Views

Fan et al. [15] proposed an approach for access control enforcement based on security views. A security view is a portion of the original document and the underlying document DTD that exposes all and only necessary schema structure and document content to authorized users. Authorized users can only pose queries over the security view by making use of the exposed DTD view to formulate their queries. The authors proposed a novel quadratic time algorithm such that given the document DTD and an access policy specification, it automatically derives a sound and complete security-view definition (i.e., a view that exposes all and only accessible data elements and schema structure).

To elaborate on certain issues left open in [15], Kuper et al. [20] studied access control and security specifications defined on general DTDs in terms of regular expressions rather than normalized DTDs of [15]. They developed a new algorithm for deriving a security view definition from more intuitive access control specification (with regard to a non-recursive DTD) without introducing dummy element types as in [15], thus preventing inference of sensitive information from the XML structure revealed by dummies. They also developed an algorithm for materializing security views, which ensures that views conform to the secure DTD views.

It is quite expensive to actually materialize and maintain multiple security views of a large XML document. To avoid constructing multiple views, Bertino et al. [8] used encryption to enforce the authorization policies on one XML document. The approach uses different keys for encrypting different portions of the same document. Each portion is encrypted with one and only one key. The same (encrypted) copy of the document is then broadcast to all subjects, whereas each subject only receives the key(s) for the portion(s) he/she is enabled to access. The encryption granularity of the document is the finest level granularity, i.e., every single attribute or element of the document is encrypted with a potentially different key. To limit the number of keys that will be generated, a method was proposed by which the portions of the document to which the same access policies apply are encrypted with the same keys.

Miklau et al. [23] also proposed a framework for enforcing access control policies on published XML documents using cryptography. In this framework each node in the XML document is guarded by positive boolean formulas, namely a *protection*, over a set of cryptographic keys, instead of only one key, as in Bertino et al. [8]. The access control policies are translated into *protections* and are applied on the XML document by encryption. The authors described a simple extension of XQuery that allows the user to access data selectively, moreover, guide the query processor to locate which keys to use where. Based on their work, Abadi et al. [1] provide a precise justification of the security guarantee of this framework against probabilistic polynomial-time adversaries with respect to a strong, computational notion of security.

Damiani et al. [13, 14] used a different approach for the implementation of the authorization view. The view that is accessible to a user is computed through a tree labeling process. The tree labeling process associates to each node a tuple as a label, whose content reflects the authorizations specified on the node. The labeling of the complete document can be obtained by starting from the root and proceeding downwards with a preorder traversal.

Access Control Index

Another method to enforce access control policies on an XML document is to represent the access control information by some data structure, i.e., the index scheme, so that the accessibility of (portion of) the XML data can be efficiently determined by exploiting the index.

Bouganim et al. [10] studied how to implement the access control model on streaming XML documents. The authors proposed an efficient access control rule evaluator in which each access control rule (in XPath syntax) is represented by a non deterministic finite automaton. This evaluator benefits from the design of a highly compact index structure, called *skip index*, which allows fast access to the authorized portion of the document and skip the irrelevant parts with respect to the access control policy and to a potential query. The skip index is encoded recursively into the XML document to allow streaming, which can be used as a new means of compressing the structural part of the document.

Gummadi et al. [17] proposed a three dimensional bitmap data structure, named *security cube*, to represent the access control policies. The three dimensions of the security cube are documents, element paths and user/group. It is fine-tuned to represent the access control at the element path level granularity (the lowest level of granularity) for multiple users. Thus the security cube can be effectively used to provide control of access to multiple users over several documents with many element paths. The security cube supports quick access, and is flexible for maintenance and updates. It's extendible to include new subjects, for example, Internet Protocol (IP) address or symbolic names, to add *write* and *append* privileges, and to express the access control on the content level. The authors also showed how to enhance the security cube in different environments, for example, mandatory access control model, discretionary access control model, role-based model and rule-based model.

Yu et al. [31] investigated the problem of efficiently determining whether or not a user has access to a particular XML element, for arbitrary access control policies. A compressed accessibility map (CAM) was proposed to resolve the problem in a way to compactly represent the data items by exploiting the locality of accessibility in hierarchical XML data. The authors presented a CAM lookup algorithm for determining if a user has access to a data item. The complexity of the lookup algorithm is proportional to the product of the depth of the item in the XML data and logarithm of the CAM size. They also developed an algorithm for building an optimal size CAM that takes time linear in the size of the XML data set. While optimality cannot be preserved incrementally under data item updates, they provided an algorithm for incrementally maintaining near-optimality.

Zhang et al. [32] presented a compact XML access control labeling scheme that exploits both access control structural locality within the XML data and correlations between access rights of different users. The physical representation of the access control labeling is a compact index scheme which can be constructed by using a single pass over an XML document with access control labels. This physical scheme can be integrated with a next-of-kin (NoK) XML query processor so that efficient and secure query evaluation is supported. The authors noted that all the updates to the access control labeling are local, i.e., the updates are confined within a contiguous region of the affected data.

Static Analysis

To apply a query securely on the access controlled data, the accessibility of each query node must be checked against the database. However, such process can be expensive for XML documents of large size. Murata et al. [24] studied the problem of how to determine whether a query expression is safe with regard to the given access control policy by static analysis, i.e., without evaluating any query expression against an actual database. Run-time checking is needed only when static analysis is unable to determine whether the access is granted or denied. The key idea of the approach is to construct the automata for queries, access control policies and schemas individually. By comparing these three automata the queries that do not satisfy access control policies are filtered out, and the "safe" queries are referred to the XML query engine for further checking and processing. If there is no schema available, schema automata will be skipped and the comparison is only between access control automata and query automata.

Query Evaluation and Rewriting

It has been noted that materializing and maintaining multiple security views of a large XML document is expensive. To avoid the overheads of view materialization and the complexities of view maintenance, Fan et al. [15] proposed a novel XML query-rewriting algorithm that transforms an input XPath query posed over a security view to an equivalent, secure query over the original document, which yields an effective querying mechanism that completely bypasses view materialization. It also introduced a new query optimization technique that leverages the structural properties of DTDs to optimize the evaluation of the transformed query.

Luo et al. [21] examined three different approaches, namely *primitive*, *pre-processing* and *post-processing* processes, to perform the access control policy on a finer granularity. The *primitive* approach is to view both the query and the access control policies as two constraints and apply both constraints to the database. The *pre-processing* approach is to first prune away the queries that conflict with the access control polices. Then the queries are rewritten with regard to the access control policies so that only the safe "revised" queries will be applied on the database. The rewriting is based a method that called *QFilter*, which is based on nondeterministic finite automata. The *post-processing* approach is to apply all queries to the database, no matter whether they are safe or not. Then the intermediate results will be verified by the *post-filtering* process and the unsafe answers will be pruned away. The authors showed that QFilter-based *pre-processing* approach significantly outperforms the *primitive* and *post-processing* approaches by their experimental results.

Our focus in this chapter is finding *optimal*, *correct* rewritings of queries against an XML database conforming to a given DAG DTD. The rewriting guarantees secure evaluation of the queries. Our model supports inheritance of security levels with overriding. The rewriting is accomplished by means of adorning query tree nodes with security check annotation labels that infer the accessibility of a given node. As discussed in the introduction, our work is inspired by, and *substantially enhances*, the work by Cho et al. [11], which focused on much simpler tree-structured DTDs.

3 Model and The Problem

3.1 Security and Authorization Model

We adopt a very general security model, where any mechanism (e.g., multi-level security, role-based access, or rules) can be used to explicitly determine which data object (XML element) is accessible by which user/subject.[4] Since it can be too tedious and cumbersome to require every element to have its security (i.e., accessibility) explicitly defined, the various proposals for XML security permit an element (whose security is not explicitly defined) to inherit its security from its closest ancestor where it is defined. We require that the root element must have its security explicitly defined. This security model permits the security of elements to be defined in a flexible way, allowing them to be inherited and overridden in an arbitrary fashion. Attribute-level security can be handled analogously to that for elements and is not considered further.

We propose a lightweight extension to schemas whereby the schema nodes can be associated with security information, declared as: (i) *mandatory* (`M`) (all instances

[4] Our primary focus being query processing, we consider only read access.

must have their security defined explicitly), or (ii) *optional* `(O)` (instances may have their security defined explicitly or inherited), or (iii) *forbidden* `(F)` (no instance may have their security defined explicitly; only inheritance is permitted). We require that the root of the schema must be specified as `(M)`. This is illustrated in Figure 1. Firstly the root of the schema is annotated `(M)`. Secondly, since the *accounts* information is sensitive, it must have its security level explicitly specified. Therefore the annotation of `Accounts` node is declared as `(M)`. Thirdly, the security level on each account varies for different customers. It is either the same security level as that is specified on the ancestor elements or specified locally. Therefore the annotation of node `Account` is declared `(O)`. The same to the `Cart` node. Lastly, the security level of all other schema nodes are labeled with `(F)`. Thus the corresponding instance nodes won't have any security level locally specified. The flexibility of the security annotations allow our model to be fit in a role-based access control environment as well.

3.2 Multi-level Security and Authorization

We assume a set of *security levels*, which may be any finite partially ordered set. For simplicity of exposition, we use total orders in all our examples. For instance, in a military environment, it is common to use the security levels $S = \{unclassified, confidential, secret, topsecret\}$, with the ordering $unclassified < confidential < secret < topsecret$. The security levels used in a commercial application may vary, and depend on the organization's policy.

The basic idea behind multi-level security is that each resource/object (e.g., XML element) is potentially assigned a security level, as is each user/subject that is authorized to access objects in the space (e.g., a collection of XML documents). Here, "user" might include an application or a human. A subject may only access an object if the security level assigned to the subject is no less than that assigned to the object. In general, separate security levels may be associated depending on the kind of access action (e.g., read or write). Since our focus is query processing, we only consider read actions, and thus leave them implicit. Thus, a subject whose security level is "secret" can access (i.e., read) objects with security level "secret", "confidential", or "unclassified".

In the context of XML data trees, security levels are assigned to elements by associating a separate attribute called, say `SecurityLevel`. Thus, a DTD needs to permit such attributes in addition to the usual content of elements. Since XML is tree structured, the security level of an element, if not specified, can be inherited from its closest ancestor. On the other hand, a security level defined at an element always overrides the inherited one. This overriding can be *monotone*, in that security levels defined at subelements are never less than those defined at their parent, or *non-monotone* where no such restriction is imposed. Clearly, non-monotone overriding is more expressive in that it permits a broader class of applications. For this reason and for brevity, in the sequel, we only consider non-monotone overriding.

3.3 DTDs, DTD Graphs, and Queries

DTDs essentially are a subset of (extended) context-free grammars, with productions of the form $A \rightarrow \alpha$, where A is a non-terminal and α is a string over the vocabulary $N \cup \{?, 1, +, *, (,), |\}$, N being the set of non-terminals. We refer to '$?, 1, *, +$' as quantifiers. They indicate optionality, 'exactly one occurrence', 'zero or more occurrences', and 'one or more occurrences' respectively. The operator '|' indicates choice. For example, the production $A \rightarrow (B?C^{+}) \mid (CD)^{*}$ uses all the said quantifiers.[5] This production contains a choice and says either $A \rightarrow (B?C^{+})$ or $A \rightarrow (CD)^{*}$. We call productions containing '|' *choice productions*. A DTD containing at least one choice production is a *choice* DTD. Otherwise, it is a *choiceless* DTD.

In the sequel, we will assume that the choice operator of a DTD is not nested with choice or with quantifiers '$?, 1, *, +$', and that quantifiers are not nested with themselves more than once. There is no loss of generality as any DTD can be rewritten into an equivalent DTD satisfying this assumption, by introducing new non-terminals to factor out such nested occurrences. Here, equivalence means both grammars generate the same language. In a production $A \rightarrow \alpha_1 \mid \cdots \mid \alpha_k$, suppose α_i is of the form $(\langle \text{string} \rangle)\ell$, where $\ell \in \{?, 1, *, +\}$. Then we refer to ℓ as the *principal quantifier* associated with α_i. This notion also extends to single non-terminals and we speak of the quantifier associated with a non-terminal in a sequence. The following example illustrates the transformation and the notions above.

Example 1. **[Unnesting Choice] :** Consider the production $A \rightarrow (((B?C^{+})^{*} \mid (CD?)^{+})^{*} \mid ((DEF)^{*})^{+})?$. This is equivalent to the set of productions $A \rightarrow G?$, $G \rightarrow H^{*} \mid I^{+}$, $H \rightarrow (B?C^{+})^{*} \mid (CD?)^{+}$, $I \rightarrow (DEF)^{*}$. These productions do not involve a nesting of choice with any quantifier or choice, and quantifiers are nested with quantifiers at most once. The principal quantifier associated with $(DEF)^{*}$ as well as with $(B?C^{+})^{*}$ is '$*$'. The quantifier associated with C in $(B?C^{+})^{*}$ is '$+$'.

Henceforth, we will assume that each production in a DTD is of the form $A \rightarrow \alpha_1 \mid \cdots \mid \alpha_k$ $(k \geq 1)$, where α_i is a regular expression over non-terminals that may involve quantifiers but not choice node. A DTD Δ can be represented in the form of a directed node- and edge-labeled graph $\mathcal{G}(\Delta) = (V, E)$, called the *DTD Graph*, as follows. The graph $\mathcal{G}(\Delta)$ contains an element node for each non-terminal. Besides, for every production in the DTD of the form $A \rightarrow [\alpha_1 \mid \cdots \mid \alpha_k]$ $(k \geq 1)$, $\mathcal{G}(\Delta)$ contains one choice node, k sequence nodes, and the following labeled edges:

- an edge (x, y) with label '1' where x is the non-terminal A and y is the choice node associated with this production.
- an edge (x, y) where x is the choice node associated with this production and y is a sequence node associated with some α_i $(1 \leq i \leq k)$. The label of this edge is the principal quantifier associated with α_i.
- an edge (x, y) where x is a sequence node associated with some α_i $(1 \leq i \leq k)$, and y is a non-terminal appearing in α_i. The label of this edge is the quantifier associated with y in α_i.

[5] Quantifier 1 is left implicit.

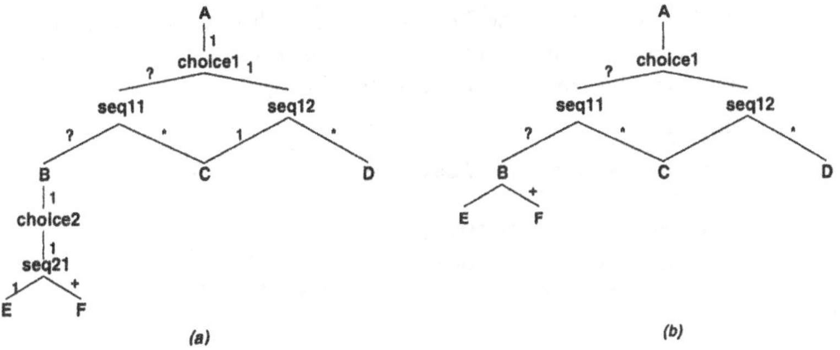

Fig. 2. DTD Graph illustrated: (a) (Original) DTD graph and (b) simplified DTD graph of $\{A \rightarrow (B?C^*)? \mid (CD^*),\ B \rightarrow (EF^+)\}$.

Figure 2(a) shows a sample DTD and its associated DTD graph. Often, it is useful to simplify a DTD graph without losing essential information. We drop the label '1' and use it as the default label of an edge. When a production does not involve choice, we can eliminate the choice node. Additionally, if the principal quantifier associated with the sequence in a choiceless production is '1', we can eliminate that sequence node. In effect, we merge the choice and sequence nodes with the non-terminal node of the production. Figure 2(b) shows the simplified DTD graph. In our examples, we usually use simplified DTD graphs.

We call a DTD a tree (resp., acyclic, cyclic) provided its DTD graph is a tree (resp., is acyclic, is cyclic). Acyclic DTDs are also called DAG DTDs.

A *tree pattern query* (TPQ) is a node-labeled and edge-labeled rooted tree with its edges labeled by pc (for parent-child) or ad (for ancestor-descendant), nodes labeled by an element tag, with leaves labeled by either an element tag or a constraint that constrains the element value, and with a subset of nodes marked as *distinguished*. Distinguished nodes abstract the notion of output nodes and are shown inside boxes in our examples, while pc-edges (ad-edges) are shown in single (double) line (e.g., see Figure 3). As such, TPQs abstract the core fragment of XPath. Answers to a TPQ are based on matchings, which are functions that map pattern nodes to data nodes, while satisfying node predicates (such as tag) and relationships between nodes.

3.4 SC Annotations and Problem Statement

Secure evaluation of a tree pattern query involves checking the (explicitly defined or inherited) security of every data tree node matching a query node to ensure that it is accessible by the user. We introduce the notion of checking additional predicates potentially at every data tree node that matches a tree pattern query node by examining the value of the `SecurityLevel` attribute in the data. These notions are RC (recursive check), LC (local check), and NC (no check). We call these *security check annotation labels* (SC annotation labels). LC merely amounts to checking the value of the `SecurityLevel` attribute at a given node, while NC is a no-op. RC, on the other hand, involves recursively checking the value of this attribute at every node starting from the given node until a nearest ancestor is reached where the attribute is defined. Consider the following function definition in XQuery:

```
DEFINE FUNCTION
self-or-nearestAncestor(element $e)
      RETURNS integer{
   IF $e/@SecurityLevel THEN
      RETURN $e/@SecurityLevel
   ELSE RETURN self-or-nearestAncestor($e/..)
}
```

This function implements RC by computing the value of the SecurityLevel attribute at the nearest ancestor of the current node where it is defined. We can now implement LC at a node by adding the predicate [@SecurityLevel ≤ $usl OR NOT @SecurityLevel] to the label of the node. Notice that in a tree pattern query, each node label, i.e., an element tag t, or value v, really stands for the predicate tag=t, or content=v. By adding the additional predicate corresponding to SecurityLevel above, we really are taking a conjunction of the two predicates. In the same way, we can implement RC at a node by adding the predicate [self-or-nearestAncestor(.)≤$usl]. As an example, the query of Figure 3(e), with SC annotation labels incorporated, corresponds to the XPath expression

```
   Accounts[@SecurityLevel ≤ $usl OR NOT
@SecurityLevel][.//Customer]
   //PaymentInfo[self-or-nearestAncestor(.)≤ $usl].
```

Thus, every tree pattern query with SC annotation labels added can be expressed as a query with function calls added for local and recursive checks and evaluated using the same evaluation engine. To formulate the optimization problem, we define the following:

Definition 1 (Minimal SC Annotation). Let Q be a tree pattern query. A *security check(SC) annotation* of Q is essentially Q with each of its nodes associated with one of the SC annotation labels RC, LC, NC. Define RC > LC > NC, reflecting the complexity of performing these checks in general. Given two different SC annotations $\mathcal{A}_1, \mathcal{A}_2$ of a TPQ Q, we say $\mathcal{A}_1$ *dominates* $\mathcal{A}_2$, written $\mathcal{A}_1 \geq \mathcal{A}_2$, provided for every node $x \in Q$, $\mathcal{A}_1(x) \geq \mathcal{A}_2(x)$. An SC annotation $\mathcal{A}$ in a set of annotations S is *minimal* provided there is no annotation $\mathcal{B} \in S$ such that $\mathcal{A} > \mathcal{B}$.

We now formalize our notion of correctness. Let Q be a query issued by a user against a database D. A tuple of data nodes that are mappings of pattern nodes of Q is a *binding tuple*. We call a binding tuple $\langle d_1, ..., d_k \rangle$ associated with Q and D *safe* provided each $d_i (1 \leq i \leq k)$ is accessible to the user. An answer tuple is *safe* provided it is the projection of a safe binding tuple. Given a query Q and a DTD Δ, an annotation $\mathcal{A}$ of Q is *correct* with regard to Δ, provided on every valid database instance D of Δ, every answer to Q on D obtained using $\mathcal{A}$ is safe.[6]

There is a trivial way to make sure we get exactly the safe and correct answers: annotate all query nodes with RC. This guarantees the evaluation of Q never accesses nodes the user with security level *usl* is not allowed to. However, it's very expensive to evaluate queries this way, since a lot of avoidable redundant security checks may be performed. Thus we seek to optimize the SC annotations on as many query nodes as possible. More precisely, we give the problem statement as follows.

Problem Statement: Given a tree pattern query Q and a DTD Δ, find a minimal SC annotation among the set of all SC annotations of Q that are correct with regard to Δ. We call this the security check annotation optimization problem (SCAOP).

In this chapter, we assume that the queries we consider are minimal. Minimizing tree pattern queries is a well-researched topic and we refer the reader to [22, 28] for minimization techniques. Note that a minimal unsatisfiable query is clearly the empty query which is always false.

4 Definitions and Conventions

Before we go to the details, we give the definitions and conventions that we will frequently used in the chapter.

Let Q be a TPQ, Δ be a DTD, and x be a node in Q with tag t. Then we use x' to denote the node in Δ with tag t. For a set of query nodes S, S' denotes the corresponding set of DTD nodes. For simplicity, we blur the distinction between a (query or DTD) node and its tag and speak of node A to mean node with tag A.[7] A node in Δ is *overriding* if it is marked (M) or (O) in Δ. A DTD path from node x' to y' is *overriding* if it contains an intermediate node that is overriding between node x' and y', otherwise it is *non-overriding*. We say an overriding node z' exists between two DTD nodes x' and y' if it occurs on a path from x' to y', where $z' \neq x', y'$. Such a node is closest to y' (x') if there is a non-overriding DTD path from z' to y' (from x' to z'). We say a DTD node x' is an *ancestor* of a DTD node y' provided there is a DTD path from x' to y'. We say a node w' is an *lowest common ancestor* of node x' and y' if (1) w' is the ancestor of x' and y', and (2) there doesn't exist a node z' that is the descendant of w' and the ancestor of both x' and y'.

A path in Δ is *optional* if at least one of the edges in it is labeled either '?' or '$*$', otherwise it is *non-optional*. A path is *unique* if all edges in it are labeled '?' or '1'. For a query node x, its query parent is the node y in Q such that Q contains an (ad- or pc-) edge (y, x). A query node x is *unconstrained* if (i) it is not a distinguished node of Q, (ii) Q has no value-based constraint of the form *content relOp value* on

6 Note that the evaluation of an annotated query always produces all safe answers against any database. However, it may produce unsafe answers, when it is incorrect.

7 In specific examples, of course both the query node x and the DTD node x' will have the same tag, say A.

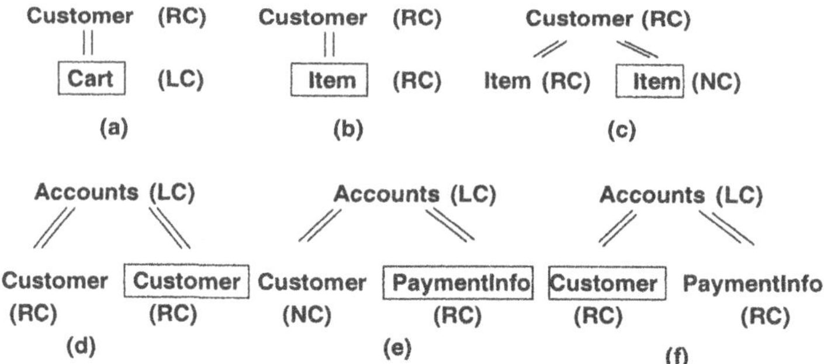

Fig. 3. Examples for Tree-Structured DTD Graph

x, and (iii) each of its query children w is (a) (recursively) unconstrained and labeled with (NC), and (b) at least one path between x' and w' is non-optional. The SC annotation decision for an unconstrained node can be made without regard to other nodes in its query subtree. Finally, in a TPQ, we say two nodes are *cousins* of each other if neither is an ancestor (proper or not) of the other. Note that cousins have a common ancestor that is different from them both. Also note that x and y may be cousins in a query but the corresponding DTD nodes x' and y' *may* have an ancestor-descendant relationship.

Let x, y be any query nodes and x', y' the corresponding DTD nodes. Suppose in any valid instance, either the security levels of corresponding matches of x and y are the same or whenever they are not, this is solely because the security level at (the match of) x is locally changed. In this case, we say that the (match of) x has *almost the same security level* as the (corresponding match of) y.

5 Tree-Structured DTD Graph

In this section, we discuss the optimization of SC annotations of arbitrary tree pattern queries, for the case of tree-structured DTD graphs. The reasoning involved in determining optimal SC annotations for this case is quite non-trivial, even though we assume the DTD is tree-structured. To reuse the DTD in Figure 1 we reason on the part of the DTD with its edges bolded in Figure 1, which can be considered as a tree-structured DTD.

5.1 Optimization on Query Root

The SC annotation of the query root can be optimized by the following: When query root x is such that the path from the DTD root to the corresponding DTD node x' is non-overriding, we can optimize the SC annotation of x: if x' is overriding, we can optimize the SC annotation of x to (LC), otherwise to (NC). Using Figure 3(e) as an example, since the path (and it's the only path) from the DTD root

(OnlineSeller) to Accounts is non-overriding, and Accounts is labeled with (M) in DTD, the SC annotation of query root Accounts is optimized as (LC).

5.2 Optimization on Non-root Query Nodes

Nodes of the tree pattern query Q are traversed top-down in some topological order. If the current node n_2 is the query root, it is dealt with as above. Otherwise, let n_2' be the node in the DTD graph corresponding to n_2 (i.e., it has the same tag). Let n_1 be the parent of n_2 in Q and let n_1' be the corresponding DTD graph node.[8] If the DTD path p from n_1' to n_2' is non-overriding, then n_2 cannot inherit its security level from an ancestor other than n_1', so if n_2' is overriding, we can set n_2's SC annotation to LC. Else we set it to NC. The more difficult case is when there is an overriding path p. In this case, if n_2' is marked (M), again, we can set n_2's SC annotation to LC. If n_2' is marked (O) or (F), then depending on whether there is a query node $n_3(\neq n_2)$ as the "witness" such that for all data tree instances of n_2' under the data tree instance of n_1' they always have the same security level as n_3', we can optimize the SC annotation on n_2 to LC if n_2' is labelled (O), or to NC if n_2' labelled (F). These intricacies are best illustrated with examples.

First, consider Figure 3(a). It's easy to see that the root is labeled with RC. Since the DTD path from Customer to Cart doesn't contain any overriding node, Cart must get a LC. This is an optimal SC annotation. Next, consider the only slightly different Figure 3(b). We can observe that the DTD path from Customer to Item contains one overriding node Cart. Thus Item must be labeled with RC.

We then consider the queries with multiple branches. Consider the query Figure 3(c). Suppose the topological order used is the root Customer, followed by the left Item, followed by the right. The SC annotation labels of the root and its two children are determined exactly as before, and are initially set to RC. However, when the second Item child is processed, we notice that it must inherit its security level from an intermediate Cart node in the DTD path from Customer to Item, and all edges on the path segment from Customer to Cart (there is only one!) are *not* labeled * or +, so all Item children must inherit their security level from a unique Cart node. This means the previously processed Item node can act as an existential witness for the second Item node, whose SC annotation label can thus be replaced by an NC. In contrast, for the query of Figure 3(d), which looks identical in structure to that of Figure 3(c), we cannot do the same optimization, since the DTD path from Accounts to Account (the node that is overriding) contains at least one edge labeled *, which destroys the uniqueness property mentioned above.

To illustrate another intricacy and subtlety, consider yet another identical looking query of Figure 3(e). Initially, both non-root query nodes get an RC. In particular, we can reason that in the DTD, the Customer node that is not overriding, must inherit its security level from the ancestor Account. So, if the PaymentInfo node in the query has an RC on it (as it does), it would ensure an accessible Account ancestor.

[8] Note that the edge (n_1, n_2) might be an ad-edge.

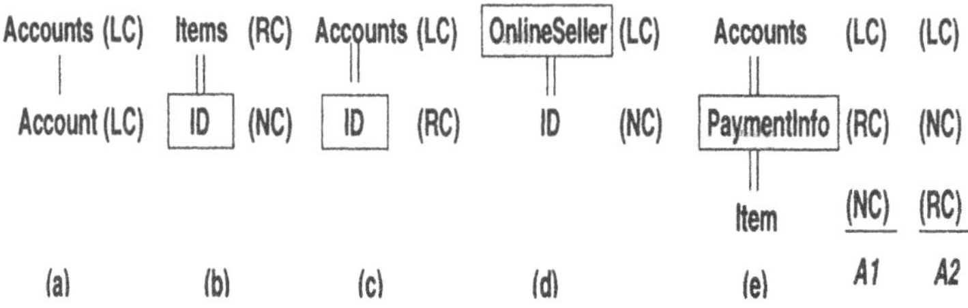

Fig. 4. Examples for DAG-Structured DTD: PC Rules

Since the DTD path from the `Account` node to `Customer` node is free from edges labeled ? or *, we know there is guaranteed to be a `Customer` descendant, which must be accessible, since its security level is inherited from the `Account` ancestor, which is accessible. So, in the query, the `Customer` node's SC annotation label can be changed to an NC. We leave it to the reader as a simple exercise to see why in yet another similar query, Figure 3(f), none of the child labels can be changed from an RC.

Algorithm `ForwardPassTree` that presents pseudo-code for optimizing SC annotations of arbitrary XML tree pattern queries, for the case of tree-structured DTD graphs, is presented in [11]. The following result is also shown in [11].

Theorem 1 (Optimality of `ForwardPassTree`). Let Q be an arbitrary XML tree pattern query, and $\triangle$ be any tree-structured DTD graph. Then the SC annotation of Q computed by Algorithm `ForwardPassTree` is the minimal SC annotations of Q on D.

6 DAG-structured DTD Graphs

There is a considerable conceptual leap from tree DTDs to DAG DTDs, since there are multiple paths between pairs of nodes, each with a different sequence of labels. A straightforward extension of the reasoning over a single schema path for tree structured DTDs to multiple schema paths for DAG DTDs would lead to an exponential-time algorithm for the case of DAG schemas. Then how can we do the reasoning efficiently over DAG DTDs? Besides, we have the following questions in mind: (1) When can we optimize a SC annotation of a query node when the context of the matching node in DTD gets more complicated due to multiple parents/ancestors? (2) In what order should we process nodes? (3) Is the minimal correct SC annotation unique? As a preview, we propose four rules for optimizing query nodes (Root, PC, CP, and CC). We show these rules are sound and complete. Based on this, we develop a *polynomial-time* algorithm that is guaranteed to reach a minimal SC annotation for a given query. In this section, we give the pseudocode for each rule and explain them separately. We use the DTD shown in Figure 1 for all examples in this section.

```
Procedure rootSCA(query root x)
Output:x with its correct SC annotation
   sc(x)=case_II(DTDroot, x);
END Procedure
Function SimplifyBelow(query node x)
   if (forbidden(x')) return "NC";
   else return "LC";
END Function
Function SimplifyAbove(query node x)
   if (mandatory(x')) return "LC";
   else return "RC";
END Function
```

Fig. 5. Root rule & Optimization

```
Function case_I(query node x)
   return SimplifyBelow(x);
END Function
Function case_II(query parent y, query node x)
if (mandatory(x')) return ''LC'';
else {if (ornodeset(y',x') != NULL) return ''RC'';
       else if (optional(x')) return ''LC'';
          else return ''NC''; }
END Function
Function case_III(query parent y, query node x)
∀ o ∈ ornodeset(y', x') closest to y'{
 assume S be the set of nodes s.t.∀ c ∈ S,
     (c' under y' or c'=y')AND c'= ancestor(o')
     AND nonoptionalnonoverriding(c', x')
     if(S.size()==0)return SimplifyAbove(x);
     if ∃ path P from y' to x' goes through o'
     s.t. P doesn't go through any node ∈ S
        return SimplifyAbove(x);}
return SimplifyBelow(x);
END Function
```

Fig. 6. Parent-Child rule

6.1 Root Rule

When the query root x is such that all paths from the DTD root to the corresponding node x' are non-overriding(see the definition of *non-overriding path* in Section 4), we can optimize the SC annotation of x: if x' is overriding, we can optimize the SC annotation of x to `(LC)`, otherwise to `(NC)`. As an example in Figure 4(a), since the path (and it's the only path) from the DTD root (`OnlineSeller`) to `Accounts` is non-overriding, and DTD node `Accounts` is labelled with `(M)`, the SC annotation of query root `Accounts` is optimized as `(LC)`.

6.2 Parent-Child(PC) Rule

Let x be a query node and y its query parent. Let x', y' be the corresponding DTD nodes. We can optimize the SC annotation on x if any data node that matches x

has almost the same security level as the corresponding match of y. There are three possible scenarios for such optimization.

Case I: The query in Figure 4(a) involves a direct pc-edge. We can optimize the SC annotation of such a query node x whenever the corresponding DTD node x' is non-overriding. This is the case for node `Account` and so its SC annotation is optimized to `(LC)` in Figure 4(a).

Case II: Consider next an ad-edge (y, x) in the query. If all DTD paths from y' to x' are non-overriding, i.e., there is no node to introduce new security level between x and y, then we can optimize node x. In the query of Figure 4(b), all DTD paths from `Items` to `ID` are non-overriding and `ID` is non-overriding, so the SC annotation of `ID` can be optimized to `(NC)`. The pseudocode can be found on lines 1-4 in Figure 6. We leave it to the reader as a simple exercise to see why in yet another similiar query, Figure 4(c), the SC annotation of node `ID` cannot be optimized.

Case III: Finally, let (y, x) be an ad-edge and suppose x is unconstrained(see the definition of *unconstrained node* in Section 4). Then we can optimize the SC annotation of x *if* a match of y in any instance is guaranteed to have a descendant that matches x which has almost the same security level as the said match of y. In terms of DTD paths, it is enough to show that on every path P from y' to x', there is a node z' (possibly $= y'$), such that there is at least one non-optional non-overriding DTD path from z' to x'(see the definition of *non-optional path* and *non-overriding path* in Section 4), and the segment of the path P from y' to z' is non-overriding. Note here if z' is an intermediate node, z' must be non-overriding. E.g., for nodes `OnlineSeller` and `ID` in the query of Figure 4(d), the path {`OnlineSeller, Items, Book, ID`} in the DTD (Figure 1) is such a path.[9] This path tells us that any data node `OnlineSeller` is guaranteed to have a descendant with tag `ID` that has the same security level as itself. So we can optimize the SC annotation of `ID` to be `(NC)`. The pseudocode can be found on lines 5-13 in Figure 6.

To sum, we have three cases for optimizing a query node based on its query parent. The first two cases apply to both constrained and unconstrained nodes while the last applies only to unconstrained nodes. We have the following result:

Lemma 1. [Completeness of PC-Rule] : Let Q be a tree pattern query, Δ be any choiceless DAG DTD, and (y, x) be an (ad- or pc-) edge in Q. Suppose D is a valid database instance of Δ. Then in every matching $\mu : Q \to D$, $\mu(x)$ and $\mu(y)$ have almost the same security levels if and only if one of the three cases above holds. .

As a fallout, if one of the cases I-III holds[10] for a query node x, but the DTD node x' is overriding, then x can be optimized to `(LC)`. The proof of Lemma 1 is shown in [26].

6.3 Child-Parent(CP) Rule

The core intuition behind optimizing a query node using the PC-rule is that it is guaranteed to have (almost) the same security level as the match of its query parent.

[9] $z' = y'$ in this case.

[10] This means we don't count the label on x' when deciding if a path to x' is overriding.

We could use the similiar reasoning to optimize a node if it has (almost) the same security level as its query child instead, whenever one of the cases I-III above holds. For example, in Figure 4(e), two correct SC annotations $\mathcal{A}_1, \mathcal{A}_2$ are shown. In both SC annotations, the root `Accounts` is optimized to `(LC)`. In $\mathcal{A}_1$, the SC annotation of node `Item` is optimized to `(NC)` using PC-rule (both case II and case III can be applied), whereas in $\mathcal{A}_2$, node `PaymentInfo` is optimized using CP-rule (with only case III can be applied). Note, however, that it is incorrect to optimize both `PaymentInfo` and `Item`! For this example, $\mathcal{A}_1$ and $\mathcal{A}_2$ are both minimal correct SC annotations. *Thus, the minimal correct solution to SCAOP is not unique.*

6.4 Cousin-Cousin(CC) Rule

It is possible to optimize a query node x even when PC- and CP-rules both fail to apply. The intuition is that x may have a cousin y in the query tree such that y is annotated `(RC)` or `(LC)` and from the DTD we can infer that in any valid database instance, any match of x has almost the same security level as a corresponding match of y.[11] Verifying this condition based on the DTD graph is somewhat complex and we break this down into two major cases.

Unconstrained Nodes

Suppose x is unconstrained and y is annotated. Let w be the lowest common ancestor of x and y in the query tree and S_x (S_y) be the set of ancestors of x (y) occurring on the path from w to x (y) in the query tree, including w. Intuitively, $S_x(S_y)$ captures the relevant query context of node $x(y)$. Let S_x'(S_y)' be set of DTD nodes corresponding to $S_x(S_y)$. We wish to optimize x whenever (a match of) x must have almost the same security level as (a corresponding match of) y. There are three possible scenarios: x' and y' are cousins(case IV.1), x' is the descendant of y'(case IV.2), and x' is the ancestor of y'(case IV.3). The details are given below.

Case IV.1: Suppose there is at least one overriding node between w' and y', and that for every overriding node z' between w' and y' that is closest to y' within context of S'_y, we see that there is a DTD path P from w' to x' that passes through this overriding node z' as well as through all nodes in S'_x, such that the segment of P from z' to x' is non-optional and non-overriding (illustrated in Figure 8(a)). This guarantees that in any valid instance, for any match of y, there *must exist* a corresponding match of x occurring in the right query context such that both matches inherit their security level from the same w.[12] So, if y is annotated `(RC)`, we can optimize x – to `(LC)` whenever x' is overriding, and to `(NC)` otherwise. The pseudo code is shown on lines 14-20 in Figure 9. Using Q_1 in Figure 7 as an example(the DTD is shown in Figure 1), `Item` has two closest overriding ancestors: `Cart` and `Account`. Since for each of them there exists a non-overriding non-optional path to node `ID`, no matter from which node `Item` inherits the security level, we can ensure such a node

[11] Thus, since the security level of y is checked, there is no need to do a recursive check on x.
[12] The match of x may override it with a local definition of security level.

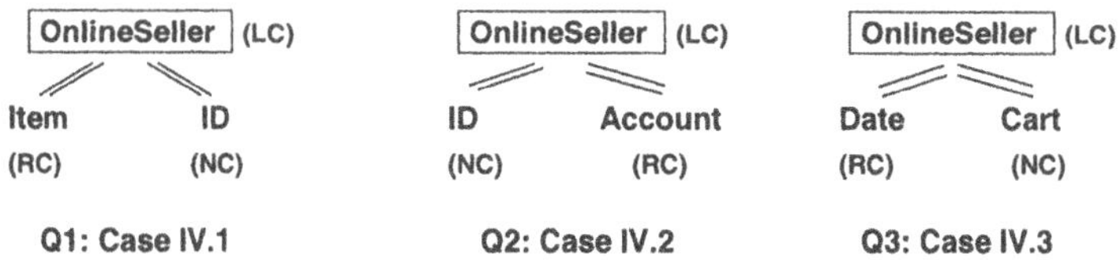

Fig. 7. CC-Rule Example for Unconstrained Nodes

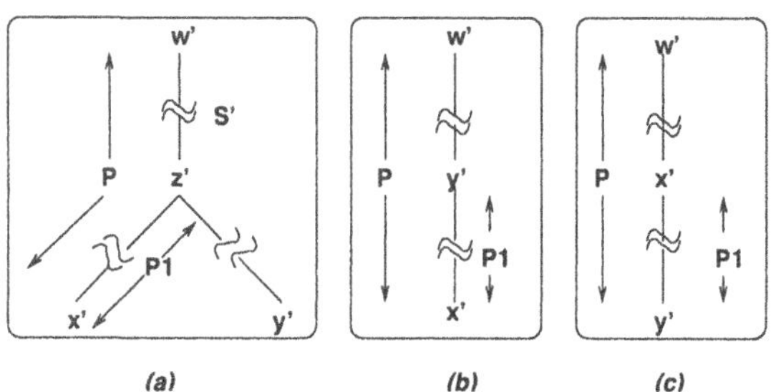

Fig. 8. CC-Rule for unconstrained nodes: (a) case IV.1; (b) case IV.2; (c) case IV.3.

must have an `ID` descendant that has the same security level as `Item`. Thus we put `(NC)` on `ID` while keep `(RC)` on `Item`.

Case IV.2: A second scenario for optimizing x is that y' occurs on some path P from w' to x', and this path passes through all nodes in S'_x, thus carrying the right query context of node x. Suppose for each P within the query context of S'_y, the segment of P from y' to x' is non-overriding and non-optional. As a result, for any match of y we are guaranteed of an existence of a match of x with almost the same security level as (the match of) y (illustrated in Figure 8(b)). Thus, if y is annotated `(RC)` or `(LC)`, we can optimize the SC annotation of x (to `(NC)` if x is not overriding and to `(LC)` otherwise). E.g. for Q_2 in Figure 7 as an example, there exists a non-optional non-overriding path from `Account` to `ID` within the query context, thus we put `(NC)` on `ID` while keeping `(RC)` on `Account`. The pseudo code is shown on lines 21-24 in Figure 9.

Case IV.3: The last scenario is that x' appears on every path P in the DTD from w' to y' and the segment P_1 of P from x' to y' is non-overriding (illustrated in Figure 8(c)). In this case, the mere existence of a match of y in the instance guarantees the existence of a corresponding match of x with almost the same security level as the match of y. Furthermore, since x' appears on *every* path from w' to y' within the query context of S'_y, the appropriate query context is also captured. In this case, we can optimize the SC annotation of x to `(NC)`, *even if x' is not overriding*. The reason is that the check performed for y subsumes the necessary check for x. The Q_3 in Figure 7 is left as the exercise for the readers. One thing to note from Q_3 is that the SC annotation of `Cart` is optimized as `(NC)`, although it's labeled as `(O)` in DTD. The pseudo code is shown on lines 25-29 in Figure 9.

```
Function case_IV(query node x, x's query cousin list Clist)
if ∃ y ∈ Clist {
     Let w be LCA of x and y;
     Let S1 be the set of ancestors of x occurring on the path
     from w to x in query;
     Let S2 be the set of ancestors of y occurring on the path
     from w to y in query;
     if (case_IV3(x, y, w, S1, S2) != NULL) return "NC";
     else if(case_IV2(x, y, w, S1, S2) != NULL) return SimplifyBelow(x);
     else if ∃ LCA l' of x' and y' in DTD
     s.t. !nonoptionalnonoverriding(l', x')
        within context S1 return SimplifyAbove(x);
else if case_IV1(x, y, w, S1, S2)!=NULL return SimplifyBelow(x);}
else return SimplifyAbove(x);
END Function
Function case_IV1 (query node x, x's query cousin y, LCA w,
x and y's query context S1 and S2)
if ∀ o ∈ ornodeset(w', y') closest to x' within context of S2
     ∃ path P from w' through o' to x' s.t. P goes through all nodes ∈ S1
     AND ornodeset(o',x')==NULL on P AND forbidden(y') AND
     nonoptionalnonoverriding(o',x') on P
Add o to output;
else return NULL;
return output;
END Function
Function case_IV2(query node x, x's query cousin y, LCA w,
x and y's query context S1 and S2)
if y' is ancestor of x' in DTD AND ∃ path P within context of S2 s.t.
     P goes through all nodes in S1 AND nonoptionalnonoverriding(y',x') on P
Return y;
else return NULL;
END Function
Function case_IV3(query node x, x's query cousin y, LCA w,
x and y's query context S1 and S2)
if x' is ancestor of y' in DTD AND forbidden(y') AND
     ∀ path P from w' to y' within context of S2
     x' is on P AND ornodeset(x', y')== NULL on P
Return y;
else return NULL;
END Function
```

Fig. 9. Cousin-Cousin rule for unconstrained nodes

Constrained Nodes

When x is constrained, we must ensure that every one of its matches that satisfies the query conditions is accessible.

Let x be a query node and w any query ancestor of x. Let S be the set of query nodes appearing on the path from w to x in the query tree. If there are no overriding nodes between w' and x' in the DTD, then we could always apply PC-rule to optimize x, so suppose there are. We can optimize x *provided* for every overriding node z' between w' and x' that is closest to x', such that z' is on a DTD path starting at w', goes through the nodes S', and ends in x',[13] we can find a cousin y of x in the query satisfying certain obligations. The first obligation is that y should be annotated (RC). The second is that w must be the lowest common ancestor(LCA) of x and y

[13] This path captures the right query context for node x.

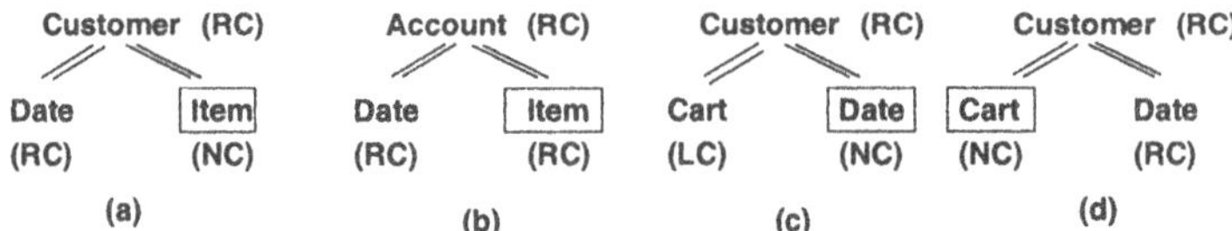

Fig. 10. CC-Rule Examples for Constrained Nodes

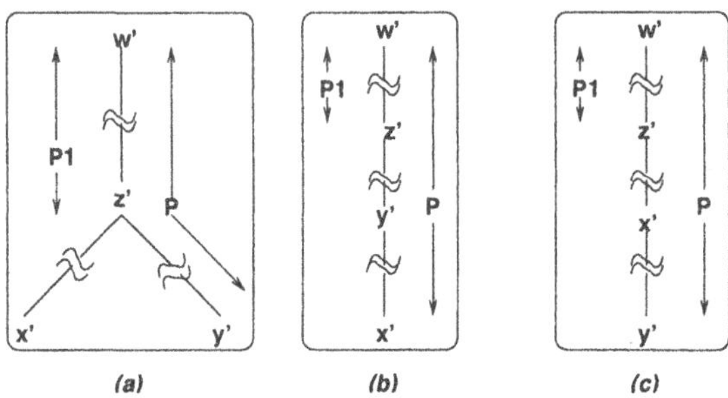

Fig. 11. CC-Rule for constrained nodes: (a) case V.1; (b) case V.2; (c) case V.3.

in the query. The remaining obligation is that one of the conditions Case V.1(x' and y' are cousins), Case V.2(x' is the descendant of y'), or Case V.3(x' is the ancestor of y'), discussed next, must hold. These conditions are similar to those discussed for Case IV for the unconstrained case. Let T be the set of query nodes appearing on the path from w to y in the query tree.

Case V.1: Suppose z' is a common ancestor of x' and y' in the DTD and furthermore there is exactly one path P from w' to y', and the segment P_1 of P from w' to z' is unique(see the definition of *unique path* in Section 4). Furthermore, suppose P goes through all nodes in T', thus carrying the right query context for y. In addition, suppose there are no overriding nodes between z' and y' nor between z' and x' (illustrated in Figure 11(a)). Under these conditions, for any match of y, we are assured that *every* corresponding match of x inherits its security level from a match of w from which y inherits its security level as well. One or more matches of x may override this locally, if at all. It follows then that x can be optimized to `(LC)` if x' is overriding and to `(NC)` otherwise. Using Figure 10(a) as an example, there exists only one DTD path from `Customer` to `Date`, on which the DTD node `Cart` is overriding. Since the DTD path from `Customer` to `Cart` is unique, there only exists one instantiated node of `Cart` under `Customer`. Note that since `Cart` is labeled with `(O)`, it may be assigned a different security level from `Customer`. However, since there is no overridng node between either `Cart` and `Date` nor `Cart` and `Item`, thus we put `(NC)` on `Item` while keeping `(RC)` on `Date`, i.e., for every accessible `Date`, it must inherit the security level from the only accessible source `Cart`, which is also true for `Item`. It's obvious that if the query root is changed to be `Account` (Fgure 10(b)), the SC annotation on neither `Date` nor `Item` can be optimized. This is because the DTD path from Account to Cart is not unique! The pseudo code is given by lines 12-17 in Figure 12.

Case V.2: Suppose y' is an ancestor of x' in the DTD and z' is an ancestor of y'. Furthermore, suppose there is only one DTD path P from w' to y' which passes through the query context nodes T', such that the segment P_1 of P from w' to z' is unique, and that there are no overriding nodes between z' and x' (illustrated in Figure 11(b)). In this case, in any valid instance, for any match of y, *every* corresponding match of x has almost the same security level as that of (the corresponding match of) z, which is also the security level of (the match of) y, and both matches appear in the right query context, so x can be optimized to (LC) if x' is overriding and to (NC) otherwise. Using Figure 10(c) as an example, there exists only one DTD path from Customer to Cart, which is also unique. Since there is no overriding node between either Cart and Date, we put (NC) on Date while keeping (LC) on Cart, i.e., there only exists one instantiated node Cart below Customer, from which node Date will inherit the security level. Thus if such a Cart is accessible, all Date nodes below Customer must be accessible as well. The pseudo code is given by lines 18-22 in Figure 12.

Case V.3: Finally, suppose x' is an ancestor of y' in the DTD and z' is an ancestor of x'. Furthermore, suppose there is exactly one path P from w' to y' which passes through the context nodes T', and the segment P_1 of P from w' to z' is unique (illustrated in Figure 11(c)). Suppose also that there are no overriding nodes between z' and y'. Then, in any valid instance, *every* match of y must be a descendant of a corresponding match of x. Since there are no overriding nodes between them, they must have the same security level, allowing us to optimize x. Just as for Case IV.3, we can optimize x to (NC), *even if x' is overriding*. The reason is that the check performed for y subsumes the necessary check for x. Figure 10(d) is left as the exercise for the readers. One thing to note from this query is that Cart is labeled as (NC), although it's labeled as (O) in the DTD. The pseudo code is given by lines 23-28 in Figure 12.

We can show the following results:

Lemma 2. [Completeness of CC – Unconstrained] : Let Q be a tree pattern query, Δ be a DTD, and x be an unconstrained node in Q. Suppose x cannot be optimized using PC- and CP-rules. Then x can be optimized if and only if one of the conditions Case IV or Case V holds. ▪

Lemma 3. [Completeness of CC – Constrained] : Let Q be a tree pattern query, Δ be a DTD, and x be a constrained node in Q. Suppose x cannot be optimized using PC- and CP-rules. Then x can be optimized if and only if Case V holds. ▪

The proof of Lemma 2 and Lemma 3 is shown in [26].

6.5 Putting It All Together

We can show that the rules Root, PC, CP, CC are complete for optimizing nodes in a tree pattern query tree. We start from Lemma 4.

```
Function case_V(query node x, x's query cousin list Clist)
if ∃ ancestor w of x in query {
  let S be the set of ancestors of x  on the path from w to x in query;
  ∀ o ∈ ornodeset(y', x') closest to x' within context of S
  ∃ y ∈ Clist in query s.t.
     y=w or y below w in query AND w is LCA of x and y AND
     (case_V1(w, x, y, o, T) != NULL OR case_V2(w, x, y, o, T) !=NULL
     OR case_V3(w, x, y, o, T) != NULL)
     (T: the set of ancestors of y  on the path from w to y in query)
     if (only case_V3 applied) return "NC";
     else return SimplifyBelow(x);
else return SimplifyAbove(x);
END Function
Function case_V1(query LCA w, query node x, x's query cousin y,
overriding node o, y's query context T)
if y' is not descendant or ancestor of x' in DTD AND
     only one path P from w' to y' within context of T AND forbidden(y')
     AND o' is ancestor of y' in DTD on P AND unique(w', o') on P
     AND ornodeset(o', y')==NULL on P
Return y;
else return NULL;
END Function
Function case_V2(query LCA w, query node x, x's query cousin y,
   overriding node o, y's query context T)
if only one path P from w' to y' within context of T
     AND y' is ancestor of x' on P AND ornodeset(y', x') == NULL on P
     AND o' is ancestor of y' on P AND unique(w', o') on P
Return y;
else return NULL;
END Function
Function case_V3(query LCA w, query node x, x's query cousin y,
   overriding node o, y's query context T)
if only one path P from w' to y' within context of T AND
     y' is descendant of x' on P AND
     forbidden(y') AND o' is the ancestor of x' on P AND
     ornodeset(x', y') == NULL on P AND unique(w', o') on P
Return y;
else return NULL;
END Function
```

Fig. 12. Cousin-Cousin rules for Constrained nodes

Lemma 4. [Redundancy of Reasoning on Query Ancestor/Descendant] : Let Q be a tree pattern query, Δ be any choiceless DAG DTD, x be an arbitrary query node in Q, y be its query parent, and z be an query ancestor of x. Suppose D is a valid database instance of Δ. Then in every matching $\mu : Q \rightarrow D$, if $\mu(x)$ and $\mu(z)$ have almost the same security levels, $\mu(x)$ and $\mu(y)$ must have the same security levels. .

The correctness of Lemma 4 is obvious: if the instantiated node x' of the query node x always has almost the same security level as the instantiated node z' of x's query ancestor z, there should be no node between x' and z' that brings into a new security level, i.e., any instantiated node y' of x's query parent y is guaranteed to have the same security level as x'.

Lemma 4 shows that if the SC annotation of any query node can be optimized based on the reasoning on its query ancestor/descendant, it should be optimized by reasoning on its query parent/child. Then we can show the following theorem.

Theorem 2. [Completeness of Rules] : Let Q be a tree pattern query with all its nodes annotated `(RC)`, and Δ be any choiceless DAG DTD. Then the SC annotation on a node x in Q is optimizable if and only if it can be optimized using one of the rules {Root, PC, CP, CC}. ▪

Proof:
The essence of the optimization of the SC annotation of a query node p is the existence of a "witness" in the query to ensure p's accessibility. Such a "witness" can be any query node other than itself. Thus it must be one of its query parent, child, cousin, ancestor or descendant. For the query root, Root rule covers the optimization. For the non-root query nodes, since the reasoning on ancestor and descendant are redundant (Lemma 4), the reasoning on the query parent (PC rule), child (CP rule), and cousin (CC rule) are enough. ▪

Unfortunately, Theorem 2 does *not* yield an efficient algorithm for SCAOP. It is not clear in what order the rules should be applied and in what order query nodes should be visited. We can show the following lemmas concerning rule applications. For convenience, we use regular expressions to denote order of rule applications. E.g., Root(PC|CC|CP)$*$ indicates applying Root first, followed by any sequence of rule applications – PC, CC, CP. For two SC annotations $\mathcal{A}$ and $\mathcal{B}$ of a query, we write $\mathcal{A} <_X \mathcal{B}$, where $X \in \{\texttt{RC}, \texttt{LC}, \texttt{NC}\}$, provided the number of query nodes mapped to X by $\mathcal{A}$ is less than the number of nodes mapped to X by $\mathcal{B}$. The relation $=_X$ is defined similarly. E.g., $\mathcal{A} <_{\texttt{RC}} \mathcal{B}$ means $\mathcal{A}$ annotates fewer nodes with an `(RC)` than $\mathcal{B}$.

Lemma 5. [Remove CP(s)] : Let Q be any query, Δ be any choiceless DAG DTD, and $\mathcal{A}$ be the SC annotation assigning `(RC)` to all nodes of Q. For any (correct) SC annotation $\mathcal{A}'$ obtained from $\mathcal{A}$ by applying {Root, PC, CP, CC}*, we can always reach a correct SC annotation $\mathcal{B}$ by applying {Root, PC, CC}*. We have either (i) $\mathcal{B} <_{\texttt{RC}} \mathcal{A}'$ or (ii) $\mathcal{B} =_{\texttt{RC}} \mathcal{A}'$ and $\mathcal{B} \leq_{\texttt{LC}} \mathcal{A}'$. ▪

E.g., in Figure 4(e), SC annotation $\mathcal{A}_1$ would be obtained using Root(PC*)(CC*), whereas $\mathcal{A}_2$ would be obtained using Root(CP*). Clearly, $\mathcal{A}_1 =_{\texttt{RC}} \mathcal{A}_2$ and $\mathcal{A}_1 =_{\texttt{LC}} \mathcal{A}_2$.

Lemma 6. [Move PC(s) Ahead] : Let Q be any query, Δ be any choiceless DAG DTD, and $\mathcal{A}$ be the SC annotation assigning `(RC)` to all nodes of Q. For any (correct) SC annotation $\mathcal{A}'$ obtained from $\mathcal{A}$ by applying {Root, PC, CC}*, we can always reach a correct SC annotation $\mathcal{B}$ by applying PC rule firstly until no more node whose SC annotation can be optimized, then applying CC rules in the same fashion. We have either (i) $\mathcal{B} <_{\texttt{RC}} \mathcal{A}'$ or (ii) $\mathcal{B} =_{\texttt{RC}} \mathcal{A}'$ and $\mathcal{B} \leq_{\texttt{LC}} \mathcal{A}'$. ▪

The correctness of Lemmas 5 and 6 are based on the study of the defined rules. More details are provided in [26]. Based on Lemmas 5 and 6 we can show the following "normal form" result:

Theorem 3. [Normal Form] : Let Q be any query, Δ be any choiceless DAG DTD, and $\mathcal{A}$ be the SC annotation assigning `(RC)` to all nodes of Q. Then the SC annotation $\mathcal{B}$ obtained by applying Root(PC*)(CC*) to query nodes, with the PC* and CC* closures applied top-down, is correct and minimal. Furthermore, for any (correct) SC annotation $\mathcal{A}'$ obtained from $\mathcal{A}$ by applying {Root, PC, CP, CC}*, we have either (i) $\mathcal{B} <_{\text{RC}} \mathcal{A}'$ or (ii) $\mathcal{B} =_{\text{RC}} \mathcal{A}'$ and $\mathcal{B} \leq_{\text{LC}} \mathcal{A}'$. ▪

In particular, the theorem shows that any SC annotation we could have obtained is equaled or bettered by applying rules according to the normal form above. The proof can be found in [26].

We can show:

Theorem 4. [Complexity] : Let Q be any query and Δ be any choiceless DAG DTD. Then a minimal correct SC annotation of Q w.r.t. Δ can be obtained in polynomial time in the size of Q and Δ. ▪

Proof:
The main intuition behind polynomiality is that Root, PC and CC rules base their reasoning on overriding nodes (referred to in the pseudocode as `ornodeset`), using which it captures all overriding paths that could potentially affect the optimizability of a query node. For each such node, it checks the existence of certain paths in the DTD. Additionally, for constrained nodes, it checks the absence of certain paths.

For these, certain paths that will be checked are listed as follows:

- we say a node z' is on every path from x' to y', OEP(x', y', z'), if this holds in a conventional graph theoretical sense; this check can be done in polynomial time by using depth first search.
- there is a non-optional non-overriding path from x' to y', NONOR(x', y'), if and only if there is a path from x' to y' such that all edges in the path are labeled '+' or '1' and all intermediate nodes are non-overriding; this check can be done in polynomial time by the following procedure: there is a non-overriding non-optional path from DTD node x' to y' if and only if: (a) nodes y' and x' are identical; or (b) $\exists$ a non-overriding child e' of x' s.t. the edge(x', e') is labeled with '+' or '1' and NONOR(e', y').
- there is a unique path from x' to y', UP(x', y'), iff there is a path from x' to y' such that all edges in the path are labeled '?' or '1'; this check can be done in polynomial time by the following procedure: there is a unique path from DTD node x' to y' if and only if: (a) nodes y' and x' are identical; or (b) $\exists$ a child e' of x' s.t. the edge(x', e') is labeled with '?' or '1' and UP(e', y').
- there is only one path from x' to y', OOP(x', y'), if and only if there is exactly one path from x' to y'. This check can be done in polynomial time by the following procedure: there is only one path from DTD node x' to y' if and only if: (a) nodes y' and x' are identical; or (b) $\exists$ only one child e' of x' that has path to y' and OOP(e', y'). The "only one child" condition is controlled by adding a counter when using recursion.

To sum up, since each path condition checking can be implemented polynomially, a minimal correct SC annotation of Q w.r.t. Δ can be obtained in polynomial time in the size of Q and Δ. ▪

7 DAG-Structured DTDs with Choice

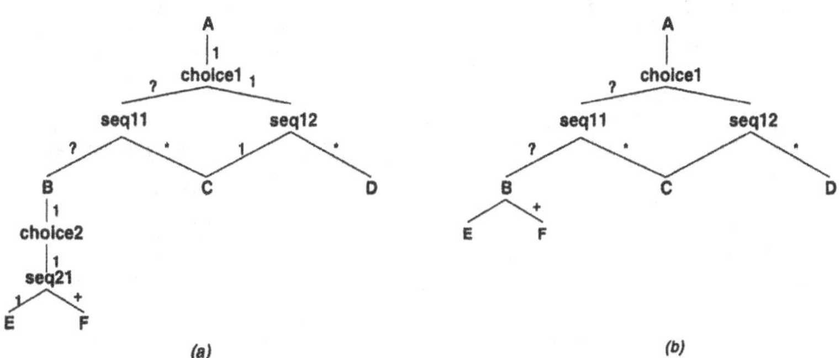

Fig. 13. DTD Graph illustrated: (a) (Original) DTD graph and (b) simplified DTD graph of $\{A \rightarrow (B?C^*)? \mid (CD^*),\ B \rightarrow (EF^+)\}$.

A DAG DTD Δ with choice nodes can be unfolded into a set of choiceless DTDs by choosing one of the sequences from each choice production. Each set of choices results in a choiceless DTD. We call the set of such DTDs *candidate DTDs* of Δ. The DTD in Figure 13 has two candidate DTDs: $\Delta_1 = \{A \rightarrow (B?C^*)?,\ B \rightarrow (EF^+)\}$ and $\Delta_2 = \{A \rightarrow (CD^*)\}$. It is straightforward to show:

Proposition 1. (Candidate DTDs) : Let Q be a tree pattern query, Δ be a choice DTD, and $cand(\Delta)$ be its associated set of candidate DTDs. Then a SC annotation on Q is correct w.r.t. Δ if and only if it is correct w.r.t. every DTD in $cand(\Delta)$. ▪

7.1 The Challenges

Unfortunately, the above result doesn't yield an efficient algorithm for optimizing the SC annotations of a query w.r.t. choice DTDs, since a choice DTD can have exponentially many candidate DTDs. E.g., the DTD in Example 2, graphed in Figure 14(a), has $2^2 = 4$ candidate DTDs.

Example 2. **[Choice DTD] :** We will use the DTD $\Delta = \{A \rightarrow B \mid C,\ B \rightarrow D^*H,\ C \rightarrow D,\ D \rightarrow E \mid F,\ E \rightarrow G,\ F \rightarrow G,\ G \rightarrow H^*I^*\}$ as the running example throughout this section. The DTD graph is shown (in simplified form, per Section 3) in Figure 14(a). In this DTD elements A and F are marked `(M)`, and D and E are marked `(O)`, all other elements being `(F)`. Figure 14(b) shows a query. All nodes are identified by tags. E.g., for a query node A, the corresponding DTD node is also shown as A.

The following example shows there is no obvious connection between optimizability of query nodes against choiceless DTDs and that w.r.t. a corresponding choice DTD.

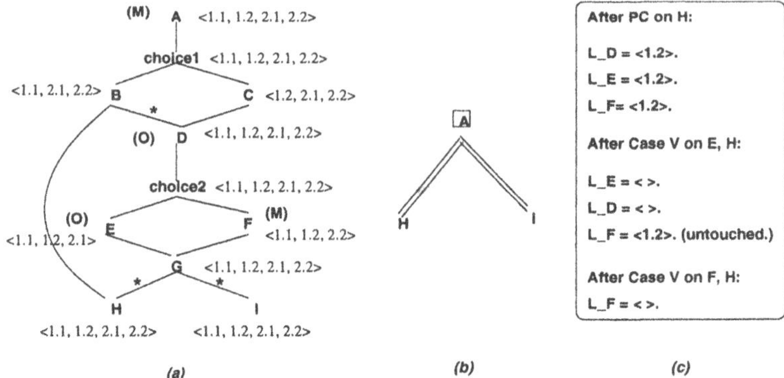

Fig. 14. A choice DTD and a query.

Example 3. **[Choiceless vs. choice DTDs] :** Consider the DTD $\Delta_1 = \{A \to BC, B \to D, C \to D\}$, with C being optional `(O)`. In the query `A[.//D]`, D can be optimized since there is a non-overriding non-optional path from A to D (Case III). If we change the first production to $A \to B \mid C$, we cannot optimize D since the optimization wouldn't be correct w.r.t. the candidate DTD $\{A \to C, C \to D\}$.

Now, consider the choice DTD $\Delta_2 = \{A \to B \mid C, B \to D^*E^*, C \to DE^*\}$, with C being optional `(O)`. In the query `A[.//D][.//E]`, we can optimize D, since in one candidate DTD, we can apply PC (Case II) and in the other we can apply CC (Case IV.1) successfully. However, if we remove the choice nodes from the DTD by changing the first production to $A \to BC$, then D can no longer be optimized. Figure 15 shows an instance demonstrating that D *must* be annotated `(RC)`.

Fig. 15. An example database instance; nodes marked × ($\surd$) inaccessible (accessible).

Thus we need a clever strategy for optimizing the SC annotations against choice DTDs.

7.2 Optimizing against Choice DTDs

For space limitations, we omit the pseudocode of our algorithm. Instead, we point out how the optimization algorithm for the schema without choice nodes (Sec 6) can be modified so as to get an efficient optimal algorithm for choice DTDs.

An important and surprising fact is that we can show that even for choice DTDs, we can give a small set of sound and complete rules – Root, PC, CP, and CC. These rules need to be suitably redefined to handle choice. The key challenge is the existence of exponentially many candidate DTDs underlying a choice DTD, where a query node may be optimizable in different candidate DTDs for different reasons. To keep track of this, we introduce a labeling scheme that assigns a label to each node.

Our labeling scheme permits us to keep track of the membership of DTD nodes in candidate DTDs *with a polynomial amount of information*. Specifically, we assign each choice node in the DTD a distinct integer. We also assign each sequence node out of the choice node a distinct integer. Labels are sets of entries of the form $i.j$ and are computed using the rules:

- Every ancestor of a choice node i (including node i) has a label that includes all entries of the form $i.j$, for every sequence node j out of node i.
- For a choice node i and a sequence node j out of node i, node j inherits the label of node i, except all entries in the inherited label of the form $i.k$, where $k \neq j$, are removed.
- Whenever y is an element node, it inherits the label of every sequence node from which there is an incoming edge into y in the DTD graph.

Any label assignment to nodes of a choice DTD, satisfying the rules above, is a *(valid) labeling*. Labeling for a (DAG) choice DTD can be computed efficiently with a backward propagation pass followed by a forward propagation. Figure 14(a) illustrates the labeling scheme.[14] Note that labeling takes up space that is linearly bounded by the DTD size.

Definition 1 [Labeling] Let Δ be a choice DTD, $\Delta_c \in cand(\Delta)$ a candidate DTD, and L be any label. Then Δ_c is *covered* by L provided for every choice node i in Δ, whenever sequence node j out of i is present in Δ_c, the entry $i.j$ is present in L.

E.g., in Figure 14(a), the label $L = \langle 1.1, 1.2, 2.1 \rangle$ covers the candidate DTD $\{A \to B,\ B \to D^*H,\ C \to D,\ D \to E, E \to G, F \to G,\ G \to H^*I^*\}$. The following result is straightforward.

Proposition 2. (Labeling) : Every choice DAG DTD Δ has a unique labeling. For any node x in Δ, a candidate DTD Δ_c of Δ contains node x if and only if the label of x covers Δ_c. ▪

E.g., in Figure 14(a), the label $L = \langle 1.1, 1.2, 2.1 \rangle$ of node E covers the candidate DTD above and is present in it.

7.3 Modified Rules

We now define the four rules Root, PC, CP, and CC, adapted for handling choice nodes in the schema. As a quick summary, the major change is that rule applications

[14] Note that the figure shows a simplified DTD graph, so some sequence/choice nodes are implicit.

also have to manipulate and update labels to reflect the reasoning employed. Additionally, some of the reasoning about paths needs to be universal, to allow for choice. Below, we assume x is the node to be optimized. We denote the label of a DTD node x' by $L_{x'}$.
Root: This rule is identical to that for choiceless DTDs.
PC: Let y be the query parent of x. Recall Cases I-III defined for choiceless DTDs. Of these, Case I, applicable when the query edge (y, x) is a pc-edge, is unchanged. Choice nodes cannot affect such direct edges. So suppose (y, x) is an ad-edge. Case II applies when there are no overriding DTD nodes between y' and x' and is also unchanged. The intuition is that there are no intervening overriding nodes in any candidate DTD. Case III is similar. Suppose there are overriding nodes between y' and x'. For every such node o' that is closest to y', for every ancestor w' of o' that is between y' and o', we test if there is a non-overriding non-optional path from y' to w'. If so, we subtract $L_{w'}$ from $L_{o'}$. At the end, if for every overriding node o' between x' and y' that is closest to y', the label $L_{o'}$ is empty, we can optimize x. The intuition is that in every candidate DTD where o' is present, there is a non-overriding non-optional path which acts as a "bypass". Here, a critical point is the test for a non-overriding non-optional path: it needs to be interpreted in a universal sense. More precisely, we have the following:

Definition 2 [Non-overriding non-optional path] There is a non-overriding non-optional path from DTD node x' to y', NONOR(x', y') , iff: (i) x' is an element node, its choice child is c' and NONOR(c', y') holds; or (ii) x' is a choice node and for each sequence child s' of x', NONOR(s', y') holds; or (iii) x' is a sequence node and $\exists$ an element child e' of x' such that the DTD label on the edge (x', e') is '1' or '+' and NONOR(e', y'); or (iv) nodes x' and y' are identical.

We can test the NONOR predicate efficiently using depth first search. Before closing on PC, we note that in addition to subtracting $L_{w'}$ from $L_{o'}$ above, we could "propagate" this change by subtracting $L_{w'}$ from the label of every overriding node that is between o' and x'. We assume this below.
CP: Just as for choiceless DTDs, CP is symmetric to PC: it uses Cases I-III but to optimize a node based on its query child. We omit the details.
CC: The key changes are (i) applying the CC rule (both for constrained and unconstrained nodes) also entails label manipulation and (ii) reasoning about the existence of "unique path", or about "only one path" between a pair of DTD nodes, and also about a node being present in "every path" between two other nodes all need to be done in the context of labels (which capture candidate DTDs). We highlight these changes next.

In a choiceless DTD, we have the following: (i) we say a node z' is on every path from x' to y', OEP(x', y', z'), if this holds in a conventional graph theoretical sense; (ii) there is a unique path from x' to y', UP(x', y'), iff there is a path from x' to y' such that all edges in the path are labeled '?' or '1'; and (iii) there is only one path from x' to y', OOP(x', y'), iff there is exactly one path from x' to y'.

In a choice DTD, each of these, OEP$_{\text{ch}}(x', y', z')$, UP$_{\text{ch}}(x', y')$, and OOP$_{\text{ch}}(x', y')$, is a function that returns a label L such that in any candidate DTD Δ_c

the corresponding predicate for choiceless DTD holds if and only if Δ_c is covered by L. Each of these functions can be implemented efficiently.

Finally, the CC rule itself is applied as follows. As with choiceless DTDs, if the node being optimized x is constrained, only Case V (see below) applies, else both Cases IV and V do. Case IV for choice DTDs is defined to be Case IV for choiceless DTDs, except that the new definitions of $\text{NONOR}_{\text{ch}}, \text{OEP}_{\text{ch}}$, above are used in place of the corresponding definitions of NONOR, OEP. Similarly, Case V for choice is essentially the same as the choiceless schema, except the new definitions of $\text{UP}_{\text{ch}}, \text{OOP}_{\text{ch}}$ are used in place of the corresponding definitions of UP, OOP. The upshot is that Case IV for choice can be regarded as a function that returns a label L such that Case IV for choiceless holds in a candidate DTD if and only if it is covered by L. Similarly for Case V. We apply these cases as follows.

For every query ancestor w of x, for every overriding node o' between w' and x' that is closest to x' in the DTD, and for every cousin y of x in the query tree, apply Case IV for the 4-tuple of nodes w', o', x', y' to obtain a label L. Then subtract L from the label of o' as well as that of all overriding nodes between w' and o'. The subtraction amounts to checking off candidate DTDs where x is optimizable using Case IV. Similarly, we apply Case V on the nodes w', o', x', y' to obtain a label L. Then subtract L from the label of o' as well as that of all overriding nodes between w' and o'. This has an analogous rationale. Finally, if all overriding nodes between w' and x' have an empty label at the end, we optimize x and exit, else try the next query ancestor w of x. Here, a small technicality is that whenever only Case IV.3 or Case V.3 is used to render labels of all overriding nodes between an ancestor w' and x' to be empty sets, then we can optimize x to `(NC)`, unconditionally, exactly like we could do for choiceless DTDs. In other cases, we optimize x to `(LC)` if x' is overriding and to `(NC)` otherwise.

7.4 Algorithm ChoiceOpt

The optimization algorithm for choice DTDs, Algorithm `ChoiceOpt`, proceeds by applying the Root rule. Then it applies each of PC and CC rules to saturation, in that order, again exactly like the algorithm for choiceless DTDs. We next illustrate the algorithm.

Example 4. **[Illustrating Algorithm ChoiceOpt] :** Consider the query in Figure 14(b). Initially let all nodes be annotated `(RC)`. The Root rule is the same as for choiceless DTDs. So, first the query root A can be optimized to `(LC)` since the corresponding DTD node is marked `(M)`. Next, consider the query node H. Let us apply the PC-rule. Consider overriding DTD nodes between A and H that are closest to A. D is the only such node. D has an ancestor B, from which there is a non-overriding non-optional path to H. So, we subtract L_B from L_D as well as from L_E and L_F as part of change propagation (see Figure 14(c)). The label $L_D = \langle 1.2 \rangle$ is non-empty, signifying that in every candidate DTD which contains node C corresponding to sequence node 2 out of choice node 1, the PC-rule (for choiceless DTDs) fails, so we cannot optimize H at this point. (If hypothetically, the DTD contained a non-overriding non-optional path from C to H then L_D would become empty and hence H could be optimized.)

Next, consider the CC rule on H and consider Case IV. The only query cousin of H is node I and its counterpart in the DTD is neither an ancestor nor a descendant of H in the DTD. Thus, Case IV.1 is the only subcase under Case IV that would apply. The only query ancestor of H is A. The overriding DTD nodes between A and H that are closest to H are E and F. But Case IV.1 fails for the 4-tuple of DTD nodes A, E, H, I, since there is no non-optional non-overriding path from E to H. Similarly, it also fails for A, F, H, I.

Let us now apply Case V. Consider Case V.1. Node I corresponding to the query cousin I of H is neither an ancestor nor a descendant of H in the DTD. First, consider the overriding node E. There is a unique path from A to E, viz., $A \to C \to D \to E$. The function $\text{UP}_{\text{ch}}(A, E)$ returns the label $L_1 = \langle 1.2, 2.1 \rangle$, which corresponds to the intersection of the labels of nodes on this path. The function $\text{OOP}(E, I)$ returns the label $L_2 = \langle 1.1, 1.2, 2.1, 2.2 \rangle$, since such a path exists in every candidate DTD. There is a non-overriding path from E to H as well as from E to I. Finally, the label L for this round of Case V is computed as the intersection $L = L_1 \cap L_2$. Then subtract L from the label L_E as well as from the label of every overriding node between A and E. The result is shown in Figure 14(c). Note that L_E becomes empty.

It is easy to check that when Case V.1 is applied for the overriding node F, we similarly end up emptying its label (see Figure 14(c)). So, finally, H can be optimized to `(NC)`. Indeed, the SC annotation $\{A : (\texttt{LC}), H : (\texttt{NC}), I : (\texttt{RC})\}$ is the optimal annotation for the query. The reader is invited to check that both PC-rule and CC-rule fail for I, even if I is considered before H for optimization.

7.5 Results

We have the following results for optimizing the SC annotations of a given query against choice DTDs. The first one shows that the modified rules are sound and complete.

Theorem 5. [Completeness] : Let Δ be a choice DTD and Q be a query. The SC annotation on a node x in Q is optimizable if and only if it can be optimized using one of the modified rules Root, PC, CP, CC.

The next result shows that it is sufficient to apply rules in a certain normal form, analogously to choiceless DTDs.

Theorem 6. [Normal form] : Let Δ be a choice DTD and Q be a query. Let $\mathcal{A}$ be the SC annotation assigning `(RC)` all nodes of Q, and $\mathcal{A}'$ be any SC annotation obtained from $\mathcal{A}$ by applying the rules {Root, PC, CP, CC} in any order. Then there is a SC annotation $\mathcal{B}$ such that $\mathcal{B}$ is correct, $\mathcal{B} \leq \mathcal{A}'$, and $\mathcal{B}$ can be obtained from $\mathcal{A}$ by applying the Root rule, then the PC rule repeatedly to saturation to nodes of Q top-down, followed by CC rule repeatedly to saturation to nodes of Q top-down.

Finally, we have:

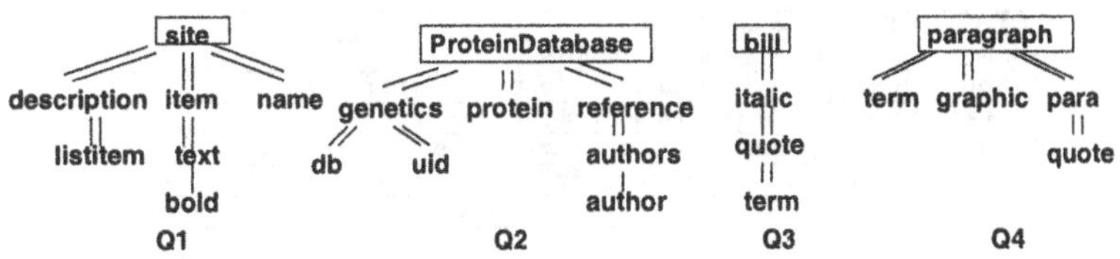

Fig. 16. Queries Used in the Experiments

Theorem 7. [Optimality] : Let Δ be a choice DTD and Q be a query. Then a minimal correct SC annotation of Q can be obtained in time polynomial in the size of Q and Δ.

The correctness of Theorems 5-7 is provided in [26].

8 Experiments

8.1 Experimental Setup

We ran our experiments on the `XMark` XML benchmark dataset [30], a `Biomedical` dataset [9] from National Biomedical Research Foundation, and U.S. `Congress Bills` dataset [25] from U.S. House of Representatives. We constructed two different security specifications for each DTD: one DTD with only three elements marked `(M)` (we call this a *sparse DTD*); the other DTD with a quarter of elements marked `(M)` and a quarter of elements marked `(O)` (we call this a *dense DTD*). We modified a few elements in the DTDs to get rid of cycles.

For each dataset, we constructed two kinds of XML documents, one on the sparse and one on the dense DTD, using IBM XMLGenerator [18] . For every DTD element marked `(M)` we assigned a value 0 or 1 to the `SecurityLevel` attribute of the corresponding instance nodes, 0 meaning "inaccessible" and 1 means "accessible". For each element marked `(O)` we used a random number generator to decide whether to assign a value to the `SecurityLevel` attribute of the corresponding instance nodes. If the generator generated an even number, then a value 0 or 1 is assigned to the `SecurityLevel` attribute of the corresponding instance nodes. Else the `SecurityLevel` attribute of the corresponding instance nodes is left as unspecified.

We used the XALAN [29] engine for query evaluation, with external function calls for security checks. SCAOP optimization algorithms were implemented in Java. Our experiments were run on a Windows PC with 512MB of memory and 2GHz CPU speed. All reported results are the average of 7 trials after the maximum and minimum were dropped.

8.2 Impact of Optimization

We used ten queries for each dataset. These queries included pc-edges and ad-edges; some were path queries and the others were branching (tree pattern) queries. Among

DTD	Type	Overriding Nodes
XMark	sparse	site, payment, people
XMark	dense	site, payment, people, regions, parlist
Biomedical	sparse	ProteinDatabase, db, header
Biomedical	dense	ProteinDatabase, gene, ProteinEntry, xrefs
Congress	sparse	bill, legis-body, formula
Congress	dense	bill, formula, legis-body, non-statutory-material

Fig. 17. DTDs w.r.t setup of overriding nodes

Query	DTD	Query Nodes Annoted NC	Query Nodes Annoted LC	Query Nodes Annoted RC
Q_1	sparse	description, item, name, listitem, text, bold	site	
Q_1	dense	description, name, text, bold	site	item, listitem
Q_2	sparse	genetics, protein, reference, authors, author, uid	ProteinDatabase, db	
Q_2	dense	protein,uid, author	ProteinDatabase	genetics, db reference, authors
Q_3	sparse		bill, italic, quote	term
Q_3	dense		bill, quote	italic, term
Q_4	sparse	term, para, quote		paragraph, graphic
Q_4	dense	term, quote		para, paragraph, graphic

Fig. 18. Optimized SC annotation on query

branching queries, some branched only at the root, while others also branched below the root. From these thirty queries, we picked the queries in Figure 16 as the examples to explain the experiment results. We pick these four queries because the optimization on those four queries covered most of the optimization rules we have discussed in the previous sections. Query Q_1 is based on auction.dtd, Q_2 on protein.dtd, and Q_3 and Q_4 on bills.dtd. Figure 17 shows the overriding nodes within the query context we used for each DTD. Figure 18 shows the optimized SC annotation we got for each query.

We varied the size of datasets from 1MB to 100MB. The size of the secure answer is obviously the same for optimized query and unoptimized query.

Figure 19 shows the query evaluation time on XMark, Biomedical and Congress datasets. First, note that the benefits of our optimization on all datasets are substantial. E.g., for the 100MB XMark dataset, the unoptimized secure evaluation on Q_1 for the sparse DTD is 20s, whereas the optimized secure evaluation took only 6s, a saving of 70%. Second, the benefit of the optimization on sparse DTD is more than the benefit on dense DTD. The reason is that for the evaluation of RC label, the recursive check needs to traverse more nodes, on the average, to reach a node that has a specified security level when the data is sparsely annotated. Thus the savings by optimizing the (RC) annotation to (LC) or (NC) gains more savings on sparse DTD than on dense DTD. And there are more such nodes that are optimized as LC or NC when there are fewer overriding nodes in the schema for sparse DTD than dense DTD. The results of other queries were similar.

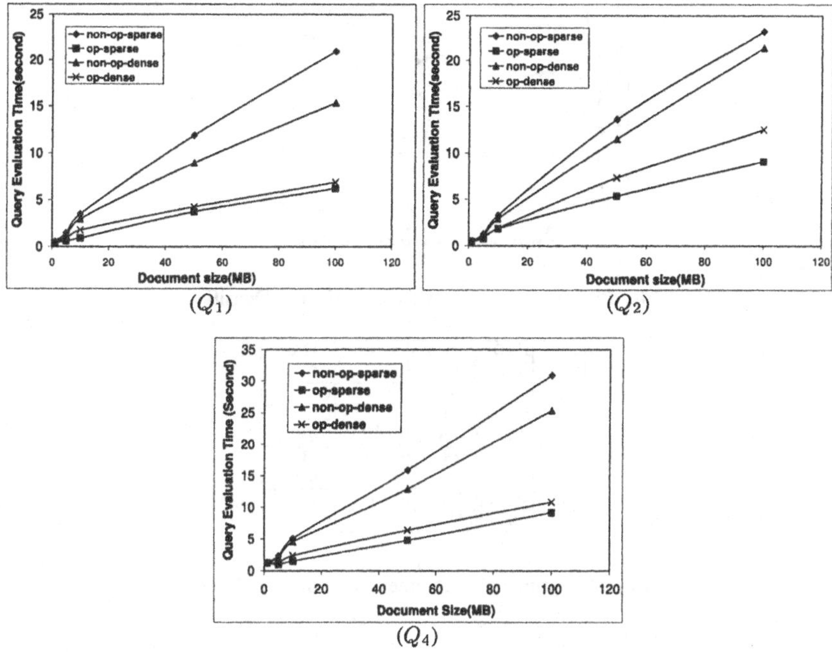

Fig. 19. Query Evaluation Time on Q_1, Q_2 and Q_4

Figure 20 reports the query evaluation time for various percentage of instance elements whose corresponding DTD nodes are assigned `(O)` so that their `SecurityLevel` attributes in the instance were assigned a value by random. We applied unoptimized and optimized Q_1 for sparse and dense DTDs on the document of size 50MB. Firstly the graph of query evaluation time on sparse DTD is flat. The reason is that the minimal SC annotation for each query node in Q_1 is `(NC)` or `(LC)`. Thus most of the security check is done locally. Secondly query evaluation time decreases as the percentage of nodes with assigned `SecurityLevel` attribute increases. This is because the recursive check needs to traverse fewer nodes to find the closest ancestors with assigned security level.

We also tested the speedup of query evaluation with optimized SC annotation versus that of unoptimized SC annotation against varying query size. A linear scaleup is observed: e.g., for a query with 40 nodes the speedup was 6.11, and at 80 nodes, we observed a speedup of 10.

8.3 Optimization Overhead

We tested how the overhead of optimization varies as query size increases. We tried on the queries whose number of nodes vary from 10 to 30. Figure 21 shows opti-

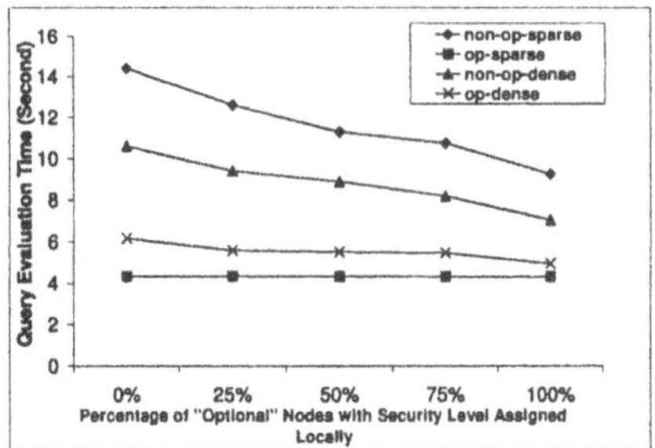

Fig. 20. Query Evaluation Time on Various Densities

Query	DTD	10 Nodes	20 Nodes	30 Nodes
Q_1	sparse	0.005	0.007	0.01
Q_1	dense	0.011	0.019	0.025
Q_2	sparse	0.016	0.025	0.0372
Q_2	dense	0.036	0.047	0.059
Q_3	sparse	0.006	0.009	0.013
Q_3	dense	0.010	0.013	0.016
Q_4	sparse	0.151	0.206	0.275
Q_4	dense	0.172	0.228	0.297

Fig. 21. Optimization Overhead w.r.t Size of Query

mization times for queries of various sizes over sparse and dense DTDs. Note that the optimization times on sparse DTDs are always smaller than on dense DTDs because there are fewer overriding nodes to check. Also note that the optimization time is very small: even for a query with 30 nodes it only took 0.297s to optimize for the worst case. In all cases, we found the overhead a negligible fraction (e.g., 0.01%-1.1%) of the actual evaluation time benefits.

The placement of overriding nodes in a DTD can make a difference to optimization time. To measure this, we tested on the `XMark`, `Biomedical` and `Congress` datasets with overriding nodes lined up versus overriding nodes scattered, as well as such nodes being leaves versus intermediate nodes in the DTD. Firstly the difference in optimization time between "scattered" versus "lined up" was substantial: e.g., 0.02324s versus 0.0141s (about 40% less) for a DTD with 15 overriding nodes. The reason is that when they line up, the reasoning for one overriding node can subsume that required for others, thus reducing the overall work. Secondly we found that overriding DTD leaves contribute very little to the SC annotation optimization overhead. This is because the optimization overhead is decided by the number of intermediate overriding nodes that are reasoned during the optimization, in which the overriding leaves never get involved. For brevity, we don't show these graphs.

Next, we varied the number of choice nodes in the choice DTD `bills.dtd` by randomly changing a few choice nodes in the query context of Q_3, Q_4 into sequence nodes. Figure 22 shows that the optimization overhead is not proportionally increasing with the number of choice nodes. This is because the time complexity of

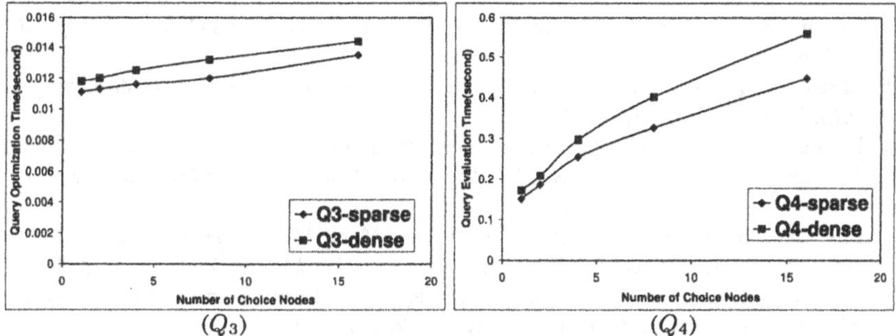

Fig. 22. Query Optimization Overhead w.r.t. Number of Choice Nodes

optimization is dependent on the number of overriding nodes in the query context, not the number of choice nodes.

9 Summary

In this chapter, we have considered the problem of secure evaluation of XML tree pattern queries, for the simple, but useful, multi-level security model. We focus on an efficient algorithm that determines an optimal set of security check annotations with tree pattern query nodes, by analyzing the subtle interactions between inheritance of security levels and the paths in the DTD graph. We experimentally validated our algorithm, and demonstrated the performance benefits to optimizing the secure evaluation of tree pattern queries.

We mention two of the many interesting questions spawned by this work. (1) How does one deal with cyclic DTDs? DTD paths corresponding to a pair of query nodes may need to traverse DTD nodes multiple times to take care of various possibilities for overriding nodes, and the algorithms presented in this paper are not directly applicable. (2) Can one design efficient security check optimization algorithms that utilize knowledge about database statistics to choose from among multiple minimal SC annotations?

References

1. Martin Abadi and Bogdan Warinschi. Security analysis of cryptographically controlled access to xml documents. *Symposium on Principles of Database Systems(PODS)*, 2005.
2. Chutiporn Anutariya, Somchai Chatvichienchai, Mizuho Iwaihara, and Yahiko Kambayashi Vilas Wuwongse. A rule-based xml access control model. *International Conference on Rules and Rule Markup Languages for the Semantic Web(RuleML)*, 2003.
3. Elisa Bertino, M. Braun, Silvana Castano, Elena Ferrari, and Marco Mesiti. Authorx: A java-based system for xml data protection. *IFIP Working Conf. Database Security*, 2000.

4. Elisa Bertino, Silvana Castano, and Elena Ferrari. On specifying security policies for web documents with an xml-based language. *ACM Symposium on Access Control Models and Technologies (SACMAT)*, 2001.
5. Elisa Bertino, Silvana Castano, and Elena Ferrari. Securing xml documents with author-x. *IEEE Internet Computing*, 2001.
6. Elisa Bertino, Silvana Castano, Elena Ferrari, and Marco Mesiti. Controlled access and dissemination of xml documents. *Workshop on Web Information and Data Management*, 1999.
7. Elisa Bertino, Silvana Castano, Elena Ferrari, and Marco Mesiti. Specifying and enforcing access control policies for xml document sources. *World Wide Web Journal*, 2000.
8. Elisa Bertino and Elena Ferrari. Secure and selective dissemination of xml documents. *ACM Transactions on Information and System Security (TISSEC)*, 2002.
9. Biomedical database, http://www.cs.washington.edu/-research/xmldatasets/www/repository.html.
10. Luc Bouganim, Francois Dang Ngoc, and Philippe Pucheral. Client-based access control management for xml documents. *Very Large Database (VLDB)*, 2004.
11. SungRan Cho, Sihem Amer-Yahia, Laks V. S. Lakshmanan, and Divesh Srivastava. Optimizing the secure evaluation of twig queries. *Very Large Database (VLDB)*, 2002.
12. Ernesto Damiani, Sabrina De Capitani di Vimercati, Stefano Paraboschi, and Pierangela Samarati. Design and implementation of an access control processor for xml documents. *Computer Networks*, 2000.
13. Ernesto Damiani, Sabrina De Capitani di Vimercati, Stefano Paraboschi, and Pierangela Samarati. Securing xml documents. *International Conference on Extending Database Technology(EDBT)*, 2000.
14. Ernesto Damiani, Sabrina De Capitani di Vimercati, Stefano Paraboschi, and Pierangela Samarati. Xml access control systems: A component-based approach. *Informatica*, 2002.
15. Wenfei Fan, Chee Yong Chan, and Minos N. Garofalakis. Secure xml querying with security views. *Special Interest Group on Management of Data(SIGMOD)*, 2004.
16. Irini Fundulaki and Maarten Marx. Specifying access control policies for xml documents with xpath. *ACM Symposium on Access Control Models and Technologies (SACMAT)*, 2004.
17. Abhilash Gummadi, Jong P. Yoon, Biren Shah, and Vijay Raghavan. A bitmap-based access control for restricted views of xml documents. *ACM Workshop on XML Security*, 2003.
18. IBM XML generator, http://www.alphaworks.ibm.com/tech/xmlgenerator.
19. Michiharu Kudo and Satoshi Hada. Xml document security based on provisional authorization. *ACM Conf. Computer and Communications Security*, 2000.
20. Gabriel Kuper, Fabio Massacci, and Nataliya Rassadko. Generalized xml security views. *ACM Symposium on Access Control Models and Technologies (SACMAT)*, 2005.
21. Bo Luo, Dongwon Lee, Wang-Chien Lee, and Peng Liu. Qfilter: Fine-grained run-time xml access control via nfa-based query rewriting. *Conference on Information and Knowledge Management(CIKM)*, 2004.
22. Gerome Miklau and Dan Suciu. Containment and equivalence for an xpath fragment. *Symposium on Principles of Database Systems(PODS)*, 2002.
23. Gerome Miklau and Dan Suciu. Controlling access to published data using cryptography. *Very Large Database (VLDB)*, 2003.
24. Makoto Murata, Akihiko Tozawa, and Michiharu Kudo. Xml access control using static analysis. *ACM Conference on Computer and Communications Security (CCS)*, 2003.
25. United States Government Bills, http://xml.house.gov.

26. Hui Wang, Divesh Srivastava, Laks V.S. Lakshmanan, SungRan Cho, and Sihem Amer-Yahia. Optimizing tree pattern queries over secure xml databases: Full paper. *http://www.cs.ubc.ca/~hwang/accesscontrol/proof.pdf*, 2005.
27. Jingzhu Wang and Sylvia L. Osborn. A role-based approach to access control for xml databases. *ACM Symposium on Access Control Models and Technologies (SACMAT)*, 2004.
28. Peter Wood. Containment for xpath fragments under dtd constraints. *International Conference on Database Theory(ICDT)*, 2003.
29. XALAN, http://xml.apache.org.
30. XMark, http://monetdb.cwi.nl/xml/.
31. Ting Yu, Divesh Srivastava, Laks V.S. Lakshmanan, and H. V. Jagadish. A compressed accessibility map for xml. *ACM Transactions on Database Systems*, 2004.
32. Huaxin Zhang, Ning Zhang, Kenneth Salem, and Donghui Zhuo. Compact access control labeling for efficient secure xml query evaluation. *International Workshop on XML Schema and Data Management(XSDM)*, 2005.

Part III

Distributed Trust Management

Rule-based Policy Specification

Grigoris Antoniou[1], Matteo Baldoni[2], Piero A. Bonatti[3], Wolfgang Nejdl[4], and Daniel Olmedilla[4]

[1] Information Systems Laboratory, Institute of Computer Science, FORTH, Greece
antoniou@ics.forth.gr
[2] Dipartimento di Informatica,Università degli Studi di Torino, Torino, Italy
baldoni@di.unito.it
[3] Università di Napoli Federico II, Naples, Italy
bonatti@na.infn.it
[4] L3S Research Center and University of Hanover, Hanover, Germany
{nejdl,olmedilla}@L3S.de

1 Introduction

For a long time, logic programming and rule-based reasoning have been proposed as a basis for policy specification languages. However, the term "policy" has not been given a unique meaning. In fact, it is used in the literature in a broad sense that encompasses the following notions:

- *Security Policies* pose constraints on the behaviour of a system. They are typically used to control permissions of users/groups while accessing resources and services.
- *Trust Management policy languages* are used to collect user properties in open environments, where the set of potential users spans over the entire web.
- *Action Languages* are used in reactive policy specification to execute actions like event logging, notifications, etc. Authorizations that involve actions and side effects are sometimes called *provisional*.
- *Business Rules* are "statements about how a business is done" [25] and are used to formalize and automatize business decisions as well as for efficiency reasons. They can be formulated as *reaction rules*, *derivation rules*, and *integrity constraints* [142, 147].

All these kinds of specification interact tightly with each other: Credential-based user properties are typically used to assign access control permissions; logging, monitoring, and other actions are part of the high-level security specification documents of many organizations; many business rules—e.g., for granting discounts or special services—are based on the same kind of user properties that determine access control decision. Moreover, this kind of business decisions and access control decisions are to be taken more or less simultaneously—e.g. immediately before service access.

There has been extensive research focusing on each of these different notions of policies. In the next four sections, we will give an overview of existing approaches for each of these notions (security policies, policy-based trust management, action languages and business rules), and will then discuss in section 6 two different efforts to integrate several aspects in a common framework. There is still a lot of work to be done in the future and this chapter provides the knowledge and pointers required for anyone planning to work on this area.

2 Security Policies

Rule-based languages are commonly regarded as the best approach to formalizing security policies. In fact, most of the systems we use every day adopt policies formulated as rules. Roughly speaking, the access control lists applied by routers are actually rules of the form: "*if a packet of protocol X goes from hosts Y to hosts Z then [don't] let it pass*". Some systems, like Java, adopt procedural approaches. Access control is enforced by pieces of code scattered around the virtual machine and the application code; still, the designers of Java security felt the need for a method called *implies*, reminiscent of rules, that causes certain authorizations to entail other authorizations [81].

The main advantages of rule-based policy languages can be summarized as follows:

- People (including users with no specific training in computers or logic) spontaneously tend to formulate security policies as rules.
- Rules have precise and relatively simple formal semantics, be it operational (rewrite semantics), denotational (fixpoint-based), or declarative (model theoretic). Formal semantics is an excellent help in implementing and verifying access control mechanisms, as well as validating policies.
- Rule languages can be flexible enough to model in a unified framework the many different policies introduced along the years as ad-hoc mechanisms. Different policies can be harmonized and integrated into a single coherent specification.

In particular, logic programming languages are particularly attractive as policy specification languages. They enjoy the above properties and have efficient inference mechanisms (linear or quadratic time). This property is important as in most systems policies have to manage a large number of users, files, and operations—hence a large number of possible authorizations. And for those applications where linear time is too slow, there exist well-established compilation techniques (materialization, partial evaluation) that may reduce reasoning to pure retrieval at run time.

Another fundamental property of logic programs is that their inference is *nonmonotonic*, due to *negation-as-failure*. Logic programs can make default decisions in the absence of complete specifications. Default decisions arise naturally in real-world security policies. For example, *open* policies prescribe that authorizations by default are granted, whereas *closed* policies prescribe that they should be denied unless stated otherwise. Other nonmonotonic inferences, such as authorization inheritance and overriding, are commonly supported by policy languages.

For all of these reasons, rule languages based on nonmonotonic logics eventually became the most frequent choice in the literature. A popular choice consists of *normal logic programs*, i.e. sets of rules like

$$A \leftarrow B_1, \ldots, B_m, \text{not}\, C_1, \ldots, \text{not}\, C_n$$

interpreted with the *stable model semantics* [73]. In general, each program may have one stable model, many stable models, or none at all. There are opposite points of view on this feature.

Some authors regard multiple models as an opportunity to write nondeterministic specifications where each model is an acceptable policy and the system makes an automatic choice between the available alternatives [31]. For instance, the models of a policy may correspond to all possible ways of assigning permissions that preserve a *Chinese Wall* policy [45]. However, the set of alternative models may grow exponentially, and the problem of finding one of them is NP-complete. There are exceptions with polynomial complexity [124, 132], though.

Some authors believe that security managers would not trust the system's automatic choice and adopt restrictions such as *stratifiability* [6] to guarantee that the canonical model be unique. The system rejects non-stratified specifications, highlighting nonstratified rules to help the security administrator in reformulating the specifications. As a further advantage, stratifiability-like restrictions yield PTIME semantics.

A nonmonotonic logic has been proposed for the first time as a policy specification language by Woo and Lam [151]. The main motivations are expressiveness and flexibility. To address complexity issues (inference in propositional default logic is at the second level of the polynomial hierarchy), Woo and Lam propose to use the fragment of default logic corresponding to *stratified, extended logic programs*, that is, stratified logic programs with two negations (negation as failure and classical negation), whose unique stable model can be computed in quadratic time. Extended logic programs can be easily transformed into equivalent normal logic programs (with only negation as failure) by means of a straightforward predicate renaming.

The approach by Woo and Lam has been subsequently refined by many authors. Some have proposed fixed sets of predicates and terms, tailored to the expression of security policies. In the language of the security community, such a fixed vocabulary is called a *model*, whereas in the AI community, it would be probably regarded as an elementary ontology. From a practical point of view, the vocabulary guides security administrators in specifying the policy.

Furthermore, the original approach has been extended with temporal constructs, inheritance and overriding, message control, policy composition constructs, and electronic credential handling. All these aspects are illustrated in detail in the following subsections. Further rule-based languages for policy specification that do not exhibit dynamic or nonmonotonic features will be discussed in the section devoted to trust management.

2.1 Dynamic Policies

Security policies may change with time. Users, objects, and authorizations can be created and removed. Moreover, some authorizations may be active only periodically. For example, an employee may use the system only during work hours. Therefore, rule-based policy languages should be able to express time-dependent behavior.

Temporal Authorization Bases

In [28] the sets of users and objects are fixed, and the temporal validity of authorizations is specified through *periodic expressions* and suitable *temporal operators*.

Periodic authorizations are obtained by labeling each rule with a *temporal expression* specifying the time instants at which the rule applies. Temporal expressions consist of pairs ⟨`[begin,end]`, `P`⟩. `P` is a *periodic expression* denoting an infinite set of time intervals (such as "*9 A.M. to 1 P.M. on working days*"). The temporal interval `[begin, end]` denotes the lower and upper bounds imposed on the scope of the periodic expression `P` (for example, `[2/2002,8/2002]`). The rule is valid at all times that lie within the interval `[begin,end]` and satisfy the periodic expression `P`.

Rules are expressions A ⟨OP⟩ $\mathcal{B}$, where A is the authorization to be derived, $\mathcal{B}$ is a Boolean composition of (ground) authorizations, and OP is one of the following operators: WHENEVER, ASLONGAS, UPON. The three operators correspond to different temporal relationships that must hold between the time t in which A is derived, and the time t' in which $\mathcal{B}$ holds. The semantics is the following:

- WHENEVER derives A for each instant in `([begin,end],P)`, where $\mathcal{B}$ holds (i.e. $t = t'$).
- ASLONGAS derives A for each instant t in `([begin,end],P)` such that $\mathcal{B}$ has been "continuously" true for all $t' < t$ in `([begin,end],P)`.
- UPON derives A for each instant t in `([begin,end],P)` such that $\mathcal{B}$ has been true in some $t' < t$ in `([begin,end],P)`.

Note that WHENEVER corresponds to classical implication, ASLONGAS embodies a classical implication and a temporal operator, and UPON works like a trigger.

In this framework, policy specifications are called *temporal authorization bases* (TABs, for short). They are sets of periodic authorizations and derivation rules. TABs are given a semantics by embedding them into *function-free constraint logic programs* over the integers, a fragment of CLP($\mathbf{Z}$) denoted by Datalog$^{\mathbf{not},\equiv_{\mathbf{Z}},<_{\mathbf{Z}}}$ [110, 143].

The semantics of negation as failure is the stable model semantics, extended to constraint logic programs. To ensure the uniqueness of the canonical model and its PTIME computability, TABs are restricted so that the corresponding logic program is locally stratified.

To implement TAB-based access control efficiently, the canonical model of the corresponding logic program is materialized, that is, it is computed in advance. In this way, access control involves no deduction and is reduced to retrieval. The technical difficulty to be solved is that the canonical model is infinite because time is unbounded. The results of [28] show that policy extensions always become periodic after an initial stabilization phase; therefore, only this phase and one period need to be materialized. The materialized view is computed using the Dred [86] and Stdel [110] approaches.

The TABs framework embodies a fixed strategy for conflict resolution (denials take precedence). The problem of specifying different strategies is not addressed in [28]. Conflict resolution in general will be dealt with in Sect. 2.2.

Active Rules

An intermediate approach between imperative and declarative dynamic policy specifications can be found in [29]. The specification language, TRBAC, is based on active rules called *role triggers*, whose head specifies actions that modify the policy extension. One difference between this language and previous approaches is that dynamic changes concern *roles*, rather than individual authorizations. Mathematically, a role can be regarded as a relation between users and permissions [133], so by activating and deactivating roles, active rules simultaneously handle entire groups of authorizations.

The syntax of role activation/deactivation policies is based on *event expressions* and *status expressions*. The former may have the form `enable` R or `disable` R, where R is a role name. Event expressions can be *prioritized* by labeling them—as in p : `enable` R—with a priority p taken from a partially ordered set. If the policy simultaneously entails two conflicting prioritized events, p_1 : `enable` R and p_2 : `disable` R, then the event with higher priority overrides the other. If $p_1 = p_2$, then the default choice is p_2 : `disable` R. This choice can be regarded as a particular instantiation of the denial-takes-precedence principle. Status expressions may have the form `enabled` R or $\neg$`enabled` R. Role triggers have the form

$$S_1, \ldots, S_n, E_1, \ldots, E_m \rightarrow p : E_0 \ \texttt{after} \ \Delta t$$

where $S_1, \ldots, S_n$ are status expressions, $E_0, \ldots, E_m$ are event expressions ($n, m \geq 0$), and Δt specifies a delay after which E_0 will be executed. Conceptually, all role triggers whose bodies are satisfied fire in parallel and schedule the event in their heads. The bodies can be made true by previously scheduled events, by events requested at run time by the security administrator, and by *periodic events*, that is, prioritized events labeled with a periodic expression of the same form as those adopted in [28] (and illustrated previously).

Semantics is modeled via a *transition function*, obtained by adapting the stable model semantics to role triggers and periodic events. A suitable form of *stratifiability* is introduced to make the system behavior deterministic and computable in polynomial time. The new form of stratifiability must take into account the priorities associated with rule heads and the temporal delays Δt.

Role triggers can be naturally implemented through the standard triggers supported by several DBMS (a prototype implementation based on Oracle is described in [29]). Periodic events are materialized like TABs, by considering only the stabilization phase and one period. The materialization, called *agenda*, is then used to generate events that activate the triggers. TRBAC gives an abstract and cleaner view of the procedural trigger mechanism supported by the DBMS. For example, the semantics of the triggers derived from TRBAC policies does not depend on the order in which triggers are fired.

Other approaches

Two recent languages, KAoS and Ponder [57,144], adopt constructs similar to active rules for expressing policies. They can formulate *obligations*, that cause an agent to execute some actions whenever a specified event triggers the rule and some precondition is satisfied. In KAoS and Ponder, however, triggers and preconditions cannot refer to other authorizations, so, for example, it is impossible to express rules like "*grant/deny A if A′ is granted/denied*". Extending KAoS and Ponder with such rules is a nontrivial problem. In particular, KAoS is based on a description logic (OWL) that extended with rules becomes easily undecidable.

Another recent approach, PROTUNE, supports actions in a significantly different way. Some predicates, called *provisional predicates*, can be made true—if desired—by executing suitable actions. The directions on how and when a provisional predicate should be made true are described in a meta-policy. PROTUNE is described later in this chapter.

2.2 Hierarchies, Inheritance and Exceptions

Since the earliest time, computer security models have supported some forms of abstraction on the authorization elements, to formulate security policies concisely. For instance, users can be collected in groups, and objects and operations in classes. The authorizations granted to a user group apply to all of its member users, and authorizations concerning a class of objects apply to all of its members. This is modelled via an authorization hierarchy derived from the hierarchies of subjects, objects and operations—called *basic hierarchies* in the following. For example, if authorizations are simply triples (*subject,object,action*), then let $(s, o, a) \leq (s', o', a')$ iff $s \leq s'$, $a \leq a'$ and $o \leq o'$. In this case, we say that the authorization (s, o, a) is *more specific* than (s', o', a'). Now, if (s', o', a') is granted by the policy, then all (s, o, a) such that $(s, o, a) \leq (s', o', a')$ are implicitly granted, too. By analogy with object-oriented languages, we say that (s, o, a) is *inherited* from (s', o', a').

The authorization hierarchy can be exploited to formulate policies in a top-down, incremental fashion. An initial set of general authorizations can be progressively refined with more specific authorizations that introduce *exceptions* to the general rules. A related benefit is that policies may be expressed concisely and manageably. Exceptions make inheritance a *defeasible* inference in the sense that inherited authorizations can be retracted (or *overridden*) as exceptions are introduced. As a consequence, the underlying logic must be nonmonotonic.

Exceptions require richer authorizations. It must be possible to say explicitly whether a given permission is granted or denied. Then authorizations are typically extended with a *sign*, '+' for granted permissions and '−' for denials.

It may easily happen that two conflicting authorizations are inherited from two incomparable authorizations, therefore a policy specification language featuring inheritance and exceptions must necessarily deal with *conflicts*. A popular conflict resolution methods—called *denial takes precedence*—consists of overriding the positive authorization with the negative one (i.e. in case of conflicts, authorization is denied), but this is not the only possible approach.

Recent proposals have worked towards languages and models able to express, in a single framework, different inheritance mechanisms and conflict resolution policies. Logic-based approaches, so far, are the most flexible and expressive.

Flexible Authorization Framework

Jajodia et al. [97] attempted to balance flexibility and expressiveness on one side, and easy management and performance on the other. Their proposal for a *flexible authorization framework* (FAF) is a fragment of stratified normal programs with polynomial (quadratic) time data complexity. In FAF, policies are divided into four decision stages, corresponding to the following policy components:

- *Authorization Table*. This is the set of explicitly specified authorizations.
- The *propagation policy* specifies how to obtain new derived authorizations from the explicit authorization table. For instance, derived authorizations can be obtained by inheritance and exceptions.
- The *conflict resolution policy* describes how possible conflicts between the (explicit and/or derived) authorizations should be solved. Possible conflict resolution policies include *no-conflict* (conflicts are considered errors), *denials take precedence* (negative authorizations prevail over positive ones), *permissions-take-precedence* (positive authorizations prevail over negative ones), and *nothing-takes-precedence* (the conflict remains unsolved). Some forms of conflict resolutions can be expressed within the propagation policy, as in the case of overriding (also known as *most-specific-takes precedence*).
- A *decision policy* defines the response that should be returned to each access request. In case of conflicts or gaps (i.e. some access is neither authorized nor denied), the decision policy determines the answer. In many systems, decisions assume either the open or the closed form (by default, access is granted or denied, respectively).

The four decision stages correspond to the following predicates. (Below s, o, and a denote a subject, object, and action term, respectively, where a term is either a constant value in the corresponding domain or a variable ranging over it).

`cando(o,s,±a)` represents authorizations explicitly inserted by the security administrator. They represent the accesses that the administrator wishes to allow or deny (depending on the sign associated with the action).

Stratum	Predicate	Rules defining predicate
0	hie-predicates rel-predicates done	Base relations. Base relations. Base relation.
1	cando	Body may contain done, hie- and rel-literals.
2	dercando	Body may contain cando, dercando, done, hie-, and rel- literals. Occurrences of dercando literals must be positive.
3	do	When head is of the form do(_, _, $+a$) body may contain cando, dercando, done, hie- and rel- literals.
4	do	When head is of the form do(o, s, $-a$) body contains just one literal ¬do(o, s, $+a$).
5	error	Body may contain do, cando, dercando, done, hie-, and rel- literals.

Fig. 1. Rule composition and stratification of the proposal in [97]

dercando(o,s,±a) represents authorizations derived by the system using logic program rules.
do(o,s,±a) handles both conflict resolution and the final decision.

Moreover, a predicate done keeps track of the history of accesses (for example, this can be useful to implement a Chinese Wall policy), and a predicate error can be used to express integrity constraints. In addition, the language has a set of predicates for representing hierarchical relationships (hie-predicates) and additional application-specific predicates, called rel-predicates. Application-specific predicates capture the possible different relationships, existing between the elements of the data system, that may need to be taken into account by the access control system. Examples of rel-predicates are owner(user, object), which models ownership of objects by users, or supervisor(user1, user2), which models responsibilities and control within the organizational structure.

Authorization specifications are stated as logic rules defined over the above predicates. To ensure stratifiability, the format of the rules is restricted as illustrated in Fig. 1. Note that the adopted strata reflect the logical ordering of the four decision stages.

The unique stable model of the given policy can be produced, stored and incrementally updated via suitable materialization techniques.

Note that the clean identification and separation of the four decision stages can be regarded as a basis for a policy specification methodology. In this sense, the choice of a precise ontology and other syntactic restrictions (such as those illustrated in Fig. 1) may assist security managers in formulating their policies.

Hierarchical Temporal Authorization Model

A general approach to authorization inheritance under the denial-takes-precedence principle can be found in [30]. In this framework, called the *hierarchical temporal authorization model* (HTAM), no distinction is made between primitive and derived authorizations. This feature required an extension to classical stratification techniques.

The syntax of the policy language is the same as the syntax of TABs [28] with one important difference: the elements of authorization triples can be arbitrary nodes of basic hierarchies. The authorization hierarchy is defined by $(s, o, a, sign, g) \leq (s', o', a', sign, g)$ iff $s \leq s'$, $a \leq a'$ and $o \leq o'$. Conflicts are resolved according to the denial-takes-precedence principle. The formal semantics is formulated by adapting the fixed-point construction underlying the stable model semantics.

The major technical difficulty to be solved in this framework is that policy specifications are always equivalent to a nonstratifiable logic program. In general, such programs do not have a unique canonical model (and may have no canonical model at all), and inference is not tractable. Stable model existence and uniqueness, as well as its PTIME computability cannot be proved by means of the usual stratification techniques. In [30] the theory of logic programming is extended by identifying a class of nonstratifiable programs—called *almost stratifiable programs*—with the same nice properties as stratifiable programs. If the policy satisfies a weakened stratification condition (ensuring that all non-stratifiable cycles are caused only by the inheritance rules), then the policy has one canonical model computable in polynomial time. These results rely on the denial-takes-precedence principle, that disambiguates the meaning of the specifications and ensures that the bodies of the inheritance rules involved in a negative cycle are always mutually inconsistent.

HTAM and FAF enjoy complementary properties. On one hand, HTAM gives a general solution to inheritance and overriding by resorting to non-stratifiable programs. In FAF, it is impossible to override an inherited authorization with a derived authorization because of the syntactic constraints enforcing stratifiability.

On the other hand, conflict resolution and decision policies are fixed in HTAM (and based on the denials take precedence principle, that is necessary for stable model uniqueness and tractability), whereas FAF supports multiple such policies. The main goal of FAF is flexibility. So far, no attempt has been made to combine the advantages of both models.

Ordered Logic Programs

A significantly different approach, inspired by *ordered logic programs* [102], can be found in [31]. There, security policies generalize the structure of an access control matrix by introducing inheritance over the matrix indexes and by allowing derivation rules in the matrix elements. The logic language is inspired by *ordered logic programs*.

More precisely, let a *reference* be a pair $(object, subject)$, and let references be structured by the natural hierarchy induced by the basic object and subject hierarchies. A rule in this framework is a pair

$$\langle\, (o, s),\ L_0 \leftarrow L_1, \ldots, L_m, \mathsf{not}\ L_{m+1}, \ldots, \mathsf{not}\ L_n \,\rangle\ ,$$

where (o, s) is a reference. Each L_i is either a standard literal (A or $\neg A$, where A is a logical atom) or a *referential literal* $(o', s').L$, where (o', s') is a reference and L is a standard literal. The authorization predicate has the form $\mathtt{auth}(p, g)$, where p is a privilege (the analogue of the *action* field of the authorizations discussed previously) and g is the grantor of the authorization. As in the previous approaches, the semantics is obtained by adapting the stable model semantics.

This syntax is just a factorized reformulation of the syntax of the other approaches. By default, subject and object are specified by the rule's reference. In rule bodies, one may refer to other subjects and objects by means of referential literals. The real difference between this approach, on one hand, and HTAM and FAF, on the other hand, is that when a policy specification has multiple stable models, the authors of [31] propose three different conflict resolution strategies:

1. Use the *well-founded* model of the policy. This (partial) model approximates the intersection of all stable models of the policy and can be computed in polynomial time.
2. Use the intersection of the stable models (called the *skeptical semantics* of the policy). Computing the intersection is a co-NP-hard problem.
3. Select dynamically a stable model that contains all authorizations granted so far and grants the current operation, if possible. Otherwise, deny the operation. The problem of finding such a stable model (called *credulous semantics*) is NP-complete (data complexity). Moreover, the history of previous authorization must be stored and maintained.

The second and third strategies are computationally demanding. Powerful engines for computing skeptical and credulous stable model semantics exist [65, 120], but so far they have not been experimentally evaluated in this context. A further difficulty related to the third strategy is that the policy cannot be materialized in advance because its extension is selected dynamically at access control time.

Other approaches

KAoS and Ponder support little more than inheritance without exceptions. As we pointed out before, preconditions cannot check whether other authorizations are granted or denied, so rules cannot be chained. Inference consists in matching requests against policies, looking for a more general authorization whose associated preconditions are satisfied. In KAoS, this means computing subsumptions between the given request and the concepts describing authorizations. Overriding is not supported.

2.3 Message Control

Many modern systems are based on distributed objects or agents that interact and cooperate by exchanging messages. A natural approach in such systems is to formulate policies at the level of the communication middleware. Messages may be delivered, blocked, or modified to enforce the security policy. For example, when the sender is not trusted, the receiver specified in the message may be replaced by a secure wrapper. The message contents may be changed, too, e.g. by weakening a service request.

This approach is pursued in a series of papers by Minsky et al., including [116, 117]. In the former paper, the policy language of the *Darwin* system is described. It adopts a Prolog-like syntax to formulate message handling and transformation rules.

The act of sending a message is denoted by the logical atom $\mathtt{send}(s, m, t)$, where s is the sender object, m is the message, and t is the target object. Note that from a mathematical viewpoint, messages have the same structure as authorization triples (subject,action,object).

Policies consist of sets of *laws*. Laws are functions that map each message $\mathtt{send}(s, m, t)$ onto an action of the form $\mathtt{deliver}(m', t')$ or `fail`. It may be the case that $t \neq t'$ (the message is redirected to another object) or $m \neq m'$ (the message contents are modified).

Each law can be composed of several rules that are interpreted according to the procedural semantics of Prolog. The syntax is inspired by definite clause grammars (the symbol '`-->`' is equivalent to '`:-`'). Consider the following example:

```
r1: send(S, ^M, T) -->
          isa(T, module) &
          T.owner=S      &
          deliver(^M,T).

r2: send(S, @M, T) -->
          isa(S,module)   &
          isa(T,module)   &
          deliver(@M,T).
```

The first rule prescribes that every object `S` can send a metamessage `^M` (such as `^new`, to create objects, or `^kill` to destroy objects) to any subclass `T` of the class `module`, provided that `S` is the owner of `T`. The second rule allows arbitrary messages between the system's modules (note that ^ and @ specify the message type). In these rules, the message and the target are not modified.

The implementation follows two approaches. In the first approach, called *dynamic*, messages are intercepted and transformed by interpreting the policy. The second approach, called *static*, is more efficient. By means of static analysis, program modules are checked to see whether the policy will be obeyed at run time. When the policy prescribes message modification, the code may have to be changed. Of course, the static approach is applicable only to local modules under the control of the security administrator.

The second paper [117] adapts these ideas to the framework of electronic commerce. Changes mainly concern the set of primitive operations; rule structure is preserved. Moreover, the language distinguishes the act of sending a message from the actual message delivery.

The level of abstraction and the expressiveness of these policy languages are appealing. Unfortunately, the semantics is described procedurally by relying on the user's understanding of Prolog interpreters. No equivalent declarative formulation is provided, even if it seems possible to give a declarative reading to law rules, for example, in abductive terms.

Another interesting option is applying a policy description language based on event-condition-action rules, such as $\mathcal{PDL}$ [51, 108], to message-handling policies. However, so far, $\mathcal{PDL}$ has been considered only in the framework of network management, and static analysis techniques have not been considered as an implementation technique.

3 Policy-Based Trust Management

The concept of *trust* has come with many different meanings and it has been used in many different contexts like security, credibility, etc. Work on authentication and authorization allows to perform access control based on the requester's identity or properties. Trust in this sense provides confidence in the source or in the author of a statement. In addition, trust might also refer to the quality of such a statement.

Typically access control systems are identity-based. It means that the identity of the requester is known and authorization is based on a mapping of the requester identity to a local database in order to check if he/she is allowed to perform the requested action. For example, given that Alice asks Bob for access to a resource, she must first authenticate to Bob. This way, Bob can check if Alice should be allowed to access that resource.

Nowadays, however, due to the amount of information and the increase of the World Wide Web, establishment of trust between strangers is needed, i.e., between entities that have never had any common transaction before. Identity-based mechanisms are not sufficient. For example, an e-book store might give a discount to students. In this case, the identity of the requester is not important, but whether he/she is a student or not. These mechanisms are property-based and, contrary to identity-based systems, provide the scalability necessary for distributed environments.

This section offers a historical review of existing research and describe in detail the state of the art of policy-based trust management.

3.1 Trust Management

Existing authorization mechanisms are not enough to provide expressiveness and robustness for handling security in a scalable manner. For example, Access Control Lists (ACL) are lists describing the access rights a principal (entity) has on an object (resource). An example is the representation of file system permissions used in the UNIX operating system. However, although ACLs are easy to understand and they have been used extensively, they lack [34]:

- Authentication: ACL requires that entities are known in advance. This assumption might not hold in true distributed environments where an authentication step (e.g. with a login/password mechanism) is needed.
- Delegation: Entities must be able to delegate to other entities (not necessarily to be a Certification Authority) enabling decentralization.
- Expressibility and Extensibility: A generic security mechanism should be extendable with new conditions and restrictions without the need to rewrite applications.
- Local trust policy: As policies and trust relations can be different among entities, each entity must be able to define its own local trust policy.

In order to solve the problems stated above and provide scalability to security frameworks, a new approach called *trust management* [36] was introduced.

In general, the steps a system must perform in order to process a request based on a signed message (e.g. using PGP [154] or X.509 [96]) can be summarized as "Is the key, with which the request was signed, authorized to perform the requested action?". However, some of the steps involved in answering such a question are too specific and can be generalized, integrating policy specifications with the binding of public keys to authorized actions. Therefore, the question can be replaced by "Given a set of credentials, do they prove that the requested action complies with a local policy?". In [34, 36] the "trust management problem" is defined as a collective study of security policies, security credentials and trust relationships. The solution proposed is to express privileges and restrictions using a programming language.

The next subsections describe systems that provided a scalable framework following these guidelines.

PolicyMaker and KeyNote

PolicyMaker [36, 37] addresses the trust management problem based on the following goals:

- Unified mechanism: Policies, credentials, and trust relationships are expressed using the same programming language.
- Flexibility: Both standard certificates (PGP [154] and X.509 [96]) as well as complex trust relationships can be used (with small modifications).
- Locality of control: Each party is able to decide whether it accepts a credential or on whom it relies on as trustworthy entity, avoiding a globally known hierarchy of certification authorities.
- Separation of mechanisms from policies: PolicyMaker uses general mechanisms for credential verification. Therefore, it avoids having mechanisms depending on the credentials or on a specific application.

PolicyMaker consists of a simple language to express trusted actions and relationships and an interpreter in charge of receiving and answering queries. PolicyMaker maps public keys into predicates that represent which actions the key are trusted to be used for signing. This interpreter processes "assertions" which confer authority on keys.

KeyNote [33,35] extends the design principles used in PolicyMaker with standardization and ease of integration into applications. Keynote performs signature verification inside the trust management engine while PolicyMaker leaves it up to the calling application. In addition, KeyNote requires credentials to be written in an assertion language designed for KeyNote's compliance checker.

In KeyNote, the calling application sends a list of credentials, policies and requester public keys to the evaluator together with an "action environment". This action environment contains all the information relevant to the request and necessary to make the trust decision. The identification of the attributes, which are required to be included in the action environment, is the most important task in integrating KeyNote into different applications. The result of the evaluation is an application-defined string which is returned to the application.

It is important to note that neither PolicyMaker nor KeyNote enforce policies but give advice to applications that make calls to them. It is up to the calling application whether to follow their advice or not. In addition, although their languages are not rule based, we included them in this section for completion and as a motivation for rule based policy languages.

REFEREE

REFEREE [52] (Rule-controlled Environment For Evaluation of Rules, and Everything Else) is a trust management system that provides policy-evaluation mechanisms for Web clients and servers and a language for specifying trust policies. Its authors define trust as "undertaking a potentially dangerous operation knowing that it is potentially dangerous". The elements necessary to make trust decisions are based on credentials and policies.

REFEREE uses PICS labels [128] as credentials. A PICS label states some properties of a resource in the Internet. In this context, policies specify which credentials must be disclosed in order to grant an action.

In REFEREE credentials are executed and their statements can examine statements made by other credentials and even fetch credentials from the Internet. Policies are needed to control which credentials are executed and which are not *trusted*. The policies determine which statements must be made about a credential before it is safe to run it.

The main difference compared with PolicyMaker [36,37] is that PolicyMaker assumes that credential-fetching and signature verification are done by the calling application. PolicyMaker receives all the relevant credentials and assumes that the signatures have been already verified before the call to the system.

SD3

SD3 [98] (Secure Dynamically Distributed Datalog) is a trust management system consisting of a high-level policy language, a local policy evaluator and a certificate retrieval system. It provides three main features:

- Certified evaluation: At the same time an answer is computed, a proof that the answer is correct is computed, too.
- High-level language: SD3 abstracts from signature verification and certificate distribution. It makes policies easy to write and understand.
- SD3 is programmable: Policies can be easily written and adopted to different domains.

SD3 language is an extension of datalog. The language is extended with SDSI global names [54]. A rule in SD3 is of the form:

T(x,y) :- K$E(x,y) ;

In the previous rule, *T(x,y)* holds if a digital credential asserting *E(x,y)* and signed with the private key of *E* was given. Whenever a global name is used, an authentication step is needed. In addition, SD3 can refer to assertions in remote computers. Given the rule

T(x,y) :- (K@A)$E(x,y) ;

the query evaluator must query a remote SD3 evaluator at an IP address *A*. This gives SD3 the possibility to create "chains of trust".

3.2 Trust Negotiation

Often, shared information in traditional distributed environments tells which parties can provide what kind of services and which parties are entitled to make use of those services. Then, trust between parties is a straightforward matter. Even if on some occasions there is a trust issue, as in traditional client-server systems, the question is whether the server should trust the client, and not vice versa. Trust establishment is often handled by uni-directional access control methods, such as having the client log in as a pre-registered user.

In contrast, in new environments like the Web parties may make connections and interact without being previously known to each other. In many cases, before any meaningful interaction starts, a certain level of trust must be established from scratch. Generally, trust is established through exchange of information between the two parties. Since neither party is known to the other, this trust establishment process should be bi-directional: both parties may have sensitive information that they are reluctant to disclose until the other party has proved to be trustworthy at a certain level. As there are more service providers emerging on the Web every day, and people are performing more sensitive transactions (for example, financial and health services) via the Internet, this need for building mutual trust will become more common.

Trust negotiation is an approach to automated trust establishment. It is an iterative process where trust is established gradually by disclosing credentials and requests for credentials. This differs from traditional identity-based access control and release systems mainly in the following aspects:

- Trust between two strangers is established based on parties' properties, which are proved through disclosure of digital credentials.

- Every party can define access control and release policies (*policies*, for short) to control outsiders' access to their sensitive resources. These resources can include services accessible over the Internet, documents and other data, roles in role-based access control systems, credentials, policies, and capabilities in capability-based systems.
- In the approaches to trust negotiation developed so far, two parties establish trust directly without involving trusted third parties, other than credential issuers. Since both parties have policies, trust negotiation is appropriate for deployment in a peer-to-peer architecture, where a client and server are treated equally. Instead of a one-shot authorization and authentication, trust is established incrementally through a sequence of bilateral credential disclosures.

A trust negotiation is triggered when one party requests to access a resource owned by another party. The goal of a trust negotiation is to find a sequence of credentials $(C_1, \ldots, C_k, R)$, where R is the resource to which access was originally requested, such that when credential C_i is disclosed, its policy has been satisfied by credentials disclosed earlier in the sequence—or to determine that no such credential disclosure sequence exists.

A detailed discussion on general criteria for trust negotiation languages as well as important features (like well-defined semantics, expression of complex conditions, sensitive policies and delegation) can be found in [137].

Regulating Service Access and Information Release

A formal framework to specify information disclosure constraints and the inference process necessary to reason over them and to filter relevant policies given a request is presented in [40]. A new language is presented with the following elements:

- *credential(c,K)* where c is a credential term and K is a public key term.
- *declaration(attribute_name=value_term)*
- *cert_authorityy(CA,K_{CA})* where CA represents a certification authority and K_{CA} its public key.
- *State predicates* which evaluates the information currently available at the site
- *Abbreviation predicates*
- *Mathematic predicates* like $=$, $\neq$, $<$.

Using the elements described above, rules can be specified in order to regulate the negotiation. There are two kind of rules: *service accessibility rules* and *portfolio disclosure rules*. A service is a functionality that a server offers in the form of e.g. an application that a client can execute. A portfolio is the set of properties that a party can disclose during a negotiation in order to obtain access to or offer services. Therefore service accessibility rules specify the requirements that a client must satisfy in order to get access to a service and portfolio disclosure rules specify the conditions a requester must satisfy in order to receive information from the portfolio.

Portfolio requisite rules define required credentials and declarations that other party must satisfy before portfolio information (credentials or declarations) are disclosed.

These basic elements and rules are all needed to perform a negotiation between a server which offers services and a client who wants to consume them. In order to allow the server to select applicable rules a policy filtering mechanism is needed. This mechanism filters the rules related to a specific request from the server's knowledge base. Those selected rules will be then pre-evaluated locally and/or sent to the client. Figure 2 shows an example scenario of the interaction process between client and server.

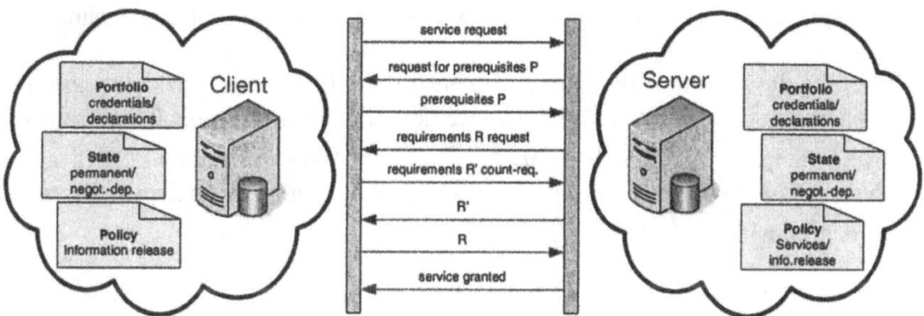

Fig. 2. Client/Server interplay

RT: Role-based Trust-Management

The RT framework [104–106] is a set of languages for representing policies and credentials. It is specially suited for "decentralized collaborative systems" (systems where they do not have to loose the authority over the resources they control) and for attribute-based access control (ABAC). Those systems must be able to express decentralized attributes, delegation of attribute authority, inference of attributes, attribute field and attribute-based delegation of attribute authority.

RT uses roles in order to represent attributes. An entity has an attribute if it is a member of the corresponding role. The RT framework consists of several components:

RT_0 It is the most basic language of the RT set. It addresses all the requirements described above except "attribute fields".
In RT_0 policy statements take the form of role definitions. Role definitions have a head of the form $K_A.R$ and a body. K_A represents a principal while R is a role term. RT_0 allows constructions for simple membership, simple containment, linking containment, intersection containment, simple delegation and linking delegation.

RT_1 In RT_0 roles do not take any paremeters. RT_1 role definitions have the same form as in RT_0 but they may contain parameterized roles. In RT_1 a role is of the form $r(p_1, \ldots, p_n)$. r is the role name and p_i can be $name = c$, $name = ?X[\in S]$ ($\in S$ is optional) or $name \in S$ where $name$ represents a name of a parameter, c represents a constant, $?X$ is a variable and S is a value set.

RT_2 RT_2 adds to RT_1 logical objects (also o-set) in order to group permissions between objects. A credential in RT_2 is either an o-set-definition or a role-definition. An o-set-definition is formed by an entity followed by an o-set identifier ($K.o(h_1, \ldots, h_n)$ and allows to constrain variables with dynamic value sets (inferred from roles or o-sets).

RT^T Sometimes it is required that two or more different entities are responsible to perform a sensitive task together for its completion. RT^T provides manifold roles and role-product operators. A manifold role defines a set of principals sets. Each of these sets is a set of principals whose collaboration satisfies the manifold role.

RT^D RT^D provides delegation of role activations which express selective use of capacities and delegation of these capacities. A delegation credential presented by a principal D takes the form of $D \overset{D\ as\ A.R}{\longleftarrow} B_0$. With it a principal D activates the role $A.R$ to use in a session B_0. In addition B_0 can further delegate this role activation with $B_0 \overset{D\ as\ A.R}{\longleftarrow} B_1$.

PEERTRUST

PEERTRUST [72, 119] builds upon previous work on policy-based access control and release for the Web and implements automated trust negotiation for such a dynamic environment.

PEERTRUST's language is based on first order Horn rules (definite Horn clauses), i.e., rules of the form "$lit_0 \leftarrow lit_1, \ldots, lit_n$" where each lit_i is a positive literal $P_j(t_1, \ldots, t_n)$, P_j is a predicate symbol, and the t_i are the arguments of this predicate. Each t_i is a term, i.e., a function symbol and its arguments, which are themselves terms. The head of a rule is lit_0, and its body is the set of lit_i. The body of a rule can be empty.

Definite Horn clauses are the basis for logic programs, which have also been used as the basis for the rule layer of the Semantic Web and specified in the RuleML effort ([83, 85]) as well as in the recent OWL Rules Draft [91]. Definite Horn clauses can be easily extended to include negation as failure, restricted versions of classical negation, and additional constraint handling capabilities such as those used in constraint logic programming. Although all of these features can be useful in trust negotiation, here we describe instead other more unusual required language extensions.

References to Other Peers

The ability to reason about statements made by other peers is central to trust negotiation. To express delegation of evaluation to another peer, each literal lit_i is extended with an additional *Authority* argument,

lit_i @ Authority

where *Authority* specifies the peer who is responsible for evaluating lit_i or has the authority to evaluate lit_i. The *Authority* argument can be a nested term containing a sequence of authorities, which are then evaluated starting at the outermost layer.

A specific peer may need a way of referring to the peer who asked a particular query. This is accomplished by including a *Requester* argument in literals, so that now literals are of the form

lit_i @ Issuer $ Requester

The *Requester* argument can be nested, too, in which case it expresses a chain of requesters, with the most recent requester in the outermost layer of the nested term.

Using the *Issuer* and *Requester* arguments, it is possible to delegate evaluation of literals to other parties and also express interactions and the corresponding negotiation process between parties.

Signed Rules

Each peer defines a policy for each of its resources, in the form of a set of definite Horn clause rules. These and any other rules that the peer defines on its own are its *local* rules. A peer may also have copies of rules defined by other peers, and it may use these rules in its proofs in certain situations.

A signed rule has an additional argument that says who signed the rule. The cryptographic signature itself is not included in the logic program, because signatures are very large and are not needed by this part of the negotiation software. The signature is used to verify that the issuer really did issue the rule. It is assumed that when a peer receives a signed rule from another peer, the signature is verified before the rule is passed to the DLP evaluation engine. Similarly, when one peer sends a signed rule to another peer, the actual signed rule must be sent, and not just the logic programmatic representation of the signed rule. More complex signed rules often represent delegations of authority.

Putting it together

Figure 3 depicts an implemented scenario in an e-learning domain [72, 140] (PEERTRUST has also been applied, among other scenarios, to Grid [21] and Semantic Web Services [123]). Alice and E-Learn obtain trust negotiation software signed by a source that they trust (PEERTRUST Inc.) and distributed by PEERTRUST Inc. or another site, either as a Java application or an applet. After Alice requests the Spanish course from E-Learn's web front end, she enters into a trust negotiation with E-Learn's negotiation server. The negotiation servers may also act as servers for the major resources they protect (the Learning Management Servers (LMS)), or may be separate entities, as in our figure. Additional parties can participate in the negotiation, if necessary, symbolized in our figure by the InstitutionA and InstitutionB servers. If access to the course is granted, E-Learn sets up a temporary account for Alice at the course provider's site, and redirects her original request there. The temporary account is invisible to Alice.

Cassandra

Cassandra [23,24] is a role-based trust management system. It uses a policy language based on datalog with constraints and its expressiveness can be adjusted by changing

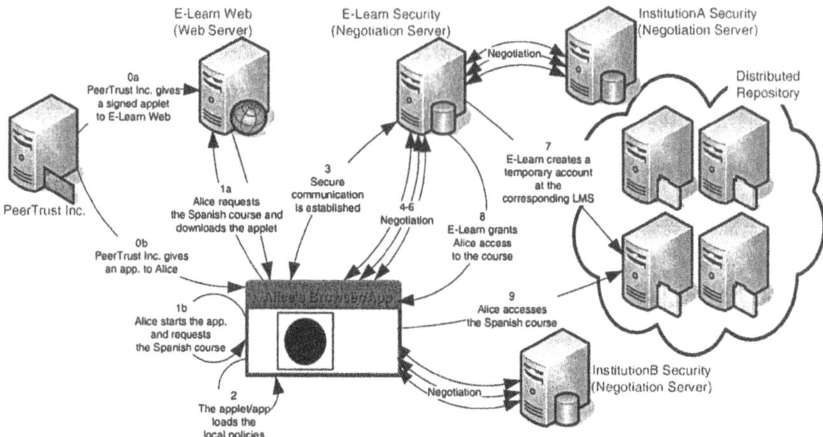

Fig. 3. PEERTRUST: Automated Trust Negotiation for Peers on the Semantic Web

the constraint domain. Policies are specified using the following predicates which govern access control decisions:

- $permits(e, a)$ specifies who can perform which action
- $canActivate(e, r)$ defines who can activate which role (e is a member of r)
- $hasActivated(e, r)$ defines who is active in which role
- $canDeactivate(e, r)$ specifies who can revoke which role
- $isDeactivated(e, r)$ is used to define automatically triggered role revocation
- $canReqCred(e_1, e_2, p(e))$ specifys the requirements that a request must satisfy in order to issue and disclose credentials

This way, policy managers can define and use new predicates as they need.

A Cassandra predicate also contains an *issuer* and a *location* like

loc @ iss.p(e)

where *location* represents the entity where the assertion applies (and therefore it allows queries over the network) and the issuer is the entity that asserts it.

Although Cassandra does not provide special constraints to specify role validity periods, auxiliary roles, role hierarchy, separation of duties, role delegation, automated trust negotiation and credential discovery, it can express these kind of policies. That way the language and its semantics are simpler and makes easier the extension of the language.

A policy rule in Cassandra is of the form:

$$E_{loc}@E_{iss}.p_0(e_0) \leftarrow loc_1@iss_1.p_1(e_1), \ldots, loc_n@iss_n.p_n(e_n), c$$

where p_i are the names of the predicates, e_i is a set of expression tuples and c is a constraint.

A rule with only a constraint c in its body like

$E_{loc}@E_{iss}.p_0(e_0) \leftarrow c$

represents a credential signed and issued by E_{iss} asserting $p_0(e_0)$ which is stored at E_{loc}.

PROTUNE

The PRovisional TrUst NEgotiation framework PROTUNE [42] aims at combining distributed trust management policies with provisional-style business rules and access-control related actions. PROTUNE's rule language extends the PAPL [40] and PEERTRUST [72] languages and it provides a powerful declarative metalanguage for driving some critical negotiation decisions, and integrity constraints for monitoring negotiations and credential disclosure. PROTUNEwill be further described in section 6.2.

4 Action Languages

Reasoning about action and change is a kind of temporal reasoning where, instead of reasoning about *time* itself, we reason on *phenomena* that take place in time. *Action theories* are formal theories for reasoning about action and change, that describe a *dynamic world* changing because of the execution of actions. Properties characterizing the dynamic world are usually specified by propositions which are called *fluents*. The word *fluent* stresses the fact that the truth value of these propositions depends on time and may vary depending on the changes which occur in the world.

The problem of reasoning about the effects of actions in a dynamically changing world is considered one of the central problems in knowledge representation theory. Different approaches in the literature took different assumptions on the temporal ontology and they developed different abstraction tools to cope with dynamic worlds. However, most of action theories describe dynamic worlds according to the so-called *state-action model*. In the state-action model the world is described in terms of states and actions that cause the transition from a state to another. More precisely, there are some assumptions that typically hold in action theories referring to the *state-action model*, that we list below:

- the dynamic world to be modeled is always in a determined state;
- change is interpreted as a transition from a world state to another;
- the world persists in its state unless it is modified by an action execution that causes the transition to a new state (*persistency assumption*).

Based on the above conceptual assumptions, the main target of action theories is to use a logical framework to describe the effects of actions on a world where *all* changes are caused by the execution of actions. More precisely, a formal theory for representing and reasoning about actions allows us to specify:

(a) *causal laws*, i.e. axioms that describe domain's actions in terms of their preconditions and effects on the fluents;

(b) action sequences that are executed from the initial state;
(c) *observations* describing the fluent's value in the *initial state*;
(d) *observations* describing the fluent's value after some action execution.

In the following, the term *domain description* is used to refer to a set of propositions that express causal laws, observations of the fluents value in a state and possibly other information for formalizing a specific problem. Given a domain description, the principal reasoning tasks are *temporal projection* (or prediction), *temporal explanation* (or postdiction) and *planning*. Intuitively, the aim of *temporal projection* is to predict action's future effects based on (even partial) knowledge about the actual state (reasoning from causes to effects). On the contrary, the target of *temporal explanation* is to infer something on the past states of the world by using knowledge about the actual situation. The third reasoning task, *planning*, is aimed at finding an action sequence that, when executed starting from a given state of the world, produces a new state where certain desired properties hold.

Usually, by varying the reasoning task, a domain description will contain different elements that provide a basis for inferring the new facts. For instance, when the task is to formalize the temporal projection problem, a domain description will contain information on (a), (b) and (c), then the logical framework will provide the inference mechanisms for reconstructing information on (d). Otherwise, when the task is to deal with the planning problem, the domain description will contain the information on (a), (c), (d) and we will try to infer (b), i.e. which action sequence has to be executed on the state described in (c) for achieving a state with the properties described in (d).

A relevant formalization difficulty is known as the *persistency problem*. It concerns the characterization of the invariants of an action, i.e. those aspects of the dynamic world that are not changed by an action. If a certain fluent f, representing a fact of the world, holds in a certain state and it is not involved by the next execution of an action a, then we would like to have an efficient inference mechanism to conclude that f still holds in the state resulting from the execution of a.

A second formalization difficulty, known as the *ramification problem*, arises in presence of the so-called indirect effects (or ramifications) of actions and concerns the problem of formalizing *all* the changes caused by an action's execution. Indeed, action's execution might cause a change not only on those fluents that represent its direct effects, but also on other fluents which are indirectly involved by the chain of events started by the action's execution.

Various approaches in the literature can be broadly classified in two categories: those choosing classical logics as knowledge representation language [101, 113] and those addressing the problem by using non-classical logics [48, 77, 136] or computational logics [15, 20, 74, 109]. In the following, we will briefly review the most popular logic-based approaches to reason about action and change.

Expressing policies by means of declarative languages is surely useful because it simplifies the verification of properties; in particular using the action metaphor for modelling policies is one of the most intuitive ways. Different to the standard use of actions, in this case there are further situations that might be taken into account. For example, as suggested in [130], it might be useful to enrich the action description by adding mid-conditions, i.e. conditions that might become true at execution time. The idea is to capture specific conditions that are relevant in modelling security. On the other hand, research in action theory has proposed extensions that deal with reasoning about complex actions that we believe are useful to increase the expressiveness of security policies.

4.1 Logical Approaches

Among the various logic-based approaches to reasoning about actions one of the most popular is still the situation calculus, introduced by Mc Carthy and Hayes in the sixties [113]. The situation calculus represents the world and its change by a sequence of *situations*. Each situation represents a state of the world and it is obtained from a previous situation by executing an action. A world is represented as a sequence of actions, called a *situation*, starting from an *initial situation* S_0. A binary function symbol $do(a, s)$ denotes the successor situation resulting from performing action a in situation s. For example, the term $do(putdown(A), do(pickup(A), S_0))$ is a situation denoting the world resulting from the sequence of actions [pickup(A), putdown(A)]. *Fluents*, i.e. relations whose truth values vary from situation to situation, are denoted by predicate symbols taking a situation as their last argument. For example $on(A, B, s)$ means that block A is on block B in situation s. An *action theory* can be defined by giving *preconditions* and *effects* for each action.

As pointed out by McCarthy and Hayes [113] formalizing an action theory requires dealing with *persistency*, by specifying those fluents which remain unaffected by a given action. Since most of the fluents do not change from a state to the next one, we want a parsimonious solution to this problem. The main idea is to minimize change from one state to the next by making use of nonmonotonic logics or of completion constructions. In particular, Reiter [127] proposed a solution which relies on the *completeness assumption* that the action theory describes all action laws affecting the truth value of any fluent f. Under this assumption, it is possible to define a *successor state axiom* for each fluent, giving the value of this fluent in the next state.

Kowalski and Sergot have developed a different calculus to describe change [101], called *event calculus*, in which *events* producing changes are temporally located and they initiate and terminate action effects. Like the situation calculus, the event calculus is a methodology for encoding actions in first-order predicate logic. However, it was originally developed for reasoning about events and time in a logic-programming setting.

Another approach to reasoning about actions is the one based on the use of modal logics. The suitability of dynamic logics or modal logics to formalize reasoning about actions and change has been pointed out in various proposals [48,60,77,136]. Modal logics adopt essentially the same ontology of situation calculus by taking the state of the world as primary and by representing actions as state transitions. In particular, actions are represented in a very natural way by modalities whose semantics is a standard Kripke semantics given in terms of accessibility relations between worlds, while states are represented as sequences of modalities. In modal logic, a primitive action a can be represented by a modal operator $[a]$, and a sequence of actions $a_1, a_2, \ldots, a_n$ by the modal operator $[a_1; a_2; \ldots; a_n]$ ($[\varepsilon]$ represents the empty sequence of actions, i.e. the initial state). Furthermore we can use a modality $\Box$ to represent an arbitrary sequence of actions. For instance , action effects can be expressed as $\Box[load]loaded$, meaning that fluent *loaded* holds after execution of action *load* in any state, or $\Box(loaded \Rightarrow [shoot]\neg alive)$ and $\Box[shoot]\neg loaded$, meaning that after action *shoot* fluent *loaded* will be false, and fluent *alive* will be false if *loaded* holds before executing the action. Although the representation with modal logic and the one with first-order logic are apparently similar, it is important to point out a significant difference between the two. In fact, if we do not assume any particular property for the modal operators representing actions (modal logic K), the two formulas $\neg[s]\phi$ and $[s]\neg\phi$ have different meanings, whereas in the situation calculus both would be represented by $\neg\phi(s)$. Thus, differently from the situation calculus, we cannot derive $\neg loaded$ from the above rules and $[shoot]alive$, i.e. action rules cannot be used contrapositively.

4.2 Computational Logic

Non-classical logics have successfully been used for developing agent theories, for representing and reasoning about action and change as well as for modeling mental attitudes as beliefs, knowledge and goals. This is due to their capability of representing *structured and dynamic knowledge*. However a wide gap between the expressive power of the formal models and the practical implementations has emerged, due to the computational effort required for verifying that properties granted by logical models hold in the systems that implement them.

For this reason there is a growing interest on the use of *computational logic*, which allows one to express formal specifications that can be directly executed, thanks to the fact that logic programs have a procedural interpretation, besides the declarative one [146]. In '93 Gelfond and Lifschitz have defined a simple declarative language for describing actions, called $\mathcal{A}$ [74]. The target is to define a logical entailment relation between a domain description and simple *queries* of the form "f **after** $a_1, \ldots, a_n$" where f is a fluent and $a_1, \ldots, a_n$ are elementary actions with the meaning of "Is it true that the fluent f holds after the execution of actions $a_1, \ldots, a_n$?". As a difference of the computational logic approach with respect to a logical approach, the domain description contains causal laws for the domain's actions and observations on fluents value in the initial state, and for all of them and for the goal it is easy to give a goal directed proof procedure, that is prolog-like. Alternatively, it is possible to translate the representation directly in Prolog. Actually, the language $\mathcal{A}$ has been formally defined by giving a translation into general logic programming extended with explicit negation. Note that the entailment relation of $\mathcal{A}$ is nonmonotonic, and this aspect is modeled by the *negation as failure* of logic programming.

Various extensions of $\mathcal{A}$ have been proposed in the last years with the intention to deal with nondeterministic actions [17, 100], concurrent actions [19], ramifications

[79, 100] or sensing actions [20, 109]. Most of the times, a sound translation of such extensions into logical languages is provided.

4.3 Executable agent specification languages

The theory of computational agents plays a central role in Artificial Intelligence, providing powerful conceptual tools for characterizing complex systems situated in dynamic environments [126, 152]. Software agents are usually designed as highly autonomous entities (each agent has an internal state -i.e. a set of attitudes like beliefs and goals- and uses it to take decisions), able to react to variations in their environments (reactivity), able to achieve their goals (proactiveness) by interacting, if necessary, with other agents (social capabilities). Thus, they must be able to perform practical reasoning such as planning, i.e. the process of deciding how to achieve a *goal* using the available means (the actions which can be performed).

One of the core research issues in this field is the definition of formal languages for specifying single agents (including the representation of their knowledge and their reasoning techniques) and for modeling communication and interaction among agents. Many theories about agency are based on *logic formalisms* [53, 56, 126, 152].

Modeling agent's internal behaviour and attitude dynamics is a difficult task. Generally speaking, it is impossible to assume either *knowledge completeness* (agents can have partial and incomplete views on the external world) or *knowledge uniqueness* (different agents can have different views on the external world). In presence of incomplete knowledge, the output of reasoning is not expected to be a fixed sequence of actions (*linear plan*), but a more general specification involving conditionals, in which the next action to perform depends on the result of a sensing actions (*conditional plan*). An agent could start in the generation of a plan from scratch, as in standard planning in AI. Alternatively, it could be provided with a *library of plans*, which have been predefined by the designer: finding a plan to achieve a goal means extracting from the library a plan that, when executed, will have the goal as a post-condition, and that is sound given the agent's current beliefs. Predefined plans can also be partially specified, by means of procedures, defining complex actions the agent can perform. In this case the planning task is interpreted as finding a terminating execution of the procedure that leads to a state where the desired goal holds. The procedure definition constrains the search space in which to look for the wanted sequence.

In order to cope with these issues, extensions of classical logics and new reasoning techniques have been studied. Most of the approaches build on the top of an action theory expressed in one of the formalisms reviewed in the previous sections. Non-classical logics (like modal logics, deontic logic and non-monotonic logics) have been successfully used for developing agent theories, both to represent and reason about actions, and to formalize mental states and their dynamics. Computational logic is often used to develop *logic-based executable agent specifications* due to its nature it also supports the verification tasks. In fact, in logic programming, logic *is* the programming language and agent programs can be specified as logical rules that can be executed by a SLD-style proof procedure.

Logic-based, executable agent specification languages have been deeply investigated in the last decade [7, 16, 68, 103]. Both situation calculus and modal action logics influenced the design of these languages, in particular, the cognitive robotic project at University of Toronto has lead to the development of a high-level agent programming language, called GOLOG, which is based on *situation calculus* [103]. A *modal action theory* has been used as a basis for specifying and executing agent behaviour in the logic programming language DyLOG [16]. The language IMPACT is an example of use of *deontic logic* for specifying agents. In the following, we will briefly recall the main features of these three languages, which seem to be particularly promising for the implementation of intelligent application systems, including security.

GOLOG is a programming language, for the specification and the execution of complex actions in dynamic domains based on the situation calculus [7]. It is a procedural language mainly designed for programming high-level robot control and intelligent software agents. Recently it has been used for allowing the automatically composition of services on the semantic web in the context of the DAML-S initiative [114, 115]. Primitive actions are specified by giving their preconditions and effects in terms of suitable axioms. Formalization of complex actions refers to an Algol-like paradigm and draws considerably from dynamic logic. In particular, action operators like sequence, nondeterministic choice and iteration are provided. Second order logic is needed for defining iteration and procedures. Once extracted, a GOLOG plan can be executed by the agent. Thus, it is possible to implement rational agents alternating planning and execution. Specific works in this direction has driven to the development of IndiGolog [75]. The problem of dealing with concurrency instead has been faced in [61, 62], by leading to the definition of CONGOLOG.

Like GOLOG, the language DyLOG is designed for specifying agents behaviour and for modeling dynamic systems. As a main difference, it is fully set inside the logic programming paradigm by defining programs by sets of Horn-like rules and giving a SLD-style proof procedure. DyLOG has been used for implementing a *virtual tutor* [14], that helps students to build personalized study curricula, while in [9–11] the capability of reasoning about interaction protocols, supported by the language, has been exploited for customizing web service selection and composition w.r.t. to the user's constraints, based on a semantic description of the services. The language is based on a modal theory of actions and mental attitudes where *modalities* are used for representing primitive and complex *actions* as well as the agent beliefs [16]. Complex actions are defined by *inclusion axioms* [8] and by making use of action operators from dynamic logic, like sequence ";", test "?" and nondeterministic choice "$\cup$". DyLOG rules can be used also for giving a local representation of interaction protocols, i.e. for defining conversation policies -building upon FIPA-like speech-acts- that the agent follows when interacting with others.

DyLOG supports planning and temporal projection, by allowing to prove existential properties of the kind "given a procedure p and a set of desiderata, is there a legal sequence of actions conforming to p that, when executed from the initial state, also satisfies the desired conditions?". In case we deal with communicative behavior, this process is meant to find an answer to the query: "given a conversation policy

p and a set of desiderata, is there a specific conversation, respecting the policy, that also satisfies the desired conditions". As in GOLOG the procedure definition constrains the search space. A goal-directed proof procedure has been developed that implements such kinds of reasoning and planning, and allows to automatically extract, from DyLOG procedures, *linear* or *conditional* plans for achieving a given goal from an incompletely specified initial state [10, 16].

The IMPACT agent architecture, introduced by Subrahmanian et al. [7], provides a framework to build agents on top of heterogeneous sources of knowledge. To agentize such sources, the authors introduce the notion of agent program. Such agent programs and their semantics resemble logic programs extended with deontic modalities. Indeed, they consist of a set of rules suitable to specify, by means of deontic modalities, agent policies in normative terms, that is what actions an agent is obliged to take in a given state, what actions it is permitted to take, and how it chooses which actions to perform. Thus, if $\alpha(\mathit{Vectorst})$ is an action with parameters *Vectorst*, then $\mathbf{O}\alpha(\mathit{Vectorst})$, $\mathbf{P}\alpha(\mathit{Vectorst})$, $\mathbf{F}\alpha(\mathit{Vectorst})$, $\mathbf{Do}\alpha(\mathit{Vectorst})$, $\mathbf{W}\alpha(\mathit{Vectorst})$, are the so-called action status atoms possibly included in IMPACT rules, which are read (respectively) as $\alpha(\mathit{Vectorst})$ is obligatory, permitted, forbidden, done, and the obligation to do $\alpha(\mathit{Vectorst})$ is waived. In IMPACT, at every state transition, the agent determines a set of actions to be executed, obeying some notion of deontic consistency. IMPACT has been used to develop real applications ranging from combat information management to aerospace applications.

4.4 Reasoning about interaction

Communication and dialogue have intensively been studied in the context of formal theories of agency [93]. In particular, great attention has been devoted to the definition of *standard agent communication languages* (ACL), such as FIPA and KQML. The crucial issue was to achieve interoperability in open agent systems, characterized by the interaction of heterogeneous agents; to this aim it is fundamental to have a universally shared semantics.

Agent communication languages are complex structures because a communicative act must specify many kinds of information. The definition of a formal semantics for individual communicative acts has been one of the major topics of research in this field. Most of the proposals are based on the philosophical theory of speech acts developed by Austin and Searle in the sixties: communications are not merely considered as the transmission of information but as *actions* that, instead of modifying the external world, affect the mental states of the involved agents. Thus, ACL semantics of individual speech acts is given in terms of preconditions and effects on the mental attitudes (as it is commonly done with action semantics). Standard techniques for reasoning about change can be exploited for proving conversation properties, for planning communication with other agents and for answer selection as in [44, 67]. Therefore, ACL-like speech act they can naturally be represented in agent programming languages based on action theories, e.g. the languages DyLOG.

Opposed to the mentalistic approach, followed by ACL-based agent languages as DyLOG, some authors have recently proposed a *social approach* to agent communication [139], in which communicative actions affect the "social state" of the system rather than the internal states of the agents. The social state records the social facts, like the *permissions* and the *commitments* of the agents, which are created and modified along the interaction. The birth of the social approach is due to the difficulty of verifying, in a mentalistic framework, that an agent acts according to a commonly agreed semantics, because its mental state cannot be accessed [149], a problem known as *semantics verification*. The social approach overcomes the semantics verification problem because it exploits a set of established commitments *between* the agents, that are stored as part of the MAS social state.

Recently the attention has been moved towards the formalization of those aspects of communication that are related to the conversational context in which communicative acts occur [111] with the introduction of *conversation policies* and *interaction protocols*. The need for the verification if a given property holds for a given protocol has recently emerged as a fundamental requirement. To such purpose formal languages and analysis tools are currently considered aspects of primary importance, especially for security protocols, where formal proofs of properties are indeed fundamental for the protocol itself [80]. The research on protocol verification has greatly benefit from some important contributions achieved in the distributed and concurrent systems research area. In particular, the results obtained in model checking [27, 55] have been proved extremely useful for the verification of protocols. A notable example is the SPIN system [89, 90] where interacting entities can be defined as finite state automata through PROMELA (PROtocol LAnguage Goal), and protocol properties can be expressed through formulas in temporal linear logic. In the area of agent languages based on logic, some examples of definition of protocols for guiding the agent communicative behavior can be found [12, 13, 66]. The logical formalization supports the definition of elegant techniques for conformance verification of agent policies w.r.t. public protocol specifications.

The basic idea is that protocols built upon a predefined set of speech acts. The social approach provides a high-level specification of the protocol, and does not require the rigid specification of all the allowed action sequences by means of finite state diagrams, which is instead typical of mental approaches. In a social framework it is possible to formally prove the correctness of public interaction protocols with respect to the specifications outcoming from the analysis phases; such proof can be obtained, for instance, by means of model checking techniques [26, 78, 125, 149]. However, when one passes from the public protocol specification to its *implementation* in some language (e.g. Java, DyLOG), a program is obtained which, by definition, relies on the information contained in the internal "state" of the agent for deciding which action to execute. In this perspective, the use of a declarative language is helpful because it allows the proof of properties of the *specific implementation* in a straightforward way. In particular, the use of a language that explicitly represents and uses the agent internal state is useful for proving to which extent certain properties depend on the agent mental state or on the semantics of the speech acts. For instance, in [9–11, 16] the hypothetical reasoning about the effects of conversations on the agent mental state is used to find conversation plans which are proved to respect the implemented protocols, achieving at the same time some desired goal.

5 Business Rules

Business rules are "statements about how a business is done, i.e. about guidelines and restrictions with respect to states and processes in an organization" [25]; they "formulate a law or custom that guides the behavior or actions of the actors connected to the organization" [145]. Business rules can be formalized and explicitly managed, but they are often implicitly captured in corporate documents, spreadsheets, workflow descriptions and information systems, scattered all over the organization.

While many business rules are (implicitly) introduced from external sources like the culture or the law, in many other cases, business rules are negotiated between the members of the organizations or their representatives. The goal of writing down those rules is to gain reliability and predictable operations of the organization.

Galbraith summarizes the main reasons in favor of using formalized rules as follows [71]: (a) *Coordination*: In complex situations, the execution of tasks may need synchronization of the work done by several persons; (b) *Precision*: The execution of as far as possible formalized tasks is precise over time, i.e. everybody knows what to do in every considered event; (c) *Efficiency*: A machine(like) consistency of the task execution may lead to more efficient production, like in the automobile industry; and (d) *Fairness*: Especially government organizations have to secure an equal treatment of every client; hence they strive to formalize their behavior in order to protect clients and also employees.

Today, a number of business rules are explicitly written down, commonly in organizational handbooks which contain systematically collected and specified business rules; they describe the static and dynamic aspects of an organization: the positions within the organization, verbal descriptions of rights and duties of the employees, and the business processes, illustrating the tasks do be accomplished, their dependencies, time restrictions, and responsibilities.

Another, usually smaller and more homogeneous subset of the business rules of an organization is captured by information systems, which often are also used to *enforce* those rules. Clearly, not all business rules are candidates of being explicitly written down and formalized. Schmidt [135] has established a series of criteria which may help to decide which types of rules and tasks are eligible of formalization. Rules that fit those criteria can be operationalized by transforming them into executable rule expressions, e.g. into a declarative logic based rule language.

5.1 Typology of Formalized Business Rules

In this section we are particulary concerned about the explicit formulation of business rules. We follow the top-level classification illustrated by [142] and [147], which bases on [47] and distinguish three families of business rules: Reaction rules, derivation rules and integrity constraints. In the following, we will characterize these types of rules and their components.

Reaction Rules

Reaction rules are concerned with the invocation of actions in response to events. They state the conditions under which actions must be taken. They define the behavior of a system (or an agent) in response to perceived environment events and to communication events [147]. Reaction rules, often called ECA (Event-Condition-Action) rules, are conceptually of the following type:

```
ON event
IF condition is fulfilled
THEN perform action
```

This concept assumes an *event controller*, which monitors certain types of events, and upon occurrence of such an event, the condition of the rule is evaluated. If the condition is true, the action associated to the rule is executed.

Production Rules

Production rules are similar to ECA rules; they may even be considered a special case of the general concept of reaction rules [147]. In rule based systems, productions rules are of the form `IF C THEN A`, where `C` is a condition and `A` is *any* kind of action, including external procedures/methods.

The inputs to production rule systems are a set of such production rules, i.e. condition-action pairs of the form if *condition* then *action*. The other two components of a production rule system are: (i) *Working memory*: The memory holds the description of the current state of the world in a reasoning process. Most production systems allow to create networks of objects, defined by object templates which have one head and one or more slots (i.e. attribute fields). (ii) *Recognize-act cycle*: The conditions (i.e. left hand side of the rules) are continuously matched against the known facts in the working memory. If one rule applies, it is fired, that is, its right hand side is executed. If more than one rules apply, the conflicting rules are added to a goal agenda, ordered and then executed sequentially. This cycle continues until all rules are satisfied.

The fact that production systems are responsible for determining the set of applicable rules at a given time relieves the programmer (rule modeler) from considering and codifying all the paths by which a rule may become applicable or inapplicable.

The most efficient algorithm for implementing such production systems is the Rete algorithm [69]. The Rete algorithm is the only known algorithm for production systems whose performance is demonstrably independent of the number of rules in the system. An algorithm similar to Rete is TREAT [118], which differs in several aspects of the organization of the internal working memory of the algorithms.

Derivation Rules

Another class of rules that is widely used for the specification of formal business rules are derivation rules. Derivation rules allow to *derive* knowledge from other knowledge by an inference or a mathematical calculation [147].

Each rule expresses the knowledge that if one set of statements happens to be true, then some other set of statements must also be true (or become true). Using a set of such rules, it is possible to specify the behavior of systems by means of logical specifications. This leads us to the term *Logic Programming* [107], which is a well-known programming paradigm based on a subset of First Order Logic, named Horn clause Logic.

The most prominent example of a language exploiting the advantageous properties of Horn clauses is *Prolog*. Prolog departs from pure logics by supporting numerous extra-logical features, e.g. numeric operations and the CUT. The CUT is a construct that can be used to steer the SLD resolution process.

A variant of Prolog, *Datalog* [49], is used to implement deductive database systems. These systems are called *deductive*, because they are able to deduce new facts from the data already stored in the database.

Datalog is used to define rules declaratively in conjunction with an existing set of relations, which are themselves treated as literals in the language [58]. A deductive database uses two main types of specifications: facts and rules. Facts can be compared to relations in RDBM systems, while rules can be compared to SQL views. One of the fundamental differences to SQL views, however, is that Datalog based views (i.e. rules), may involve recursion and hence may yield virtual relations that cannot be defined in terms of standard relational views [58].

Integrity Constraints

An integrity constraint is an assertion that must be satisfied in all evolving state and state transition histories of an enterprise viewed as a discrete dynamic system [142].

In the literature, the following types of integrity constraints are mentioned:

- *State constraints*: These constraints must hold at any point in time. An example of a state constraint is "a customer of the car rental company EU-Rent must be at least 25 years old" [142].
- *Structural assertions*: An important type of state constraints are structural assertions [88]. A structural assertion is a statement that something of importance to the business either exists as a concept of interest or exists in relationship to another thing of interest. It details a specific, static aspect of the business, expressing things known or how known things fit together.
- *Process constraints*: These refer to the dynamic integrity of a system; they restrict the admissible transitions from one state of the system to another. An process constraint may, for example, declare that the admissible state changes of a RentalOrder object are defined by the following transition path: $reserved \rightarrow allocated \rightarrow effective \rightarrow dropped - off$ [142].

Integrity constraints can be found in many different systems and use very different notations; Constraints can be expressed as IF-THEN statements in programming languages, as explicit assertion statements supported by programming languages such as C++, Eiffel or in the recent Java 2 version 1.5, as CHECK and CONSTRAINT clauses in SQL table definitions and as CREATE ASSERTION statements in SQL database schema definition [142], c.f. also Section "Rules in Active DBMS" below. Finally, structural assertions can be modeled as UML or entity/relationship diagrams and can be augmented by state constraints represented as OCL (Object Constraint Language)

Integrity constraints can also be seen as a special case of ECA rules, because they perform a certain *action* (e.g. repair the database) in the *event* of a violated integrity constraint.

5.2 Implementation of Business Rules

Rules in Active DBMS

Active DBMS on the other hand, use rules – mainly based on the ECA paradigm – to describe activities to be carried out by the system. Active DBMS monitor events and then react appropriately; hence, active databases present a *reactive* behavior (compared to the passive behavior of typical DBMS): they execute not only user transactions, but also the rules specified.

Many commercial relational systems like Oracle, DB2 Sybase offer this functionality, in the form of triggers (standardised in SQL-3); other examples for active relational DBMS are Ariel [87], Postgres [141] and Starbust [150]. There also exists object oriented active databases such as HiPac [59], Sentinel [50] and EXACT [63].

Besides the reactive behavior, modern database systems are able to capture and enforce another type of rules, i.e. integrity constraints. Constraints are declarations of conditions about the database that must remain true. These include attributed-based, tuple-based and referential integrity constraints. The database system checks for the violation of the constraints on actions that may cause a violation and aborts the action accordingly.

Rule-Based Programming Environments

In the following we briefly review popular rule engines.

Mandarax

Mandarax [64] is an open source java library for business rules. This includes the representation, persistence, exchange, management and processing (querying) of rule bases. The main objective of Mandarax is to provide a pure object oriented platform for rule-based systems.

In Mandarax, rules are presented as clauses that consist of a body (the prerequisite or antecedent of the rule) and a head (i.e. the consequence of the rule). The prerequisites and the conclusion are *facts*, which themselves consist of *terms* and *predicates* associating those terms. Under the object oriented notation supported by Mandarax, terms represent objects while predicates on the other hand represent relationships between terms. Terms can be constants, variables or complex terms; complex terms are terms that can be computed from other terms (functions).

The Mandarax engine uses an object oriented version of backward chaining mechanism similar to Prolog; this is in contrast to popular rule engines like ILOG or JESS, which use the forward chaining Rete algorithm [69]. The Mandarax project offers several rule engines which slightly differ in some implementation aspects (e.g. support of Prolog-like Cut, negation as failure).

The Mandarax project is also developing a reactive variant of the Mandarax rule engine. The engine – called Mandarax ECA – is an extension that can be used to program reactive agents; events have registered event listeners (handlers), these listeners query the knowledge base for the next action that must be performed.

ILOG

ILOG [94] is a rule engine and programming library that allows developers to combine rule-based and object-oriented programming to add business rules to new and existing applications. The ILOG rule engine is exposed to Java[5] and C++ code via an application programmer interface (API). Rules can be dynamically added, modified, or removed from the engine on the fly, i.e. without shutting down or recompiling the application.

ILOG uses an optimized variant of the Rete algorithm, which makes it capable of handling large numbers of rules within an application and achieving a high performance in handling rules. Further, ILOG offers a wide range of enhancements, such as automatic rule optimizations which occur transparently to the developer, auto hashing and indexing.

ILOG rules employs the ILOG Rule Language, which has a Java-like syntax and a variety of language extensions. Developers have at their disposal full support of operators in expressions and tests, Java-like syntax for interfaces, arrays, and variable scope management.

The ILOG Rules rule engine can directly parse and output rules in an XML representation, allowing the management of rules by standard XML tools. Further, the ILOG tool suite offers a point-and-click editor to manipulate the rule base.

Jess

Jess [70] is a Java based rule engine and scripting environment inspired by the CLIPS [76, 129] expert system shell with its OPS5 [46] production rule language. Just like Mandarax, Drooles and ILOG, Jess is augmented by an object oriented language (i.e. Java) to increase its applicability for commercial projects (which often have a large legacy code base to support).

Jess can directly make use and manipulate Java objects. Moreover, it is a reference implementation for the JSR-94 standardization proposal, which aims at providing a uniform Java application programming interface to rule engines.

Like CLIPS, Jess is based on the Rete algorithm [69], the forward chaining mechanism for production rule systems. Like all production rule-based systems, the functionality of Jess is comprised of the rule base, the working memory and the recognize-act cycle (cf. Section "Production Rules").

[5] The engine for Java is branded *JRules*.

Rule Markup Language (RuleML)

RuleML [39,95] is a standardization initiative that was started in 2000 with the goal to establish an open, vendor neutral XML based rule language standard, permitting both forward (bottom-up) and backward (top-down) rules in XML for deduction, rewriting, and further inferential-transformational tasks.

RuleML foresees a classification of the rule it supports. RuleML encompasses a hierarchy of rules, from reaction rules, via integrity constraints and derivation rules to facts (i.e. premiseless derivation rules). For these top-level families, XML DTDs are provided, reflecting the structures of the rule families.

In the first two years of RuleML, the emphasis has been on the expression of derivation rules XML. Another goal of RuleML is to integrate the rule markup language with ontology languages like DAML+OIL and subsequently OWL. The current outcome of these efforts is a draft for SWRL (Semantic Web Rule Language) [92], which is based on a combination of the OWL DL and OWL Lite sublanguages of OWL with the Unary/Binary Datalog sublanguages of RuleML.

Another goal has been to provide an object oriented extension to rule modeling, as already showcased by several rule engines (c.f. Section "Implementation of Rules in Information Systems"). To date (Summer 2004) there exists a system of XML DTDs for *slotted* (i.e. frame-based) RuleML sublanguages including the Object-Oriented RuleML (OO RuleML) [38]. Recent efforts also went into defining MOF-RuleML [148], the abstract syntax of RuleML as an MOF Model and aligning RuleML with UML's Object Constraint Language (OCL).

A critical review of RuleML is given in [147]. One of the weaknesses identified by that paper is the lack of support of ECA rules. This limitation is currently being addressed by a working devoted to Reactive RuleML [1].

5.3 Dealing with Rule Conflicts and Inconsistency

Conflicts Among Rules - Causes

In many logical systems, like Horn logic, there can be no conflicts between rules: once the premises of a rule are satisfied, the rule is executed and its conclusion is drawn. This is due to the fact that negation in the rule heads is not allowed.

Once we allow negation to appear in the rule head, the situation becomes more complicated because it is possible that two rules may lead to contradictory conclusions. Conflicting rules are not necessarily indications of an error in the knowledge base, but may arise naturally in different ways.

Conflicting rules are useful as a modeling feature. For example, rules with exceptions, found in many policies, can be expressed naturally using a set of conflicting rules: a rule describing the general case, and rules expressing exceptions. For example, the general rule may say that all professors are tenured, while an exception rule may say that visiting professors are not tenured.

Another type of application scenarios is reasoning with incomplete information. In these scenarios, the available knowledge is insufficient to mace certain decisions, but we have to make conclusions based on "rules of thumb". A typical scenario is emergency medical diagnosis, where initial diagnosis and treatment needs to be made before the results of medical tests become available. Note that new information may lead to a revision of the initial decisions. These scenarios are closely linked to the area of nonmonotonic reasoning [3, 112].

Conflicting rules also naturally arise in knowledge integration, when knowledge from different sources (and possibly authors) is combined. This scenario is expected to be particularly wide-spread on the Semantic Web, where a key idea is to import knowledge from various sources and adapt it for own purposes.

Dealing with Conflicting Rules

The question is how to deal with situations where rules with conflicting heads can potentially be applied. In first-order logic and related approaches, contradictory conclusions may be drawn but have trivialization effects: every conclusion can be drawn from a contradictory set of premises.

This behaviour is deemed to be unacceptable for practical purposes. It considers contradictions as error situations, but we explained previously that this is not necessarily the case.

Reasoning systems falling in this category are wide-spread in logic programming, knowledge representation and the Semantic Web [2, 4, 82, 127].

One way of resolving conflicts is to use priorities among rules. For example, the rule stating that visiting professors are not tenured is stronger than the rue stating that professors are tenured. With this information incorporated in the knowledge base, the conclusion that a particular visiting professor is not tenured can be drawn even sceptically. The aforementioned works make use of such priorities.

Obviously, we need ways of incorporating priorities in the reasoning process even in complex cases. An extensive body of work is available in this directions [2, 4, 82, 121, 134]. We should also mention work on developing rules systems tailored to the Semantic Web that are able of dealing with inconsistent and incomplete information, among them [22, 84].

The Origin of Priorities

Priorities may arise from internal or external sources. Internal priorities are computed from a set of rules based on the idea of specificity: a more specific rule is viewed as an exception to a more general rule and should therefore be deemed to be stronger. For a system that computes priorities based on specificity of rules see [32].

While useful, specificity is only one prioritization principle. To capture other principles, most logical systems rely on priorities that are made available externally. That is, priorities are considered to be a part of the knowledge base, as are rules and facts. External priority information may be based on a number of principles:

- One rule may be preferred to another rule because it is an exception to another rule. Such information is often stated explicitly in policies and business rules [5].

- One rule may be preferred to another because it is more recent. This principle is often used in law and regulations.

Apart from these principles which apply to pairs of individual rules, priority information may be based on comparing groups of rules. For example, in business administration the rules originating from higher management have higher authority than those originating from middle management. Or in knowledge integration, one source of rules may be known to be more reliable than the other. This preference of groups is propagated to individual rules.

6 Unifying Frameworks

Cleary all specifications we have described in the previous sections interact tightly with each other. Trust management policy languages need to express security policies and actions, business rules and action languages describe how "things are done", security specifications play an important role for business rules and decisions. While it is hard or maybe even impossible to really integrate all aspects described in the previous chapters in one framework, unifying several of these aspects in one framework is necessary for comprehensive applications of rule-based policy specifications, and makes explicit the interaction between the various features treated separately in many previous approaches. In this section, we will therefore describe two different approaches towards a unifying framework: XACML and PROTUNE.

6.1 XACML

The eXtensible Access Control Markup Language (XACML) [122] is an OASIS standard that describes both a policy language and an access control decision request/response language (both in XML).

The policy language allows to specify access control conditions that must be fulfilled by a requester. There are three kind of top-level elements:

<Rule> It is a boolean expression which is not intended to be evaluated in isolation but can be reused by several policies.

<Policy> It is a set of rules and obligations that apply to a request. It contains a set of rules and an algorithm describing how to combine the results of their evaluation.

<PolicySet> It contains a set of policy and policy set elements together with an algorithm describing how to combine the results of their evaluation.

The request/response language allows to send queries in order to check whether a specific request should be allowed. There are four different valid values for the answer in the response: Permit, Deny, Indeterminate (a decision could not be made) or Not Applicable (the request can't be answered by this service)

They provide the basis for the separation of the so called Policy Enforcement Point (PEP) which is the entity in charge of protecting a resource and the Policy

Decision Point (PDP) which is responsible for checking whether a request is conformant with a given policy. In order to include the execution of actions within the standard, the authors define the *<Obligation>* element. An obligation is "an action that must be performed in conjunction with the enforcement of an authorization decision". In the current version of XACML 2.0 there are no standard definitions for these actions.

XACML is a standard, so it includes many features among which we higlight the following:

- The language allows the use of attributes in order to perform authorization decisions without relying exclusively on the identity of requester.
- Different arithmetic, set and boolean operators, and built-in functions are provided as well as a method to extend the language with non-standard functions.
- The language includes a *<Target>* element in each rule, policy or policy set in order to allow indexing and increase performance.
- Different combination algorithms are provided for rule and policy composition: `deny-overrides`, `ordered-deny-overrides`, `permit-overrides`, `ordered-permit-overrides`, `first-applicable` and `only-one-applicable`.
- An *XACML context* is define in order to provide a canonical form for representing requests and responses. As it is encoded in XML, it is possible to extract information from the context using XPath 2.0.

However, the current specification of XACML (v2.0 at the time being) is not suitable as a policy language for protocols like trust negotiation (see section 3.2). It still lacks some required expressivity like delegation of authority (see [138] for a discussion on requirements for trust negotiation) which have to be taken into consideration for next versions of the specification.

6.2 Protune

The PRovisional TrUst NEgotiation framework PROTUNE [42] aims at combining distributed trust management policies with provisional-style business rules and access-control related actions. PROTUNE's rule language extends two previous languages: PAPL [40], that until 2002 was one of the most complete policy languages for trust negotiation [137], and PEERTRUST [72], that supports distributed credentials and a more flexible policy protection mechanism. In addition, the framework features a powerful declarative metalanguage for driving some critical negotiation decisions, and integrity constraints for monitoring negotiations and credential disclosure.

PROTUNE provides a framework with:

- A trust management language supporting general provisional-style actions (possibly user-defined).
- An extendible declarative metalanguage for driving decisions about request formulation, information disclosure, and distributed credential collection.

- A parameterized negotiation procedure, that gives a semantics to the metalanguage and provably satisfies some desirable properties for all possible metapolicies.
- Integrity constraints for negotiation monitoring and disclosure control.
- General, ontology-based techniques for importing and exporting metapolicies and for smoothly integrating language extensions.

The PROTUNE rule language is based on normal logic program rules "$A \leftarrow L_1, \ldots, L_n$" where A is a standard logical atom (called the *head* of the rule) and $L_1, \ldots, L_n$ (the *body* of the rule) are literals, that is, L_i equals either B_i or $\neg B_i$, for some logical atom B_i.

A *policy* is a set of rules, such that negation is applied neither to *provisional predicates* (defined below), nor to any predicate occurring in a rule head. This restriction ensures that policies are *monotonic* in the sense of [137], that is, as more credentials are released and more actions executed, the set of permissions does not decrease. Moreover, the restriction on negation makes policies *stratified programs*; therefore negation as failure has a clear, PTIME computable semantics that can be equivalently formulated as the perfect model semantics, the well-founded semantics or the stable model semantics [18].

The vocabulary of predicates occurring in the rules is partitioned into the following categories: *Decision Predicates* (currently supporting "allow()" which is queried by the negotiation for access control decisions and "sign()" which is used to issue statements signed by the principal owning the policy, *Abbreviation/Abstraction Predicates* (as described in [40]), *Constraint Predicates* (which comprise the usual equality and disequality predicates) and *State Predicates* (which perform decisions according to the state). State Predicates are further subdivided in *State Query Predicates* (which read the state without modifying it) and *Provisional Predicates* (which may be made true by means of associated actions that may modify the current state like e.g. $credential(C, K), declaration(), logged(X, logfile\_name)$).

Furthermore, metapolicies consist of rules similar to object-level rules. They allow to inspect terms, check groundness, call an object-level goal G against the current state (using a predicate $holds(G)$), etc. In addition, a set of reserved attributes associated to predicates, literals and rules (e.g., whether a policy is public or sensitive) is used to drive the negotiator's decisions. For example, if p is a predicate, then p.`sensitivity : private` means that the extension of the predicate is private and should not be disclosed. An assertion p.`type : provisional` declares p to be a provisional predicate; then p can be attached to the corresponding action α by asserting p.`action :`α. If the action is to be executed locally, then we assert p.`actor : self`, otherwise assert p.`actor : peer`.

7 Summary and Open Research Issues

The term *policy* is used with different meanings in the existing literature but generally refers to the "specification of the behaviour of a system". The most important aspect of policy specification is the language issue, i.e. which language to use to express those policies. In this chapter we provided an exhaustive overview on rule based policy specification encompassing security and trust management policies, action languages and business rules.

Security Policies pose constraints on the behaviour of a system. They are typically used to control permissions of users/groups while accessing resources and services. The languages for specifying security policies are more and more focussing on logic-based, and especially rule-based languages. After exploring a number of different constructs (such as negation as failure, temporal operators, deontic modalities, etc.) and different semantics (top down, tabled, abductive, and dynamic, like event-condition-action rules) it is clear that such languages are extremely flexible and capable of capturing the most diverse policies arising in real application scenarios.

The term trust management refers to reputation based metrics and models, or to policy based trust. *Trust Management policy languages* are used to collect user properties in open environments, where the set of potential users spans the entire web. In this section we offered an extensive review of existing research on policy-based trust management. Among other properties, all current languages have in common that they do not consider authorization as a one-shot process anymore but instead rely on trust negotiations in order to establish trust between strangers.

Action Languages are used in reactive policy specification to execute actions like event logging, notifications, etc. Authorizations that involve actions and side effects are sometimes called provisional. Action languages also allow to reason about phenomena that take place in time and to describe a dynamic world changing because of the execution of actions. Proposals based on (classical and non-classical) logics and computational logic are the most successful ones. Besides the representation used, an action theory is formed by a set of action laws that describe actions in term of preconditions and effects on the world. Typical kinds of reasoning performed on an action theory are temporal projection, temporal explanation, and planning.

Business Rules are "statements about how a business is done" and are used to formalize and automatize business decisions as well as for efficiency reasons. We provided an overview of formal languages and approaches for expressing such rules, to gain readability and predictable operation of an organization. In particular, we provided a typology of formalized business rules and described the main approaches.

All these kinds of specification interact tightly with each other and new approaches are appearing aiming at their unification in a single language/framework.

However, although the research community has achieved great advances in the area, there still exist several open issues and challenges for policy specification. Some of the main research issues concern *integration*, *ease of use* and *implementation*.

A major integration issue concerns the harmonization of the different semantics mentioned above (top down, tabled, etc.), when the policy comprises both declarative and ECA rules. The problem is even more subtle in trust negotiation, where action execution must be scheduled appropriately during multiple negotiation steps.

Integration is also related to implementation. The powerful rule-based policy languages being developed might have a fast and widespread impact if we could (sometimes) translate high-level rules into policies supported by common mechanisms (such as firewalls and the access control mechanisms of DBMSs and web servers). Then high-level policy specifications would let security managers organize their policies in a homogeneous and coherent way, without giving up the efficiency and robustness of lower-level security mechanisms. It would be possible to have a centralized, global view of the system's policy without necessarily introducing bottlenecks such as centralized security monitors.

One of the few open representation problems that has not yet been extensively explored concerns *delegation*: what can a peer do with a piece of information it receives? These policies should express in a simple and compact way the requirements which the information owner poses on subsequent disclosures, as well as allow the receiver to add its own constraints (when possible) [99, 119, 153]. Expressing this kind of dynamic behavior appropriately in a declarative way, accessible to a vast class of users, is a nontrivial challenge. The same is true of the development of a (cryptographic?) infrastructure capable of enforcing this kind of policies, that otherwise would be left to voluntary compliance. Another issue is integration with trust and reputation models [41, 140] and with other security approaches and new applications (e.g., Grids [21, 131]).

On the other hand, in the context of business rules, formal representation is still an open problem. Work will continue on developing formal languages combining sufficient expressive power, efficient reasoning support, and naturalness of expression.

Last but not least, it will be important to give common users the ability of understanding and personalizing their systems' policies. This is essential to bring the existing security mechanisms to their full potential, and increasing user awareness about security problems. Adopting a rule language is not enough for this purpose, because common users typically have no knowledge about logics (and nonmonotonic logics in particular). It is necessary to provide user-friendly front-ends that illustrate the policy in a language familiar to the user, such as a graphical language, or maybe natural language. Actually, there are already lines of research pursuing the formulation of policy rules in a controlled fragment of natural language. Moreover, very recent work is tackling explanation mechanisms that support advanced queries to policies [43]. Such an explanation tool is meant to guide the user in acquiring the permissions necessary to get the desired services. This kind of support is crucial in e-business applications: a *cooperative way of enforcing policies* may be the key to success in such application scenarios.

8 Acknowledgements

The authors would like to thank the contribution of Cristina Baroglio, Alberto Martelli, and Viviana Patti to the Section 4.

References

1. A. Adi, Z. Sommer, A. Biger, S. Ross-Talbot, and G. Wagner. Reactive ruleml, `http://groups.yahoo.com/group/reactive-ruleml/`, 2004.
2. J. Alferes and L. Pereira. *Reasoning with logic programming*, volume 1111 of *LNAI*. Springer-Verlag, 1996.
3. G. Antoniou. *Nonmonotonic Reasoning*. The MIT Press, 1997.
4. G. Antoniou, D. Billington, G. Governatori, and M. Maher. Representation results for defeasible logic. *ACM Transactions on Computational Logic*, 2:255–287, 2001.
5. G. Antoniou, D. Billington, and M. Maher. On the analysis of regulations using defeasible rules. In *Proc. of HICSS'99*, 1999.
6. K. R. Apt, H. A. Blair, and A. Walker. Towards a theory of declarative knowledge. In *Foundations of Deductive Databases and Logic Programming.*, pages 89–148. Morgan Kaufmann, 1988.
7. K. Arisha, T. Eiter, S. Kraus, F. Ozcan, R. Ross, and V. Subrahmanian. IMPACT: a platform for collaborating agents. *IEEE Intelligent Systems*, 14(2):64–72, 1999.
8. M. Baldoni. Normal Multimodal Logics with Interaction Axioms. In D. Basin, M. D'Agostino, D. M. Gabbay, S. Matthews, and L. Viganò, editors, *Labelled Deduction*, volume 17 of *Applied Logic Series*, pages 33–53. Applied Logic Series, Kluwer Academic Publisher, 2000.
9. M. Baldoni, C. Baroglio, L. Giordano, A. Martelli, and V. Patti. Reasoning about communicating agents in the semantic web. In F. Bry, N. Henze, and J. Maluszynski, editors, *Proc. of the 1st International Workshop on Principle and Practice of Semantic Web Reasoning, PPSWR 2003*, volume 2901 of *LNCS*, pages 84–98, Mumbai, India, December 2003. Springer.
10. M. Baldoni, C. Baroglio, A. Martelli, and V. Patti. Reasoning about self and others: communicating agents in a modal action logic. In *Proc. of ICTCS'2003*, volume 2841 of *LNCS*, pages 228–241. Springer, 2003.
11. M. Baldoni, C. Baroglio, A. Martelli, and V. Patti. Reasoning about interaction protocols for web service composition. In M. Bravetti and G. Zavattaro, editors, *Proc. of 1st Int. Workshop on Web Services and Formal Methods, WS-FM 2004*, volume 105 of *Electronic Notes in Theoretical Computer Science*, pages 21–36. Elsevier Science Direct, 2004.
12. M. Baldoni, C. Baroglio, A. Martelli, and V. Patti. Verification of protocol conformance and agent interoperability. In F. Toni and P. Torroni, editors, *Proc. of Sixth International Workshop on Computational Logic in Multi-Agent Systems, CLIMA VI*, London, UK, June 2005.
13. M. Baldoni, C. Baroglio, A. Martelli, V. Patti, and C. Schifanella. Verifying protocol conformance for logic-based communicating agents. In J. Leite and P. Torroni, editors, *Post Proc. of Fifth International Workshop on Computational Logic in Multi-Agent Systems, CLIMA V*, LNAI. Springer, 2005.
14. M. Baldoni, C. Baroglio, and V. Patti. Web-based adaptive tutoring: an approach based on logic agents and reasoning about actions. *Artificial Intelligence Review*, 22(1):3–39, 2004.
15. M. Baldoni, L. Giordano, A. Martelli, and V. Patti. An Abductive Proof Procedure for Reasoning about Actions in Modal Logic Programming. In J. D. et al., editor, *Proc. of NMELP'96*, volume 1216 of *LNAI*, pages 132–150. Springer-Verlag, 1997.
16. M. Baldoni, L. Giordano, A. Martelli, and V. Patti. Programming Rational Agents in a Modal Action Logic. *Annals of Mathematics and Artificial Intelligence, Special issue on Logic-Based Agent Implementation*, 41(2-4):207–257, 2004.

17. C. Baral. Reasoning about actions: non-deterministic effects, constraints, and qualification. In *Proc of IJCAI'95*, pages 2017–2023, 1995.
18. C. Baral. *Knowledge representation, reasoning and declarative problem solving*. Cambridge University Press, Cambridge, 2003.
19. C. Baral and M. Gelfond. Reasoning about effects of concurrent actions. Journal of Logic Programming, 31(1-3):85–117, May 1997.
20. C. Baral and T. C. Son. Formalizing Sensing Actions - A transition function based approach. *Artificial Intelligence*, 125(1-2):19–91, January 2001.
21. J. Basney, W. Nejdl, D. Olmedilla, V. Welch, and M. Winslett. Negotiating trust on the grid. In *2nd WWW Workshop on Semantics in P2P and Grid Computing*, New York, USA, may 2004.
22. N. Bassiliades, G. Antoniou, and I. Vlahavas. DR-DEVICE: A defeasible logic system for the semantic web. In *Proc. 2nd International Workshop on Principles and Practice of Semantic Web Reasoning*, LNCS. Springer Verlag, 2004.
23. M. Y. Becker and P. Sewell. Cassandra: distributed access control policies with tunable expressiveness. In *5th IEEE International Workshop on Policies for Distributed Systems and Networks*, Yorktown Heights, June 2004.
24. M. Y. Becker and P. Sewell. Cassandra: flexible trust management, applied to electronic health records. In *17th IEEE Computer Security Foundations Workshop*, Pacific Grove, CA, June 2004.
25. J. Bell, D. Brooks, E. Goldbloom, R. Sarro, and J. Wood. Knowledge representation, reasoning and declarative problem solving. Technical report, US West Information Technologies Group, Bellevue Golden, 1990.
26. J. Bentahar, B. Moulin, J. J. C. Meyer, and B. Chaib-Draa. A computational model for conversation policies for agent communication. In J. Leite and P. Torroni, editors, *Pre-Proc. of CLIMA V*, pages 66–81, Lisbon, Portugal, September 2004.
27. B. Berard, M. Bidoit, A. Finkel, F. Laroussinie, A. Petit, L. Petrucci, and P. Schnoebelen. *Systems and Software Verification. Model-Checking Techniques and Tools*. Springer, 2001.
28. E. Bertino, C. Bettini, E. Ferrari, and P. Samarati. An access control model supporting periodicity constraints and temporal reasoning. *ACM TODS*, 23(3), 1998.
29. E. Bertino, P. Bonatti, and E. Ferrari. Trbac: A temporal role-based access control model. *ACM Trans. on Information and System Security*, 4(3):191–223, 2001.
30. E. Bertino, P. A. Bonatti, E. Ferrari, and M. L. Sapino. Temporal authorization bases: From specification to integration. *Journal of Computer Security*, 8(4), 2000.
31. E. Bertino, E. Ferrari, F. Buccafurri, and P. Rullo. A logical framework for reasoning on data access control policies. In *Proc. of the 12th IEEE Computer Security Foundations Workshop (CSFW'99)*, pages 175–189. IEEE Computer Society, 1999.
32. D. Billington, K. de Coester, and D. Nute. A modular translation from defeasible nts to defeasible logics. *Journal of Experimental and Theoretical Artificial Intelligence*, pages 151–177, 1990.
33. M. Blaze, J. Feigenbaum, J. Ioannidis, and A. Keromytis. The KeyNote Trust Management System Version 2. In *Internet Draft RFC 2704*, Sept. 1999.
34. M. Blaze, J. Feigenbaum, J. Ioannidis, and A. D. Keromytis. The role of trust management in distributed systems security. *Lecture Notes in Computer Science*, 1603:185–210, 1999.
35. M. Blaze, J. Feigenbaum, and A. D. Keromytis. KeyNote: Trust Management for Public-Key Infrastructures. In *Security Protocols Workshop*, Cambridge, UK, 1998.
36. M. Blaze, J. Feigenbaum, and J. Lacy. Decentralized Trust Management. In *IEEE Symposium on Security and Privacy*, Oakland, CA, May 1996.

37. M. Blaze, J. Feigenbaum, and M. Strauss. Compliance Checking in the PolicyMaker Trust Management System. In *Financial Cryptography*, British West Indies, Feb. 1998.
38. H. Boley, B. Grosof, M. Sintek, S. Tabet, and G. Wagner. Object-Oriented RuleML, version 0.85 of 15 march 2004,`http://www.ruleml.org/indoo`, 2004.
39. H. Boley, S. Tabet, and G. Wagner. Design rationale of RuleML: A markup language for semantic web rules. In *International Semantic Web Working Symposium (SWWS)*, 2001.
40. P. Bonatti and P. Samarati. Regulating service access and information release on the web. In *CCS '00: Proceedings of the 7th ACM conference on computer and communications security*, pages 134–143. ACM Press, 2000.
41. P. A. Bonatti, C. Duma, D. Olmedilla, and N. Shahmehri. An integration of reputation-based and policy-based trust management. In *Semantic Web Policy Workshop in conjunction with 4th International Semantic Web Conference*, Galway, Ireland, nov 2005.
42. P. A. Bonatti and D. Olmedilla. Driving and monitoring provisional trust negotiation with metapolicies. In *6th IEEE International Workshop on Policies for Distributed Systems and Networks (POLICY 2005)*, pages 14–23, Stockholm, Sweden, jun 2005. IEEE Computer Society.
43. P. A. Bonatti, D. Olmedilla, and J. Peer. Advanced policy queries. Project Deliverable D4, Working Group I2, EU NoE REWERSE, Sept. 2005.
44. P. Bretier and D. Sadek. A rational agent as the kernel of a cooperative spoken dialogue system: implementing a logical theory of interaction. In J. Müller, M. Wooldridge, and N. Jennings, editors, *Intelligent Agents III, proc. of ECAI-96 Workshop on Agent Theories, Architectures, and Languages (ATAL-96)*, volume 1193 of *LNAI*. Springer-Verlag, 1997.
45. D. F. C. Brewer and M. J. Nash. The chinese wall security policy. In *IEEE Symposium on Security and Privacy*, pages 206–214, 1989.
46. L. Brownston, R. Farrell, E. Kant, and N. Martin. *Programming expert systems in OPS5: an introduction to rule-based programming*. Addison-Wesley Series In Artificial Intelligence. Addison-Wesley, 1985.
47. J. Bubenko, D. Brash, and J. Stirna. Ekd - enterprise knowledge development user guide, 1998.
48. M. Castilho, O. Gasquet, and A. Herzig. Modal tableaux for reasoning about actions and plans. In S. Steel, editor, *Proc. ECP'97*, LNAI, pages 119–130, 1997.
49. S. Ceri, G. Gottlob, and L. Tanca. Logic programming and databases. In *Surveys in Computer Science*, Berlin, Heidelberg, New York, 1990. Springer-Verlag.
50. S. Chakravarthy, E. Anwar, L. Maugis, and D.Mishra. Design of Sentinel: An object-oriented DBMS with event-based rules. *Information and Software Technology*, 9:559–568, 1994.
51. J. Chomicki, J. Lobo, and S. Naqvi. A logic programming approach to conflict resolution in policy management. In *Proc. of the Seventh International Conference on Principles of Knowledge Representation and Reasoning (KR 2000)*, pages 121–132. Morgan Kaufmann, 2000.
52. Y.-H. Chu, J. Feigenbaum, B. LaMacchia, P. Resnick, and M. Strauss. REFEREE: Trust management for Web applications. *World Wide Web Journal*, 2:127–139, 1997.
53. A. Ciampolini, E. Lamma, P. Mello, and P. Torroni. Expressing collaboration and competition among abductive logic agents. In K. Satoh and F. Sadri, editors, *CL-2000 Workshop on Computational Logic in Multi-Agent Systems (CLIMA-00)*, 2000.
54. D. Clarke, J.-E. Elien, C. Ellison, M. Fredette, A. Morcos, and R. L. Rivest. Certificate chain discovery in spki/sdsi. *Journal of Computer Security*, 9(4):285–322, 2001.
55. E. Clarke, O. Grumberg, and D. Peled. *Model Checking*. MIT Press, 2000.

56. P. Cohen and H. Levesque. Intention is choice with commitment. *Artificial Intelligence*, 42:213–261, 1990.
57. N. Damianou, N. Dulay, E. Lupu, and M. Sloman. Ponder: A language for specifying security and management policies for distributed systems. Technical report, Imperial College, October 2000.
58. C. Date. *An Introduction to Database Systems*. Addison-Wesley, 1995.
59. U. Dayal, B. Blaustein, A. Buchmann, and S. Chakravarthy. The HiPAC project: Combining active databases and timing constraints. In *ACM SIGMOD*, pages 51–70, 1988.
60. G. De Giacomo and M. Lenzerini. PDL-based framework for reasoning about actions. In *Proc. of AI*IA '95*, volume 992 of *LNAI*, pages 103–114, 1995.
61. G. De Giacomo, Y. Lespérance, and H. J. Levesque. Reasoning about concurrent execution, prioritized interrupts, and exogenous actions in the situation calculus. In *Proceedings of IJCAI'97*, pages 1221–1226, Nagoya, August 1997.
62. G. De Giacomo and H. J. Levesque. An Incremental Interpreter for High-Level Programs with Sensing. In *Proceedings of the AAAI 1998 Fall Symposium on Cognitive Robotics*, Orlando, Florida, USA, October 1998.
63. O. Diaz, N. Paton, and P. Gray. Rule management in object oriented databases: A uniform approach. In *Seventeenth International Conference on Very Large Data Bases*, Barcelona, Spain, 1991.
64. J. Dietrich. The mandarax manual, `http://mandarax.sourceforge.net/docs/mandarax.pdf`, 2003.
65. T. Eiter, N. Leone, C. Mateis, G. Pfeifer, and F. Scarcello. A deductive system for nonmonotonic reasoning. In *Logic Programming and Nonmonotonic Reasoning, 4th International Conference, LPNMR'97*, volume 1265 of *Lecture Notes in Computer Science*, pages 364–375. Springer, 1997.
66. U. Endriss, N. Maudet, F. Sadri, and F. Toni. Logic-based agent communication protocols. In F. Dignum, editor, *Advances in agent communication languages*, volume 2922 of *Lecture Notes in Artificial Intelligence (LNAI)*, pages 91–107. Springer-Verlag, 2004.
67. FIPA. FIPA 2000. Technical report, FIPA (Foundation for Intelligent Physical Agents), November 2000.
68. M. Fisher. A survey of concurrent metatem - the language and its applications. In D. Gabbay and H. Ohlbach, editors, *Proc. of the First International Conference on Temporal Logic, ICTL '94*, volume 827 of *LNAI*, pages 480–505. Springer-Verlag, July 1994.
69. C. L. Forgy. RETE: A fast algorithm for the many pattern/many object pattern matching problem. *Artificial Intelligence*, 19:17–37, 1982.
70. E. Friedman-Hill. *Jess in Action*. Manning Publications Co., 2003.
71. J. Galbraith. *Organization Design*. Addison-Wesley, 1997.
72. R. Gavriloaie, W. Nejdl, D. Olmedilla, K. E. Seamons, and M. Winslett. No registration needed: How to use declarative policies and negotiation to access sensitive resources on the semantic web. In *1st European Semantic Web Symposium (ESWS 2004)*, volume 3053 of *Lecture Notes in Computer Science*, pages 342–356, Heraklion, Crete, Greece, may 2004. Springer.
73. M. Gelfond and V. Lifschitz. The stable model semantics for logic programming. In *Proc. of the 5th ICLP*, pages 1070–1080. MIT Press, 1988.
74. M. Gelfond and V. Lifschitz. Representing action and change by logic programs. *Journal of Logic Programming*, 17:301–321, 1993.
75. G. D. Giacomo, Y. Lespérance, H. J. Levesque, and S. Sardina. On the semantic of deliberation in Indigolog: from theory to implementation. In *Proc. of KR 2002*, pages 603–614. Academic Press, 2002.

76. J. Giarratano and G. Riley. *Expert Systems: Principles and Programming, 3rd Edition*. PWS Publishing Co., Boston, MA, USA, 1998.
77. L. Giordano, A. Martelli, and C. Schwind. Dealing with concurrent actions in modal action logic. In *Proc. ECAI-98*, pages 537–541, 1998.
78. L. Giordano, A. Martelli, and C. Schwind. Verifying communicating agents by model checking in a temporal action logic. In *JELIA'04*, volume 3229 of *LNAI*, pages 57–69, Lisbon, Portugal, 2004. Springer-Verlag.
79. E. Giunchiglia, G. N. Kartha, and V. Lifschitz. Representing actions: indeterminacy and ramifications. *Artificial Intelligence*, 95:409–443, 1997.
80. D. Gollman. Analysing security protocols. In A. E. Abdallah, P. Ryan, , and S. Schneider, editors, *Proc. of FASec 2002*, volume 2629 of *LNCS*, pages 71–80. Springer-Verlag, 2003.
81. L. Gong. *Inside Java 2 Platform Security: Architecture, API Design, and Implementation*. Addison-Wesley, 1999.
82. B. Grosof. Prioritized conflict handling for logic programs. In *International Symposium on Logic Programming (ILPS-97*, 1997.
83. B. Grosof. Representing e-business rules for the semantic web: Situated courteous logic programs in RuleML. In *Proceedings of the Workshop on Information Technologies and Systems (WITS)*, New Orleans, LA, USA, Dec. 2001.
84. B. Grosof, M. Gandhe, and T. Finin. Sweetjess: Translating damlruleml to jess. In *International Workshop on Rule Markup Languages for Business Rules on the Semantic Web, held in conjunction with the First International Semantic Web Conference (ISWC-2002)*, 2002.
85. B. Grosof and T. Poon. SweetDeal: Representing agent contracts with exceptions using XML rules, ontologies, and process descriptions. In *Proceedings of the 12th World Wide Web Conference*, Budapest, Hungary, May 2003.
86. A. Gupta, I. S. Mumick, and V. S. Subrahmanian. Maintaining views incrementally. In *SIGMOD Conference*, pages 157–166, 1993.
87. E. Hanson. Rule condition testing and action execution in ariel, 1992.
88. D. Hay and K. Healy. Defining business rules – what are they really?, 2000.
89. G. Holzmann. *Description and Validation of Computer Protocols*. Prentice Hall, 1992.
90. G. J. Holzmann. The model checker spin. *IEEE Trans. Software Eng.*, 23(5):279–295, 1997.
91. I. Horrocks and P. Patel-Schneider. A proposal for an owl rules language. http://www.cs.man.ac.uk/ horrocks/DAML/Rules/, Oct. 2003.
92. I. Horrocks, P. Patel-Schneider, H. Boley, S. Tabet, B. Grosof, and M. Dean. A semantic web rule language combining OWL and RuleML, version 0.5 of 19 november 2003, `http://www.daml.org/2003/11/swrl/`, 2003.
93. H. Huget, editor. *Communication in Multiagent Systems*, volume 2650 of *LNAI*. Springer, 2003.
94. ILOG web site, http://www.ilog.com, 2004.
95. R. Initiative. The Rule Markup Initiative Web Site, `http://ruleml.org/`, 2004.
96. International Telecommunication Union. *Rec. X.509 - Information Technology - Open Systems Interconnection - The Directory: Authentication Framework*, Aug. 1997.
97. S. Jajodia, P. Samarati, M. Sapino, and V. Subrahmanian. Flexible supporting for multiple access control policies. *ACM Transactions on Database Systems*, 26(2):214–260, 2001.
98. T. Jim. SD3: A Trust Management System With Certified Evaluation. In *IEEE Symposium on Security and Privacy*, Oakland, CA, May 2001.

99. G. Karjoth, M. Schunter, and M. Waidner. The platform for enterprise privacy practices - privacyenabled management of customer data, 2002.
100. G. N. Kartha and V. Lifschitz. Actions with Indirect Effects (Preliminary Report). In *Proc. of the KR'94*, 1994.
101. R. Kowalski and M. Sergot. A Logic-based Calculus of Events. *New Generation of Computing*, 4:67–95, 1986.
102. N. Leone and P. Rullo. Ordered logic programming with sets. *J. Log. Comput.*, 3(6):621–642, 1993.
103. H. J. Levesque, R. Reiter, Y. Lespérance, F. Lin, and R. B. Scherl. GOLOG: A Logic Programming Language for Dynamic Domains. *J. of Logic Programming*, 31:59–83, 1997.
104. N. Li and J. Mitchell. RT: A Role-based Trust-management Framework. In *DARPA Information Survivability Conference and Exposition (DISCEX)*, Washington, D.C., Apr. 2003.
105. N. Li, J. Mitchell, and W. Winsborough. Design of a role-based trust-management framework. In *SP '02: Proceedings of the 2002 IEEE Symposium on Security and Privacy*, page 114. IEEE Computer Society, 2002.
106. N. Li, W. Winsborough, and J. Mitchell. Distributed credential chain discovery in trust management. *Journal of Computer Security*, 11(1):35–86, Feb. 2003.
107. J. Lloyd. *Logic Programming*. Springer Verlag, 1984.
108. J. Lobo, R. Bhatia, and S. Naqvi. A policy description language. In *Proc. of the 16th National Conference on Artificial Intelligence (AAAI'99)*, pages 291–298. AAAI Press, 1999.
109. J. Lobo, G. Mendez, and S. R. Taylor. Adding Knowledge to the Action Description Language $\mathcal{A}$. In *Proc. of AAAI'97/IAAI'97*, pages 454–459, Menlo Park, 1997.
110. J. J. Lu, G. Moerkotte, J. Schü, and V. S. Subrahmanian. Efficient maintenance of materialized mediated views. In *SIGMOD Conference*, pages 340–351, 1995.
111. A. Mamdani and J. Pitt. Communication protocols in multi-agent systems: A development method and reference architecture. In *Issues in Agent Communication*, volume 1916 of *LNCS*, pages 160–177. Springer, 2000.
112. V. Marek and M. Truszczynski. *Nonmonotonic Reasoning*. Springer Verlag, 1993.
113. J. McCarthy and P. Hayes. Some, Philosophical Problems from the Standpoint of Artificial Intelligence. *Machine Intelligence*, 4:463–502, 1963.
114. S. McIlraith and T. Son. Adapting Golog for composition of semantic web services. In *Proceedings of the Eighth International Conference on Knowledge Representation and Reasoning (KR2002)*, pages 482–493, Trento,Italy, 2002.
115. S. McIlraith, T. Son, and H. Zeng. Semantic web services. *IEEE Intelligent Systems. Special Issue on the Semantic Web*, 16(2):46–53, 2001.
116. N. Minsky and D. Rozenshtein. A software development environment for law-governed systems. In *ACM SIGSOFT/SIGPLAN Software Engineering Symposium on Practical Software Development Environments (SDE'88)*. P.B. Henderson (ed.), 1988.
117. N. Minsky and V. Ungureanu. A mechanism for establishing policies for electronic commerce. In *Proc. of the 18th International Conference on Distributed Computing Systems (ICDCS 1998)*, pages 322–331. IEEE Computer Society, 1998.
118. D. Miranker. Treat: A better match algorithm for ai production systems. In *Proceedings of the National Conference on Artificial Intelligence*, American Association for Artificial Intelligence, pages 42–47, 1987.
119. W. Nejdl, D. Olmedilla, and M. Winslett. Peertrust: Automated trust negotiation for peers on the semantic web. In *VLDB Workshop on Secure Data Management (SDM)*,

volume 3178 of *Lecture Notes in Computer Science*, pages 118–132, Toronto, Canada, aug 2004. Springer.

120. I. Niemelä and P. Simons. Smodels - an implementation of the stable model and well-founded semantics for normal lp. In *Logic Programming and Nonmonotonic Reasoning, 4th International Conference, LPNMR'97*, volume 1265 of *Lecture Notes in Computer Science*, pages 421–430. Springer, 1997.
121. D. Nute. *Handbook of Logic for Artificial Intelligence and Logic Programming, Vol. III*, chapter Defeasible logic, pages 353–395. Oxford University Press, 1994.
122. extensible access control markup language (XACML) version 2.0. oasis standard, feb 2005.
123. D. Olmedilla, R. Lara, A. Polleres, and H. Lausen. Trust negotiation for semantic web services. In *1st International Workshop on Semantic Web Services and Web Process Composition (SWSWPC)*, volume 3387 of *Lecture Notes in Computer Science*, pages 81–95, San Diego, CA, USA, jul 2004. Springer.
124. L. Palopoli and C. Zaniolo. Polynomial-time computable stable models. *Ann. Math. Artif. Intell.*, 17(3-4):261–290, 1996.
125. L. R. Pokorny and C. R. Ramakrishnan. Modeling and verification of distributed autonomous agents using logic programming. In *Pre-Proceedings of the Workshop on Declarative Agent Languages and Technologies (DALT'04)*, pages 172–187, 2004.
126. A. Rao and M. Georgeff. Modeling rational agents whithin a bdi-architecture. In *Proceedings of KR'91*, pages 473–484, 1991.
127. R. Reiter. A logic for default reasoning. *Artificial Intelligence*, 13:81–132, 1980.
128. P. Resnick and J. Miller. PICS: Internet access controls without censorship. *Communications of the ACM*, 39(10):87–93, Oct. 1996.
129. G. Riley. Clips - a tool for building expert systems, web site, `http://www.ghg.net/clips/clips.html`, 2004.
130. T. Ryutov and C. Neuman. The Specification and Enforcement of Advanced Security Policies. In *Proc. of the Conference on Policies for Distributed Systems and Networks, POLICY 2002*, Monterey, California, June 5–7 2002.
131. T. Ryutov, L. Zhou, C. Neuman, T. Leithead, and K. E. Seamons. Adaptive trust negotiation and access control. In *SACMAT '05: Proceedings of the tenth ACM symposium on Access control models and technologies*, pages 139–146, New York, NY, USA, 2005. ACM Press.
132. D. Saccà and C. Zaniolo. Stable models and non-determinism in logic programs with negation. In *Proc. of the Ninth ACM SIGACT-SIGMOD-SIGART Symposium on Principles of Database Systems (PODS'90)*, pages 205–217, 1990.
133. R. S. Sandhu, E. J. Coyne, H. L. Feinstein, and C. E. Youman. Role-based access control models. *IEEE Computer*, 29(2):38–47, 1996.
134. T. Schaub and K. Wang. A semantic framework for preference handling in answer set programming. *Logic Programming Theory and Practice*, 3:569–607, 2003.
135. J. Schmidt. Planvolle steuerung gesellschaftlichen handelns. *Verlag für Sozialwissenschaften*, 1983.
136. C. B. Schwind. A logic based framework for action theories. In J. Ginzburg et al., editor, *Language, Logic and Computation*, pages 275–291. CSLI, 1997.
137. K. Seamons, M. Winslett, T. Yu, B. Smith, E. Child, J. Jacobson, H. Mills, and L. Yu. Requirements for policy languages for trust negotiation. In *Proceedings of the 3rd International Workshop on Policies for Distributed Systems and Networks (POLICY'02)*, Monterey, CA, June 2002. IEEE Computer Society.
138. K. Seamons, M. Winslett, T. Yu, B. Smith, E. Child, J. Jacobson, H. Mills, and L. Yu. Requirements for policy languages for trust negotiation, 2002.

139. M. P. Singh. A social semantics for agent communication languages. In *Proc. of IJCAI-98 Workshop on Agent Communication Languages*, Berlin, 2000. Springer.
140. S. Staab, B. K. Bhargava, L. Lilien, A. Rosenthal, M. Winslett, M. Sloman, T. S. Dillon, E. Chang, F. K. Hussain, W. Nejdl, D. Olmedilla, and V. Kashyap. The pudding of trust. *IEEE Intelligent Systems*, 19(5):74–88, 2004.
141. M. Stonebraker, E. Hanson, and C. Hong. The design of the postgres rule system. In *3rd International IEEE Conference on Data Science*, 1987.
142. K. Taveter and G. Wagner. Agent-oriented enterprise modeling based on business rules. In *ER '01: Proceedings of the 20th International Conference on Conceptual Modeling*, pages 527–540. Springer-Verlag, 2001.
143. D. Toman, J. Chomicki, and D. S. Rogers. Datalog with integer periodicity constraints. In *SLP*, pages 189–203, 1994.
144. A. Uszok, J. M. Bradshaw, and R. Jeffers. Kaos: A policy and domain services framework for grid computing and semantic web services. In *Trust Management, Second International Conference, iTrust 2004, Oxford, UK, March 29 - April 1, 2004, Proceedings*, volume 2995 of *Lecture Notes in Computer Science*, pages 16–26. Springer, 2004.
145. F. van Assche. Information systems developement: a rule-based approach. *Knowledge-based Systems*, 4:227–234, 1988.
146. M. van Emden and R. A. Kowalski. The semantics of predicate logic as a programming language. *Journal of the ACM*, 23(4), 1976.
147. G. Wagner. How to design a general rule markup language? In *XML Technologien für das Semantic Web - XSW 2002, Proceedings zum Workshop*, pages 19–37. GI, 2002.
148. G. Wagner, S. Tabet, and H. Boley. MOF-RuleML: The abstract syntax of RuleML as a MOF model. In *Integrate 2003*, 2003.
149. C. Walton. Model checking agent dialogues. In *Proceedings of the Workshop on Declarative Agent Languages and Technologies (DALT'04)*, volume 3476 of *LNAI*. Springer-Verlag, 2005.
150. J. Widom and S. Ceri. *Active Database Systems: triggers and rules for advanced database processing*. Morgan Kaufmann Publishers Inc., 1996.
151. T. Y. C. Woo and S. S. Lam. Authorizations in distributed systems: A new approach. *Journal of Computer Security*, 2(2-3):107–136, 1993.
152. M. Wooldridge and N. R. Jennings. Agent Theories, Architectures, and Languages: A survey. In *Proc. of the ECAI-94 Workshop on Agent Theories*, volume 890 of *LNAI*, pages 1–39. Springer-Verlag, 1995.
153. C. Zhang, M. Winslett, and P. A. Bonatti. Peeraccess: A logic for distributed authorization. In *12th ACM Conference on Computer and Communication Security (CCS 2005)*, Alexandria, VA, USA, nov 2005. ACM Press.
154. P. Zimmerman. *PGP User's Guide*. MIT Press, 1994.

Automated Trust Negotiation in Open Systems

Adam J. Lee[1], Kent E. Seamons[2], Marianne Winslett[1], and Ting Yu[3]

[1] University of Illinois at Urbana-Champaign
{adamlee, winslett}@csc.ucsu.edu
[2] Brigham Young University
seamons@cs.byu.edu
[3] North Carolina State University
yu@csc.ncsu.edu

1 Introduction

To *trust* an entity means to have strong confidence in the integrity and ability of that entity to perform according to one's expections [24]. Trust relationships between entities are particularly important when one entity's action or service may have a great impact on the interests of others. In this chapter, we study how to establish such trust relationships between entities. In particular, we are interested in the establishment of trust relationships between service providers and service requesters in open distributed computing environments.

In traditional distributed environments, service providers and requesters are usually known to each other. Often shared information in the environment tells which parties can provide what kind of services and which parties are entitled to make use of those services. Thus, trust between parties is a straightforward matter. In an open computing environment, however, the goal is to allow (qualified) strangers to access the resources available in the environment. Since these outsiders are unknown to the service providers in the open environment and vice versa, there is no easy way to tell which outsiders are qualified to gain access to services or which service providers are trustworthy. Open computing has imposed new requirements on trust establishment and access control.

For example, suppose a parent wants to register online her child for the local public kindergarten. In order to be qualified for the registration, the following conditions must be satisfied. First, the requester needs to prove that the child will be age 5 or greater on September 1, 2007. This can be done by showing the child's birth certificate. Second, the requester has to be a parent or a legal guardian of the child. This can be proved by showing the child's birth certificate or a valid court order. Third, the requester should be living in the school district of the kindergarten. This can be proven by showing the requester's driver's license. Finally, the child should have had all the required immunizations. This can be proven by showing valid clinic records.

Currently on the Internet, the prevailing approach is still the traditional identity-based access control method, where clients are required to pre-register with a server, in order to obtain a local login, capability, or identity certificate before requesting that service. There are several disadvantages of this approach. First, such practices are usually offered in a "take-it-or-leave-it" fashion, i.e., the clients either *unconditionally* disclose their information to the server in the pre-registration phase, or do not get the service at all. There is little chance for the clients to apply their own access control policies for their information, and decide accordingly whether the server is trustworthy enough so that sensitive information can be disclosed.

Second, when the clients fill out the online registration form, it is very hard for the server to verify whether the provided information is valid. More generally, the problem of a large amount of dirty data in commercial databases is becoming a major factor that lowers the effectiveness of commercial information analysis.

Third, often, much of the information required in online registration forms does not seem directly related to the service that clients request to access. However, since the clients have to unconditionally provide the information, there is no way that they can discuss their misgivings with the server.

Property-based *digital credentials* [4] (or simply *credentials*) make it feasible to manage trust establishment efficiently and bi-directionally on the Internet. Digital credentials are the on-line counterparts of paper credentials that people use in their daily life, such as drivers licenses. By showing appropriate credentials to each other, a service requester and provider can both prove their qualifications. In detail, a credential is a digitally signed assertion by the *credential issuer* about the properties of one or more entities [4, 35]. Using modern encryption technology, the issuer signs a credential, which describes one or more attributes of the entities, using its own private key. The public key of the issuer can be used to verify that the credential was actually issued by the issuer. The signed credential can also include the public keys of the entities referred to in the credential. This allows an entity to use her private key to authenticate herself as one of the entities referred to in the credential [27]. So digitally signed credentials can be verifiable and unforgeable. In practice, digital credentials can be implemented as X.509 certificates or signed XML statements.

When credentials do not bear sensitive information, the trust establishment procedure is very simple. A requester can simply present her credentials to prove her qualification to get a service. However, in many situations, especially in the context of e-business, credentials themselves carry some sensitive information.

For example, suppose that a landscape designer wishes to order plants from Champaign Prairie Nursery (CPN). She fills out an order form on the web, checking an order form box to indicate that she wishes to be exempt from sales tax. Upon receipt of the order, CPN will want to see a valid credit card or her account credential issued by CPN, and a current reseller's license. The designer has no account with CPN, but she does have a digital credit card. She is willing to show her reseller's license to anyone, but she will only show her credit card to members of the Better Business Bureau.

To deal with such scenarios, a more complex procedure needs to be adopted to establish trust through negotiation. In our approach to automated trust establishment, trust is established gradually by disclosing credentials and requests for credentials, an iterative process known as *trust negotiation*. It differs from traditional identity-based access control systems mainly in the following aspects.

First, trust between two strangers is established based on parties' properties, which are proven through disclosure of digital credentials. A digital credential is a verifiable, unforgeable, digitally signed assertion by a credential issuer about the properties of the parties mentioned in the credential. A credential often contains a public key of one or more of the parties it mentions, so that those parties can prove that the credential describes them.

Second, every party can define access control policies to control outsiders' access to their sensitive resources. These resources can include services accessible over the Internet, roles in role-based access control systems, credentials, policies, and capabilities in capability-based systems.

Third, in the approaches to trust negotiation developed so far, two parties establish trust directly without involving trusted third parties, other than credential issuers. Since both parties have access control policies, trust negotiation can employ a peer-to-peer architecture, where a client and server are treated equally. Instead of a one-shot authorization and authentication, trust is established incrementally through a sequence of bilateral credential disclosures. Less sensitive credentials are disclosed first. Later on, when a certain level of trust has been established, more sensitive credentials can be disclosed.

The practical deployment of automated trust negotiation raises many new issues, including the guarantee of negotiation success, policy languages and specification, privacy protection, resilience and usability. In this chapter, we focus our discussion on the following problems:

Negotiation Strategies Different parties might have different requirements for how much computation they are willing to do, how freely they disclose resources, how interested they are in extracting information from the other party during negotiation, and other strategic decisions. For such decisions, each party relies on its *trust negotiation strategy*, an algorithm that determines what information to disclose to others and when to do so. Because the Internet is a free-wheeling place with decentralized control, all parties should be free to choose whatever strategies meet their needs. On the other hand, it is desirable for two parties always to be able to establish trust whenever it is allowed by their access control policies. These two requirements conflict with each other. How to nicely balance the requirements from the two conflicting aspects is a challenging problem.

Resource Protection In contrast to traditional trust management systems, trust negotiation typically involves multiple rounds of credentials and policy disclosures. Therefore, information may flow between two parties in a variety of forms. The basic model of trust negotiation uses access control policies to govern the disclosure of sensitive credentials. This model implicitly makes the assumption that sensitive information can flow to others only when credentials are disclosed. Such an assumption does not always hold in practice. It has been shown that, without proper protection, policy disclosure itself might reveal sensitive information unintentionally.

System Design Trust negotiation may be deployed in a variety of platforms, from powerful servers to resource contrained thin clients such as cell phones and smart cards. Meanwhile, trust negotiations often involve many expensive operations, including policy evaluation and credential chain verification. Without careful design of trust negotiation components and their interactions, it may easily become performance bottleneck. Further, trust negotiation systems need to be designed reusable so that it can be easily tailored to support a variety of services.

The rest of the chapter is organized as follows. In section 2 we present in detail the key concepts and components of trust negotiation. Major research issues in trust negotiation will also be discussed in this section. In section 3, we give a formal definition of negotiation strategies and propose the concept of strategy families. We further discuss how to guarantee that two parties can always establish trust wheneve possible, even when they are using different strategies. In section 4, we discuss the problem of sensitive policies and a unified scheme for resource protection during trust negotiation. Section 5 presents a system design for trust negotiation. We conclude this chapter in section 6.

2 Basic Concepts of Automated Trust Negotiation

Figure 1 shows the general architecture for trust negotiation. Each participant in the negotiation adopts a security agent that interacts with the other party's security agent and manages the negotiation. The security agent mediates access to local protected *resources*, i.e., services, policies, and credentials — the three kinds of resources that may be opened up to access by strangers in our work. We say a credential or access control policy is *disclosed* if it has been sent to the other party in the negotiation, and that a service is disclosed if the other party is given access to it. Disclosure of each resource is governed by an access control policy that specifies what credentials the other party must possess if the resource is to be disclosed.

As shown by previous examples, in trust negotiation, trust between two parties is often established through bilateral, incrementail credential and policy disclosures. Different parties might have different requirements for how much computation they are willing to do, how freely they disclose resources, how interested they are in extracting information from the other party in the negotiation, and other such strategic decisions. For such decisions, each party relies on its trust negotiation *strategies*. During a trust negotiation, once enough trust has been established that a particular credential can be disclosed to the other party, a local strategy determines whether the credential is relevant to the current stage of the negotiation and whether it should be sent to the other party. In other words, a negotiation strategy controls the exact content of the messages that a party sends to others, i.e., which credentials to disclose, when to disclose them, and when to terminate a negotiation.

Another important concept in the architecture of trust negotiation is *trust negotiation protocols*. A trust negotiation protocol defines the ordering of messages and

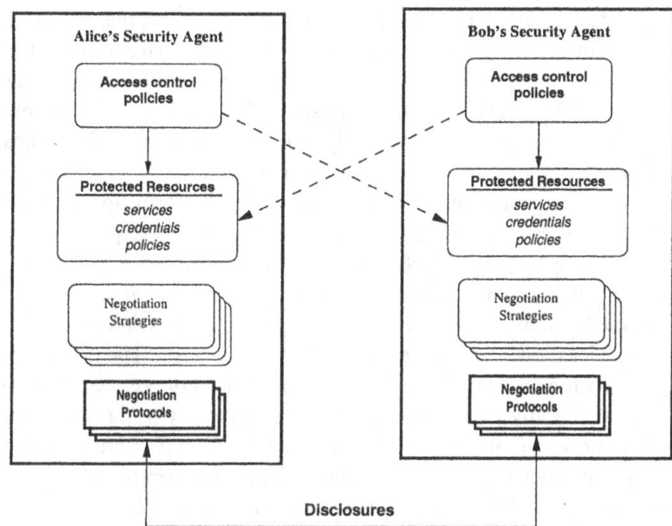

Fig. 1. An architecture for automated trust negotiation.

the type of information that messages will contain. Before a trust negotiation starts, two parties should agree on the negotiation protocol that will be used. Otherwise, they will not be able to understand each other. Note the difference between a trust negotiation protocol and a communication protocol. A trust negotiation protocol is independent of the choice of communication protocol, such as HTTP, SSL/TLS , IP, SOAP [8], etc. However, a strategy written for one negotiation protocol may not work with another negotiation protocol, as will become clear when we discuss strategies and negotiation protocols in later sections.

The architecture in figure 1 supports multiple protocols for establishing trust, and assumes there will be a variety of negotiation strategies that must be supported. Note that we adopt a peer-to-peer architecture for trust negotiation, i.e., we assume there is no third party which knows both parties' access control policies. We will come back to this assumption later in this section. Although all our trust negotiation algorithms are peer-to-peer, for simplicity we will use the term *server* to refer to owner of the service, and client to refer to the entity that tried to access the service.

2.1 Access Control Policies

We assume that the information contained in access control policies and credentials can be expressed as finite sets of statements in a language with a formal semantics, so that two strategies can agree on the interpretation of a credential or policy. For purely practical reasons, we require that the language be *monotonic*, i.e., if a set of statements X satisfies policy P, then any superset of X will also satisfy P; that way, once a negotiation strategy has determined that the credentials disclosed by a participant satisfy the policy of a resource, the strategy knows that the same policy will be satisfied for the rest of the negotiation, and does not have to be rechecked.

For simplicity, we will treat resources as propositional symbols — black boxes that have an externally visible key (the propositional symbol) but no other externally visible structure. Each resource has exactly one access control policy, whose body is a Boolean expression involving only credentials $C_1, \ldots, C_k$ that the other party may possess, Boolean constants $true$ and $false$, the Boolean operators $\wedge$ and $\vee$, and parentheses as needed. C_i is *satisfied* if and only if the other party has disclosed credential C_i. Resource C is *unlocked* if its access control policy is satisfied by the set of credentials disclosed by the other party. A resource is *unprotected* if its policy is always satisfied. An intuitive observation is that two parties cannot establish trust unless there is at least one unprotected resource at either party. The *denial policy* has the body $false$, which means that either the party does not possess C, or else will not disclose C under any circumstances. A party implicitly has a denial policy for each credential it does not possess. If the disclosure of a set S of credentials satisfies resource R's policy, then we say S is a *solution* for R. Further, if none of S's proper subsets is a solution for R, we say S is a *minimal solution* for R. The *size* of a policy is the number of symbol occurrences in it.

Given a resource R, we say a resource C is *syntactically relevant* to R if and only if (1) C appears in R's policy; or (2) C appears in the policy of a resource C' which is syntactically relevant to R. If C appears in one of R's minimal solutions, then we say C is *semantically* relevant to R.

Given sequence $G = (C_1, \ldots, C_n)$ of disclosures of resources, if each C_i is unlocked at the time it is disclosed, $1 \leq i \leq n$, then we say G is a *safe disclosure sequence*. The goal of trust negotiation is to find a safe disclosure sequence $G = (C_1, \ldots, C_n = R)$, where R is the resource to which access was originally requested. When this happens, we say that trust negotiation succeeds. If $C_i = C_j$ and $1 \leq i < j \leq n$, then we say G is *redundant*. Since the language used to represent policies and credentials is monotonic, we can remove the later duplicates from a redundant safe disclosure sequence and the resulting sequence is still safe. Figure 2 shows a safe disclosure sequence an abstract example.

3 Interoperable Strategies

Early work on trust negotiation assumed that two negotiation participants were willing to use the same strategy to establish trust [36]. However, considering the autonomous nature of entities in open systems, such an assumption is unlikely to hold in practice. Different entities will have different requirements when choosing their trust negotiation strategies. For example, service providers (e.g., certificate authorities and e-business and e-medical servers) tend to possess many sensitive resources along with adequate computation power. Therefore, cautious strategies, which carefully analyze ongoing negotiation and only disclose relevant information to others, may be appropriate. On the other hand, thin clients like smart cards have limited

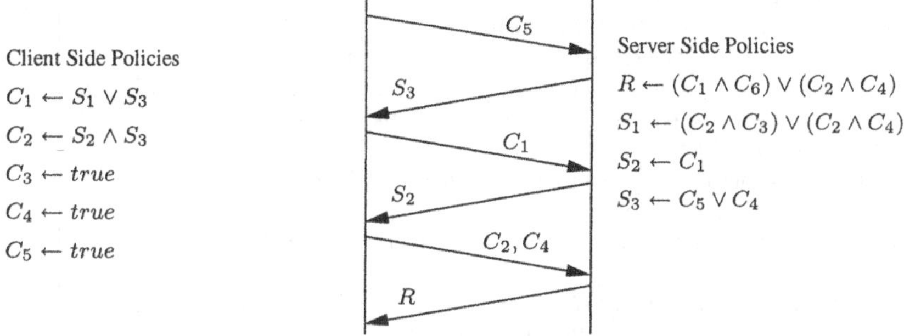

Client Side Policies
$C_1 \leftarrow S_1 \vee S_3$
$C_2 \leftarrow S_2 \wedge S_3$
$C_3 \leftarrow true$
$C_4 \leftarrow true$
$C_5 \leftarrow true$
C_5
S_3
C_1
S_2
C_2, C_4
R
Server Side Policies
$R \leftarrow (C_1 \wedge C_6) \vee (C_2 \wedge C_4)$
$S_1 \leftarrow (C_2 \wedge C_3) \vee (C_2 \wedge C_4)$
$S_2 \leftarrow C_1$
$S_3 \leftarrow C_5 \vee C_4$

Fig. 2. An example of access policies and a safe disclosure sequence that establishes trust between the server and the client.

computation ability. They may choose simpler strategies which may disclose irrelevant credentials. Therefore, interoperation between different strategies with a variety of properties should be supported in automated trust negotiation.

As defined in section 2, a trust negotiation protocol defines the ordering of messages and the type of information messages will contain, while a trust negotiation strategy controls the exact content of the messages, i.e., which credentials to disclose, when to disclose them, and when to terminate a negotiation. Early works did not define negotiation protocols explicitly since they are implied by the same strategies used by two negotiation participants. This is one reason why no two different strategies from the early literature on automated trust negotiation can interoperate — their underlying protocols are totally different.

We remedy this problem by defining a simple protocol for TrustBuilder, shown in figure 3. Formally, a *message* in TrustBuilder Protocol is a set $\{R_1, \ldots, R_k\}$ where each R_i is a disclosure of a local credential, a local policy, or a local service. When a message is the empty set $\emptyset$, we also call it a *failure message*. Further, to guarantee the safety and timely termination of trust negotiation no matter what policies and credentials the parties possess, the TrustBuilder Protocol requires the negotiation strategies used with it to enforce the following three conditions throughout negotiations:

1. Every disclosure must be safe.
2. If a message contains a denial policy disclosure $C \leftarrow false$, then C must appear in a previously disclosed policy. This helps to focus the negotiation and helps prevent infinite negotiations.
3. A credential or policy can be disclosed at most once. Again, this helps focus the negotiation.

We assume that policies are unprotected.

Before the negotiation starts, Alice sends the original resource access request message to Bob, indicating her desire to access Bob's service R. This request triggers the negotiation, and Bob invokes his local security agent with the call security_agent(L, R), where L is the set of Bob's credentials and policies. Meanwhile,

```
security_agent(L,R)
Input: L is the set of local resources.
       R is the resource to which access was originally requested.
Output: the result of the negotiation, which can either be FAIL or SUCCEED.
Let M be an empty disclosure message sequence.
r ← NOT_TERMINATED.
If (R is a local resource) then //Negotiation is initiated by the other party.
    r ←send_response(M,L,R).
    If (r=SUCCEED or r=FAIL) //Negotiation has terminated.
        then return r.
While (r=NOT_TERMINATED)
    Receive message m from the other party.
    Add m to the end of M.
    r ← check_for_termination(m,R).
    If (r=SUCCEED or r=FAIL)
        the return r.
    r ← send_response(M,L,R).
    If (r=SUCCEED or r=FAIL)
        then return r.
End of security_Agent.

send_response(M,L,R)
S_m ← local_strategy(M,L,R).
//S_m contains the candidate messages that the local strategy suggests.
Choose any single message m' from S_m.
Send m' to the remote party.
Add m' to the end of M.
r ← check_for_termination(m',R).
Return r.
End of send_response.

check_for_termination(m, R)
If (m = ∅)
    the return FAIL. //Negotiation has failed.
If (R ∈ m)
    the return SUCCEED. //Negotiation has succeeded.
Return NOT_TERMINATED.
End of check_for_termination.
```

Fig. 3. Pseudocode for TrustBuilder Protocol

Alice also invokes her security agent. Then Alice and Bob exchange messages until either the service R is disclosed by Bob or one party sends a failure message. The whole negotiation process is shown in figure 3.

In the remainder of this section, unless otherwise noted, we discuss only strategies that can be called from TrustBuilder Protocol and satisfy the three conditions above. A formal definition of a negotiation strategy is given below. Intuitively, based on the sequence of disclosures made so far, plus the set of all local resources, a negotiation strategy will suggest the next set of disclosures to send to the other party.

Definition 1. *A* strategy *is a function f which takes three parameters $\mathcal{M}$, L and R, where R is a resource name, $\mathcal{M} = (m_1, \ldots, m_k)$ is a sequence of disclosure messages such that $m_i \neq \emptyset$ and $R \notin m_i$ for $1 \leq i \leq k$, and L is a set of resources. The output of f is a set S_m of disclosure messages. Further, every disclosure in a message in S_m must occur in L, as must be all the disclosures in m_{k-2i}, for $1 \leq k - 2i < k$. The remaining disclosures in $\mathcal{M}$ cannot occur in L.*

Note that a strategy returns a *set* of possible disclosure messages, rather than a single message. Practical negotiation strategies will suggest a single next message, but the ability to suggest several possible next messages will be very convenient in our formal analysis of strategy properties, so we include it both in the formal definition of a negotiation strategy and also in the TrustBuilder Protocol pseudocode in figure 3.

Definition 2. *Strategies s_1 and s_2 are* compatible *if whenever there exists a safe disclosure sequence for a party Alice to obtain access to a resource owned by a party Bob, the trust negotiation will succeed when Alice uses s_1 and Bob uses s_2. If $s_1 = s_2$, then we say that f_A is* self-compatible.

Definition 3. *A* strategy family *is a set $\mathcal{F}$ of mutually compatible strategies, i.e., $\forall s_1 \in \mathcal{F}, s_2 \in \mathcal{F}$, s_1 and s_2 are compatible. We say a set $\mathcal{F}$ of strategies is* closed *if given a strategy s, if s is compatible with every strategy in $\mathcal{F}$, then $s \in \mathcal{F}$.*

One obvious advantage of strategy families is that a security agent (SA) can choose strategies based on its needs without worrying about interoperability, as long as it negotiates with other SAs that use strategies from the same family. As another advantage, under certain conditions, an SA does not need to stick to a fixed strategy during the entire negotiation process. It can adopt different strategies from the family in different phases of the negotiation. For example, during the early phase, since the trust between two parties is very limited, an SA may adopt a cautious strategy for disclosing credentials. When a certain level of trust has been established, in order to accelerate the negotiation, the SA may adopt a less cautious strategy. However, without the closure property, a family may not be large enough for practical use. As an extreme example, given any self-compatible strategy s, $\{s\}$ is a strategy family. The closure property guarantees the maximality of a strategy family.

3.1 Characterizing Safe Disclosure Sequences

In this section, we define the concepts that we use to describe the progress of a negotiation and to characterize the behavior of different strategies. More precisely, we define the trees and tree operations that give meaning to strategies' actions. Negotiation strategies do not need to materialize these trees; rather, the trees provide the formal basis for what a strategy does. This section is the heart of our discussion

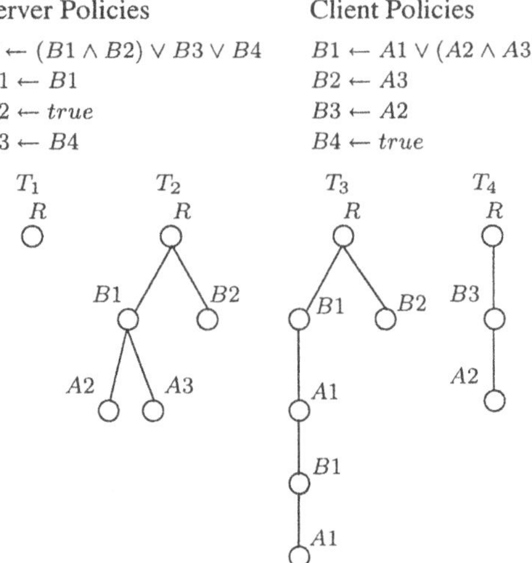

Fig. 4. Example disclosure trees for a set of policies

on interoperable strategies, and readers who survive its onslaught of definitions and examples will understand why some strategies interoperate and others do not. This section also shows how to generate a set of strategies based on the set's member who is the most reluctant to disclose information. The concepts introduced in this section will be used to define a useful strategy family.

In the remainder of this section, we use R to represent the resource to which access was originally requested, unless otherwise noted.

Definition 4. *A* disclosure tree *for R is a finite tree satisfying the following conditions:*

1. *The root is labeled with R.*
2. *Except for the root, each node is labeled with a credential. When the context is clear, we refer to a node by its label. If two nodes are labeled with the same credential, we will explicitly distinguish them when we refer to them.*
3. *The labels of the children of a node C form a minimal solution for C.*

When all the leaves of a disclosure tree T are unprotected credentials, we say T is a full *disclosure tree. Given a disclosure tree T, if there is a credential appearing twice in the path from a leaf node to the root, then we call T a* redundant *disclosure tree.*

Figure 4 shows example disclosure trees. Note that T_3 is redundant and T_4 is a full disclosure tree. We use abstract examples because they are much more concise and can be easily manipulated to show all the different cases that the theory must cover.

The following theorems state the relationship between disclosure trees and safe disclosure sequences that lead to the granting of access to resource R.

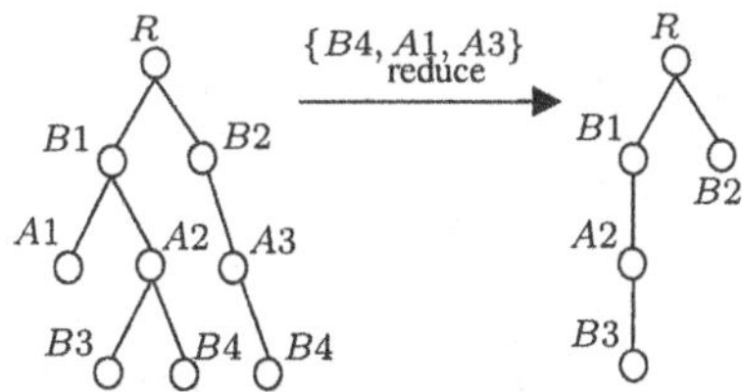

Fig. 5. Example of a disclosure tree reduction.

Theorem 1. *Given a non-redundant safe disclosure sequence $\mathcal{Q} = (C_1, \ldots, C_n = R)$, there is a full non-redundant disclosure tree T such that the following both hold:*

1. *The nodes of T are a subset of $\{C_1, \ldots, C_n\}$.*
2. *For all credential pairs (C_1', C_2') such that C_1' is an ancestor of C_2' in T, C_2' is disclosed before C_1' in $\mathcal{Q}$.*

Theorem 2. *Given a full disclosure tree for R, there is a non-redundant safe disclosure sequence ending with the disclosure of R.*

By theorems 1 and 2, we get the following corollary immediately.

Corollary 1. *There is a safe disclosure sequence ending with the disclosure of R if and only if there is a full non-redundant disclosure tree.*

Without loss of generality, from now on, we consider only non-redundant disclosure sequences.

Since there is a natural mapping between safe disclosure sequences and disclosure trees, during the negotiation, theoretically one could determine whether a potential credential or policy disclosure is helpful by examining all the disclosure trees for R. At the beginning of a negotiation, before disclosures begin, the only relevant disclosure tree for the client contains a single node R. As the negotiation proceeds, other trees may become relevant. The following definitions help us describe the set of relevant trees.

Definition 5. *Given a disclosure tree T and a set $\mathcal{C}$ of credentials, the* reduction *of T by $\mathcal{C}$, $reduce(T, \mathcal{C})$, is the disclosure tree T' which is obtained by removing all the subtrees rooted at a node labeled with resource $C \in \mathcal{C}$. Given a set $\mathcal{T}$ of disclosure trees, $reduce(\mathcal{T}, \mathcal{C}) = \{reduce(T, \mathcal{C}) \mid T \in \mathcal{T}\}$.*

If $\mathcal{C}$ is the set of credential disclosures made so far, then reducing T by $\mathcal{C}$ prunes out the part of the negotiation that has already succeeded. Intuitively, if a credential C has been disclosed, then we already have a safe disclosure sequence for C. We do not need to disclose additional credentials or policies in order to get a full disclosure tree rooted at C. Tree reduction can be viewed as a reformulation of partial evaluation [5] in the context of disclosure trees. An example of a disclosure tree reduction is shown in figure 3.1.

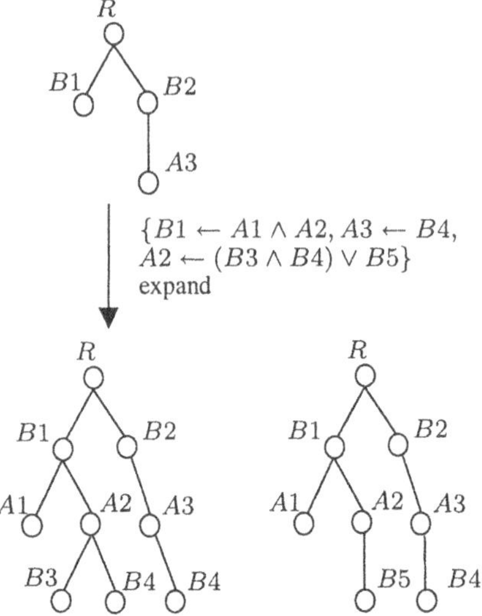

Fig. 6. Example of a disclosure tree expansion.

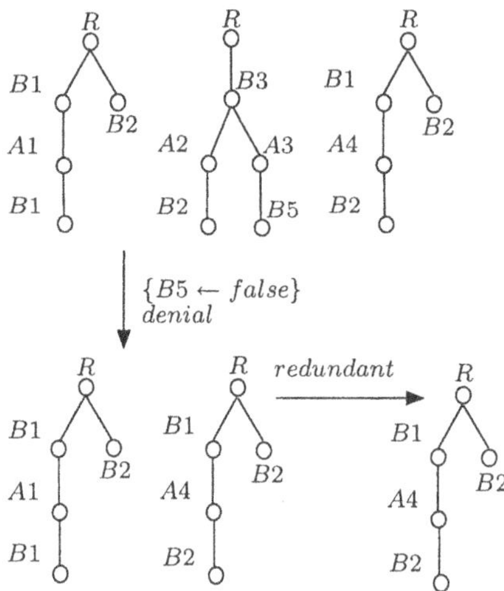

Fig. 7. Example of denial pruning and redundancy pruning.

Definition 6. *Given a disclosure tree T and a policy set $\mathcal{P}$ containing no denial policies, the* expansion *of T by $\mathcal{P}$, $expand(T, \mathcal{P})$, is the set of all disclosure trees T_i such that*

1. *T_i can be reduced to T, i.e., there exists a set $\mathcal{C}$ of credentials such that $reduce(T_i, \mathcal{C}) = T$.*

$$\begin{aligned} \mathcal{S} = \{&A2, B4,\\ &R \leftarrow (B1 \wedge B2) \vee (B3 \wedge B4) \vee B5,\\ &B1 \leftarrow A1 \vee (A2 \wedge A3),\\ &B3 \leftarrow A2, B5 \leftarrow A6 \wedge A7,\\ &A1 \leftarrow B1, A3 \leftarrow B4, A6 \leftarrow false\} \end{aligned}$$

$trees(\mathcal{S})$ contains the following derivation trees:

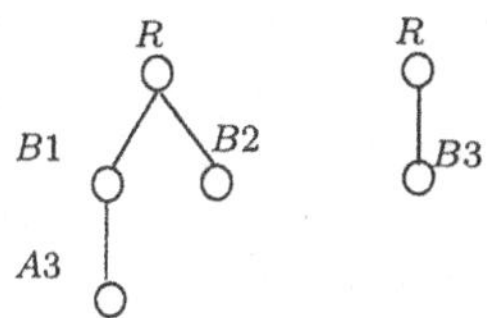

Fig. 8. Example of a disclosure tree evolution.

2. *For each edge (C_1, C_2) in T_i, if (C_1, C_2) is not an edge of T, then C_1's policy is in $\mathcal{P}$.*
3. *For each leaf node C of T_i, either $\mathcal{P}$ does not contain C's policy, or T_i is redundant.*

Given a set of disclosure trees $\mathcal{T}$, $expand(\mathcal{T}, \mathcal{P}) = \bigcup_{T \in \mathcal{T}} expand(T, \mathcal{P})$.

A disclosure tree can expand when a party receives new policy disclosures. An example of a disclosure tree expansion is shown in figure 3.1.

Definition 7. *Given a set $\mathcal{T}$ of disclosure trees and a set $\mathcal{P}$ of denial policies, the* denial pruning *of $\mathcal{T}$ by $\mathcal{P}$, denoted $deny(\mathcal{T}, \mathcal{P})$, is the set*

$$\{T \mid T \in \mathcal{T} \text{ and } T \textit{ contains no resource whose policy is in } \mathcal{P}\}.$$

Since a full disclosure tree contains only credentials that the two parties possess, if a disclosure tree node is labeled with a credential with a denial policy, that tree cannot evolve into a full disclosure tree, and is no longer relevant.

Definition 8. *Given a set $\mathcal{T}$ of disclosure trees, the* redundancy pruning *of $\mathcal{T}$, denoted $redundant(\mathcal{T})$, is the set*

$$\{T \mid T \in \mathcal{T} \text{ and } T \textit{ is not a redundant disclosure tree}\}.$$

The rationale for redundancy pruning will be shown after we introduce more operations on disclosure trees. Examples of denial and redundancy pruning are shown in figure 3.1.

Definition 9. *Given a disclosure tree T and a set $\mathcal{D}$ of denial policies, a set $\mathcal{P}$ of non-denial policies, and a set $\mathcal{C}$ of credentials, let $\mathcal{S} = \mathcal{D} \cup \mathcal{P} \cup \mathcal{C}$. The* evolution *of T by $\mathcal{S}$, denoted $evolve(T, \mathcal{S})$, is*

$$redundant(deny(reduce(expand(T, \mathcal{P}), \mathcal{C}), \mathcal{D}).$$

Given a set $\mathcal{T}$ *of disclosure trees,* $evolve(\mathcal{T}, \mathcal{S}) = \bigcup_{T \in \mathcal{T}} evolve(T, \mathcal{S})$. *As a special case, when* T *is the disclosure tree containing only a root node* R, *then we say* $evolve(T, \mathcal{S})$ *is the* trees *of* $\mathcal{S}$, *denoted* $trees(\mathcal{S})$.

During the negotiation, let $\mathcal{S}$ be the set of credentials and policies disclosed so far and L be the local policies of a negotiation party. Then $trees(S \cup L)$ contains all the relevant disclosure trees which can be seen by this party. An example set of trees is shown in figure 3.1.

Sometimes even though a tree may evolve into a full tree later in the negotiation, it is nonetheless redundant and can be removed by redundancy pruning, whose correctness is guaranteed by the following theorem.

Theorem 3. *Let* T *be a full but redundant disclosure tree. Then there is a full disclosure tree* T' *that is not redundant.*

Suppose $\mathcal{S}$ is the set of currently disclosed credentials and policies. By theorem 3, if a redundant tree may evolve into a full tree, then the corresponding non-redundant tree is already included in $trees(\mathcal{S})$. So the redundant trees are not relevant for the remainder of the negotiation.

In order to make a negotiation successful whenever the policies of the two negotiation parties allow, the negotiation strategy should make sure no possible full disclosure trees have been overlooked. A disclosure tree also tells a party what may contribute to the success of a negotiation. As an example, suppose Bob requests to access Alice's resource R. $\mathcal{S}$, the set of disclosures so far, and $trees(\mathcal{S})$ are shown in figure 9. Suppose now it is Alice's turn to send a message to Bob. From the disclosure tree, it is clear to an outside observer that credentials $A1$ and $A2$ must be disclosed if the negotiation is to succeed. So Alice's negotiation strategy can now disclose $A1$'s and/or $A2$'s policy. This example shows that in order to let Alice know what might be the next appropriate message, a disclosure tree should have at least one leaf node that is a credential that Bob wants Alice to disclose. We have the following definition:

Definition 10. *Disclosure tree* T*'s* evolvable leaves *for party* A, *denoted as* $evolvable(T, A)$, *are the set of leaf nodes* C *of* T *such that either* $C = R$ *and* A *is the server, or* C *appears in a policy that party* B *disclosed to* A. *If* $evolvable(T, A) \neq \emptyset$, *we say* T *is* evolvable *for* A.

The disclosure tree in figure 9 is evolvable for both Alice and Bob. If there is no evolvable tree, then a cautious party will choose to end the negotiation even if the policies of the two parties allow success. Therefore, to ensure that negotiations succeed whenever possible, a strategy must ensure that the other party will have an evolvable tree when the other party needs to make its next disclosure. The only exception is when the strategy knows that no disclosure tree can evolve into a full tree. If a negotiation reaches a point where every leaf node of some disclosure tree is unlocked, then the tree is a full tree and corresponds to a safe disclosure sequence.

If $\mathcal{F}$ is a strategy family, then intuitively, every strategy in $\mathcal{F}$ always discloses enough information to keep the negotiation moving toward success, if success is possible. If $\mathcal{F}$ is also closed, then $\mathcal{F}$ must also contain those strategies that disclose only

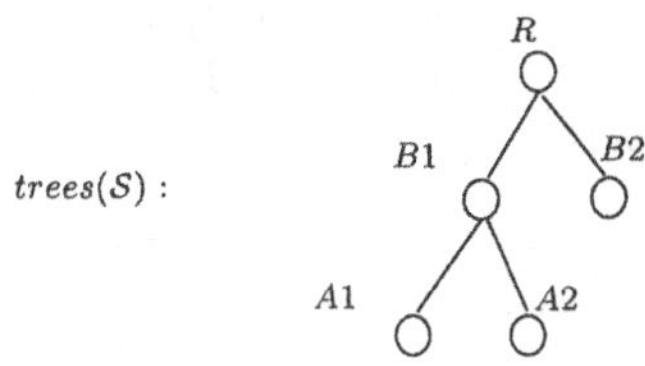

Fig. 9. $trees(\mathcal{S})$

the minimal amount of information needed to continue negotiations. Therefore it is helpful to formally define a relationship between strategies based on the information they disclose.

Definition 11. *Given two negotiation strategies s_1 and s_2, if for all possible inputs $\mathcal{M}$, L, and R to s_1 and s_2, we have*

$$\forall m \in s_2(\mathcal{M}, L, R)\ \exists m' \in s_1(\mathcal{M}, L, R) \text{ such that } m' \subseteq m$$

then we say s_1 is at least as cautious as *f_2, denoted as $s_1 \preceq s_2$ or $s_2 \succeq s_1$.*

Caution defines a partial order between strategies. Intuitively, if $s_2 \succeq s_1$ then s_2 always discloses at least as much information as s_1 does.

Definition 12. *Given a strategy f, the set of strategies* generated *by f, is the set $\mathcal{F} = \{s' | s' \succeq s\}$. f is called the* generator *of $\mathcal{F}$.*

3.2 The Disclosure Tree Strategy Family

In this section, we present the *disclosure tree strategy* (DTS), and prove that DTS generates a closed family. DTS can be thought of as a strategy that is willing to reason very carefully about the trees presented in the previous section, in order to avoid making any unnecessary disclosures. Though DTS is mainly of theoretical interest, the family DTS generates contains many highly practical strategies. We will give two example practical strategies belonging to the family DTS generates.

Throughout this section, we assume that $\mathcal{M} = (m_1, \ldots, m_k)$ is a sequence of messages such that $m_i \neq \emptyset$ and $R \notin m_i$ for $1 \leq i \leq k$. We assume L_A and L_B are the local policies of parties Alice and Bob, respectively, and $\mathcal{S}_\mathcal{M} = \bigcup_{1 \leq i \leq k} m_i$. Without loss of generality, we assume Alice will send the next message to Bob.

Definition 13. *The* Disclosure Tree Strategy *(DTS for short) is a strategy $DTS(\mathcal{M}, L_A, R)$ such that:*

1. *$DTS(\mathcal{M}, L_A, R) = \{\emptyset\}$ if and only if $trees(\mathcal{S}_\mathcal{M} \cup L_A) = \emptyset$ or $trees(\mathcal{S}_\mathcal{M})$ has no evolvable tree for Alice.*
2. *Otherwise, $DTS(\mathcal{M}, L_A, R)$ contains all messages m' such that one of the following conditions holds:*

- *$m' = \{R\}$, if R is unlocked by credentials in $S_{\mathcal{M}}$;*
- *m' is a non-empty set of credentials and policies such that $trees(S_{\mathcal{M}} \cup m')$ contains at least one evolvable tree for Bob, and no non-empty proper subset of m' has this property.*

Condition 1 states under what circumstances the DTS strategy will terminate the negotiation with a failure message. Condition 2 guarantees that the other party will have an evolvable tree. Therefore, the other party can always send a message back that evolves a disclosure tree. Thus, no failure message will be sent unless there is no disclosure tree at all, in which case the negotiation cannot succeed anyway. Formally, we have the following theorems:

Theorem 4. *The set of strategies generated by DTS is a family.*

Theorem 5. *If a strategy s and DTS are compatible, then $f \succeq DTS$.*

We call the family generated by DTS the *DTS family*. By theorems 4 and 5, we get the following corollary immediately.

Corollary 2. *The DTS family is closed.*

As we mentioned before, one advantage of a strategy family can be the ability to adopt different strategies from a family in different phases of the negotiation. Correct interoperability is guaranteed as long as both parties' strategies are from the same family.

Definition 14. *Let s_1 and s_2 be two strategies. A strategy s' is a* hybrid *of s_1 and s_2 if for all choices of $\mathcal{M}$, L and R, we have $s'(\mathcal{M}, L, R) \subseteq s_1(\mathcal{M}, L, R) \cup s_2(\mathcal{M}, L, R)$ and $s' \neq s_1$ and $s' \neq s_2$.*

If a security agent adopts different DTS family strategies in different phases of trust negotiation, it is equivalent to adopting a hybrid of those strategies.

Theorem 6. *Let s_1 and s_2 be strategies in the DTS family and let s' be a hybrid of s_1 and s_2. Then s' is also in the DTS family.*

Therefore, as long as both parties use strategies from the DTS family, they can switch between different practical strategies as often as they like, and trust negotiation will still succeed whenever possible.

Although disclosure trees are a useful tool for understanding strategy properties, it could require exponential time and space to materialize all the disclosure trees during a negotiation. Fortunately, many strategies in the DTS family are quite efficient, such as TrustBuilder-Simple and TrustBuilder-Relevant in figures 10 and 11.

The TrustBuilder-Simple strategy (Figure 10) puts all undisclosed policies and unlocked credentials in the next message to the other party. If all the policies and unlocked credentials have already been disclosed, it will send a failure message.

The TrustBuilder-Relevant strategy (figure 11) discloses a credential C's policy only if C is syntactically relevant to R. Similarly, TrustBuilder-Relevant only discloses syntactically relevant unlocked credentials.

The TrustBuilder-Simple Strategy

Input:

$\mathcal{M} = (m_1, \ldots, m_k)$: a sequence of safe disclosure messages.

L: the local resources and policies of this party.

R: the resource to which access was originally requested.

Output:

A set containing a single disclosure message m.

Pre-condition:

R has not been disclosed and $m_k \neq \emptyset$.

```
S_M ← ⋃_{1≤i≤k} m_i.
m ← ∅.
For every local credential C that is unlocked by S_M
    m ← m ∪ {C}.
For every local locked credential C
    if (C's policy P is not a denial policy)
        then m ← m ∪ {P}.
For every policy P' ∈ S_M such that P' ∉ L
    For every credential that C appears in P' and has a denial policy
        m ← m ∪ {C ← false}.
m ← m − S_M.
Return {m}.
```

Fig. 10. Pseudocode for the TrustBuilder-Simple strategy

Lemma 1. *If a credential C appears in a disclosure tree for R, then C is relevant to R.*

Theorem 7. *TrustBuilder-Simple and TrustBuilder-Relevant belong to the DTS family.*

4 A Unified Scheme for Resource Protection in Trust Negotiation

Access control policies play a key role in trust negotiation. Unlike traditional decentralized systems, where access control policies are either publicly visible (such as in traditional file systems) or completely hidden (such as the configuration of a firewall for a local network), one's access control policies may need to be dynamically disclosed during the process of trust establishment. In many situations, either because the trust between two strangers is so limited, or because of the nature of the ongoing transactions, disclosing the contents of an access control policy to a stranger may leak valuable business information or jeopardize one's privacy. For example, suppose

The TrustBuilder-Relevant Strategy
Input:
$G = (m_1, \ldots, m_k)$: a sequence of safe disclosure messages.
L: the local resources and policies of this party.
R: the resource to which access was originally requested.
Output:
A set containing a single disclosure message m.
Pre-condition:
R has not been disclosed and $m_k \neq \emptyset$.

$\mathcal{S}_{\mathcal{M}} \leftarrow \bigcup_{1 \leq i \leq k} m_i$.
$m \leftarrow \emptyset$.
For every local credential C syntactically relevant to R
if (C is unlocked by $\mathcal{S}_{\mathcal{M}}$)
then $m \leftarrow m \cup \{C\}$.
else $m \leftarrow m \cup \{C\text{'s policy}\}$.
For every policy $P' \in \mathcal{S}_{\mathcal{M}}$ such that $P' \notin L$
For every credential C that appears in P' and has a denial policy
$m \leftarrow m \cup \{C \leftarrow false\}$.
$m \leftarrow m - \mathcal{S}_{\mathcal{M}}$.
Return $\{m\}$.

Fig. 11. Pseudocode for the TrustBuilder-Relevant strategy

that an online store gives a special discount to employees of its business partners. If the policy, which contains the list of its business partners, is shown to arbitrary requesters for the service, then by merely looking at the policy, an outsider will know who is partnering with the store.

To give access control policies the protection they need, in this chapter we propose UniPro, a Unified Resource Protection Scheme for trust negotiation. We first introduce desiderata for protection of sensitive access control policies, and show how previously proposed approaches measure up to the desiderata. We then present UniPro and show that unlike previous proposals, UniPro treats access control policies as first-class resources, provides fine-grained control over policy disclosure, and clearly distinguishes between policy disclosure and policy satisfaction. We also prove that UniPro generalizes two previous proposals, and explain why in spite of this, we believe that other ways of protecting policies still have an important role to play in trust negotiation.

4.1 Sensitive Policies and Their Protection

Realistic access control policies tend to contain sensitive information, because the details of Alice's policy P for disclosure of credential C tend to give hints about C's contents. For example, if there is any information in C that is so sensitive that Alice chooses to control its disclosure very tightly, then it is possible to guess at the nature of that information by looking at P: is her parole officer allowed to see C? Her welfare case worker? The local HIV, cancer, or mental health clinic? An Enron employees' stock sale web page whose policy spelled out exactly who could sell stock and when might have raised many eyebrows. More generally, a company's internal and external policies are part of its corporate assets, and it will not wish to indiscriminately broadcast its policies in their entirety.

Example 1. [28] Suppose a web page's access control policy states that in order to access documents of a project in the site, a requester should present an employee ID issued either by Microsoft or by IBM. If such a policy can be shown to any requester, then one can infer with high confidence that this project is a cooperative effort of the two companies.

Example 2. (Inspired by examples in [5]) Coastal Bank's loan application policy says that a loan applicant must be a customer of the bank who is not on the bank's bad-customer list. If this policy is fully disclosed to a requester, then an outsider can easily learn who the bank's bad customers are, which is very sensitive business information.

In the first example, the correlation between two constraints in a single policy reveals certain properties of the protected resource. The policy in the second example directly refers to sensitive local information that should be protected. One obvious way to prevent such information leakage is to selectively disclose part of a policy. For instance, in Example 1, we can first ask the requester to show an employee ID. After receiving the credential, we check whether it is issued by either Microsoft or IBM. Similarly, in Example 2, Coastal Bank may only ask for a customer ID and perform the check on the bad customer list after the credential is received. However, this approach may cause a dispute between the two negotiating parties. If we simply remove those sensitive constraints when disclosing a policy, Alice may disclose some credentials and believe that Coastal Bank's policy has been satisfied, while Coastal Bank believes the opposite because the sensitive constraints of the bank's policy are not satisfied.

A key observation is that since policies may be sensitive and need to be protected from unauthorized disclosure, there is no essential difference between policies and other resources, from the point of view of resource protection. That means that when we protect a sensitive policy, we can protect it in the same way as any other resource. Therefore a resource protection scheme that satisfies the following desiderata is desirable.

1. When Alice requests access to Bob's resource R, Bob may disclose R's access control policy P to Alice so that Alice can learn how to gain access to R. Once

Alice has disclosed credentials that satisfy P, Bob will grant Alice access to R. One underlying assumption in this process is that the two parties have the same understanding of the semantics of policies. When one party believes that a policy has been satisfied by disclosed credentials, the other party should believe the same. Otherwise, a dispute may arise even though the two parties negotiate trust in good faith. We call this the *satisfaction-agreement* assumption.
2. Protection of sensitive policies should be as flexible as for any other kind of resource, allowing any kind of constraint that is used for protecting other resources. Because different parts of a policy may be sensitive in different ways, the policy protection approach should allow fine-grained control of the protection applied to each part of a policy.
3. Let R be a resource with access control policy P. The resource protection scheme should decouple the protection of R and P. R's accessibility should only depend on P's satisfaction. Whether P is disclosed or not should not affect R's accessibility. In other words, the scheme should be able to model the situation where the client presents the right credentials, satisfies P and gains access to R, without becoming eligible to see the actual contents of P during a negotiation. Taken to the extreme, this will allow servers to offer private services whose existence and access control policies are never made public, but whose location and policies can be pushed privately to selected clients.
4. The design of interoperable strategies is an important issue in research on trust negotiation, and the resource protection scheme should not become an obstacle to interoperation. The resource protection scheme must allow a wide variety of practical negotiation strategies that will interoperate correctly with one another.
5. The resource protection scheme must allow a human-friendly interface for policy capture and maintenance. We believe that the challenge of policy capture and maintenance is perhaps the biggest obstacle to widespread deployment of systems that are open to access by outsiders. Businesses and individuals must have confidence in their policies, but policies are hard to write and will require updates in a changing world. While these issues are the focus of work by other researchers [6,11,22,31,32] and are largely outside of the scope of this chapter, we believe that they must be kept in mind when designing a unified resource protection scheme.

4.2 Related Work on Sensitive Policy Protection

Service Accessibility Rules

Bonatti and Samarati [5] proposed a framework for regulating service access and information release on the web. The framework is targeted at environments where no single centralized security domain exists. Their framework contains a policy language for access control specification, and a filtering mechanism to identify the relevant policies for a negotiation. A service accessibility rule in their model is composed of two parts: a prerequisite rule and a requisite rule. Service prerequisite rules state the conditions that a requester must satisfy before she can be considered for the service. Service requisite rules state sufficient conditions for obtaining access to the service, i.e., if a requester also satisfies a requisite rule, she will be entitled to access the service. To protect both the server and client's privacy, the model enforces a specific ordering between a service's prerequisite and requisite rules. The server will not disclose a requisite rule until after the requester satisfies a corresponding prerequisite rule. Prerequisite rules can contain constraints that are hidden from strangers.

For instance, to get a special offer from an auto insurance company, suppose that a requester is first required to show a valid driver's license which contains basic personal information such as gender, age and address. Based on such information, the insurance company will determine whether the requester is likely to be in a high risk group. How the company makes its decision should not be disclosed to the requester. If the requester does not belong to a high risk group, the insurance company will require disclosure of the title of the vehicle to verify that the requester is actually the owner of the insured vehicle. By using the model in [5], we have the following rules:

1. $service\_prereqs(special\_offer()) \leftarrow credential(drivers\_license(gender = X, age = Y, issuer =$"DMV"$)) \mid high\_risk(gender = X, age = Y) = false$. (The constraint $high\_risk(gender = X, age = Y) = false$ is hidden when the prerequisite rule is disclosed.)
2. $service\_reqs(special\_offer()) \leftarrow credential(vehicle\_title(owner = X, issuer =$"DMV"$)), credential(drivers\_license(name = Y)), X = Y$.

For simplicity, we have omitted several details in the above service rules. In particular, issuers of these credentials should be principals that the server trusts, and the requester should authenticate to the owner of each credential. We would expect the credential issuer to be identified not by a string, but by a public key lookup. Further, a party must verify that each credential it receives during trust negotiation has contents that correspond to its signature. Also, trust negotiation should be conducted over a secure channel to prevent certain attacks. We will also omit these important details in all later examples in this chapter.

By explicitly indicating whether a policy is a prerequisite or requisite rule, a requester can be made to understand the consequences of disclosing particular credentials. Thus, the satisfaction-agreement assumption holds in this model.

A prerequisite rule serves two functions at the same time: controlling the disclosure of the service requisite rules and controlling access to the service. The scheme does not decouple policy disclosure from policy satisfaction. Thus, desideratum 3 is not satisfied. Also, the only way to protect a sensitive policy is to keep it completely inaccessible to a requester. This makes it difficult to use service accessibility rules to express complex authorization requirements. Therefore desideratum 2 is not met. On the other hand, examples 1 and 2 can be easily expressed using service accessibility rules.

Example 3. McKinley Clinic makes its patient records available for online access. Let R be Alice's record. To gain access to R, R's policy states that a requester must either present Alice's patient ID for McKinley Clinic, or present a California social worker license and a release-of-information credential issued to the requester by Alice. Knowing that Alice's record specifically allows access by social workers will help people infer that Alice may have a mental or emotional problem. Alice will probably want to keep this constraint inaccessible to strangers. However, employees of McKinley Clinic should be allowed to see the contents of this policy. Note that this does not mean that to satisfy R's policy, a requester has to work for McKinley Clinic. Any licensed social worker can access Alice's patient record as long as the social worker has obtained a release-of-information credential from Alice and pushes the relevant credentials to the server.

In example 3, if the social worker constraint is put in a prerequisite rule, then it must be made inaccessible to everybody or accessible to everybody. On the other hand, if the constraint is put in the requisite rule, then the constraint on working for McKinley Clinic has to appear in the prerequisite rule, which means that anyone other than Alice who accesses Alice's record has to be employed by McKinley Clinic. In either case, we do not capture the original intent of the policy.

If the social worker is not working for McKinley Clinic, how could she know that she should present her social worker license and the release-of-information credential from Alice? In practice, we expect that Alice will have disclosed a version of R's policy to the social worker at the same time as Alice gave out the release-of-information credential. The social worker can cache both the credentials and the policy fragment for later use during trust negotiation. More generally, we expect advance disclosure and caching of policies to be useful whenever policies are invisible to all but a targeted audience.

Policy Graphs

The concept of policy graphs was proposed by Seamons et al. [28]. In their scheme, a resource's access control is expressed as a policy graph instead of a single policy. A policy graph is a directed acyclic graph with a single source node N_0 and a single sink node R. The sink node represents a sensitive resource, while all the other nodes represent policies. In a policy graph, if there is an edge from node N_i to N_j ($N_i \rightarrow N_j$), then we say N_i is a predecessor of N_j. The policy represented by the source node N_0 is not protected, thus can be disclosed to any requester. All other policies and resources N_k can be accessed only if there exists a directed path $(N_0, \ldots, N_j, N_k)$, such that every policy in the subpath $(N_0, \ldots, N_j)$ is satisfied by the credentials disclosed by the requester. The essential idea of policy graphs is to protect access control policies through gradual disclosure of constraints. For example, suppose a special insurance promotion is offered to graduate students whose age is over 25 or whose GPA is over 3.0. The access control policy graph may be as shown in figure 12.

During a negotiation, if a requester cannot present a valid student ID proving she is a graduate student, then the insurance company can just terminate the negotiation and does not need to disclose further constraints (P_1 and P_2). If the insurance company regards the constraints on age and GPA as sensitive information, then, to

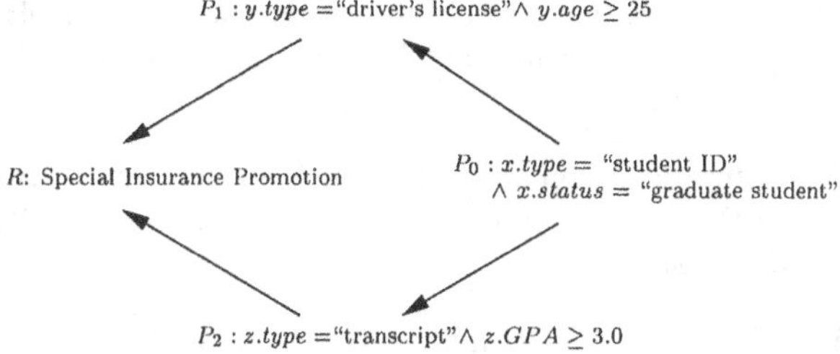

Fig. 12. An example of policy graphs.

some extent, policy P_0 in the source node helps to prevent the disclosure of P_1 and P_2 to arbitrary strangers. Based on this observation, Seamons et al. claim [28] that by dividing access control requirements into layers and organizing them as a policy graph, one can effectively protect sensitive policies.

However, from the semantics of policy graphs, we can see that each policy in a policy graph not only controls its direct successor's accessibility, but also that of its indirect successors. In the above example, P_0 controls when P_1 and P_2 can be disclosed. Further, to gain access to R also requires a requester to satisfy P_0 in the first place. Thus, the concept of policy graphs couples a policy's satisfaction tightly with the policy's disclosure, which makes it difficult to use policy graphs to express certain access control requirements.

In example 1, if we treat the policy requiring an employee ID as the source node P_0 and regard constraints on the issuer of the employee ID as its successor P_1, then anyone who can produce an employee ID may be able to see the contents of P_1, which is obviously not desired. On the other hand, if we put $false$ in the policy graph as P_1's predecessor, indicating that nobody is allowed to see the contents of P_1, then no one will be able to gain access to the project documents, which is not consistent with the original access control requirements either. Similarly, policy graphs cannot be used to capture the intent of examples 2 and 3.

In summary, policy graphs preserve the satisfaction-agreement assumption: once a policy P is satisfied, a requester knows that either she gains access to R or she will see the content of one of P's successors. But policy graphs couple policy disclosure with policy satisfaction, which limits their expressiveness and violates desiderata 2 and 3.

4.3 A Unified Scheme for Resource Protection

The lack of centralized authority on the Internet suggests that more than one general-purpose language may become popular for expressing policies. Specialized sublanguages may evolve by, for example, making it easier to capture and maintain common access control constraints for certain kinds of resources. Thus our goal is to provide a general-purpose way to protect policies without dictating the choice of policy languages, beyond certain minimal requirements described later.

In the examples we give in the rest of this section, we use symbols in the calligraphic font to represent policies in the underlying policy language: $\mathcal{P}$, $\mathcal{P}_1$, $\mathcal{P}_2$, etc. We begin by reifying policies.

Definition 15. *A* policy definition *takes the form $P \leftrightarrow \mathcal{P}$, where P is a unique ID for this policy and $\mathcal{P}$ is a policy in the underlying policy language. We call $\mathcal{P}$ the* content *of the policy, denoted as $content(P)$.*

Definition 16. *A set $\mathcal{C}$ of credentials* minimally satisfies *$\mathcal{P}$ if no proper subset of $\mathcal{C}$ satisfies $\mathcal{P}$.*

For example, consider the policy stating that the requester must be a social worker licensed by the state of California, and have a release form signed by Alice. The sets of credentials minimally satisfying $\mathcal{P}$ will contain exactly two credentials.

Definition 17. *Given policy definition $P \leftrightarrow \mathcal{P}$ and policy content $\mathcal{P}'$, we say a set $\mathcal{C}$ of credentials satisfies $(\mathcal{P}') \wedge P$ if $\mathcal{C}$ satisfies $(\mathcal{P}') \wedge (\mathcal{P})$. Similarly, $\mathcal{C}$ satisfies $(\mathcal{P}') \vee P$ if $\mathcal{C}$ satisfies $(\mathcal{P}') \vee (\mathcal{P})$.*

Definition 17 allows policy IDs to appear in policy definitions, to give finer-grained greater control over policy protection. In the remainder of the paper, policy contents will be written in this *augmented policy language.* Definition 17 also introduces a very simple type of policy composition. The definition can be viewed as stating what it means to satisfy two policies in the underlying language simultaneously, or to satisfy one of two policies. This kind of policy reuse and composition [6,31,32] is an effective way to help users design and maintain their policies. We will use it to translate policy graphs and service accessibility rules into UniPro.

Although Definition 17 may seem trivial at first glance, it must be formulated very carefully for underlying policy languages that allow free variables to appear in policies; conjoining two policies may force two variables to refer to the same resource or attribute value. Definition 17 is appropriate for the policy languages used by Seamons et al. and Bonatti and Samarati, but it may need to be tailored to meet the needs of other policy languages developed in the future.

For example, let P_1 be the ID of a seat upgrade policy that requires a requester to be a Platinum Frequent Flyer with a seat upgrade certificate. Then we have $P_1 \leftrightarrow x.type$ = "Platinum Frequent Flyer" $\wedge$ $x.issuer$ = "CheapAir" $\wedge$ $y.type$ = "Seat Upgrade Certificate" $\wedge$ $y.issuer$ = "CheapAir". Let P_2 be the ID of a seat upgrade policy that requires the requester to be a gate agent: $P_2 \leftrightarrow z.type$ = "Employee ID" $\wedge$ $z.issuer$ = "CheapAir" $\wedge$ $z.jobTitle$ = "Gate Agent". Now we want to have a policy ID P whose content says that a requester needs to either be a gate agent or be a Platinum Frequent Flyer with an upgrade certificate. There are several possible ways to get P through policy composition; each of these ways offers different possibilities for protecting the policies.

1. We may have $P \leftrightarrow P_1 \vee P_2$. In this case, P, P_1, and P_2 can have entirely different access control policies. For example, P may be made freely accessible, so that all can see P's internal disjunctive structure. P_1 may be accessible to all

Platinum Frequent Flyers and airline employees, while P_2 is only accessible to airline employees.

2. We may have $P \leftrightarrow content(P_1) \vee content(P_2)$. In this case, anyone who can satisfy P's access control policy—say, all Platinum flyers—will be able to see the full policy for seat upgrades. This may be undesirable, as Platinum passengers may beg the gate agent for free upgrades, once they learn about this policy.
3. We may also have $P \leftrightarrow content(P_1) \wedge P_2$. In this case, anyone who satisfies P's policy can learn the standard way of obtaining an upgrade. The fact that gate agents can perform a free upgrade can be hidden from everyone but airline employees, if desired.

Definition 18. *A* policy declaration *takes the form $R : P$, where P is the ID of the access control policy for resource R. A requester is entitled to gain access to R only if she has disclosed credentials that satisfy P.*

Under UniPro (**Unified** Resource **Protection** Scheme), each resource R is protected by exactly one policy ($R : P$), and each policy ID P has exactly one policy definition $P \leftrightarrow \mathcal{P}$. Further, the fact that R is protected by a policy with a particular ID ($R : P$) is freely disclosable to all, because P and R are both just resource IDs. In UniPro, policies can be protected by policies which can be protected by policies and so on, but the chain of protection must bottom out with a policy that is either always hidden or always disclosable. These special policies have IDs *true* and *false*, their contents are always and never satisfied, respectively, and they are freely disclosable. In particular, assume R is not a policy. We use $R : true$ to denote that a resource R is not protected, and $R : false$ for a resource that a party does not possess or that will not be disclosed under any circumstances. We say $R : false$ is a denial policy declaration.

Let us revisit the examples given in the beginning of this section.

Example 1. The access control policy for the project documents R is $R : P$, where $P \leftrightarrow x.type =$ "Employee ID"$\wedge$ P_1 and $P_1 \leftrightarrow x.issuer =$ "Microsoft" $\vee\, x.issuer =$ "IBM". We also have $P : true$ and $P_1 : false$. Since P's policy is always satisfied, any requester can see P's content. However, P_1's policy is never satisfied, which means P_1's content should not be shown to anybody. Assume Alice is an employee of Sun Microsystems and wants to access the project's documents. After P's content has been disclosed, she may disclose her Sun employee ID. But since Alice knows that P refers to an inaccessible policy P_1 (because $P_1 : false$ is freely disclosable), she knows that her employee ID may not be enough to satisfy P. Therefore, the satisfaction-agreement assumption holds in this situation.

Example 2. Coastal Bank's loan application policy definition is $P \leftrightarrow x.type =$ "Customer ID" $\wedge\, x.issuer =$ "Coastal Bank" $\wedge\, P_1$. We also have $P_1 \leftrightarrow x.ID \notin BadCustomerList$, $P : true$, and $P_1 : false$. After a loan applicant discloses her Coastal Bank customer ID, since P_1 is a conjunct in the content of P, and the content of P_1 will never be disclosed, she should wait for Coastal Bank to decide whether P is satisfied instead of taking it for granted that she is qualified for the loan.

Example 3. Let R be Alice's patient record. We have

1. $R : P$.
2. $P \leftrightarrow P_1 \vee P_2$ and $P : true$. Everyone can see that there are two ways to get access to Alice's record.
3. $P_1 \leftrightarrow x.type =$ "patient ID" $\wedge\ x.name =$ "Alice" $\wedge\ x.issuer =$ "McKinley Clinic", and $P_1 : true$. Everyone can see that Alice can access her own records.
4. $P_2 \leftrightarrow x.type =$ "Professional License" $\wedge\ x.profession =$ "Social Worker" $\wedge\ x.issuer =$ "State of California" $\wedge\ y.type =$ "Medical Records Release"
   $\wedge\ y.issuer =$ "Alice" $\wedge\ y.institution =$ "McKinley Clinic". Alice can also authorize social workers to look at her records.

To prevent the inappropriate disclosure of P_2's content, we also have $P_2 : P_3$, $P_3 \leftrightarrow z.type =$ "Employee ID" $\wedge\ z.issuer =$ "McKinley Clinic", and $P_3 : true$. Then everyone can see that McKinley employees can see another way to gain access to Alice's records.

[itemsep=0pt]

Next we analyze UniPro according to the first identified three desiderata.

1. In UniPro, if a requester submits credentials that satisfy a resource's policy, then she is entitled to access that resource. On the other hand, because of the explicit appearance of policy IDs in a policy, a requester will be aware of parts of a policy that have not been disclosed yet. Without seeing those parts, she will not always be able to tell whether the policy has been satisfied by the credentials she has disclosed. Therefore, there will be no disagreement between two parties over whether a policy has been satisfied, given that they both understand the semantics of the underlying policy language.
2. UniPro explicitly protects policies in the same way as other resources. Users can design policies that provide fine-grained control of sensitive policies' disclosure. In fact, by looking at a resource's policy, $R : P$, we cannot tell whether R is a policy, a credential or a service.
3. The semantics of UniPro explicitly separates a policy's satisfaction from its disclosure. If a resource is protected by a policy P, then as long as P is satisfied, R can be accessed. Whether P has been disclosed or not is irrelevant to R's disclosure.

Regarding desideratum 5, probably no policy language with roots in mathematical logic will ever be regarded as user-friendly by the average corporate programmer. We view the previously proposed policy languages for trust negotiation as efforts to put a firm semantic foundation under trust negotiation, and to understand the requirements for policy languages for trust negotiation. They have served admirably in this capacity, and UniPro builds directly upon them. More generally, we view UniPro not as a replacement for other policy languages, but rather as an underlying foundation that other, more programmer-friendly, policy capture tools can be hooked into. A programmer can use the friendliest capture tool with sufficient modeling power for a new/updated policy, and then the captured policy can be translated into UniPro-style policy definitions in a well-known, general-purpose policy language, to provide portability and mutual comprehension of policies written by strangers. To show the promise of this approach, the following two theorems show how UniPro generalizes service accessibility rules and policy graphs.

Theorem 8. *Given a policy graph G protecting resource R, there is a set of UniPro policy definitions with the same semantics as G. More precisely,*

1. *If R's UniPro policy is satisfied by a set of disclosed credentials, then there exists a path from the source node of G to an immediate predecessor of R in G, such that every policy along the path is satisfied by the set of disclosed credentials.*
2. *For any policy node N in the policy graph, if N's content is disclosed, then there exists a path from the source node of G to an immediate predecessor of N in G, such that every policy along the path is satisfied by the set of disclosed credentials.*

Theorem 8 shows that UniPro is at least as expressive as policy graphs. As shown in Examples 1 and 2 in this section, there are realistic cases whose access control requirements cannot be expressed with policy graphs. Thus UniPro generalizes policy graphs. However, as mentioned earlier, policy graphs or another graphical interface to an underlying policy language can be used as a friendly interface on top of UniPro for capturing and maintaining access control requirements that do not require all of UniPro's modeling power.

Theorem 9. *Given a service prerequisite rule $service\_prereqs(s) \leftarrow q_1, \ldots, q_n \mid p_1, \ldots, p_m$ and a service requisite rule $service\_reqs(s) \leftarrow q'_1, \ldots, q'_t$, where q_i $(1 \leq i \leq n)$, p_i $(1 \leq i \leq m)$, and q'_i $(1 \leq i \leq t)$ are all predicates, there is a set of UniPro policy definitions with the same semantics as the service accessibility rules. More precisely:*

1. *Service s's UniPro policy is satisfied by a set of credentials disclosed by Alice if and only if those credentials satisfy $q_1 \wedge \cdots \wedge q_n$, $p_1 \wedge \cdots \wedge p_m$, and $q'_1 \wedge \cdots \wedge q'_t$.*
2. *If the contents of any $q'_i, 1 \leq i \leq t$, are disclosed to Alice, then $q_1 \wedge \cdots \wedge q_n \wedge p_1 \wedge \cdots \wedge p_m$ are satisfied by credentials Alice has already disclosed.*
3. *The contents of p_i, $1 \leq i \leq m$, are never disclosed.*

As shown by Example 3 in this section, there are realistic access control requirements that cannot be expressed using service accessibility rules. Thus UniPro generalizes service accessibility rules.

5 Trust Negotiation System Design

Recent research in trust negotiation has focused on a number of important issues including languages for expressing resource access policies (e.g., [1,3,13,23]), protocols and strategies for conducting trust negotiations (e.g., [2,17,18,37]), and logics for reasoning about the outcomes of these negotiations (e.g., [7,34]). The foundational results presented in these works have also been shown to be viable access control solutions for real-world systems through a series of implementations (such as those presented in [2,14,16,33]) which demonstrate the utility and practicality of these theoretical advances. Most of these implementations exist mainly as proofs of concept and were not designed to meet the needs of large-scale distributed systems. The strong theoretical foundation underlying trust negotiation along with these proof of concept systems indicate that access control solutions based on trust negotiation stand to revolutionize the way that information sharing occurs in distributed systems.

Prior to deploying access control systems based on trust negotiation, their systems and architectural properties must be fully explored. Several important areas of investigation include protocol compatibility, system scalability, feature extensibility, and external party interactions. With regard to external party interactions, researchers must be able to design and test effective strategies for credential search and discovery, develop mechanisms for the automatic generation of proof hints, and explore systems for establishing confidence in results obtained from the various "helpful third parties" with whom trust negotiation agents are likely to interact. To adequately answer questions such as these, we require a general-purpose framework in which access control systems based on trust negotiation can be implemented and tested.

Our goal in this section is to formalize a set of requirements for future trust negotiation architectures and propose interesting directions for future research in this area. We begin by first describing set of core logical components required by any trust negotiation architecture, including the prototype implementations available today. We then analyze several interesting use cases in which access control systems based on trust negotiation could be extremely beneficial. Rather than limiting our view of trust negotiation to a particular domain, we examine use cases from the realms of client-server interactions taking place on the World Wide Web, access control for scientific grid computing systems, and information sharing in high-assurance environments. These use cases are then used to derive a set of functional requirements for flexible next-generation trust negotiation architectures. While this is by no means an exhaustive list of possible usage scenarios, the union of the requirements exposed by these cases covers a much larger set of usage scenarios. We conclude this section with a discussion of the areas in which existing trust negotiation architectures satisfy our set of requirements and propose several directions of research relevant to the investigation of next-generation trust negotiation architectures.

5.1 Core Components

At its core, any trust negotiation system consists of at least five logical components: a strategy module, compliance checker, credential verifier, policy database, and profile manager. By varying the properties of these five components, a variety of interesting systems with widely varying properties can be developed. A basic understanding of these core components is prerequisite for later discussion which aims to derive requirements for next-generation flexible trust negotiation architectures.

The most basic components of a trust negotiation system are the *policy database* and *profile manager*. The policy database is simply some structure that holds the policies used to protect access to system resources. Likewise, the profile manger is a data structure that contains credentials and assertions about a given entity. Current trust negotiation prototypes tend to support policies written in a single policy language (such as Cassandra [1], X-TNL [3], TPL [13], or RT [23]) and credentials encoded in a single, specific format such as X.509 [15] or SAML [10].

Trust negotiation is a strategy-driven interaction in which two parties exchange policies and credentials when one party wishes to convince another that she should be permitted to access some networked resource. Previous sections in this chapter highlighted several families of interoperable strategies that can be used during a trust negotiation session. Entities can choose strategies from families such as these that satisfy their particular goals, for instance, maximizing the speed of a negotiation or preserving privacy. The *strategy module* component of a trust negotiation system is responsible for making decisions regarding information disclosure and resource access at each step of the negotiation. The strategy modules implemented in existing trust negotiation systems tend to support a single negotiation strategy or, at best, a fixed set of negotiation strategies that can be used during a negotiation.

At each step of a negotiation, the strategy module communicates with the *credential verifier* to validate any new credentials received. This typically involves checking that credential is formatted properly, i.e., that it has a valid digital signature and that the entity that disclosed the credential could demonstrate proof of ownership. To the best of our knowledge, no existing trust negotiation prototypes implement any sort of online check to determine if a credential has been revoked. It will be important for production trust negotiation architectures to enable these types of checks either through the use of certificate revocation lists, OCSP [25], or online CAs such as COCA [38].

The last core trust negotiation component is the *compliance checker*. The job of the compliance checker is to determine whether a certain set of credentials can satisfy a given policy or policy fragment. This component is important when the strategy module must decide either if its local collection of credentials can satisfy a remote policy or if a set of credentials disclosed by the remote party can satisfy a local policy. More formally, given a set of credentials, C and a policy P, a compliance checker returns either `true` if C satisfies P or $\langle$`false`, *justification*$\rangle$ if C does not satisfy P where *justification* describes why C did not satisfy P. For examples, *justification* could be a sub-policy of P that has yet to be satisfied. Some compliance checkers can also determine a minimal satisfying set of C which satisfies P and also return this when P is satisfied [29].

Figure 13 illustrates the interactions between these core components graphically. At this point, it should be clear that the trust negotiation functionalities described earlier in this chapter can be encapsulated using only these five components. In the remainder of this section, we explore a number of use cases through which we extend this basic notion of a trust negotiation architecture. We derive new requirements for these core system components and find that the flexibility to incorporate support for

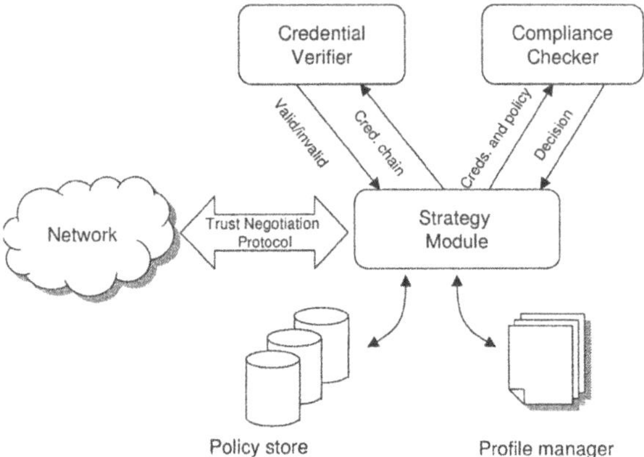

Fig. 13. The core components of a trust negotiation architecture and their interactions.

a variety of other functionalities will be critical to the long-term success of next-generation trust negotiation architectures.

5.2 Use Case Analysis

Having explored the basic components of a trust negotiation architecture, we now discuss three interesting use cases for access control systems based on trust negotiation. In particular, we explore client-server information sharing on the World Wide Web, scientific grid computing, and information sharing in high-assurance environments. It should be noted that most research to date has focused on two-party trust negotiations. In this section, however, we relax this assumption and consider cases in which multi-party interactions could be useful in hopes of deriving requirements that will lead to trust negotiation architectures with increased levels of flexibility.

The World Wide Web

The World Wide Web is an almost endless source of examples of client-server interactions ranging from e-commerce to research applications. Rather than examining a particular client-server interaction in detail, we will discuss this problem more generally. Consider the case in which some service provider wishes to offer their service, S, to any clients who satisfy some access control policy, P, which is specified in any one of a number of trust negotiation languages (e.g., Cassandra [1], X-TNL [3], TPL [13], or RT [23]). Upon requesting access to S, the client and the server begin a trust negotiation to determine whether the client satisfies P and should be granted access to the service.

In such interactions, the client and server are likely to have different requirements governing the execution of the trust negotiation. From the client's perspective, the following assumptions may hold true:

- To prevent identity theft, the client is likely to have few credentials which are freely disclosable. That is, most of the clients credentials will be protected by release policies.
- Clients will not often be concerned with the threat of denial of service (DoS) attacks being launched on their trust negotiation agents by the services that they contact. However, information gathering attacks will be expected.
- To ensure access to S, the client will often be willing to do extra work. For instance, if a client does not possess a credential required by P, they may be willing to try to locate the missing credential (within certain constraints).
- Technically savvy clients may wish to be involved directly in the trust negotiation process. This could take the form of either the clients writing their own credential release policies or making strategic decisions at the time of negotiation. Naive clients may wish to have "reasonable" policies provided to them and allow their user agent to perform the entirety of the negotiation process using these policies.

In contrast to these points, the following assumptions are likely to hold true at the server:

- Many servers are public interfaces to resources and will likely have very few credentials protected by release policies.
- Due to the heavyweight nature of trust negotiation, servers will be concerned with the threat of DoS attacks. However, information gathering attacks will not be a concern, as most credentials held by the server will be publicly available.
- Due to the threat of DoS, servers are unlikely to engage in expensive external efforts to ensure the success of a negotiation (such as searching for requested credentials). However, under certain constraints, servers may wish to carry out some external actions.
- The negotiation protocol executed by the server must be entirely automated, as there is no human operator present to make decisions at runtime.
- To increase revenue or information dissemination, servers will likely wish to have a robust trust negotiation configuration which will maximize the number of clients who can access the system while minimizing the cost of a negotiation to the server.

In examining these points, we notice two main discrepancies that exist between the client and server. First, servers wish to maximize the number of trust negotiations that can be conducted per unit time, while the client is often willing to allow this process to take longer in hopes of ensuring success. Second, the fact that servers are public entities is in direct contrast with the private nature of individuals. Several interesting features will be derived from these differences later in this section.

Scientific Grid Computing

In scientific grid computing, researchers utilize geographically and administratively distributed resources to solve complicated research and simulation problems. For example, a scientist in Utah might wish to allocate processor time on computing clusters in Illinois and California, access a wave tank owned by a university in Florida, and use a data set collected by colleagues in Maine to analyze various characteristics of a tsunami. In order to successfully submit such a job for execution on a grid, the scientist must establish the right to access resources owned by multiple resource providers.

The nature of the interactions that must occur to successfully negotiate for access to a computational grid lead users to make the following assumptions regarding trust negotiation:

- The integrity of jobs submitted to these systems is of the utmost importance to users, as resource constraints and deadlines often prohibit running a job multiple times. Users will likely have stringent requirements that must be satisfied by resource providers and may even require interaction with third-party reputation services to ensure that the results that they obtain will be accurate.
- The time required to run many grid computing jobs is measured in hours or days. This implies that users will be willing to spend extra time and effort to ensure the success of their trust negotiation sessions, as this cost can be amortized over the duration of the job.
- Even though users may be willing to interact with third parties to help ensure the success of their negotiations, this must be done with care, as third parties may give incorrect answers either accidentally or maliciously (particularly if there is a high demand for resources, as there tends to be near deadlines).
- Users will have many sensitive credentials detailing their research and organizational memberships, especially if they are employed in government or industry research labs where need-to-know is often limited.

Though at first glance the resource providers in computational grids seem equivalent to the servers discussed in the World Wide Web use case, they are in fact quite different. Resource providers in computational grids are likely to make the following assumptions regarding trust negotiation:

- Maximizing system utilization is key. Many resources attached to computational grids are expensive to own and operate, thus it is in the best interest of resource providers to ensure that a maximum number of authorized users gain access to help pay the cost of operating the resources. This implies that resource providers will be configured to maximize the number of clients able to access the system successfully and will be concerned less with the speed with which trust negotiation sessions occur.
- The length of time required to run a grid job implies that resource providers will be carrying out fewer trust negotiation sessions than, for example, e-commerce

web sites. As a result, resource providers will be more open to the idea of doing extra work to ensure the success of a negotiation. For instance, resource providers may attempt to locate credentials requested by a particular client.

- Resource providers will likely have many public credentials, as was the case with servers on the World Wide Web, though they will likely have other more sensitive credentials that will be protected by release policies (particularly in government computing environments).

While the grid computing application domain has some similarities with the client-server environment, the inherently collaborative nature of this environment gives rise to several differing assumptions. These contrasting assumptions will elicit requirements for features not needed in the client-server domain.

High Assurance Environments

High-assurance environments such as disaster management networks or critical infrastructures, like the electric power grid, tend to have stringent requirements on information sharing. In particular, it is of the utmost importance that *qualified* individuals gain access to all necessary information in a timely manner, even if those qualified individuals happen to be *outsiders*. For instance, during a time of crisis, it is important that police, fire, and rescue workers can access status information about the incident to which they are responding, even if they happen to be volunteers from another district. In the case of the electric power grid, there are when that otherwise market-sensitive information should be released to competing entities to enable proper response to changing conditions in the grid and avoid cascading blackouts or other failure situations.

As with the previous two use cases, we examine characteristics of this environment from the perspective of both clients (information consumers) and servers (information producers). From a client viewpoint, the following assumptions are likely to hold true:

- Emergencies and other situations in which information sharing is likely to occur in high-assurance environments are usually highly context-dependent. The variability that this introduces can make it difficult for users to understand why their access requests are permitted or denied. The reasons for the success and failure of any access control decisions should be explained carefully by the underlying trust negotiation architecture.
- Many times critical decisions must be made quickly. Users will not tolerate high delays when requesting information in this environment.
- The criticality of these systems implies that users want their interactions to succeed if at all possible. Interactions with external parties that would increase the likelihood of a successful negotiation will be tolerated, though they will be subjected to stringent timing constraints.
- Users will likely act in uncharacteristic ways during times of crisis or when adverse conditions arise in the system. Since these environments have stringent

security requirements, users may be investigated after atypical actions are taken. To protect themselves, users will require verifiable audit trials be stored locally. These records must include information about both the external environment (i.e., system context) and specific records detailing the negotiations carried out by the user.

With respect to information producers in high-assurance environments, the following assumptions regarding information sharing are likely to hold true:

- The high-security nature of these environments implies that in many ways they are more constrained than the World Wide Web or grid computing environments discussed previously. Support for a wide array of configuration options regarding supported credential types and strategies is likely to be unnecessary; a preordained set of these options should suffice.
- Since flow of information is key to the operation of these environments, information providers will require that their trust negotiation systems be fast and denial of service resistant.
- In general, high-assurance environments have very stringent requirements on the flow of information. However, under certain circumstances (e.g., emergency conditions) information providers may take a more permissive approach to information dissemination in hopes of solving problems of critical importance. To help detect patterns of abuse, information providers will need strong audit trails detailing exactly what information was released and to whom it was released.

5.3 Derived Requirements

We now examine the assumptions made in the previously presented use cases and derive functional requirements for a general-purpose trust negotiation framework. These requirements fall naturally into four categories: requirements placed on core trust negotiation components, requirements relating to external interactions, audit and accountability requirements, and performance and extensibility requirements. In all cases, we examine both the derivation and implications of each requirement.

Core Components

The most obvious requirements for any trust negotiation system relate to the functionalities that should be provided by the core components discussed earlier in this Section. Upon examining our three use cases, it immediately becomes clear that the goals of the participants in the system can vary widely from situation to situation. To account for this, the functionality provided by the core system components needs to be as flexible as possible. In particular, the core components should satisfy the following requirements:

Arbitrary policy languages In the World Wide Web and scientific grid computing use cases, it was noted that servers and resource providers will wish to be accessible to as many potential clients as possible. To facilitate this, these entities should be able to parse access policies written in a variety of formats. This includes both allowing support for policy languages with tunable constraint domains (e.g., Cassandra [1]), as well as supporting the use of multiple unrelated policy languages (e.g., supporting X-TNL [3], TPL [13], and RT [23]). It should be possible to add support for new policy languages to deployed systems easily.

Arbitrary credential formats To further enable interactions with a maximal set of users, the system should support the use of multiple credential formats such as X.509 certificates [15] and SAML assertions [10]. It should also be possible to add support for new credential formats to deployed systems easily.

Interchangeable negotiation strategies Trust negotiation is by nature a strategy-driven process. Entities should be able to choose negotiation strategies that direct the execution of a trust negotiation session to meet their particular goals (e.g., maximizing privacy or minimizing latency). As is the case in client-server negotiations on the World Wide Web, the goals of negotiation participants may often be conflicting. The use of families of interoperable strategies that allow negotiation participants to choose different, yet compatible, strategies (e.g., as in [37]) should be supported. It should be possible to add support for new negotiation strategies to deployed systems.

Flexible policy and credential stores In many situations, clients are likely to utilize several computing devices, such as desktop computers, laptops, PDAs, and smart phones. It is therefore important that the trust negotiation architecture support interactions with a variety of flexible policy and credential stores (e.g., [26, 30]) that will enable users to effectively manage their digital identities across multiple devices.

It should again be noted that the core system components discussed earlier in this section are only logical components and that the functionality of multiple components may be handled by a single object in the system. However, the above requirements suggest that these components are perhaps best implemented as separate objects within the system. This increases the ease with which new functionality can be added to the system by eliminating redundant code and subtle dependencies that could hinder the level of extensibility discussed above.

External Interactions

Though the majority of a trust negotiation can take place within the confines of the core system components discussed in Section 5.1, the inclusion of external functionality can be quite helpful in many cases. For instance, the World Wide Web use case highlighted the need for users to be able to request help locating missing credentials from external entities (e.g., as in [34]). Similarly, the grid computing use case introduced the need to support a wider array of helpful third parties, such as reputation systems. In yet other cases, the active participation of the human on whose behalf a negotiation is initiated may be desired. Unfortunately, the naive inclusion of these features can lead to a variety of problems. The following requirements help to safely enable beneficial external interactions:

Strategy-driven external interactions It is clear that negotiation participants must have the ability to interact with a wide range of external entities who can help solve difficult problems which may arise during the negotiation. These interactions should be strategy-driven to allow participants to control the amount of time and resources spent in pursuing and validating the results of these interactions.

Tunable human involvement In some instances, humans may wish to be involved directly in the negotiation process. For example, users may want to specify an "ask me" release policy for a sensitive credential, see a visual representation of the negotiation process for policy evaluation purposes, or be involved in the decision-making process when the negotiation comes to a point where there are multiple execution paths that could be followed rather than relying on a predefined strategy. The framework should support extensions which can add a human "in the loop" if such features are requested.

Audit and Accountability

Depending on their deployment model, trust negotiation systems can place interesting restrictions on the way that users are identified in the system. For instance, unless a user's attribute certificates each contain a reference to some global identifier describing the user, it is possible for a user to gain access to some resource without ever disclosing an identity that can be used to hold the user accountable for her actions. In high assurance environments in particular, this can be problematic. The following requirement ensures that users can be linked to transactions carried out on their behalf:

Identifiability In the event that such functionality is required, a trust negotiation architecture should have some means of linking negotiations carried out by a single individual. This may occur through forced usage of credentials containing a globally verifiable user identifier (e.g., requiring that all attributes be linked to a single X.509 identity certificate) or through the use of a more privacy-preserving method such as virtual fingerprinting [19].

Given some means of linking transactions, as described above, it is then important to allow entities to maintain records that can be used to ensure that the system is being used as intended. This includes tasks such as looking for patterns of resource abuse (particularly in high-assurance environments) and verifying that policies are being enforced as expected.

Advanced logging capabilities The architecture should have a robust logging service which can record any aspect of the negotiation process. It is possible that such a high degrees of logging might be excessive in some cases; to address this, the logging subsystem should support the recording of logs at various granularities.

Performance and Extensibility

For a trust negotiation architecture to be widely adopted, it should have tunable performance guarantees and be reasonably extensible and configurable. These goals enable the architecture to be applicable to a wider range of scenarios and tolerate high levels of demand under both both legitimate and malicious conditions. In particular the following requirements help to meet these goals:

Selective feature activation To enable more efficient or more secure trust negotiation sessions (as indicated in the World Wide Web and high-assurance computing use cases, respectively), the features enabled by the framework should be fully configurable. For instance, disabling support for visualization features and external interactions might increase the performance of the system, while disabling third-party plug-ins might increase overall system security and trustworthiness.

Feature ordering To enhance performance of the system, entities should have the ability to choose the order in which certain functionalities are invoked. For instance, it should be possible for a negotiation strategy to choose the time at which credentials are validated. Since clients in the World Wide Web use case are not expecting DoS attacks, it makes sense for them to validate credentials prior to checking for policy satisfaction, as each credential received is likely to be both *valid* and *relevant* to the current negotiation. However, servers should not adopt this strategy, as clients could then easily conduct a DoS attack by sending spurious credentials to the server, which would then waste time attempting to validate them. In this case, it is perhaps best to validate only those credentials which can be used to satisfy a given policy.

Clearly, it would be impossible to derive a complete set of functional requirements for trust negotiation systems based upon the examination of only three use cases. Despite the general nature of the use cases presented in this section, the requirements extracted above cannot possibly cover the requirement space for all future applications of trust negotiation. It is important that future trust negotiation architectures account for the impossibility of deriving a complete set of functional requirements.

Sustainability The framework must support the addition of new functionality after deployment without requiring modifications to the existing code base. Example features may include (but are not limited to) the inclusion of new local data processing rules, the enforcement of obligations, the use of new strategies, policy languages, or data types during negotiations, or support for new forms of external-party interaction.

5.4 Into the Future

In recent years, we have seen a surge of interest in the theoretical aspects of trust negotiation. This has led to significant advances in the areas of languages for trust negotiation policies, negotiation strategies, and logics for reasoning about this new form of access control. To date, the implementations of trust negotiation systems that have been produced have been mainly proof-of-concept systems meant to demonstrate the practicality of the aforementioned theoretical advances. Though these implementations show that the theoretical benefits of trust negotiation are practically realizable, they fail to meet even the simple flexibility requirements for core components derived in this section. The theoretical foundations of trust negotiation have matured to a point at which exploring the systems and implementation issues associated with this more flexible form of access control is necessary to enable the adoption of this promising new technology.

There are several important directions for future work regarding the systems and architectural aspects of trust negotiation that must be explored. Clearly, designing and implementing a framework for trust negotiation that embodies, at a minimum, the requirements presented in this section is an important task. Such an architecture would allow researchers to quickly prototype and experiment with new trust negotiation strategies and protocols. A sufficiently general protocol within such a framework would allow a wide array of trust negotiation systems to interoperate with one another and could ease the adoption of trust negotiation technologies into existing systems. Currently, an effort to develop such a framework is underway at the University of Illinois at Urbana-Champaign.

Other important systems-level considerations emerge when one considers the changes to current security practices that a more flexible authorization system, such as trust negotiation, will introduce. It is clear that trust negotiation is a much more heavyweight process than checking the validity of a ⟨username, password⟩ pair. As such, trust negotiation is likely to become a bottleneck in highly-utilized systems. The investigation of both theoretical and systems-level advances to enhance the scalability of these systems while under heavy load and attack are required. The Trust-X [2] system enables the use of "trust tickets" that can be used to bypass recently executed portions of a negotiation for a limited window of time. This enhances the speed with which repeated negotiations can be executed, though it only scratches the surface of the scalability problem. Another interesting avenue for research in the scalability and DoS-resistance arenas is the development of credential chain validation strategies that are difficult to exploit during denial of service attacks. Also, as the open systems which adopt trust negotiation grow in size, it will become important for researchers to investigate effective means for audit and collusion detection across organizational boundaries.

In addition to these architectural research problems, there are still many other open issues in trust negotiation; several of these will be discussed in the concluding section of this chapter.

6 Conclusion

Automated trust negotiation is a new approach to authorization and authentication in open, flexible systems. It has the potential to provide nimble security facilities that will help organizations and individuals to rapidly and efficiently access each other's resources and integrate the information provided by the resources, while offering specific privacy guarantees.

In this chapter, we have introduced the basic concepts of automated trust negotiation, and present the state of the art of the research on negotiation strategies, resource protection and system design. As mentioned before, the full deployment of trust negotiation relies on the resolution of many challenging problems. In section 5, we have discussed several research issues in the aspect of system development. Next we will briefly discuss issues in other aspects of trust negotiation.

First, trust is a very broad concept. Depending on the specific context, applications may have different understandings of and requirements for trust and trust management. We believe that trust negotiation is only one step toward building a secure open computing environment. Specifically, trust negotiation enables strangers from different security domains to get familiar with each other. The trust built during this step may be strengthened in their future interactions through a different trust model.

For example, consider a carefully managed online auction system. Trust negotiation will enable Alice to gain local identities, capabilities or roles, so that Alice has the privilege to do business inside the community. Meanwhile, inside the auction system, a reputation-based trust model may be more appropriate to ensure that transactions are conducted properly. On the other hand, trust negotiation may also take place between users inside the auction system, where a user's reputation is taken as a special credential certified by the auction system.

As a future direction, we believe that it is important to investigate the **integration of different trust models** and provide a more comprehensive trust management framework for secure open computing.

Second, in our current discussion, we model trust negotiation as a two-party computation problem. One important direction is to investigate whether the theory of **secure multi-party function computation** can be applied to trust negotiation.

The problem of secure multi-party function computation is as follows: n players, $P_1, \ldots, P_n$, wish to evaluate a function $F(x_1, \ldots, x_n)$, where x_i is a secret value provided by P_i. The goal is to preserve the privacy of the player's inputs and guarantee the correctness of the computation. Trust negotiation maps naturally to this formulation. We have players Alice and Bob, each of which has a set of credentials and corresponding access control policies. The output of the function they compute is a safe disclosure sequence. It is interesting to investigate how well privacy is protected under this model and whether there is an efficient way to conduct this secure two-party function computation. Current, several work has been done toward realizing this goal [9, 12, 20, 21].

Third, inference protection is a hard problem in trust negotiation. Currently our approach to this problem is quite ad hoc, in the sense that we identify one possible way for an attacker to infer one kind of sensitive information, then we propose a solution to that problem. Such an approach cannot give us any guarantee of how good the protection really is. It is important to **formally model the information flow** between two negotiation participants so that we can study inference prevention in a systematic way.

Forth, access control policies are a cornerstone of trust negotiation. Organizations and individuals must have faith in their resources' policies, or they will be afraid to open their systems to access from outside. To instill confidence in policies, the person in charge of security for a resource will need a policy editor, access to canned, composable, and reusable policies (e.g., the definitions of a non-profit company, a full-time student at an accredited university, a minority-owned business); and ways to analyze, understand, and test policies before they are deployed. Security managers will want tools for regression testing (comparison of policy coverage under old and new sets of policies), consistency checking, and comparison of policies against higher-level specifications (when available). Without such tools, many organizations will be unable to change their security policies for fear that alterations will create security holes that leave them vulnerable. These concerns arise in automated trust negotiation and also in the growing number of other computational realms that rely on policies.

It is important to investigate the **design of policy management systems**. In particular, it is interesting to study the infrastructure for policy template distribution, the model for policy reuse and customization, and the analysis of policy correctness according to high-level policy requirements.

References

1. Moritz Y. Becker and Peter Sewell. Cassandra: Distributed access control policies with tunable expressiveness. In *Proceedings of the 5th IEEE International Workshop on Policies for Distributed Systems and Networks (POLICY '04)*, pages 159–168, 2004.
2. E. Bertino, E. Ferrari, and A.C. Squicciarini. Trust-χ: A Peer-to-Peer Framework for Trust Establishment. *IEEE Transactions on Knowledge and Data Engineering*, 16(7), July 2004.
3. Elisa Bertino, Elana Ferrari, and Anna Cinzia Squicciarini. X -TNL: An XML-based language for trust negotiations. In *Proceedings of the 4th IEEE International Workshop on Policies for Distributed Systems and Networks (POLICY '03)*, 2003.
4. E. Bina, V. Jones, R. McCool, and M. Winslett. Secure Access to Data Over the Internet. In *Conference on Parallel and Distributed Information Systems*, September 1994.
5. P. Bonatti and P. Samarati. Regulating Service Access and Information Release on the Web. In *Conference on Computer and Communications Security*, Athens, November 2000.
6. P. Bonatti, S. Vimercati, and P. Samarati. A Modular Approach to Composing Access Control Policies. In *ACM Conference on Computer and Communication Security*, Athens, Greece, November 2000.
7. Piero Bonatti and Pierangela Samarati. Regulating service access and information release on the web. In *7th ACM Conference on Computer and Communications Security*, pages 134–143, 2000.
8. D. Box, D. Ehnebuske, G. Kakivaya, A. Layman, N. Mendelsohn, H.F. Nielsen, S. Thatte, and D. Winer. *Simple Object Access Protocol (SOAP) 1.1*. World Wide Web Consortium, May 2000.
9. R.W. Bradshaw, J.E. Holt, and K.E. Seamons. Concealing complex policies with hidden credentials. In *ACM conference on Computer and communications security*, Washington DC, USA, 2004.

10. Scott Cantor, John Kemp, Rob Philpott, and Eve Maler (Editors). Assertions and protocols for the OASIS security assertion markup language (SAML V2.0). OASIS Standard, Mar. 2005. ⟨http://docs.oasis-open.org/security/saml/v2.0/saml-core-2.0-os.pdf⟩.
11. D. Damianou, N. Dulay, E. Lupu, and M. Sloman. The Ponder Policy Specification Language. In *2nd International Workshop on Policies for Distributed Systems and Networks*, Bristol, UK, January 2001.
12. K.B. Frikken, M.J. Atallah, and J. Li. Hidden Access Control Policies with Hidden Credentials. In *ACM Workshop on Privacy in Electronic Societies*, Washington, DC, October 2004.
13. Amir Herzberg, Yosi Mass, Joris Michaeli, Dalit Naor, and Yiftach Ravid. Access control meets public key infrastructure, or: assigning roles to strangers. In *IEEE Symposium on Security and Privacy*, May 2000.
14. Adam Hess, Jared Jacobson, Hyrum Mills, Ryan Wamsley, Kent E. Seamons, and Bryan Smith. Advanced client/server authentication in TLS. In *Network and Distributed Systems Security Symposium*, Feb. 2002.
15. Russell Housely, Warwick Ford, Tim Polk, and David Solo. Internet X.509 Public Key Infrastructure Certificate and CRL Profile. IETF Request for Comments RFC-2459, Jan. 1999.
16. H. Koshutanski and F. Massacci. Interactive access control for web services. In *19th IFIP Information Security Conference (SEC)*, pages 151–166, Aug. 2004.
17. H. Koshutanski and F. Massacci. An interactive trust management and negotiation scheme. In *2nd International Workshop on Formal Aspects in Security and Trust (FAST)*, pages 139–152, Aug. 2004.
18. H. Koshutanski and F. Massacci. Interactive credential negotiation for stateful business processes. In *3rd International Conference on Trust Management (iTrust)*, pages 257–273, May 2005.
19. Adam J. Lee and Marianne Winslett. Virtual fingerprinting as a foundation for reputation in open systems. In *4th International Conference on Trust Management (iTrust 2006)*, May 2006.
20. J. Li and N. Li. OACerts: Oblivious Attribute Certificates. In *International Conference on Applied Cryptography and Network Security*, New York, NY, June 2005.
21. N. Li, W. Du, and D. Boneh. Oblivious Signature-Based Envelope. In *Proceedings of the 22nd ACM Symposium on Principles of Distributed Computing (PODC 2003)*. ACM Press, July 2003.
22. N. Li, W. Winsborough, and J.C. Mitchell. Beyond Proof-of-compliance: Safety and Availability Analysis in Trust Management. In *IEEE Symposium on Security and Privacy*, Berkeley, California, May 2003.
23. Ninghui Li and John Mitchell. RT: A role-based trust-management framework. In *Third DARPA Information Survivability Conference and Exposition*, Apr. 2003.
24. MANBIZ IPP LLC. *Frequent Asked Questions*.
25. M. Myers, R. Ankney, A. Malpani, S. Galperin, and C. Adams. X.509 internet public key infrastructure online certificate status protocol–OCSP. IETF Request for Comments RFC 2560, Jun. 1999. ⟨http://www.ietf.org/rfc/rfc2560.txt⟩.
26. Jason Novotny, Steven Tuecke, and Von Welch. An online credential repository for the grid: MyProxy. In *Tenth International Symposium on High Performance Distributed Computing (HPDC-10)*, Aug. 2001.
27. B. Schneier. *Applied Cryptography, second edition*. John Wiley and Sons. Inc., 1996.

28. K. Seamons, M. Winslett, and T. Yu. Limiting the Disclosure of Access Control Policies during Automated Trust Negotiation. In *Network and Distributed System Security Symposium*, San Diego, CA, February 2001.
29. Bryan Smith, Kent E. Seamons, and Michael D. Jones. Responding to policies at runtime in TrustBuilder. In *5th International Workshop on Policies for Distributed Systems and Networks (POLICY 2004)*, Jun. 2004.
30. Tim W. van der Horst and Kent E. Seamons. Short paper: Thor — the hybrid online repository. In *First IEEE International Conference on Security and Privacy for Emerging Areas in Communications Networks*, Sept. 2005.
31. D. Wijesekera and S. Jajodia. Policy Algebras for Access Control - The Propositional Case. In *ACM Conference on Computer and Communication Security*, Philadelphia, PA, November 2001.
32. D. Wijesekera and S. Jajodia. Policy Algebras for Access Control - The Predicate Case. In *ACM Conference on Computer and Communication Security*, Washington, DC, November 2002.
33. Marianne Winslett, Ting Yu, Kent E. Seamons, Adam Hess, Jared Jacobson, Ryan Jarvis, Bryan Smith, and Lina Yu. The TrustBuilder architecture for trust negotiation. *IEEE Internet Computing*, 6(6):30–37, Nov./Dec. 2002.
34. Marianne Winslett, Charles Zhang, and Piero Andrea Bonatti. PeerAccess: A logic for distributed authorization. In *Proceedings of the 12th ACM Conference on Computer and Communications Security (CCS 2005)*, Nov. 2005.
35. W. Winslett, N. Ching, V. Jones, and I. Slepchin. Using Digital Credentials on the World-Wide Web. *Journal of Computer Security*, pages 255–267, 1997.
36. T. Yu, X. Ma, and M. Winslett. PRUNES: An Efficient and Complete Strategy for Automated Trust Negotiation over the Internet. In *ACM Conference on Computer and Communication Security*, Athens, Greece, November 2000.
37. Ting Yu, Marianne Winslett, and Kent E. Seamons. Supporting structured credentials and sensitive policies through interoperable strategies for automated trust negotiation. *ACM Transactions on Information and System Security*, 6(1), Feb. 2003.
38. Lidong Zhou, Fred B. Schneider, and Robbert van Renesse. COCA: A secure distributed on-line certification authority. *ACM Transactions on Computer Systems*, 20(4):329–368, 2002.

Building Trust and Security in Peer-to-Peer Systems

Terry Bearly[1] and Vijay Kumar[2]

[1] IBM
bearly@ibm.com
[2] School of Computing and Engineering
University of Missouri-Kansas City
kumarv@umkc.edu

1 Introduction

The popularity and wide spread usage of peer-to-peer (P2P) systems has soared over the past several years. Throughout the evolution of P2P systems the definition of P2P has changed along with the software architecture of the various P2P applications. While the initial popular usage of P2P systems was for file sharing (more *specifically* the sharing of music files in mp3 format) [4] the problem domain that P2P systems address today cover the range from data sharing to collaboration to distributed computing and beyond. For the continued increased usage of P2P systems, the need for security and trust arises. This chapter covers evolution of P2P systems through the examination of Napster, Gnutella, KaZaa, and BitTorrent [9], system capabilities and shortcomings, and security needs, which highlights the need for trust in P2P systems. With this basis we then present our vision for trust and security followed by a literature review of trust in P2P systems. We then introduce and develop a Universal Trust Set as a foundation for building trustworthy environment, and then our approach for implementing the set, and the future of P2P systems where we will discuss other open issues that need addressing. We close this chapter with some concluding remarks.

The notion of peer-to-peer networking has its root in Usenet, Fidonet [26] and Arpanet [28]. Its potential as a files and music sharing network was actually recognized in 1990s. Since then there have been many definitions of P2P ranging from "simply the opposite of Client/Server" architectures" to "a distributed network architecture may be called Peer-to-Peer (P-to-P, P2P,...) network if the participants share a part of their own hardware/software resources (processing power, storage capacity, network link capacity, printers, ...) that comprise the network. These shared resources are necessary to provide the service and content offered by the network (e.g. file sharing or shared workspaces for collaboration). They are accessible by other peers directly, without passing intermediate entities. The participants of such a network are thus resource (service and content) providers as well as resource (service and content) requestors" [55]. [56] contends that true P2P need to provide support for machines without DNS (Domain Name Server) entries and that are sporadically connected to the Internet. Additional background on P2P can be found [43, 44, 45, 57, 58].

Our work on trust in P2P systems is able to use any of these definitions. But to be precise, unless otherwise indicated, we will use the following definition.

We regard P2P as a special distributed system, which provides a global information search and exchange space. Peers in P2P systems function as autonomous nodes or sites. Each peer can communicate, share and download information from any other peer that could be located anywhere in the geographical space. Peers can provide redundant resources, can have low download latency, and can increase reliability and fault tolerance in the event of disconnections. Formally:

$P_2P = \{P_1, P_2, \ldots, P_n\}$ *where* P_i*is a peer. We define a capability set* C_s *indicating the capability of a P2P system.* $C_s = \{C_1, C_2, \ldots, C_m\}$ *where* C_i *is a capability. The capability set* C_{Pi} *of a peer Pi is then* $C_{Pi} \subset C_s$*. We also define a minimum capability set of* P_2P *as* $C_{s(min)}$= *minimum capability set which must be satisfied by a peer to be in* P_2P*. Thus for Pi and Pj to be peers* $C_{Pi} \cap C_{Pj} \geq C_{s(min)}$

There are several benefits to community-based redundancy. First, each peer is able to take advantage of a system with large aggregate resources by contributing its own relatively small set of resources. Second, the distribution of resources in the system means that the utility of the aggregate resources is larger than the sum of the individual contributions. Third, the damage to a subset of peers is usually localized, thus, if one site experiences a failure, a hardware fault, a malicious attack such as a virus or a Trojan, or a natural disaster, the resources at unaffected peers can be used safely; and the sharing in collaborative system can save bandwidth, decrease communication latency, and optimize storage.

2 Evolution of P2P

Napster [29], the popular MP3 file-sharing P2P system of the late 1990s through the early 2000s, brought the P2P technology into mainstream usage. While the architecture of Napster can be described as a server-based P2P, it did provide the force to get the technology into the hands of college students and teenagers, enabling sharing of music files. This system is considered server-based P2P as there was a central server that maintained an index of which files were located at which peer. When a peer wanted to share files, it would upload files indices to the central server, which made these files available to the entire Napster community. To download a specific file, a peer would query the central server for a specific file and the central server would respond with one or more peers that had the requested file. Then the requesting peer would choose a peer to download the file from, and this part of the Napster protocol was peer-to-peer. It is the combination of server based query processing and peer-to-peer file exchange that cause this to be called a server based P2P system. The choice as to which peer to pick may be based on prior experience with the peer, or a random selection from the list of peers with the requested file.

The downfall of Napster was that the files most actively being traded were copyrighted songs, and the recording industries sued Napster [29] as they were losing money. The courts ruled in favor of the recording industry and ordered Napster to shut down the central server. Without the ability to process queries, the system was shut down. Thus the single point of failure of the query processing was utilized to stop the illegal trading of music files.

The next P2P system to experience wide spread usage was Gnutella [22, 23], released in March 2000. It is a fully distributed system, which prevents the courts from shutting down the Gnutella network by removing the central server as they did in the case of Napster. Justin Frankel and Tom Pepper of Nullsoft (a division of AOL) developed Napster. The program was available for download for one day from Nullsoft's servers. The next day AOL stopped the availability of the program due to legal concerns [32]. But the genie was out of the bottle, and within several days the protocol had been reverse engineered and several open source projects began. Instead of having a centralized server with a list of files, each peer kept its own list. A new queries were forwarded to all peers a node has connections with except for the node that originated the query. While this kept the courts from being able to stop the Gnutella network by shutting down one computer, the networking load produced by the overly simplistic query processing adversely impacted the network as the number of peers grew. It was shown that for a dial up Internet user with a 56 Kbs connection, a rate of 10 queries per second would use all the available bandwidth [49]. This just did not scale to very large number of peers. Today the term Gnutella is used to refer to the protocol, and there are many clients such as LimeWire, BearShare, Mutella, Gnotella, gtk-gnutella, and Acquistionx [3, 7, 21, 24, 37, 46, 59].

Following Gnutella in March 2001 came Kazaa [33]. It can be downloaded freely, but is financed via the accompanying spyware and adware (the vendor claims only adware is included). Software containing either adware or spyware raises trust and security concerns. There is software, Kazaa Lite, that is compatible with Kazaa, but without the adware and/or spyware. Fast download speed is one of Kazaa's features. The vendor used the ability to change the protocol to cut off access of clients who did not pay license fees.

The application Kazaa (initially written KaZaA) arrived in March 2001. Developed by Niklas Zennstrom and Janus Friis of the Dutch company Consumer Empowerment [15], Kazaa utilizes the FastTrack protocol. In 2004 there were three FastTrack based networks: Kazaa, Grokster, and iMesh [20], using mutually exclusive versions of the protocol. Kazaa has two classes of nodes, regular peer nodes and supernodes. Queries are sent to the supernode, and supernodes can communicate with other supernodes [39]. This is to limit the bandwidth used by Kazaa queries. The communication is encrypted, but the peer to supernode portion has been reverse engineered, which is one of the reasons that the second and third implementation of FastTrack networks came about. Another reason was that the vendor used the ability to change the protocol to cut off access of clients who did not pay license fees.

The last P2P file transfer system we examine here is BitTorrent, which debuted in 2002 [9]. This is, as of June 2004, the most widely used file transfer system on the Internet [11]. It is especially good at transferring large files, by breaking the file up into typically $^1/_4$ megabyte size fragments and uploading those to different peers. The peer downloading the file takes advantage of the best connection to the missing fragments in order to reassemble the entire file. BitTorrent is distributed under an open source license. The protocol's primary objective is the fast transfer of files. To reach this goal bandwidth is used whereever it can be found, even without the explicit permission of the bandwidth owner.

A highly unusual approach to query processing is utilized within BitTorrent. The protocol does not support it, nor was it designed for privacy. No attempt is made to mask the peer that has a file available for download. One of the reasons is to reduce the chances of getting sued. When asked about the lack of a search engine, the reply is to use Google. However, in late May 2005 it was announced that a BitTorrent search engine would be made available in June 2005.

User anonymity has been an important category, especially in the file-sharing systems. Users in Napster, Gnutella, and Kazaa are all anonymous, but not so in BitTorrent. Since a user is anonymous, you cannot tell if the user's machine that you are downloading a file from belongs to a specific person or organization, nor can the download side insure who is actually downloading the file. The IP address may provide what organization the user belongs to, but this can't be relied upon in all situations. In some applications, such as licensed media distribution, the knowledge that a user belongs to a group member is required, but it may not be necessary to identify the user specifically. Finally there are times when you want to be able to identify the actual person that the peer in the transaction is. In other P2P applications there may not be a requirement for anonymity. Scientific collaboration does not need anonymity, outside of the anonymous review of proposed papers. One can argue that this piece is not part of the collaboration process and thus the scientific collaboration can do without anonymity completely. The preceding systems are not a complete list. Other systems have been proposed [19, 35, 52, 64, 67] and [36] compare several P2P systems.

2.1 Issues added by mobility

Within the context of P2P data replication services the impact of mobile peers is just starting to be addressed [34]. Data consistency problems can arise from the ability of peers to arbitrarily join or leave the network, or portion of the network either by choice or by movement of either the peer or the movement of the rest of the network. With mobile networks, the lack of global knowledge could give rise to new types of consistency. These include:

Location consistency It indicates that the value of a data item is correct for a particular location,

Proxy consistency It indicates that the value of a data item is based upon a specific peer,

Application consistency It indicates that the data item value is acceptable to certain applications, and

Temporal consistency It indicates that the data item value is based on a time period.

Within a P2P application the placement of data, updating of data, caching of data, amount of data replication within the network will all have impacts on the P2P system. How should network communication lapses be handled? Will the P2P system try to replicate the data held by the lost peer onto other peers right away, or will that happen later, after a certain number of data requests to the lost peer happen, without the lost peer re-establishing communications? Will the mobility of a peer that has replicated data and if leaves its designated location cause the replicated data to become invalidated? Peer pairing (identifying a partner peer for information sharing) for performance in a MANET (Mobile Ad hoc Network) needs addressing. Should the pairing be based solely on content, or will network topology have too great of an impact to ignore?

Trust issues in mobile P2P networks also need to be addressed. If a peer stops participating in a P2P network, is it because that peer is hostile, or is it due to a mobility issue that has taken the peer out of range of the communications channel? If the peer is under a denial of service attack, should this decrease that peer's trust score? This last point needs to be addressed within wired networks as well. Within a structured P2P network, one would expect the peers to be connected all the time, versus the connections and disconnections commonly experienced in a non-structured P2P system with a large number of dialup Internet users. A structured peer-to-peer network such as overlays like [50, 53] provides a self-organizing and a powerful platform for the construction of a variety of decentralized services. Structured overlays allow applications to locate any object in a probabilistically bounded, small number of network hops, while requiring per-node routing tables with only a small number of entries. Moreover, the systems are scalable, fault-tolerant and provide effective load balancing [13].

Hardware resources are typically listed as an area for concern for mobile users, or mobile devices. However, with the ever-increasing capabilities this will become less of an issue. Presently 1 GB memory cards can be purchased for under $100. Processor speeds go up and power consumption falls with each new generation. If WiMAX networking lives up to expectations then mobile bandwidth will get a significant boost. Even battery power lifetime is on the rise. These issues, while still significant in applications such as sensor networks, will become less and less of a concern as technology keeps advancing.

2.2 Sophisticated information sharing system

The existing P2P systems support many differing application types. Table 1 is a P2P category topology present on the openp2p web site. There is considerable overlap within this listing. For instance some P2P applications are listed in several categories – file sharing, messaging frameworks is one common overlapping pair. The application types in Table 1 enjoying the most wide-spread usage are the file sharing and messaging systems. While improvements to the protocols for file sharing have been made to distribute the metadata, which changed the architecture from a hybrid peer-to-peer system of Napster, to a true pure peer-to-peer system of Gnutella. The next major changes were made in decreasing the download times, which covers both

Kazaa and BitTorrent. The various P2P file sharing systems offer very basic functionality – file transfer, and in some cases file search. Usually the P2P file sharing system operates as a download only system, but the occasional systems exist that supports upload as well.

When one considers the activities that a user typically does either on their own PC or on a multi-user computer system the creation of a file or copying a file from one machine to another is a very small percentage of most applications. Therefore we anticipate that similar functionality will be added to P2P applications. Within certain categories of P2P systems, such as collaboration, and development frameworks this is becoming the case.

Table 1. Representation of trust

Agents as peers	Collaboration
Development frameworks	Devices as peers
Distributed computation	Distributed objects
Distributed search engines	File-sharing
Gaming	Infrastructure
Internet operating systems	Licensed media distribution
Messaging frameworks	Metadata
Reputation and asset management	Security
Servers/services as peers	Superdistribution
Writeable web	

It is our goal to provide a trust infrastructure for P2P systems that will extend trust past solely the user reputation that has been the primary focus to date. To allow P2P systems to evolve to a point where the Internet can become an on demand ad-hoc sophisticated information sharing system where the user (peer) can enter into a transaction with the peer that provides the best combination of resources and personal trust or reputation that allows the originating peer to have the highest trust possible that the transaction will be successful. We call this universal P2P, and the typical P2P applications that exist presently we term simple P2P.

The existing file sharing systems do not take trust into account. There is no reputation system that has been deployed and is in use by the existing file-sharing systems. Users may try and utilize peers that they have previously had success with. Gnutella had a bandwidth parameter that was used in the query that restricted system from responding if they did not have at least the requested bandwidth. Our system, which will be discussed in a later section, will expand on these ideas and present a trust scoring protocol that can be utilized in the query phase of P2P transaction to allow a peer to select the best peer (or a peer that meets a minimum trust level if load balancing is also considered) to interact with. For example both bandwidth and location or proximity may be parameters used to select a peer to download from. This same approach will allow the requested system to determine if the requestor has a sufficient trust score to be allowed to perform the requested operation. If a peer requests distributed computing and it would require running code provided by the requestor, a new peer making the request would need additional references as opposed to an existing peer that had made similar requests in the past and completed those with no adverse impacts.

3 System Architectures and Need for Security

Before the Internet was accessible via web browsers, to get access to a server (UNIX, VMS, MVS, and all the others) a login id was needed. The system administrator, or administration group, provided this after some form of login request was filled out and approved by an authorized agent. Traditionally the request form indicated which group(s) the user should be included in, what his/her role was, and which applications that the user is authorized to use. This allowed for role based security to be implemented, and this allowed the user to perform his or her duties. Depending on the level of security needed the entire user's session may be logged, or maybe only certain activities performed by the user may be logged. By assigning the user an id and password, and not having users share ids, it is easy to track who did what.

Then the Internet age arrived. Web sites were created, and now the users could generate anonymous accounts. Some of these accounts are long lifetime accounts, used for many years. Others are one-time only accounts where the user may in fact use the account once and abandon it, or use it for a few days or weeks and then abandon it. The primary reason for anonymous accounts is the protection of the user's privacy. Other uses would be to prevent unwanted email, to provide an avenue to get honest feedback, to be able to read items without censorship or persecution. It is possible that the anonymity is being used for illegal activities also.

Within P2P communities how can security be implemented with all of the anonymous users? What type of security can we implement that allows for anonymous users? There will be certain instances where the desired security cannot be achieved with anonymous users. The general approach is to create an anonymous id and password. The password can be used to validate the user in the future, but the user is still anonymous. The application needs to address what happens to the account if the user forgets her/his password? Is there a recovery process that would allow only the legitimate user to reset the password or to obtain it?

4 Need for Trust in P2P Systems

To justify the scope and objectives for trust in P2P systems we identify the situations and events, which could threaten trust. The list, to a large extent, defines the scope of our investigation for the design, development and evaluation of necessary schemes.

Unknown peers: In P2P environment peers are usually unknown to each other [31, 61], which restricts us to replicate information at nodes until their trust is established. Reputation systems have been utilized to handle interactions between previously unknown peers. The trust in a peer can be based solely on either on first hand trust knowledge of the peer, or on reputation knowledge from the reputation system, or on a combination of the two.

Cheater identification: A new peer can be malicious or an existing peer can cast negative feedback or turn malicious. The new user problem hasn't been handled well. Generally the new user is permitted to do a limited amount of the system functionality, and must build its trust score over time. This is a defensive approach and it protects the established users at the expense of the new user. To handle the possibility of existing users going bad, frequent updates to the reputation system must be made and the reputation value should decrease rapidly on bad behavior and take a relatively long time to repair the reputation damage. Utilizing negative feedback to lower another peer's reputation can be addressed within the reputation system. To accomplish this the reputation system needs to track not only peers' reputation values, but also which peers have been evolved in creating the reputation value.

Scalability: P2P systems should be scalable, however, this facility may threaten trust. Systems that are known to have very small user groups can get away without much attention to scalability. When their protocol is being developed, attention should be paid to avoid P2P scalability problems with known solutions. Adding trust management within a P2P protocol will add overhead and impact performance if care isn't used in the design and implementation of the trust protocol. If small systems utilize the same trust protocol implementation as are used in large P2P systems then the trust portion of the small P2P system will not be a scalability problem.

Replication: The first problem we face is where to partially replicate desired data in the presence of malicious peers. We need the trust and reputation system to quickly identify these peers as malicious so that they can be avoided, and any data that has been replicated to a malicious peer can be replicated to a non-malicious peer – either immediately or after some replication period. If it is not done immediately, then the data access must go to another peer, which may take longer, or bad data could be used.

Peer's capability: Due to the non-homogenous composure of a P2P network, the capabilities vary widely between peers. If the P2P system is supporting a distributed computing environment, two peers should have different trust scores based on their hardware, and software resources. It is logical to assume a machine with a 3.0 GHz processor with 512MB of DRAM could perform the task much quicker that a 400 MHz processor with 128 MB of DRAM. If the finish date of the task to be performed isn't crucial, then perhaps for load balancing the slower machine could be used without adverse impacts.

Both cheating peers and malicious peers have the implication that the action is being done on purpose. However hardware or software problems could cause a "good" peer to appear bad. They should be treated as a "bad" peer until the problem is fixed. Afterwards, the issue will be if their reputation should be restore to its previous value, or if it will take a long time to build the reputation score back up. One problem would be verification, how can this be done to determine if the actions were intentional or the result of a hardware or software problem. This decision must be balanced with the level of defense from attacks.

5 A Vision of Trusted P2P Systems

For universal P2P systems to be able to support more complex interactions than the existing simple P2P system of today, do the trust between peers must be increased over that which is present today. For the majority of P2P systems the peers' anonymity is highly valued. To perform the type of tasks that certain applications will entail, the peer must be a group member. How the groups are formed can be part of the process of forming an ad-hoc P2P group. The peers could come together and decide that they should form a group, and that any additional members would need to be approved by some majority of the group. One example of this could be an inter-disciplinary collaboration team on a research item of interest to the group of peers. Peers would exchange information, perform analysis on the research area, perhaps even share computing resources across the peers, and co-author papers on their results. This would be restricted to the group of peers, and until the paper was published only this peer group could work on it. The peer group would then disband when the project was finished.

Alternatively, the peer group membership may be established by other means. However a peer's membership must be able to be confirmed via a non-repudiation system. Without the verification of the peer's membership in the group, the peer will be denied access to this P2P application.

In real life people may overstate their qualifications. To guard against this in the universal P2P system an approach of "trust but verify" should be used. For instance in a distributed computing application, a peer may claim to have a CPU of a given speed and a certain amount of memory. We will trust the peer (unless we have had a previous experience with that peer that would result in a lack of trust in that peer), however if we utilize the service of that peer we should attempt a quick verification of the claims.

For a new peer to attempt to join an existing group one of three cases is likely, assuming the peer is permitted to join. First is to assign the new peer a new peer default trust level. This may restrict it from performing certain functions. Another method is to have an existing peer vouch for the new peer and get a higher than new peer default trust level assigned. The final method will be to utilize trust level data from other peer groups the new peer is in. If the trust parameters from the other groups overlap with ones employed in the group the peer is trying to join, then a trust value for the new peer may be obtained. The more parameters in common the two system use, the new trust value should be closer to the peers existing trust value than to the new peer default trust value. Of course there are extenuating circumstances when this should not be used. A peer with a great trust value and reputation in one government's grouping of P2P systems, should not be awarded a similar trust level in another government's P2P systems, especially when hostilities exist between the two governments. Even friendly governments keep secrets from each other.

For a new peer to join a small ad-hoc P2P system, the new peer must locate a group member first. In the file sharing examples discussed earlier the IP address of Napster was included in the software. Likewise for Kazaa, the addresses of a few super peers were seeded in the client software. For small groups to be easily joinable, a web page describing the group, and containing contact information is a solution. New peers can use a search engine of their choice and locate groups willing to accept new peers. If you want a closed P2P group, then simply do not advertise it via a robot searchable web page or at all. If security is a major concern, then all traffic should be encrypted. For trust values, user authentication, and certain other operations the data should be digitally signed at a minimum.

6 Literature Review

In this section we will present several definitions of trust as well as the various types of trust. The literature treatment of how trust is represented, the difference between distrust and no trust, the context sensitivity of trust and the temporal nature of trust will be presented. Next we will review the several trust in P2P system proposals in the literature.

6.1 Trust definitions

Before we give a definition of trust, let us review when trust is needed and when trust is not needed. The scope we are looking at here is the interaction between two peers. When is trust needed in this situation? Whenever there is something at risk. According to [48] there must be an element of harm or vulnerability in the interaction, for "without vulnerability, there is no need for trust". It makes sense then to manage the level of trust, or specify the level of trust needed before beginning an interaction, based upon the amount of vulnerability

There are several aspects of trust [42]. Marsh was working in the agent area, but this can be appropriate for P2P systems also. These aspects are basic trust, general trust and situational trust. Basic trust is the representation of how high the basic trusting disposition is. General trust represents the trust one agent has in another agent. Marsh used a continuous range trust scale of [-1,+1), with –1 meaning a complete distrust, and +1 would be complete trust. Situational trust, (other may use the term contextual trust), introduces the fact that the situation under examination will impact the trust level. The cited example is "whilst I may trust my brother to drive me to the airport, I most certainly would not trust him to fly the plane" which is understandable.

Another trust definition has been offered by [abd00]. It is "... trust (or symmetrically, distrust) is a particular level of subjective probability with which an agent will perform a particular action, both before we can monitor such action (or independently of his capacity of ever to be able to monitor it) and in a context in which it affects our own action."

It was stated in [42] that no trust and distrust are different. No trust is also zero trust, and assigned the value 0. A value of zero could arise from 4 situations, the trusting peer may not know the trusted agent; the trusting agent may be impartial with respect to the trusted agent; the two agents have just met and the basic trust of the agent is 0; or the trust value may have been increased or decreased via a prior experience and the resulting value is 0.

The trust scale of [-1,+1) is arbitrary. Some other proposed trust ranges have been binary, different continuous ranges [0,+1] [63], and differing discrete value ranges [1]. In fact [1] argues that probabilities are transitive, whereas trust is not. If Alice trusts Bob and Bob trusts Cathy, it does not follow that Alice will trust Cathy; however the probability would indicate this trust exists.

Trust values should have a temporal aspect. The longer it has been since one peer has interacted with another peer should cause a positive trust score to decay. For systems with negative trust, no trust, and positive trust the temporal trust decay (assuming the trust value was positive to start) should stop when a value of no trust is reached. It seems appropriate to allow a negative value to remain in place and not to decay the score towards no trust. It should require positive actions by a peer to raise it's trust value.

A great deal of literature has been created on trust as it relates to computer systems in general [10, 40] and for P2P systems [5, 8, 62, 68].

6.2 Trust and Reputation in P2P systems

Several reputation based trust systems have been proposed [6, 8, 15, 14, 16, 41, 51, 62, 66]. In [63] it has been proposed one that involves feedback in terms of amount of satisfaction, number of transactions, credibility of feedback source, transaction context factor, and community context factor. The system is name PeerTrust. They suggest a temporal aspect by weighting the more recent transactions move heavily. Here a shortcoming is that no accounting for actual time is used, so there is no guarantee that the past several transactions are current. A common problem is getting peers to provide feedback of their satisfaction with the transaction. Encouragement is provided by boosting the rating of the peer providing the feedback, with a limit on the maximum amount of increase that can be obtained in this manner. The trust rule presented here is if the trust value is greater than the trust threshold specified by the requesting peer then trust the peer.

PeerTrust has on going research into several defensive areas. An attempt is underway to strengthen the system against malicious behaviors, such as collusion among peers. Also being addressed is the response to sudden and malicious attacks. Finally PeerTrust is being incorporated into two P2P applications under development at Georgia Tech.

Another reputation-based system has been proposed by [30]. In this system three parameters are used, user ranking, compliance and verity. User ranking is the input from other users based on their view of the transactions. Kalepu argues that this is a perception with no objective indication of performance. To add objectivity, the term verity is introduced as a measurement of the variance in compliance values. It attempts to translate the outcome of meeting service levels into a numerical value. Compliance covers both attribute compliance – bandwidth, response time, availability, and service compliance. Thus a vector of user ranking, compliance and verity is used to calculate reputation.

Kalepu showed an interesting point experimentally. They had a web service running in their lab, and the local reputation vector is shown to produce a ranking much higher than the same web service provide a user that isn't local to the lab. So local reputations versus global reputations will provide differing views of the same peer. But this mirrors life in general; two people can rate the same item and give it two different values.

This problem of reputation values being different introduces a problem in how to use the reputation. In [1] a scheme is proposed in which the reputation value is adjusted to match your viewpoint. This requires that there be some peers in common that we can calculate an adjustment factor to apply to a reputation. These adjustment factors are context specific and apply to the given peer that made the recommendation. In [15] also the problem of using reputations is addressed, and it introduces the concept of building reputations for raters. One problem of a rating system that uses the reputation of the raters is the privacy issue. Allowing feedback to be tied to a user may prevent the user from providing feedback. Allowing anonymous feedback degrades the reliability of the feedback data. An effective compromise is to tie the feedback data to the reputation of the user, and not to the user. The feedback provider can remain anonymous and yet peers can gauge the appropriate emphasis to place on the feedback via the reputation of the feedback provider.

7 Universal Trust Set

There are a few trust schemes proposed in the literature [1, 2, 32, 63], however, they have some limitations. Our aim is to develop a general trust model with the help of activity-related information. Activity-related information helps to understand the needs, the behavior and position of a peer in the network. We emphasize local sufficiency, that is, our trust and security scheme will be achieved mainly through components of the network locally. If it is absolutely necessary to bring outside intervention, then it will follow a quorum approach. We propose to address the following issues.

1. Identification and creation of a Universal Trust Set (UTS), which will include all necessary parameters, which define the capability of a peer such as CPU power, data bit rate, RAM size, etc., for developing trust. While the UTS will be quite large, not all parameters will be utilized within a given P2P application. Furthermore, not all parameters will impact a trust calculation and can be excluded from the UTS, for example trivial items such as monitor size, system enclosure color, etc., would be excluded.
2. Identification and creation of an ontology of trust levels. In real life different trust levels for different activity exist. For example, a customer buys a computer of one brand but may trust another company for peripherals.

3. Identification of trust levels that can be generated mutually and trust which may need additional help that can be provided locally. An existing member of P2P family is more aware of the entire network status than any external agent or node such as a system used as a third party for monitoring system activities.
4. Scheme for detecting that a peer has not tampered with the trust value obtained from other peers and to avoid collusion of distrusted peers, or the attempt at collusion by one peer masquerading as multiple peers. Digital signatures, and other cryptographic techniques will be employed.
5. Reliable scheme for storing trust data and a scheme for verifying trust values of peers in decentralized environment. If the trust system is itself a P2P application, then the issue we address here will also apply to the trust application.
6. Scheme for managing the departure and arrival of peers and their self-reconfiguration.
7. Scheme for dissemination of trust values to other peers. Here we will monitor trade offs between efficiency and successful peer interactions.
8. Scheme for creation of a localized trust group. This will help to minimize work involved in establishing a trust environment.

We identify a P2P system as a set of countable infinite fully functional and self sufficient processing nodes (agents), i.e., $P2P = \{P_1, Pp_2, \ldots, P_\infty)$; where $P_i's$ are fully connected peer nodes. The information exchange between $P_i$and P_j ($i = j$ or $i \neq j$) is free from temporal and spatial constraints and can take place through wired and wireless medium without the mediation of any central or distributed servers [65]. At any time a nodecan leave or join the network. Special consideration will be given to mobile peers, where short breaks in connectivity due to mobility may otherwise appear to be a session of rapid disconnects and reconnects.

The question of trust is inherent in any information-sharing environment. We introduce our concept of a "fully trusted" P2P network through a directed cyclic graph (DCG). A node of DCG represents a peer and a directed edge between a pair of nodes ($p_i$and p_j) represents the presence of one-sided trust. The head of the directed edge points to the trusted node. Figure 1 illustrates this concept where 1a is untrusted P2P, 1b represents *one sided trust* where p_i trust p_j but p_j may not trust p_i, 1c represents *full trust* between p_i and p_j, and 1d represents a fully trusted P2P network where a cycle exist between any pair of nodes. Our aim is to continuously maintain a fully connected DCG (any node pair has a cycle). Note that a cycle merely indicates trust between any two peers and it does not identify a trust level between them.

We define a *Universal Trust Set* (*UTS*) = $\{e_1, e_2, \ldots, e_n\}$; where e_i is a trust parameter. A parameter is a characteristic of a peer. For example RAM size of a peer may be one of its e_i's. Our first task, therefore, is the identification of members of UTS, which will suffice for all P2P systems. Since a P2P could be highly heterogeneous, each peer would have its own subset drawn from UTS. The work by others on trust parameters will be utilized in the initial seeding of the UTS. Most of the work to date has focused on file transfer or service oriented systems, out goal is to be able to provide support for what we term Universal P2P systems, as compared to the simple P2P systems that have been done.

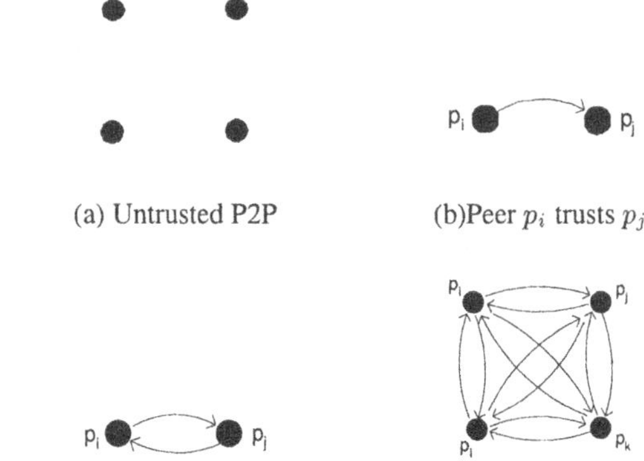

(a) Untrusted P2P (b)Peer p_i trusts p_j

(c) Mutual trust between p_i and p_j (d) Fully trusted P2P system

Fig. 1. Representation of trust.

Without any loss of generality, consider a P2P network of different types of peers where each peer is fully connected to all other peers of the network but each stores different types of information for sharing. For example, pipeer may store weather records, p_j medical records, p_k yet to be published research papers and proposals, and so on. In this setup it would not be appropriate to associate the same level of trust with each peer. Thus, the status (responsibility, contents, etc.) of a peer will be fixed or identified by the values of a subset of parameters drawn from UTS. Figure 2 illustrates such mapping to identify the trust level of a peer node. The figure does not identify the trust category such as "fully trusted" or "one-side trust", it merely indicates if a node is highly trusted or less trusted. This level is evaluated using values of e_i's of a peer.

The concept of security hierarchy is not new and has been used in databases [12]; however, this has not been widely used in trust management. Ontology has been successfully used in semantic web and has established itself as a powerful tool for level management in data access and web security.

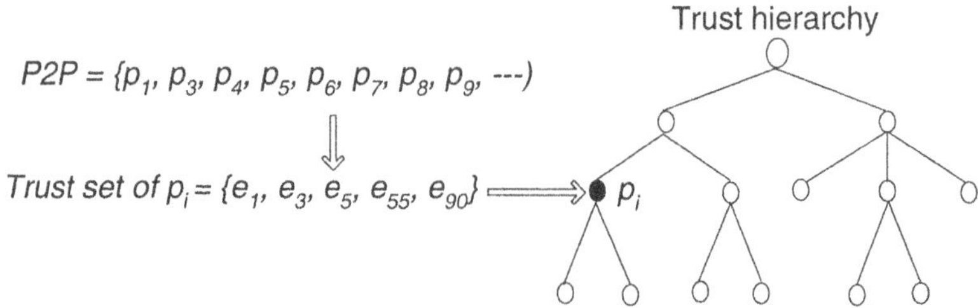

Fig. 2. Identification of peer trust level through mapping

8 Our Approach to Trust and Security

While the goal is to get to a point where the trust parameters and trust function, which indicates the level of trust one can put in its operation, for an arbitrary peer–to-peer system can be generated dynamically, the task of getting there will be broken down into two phases. The first phase will be to define several peer-to-peer systems, and develop a subset of trust parameters appropriate for the given P2P system and then come up with trust scoring functions. These will be evaluated for performance and the best ones will be retained. During this phase the parameters selected will be based on semantic arguments. Our view is that we should be able to come up with a trust score for a given peer-to-peer interaction, which will be such that a successful outcome will be more likely from peers with higher trust values.

Using the trust score values we can then choose which of several peer to interact with. Possible implementations would provide a list of peers that can perform the task with their trust scores and the highest one would be chosen. For a large system instead of listing all the peers, an arbitrary number could be used to decrease the messaging load on the network. Here again the peer with the highest trust score value would be selected. Alternately, a random peer out of the arbitrarily sized list could be chosen as a simple load-balancing scheme. Some peers may prefer to choose a peer that they have utilized in the past with good success even if that peer isn't the peer with the highest trust score.

At the end of the first phase the best performing parameters and the P2P services they support, the trust scoring function and the system performance will be loaded into system that will interact with a designer of a P2P application. Also the worst performing parameters, and trust scoring functions will also be loaded. The system will take in requirements for a new P2P system and construct a list of trust parameters and a trust scoring function for the new system. The user will be free to accept the suggested values, or they can customize the system by including other parameters, omitting suggested parameters or changing the scoring function. Also peers will be able to utilize a peer suggested by the system, or they can rely on their own knowledge in selecting a peer to interact with.

When the user is satisfied with the new system it is given a name so that it can be described to other users that may wish to join in the future. As the system gains usage, feedback on the performance of the system versus the trust score will be tracked, to enable the system to improve in the future.

It is our intention to specify a trust protocol that can be incorporated into arbitrary P2P systems. This means that points at which a user has a decision to make, the appropriate system parameters are available to calculate the trust scores. There will be protocol for the P2P application in which trust does not factor into. For instance the uploading of metadata to support query processing is outside of the trust realm, however, in some cases this may be quite important for preserving trust. If we are discussing an unstructured P2P system, then the choice of which peer to upload metadata to (assuming that there is more than one choice) is a place where trust would come into play.

So far we have viewed the trust score as something that is evaluated for each interaction, to make the best choice. There will be P2P applications that require the peer providing the service needs to know if the requesting peer should be trusted. We envision supporting two different methods. One is registration time trust scoring and the other is run time trust scoring. The registration time trust scoring is when a new peer joins, and provides their UTS parameters, a trust level is assigned and that maps to being able to perform certain activities. Peers will be able to "re-register" after belonging to the P2P group for some time in order to raise their trust score and get privileges. This is traditional role based security. Run time trust scoring is on an interaction-by-interaction basis. If the trust score is greater than the minimum needed for the interaction in question, then it is allowed to go forward, if it is lower that the minimum the interaction is prohibited for this peer.

How should feedback be provided? Should it be good to bad? If it is good does that necessarily suggest that the trust rating of the provider should be increased? Should multiple values be used? If the peer chosen was not one of the highest trust scoring peers, should the feedback be the same as if the highest value peer had been chosen? Should the requesting peer have his/her trust score impacted for picking a less capable node?

At the conclusion of the interaction either or both peers in the interaction can report the outcome of the interaction to the reputation system. This feedback is used to modify a peer's reputation value, which is one of the UTS parameters. Peers will update their own trust value for the other peer also. We anticipate that local trust values of other peers will be used where available and will be augmented with reputation values as needed. The P2P system may have its reputation system as part of the application, or it can use an external reputation system. This is determined at the time the P2P application is defined.

If the system has some levels of authorization, a peer may ask to be assigned to a given level. This would require either a minimum number of peers at the highest security level to concur, or a certain percentage of the peers at the highest level to concur. The requirement number or percentage may increase with increasing level requested. This will also work in the reverse direction. If a peer is detected to be malicious, a request to lower the level of authorization can be made. This request can range from lowering the authorization level one step to removing the peer from this P2P community.

8.1 Development of Universal Trust Set (UTS)

UTS is a finite set of relevant parameters for building trust on a peer [6]. We define $UTS = \{e_1, e_2, \ldots, e_n\}$; where e_i is a trust parameter. Some examples of e_i's could be RAM size, CPU speed, I/O speed, geographical location of the peer, etc. The quality of UTS will depend on its member selection scheme. We propose to include different categories of parameters such as the geographical location of the peer, the user group of the peer, in case of a mobile peer its geographical movement domain, its past and present activity history, and so on. Note that the activity domain, e.g., MC-P2P (m-commerce-P2P), EC-P2P (e-commerce-P2P [15, 16]), etc., plays a significant role in this categorization. The UTS will select parameters from all possible real environments where a P2P can exist. We argue that it would be useful to define an upper limit of UTS cardinality and we want to identify this limit using some semantic analysis of UTS parameters. Thus, our algorithm will use a set of association rules to identify parameters that are (a) complementary, (b) related, and (c) dependent. For example, RAM size is related to application execution speed, disk storage space is related to database size, and so on. If a parameter does not satisfy (a) or (b) or (c) then it will be rejected. We will explore the use of data mining association rules for UTS development. We propose to define a "Measure of Satisfaction (MoS)" which will help to identify the maximum cardinality of UTS sufficient for evaluating highest level of trust for a peer.

One way to define MoS is to study the interaction of application with a peer. Note that an application interacts with system that executes it in many different ways and with different frequencies. For example a debit/credit transaction application interacts with databases in a variety of ways at variety of locations and different times. A careful study of such interaction will reveal useful information about application interaction with systems. In fact, still now no detail study exists about such interaction among peers for improving system performance. In fact it is relatively more useful for high application traffic system such as P2P. We propose to study carefully such interaction and use the information to define MoS. In addition to UTS, each peer will have its own MoS, which must be satisfied to create its trust level. Note that each parameter will have a maximum and a minimum value. For example, if RAM (Random Access Memory) is a trust parameter, then it will have a minimum and a maximum value. The minimum value will decide if the peer should be included in the network. This means a peer must satisfy minimum values of all its parameters.

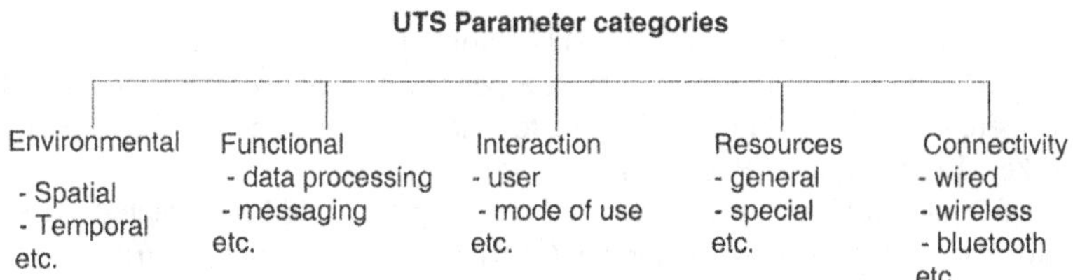

Fig. 3. UTS Parameter categories

8.2 Building UTS

UTS will have five parameter categories initially and new ones could be added whenever necessary (Figure 3). Each category will have a set of parameters and each parameter will be associated with a domain. For example, the environment category will have location as one of the parameters and Domain (location) = {Lab, Office, Shop, Car, etc.}. Note that this domain includes mobility aspect as well. Similarly,

Domain (time) = {1 hour to 30 hours} which means a peer will allow its use by others from 1 hour to 30 hours before it becomes unavailable.

Initially the UTS will be populated manually with a basic set of parameters each with a basic value set. Of course initial population will require careful selection and a heuristic approach will be the best way to achieve this. The development of such heuristic requires further investigation. One approach could be to monitor the frequency of reference of trust parameters of user's and system initiated tasks and use the result to identify its importance. For example, if a workload (e.g. games) makes extensive use of the graphic card, then this resource can be comparatively more important than I/O devices. With time along with the movement of peers (leaving and joining) the system will learn to refine and expand. For example, if a new peer arrives then the system will learn the characteristics of the peer and will enrich itself and compute and assign a trust value to the peer. We propose to develop a scheme for this learning process which will use some association rules for parameter discovery and identification.

The question who will manage the UTS is a part of our investigation. We wish to identify an existing peer and one solution would be to delegate the work to a peer with highest trust level. If we go with this, then we will have to clearly define the status of this peer in the network. Obviously, this peer must be well-protected and secured. We will also study the use of a third party trusted node, but our aim is to develop a solution using local resources. This needs a mechanism for the identification of malicious nodes. Of course this approach suffers with all problems of a centralized scheme, however, it would provide us useful information for the development of a fully distributed scheme.

8.3 Detection of malicious nodes

We propose to use digital signature (DS) [17] for detecting malicious peers. The DS could be used to secure the trust data in a peer-to-peer network. In a normal DS mechanism, a certifying authority is used to associate a prospective signer with the public key. However, in P2P we propose to do away with the certifying authority as the peer-ID and its IP address are unique and the peer could be contacted to verify the information. Our scheme maintains (a) trust score log, (b) local trust log, and (c) global trust log. Under this scheme each peer maintains its trust score log which stores all feedback sent by those peers which received data from this peer. The received feedback is encrypted using the public key of the receiving peer. As a result the feedback cannot be modified unless the peer acquires a private key. This log file helps in authenticating the trust score of each peer for detecting its status (malicious or clean).

The local trust log is maintained by each peer to keep a history of its own feedback to others (positive or negative) for the files it received. The local trust log gives a direct way of detecting whether a particular peer can be identified as malicious.

The global trust log contains the trust information with specific score that is exchanged between the peers. The score helps to determining a global view of a peer that could be malicious. A peer P_1 accepts global trust log from another peer P_2

only if P_1 has left a positive feedback to P_2. P_1 then performs a union operation on its own global trust log and the trust log received from P_2. This simple mechanism along with the digital signatures helps in making sure that the global trust log cannot be tampered with by any malicious node.

8.4 Detection of a malicious peer

A peer spreading malicious content or tampering with trust logs needs to be identified. Each peer stores it's own trust score that is based on all its previous file transfers. A trust score consists of two values, the number of positive and negative feedbacks it received. This information is stored in trust score log. The trust score along with the "query-hit" (hit-yes I have the file) message to the peer querying for a file. This peer can decide on these two values whether a peer is malicious. If the peer misrepresents its trust score, this could be easily verified using the trust score log sent by the sender. As trust log contains all the previous feedback that it received, and each feed back entry is digitally signed by the peer giving the feed back, this information could not be tampered with. The trust log entries could be easily verified by sending a trust query to the peer from where the feedback originated. Thus any peer tampering with its own trust log could easily be detected as malicious node.

Local trust score log keeps history of nodes with which a peer already interacted. This directly gives a way to find whether a peer could be trusted or not, if we already have some interaction with it. On the other hand, the global trust score log helps in finding out any malicious nodes based on others experiences with a particular node. As both these logs are also secured using digital signatures, these log files cannot easily be tampered with. Our scheme can be easily incorporated in any P2P system such as Gnutella [22].

8.5 Managing Trust Tree

The concept of security hierarchy is not new and has been used in databases [12]; however, this has not been used in trust management [38]. Trust tree (Figure 2) contains a number of nodes and with each node a trust level, MoS, and list of activities the node is allowed to perform will be associated. The root of the tree has the highest trust level and it decreases with downward travel. A parent "includes" its descendants' trusts but the opposite is not true. The creation of such trust hierarchy is challenging mainly because it not only requires logical relationship but also parameters' semantics. We propose to compose some form of association rules for the development of this tree. It is also true that the activities and state of peers will not be identical. Some peers may be handling more confidential activities compared to other peers, some peers may be involve in common public data repositories, and so on. An efficient management of this realistic situation may also need peer-specific attention. The peer status information will be necessary to develop this tree and also the management policies. We propose to define a number of policies that may find it appropriate to override some decisions which were taken based on technical considerations only.

8.6 Development of a Local Trust Set (LTS) for a Peer

Our P2P network is highly heterogeneous but there may exist homogeneous pair of nodes. As argued earlier, each peer in the network will have its own trust level and must be computed individually. The computation will require a proper subset of UTS which will be computed for each node.

We propose to define a Local Trust Set (LTS) $\subset$ UTS for any new peer that joins the network. This approach will take care of the handling the inclusion of any new node to P2P network. When a new node arrives, it presents its credentials and parameters values to the system. The system matches this set with UTS, creates a LTS (Figure 2) for this node and computes its trust level. The creation of LTS will determine its inclusion into the network and the values of its parameter will decide the trust level. Note that if an LTS for a new peer cannot be created, then it is obvious that it cannot be included in the P2P network.

8.7 Generation of One Sided and Mutual Trust

We propose to use LTSs of a pair of peers for establishing trust link (Figure 1). If $LTS\ (p_i) \cap LTS\ (p_j) = \emptyset$, then p_i and p_j may not create a trust link because p_i and p_j have nothing in common. If it is necessary to establish trust link, then their LTSs must be revised. We investigate how to establish one sided and mutual trust link (Figure 1). One way would be to see the values of LTS parameters of the two peers. The lower value parameters can trust a higher value parameter which will create one-sided trust. Similarly one way of establishing mutual trust link is to guarantees that the two peers have identical LTS and their values are also same. This is not the only way for creating one sided and mutual trust and it needs further investigation for developing a general algorithm. We have just indicated our intended approach with these simple examples.

8.8 Mapping of a Peer's Trust to Trust Hierarchy

We propose to map a peer trust to the tree using its LTS for identifying its trust level. This mapping will also help us to establish one sided or mutual trust link. If a pair of peers maps to the same level and to the same node of the tree (Figure 2), then they may be candidates for one sided or mutual trust link. A complete mapping (mapping of all nodes to the tree) will provide us a good sense of the state of all nodes and the state of P2P network. It is possible that the tree may shrink or expand, in which case the trust mappings will also change. We may experiment with an external trusted agent just to run a background process mainly to continuously monitor the dynamics of P2P network. This will help to revise peers' mappings with the tree and their trust links. Note that some trust links will continuously change (one sided to mutual and vice versa) and some may be eliminated because of peer migration (mobile peers). This will require a continuous monitoring without the help of a centralized peer. In addition to the use of external agent, we propose to use the concept of self-monitoring and status multicast to one sided and mutually connected peers. In this way every peer has the information about the state of other peers. Note that this task will also be necessary for P2P reconfiguration for maintaining the highest confidence level.

8.9 Information Replication Model

It is out of the question to replicate information among untrusted set of peers. Thus the replication problem is confined to one sided and mutually trusted peers. The classical data distribution problems in distributed systems exist here but their solutions may not be satisfactory. Besides this, some nodes are mobile and information may also be replicated there (cached) for mobile users. What happens if some confidential information is replicated at a mobile peer and the peer is untraceable? We propose to enforce specific restrictions on all mobile peers and one way to enforce them is to define a trust-cell boundary (not cellular cell area) for each mobile unit. If any mobile peer crosses its defined trust-cell boundary without surrendering its cached information, then that information is made obsolete. Of course this simple solution will not suffice and further investigation is required to tackle this problem.

The proposed replication scheme is to consider the number of queries per object, document size, and trust of the peers and the quality of service requested by peers who access the documents. The document size should be taken into consideration, as low-resolution (smaller size) documents require less memory. The proposed approach is to consider the probability of access frequency P_{ij}, where i is the peer accessing the document j. The probability of access can be combined with the average time interval T of access. Let the trust of the peer for a document D with a resolution r be D_r. Let S_r be the size of the document with resolution r. Thus, a function for a replicating factor (RF) for a document j can be given by the following function:

$$RF = (P_{ij} * T * D_r)/S_r$$

We propose to cluster the documents with similar RF and trust values. In addition, if fragments of a document are replicated then we need to first find the cluster so that all the fragments are available in close proximity with trust values in a close range. One technique is to form the bipartite graph of the nodes hosting the fragments of the related documents with similar resolution and trust. We will explore this technique in addition to our work [27] and evaluate by varying different size, resolution, hops, and access probability of documents. Once clusters are identified, we will replicate the clusters and relocate the replicas over a period of time based on the parameters discussed. We propose to replicate the documents with similar RF factor in a cluster with the similar trust within some reasonable hops (decided by the extensive simulations) to provide reasonable response time. The higher resolution data will be closer from the hosts whereas low resolution data will be kept far from the peers. The immediate update scheme will be used to update the replicas with higher resolution and lazy-replication will be used for lower resolution data. Thus, the cost of updates will be lower for lower resolution data. We will also investigate the integration of QoS requested by users to decide the location of replicas. As users are at fixed locations, we will design heuristics to balance the replica allocation with the QoS and trust requested by the users based on the current users' locations and the bandwidth available. We will consider different P2P architectures [64] and evaluate the schemes designed.

8.10 Trust and Distrust Propagation

If peer A does not trust peer B then should A broadcast its intention to all P2P nodes? In reality this is not be allowed. Peer *Pi* may distrust *Pj* but other may not distrust Pi. Similarly should no communication between two peers be an indication of distrust between them? This raises the question of trust and distrust propagation. It is not easy to make a decision just by looking at one aspect of P2P network. Our objective is to establish that if trust or distrust is propagated, then this propagation is justified and correct and there is no side effect. Furthermore, this process should also be a part of P2P reconfiguration for maintaining the highest level of trust and security. One examination of this has been presented in [25].

8.11 Policy development and enforcement

We believe that mere technical schemes and protocols would not be sufficient to develop a highly desirable trust system. A set of policies must also be defined. This is especially true with the issue of distrust. We propose to develop policies related to distrust and the propagation of distrust to other peers. Technical solutions provide effective ways to tackle a problem but they cannot decide the mode (time, place, etc.) of their deployment. This can be managed by a set of well-defined policy that must contain the nature of external environment and may also use market condition. The technical solution approves the inclusion of a trusted node in P2P but this may not be correct from external viewpoint. We propose to study the human interaction aspect, the application interaction with the system, and resource constraints for the development of useful policies.

9 P2P for the Future and Open Issues

It is our belief that P2P systems will continue to evolve, supporting both wide-spread large-scale usage, and smaller niche setting where small groups come together to collaborate on a problem and then disband. To support this there are many issues in P2P systems that need to be addressed. Some P2P applications may actually use a combination of P2P systems, with the application being the primary one, and a user reputation application being another, and a distributed search being a third. Without some system that has knowledge of a peers reputation, then any new P2P system, or a "new" peer joining an existing P2P community the new user would be defaulted to a new user low level of trust. Where this isn't desirable there must be another system with prior knowledge of the peer.

Defense against attacks on P2P reputation systems needs additional work. To counter the peer that behaves, increases the trust level and then does a malicious act, and has his/her trust level lowered the defense is to lower the trust level greatly and to increase it very slowly in the future. When carried to extremes this attack is the Sybil attack where one peer creates the appearance of many peers [18]. Each of the peer instances behaves until they have a sufficient trust level to do something malicious. The peer then discards that peer instance and uses another. These peer instance may even work together raising their trust levels by way of reporting valid interactions with one another.

9.1 Issues with file sharing P2P systems

With file-sharing P2P systems there are several issues in addition to trust that need to be addressed. Some of these are apparent from the brief history of file-sharing P2P applications in section 2 in this chapter. The issues that we will discuss here are application protocol; search mechanism and related topics; autonomy, efficiency, and robustness, file authenticity, anonymity, and access control.

The application protocol will have a great deal of impact on performance of the P2P system, and on whether or not the P2P application will scale to large number of users. The original Gnutella protocol utilized frequent messages to keep status of other nodes in the network. It is shown in [49] that even a low rate of 1 peer discover per minute in a 4000 node network the average bandwidth per node is 68.20 kBit/s, which exceeds the bandwidth of a 56 kBit/s dialup connection. Even more discouraging is that this is not linear with the number of nodes in the network, but super-linear, with a bandwidth of 194.90 kBit/s in an 8000 node network. Clearly, flooding, or even limited flooding does not scale.

The term search mechanism covers a great deal of ground in P2P systems. The file sharing system may be either structure or unstructured with respect to the data placement. Structured systems generally increase the efficiency at the cost of decreasing autonomy. The network topology of how the peers connect is logical connections as the peers are physically located somewhere in the Internet. For structured systems, utilizing the physical connection information in determining logical connections could be examined for increased performance.

Data placement has a large impact on search mechanism. This includes both actual data and metadata (or indexing information). Is the data located randomly throughout the network, which may lead to searching through a lot of the nodes, or is metadata centralized onto a few peers. Is the data replicated?

How to access the metadata is the next question, how does the system route messages? If it is random what type of search is done – breadth first search, depth first search, or random search. If there is a concentration of the metadata onto a subset of the peers what is the protocol for accessing it? How much of the data to access is the next question. If a user want to download a certain song, how many peers with that song should be returned? The answer probably is somewhere between the two extremes of the first peer found and all of them. For efficiency it would be nice if the query propagated just far enough to get the reply, and could be stopped when enough hits were obtained. The negative impact of limiting the reply set is an increase query time as parallelism is avoided to keep the result set at the desired size. Of course if you ignore answer above the limit value, then you could do parallelism and ignore the extra work.

Within a P2P system what level of autonomy should each peer enjoy? Allowing them to choose which peers to interact with seems appropriate, especially in an unstructured system. Within a structured system a peer may be the only one with certain data. In this case, should the peer be allowed to decide if another peer could have access to the data? Should a peer's trust score be impacted by the amount of time the peer is not connected to the Internet? Should a peer be allowed to disqualify itself for a super-peer role, where the issue is the peer has sufficient resources to perform the super-peer role, but does not want to perform the super-peer role. If this is allowed, should a peer that avoids the super-peer role be treated differently from peers that do not have the resources necessary to be a super-peer?

The original Gnutella network is a prime example of why efficiency is important in P2P systems. Subsequent systems have solved the scaling issues found in Gnutella, however additional work on efficiency is always possible. Trade offs made in storage usage for replication versus decreased query times, can be continually fine tuned as the resources of the peers change over time. Additionally, very small peer groups that will be in existence only for a short while will rarely need efficiencies required by a very large user population system with frequent usage. If the application doesn't scale, what happens at the point where the network grows too large? Does it cease working all together or does it segment itself into smaller networks that may overlap? Does the segmentation cause some files to become unavailable. If the fragmentation is predictable, can replication of data overcome the segmentation?

The robustness of the system is critical; this includes system performance as peers join the system, leave the system, or fail. Additionally robustness to attacks needs to be considered. Could an attacker ask a file sharing system for 5 peers that have a certain file that the attacker knows does not exist? Could several queries of this sort lock out query processing for other peers? Is there anyway for the P2P system to be able to distinguish hostile queries from non-hostile queries?

In a file sharing system how is file authenticity determined? Several proposals exist – oldest document, expert-based authentication via digital signatures, voting based by expert nodes (that may include human experts input) and reputation-based authentication. The Kazaa system uses a fast checksum approach to verify file is correct, however the checksum process is such that massive file corruption is possible. The music recording industry has made use of this my planting corrupt copies of song in the Kazaa system, hoping that users will become frustrated downloading corrupt files and end up paying for the music. In this case it is easy for the peer to determine if the file is authentic simply by listening to it.

Anonymity has a bad reputation, as it seems the major use for it is in trading (or for some viewpoints - stealing) MP3 files. However there are uses that include censorship resistance, freedom of speech and privacy protection. There are four types of anonymity, document, server, reader, and author. Document anonymity hides which documents a node stores. Server anonymity conceals which node(s) store a given document. Reader and author anonymity conceal who read a document and who wrote the documents respectively. In a given P2P system the question needs to be asked if anonymity is required.

The issue of access control has not been addressed to date in the popular P2P file sharing systems. These systems let anyone download a file, and do not allow updates to the file nor file deletion. Some systems allow (require) peers to add files, which is a method to insure continued expansion of the system resources. The legal reasons that shut down the original Napster was that the central server provided the control over locating copyright files for download. Clearly the copyright holders want some sort of digital rights management (DRM) so that they can collect fees. This is at odds with the issue of autonomy. Several P2P application types – licensed media distribution, writeable web, and collaboration and most likely others, will need various access control items addressed.

Let us examine issues in file-sharing music systems. There are several music sites that allow downloading music files on either a fee per song basis or on a monthly subscription basis. An unsolved issue is should P2P systems incorporate DRM, or should this happen at the end-user peer? Issues within the DRM space will need to address if the peer who downloads the song can store it on his/her PC, burn it to a CD, download it to an MP3 player and a MP3 enabled cell phone all for the same fee. If there are several PCs networked in a home, can the downloaded song be played on any of the PCs? What happens if a user's hard disk crashes and he doesn't have a back up – will the system allow him to re-download the songs again without paying for them again?

9.2 Mobility issues in file sharing P2P systems.

In addition to the issues listed in the previous section, mobility adds additional concerns. To improve access to data in mobile P2P systems replication of data has been proposed. One ongoing research item is the validation of the replica data. Heuristics for replica allocation can be either based upon access frequencies or based upon Read/Write Ratio (RWR). The first method replicates data that will probably be accessed by a node or by nodes in a cluster before the lifetime of the data item expires. A weather forecast may be updated hourly, and if a peer is likely to access that data before the hourly update is made then during a relocation period. The ability to accurately forecast access probabilities has great impacts on performance. The RWR ratio allows for replication of data with a high RWR values. The write portion of the ratio is the write by the peer who owns the data. Therefore data with high values of RWR are lees likely to be inconsistent than those with low values of RWR. The reason that the above strategies are heuristics is that the calculations needed to perform this depend on the network topology, which is impacted by peer mobility. The computation is expensive and the calculations for data replication would need to be performed when triggered by peer mobility.

Performance studies of the RWR heuristic have been proposed. These will look at replication based on static access frequencies by peers which will be simple to implement but with a low amount of sharing; avoid replica duplication among peers which will increase the protocol overhead while increasing data sharing; or replicate data in much large group of peers which is expected to have the highest overhead, but with sharing of replicas over larger groups which hopefully can provide stability, and can support higher data accessibility.

10 Conclusions

In order to achieve the objective of enabling P2P systems to be a rich environment in which ad-hoc information exchange and collaboration is possible there needs to be an effective method in which a peer selects which peers to interact with. To allow the fullest set of interactions, while still allowing for anonymity, trust must be utilized, furthermore trust is needed in known user situations also. Not only will the level of trust determine what the peer is allowed to do, but also the level of trust will be used to pick a peer to interact with. We are developing a system to allow trust to be extended over the entire interaction, from both the requesting peer and the requested peer. In order to achieve this we have designed the universal trust set to be the parameters on which the trust score is calculated. For a given P2P system, a trust score function is derived, and a subset of parameters from the UTS are chosen to the input parameters to the trust function. We can utilize the trust scores for both sides of the P2P interaction. The peer providing the service can use the trust score of the requesting peer to decide what privileges the requesting peer should be allowed; and the requesting peer can utilize the trust score of the peers offering to perform the service in determining which peer to select.

The trust value of the peer itself is a very important piece of data. We are proposing that local values of trust be utilized if available, otherwise a reputation service will be needed. This can either be integrated into the P2P application, or a stand-alone P2P reputation system can be accessed. Differing levels of security will have impact on the protocol performance. This is important to consider from the initial design phase of a P2P protocol, as performance and scalability along with security and trust are important aspects of the P2P application.

References

[1] Abdul-Rahman, A., and Hailes, S., 2000, Supporting trust in virtual communities. In: Proceedings of the 33rd Hawaii International Conference on Systems Sciences.

[2] Aberer, K., and Despotovic, Z., 2001, Managing trust in a peer-2-peer information system, CIKM'01, Atlanta, Georgia.

[3] acquisitionx.borgfind.com/

[4] Alexander, Peter J. Peer-to-Peer File Sharing: The Case of the Music Recording Industry, Review of Industrial Organization. Springer Science and Business Media B.V., Issue: Volume 20, Number 2, March 2002

[5] Assedin, F., and Mahewsaran, M., 2003, Trust modeling for peer-to-peer based computing systems, Proc. Intl. Parallel and Distributed Processing Symposium.

[6] Bearly, T., Kumar, V., Expanding Trust Beyond Reputation in Peer-To-Peer Systems. In: Proceeding of 15th Intl. Workshop on Database and Expert Systems Applications (DEXA 2004). Vol 00, Zaragoza, Spain.

[7] www.freepeers.com/products.htm

[8] Bhargava, B., and Zhong, Y., 2002, Authorization Based Evidence and Trust, in Proceedings of International Conference on Data Warehousing and Knowledge Discovery (DAWAK'2002), LNCS, Vol. 2454, France.

[9] BitTorrent - Wikipedia, 2003, http://en.wikipedia.org/wiki/Bittorrent.

[10] Blaze, M., Lacy, J., London, T., and Reiter, M., 1994, Issues and Mechanisms for Trustworthy Systems: Creating Transparent Mistrust. AT&T Technical Journal, 73(5).

[11] CacheLogic press release, 2004, http://www.cachelogic.com /news/pr040715.php.

[12] Castano, S., Fugini, M., Martella, G., and Samarati, P., 1994, Database Security, Addison Wesley & ACM Press, Reading, MA.

[13] Castro1, Miguel, Peter Druschel2, Ayalvadi Ganesh1, Antony Rowstron1 and Dan S. Wallach2, Secure routing for structured peer-to-peer overlay networks_Proc. of the 5th Usenix Symposium on Operating Systems Design and Implementation, Boston, MA, December 2002.

[14] Chen, M., and Singh, J.P., 2001, Computing and using reputations of internet ratings, in Proceedings of 3rd ACM International Conference on E-Commerce.

[15] Chen, R., and Yeager, W., 2000, Poblano: A Distributed Trust Model for Peer-to-Peer Networks, Sun Microsystems Technical Paper www.jxta.org/project/docs/trust.pdf.

[16] Datta, A., Hauswirth, M., and Aberer, K., 2003, Beyond "web of trust": Enabling P2P E-commerce. CEC.

[17] en.wikipedia.org/wiki/Digital_signature

[18] Douceur, J. 2002, The Sybil Attack, Proc. of First International Workshop on Peer-to-Peer Systems '02, Cambridge, MA.

[19] Druschel, P., and Rowstron, A., 2001, PAST: A large scale, persistent peer-to-peer storage utility, HotOS VIII, Schloss Elmau, Germany.

[20] FastTrack-Wikipedia; http://en.wikipedia.org/wiki/FastTrack.

[21] taxster.fateback.com/gnotella.htm

[22] Gnutella - Wikipedia, http://en.wikipedia.org/wiki/Gnutella.

[23] Gnutella 0.6-Defining a standard, http://rfc-gnutella.sourceforge.net/developer/index.html.

[24] en.wikipedia.org/wiki/Gtk-gnutella

[25] Guha, R., Kumar, R., Raghavan, P., and Tomkins, A., 2004, Propagation of trust and distrust, WWW 2004, New York.

[26] Guillarmod, F. Jacot, From FidoNet to Internet: the evolution of a national network", Proceedings of INET'92, H. Ishida Editor.

[27] Hara, T. and Madria, S. 2004. Dynamic Data Replication Schemes for Mobile Ad-hoc Network Based on Aperiodic Updates, to appear in DASFAA'04, Jeju, Korea, March, 2004, extended version is under communication in IEEE TMC.

[28] Hauben, Michael. History of ARPANET, www.dei.isep.ipp.pt/ docs/arpa.html

[29] Honigsberg, Peter Jan The Evolution and Revolution of Napster University of San Francisco Law Review, Vol. 36, 2002.

[30] Kalepu, S., Krishnaswamy, S. and Loke, S. 2004, Reputation = Uer Ranking, Compliance, Verity, Proc. IEEE Intl Cong on Web Services.

[31] Kamvar, S.D., Schlosser, M.T., and Garcia-Molina, H., 2003, The EigenTrust algorithm for reputation management in P2P networks, in Proc. 12th Intl WWW Conference.

[32] Karl, A., et. al., 2002, Advanced peer-to-peer networking: The P-Grid systems and its applications, http://www.p-grid.org/Papers/TR-IC-2002-73.pdf.

[33] KaZaA - Wikipedia, http://en.wikipedia.org/wiki/KaZaA.

[34] Klemm, A., Lindemann, C., and Waldhorst, O., 2003, A special-purpose peer-to-peer file sharing system for mobile ad hoc networks, Proc. IEEE Semiannual Vehicular Technology Conference (VTC2003-Fall), Orlando, FL.

[35] Kubiatowicz, J., Bindel, D., Chen, Y., Czerwinski, S., Eaton, P., Geels, D., Gummadi, R., Rhea, R., Weatherspoon, H., Weimer, W., Wells, C., and Zhao, B., 2000, OceanStore: An architecture for global-scale persistent storage, Proceedings of 9th International Conference On Architectural Support for Programming Languages and Op. Sys (ASPLOS 2000).

[36] Kwansei, www.ksc.kwansei.ac.jp/researchfair02/03/website/ history.htm, 2002.

[37] www.limewire.com/english/content/home.shtml

[38] Li, N., Winsborough, W.H.,and Mitchell, J.C., Distributed credential chain discovery in trust management: extended abstract, ACM Conference on Computer and Communications Security, 2001

[39] Liang J., Kumar R. and Ross K.W., 2004a, Understanding KaZaA, Working Paper.

[40] Maher, D., Trust in the new information age,. AT&T Technical Journal, 73(5), 1994

[41] Malaga R.A., 2001, Web-based reputation management systems: problems and suggested solutions, Electronic Commerce Research, 1(4).

[42] Marsh, S. 1994, Formalising Trust as a Computational Concept, PhD Dissertation, University of Stirling.

[43] Milojicic D. S., Kalogeraki V., Lukose R., Nagaraja K., Pruyne J., Richard B., Rollins S., and Xu, Z., 2002, Peer-to-Peer computing, HP Labs Technical Report, http://www.hpl.hp.com/techreports/2002/HPL-2002-57.pdf.

[44] Nadeau, B., What is peer-to-peer networking? http://anet.sourceforge.net/ docs/devel/intro/p2p.html, 2001.

[45] Mac-P2P.com, 2003, Peer to Peer (P2P) Introduction and History, http://www.mac-p2p.com/p2p-history.

[46] mutella.sourceforge.net/

[47] Noam, Eli M (ed), Ithiel de Sola Pool, *Technologies Without Boundaries,* Cambridge, Mass.: Harvard University Press, 1990.

[48] Patrick, A. 2002. Building Trustworthy Software Agents. IEEE Internet Computing, Nov-Dec 02, 46-53.

[49] Portman, M. Sookavatana, P. Ardon, S. and Seneviratne, A. 2001. The Cost of Peer Discovery and Searching in the Gnutella Peer-to-peer File Sharing Protocol, In Proceedings to the IEEE International Conference on Networks, Vol. 1.

[50] Ratnasamy , Sylvia, Paul Francis, Mark Handley, Richard Karp, and Scott Shenker. A scalable content-addressable network. In *Proc. ACM SIGCOMM'01*, San Diego, California, August 2001.

[51] Resnick, P., Kuwabara, K., Zeckhauser, R., and Friedman, E., 2000, Reputation systems, Communications of the ACM, 43(12).

[52] Rhea, S., Wells, C., Eaton, P., Geels, D., Zhao, B., Weatherspoon, H., and Kubiatowicz, J., 2001, Maintenance-free global data storage, Internet Computing, 5(4).

[53] Rowstron , Antony and Peter Druschel. Pastry: Scalable, distributed object location and routing for large-scale peer-to-peer systems. In *Proc. IFIP/ACM Middleware 2001*, Heidelberg, Germany, November 2001.

[54] De Santis, L., Scannapieco, M., and Catarci, T., 2003, A trust model for tightly coupled P2P systems. SEBD.

[55] Schollmeier, R., 2001, A definition of peer-to-peer networking for the classification of peer-to-peer architecture and applications. Proc. 1st Int. Conf. On Peer-to-Peer Computing Linköping, Sweden, August 27-29, 2001.

[56] Shirky, C., 2000, What's P2P and what's not, www.openp2p.com/pub/a/p2p/2000/11/24/shirky1-whatisp2p.html.

[57] Simon, S., 1991, Peer-to-Peer Network Management in an IBM SNA Network, IEEE Network Magazine.

[58] Sims, D., (ed), 2000, O'Reilly P2P directory www.openp2p.com/pub/q/p2p_category.

[59] SourceForge, The Annotated Gnutella Protocol Specification v0.4, http://rfc-gnutella.sourceforge.net/developer/stable/index.html .

[60] SourceForge, 2005, RFC-Gnutella 0.6, http://rfc-gnutella.sourceforge.net/developer/testing/.

[61] Vassileva, J., 2002, Supporting Peer-to-Peer User Communities, in Proc of Confederated Intl Conferences (CoopIS/DOA/ODBASE 2002), Irvine, California, USA, October 30 - November 1, 2002, LNCS, Vol. 2519, Springer.

[62] Wang, Y., and Vassileva, J., 2003, Trust and reputation in peer-to-peer networks, Proc Third Intl Conference on Peer-to-Peer Computing (P2P'03), Linköping, Sweden.

[63] Xiong, L., and Ling Liu., 2004, PeerTrust: Supporting Reputation Based Trust for Peer-to-Peer Electronic Communities, IEEE Transactions on Knowledge and Data Engineering (TKDE), Special Issue on Peer-to-Peer Based Data Management, 16(7).

[64] Yang, B., and Garcia-Molina, H., 2001, Comparing Hybrid Peer-to-Peer Systems, in Proceedings of 27th International Conference on Very Large Data Bases, Rome Italy.

[65] Young, K., 1993, Look no Server (peer-to-peer networks), Network, 21(2).

[66] Yu, B., and Singh, M.P., 2000, A Social Mechanism of Reputation Management in Electronic Communities, in Proc of 7th Intl Conference on Cooperative Information Systems (Coopis'00), Israel.

[67] Zhao, B., and Joseph, A., 2001, Tapestry: An infrastructure for fault-tolerant wide-area location and routing, Computer Sc. Division, Univ. of California, Berkeley, TR UCB/CSD-01-1141.

[68] Zhong, Y., Lu, Y., and Bhargava, B., 2003, Dynamic trust production based on interaction sequence, Technical Report CSD TR 03-006, Department of Computer Sciences, Purdue University.

Part IV

Privacy in Cross-Domain Information Sharing

Microdata Protection

V. Ciriani, S. De Capitani di Vimercati, S. Foresti, and P. Samarati

Università degli Studi di Milano
{ciriani, decapita, foresti, samarati}@dti.unimi.it

1 Introduction

The increased power and interconnectivity of computer systems available today provide the ability of storing and processing large amounts of data, resulting in networked information accessible from anywhere at any time. This information sharing and dissemination process is clearly selective. Indeed, if on the one hand there is a need to disseminate some data, there is on the other hand an equally strong need to protect those data that, for various reasons, should not be disclosed. Consider, for example, the case of a private organization making available various data regarding its business (products, sales, and so on), but at the same time wanting to protect more sensitive information, such as the identity of its customers or plans for future products. As another example, government agencies, when releasing historical data, may require a sanitization process to "blank out" information considered sensitive, either directly or because of the sensitive information it would allow the recipient to infer. Effective information sharing and dissemination can take place only if the data holder has some assurance that, while releasing information, disclosure of sensitive information is not a risk.

Many techniques have been developed for protecting data released publicly or semi-publicly from improper disclosure. These techniques depend on the method in which such data are released. In the past, data were principally released in tabular form (*macrodata*) and through *statistical databases* [1]. Macrodata are aggregate information (statistics) on users or organizations usually presented as two-dimensional tables while a statistical database is a database whose users may retrieve only aggregate statistics. Macrodata protection techniques are based on the *selective obfuscation of sensitive cells.* Techniques for protecting statistical databases follow two main approaches. The first approach restricts the statistical queries that can be made (e.g., queries that identify a small/large number of tuples) or the data that can be published. The second approach provides protection by returning to the user a modified result. The modification can be enforced directly on the stored data or run time in the process of computing the result to be returned to the user.

However, many situations require today that the specific stored data themselves, called *microdata*, be released. The advantage of releasing microdata instead of specific pre-computed statistics is an increased flexibility and availability of information for the users. To protect the anonymity of the entities, called *respondents*, to which information refers, data holders often remove or encrypt explicit identifiers such as names, addresses, and phone numbers. De-identifying data, however, provides no guarantee of anonymity. Released information often contains other data, such as race, birth date, sex, and ZIP code, that can be linked to publicly available information to reidentify respondents and inferring information that was not intended for disclosure [7,20,22]. Disclosure can be categorized as: *identity disclosure*, *attribute disclosure*, and *inferential disclosure*. Identity disclosure occurs when using a combination of identifying attributes (e.g., social security number, name, and address), an individual's identity can be reconstructed. Attribute disclosure occurs when using a combination of indirect identifying attributes, a given attribute value (or restricted set thereof) can be associated with an individual. Inferential disclosure occurs when information can be inferred with high probability from statistical properties of the released data. A first step in protecting the privacy of the *respondents* (individuals, organizations, associations, business establishments, and so on) to which the data refer, consists in releasing data that are generally "sanitized" by removing all explicit identifiers such as names, addresses, and phone numbers. Although apparently anonymous, the de-identified data may contain other data, such as race, birth date, sex, and ZIP code, which uniquely or almost uniquely pertain to specific respondents and make them stand out from others [22]. By linking these identifying characteristics with publicly available databases (e.g., databases maintained and released by the Department of Motor Vehicles, Health Maintenance Organizations, insurance companies, public offices, commercial organizations, and so on) associating these characteristics to the respondent's identity, the data recipients can determine to which respondent some pieces of released data refer, or restrict their uncertainty to a specific subset of individuals. This has created an increasing demand to devote resources for an adequate protection of sensitive data. As we will see, the microdata protection techniques usually applied to protect sensitive data follow two main strategies. The first strategy consists in reducing the information content of the data provided to the data recipients. The second strategy consists in changing the data before their release in such a way that the information content is maintained as much as possible.

In this chapter, we survey the main microdata disclosure protection techniques. Section 2 provides a brief overview of the difference between macrodata and microdata (this latter being the focus of this chapter). Section 3 provides a characterization of the main microdata disclosure protection techniques. Sections 4 and 5 describe masking techniques and synthetic data generation techniques, respectively. Section 6 provides a discussion on possible measures to evaluate how much the released microdata are protected and, at the same time, informative. Finally, Sect. 7 gives our conclusions.

	Hypertension	Obesity	Chest Pain	Short Breath	Tot
M	1	2	2	1	6
F	1	2	0	2	5
Tot	2	4	2	3	11

(**a**) number of respondents with a disease

	Hypertension	Obesity	Chest Pain	Short Breath	Tot
M	9.1	18.2	18.2	9.1	54.6
F	9.1	18.2	0	18.2	45.4
Tot	18.2	36.4	18.2	27.2	100

(**b**) percentage of respondents with a disease

	Hypertension	Obesity	Chest Pain	Short Breath	Tot
M	2	8.5	23.5	3	37
F	3	30.5	0	5	38.5
Tot	5	39	23.5	8	75.5

(**c**) average number of days spent in the hospital by respondents with a disease

Fig. 1. An example of count (**a**), frequency (**b**), and magnitude (**c**) macrodata tables

2 Macrodata Versus Microdata

Data are collected and shared in many different forms. A broad classification can distinguish release in two main classes: *macrodata* and *microdata*. Macrodata consist of data that have been aggregated (e.g., the population of a county is an aggregate of the populations of the cities), while microdata are the base information reporting data on single *respondents*. In this section, we briefly discuss the major characteristics of macrodata versus microdata.

2.1 Macrodata

Macrodata represent estimated values of *statistical characteristics* concerning a given population. A statistical characteristic is a measure that summarizes the values of one or more *properties/attributes* (*variables*, in statistical terminology) of respondents. An example of a statistical characteristic can be the average age of people living in each continent. Macrodata can be represented as tables, where each cell of the table is the aggregate value of a quantity over the considered properties. For instance, Figs. 1(a)-(c) illustrates macrodata tables that contain measures computed over properties `Sex` (M,F) and `Disease` (hypertension, obesity, chest pain, and short breath). Macrodata tables can be classified into the following three groups (types of tables).

- *Count.* Each cell of the table contains the *number of respondents* that have the same value over all attributes of analysis associated with the table. For instance, the table in Fig. 1(a) contains the number of males and females for each given disease.

- *Frequency.* Each cell of the table contains the *percentage of respondents*, evaluated over the total population, that have the same value over all the attributes of analysis associated with the table. For instance, the macrodata table in Fig. 1(b) contains the percentage of males and females for each given disease.
- *Magnitude.* Each cell of the table contains *an aggregate value of a quantity of interest* over all attributes of analysis associated with the table. For instance, the macrodata table in Fig. 1(c) contains the average number of days that males and females have spent in the hospital for each given disease.

Several macrodata protection techniques have been developed to guarantee the *confidentiality* of the data, that is, the assurance that information about single respondents cannot be derived from macrodata. The first step in protecting a macrodata table consists in discovering *sensitive cells*, that is, cells that can be easily associated with a specific respondent. The strategies for discovering and consequently protecting sensitive cells vary depending on the type of macrodata (count and frequency tables versus magnitude tables). For count and frequency tables, the most important strategy used to detect sensitive cells is the *threshold rule*, according to which a cell is sensitive if the number of respondents is less than a given threshold. As an example, consider the macrodata table in Fig. 1(a) and suppose that the threshold is 2. The first cell and the last cell in the first tuple, and the first cell and the third cell in the second tuple are sensitive because their value is below the threshold. Some of the most important strategies for protecting sensitive cells are *cell suppression*, *rounding*, *roll up categories*, *sampling*, and the *controlled tabular adjustment function* (CTA) [9, 22, 28]. Cell suppression is a well-known technique that consists in protecting sensitive cells by removing their values. These suppressions are called *primary suppressions*. However, a problem can arise when also the marginal totals of the table are published. In this case, even if it is not possible to exactly recalculate the suppressed cell, it can be possible to calculate an interval that contains the suppressed cell. If the size of such an interval is small, then the suppressed cell can be estimated rather precisely. To block such inferences, additional cells may need to be suppressed (*secondary suppression*) to guarantee that the intervals are sufficiently large. To minimize the number of cells to be suppressed, linear programming techniques have been proposed. Such techniques are suitable for small tables, although they are usually not applicable to more complex structures [6,8,13,22,28]. Rounding consists in choosing a *base number* and in modifying the original value of sensitive cells by rounding it up or down to a near multiple of the base number. Roll up categories reduces the size of the table: instead of releasing a table with N tuples and M columns, a less detailed table (e.g., a table with $N-1$ tuples and $M-1$ columns) is released. Sampling means that the table is obtained with a sample survey rather than a census. The CTA technique is based on the selective adjustment of cell values. In other words, the value of sensitive cells is replaced by a *safe value*, that is, a value that satisfies the rule chosen to detect sensitive cells, and then uses linear programming to adjust the values of the nonsensitive cells to restore the additivity property.

SSN	Name	Race	DoB	Sex	ZIP	MarStat	Disease	DH	Chol	Temp
		Asian	64/09/27	F	94139	Divorced	Hypertension	3	260	35.2
		Asian	64/09/30	F	94139	Divorced	Obesity	1	170	37.7
		Asian	64/04/18	M	94139	Married	Chest pain	40	200	38.1
		Asian	64/04/15	M	94139	Married	Obesity	7	280	37.4
		Black	63/03/13	M	94138	Married	Hypertension	2	190	35.3
		Black	63/03/18	M	94138	Married	Short breath	3	185	38.2
		Black	64/09/13	F	94141	Married	Short breath	5	200	36.5
		Black	64/09/07	F	94141	Married	Obesity	60	290	39.8
		White	61/05/14	M	94138	Single	Chest pain	7	170	37.6
		White	61/05/08	M	94138	Single	Obesity	10	300	40.1
		White	61/09/15	F	94142	Widow	Short breath	5	200	36.9

Fig. 2. An example of de-identified medical microdata table

For magnitude macrodata, there are many rules that can be used to detect sensitive cells. For instance, the *(n,k)-rule* states that a cell is sensitive if less than n respondents contribute to more than $k\%$ of the total cell value. As an example, consider the macrodata table in Fig. 1(c) and suppose to apply the (1,50)-rule. A cell is therefore sensitive if one respondent contributes to more than 50% of its value. The first cell and the last cell in the first tuple as well as the first cell in the second tuple are sensitive because, according to the macrodata table in Fig. 1(a), there is only one male and one female with hypertension and one male with short breath and therefore their contribution to these cells is 100%. Other similar rules are the *p-percentage* rule and the *pq-rule* [22]. The *p-percentage* states that a cell is sensitive if the total value t of the cell minus the largest reported value v_1 minus the second largest reported value v_2 is less than $(p/100) \cdot v_1$. Intuitively, this rule means that a user can estimate the reported value of some respondent too accurately. In the *pq-rule*, q represents how accurately respondents can estimate another respondent's value ($p < q < 100$). Note that some of the techniques used for protecting count and frequency tables can also be used for protecting magnitude tables (e.g., cell suppression, roll up categories, and CTA).

2.2 Microdata

Microdata contain a set of attributes relating to single respondents in a sample or in a population. Microdata can be represented as tables composed of tuples (records) with values from a set of attributes. Figure 2 illustrates an example of microdata table with 11 tuples and with attributes `SSN` (social security number), `Name`, `Race`, `DoB` (date of birth), `Sex`, `ZIP` code, `MarStat` (marital status), `Disease`, `DH` (days in hospital), `Chol` (cholesterol), and `Temp` (temperature).[1] In the remainder of this chapter, we refer our examples to this microdata table.

The attributes in an initial microdata table are usually classified as follows.

- *Identifiers.* Attributes that uniquely identify a microdata respondent. For instance, attribute `SSN` uniquely identifies the person with which is associated.
- *Quasi-identifiers.* Attributes that, in combination, can be linked with external information to reidentify, all or some of the respondents to whom information refers or reduce the uncertainty over their identities. For instance, attributes `DoB`, `ZIP`, and `Sex` are quasi-identifiers: they can be linked to external public information to reveal the name and address of the corresponding respondents or to reduce the uncertainty to a specific set of respondents.
- *Confidential attributes.* Attributes of the microdata table that contain sensitive information. For instance, attribute `Disease` can be considered sensitive.
- *Non confidential attributes.* Attributes that the respondents do not consider sensitive and whose release do not cause disclosure. For instance, attribute `Race` can be considered non confidential.

In general, protecting microdata from *reidentification* of respondents is a more difficult task than protecting macrodata from disclosure because each tuple of the microdata table contains actual data of single respondents. In the remainder of this chapter, we will focus on the microdata disclosure protection techniques (data protection techniques, for short).

3 Classification of Microdata Disclosure Protection Techniques

Disclosure control of microdata is an important practical issue in the private as well as in the public and governmental sectors. Microdata protection techniques have two apparently contrasting objectives. On the one side, they should avoid *reidentification* that happens whenever the information of a respondent appearing in a microdata table is identified, that is, is associated with the identity of the corresponding respondent. On the other side, the application of such techniques should preserve the *key statistical properties* of the original data that data recipients have indicated as important. More precisely, given a microdata table T, a data protection technique should transform this original table into another microdata table T' in a way that: *i)* the risk that a malicious user can use T' to determine confidential information or to identify a respondent should be low; *ii)* the statistical analysis over T and over T' should produce similar results.

In general, the following main factors contribute to disclosure risks [22].

- The existence of high visibility tuples (i.e., tuples with unique characteristics such as a high income).

[1] Note that in this table data have been de-identified by suppressing names and social security numbers so not to directly disclose the identities of the respondents to whom the data refer (see Sect. 3 for more details).

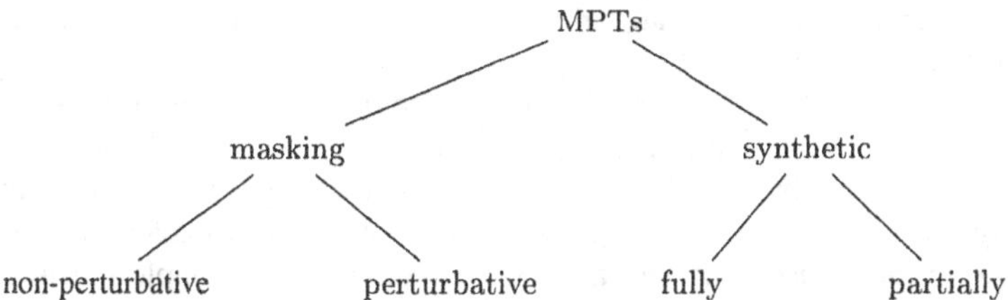

Fig. 3. Classification of microdata protection techniques (MPTs)

- The possibility of matching the microdata table with external information. For instance, suppose that a public voter list includes names, social security numbers, sex, birth dates, and addresses. Attributes `DoB`, `ZIP`, and `Sex` in Fig. 2 can then be linked to the voter list to reveal the names and social security numbers.
- The existence of a high number of common attributes between the microdata table and the external sources, which may increase the possibility of linking or make it more precise.

By contrast, the main factors that decrease the disclosure risks can be summarized as follows.

- A microdata table often contains a subset of the whole population. This implies that the information of a specific respondent, which a malicious user may want to know, may not be included in the microdata table.
- The information specified in microdata tables released to the public are not always up-to-date (often at least one or two-year old). This means that the values of the attributes of the corresponding respondents may have been changed in the meanwhile. In addition, the age of the external sources of information used for linking may be different from the age of the information contained in the microdata table.
- A microdata table and the external sources of information naturally contain noise that decreases the ability to link the information.
- A microdata table and the external sources of information can contain data expressed in different forms thus decreasing the ability to link information.

In general, to limit the disclosure risk of a microdata table it is first necessary to suppress explicit and implicit identifiers (e.g., `SSN` and `Name` in Fig. 2). This process is also known as *de-identification*. Note that de-identification does not necessarily make a tuple anonymous [44,47], as it may be possible to reidentify the tuple using external information. For instance, consider the microdata in Fig. 2, where all the identifiers have been removed and suppose to link the information in this table with the voter list that is a public non-anonymous dataset. The microdata table contains, for the last tuple, a unique combination of values for attributes `DoB`, `Sex`, `ZIP`, and `MarStat`. This combination, if unique in the voter list as well, uniquely identifies the corresponding tuple in the microdata table as pertaining to a specific respondent. In addition, it is necessary to limit geographical details as well as the number of attributes in microdata tables to reduce the probability of reidentification of respondents.

Several microdata disclosure protection techniques have been proposed in the literature. Basically, these techniques are based on the principle that reidentification can be counteracted by reducing the amount of released information, masking the data (e.g., by not releasing or by perturbing their values), or by releasing plausible but made up values instead of the real ones. According to this principle, the microdata protection techniques can be classified into two main categories: *masking techniques*, and *synthetic data generation techniques* (see Fig. 3).

- *Masking techniques.* The original data are transformed to produce new data that are valid for statistical analysis and such that they preserve the confidentiality of respondents. Masking techniques can be classified as:
  - *non-perturbative*, the original data are not modified, but some data are suppressed and/or some details are removed;
  - *perturbative*, the original data are modified.
- *Synthetic data generation techniques.* The original set of tuples in a microdata table is replaced with a new set of tuples generated in such a way to preserve the key statistical properties of the original data. The generation process is usually based on a statistical model and the key statistical properties that are not included in the model will not be necessarily respected by the synthetic data. Since the released microdata table contains synthetic data, the reidentification risks is reduced. Note that the released microdata table can be entirely synthetic (i.e., *fully* synthetic) or mixed with the original data (i.e., *partially* synthetic).

Another important feature of microdata protection techniques is that they can operate on different data types. In particular, data types can be categorized as follows.

- *Continuous.* An attribute is said to be continuous if it is numerical and arithmetic operations are defined on it. For instance, attributes date of birth and temperature are continuous attributes.
- *Categorical.* An attribute is said to be categorical if it can assume a limited and specified set of values and arithmetic operations do not have sense on it. Note that an order relationship can be defined over a categorical attribute. For instance, attributes marital status and race are categorical attributes.

In the following, we describe the principal microdata protection techniques indicating also whether they are applicable to continuous data, categorical data, or both.

4 Masking Techniques

We present some of the most popular non-perturbative and perturbative masking techniques. Figure 4 and Fig. 5 lists the techniques indicating whether they are applicable (yes) or not (no) to continuous or categorical data types.

Technique	Continuous	Categorical
Sampling	yes	yes
Local suppression	yes	yes
Global recoding	yes	yes
Top-coding	yes	yes
Bottom-coding	yes	yes
Generalization	yes	yes

Fig. 4. Applicability of non-perturbative masking techniques to the different data types

Technique	Continuous	Categorical
Resampling	yes	no
Lossy compression	yes	no
Rounding	yes	no
PRAM	no	yes
MASSC	no	yes
Random noise	yes	yes
Swapping	yes	yes
Rank swapping	yes	yes
Micro-aggregation	yes	yes

Fig. 5. Applicability of perturbative masking techniques to the different data types

4.1 Non-Perturbative Techniques

Non-perturbative techniques produce protected microdata by eliminating details from the original microdata. We discuss these techniques illustrating as examples their application to the protection of the table in Fig. 2. The result of the application of the techniques is illustrated in Fig. 7.

Sampling [22]

The protected microdata table is obtained as a sample of the original microdata table. In other words, the protected microdata table includes only the data (tuples) of a sample of the whole population. Since there is an uncertainty about whether or not a specific respondent is in the sample, the risk of reidentification in the released microdata decreases. For instance, we can decide to publish only the even tuples of the original microdata table. This technique operates on categorical attributes only.

Local Suppression [5,44]

It suppresses the value of an attribute (i.e., it i replaces it with a missing value) thus limiting the possibilities of analysis. Basically, this technique blanks out some attribute values (sensitive cells) that are likely to contribute significantly to the disclosure risk of the tuple involved. For instance, we can suppress attributes `ZIP` and `MarStat` in the last tuple.

Global Recoding (or Recoding into Intervals) [17, 18, 49]

The domain of an attribute is partitioned into disjoint intervals, usually of the same width, and each interval is associated with a label. The protected microdata table is obtained by replacing the values of the attribute with the label associated with the corresponding interval. Intuitively, global recoding decreases the details in the microdata table and therefore it should reduce the risk of reidentification. For instance, suppose that the values of attribute `Temp` are partitioned into three intervals: [35.0,36.9] with label *no fever* (nf); [37.0,38.9] with label *fever* (f); and [39.0,40.9] with label *high fever* (hf). The value in the first tuple is then replaced by label "nf"; the second, third, and fourth value are replaced by label "f"; and so on. Note that if the original domain of the considered attribute is continuous, it becomes discrete after the application of this technique.

Two particular global recoding techniques are the top-coding and the bottom-coding described in the following.

Top-Coding [17, 18]

It is based on the definition of an upper limit, called *top-code*, for each attribute to be protected. Any value greater than this value is replaced with the top-code. For instance, consider attribute `DH` and suppose that the top-code is 30. In this case, rather than publishing the third and eighth tuple showing a number of days in a hospital equal to 40 and 60, respectively, these two tuples may only show that the number of days is "> 30". The idea is that long periods in the hospital can be easily associated with specific respondents. Top-coding can be applied to categorical attributes that can be linearly ordered as well as to continuous attributes.

Bottom-Coding [17, 18]

It is similar to top-coding. It consists in defining a lower limit, called *bottom-code*, for each attribute to be protected. Therefore, any value lower than this limit is not published and is replaced with the bottom-code. For instance, consider attribute `Chol` and suppose that the bottom-code is 195. The second, fifth, sixth, and ninth tuples are modified in such a way that the value published for attribute `Chol` is "< 195". Basically, since low cholesterol values for people having obesity or hypertension problems are uncommon, they have to be obfuscated to avoid a possible reidentification. Like for top-coding, this technique can be applied to categorical attributes that can be linearly ordered as well as to continuous attributes.

Generalization [44]

It consists in representing the values of a given attribute by using more general values. This technique is based on the definition of a *generalization hierarchy*, where the most general value is at the root of the hierarchy and the leaves correspond to the most specific values. A generalization process therefore proceeds by replacing the values represented by the leaf nodes with one of their ancestor nodes at a higher

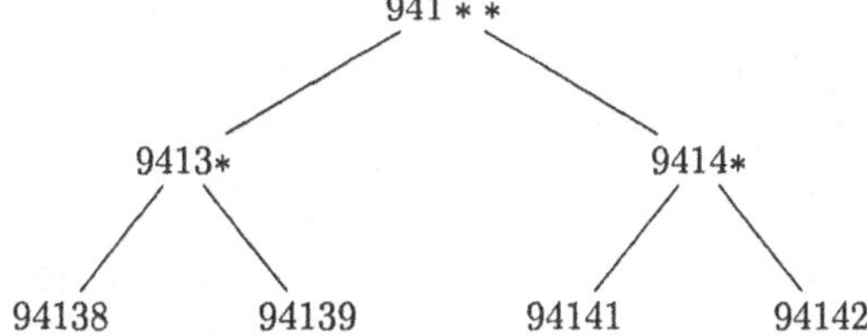

Fig. 6. Generalization hierarchy for attribute `ZIP`

SSN	Name	Race	DoB	Sex	ZIP	MarStat	Disease	DH	Chol	Temp
		Asian	64/09/27	F	9413*	Divorced	Hypertension	3	260	nf
		Asian	64/09/30	F	9413*	Divorced	Obesity	1	<195	f
		Asian	64/04/18	M	9413*	Married	Chest pain	>30	200	f
		Asian	64/04/15	M	9413*	Married	Obesity	7	280	f
		Black	63/03/13	M	9413*	Married	Hypertension	2	<195	nf
		Black	63/03/18	M	9413*	Married	Short breath	3	<195	f
		Black	64/09/13	F	9414*	Married	Short breath	5	200	nf
		Black	64/09/07	F	9414*	Married	Obesity	>30	290	hf
		White	61/05/14	M	9413*	Single	Chest pain	7	<195	f
		White	61/05/08	M	9413*	Single	Obesity	10	300	hf
		White	61/09/15	F			Short breath	5	200	nf

Fig. 7. Microdata table of Fig. 2 obtained by applying the non-perturbative techniques listed in Fig. 4

level. Different generalized microdata tables can be built, depending on the number of generalization steps applied on the considered attribute. For instance, consider attribute `ZIP` and the corresponding generalization hierarchy in Fig. 6. Each generalization step consists in suppressing the least significant digit in the `ZIP` code. In this case, if we choose to apply one generalization step, values 94138, 94139, 94141, and 94142 are generalized to 9413* and 9414*. This technique is applicable on both continuous and categorical attributes. Note also that the global recoding technique can be seen as a particular case of generalization.

Figure 7 contains the protected microdata table obtained from the microdata table of Fig. 2 by applying, as discussed, the top-coding technique on attribute `DH`, the bottom-coding technique on attribute `Chol`, the global recoding technique on attribute `Temp`, the local suppression technique on the last tuple, and one generalization step on attribute `ZIP`.

4.2 Perturbative Techniques

With perturbative techniques, the microdata table is modified for publication. Modifications can make unique combinations of values in the original table disappear as well as introduce new combinations.

S_1	S_2	S_3	S_4
260	220	170	210
170	280	290	190
200	210	220	230
280	310	270	200
190	290	185	185
185	180	300	260
200	285	250	220
290	265	260	290
170	150	190	230
300	270	270	310
200	298	200	170

(a) Initial samples

S_1	S_2	S_3	S_4	Average
170	150	170	170	165
170	180	185	185	180
185	190	190	190	188.75
190	210	200	200	200
200	220	220	210	212.5
200	265	250	220	233.75
200	270	260	230	240
260	280	270	230	260
280	285	270	260	273.75
290	290	290	290	290
300	310	300	310	305

(b) Ordered samples

Original value (S_1)	Released value
260	260
170	165
200	212.5
280	273.75
190	200
185	188.75
200	233.75
290	290
170	180
300	305
200	240

(c) Released data

Fig. 8. An example of resampling over attribute `Chol`

Resampling [14, 17]

This technique consists in replacing the values of a sensitive continuous attribute with the average value computed over a given number of samples taken from the original population. More precisely, let N be the number of tuples in a microdata table and $S_1, \ldots, S_t$ be t samples of size N. Each sample is independently ranked (using the same ranking criterion for all samples) and the average of the j-th ranked values in $S_1, \ldots, S_t$ is computed. The obtained averages are then re-ordered by taking into consideration the order of original values; the first average value then replaces the first original value, the second average replaces the second original value, and so on. For instance, suppose that attribute `Chol` is protected by applying this technique and that we choose $t = 4$ samples. Figure 8 illustrates the different steps in protecting attribute `Chol`. Note that the first sample (column S_1) corresponds to the `Chol` values in the original microdata table.

Lossy Compression [16, 17]

It is a recent technique that exploits image compression algorithms. A continuous microdata table is interpreted as an image, and a lossy compression algorithm (e.g., jpeg) is applied on it. The result is the protected microdata table. Depending on the lossy compression algorithm used, it is necessary to detect an appropriate correspondence between attribute ranges and color scales. This technique can only be applied on continuous data and the compression rate coincides with the obfuscation parameter: the higher the compression rate, the more protected the data.

Rounding [13]

It is similar to the homonymous technique used for protecting macrodata and is applicable only on continuous attributes. It replaces the original values of the considered attribute with rounded values. Rounded values are chosen among a set of *rounding points* p_i each of which defines a *rounding set*. As an example, the rounding points could be chosen as multiples of a base value b, that is, $p_{i+1} - p_i = b$, and the rounding sets could be defined as $[p_i - b/2, p_i + b/2)$, $i = 2 \ldots r - 1$, $[0, p_1 + b/2)$, and $[p_r - b/2, X_{max}]$ (X_{max} is the largest possible value for attribute X) for p_1 and p_r, respectively. An original value v of X is then replaced by the rounding point corresponding to the rounding set where v lies. For instance, consider attribute Temp, $b = 1$, and the rounding points 36, 37, 38, and 39. The corresponding rounding sets are: $[0, 36.5)$; $[36.5, 37.5)$; $[37.5, 38.5)$; and $[38.5, 40.1]$, respectively. The value 35.2 in the first tuple is replaced by 36, the second value 37.7 is replaced by 38, and so on. Note that this rounding technique is usually performed on one attribute at a time (univariate rounding); although multivariate rounding operating on whole tuples is also possible [53].

PRAM (Post RAndomized Method) [18, 29, 35]

It consists in replacing the categorical value for one or more attributes in each tuple with another categorical value based on some probability mechanism. For instance, a *Markov matrix* $P = [p_{ij}]$ (i.e., a real $n \times n$ matrix, where all elements p_{ij} are greater than or equal to 0 and $\sum_{j=1}^{n} p_{ij} = 1, i = 1, \ldots, n$) can contain the probability to replace categories in the original microdata table with other categories. In other words, p_{ij} is the probability that category c_i in the original microdata is substituted by category c_j in the protected microdata.

MASSC (Micro-Agglomeration, Substitution, Sub-sampling and Calibration) [46]

It is a technique that consists of four steps that work as follows.

- *Micro-agglomeration.* Tuples in the original microdata table are partitioned into different groups characterized by a similar risk of disclosure. Each group is formed on the basis of their quasi-identifier. Intuitively, tuples with rare combinations of values for quasi-identifier attributes are at a higher risk and should be in the same group.

- *Substitution.* Original data are perturbed by following an optimal probabilistic strategy.
- *Sub-sampling.* Some cells or whole tuples are suppressed according to an optimal probabilistic subsampling strategy.
- Optimal *calibration.* The sampling weights, used in the previous step, are calibrated to preserve a certain statistical property. In particular, this calibration involves attributes that are to be used by data recipients for surveys.

This technique has been originally proposed for reducing the disclosure risk due to the linkage of categorical attributes with external sources. It is therefore not suitable for tables that contain continuous attributes.

Random Noise [22]

It perturbs a sensitive attribute by adding or by multiplying it with a random variable with a given distribution. The *additive noise* [3, 17] is more frequently used than *multiplicative noise* and can be formally expressed as follows. Let X_j be the j-th column of the original microdata table corresponding to a sensitive attribute and suppose that there are N tuples. Each value $x_{ij}, i = 1, \ldots, N$, is replaced by $x_{ij} + \varepsilon_{ij}$, where ε_j is a vector of normally distributed errors drawn from a random variable with mean equals to zero and, in general, with a variance that is proportional to those of the original attributes (i.e., $\varepsilon_j \approx N(0, \sigma^2_{\varepsilon_j})$ and $\sigma^2_{\varepsilon_j} = \alpha \cdot \sigma^2_{X_j}$, where α is the proportional coefficient). This method, also called *uncorrelated additive noise*, preserves the mean and the co-variance of the original data while variances and correlation coefficients are not preserved. *Correlated additive noise* is another technique that preserves the mean and can allow preservation of correlation coefficients. The difference with the previous method is that the co-variance matrix of the errors is proportional to the co-variance matrix of the original data.

In general, masking by correlated additive noise produces masked data with higher analytical validity than masking by uncorrelated additive noise. However, additive noise is seldomly used by itself because of the low level of protection it provides [50,51]. Rather, it is often combined with *linear* (for continuous attributes [34]) or *non linear* (for categorical attributes [48]) transformations. This means that the microdata obtained after the application of the additive noise technique are then linearly (or non linearly) transformed before release. Such an additional transformation must preserve mean and co-variance. Note that the parameters used in the linear transformation should not be revealed because their knowledge allows the inversion of the function used: the released microdata would have the same degree of protection as if they were protected only by additive noise. The additive noise technique is suitable to protect continuous data since no assumption on the possible values of sensitive attributes can be made, and because no exact matching with external sources of information is possible. Additive noise is usually not suitable to protect categorical data.

To illustrate, consider attribute DH and suppose to protect such an attribute by applying uncorrelated additive noise. We first need to compute the mean and the variance of the original attribute: $\sigma^2_{\mathrm{DH}} = 328.36$ and $\mu_{\mathrm{DH}} = 13$. We then set α to

Original value	Error	Released value
3	+2	5
1	+1	2
40	−10	30
7	+3	10
2	+5	7
3	+8	11
5	+4	9
60	−11	49
7	−2	5
10	−3	7
5	+3	8

Fig. 9. An example of uncorrelated additive noise over attribute DH

0.1 and obtain that $\sigma^2_{\varepsilon_j} \cong 33$. We now draw the error vector (ε) from the normal distribution $N = (0, 33)$, that is, a distribution with mean equals to zero and variance equals to 33. Figure 9 illustrates the original values, the error, and the released values. Note that the mean of the released data is equal to the mean of the original one, while the variance is not preserved.

Swapping [10, 13, 33]

It consists in modifying a subset of the tuples in a microdata table by swapping the values of a set of sensitive attributes, called *swapped attributes*, between selected pairs of tuples (the pairs are selected according to a well-defined criteria). Intuitively, this technique reduces the risk of reidentification because it introduces uncertainty about the true value of a respondent's data. As an example, suppose that the swapped attributes are `Disease`, DH, `Chol`, and `Temp` and that the selected pairs of tuples must have a matching on attributes `Sex` and `MarStat`. Figure 10 illustrates the table obtained by swapping tuple t_3 with t_5, t_7 with t_8, and t_9 with t_{10} (the swapped values are reported in *italic*). Although this technique is easy to apply, in general it has the disadvantage of not preserving statistical properties on subdomains. The original technique has been presented for categorical attributes only. However, in [42] data swapping has been extended to continuous data.

Rank Swapping [17, 30, 55]

It is a variation of swapping that can be applied to continuous and categorical attributes with an order relationship. Basically, the values of an attribute X are ranked in ascending order, and each value is swapped with another value in such a way that the swapped tuples are guaranteed to be within a specified *rank-distance* of one another (i.e., the swapped values should be in a range of $p\%$ of the total range). For instance, suppose to apply this technique on attribute `Temp` and assume $p = 10\%$. The range of this attribute is [35.2,40.1] and therefore the difference between the swapped values should be equal to o lesser than ((40.1−35.2)·10)/100 = 0.49. We

SSN	Name	Race	DoB	Sex	ZIP	MarStat	Disease	DH	Chol	Temp
		Asian	64/09/27	F	94139	Divorced	Hypertension	3	260	35.2
		Asian	64/09/30	F	94139	Divorced	Obesity	1	170	37.7
		Asian	64/04/18	M	94139	Married	*Hypertension*	*2*	*190*	*35.3*
		Asian	64/04/15	M	94139	Married	Obesity	7	280	37.4
		Black	63/03/13	M	94138	Married	*Chest pain*	*40*	*200*	*38.1*
		Black	63/03/18	M	94138	Married	Short breath	3	185	38.2
		Black	64/09/13	F	94141	Married	*Obesity*	*60*	*290*	*39.8*
		Black	64/09/07	F	94141	Married	*Short breath*	*5*	*200*	*36.5*
		White	61/05/14	M	94138	Single	*Obesity*	*10*	*300*	*40.1*
		White	61/05/08	M	94138	Single	*Chest pain*	*7*	*170*	*37.6*
		White	61/09/15	F	94142	Widow	Short breath	5	200	36.9

Fig. 10. Microdata table of Fig. 2 protected through swapping over attributes `Disease`, `DH`, `Chol`, and `Temp`

can then, for instance, swap the value in the first tuple with the value in the fifth tuple; the value in the second tuple with the value in the fourth tuple; and so on. Figure 11 illustrates the resulting microdata table.

Micro-Aggregation (or Blurring) [12, 17]

It consists in grouping individual tuples into small aggregates of a fixed dimension k: the average over each aggregate is published instead of individual values. Groups are formed by using maximal similarity criteria. Although different functions can be defined to measure the similarity, it can be difficult to find an optimal grouping solution [39] and recently some heuristic algorithms have been proposed to maximize similarity [12].

There are different variations of micro-aggregation. For instance, the average can substitute the original value only for a tuple in the group or for all of them; different attributes can be protected through micro-aggregation using the same or different grouping; and the group size may be fixed or variable with a fixed minimum size. As an example, consider attribute `Chol`, and suppose to group tuples according to their value over attribute `Disease` and that the size of each group is variable (while the minimum size is set to 2). The groups are: $\{t_1, t_5\}$, $\{t_2, t_4, t_8, t_{10}\}$, $\{t_3, t_9\}$, and $\{t_6, t_7, t_{11}\}$. Figure 11 illustrates the resulting table. Note that micro-aggregation was first proposed only to protect continuous attributes, but recently some variants for categorical data have been studied. These solutions are based on existing clustering and aggregation definitions such as the c-means [52].

5 Synthetic Data Generation Techniques

The generation of synthetic data is an alternative option for protecting microdata. The basic principle on which such techniques are based is that since the statistical content

SSN	Name	Race	DoB	Sex	ZIP	MarStat	Disease	DH	Chol	Temp
		Asian	64/09/27	F	94139	Divorced	Hypertension	3	*225*	*35.3*
		Asian	64/09/30	F	94139	Divorced	Obesity	1	*260*	*37.4*
		Asian	64/04/18	M	94139	Married	Chest pain	40	*185*	*38.2*
		Asian	64/04/15	M	94139	Married	Obesity	7	*260*	*37.7*
		Black	63/03/13	M	94138	Married	Hypertension	2	*225*	*35.2*
		Black	63/03/18	M	94138	Married	Short breath	3	*195*	*38.1*
		Black	64/09/13	F	94141	Married	Short breath	5	*195*	*36.9*
		Black	64/09/07	F	94141	Married	Obesity	60	*260*	*40.1*
		White	61/05/14	M	94138	Single	Chest pain	7	*185*	37.6
		White	61/05/08	M	94138	Single	Obesity	10	*260*	*39.8*
		White	61/09/15	F	94142	Widow	Short breath	5	*195*	*36.5*

Fig. 11. Microdata table of Fig. 2 protected through rank-swapping over attribute `Temp` and micro-aggregation over attribute `Chol`

Technique	Continuous	Categorical
Bootstrap	yes	no
Cholesky decomposition	yes	no
Multiple imputation	yes	yes
Maximum entropy	yes	yes
Latin Hypercube Sampling	yes	yes

Fig. 12. Applicability of fully synthetic techniques to the different data types

Technique	Continuous	Categorical
IPSO	yes	no
Hybrid masking	yes	no
Random response	no	yes
Blank and impute	yes	yes
SMIKe	yes	yes
Multiply imputed partially synthetic dataset	yes	yes

Fig. 13. Applicability of partially synthetic techniques to the different data types

of the data is not related with the information provided by each respondent, a model well representing the data could in principle replace the data themselves [4]. An important requirement for the generation of synthetic data, which makes the generation process a complicate issue, is that the synthetic and original data should present the same quality of statistical analysis. The main advantage of this class of techniques is that the released synthetic data are not referred to any respondent and therefore their release cannot lead to reidentification. These techniques allow the data holders to pose their attention on the quality of the released data instead of posing attention on the reidentification problem.

In the remainder of this section we describe the main synthetic data generation techniques. Figure 12 and Fig. 13 lists the techniques indicating whether they are applicable (yes) or not (no) to continuous or categorical data types. The techniques are divided into two categories: *fully synthetic* techniques and *partially synthetic* techniques. The first category contains techniques that generate a completely new set of data, while the techniques in the second category merge the original data with synthetic data.

5.1 Fully Synthetic Techniques

We describe some significant *fully synthetic* generation techniques that release only synthetic data.

Bootstrap [24]

Given a microdata table with p attributes, this technique first computes the corresponding *p-variate cumulative distribution function F*. A p-variate cumulative distribution function is a function that completely describes the probability distribution of a set of p real-valued random variables (e.g., the *Gaussian function*). The parameters that characterize F can be determined by using the bootstrap technique. Basically, bootstrap estimates each parameter of the population by using a set of synthetic samples, obtained from the original sample through a resampling with replacement. Once the parameters have been estimated, the corresponding function F on the population is modified to obtain a similar function F'. This new function is then sampled to obtain a set of synthetic data. The modifications on function F should however preserve the statistical properties of the original data. Note that this technique can be applied only on continuous attributes because it is not possible to compute function F on categorical data.

Cholesky Decomposition [38]

This technique, which operates only on continuous attributes and in time linear in the sample size, preserves mean, variance, and co-variance of the original data and is based on the *Cholesky matrix decomposition* method. Given a microdata table T, that can be represented as a matrix of $N \times M$ elements, where rows are tuples and columns are attributes, it is first necessary to compute the co-variance matrix C over T. The next step consists in generating a random matrix, denoted as R, of size $N \times M$, such that the identity matrix I is the co-variance matrix. Then, the Cholesky decomposition U of C is determined, where $C = U^t \times U$. The synthetic microdata matrix is then computed as $R \cdot U$, and it has exactly the same co-variance matrix as T.

Multiple Imputation [41,43]

Given a microdata table with N tuples (i.e., a sample of N respondents) obtained from a much larger population of M individuals, attributes in the table are partitioned into three sets: a set A of *background* attributes (e.g., age, address), a set B of *non confidential* attributes, and a set C of *confidential* attributes. The values of attributes in A are known for the whole population while the values of attributes in B and C are known for the sample only. The multiple imputation method consists of the following three steps.

- Starting from the sample, a *multiple imputed population* of size M is constructed.[2] Such a population contains the N tuples of the microdata table plus p matrices of (B,C) data (p is the multiply-imputed parameter) for the $M - N$ individuals that do not belong to the sample.
- Starting from the known values in A, a set of couples (B,C) is predicted. In this way, the whole population has a value (original or imputed) for A, B, and C. Couples (B,C) are generated using a prediction model.
- A sample of N tuples on the multiply-imputed population is then drawn. This step is repeated p times to create p replicates of (B,C) values. As a result, we obtain p multiply-imputed synthetic datasets. To avoid the inclusion of the original sample (i.e., the N tuples in the microdata table), the samples can be drawn from the multiply-imputed population excluding the N original tuples from it.

This technique operates on both continuous and categorical attributes.

Maximum Entropy [4,40]

It is based on the consideration that by knowing the exact distribution of actual data, it is possible to generate an optimal sample by correctly tuning the parameters of the distribution function and randomly drawing tuples from it. However, the main problem is that since the exact distribution function is not known, it has to be estimated on the basis of the original sample. Therefore, we need to detect the family of distribution functions to which the original data distribution belongs. Then, a specific function is chosen from the family as the one having the *maximum entropy distribution* (such a function exists and is unique). Entropy is defined as the measure of data conformity to a set of constraints. The main task for the data holder is to find out a suitable set of constraints. Typically, constraints are defined on the value of certain statistics, that is, the release synthetic data preserve on average some selected sample characteristics. This technique operates on both continuous and categorical attributes.

Latin Hypercube Sampling (LHS) [25,32]

It produces a synthetic microdata sample reproducing the univariate (i.e., related to a single attribute) statistics of interest, which usually are mean and variance of the values of an attribute. This technique can be applied to a single attribute or to a set of uncorrelated attributes. Recent refinements of this technique reproduce, on synthetic data, the rank correlation structure of the original sample. To this aim, if the sample is composed of a number of attributes or if there are different observations on the same

[2] Imputation is the practice of filling in missing data with plausible values. Multiple imputation means that the missing values are replaced with p simulated values, where p usually varies between 3 and 10.

attributes for the same sample of respondents, it is necessary to iteratively refine the rank correlation matrix used to minimize the difference between the rank correlation of the original and the synthetic data. If the rank correlation matrix is well tuned, the rank correlation between subsets of attributes is better preserved. The main drawback is that it is computationally expensive to produce the synthetic sample and such a complexity depends on the number of statistics to preserve in the synthetic sample and on their value. The technique can be used on both continuous and categorical data.

5.2 Partially Synthetic Techniques

Since it may be difficult to generate plausible synthetic data for all attributes, techniques that generate partially synthetic datasets have also been considered. Basically, these techniques produce a mix of synthetic and original values. We now describe the main partially synthetic techniques.

IPSO (Information Preserving Statistical Obfuscation) [4]

It is based on the distinction of two categories of attributes: *public data* Y and *specific survey data* X. It releases a subset of the original sample after a perturbation operation performed only over public attributes, thus obtaining a new set of values Y'. Since the main purpose of this technique is to release as many values as possible collected in the specific survey, preventing reidentification, only some information in Y is released to preserve the most important statistics S on these data. More precisely, set Y' is generated in such a way to preserve X unaltered and to maintain the set S of statistics over Y. At the end, the new sample (X, Y') is released. This technique operates on continuous attributes only.

Hybrid Masking [11]

This class of techniques combines original data with synthetic data. In particular, after the generation of a simulated sample, each tuple in the original microdata table is matched with a tuple in the simulated one. Then, all the paired tuples are linearly combined, by adding or multiplying their values, and the values obtained are published. These techniques have the advantage of preserving data analytical validity. They operate on continuous attributes only.

Random Response [2, 13]

It is used in situations where sensitive data are collected from a population and there is the possibility that individuals do not respond truthfully. For instance, if an individual has to respond to the question: "Have you ever taken drugs for depression?," the individual may lie and may respond "NO". To avoid this problem, a set of questions is prepared, where some of them are sensitive and some others are not. An individual is requested to respond to one of these questions without indicating what question has been chosen. In this way, if the distribution of the answers to the non sensitive

SSN	Name	Race	DoB	Sex	ZIP	MarStat	Disease	DH	Chol	Temp
		Asian	64/09/27	F	94139	Divorced	Hypertension	3	260	35.2
		Asian	64/09/30	F	94139	Divorced	Obesity	1	170	37.7
		Asian	64/04/18	M	94139	Married	Chest pain	*24*	*228*	*37.7*
		Asian	64/04/15	M	94139	Married	Obesity	7	280	37.4
		Black	63/03/13	M	94138	Married	Hypertension	*2*	*216*	*36.7*
		Black	63/03/18	M	94138	Married	Short breath	3	185	38.2
		Black	64/09/13	F	94141	Married	Short breath	5	200	36.5
		Black	64/09/07	F	94141	Married	Obesity	*20*	*216*	*37.2*
		White	61/05/14	M	94138	Single	Chest pain	7	170	37.6
		White	61/05/08	M	94138	Single	Obesity	10	300	40.1
		White	61/09/15	F	94142	Widow	Short breath	*4*	*223*	*37.2*

Fig. 14. Microdata table of Fig. 2 protected through blank and impute over attributes DH, Chol, and Temp

questions is known, the percentage of positive responses on the sensitive question can be deducted from the number of positive answers. Since this technique can only be applied if the distribution of answers is known and if the questions have the same set of possible answers, it is usually adopted for boolean attributes only.

Blank and Impute [22]

It is a technique also used for protecting macrodata and consists in randomly choosing a set of tuples, either sensitive or not, deleting their original values for a given pre-determined set of attributes, and replacing them with a value computed using a suitable function (e.g., the average). For instance, suppose we choose to blank and impute attributes DH, Chol, and Temp, and that the randomly selected tuples are the third, the fifth, the eighth, and the eleventh. The new values for attribute DH are computed as the average over patients having the same health problem; the new values for Chol are computed as the average over patients of the same race; the new values for Temp are computed as the average over patients that were born in the same month and year. Figure 14 illustrates the resulting microdata table; the new values are reported in *italic*. This technique operates on both continuous and categorical attributes.

SMIKe (Selective Multiple Imputation of Keys) [36]

It releases multiple sets of modified data rather than just one set. Let X be the set of quasi-identifiers in the original microdata table, and Y be the set of the other attributes (either sensitive or not). First, it is necessary to introduce the concept of *sensitive case*. If the number of tuples with a specific combination on attributes X is lesser that a predefined sensitive threshold, that combination is a sensitive case. SMIKe executes the following four steps before data publication.

- Each sensitive tuple t is associated with the non sensitive tuples closest to it, where the distance is computed on the basis of the values of attributes in Y.

These tuples are inserted in the i-th mixing set M_i, where i is the i-th sensitive case of tuple t. The mixing sets for different sensitive cases may overlap.
- Let M be the union of sensitive cases and selected non sensitive cases. A completely *random imputation model* (i.e., a model that generates imputations for the missing values) for X is built. X' is the value imputed to X.
- A randomly set of tuples is chosen, where attribute values in X will be imputed synthetically, and randomly draws the new values from the distribution X' just defined.
- The quality of the synthetic sample is evaluated and, if it is too low, the process restarts from the beginning, trying to better tune the size of M_i.

This technique imputes only quasi-identifiers and substitutes a subset of the sensitive tuples with simulated tuples. It operates on both continuous and categorical attributes.

Multiply Imputed Partially Synthetic Dataset [27]

This class of techniques is based on the assumption that only sensitive attributes are to be protected through simulation, while other attributes can be published as in the original microdata table. The sensitive attributes can be simulated by using the multiple imputation technique above-mentioned.

In addition to the techniques here described for data generation, which can be applied to any kind of data, there are also some techniques for the protection of specific categories of data. For instance, specific regression models have been studied for the correct release of business microdata collected by census agencies [4]. Also, since the microdata release problem has become of great importance, different software solutions have been developed to protect microdata. For instance, μ-ARGUS is a software that exploits global recoding, local suppression, PRAM, additive noise, and micro-aggregation [31].

6 Measures for Assessing Microdata Confidentiality and Utility

As discussed in the previous sections, there is a broad choice of techniques for protecting microdata. A microdata protection technique has to be chosen in such a way to balance two contrasting needs: the need for data and the need for confidentiality protection. To this purpose, the performance of any protection technique is usually measured in terms of *information loss* and *disclosure risk*. Information loss is the amount of information that exists in the original microdata and because of the protection technique does not occur in protected microdata. Disclosure risk is the risk that a disclosure will be encountered if protected microdata are released. Two extreme solutions for releasing microdata are:

- the encryption of the original data (no disclosure risk and maximal information loss);

- the release of the original data (maximal disclosure risk and no information loss).

On the other hand, the application of any of the techniques presented in this chapter can provide means to balance the two. In the following, we describe some of the most important methods used for quantifying disclosure risk and information loss.

6.1 Disclosure Risk

In general, there are two types of disclosure: *identity* disclosure and *attribute* disclosure [21]. Identity disclosure means that a specific identity can be linked to a tuple in the microdata table. Attribute disclosure means that information has been disclosed about an attribute of an individual. In general, two factors may have an impact on identity disclosure:

- *population uniqueness* means that the probability of identifying a respondent who is the unique respondent with a specific combination of attributes is high if those attributes are present in the microdata table;
- *reidentification* means that the released microdata is linked to another published table, where the identifiers have not been removed.

Different methods have been proposed to measure the disclosure risk of released microdata. For instance, the *minimum unsafe combination of attributes* [49] returns the number of attributes with a unique combination in a specific microdata tuple. This method can be adopted only with non-perturbative masking techniques and the higher such a value, the lower the disclosure risk. Other specific methods have been proposed in [4,55]. In the remainder of this section we focus on the main methods for measuring the risk of identity disclosure, which are *uniqueness* and *record linkage*, and the main method to measure attribute disclosure, which is *interval disclosure* [15, 17].

Uniqueness

Whenever a sample unique is also a population unique, identity disclosure becomes much more likely. There are different methods for evaluating the uniqueness risk and all the methods rely on probability evaluations.

The first method measures the probability of *population uniqueness* (*PU*), that is, the probability that there is only an individual in the population having a certain combination of values over a certain set of attributes. This probability is measured as: $Pr(PU) = \sum_j I(F_j = 1)/N$, where N is the population size, F_j is the number of individuals in the population with the j-th combination over the considered attributes, and $I()$ is a function where $I(A)$ is equal to 1 if A is true; 0 otherwise.

The second method measures the probability that *a sample unique* (*SU*) is also a *population unique* (*PU*). This probability is measured as: $Pr(PU|SU) = \sum_j I(f_j = 1, F_j = 1)/\sum_j I(f_j = 1)$, where f_j is the number of individuals in the sample with the j-th combination over the considered attributes. These two methods are called *file-level* measures because assign the same risk to all tuples [47]. *Tuple-level* disclosure risk measure is the probability that the identity of a specific individual is disclosed [26]. This measure has been introduced because the risk of reidentification is not homogeneous over the whole microdata table. Suppose that there are K different combinations of quasi-identifier values in a population. These combinations produce a partition both on the population and on the sample. Let F_k be the frequency of the k-th partition, the disclosure risk for a tuple in the sample with the k-th combination is $1/F_k$. The problem of this method is that F_k is generally not known for the population. Since the sample distribution frequencies f_k are known, the distribution of frequencies F_k, given f_k, is considered ($F_k|f_k$ can be modeled as a negative binomial).

Note that uniqueness can be used as a measure of disclosure risk only if the microdata have been protected through a non-perturbative masking technique. Perturbative techniques change data values and therefore it is not possible to establish correctly the frequency of a value in the released sample because new unique combinations may be introduced and original unique combinations may disappear.

Record Linkage

Record linkage consists in finding a matching between a tuple in the protected microdata table and a tuple in a public and non anonymous external source of information (e.g., a voter list that contains the registry of all the electors of a region or a town). Since it is not possible to know a priori all the external sources of information that can be used by a possible malicious user, a probabilistic check on the protected microdata is performed. Different record linkage methods have to be adopted depending on whether or not the microdata table and the external information have common attributes. If there are common attributes, it is first necessary to adopt a unique representation for the common attributes. For instance, different abbreviations in the name of a person would lead to the conclusion that two tuples are not related, while actually they refer to the same respondent. It is then possible to adopt a strategy for record linkage [17, 18, 23]. Record linkage methods can be partitioned into three broad categories: *deterministic*, *probabilistic*, and *distance-based*.

- *Deterministic.* It looks for an exact match on one or more attributes between tuples in different datasets. The main disadvantage of this method is that it does not take into consideration the attribute relevance in finding a link.
- *Probabilistic.* Given two datasets, D_1 and D_2, the set of all possible pairs of tuples (d_{1i}, d_{2j}) is computed, where $d_{1i} \in D_1$ and $d_{2j} \in D_2$. Each pair is associated with a probability that represents whether the pair is a real match. If the probability is lower than a fixed threshold T_1, the pair is discarded because the tuples are considered not linked; if the probability is greater than a second fixed threshold T_2 the pair is considered a real match; if the probability is between T_1 and T_2, it is needed a human evaluation to verify whether it represents a match or not. Such a probability is computed considering different weights for different attributes and the agreement or partial agreement over the attribute values.

The weights associated with the attributes and the two thresholds T_1 and T_2 are established by the data holder.

- *Distance-based.* Given two datasets, D_1 and D_2, each tuple $d_{1i} \in D_1$ is matched to the nearest tuple $d_{2j} \in D_2$. This method requires the definition of a distance function f between couples of tuples. For instance, the definition of f can exploit distance functions defined on attributes and may assign different weights to each attribute, depending on its importance in the linking process. An example of distance function is the *Euclidean Distance* that considers each tuple as a vector and assigns the same weight to each attribute. This record linkage method is not suitable for categorical attributes, because it is difficult to define the distance between two categories, in particular if their domain is not ordered.

Other methods are used when there are datasets without common attributes. In these cases, the reidentification is more difficult. One method recently proposed is based on *clustering* [19]. Basically, a clustering method is applied on the considered datasets. The result is a set of clusters of tuples and each cluster within a dataset is mapped onto a cluster within the other dataset. Such a mapping is performed by using a *similarity function*.

Note that although record linkage is considered a threat, there are many situations where it can be useful. Record linkage can be used in the management of large databases to extract important information about the same subject. This is particularly useful when data are distributed on different servers (e.g., the medical information of the population is usually distributed on different systems and a record linkage technique can be exploited for reconstructing the information associated with a given individual) [45].

Interval Disclosure

The interval disclosure measure is computed in different ways, depending on the data type of the attribute (continuous or categorical). In case of a categorical attribute, for each tuple in the microdata table, *ranked intervals* are constructed as follows. Each attribute is independently ranked and a rank interval is defined around the value assumed by the attribute in each tuple t. The ranks of values within the interval constructed around tuple t should differ less than $p\%$, of the total number of tuples. Also, the rank in the center of the interval should correspond to the value assumed by the considered attribute in tuple t. The disclosure risk is then the proportion of the original values that fall into the interval centered around the corresponding protected value. If such a proportion is equal to 100%, a potential attacker is sure that the original value lies in the interval around the protected value. In case of continuous data, the method is similar to the previous one. The main difference is how ranked intervals are constructed: it is not possible to exploit ranking and the construction is based on the standard deviation of the attribute.

6.2 Information Loss

The information loss measure is strictly connected to the *purpose* for which the information will be used. Since the purposes may be different and not known a priori, it is not possible to establish a general information loss measure based on purpose. The methods used are therefore based on the concepts of *analytically valid* and *analytically interesting*, which are defined as follows [54]:

- a protected microdata table is *analytically valid* if it approximately preserves statistical analyzes (e.g., mean and co-variance) that can be produced with the original microdata;
- a protected microdata table is *analytically interesting* if it contains a sufficient number of attributes that can be validly analyzed.

In general, there are two strategies for computing information loss: *i)* directly comparing the tuples of the protected microdata with the tuples in the original microdata; *ii)* comparing the statistics computed on the protected microdata with the same statistics evaluated on the original microdata. We now describe the basic idea of some of the most common information loss measures that are partitioned into two categories according to the data type of the attributes. Other methods have been proposed, both for specific microdata protection techniques and for generic cases [4,55].

Continuous Data

To measure information loss, the statistic of interest (e.g., co-variance matrices, correlation matrices, or variants of them) is evaluated on both the original and protected data, the difference between the two values is computed. The discrepancies between the two statistics can be evaluated in three different ways: *mean square error*, *mean absolute error*, and *mean variation*. In addition to statistical measures, data can be compared, before and after the application of a microdata protection technique, by computing again the difference using one of the three methods above-mentioned.

It is important to note that the value of information loss should have a maximal value (e.g., 100 if a percentage notation is used) to compare different methods having the same scale for information loss computation [15–17,37].

Categorical Data

The information loss measures briefly introduced for continuous attributes are not directly applicable for categorical attributes. In this case, there are three main measures [16]: *direct comparison*, *contingency tables comparison*, and *entropy measure*. The direct comparison of the values of categorical attributes requires the definition of a *distance function* between the categories. In case of non ordered categories, the distance between category c_1 in the original microdata and the corresponding category c_2 in the protected microdata is equal to 0, if the two categories are the same; 1, otherwise. By contrast, if there is an ordering between the categories, the distance between categories c_1 and c_2 is equal to the number of categories between c_1 and c_2 divided by the total number of categories. The contingency tables comparison measure consists in comparing the corresponding contingency tables. An entropy-based measure [35,53] can be used whenever a microdata table has been protected by applying the local suppression, global recoding, or PRAM techniques. The idea is that the information loss can be measured using the *Shannon Entropy* because the masking process is modeled as the noise added to the original microdata when transmitted through a noisy channel. The information loss measure uses the conditional probability (the probability of a value in the original microdata, once the value in the protected microdata is given).

6.3 Disclosure Risk and Information Loss Combination

The microdata protection techniques described in this chapter have a different impact on data utility and disclosure risk. To be able to assess alternative microdata protection techniques, we first need a framework for assessing how good a protection technique is. Disclosure risk and information loss therefore need to be combined. A simple method consists in computing the average of the 2 values and choosing the technique (and the parameter setting) that has the highest score value [17]. Another method is the *R-U confidentiality maps* [20], which is a graph where the measure of data utility (the inverse of information loss) is reported on the x axis, and the disclosure risk is reported on the y axis. For each microdata protection technique, a line is drawn on the Cartesian plane with a point for each parameter setting. On the basis of the graphic obtained, it is possible to compare the various protection techniques and choose the most suitable. Once a protection technique has been chosen, the R-U confidentiality maps can also be used for selecting the parameters. It is important to note that a R-U map is only a method for correlating disclosure risk and information loss and such measures have to be computed using one of the methods above-mentioned.

Another approach for balancing data utility and disclosure risk is represented by the concept of k-minimal table with the k-anonymity (see Chap. "k-anonymity" and [44]). k-anonymity establishes a lower bound threshold of disclosure risk for a table, by ensuring that every tuple in the table cannot be related to fewer than k respondents. The k-anonymity approach aims at finding (by applying generalization and suppression techniques) a k-minimal table, that is, one that does not generalize more than it is needed to reach the threshold k. In other words, a k-minimal table is one that minimizes information loss.

The measures described should be used before releasing the data to verify whether the protection is adequate to the respondents' requests of confidentiality and to the data recipients' needs of information. After the application of a protection technique, the protected microdata can be checked and released only if they present a certain degree of protection. These measures can also be used by the data recipient to evaluate respondents' identity protection and data utility.

7 Conclusions

Today's globally networked society places great demand on the dissemination and sharing of information. While in the past released information was mostly in tabular and statistical form, many situations call today for the release of specific microdata.

To address this issue, a wide variety of protection techniques have been proposed. In this chapter, we have described the basic microdata disclosure protection techniques, classifying them as masking techniques and synthetic data generation techniques. Masking techniques protect data by transforming their values. Synthetic data generation techniques protect data by replacing them with new data that preserve the original statistical properties. We have also illustrated the main measures usually adopted for assessing data confidentiality and data utility of the protected microdata.

8 Acknowledgments

This work was supported in part by the European Union within the PRIME Project in the FP6/IST Programme under contract IST-2002-507591 and by the Italian MIUR within the KIWI and MAPS projects.

References

1. Adam NR, Wortman JC (1989). Security-control methods for statistical databases: A comparative study. ACM Computing Surveys, 21(4):515–556.
2. Bourke PD, Dalenius T (1975). Some new ideas in the realm of randomized inquiries. Technical Report 5, Detpartment of Statistics, University of Stockholm, Stockholm, Sweden.
3. Brand R (2002). Microdata protection through noise addition. In Domingo-Ferrer J, editor, Inference Control in Statistical Databases, vol. 2316 of LNCS, pp. 97–116. Springer, Berlin Heidelberg.
4. Burridge J, Franconi L, Polettini S, Stander J (2002). A methodological framework for statistical disclosure limitation of business microdata. Technical Report 1.1-D4, CASC Project.
5. Cox LH (1980). Suppression methodology and statistical disclosure analysis. Journal of the American Statistical Association, 75(370):377–385.
6. Cox LH (1981). Linear sensitivity measures in statistical disclosure control. Journal of Statistical Planning and Inference, 5(2):153–164.
7. Cox LH (1987). A constructive procedure for unbiased controlled rounding. Journal of the American Statistical Association, 82(398):520–524.
8. Cox LH (1995). Network models for complementary cell suppression. Journal of the American Statistical Association, 90(432):1453–1462.
9. Cox LH, Dandekar RA (2002). Synthetic tabular data – An alternative to complementary cell suppression. Unpublished manuscript.
10. Dalenius T, Reiss SP (1978). Data-swapping: a technique for disclosure control (extended abstract). In Proc. of the ASA Section on Survey Research Methods, pp. 191–194, Washington DC.
11. Dandekar R, Domingo-Ferrer J, Sebé F (2002). LHS-based hybrid microdata vs rank swapping and microaggregation for numeric microdata protection. In Domingo-Ferrer J, editor, Inference Control in Statistical Databases, vol. 2316 of LNCS, pp. 153–162. Springer, Berlin Heidelberg.

12. Defays D, Nanopoulos P (1993). Panels of enterprises and confidentiality: the small aggregates method. In Proc. of the 92nd Symposium on Design and Analysis of Longitudinal Surveys, pp. 195–204, Ottawa.
13. Denning DE (1982). Inference controls. In Cryptography and Data Security, pp. 331–392. Addison-Wesley Publishing Company, Reading, Massachusetts; Menlo Park, California; London; Amsterdam; Don Mills, Ontario; Sydney.
14. Domingo-Ferrer J, Mateo-Sanz JM (1999). On resampling for statistical confidentiality in contingency tables. Computers & Mathematics with Applications, 38(11-12):13–32.
15. Domingo-Ferrer J, Mateo-Sanz JM, Torra V (2001). Comparing SDC methods for microdata on the basis of information loss and disclosure risk. In Pre-proceedings of ETK-NTTS 001, vol. 2, pp. 807–826, Luxemburg. Eurostat.
16. Domingo-Ferrer J, Torra V (2001). Disclosure protection methods and information loss for microdata. In Doyle P, Lane JI, Theeuwes J, Zayatz L, editors, Confidentiality, Disclosure and Data Access: Theory and Practical Applications for Statistical Agencies. North-Holland, Amsterdam.
17. Domingo-Ferrer J, Torra V (2001). A quantitative comparison of disclosure control methods for microdata. In Doyle P, Lane JI, Theeuwes J, and Zayatz L, editors, Confidentiality, Disclosure and Data Access: Theory and Practical Applications for Statistical Agencies. North-Holland, Amsterdam.
18. Domingo-Ferrer J, Torra V (2002). Distance-based and probabilistic record linkage for re-identification of records with categorical variables. Butlleti de l'Associacio Catalana d'Intelligencia Artificial, 27.
19. Domingo-Ferrer J, Torra V (2003). Disclosure risk assessment in statistical microdata protection via advanced record linkage. Statistics and Computing, 13(4):343–354. Kluwer Academic Publishers.
20. Duncan GT, Keller-McNulty SA, Stokes SL (2001). Disclosure risk vs. data utility: The R-U confidentiality map. Technical report, Los Alamos National Laboratory. LA-UR-01-6428.
21. Duncan GT, Lambert D (1989). The risk of disclosure for microdata. Journal of Business and Economic Statistics, 7:207–217.
22. Federal Committee on Statistical Methodology (1994). Statistical policy working paper 22. USA. Report on Statistical Disclosure Limitation Methodology.
23. Fellegi IP, Sunter AB (1969). A theory for record linkage. Journal of the American Statistical Association, 64(328):1183–1210.
24. Fienberg SE (1994). A radical proposal for the provision of micro-data samples and the preservation of confidentiality. Technical Report 611, Carnegie Mellon University Department of Statistics.
25. Florian A (1992). An efficient sampling scheme: updated latin hypercube sampling. Probabilistic Engineering Mechanics, 7(2):123–130.
26. Franconi L, Polettini S (2004). Individual risk estimation in μ-ARGUS: a review. In Domingo-Ferrer J, Torra V, editors, Privacy in Statistical Databases, vol. 3050 of LNCS, pp. 262–372. Springer, Berlin Heidelberg.
27. Franconi L, Stander J (2002). A model based method for disclosure limitation of business microdata. Journal of the Royal Statistical Society D-Statistician, 51(1):1–11.
28. Gonzalez JF, Cox LH (2005). Software for tabular data protection. Statistics in Medicine, 24(4):65–669.
29. Gouweleeuw JM, Kooiman P, Willenborg RCLJ, DeWolf PP (1997). Post randomization for statistical disclosure control: Theory and implementation. Technical Report 9731, Voorburg: Statistics Netherlands, Netherlands.

30. Greenberg B (1987). Rank swapping for ordinal data. Technical report, U. S. Bureau of the Census (unpublished manuscript), Washington, DC.
31. Hundepool A, Van deWetering A, Ramaswamy R, Franconi L, Capobianchi A, DeWolf PP, Domingo-Ferrer J, Torra V, Brand R, Giessing S (2003). μ-ARGUS version 3.2 software and user manual. Statistics Netherlands. http://neon.vb.cbs.nl/casc.
32. Huntington DE, Lyrintzis CS (1998). Improvements to and limitations of latin hypercube sampling. Probabilistic Engineering Mechanics, 13(4):245–253.
33. Karr AF, Sanil AP (2004). Data quality and data confidentiality for microdata: Implications and strategies. Technical Report 149, National Institute of Statistical Sciences, Research Triangle Park, NC 27709-4006 USA.
34. Kim JJ (1986). A method for limiting disclosure in microdata based on random noise and transformation. In Proc. of the Section on Survey Research Methods, pp. 303–308, Alexandria VA.
35. Kooiman PL, Willenborg L, Gouweleeuw J (1998). PRAM: A method for disclosure limitation of microdata. Technical report, Statistics Netherlands, Voorburg, NL.
36. Little RJA, Liu F (2002). Selective multiple imputation of keys for statistical disclosure control in microdata. In Proc. of the Section on Survey Research Methods.
37. Mateo-Sanz JM, Domingo-Ferrer J, Sebé F (2004). Probabilistic information loss measures for continuous microdata. Technical report, University of Tarragona, Department of Computer Engineering and Mathematics, Research Triangle Park, NC 27709-4006 USA.
38. Mateo-Sanz JM, Martìnez-Ballesté A, Domingo-Ferrer J (2004). Fast generation of accurate synthetic microdata. In Domingo-Ferrer J, Torra V, editors, Privacy in Statistical Databases, vol. 3050 of LNCS, pp. 298–306. Springer, Berlin Heidelberg.
39. Oganian A, Domingo-Ferrer J (2001). On the complexity of optimal microaggregation for statistical disclosure control. Statistical Journal of the UNECE, 18(4):345–354.
40. Polettini S, Franconi L (2002) Simulation methods in data protection: an approach based on maximum entropy. In Proc. of the International Conference of the Royal Statistical Society, Plymouth.
41. Raughnathan TE, Reiter JP, Rubin DB (2003). Multiple imputation for statistical disclosure limitation. Journal of Official Statitsics, 19(1):1–16.
42. Reiss S (1982). Non-reversible privacy transform. In Proc. of the ACM Symposium on Principles of Database Systems, Los Angeles, CA, USA.
43. Rubin DB (1993). Discussion of statistical disclosure limitation. Journal of Official Statistics, 9(2):461–468.
44. Samarati P (2001). Protecting respondents' identities in microdata release. IEEE Transactions on Knowledge and Data Engineering, 13(6):1010–1027.
45. Computer Science and Telecommunications Board National Research Council, editors (1997). For the record protecting electronic health information. National Accademy Press, Washington, D.C., USA.
46. Singh AC, Yu F, Dunteman GH (2004). MASSC: A new data mask for limiting statistical information loss and disclosure. In Linden H, Riecan J, Belsby L, editors, Work Session on Statistical Data Confidentiality 2003, pp. 373–394. Eurostat, Luxemburg. Monographs in Official Statistics.
47. Skinner CJ, Elliot MA (2001). A measure of disclosure risk for microdata. Journal of the Royal Statistical Society, 64(4):855–867.
48. Sullivan GR (1989). The use of added error to avoid disclosure in microdata releases. Master's thesis, Iowa State University.
49. Takemura A (2001). On recent developments in statistical disclosure control techniques. In Proc. of the IAOS Satellite Meeting on Statistics for the Information Society, Tokyo, Japan.

50. Tendick P (1991). Optimal noise addition for preserving confidentiality in multivariate data. Journal of Statistical Planning and Inference, 27(3):341–353.
51. Tendick P, Matloff N (1994). A modified random perturbation method for database security. ACM Transactions on Database Systems, 19(1):47–63.
52. Torra V (2004). Microaggregation for categorical variables: a median based approach. In Domingo-Ferrer J, Torra V, editors, Privacy in Statistical Databases, vol. 3050 of LNCS, pp. 162–174. Springer, Berlin Heidelberg.
53. Willenborg L, DeWaal T (2001). Elements of Statistical Disclosure Control. Springer-Verlag, New York, USA.
54. Winkler WE (1999). Re-identification methods for evaluating the confidentiality of analytically valid microdata. In Domingo-Ferrer J, editor, Statistical Data Protection. Office for Official Publications of the European Communities, Luxemburg.
55. Winkler WE (2004). Masking and re-identification methods for public-use microdata: Overview and research problems. In Domingo-Ferrer J, editor, Privacy in Statistical Databases 2004. Springer, New York.

k-Anonymity

V. Ciriani, S. De Capitani di Vimercati, S. Foresti, and P. Samarati

Università degli Studi di Milano
{ciriani, decapita, foresti, samarati}@dti.unimi.it

1 Introduction

Today's globally networked society places great demand on the dissemination and sharing of information, which is probably becoming the most important and demanded resource. While in the past released information was mostly in tabular and statistical form (*macrodata*), many situations call today for the release of specific data (*microdata*). Microdata, in contrast to macrodata reporting precomputed statistics, provide the convenience of allowing the final recipient to perform on them analysis as needed.

To protect the anonymity of the entities, called *respondents*, to which microdata undergoing public or semipublic release refer, data holders often remove or encrypt explicit identifiers such as names, addresses, and phone numbers. De-identifying data, however, provides no guarantee of anonymity. Released information often contains other data, such as race, birth date, sex, and ZIP code, which can be linked to publicly available information to re-identify (or restrict the uncertainty about) the data respondents, thus leaking information that was not intended for disclosure. The large amount of information easily accessible today, together with the increased computational power available to the attackers, make such linking attacks a serious problem. Indeed, the restricted access to information and its expensive processing, which represented a form of protection in the past, do not hold anymore. Information about us is collected every day, as we join associations or groups, shop for groceries, or execute most of our common daily activities [8, 10]; the amount of privately owned records that describe each citizen's finances, interests, and demographics is increasing every day. Information bureaus such as TRW, Equifax, and Trans Union hold the largest and most detailed databases on American consumers. Most municipalities sell population registers that include the identities of individuals along with basic demographics; examples include local census data, voter lists, city directories, and information from motor vehicle agencies, tax assessors, and real estate agencies. Typical data contained in these databases may include names, social security numbers, birth dates, addresses, telephone numbers, family status, and employment/salary histories. These data, which are often publicly distributed or sold, can be used for linking iden-

SSN	Name	Race	Date of birth	Sex	ZIP	Marital status	Disease
		asian	64/04/12	F	94142	divorced	hypertension
		asian	64/09/13	F	94141	divorced	obesity
		asian	64/04/15	F	94139	married	chest pain
		asian	63/03/13	M	94139	married	obesity
		asian	63/03/18	M	94139	married	short breath
		black	64/09/27	F	94138	single	short breath
		black	64/09/27	F	94139	single	obesity
		white	64/09/27	F	94139	single	chest pain
		white	64/09/27	F	94141	widow	short breath

Fig. 1. De-identified private table (medical data)

Name	Address	City	ZIP	DOB	Sex	Status
....	....	....	....	....	....	....
....	....	....	....	....	....	....
Sue J. Doe	900 Market St.	San Francisco	*94142*	*64/04/12*	*F*	*divorced*
....	....	....	....	....	....	....

Fig. 2. Non de-identified public available table

tities with de-identified information, thus allowing re-identification of respondents. This situation has raised particular concerns in the medical and financial fields, where microdata, which are increasingly released for circulation or research, can be or have been subject to abuses, compromising the privacy of individuals [4, 10, 35].

To illustrate the concept, consider the table in Fig. 1, which exemplifies medical data to be released. In this table, which we refer to as *Private Table* (PT), data have been de-identified by suppressing names and Social Security Numbers (SSNs) so not to explicitly disclose the identities of respondents. However, values of other released attributes, such as `Race`, `Date of birth`, `Sex`, `ZIP` and `Marital status` can also appear in some external table jointly with the individual identity, and can therefore allow them to be tracked. For instance, `ZIP`, `Date of birth`, `Sex`, and `Marital status` can be linked to the Voter List in Fig. 2 to reveal `Name`, `Address`, and `City`. In the private table, for example, there is only one divorced female (`F`) born on `64/04/12` and living in the `94142` area. This combination, if unique in the external world as well, uniquely identifies the corresponding tuple as pertaining to "`Sue J. Doe`, `900 Market Street`, `San Francisco`", thus revealing that she has reported `hypertension`. (Notice that the medical information is not assumed to be publicly associated with individuals, and the desired protection is to release the medical information in a way that the identities of individuals cannot be determined. However, the released characteristics for `Sue J. Doe` leads to determine which medical data among those released are hers.) While this example demonstrates an exact match, in some cases, linking allows one to detect a restricted set of individuals among whom there is the actual data respondent. To avoid the release of de-identified microdata still exposed to linking attacks, different microdata protection techniques can be applied (see chap. "Microdata Protection" for a survey of these different techniques). Among them, there are the commonly used approaches like sampling, swapping values, and adding noise to the data while maintaining some overall statistical properties of the resulting table. However, many uses require release and explicit management of microdata while needing *truthful* information within each tuple. This "data quality" requirement makes inappropriate those techniques that disturb data and therefore, although preserving statistical properties, compromise the correctness of single tuples. *k-anonymity*, together with its enforcement via *generalization* and *suppression*, has been therefore proposed as an approach to protect respondents' identities while releasing truthful information [26].

In this chap. we discuss k-anonymity, starting from its original proposal and surveying then the different algorithms proposed for its enforcement. Also, we will illustrate existing proposals enriching and refining the original definition of k-anonymity. The remainder of this chap. is organized as follows. Section 2 illustrates the basic concepts on k-anonymity and describes the original k-anonymity definition with attribute generalization and tuple suppression. Section 3 introduces a taxonomy for classifying existing k-anonymity approaches. Section 4 and Sect. 5 describe the algorithms proposed in literature for producing k-anonymous tables. Section 6 briefly presents further studies based on the k-anonymity. Finally, Sect. 7 concludes the chapter.

2 k-Anonymity and k-Anonymous Tables

The concept of k-anonymity [27] tries to capture, on the private table PT to be released, one of the main requirements that has been followed by the statistical community and by agencies releasing the data, and according to which the released data should be indistinguishably related to no less than a certain number of respondents.

The set of attributes included in the private table, also externally available and therefore exploitable for linking, is called *quasi-identifier*. The requirement just stated is then translated in [26] in the k-anonymity requirement below, which states that every tuple released cannot be related to fewer than k respondents.

Definition 1 (k-anonymity requirement). *Each release of data must be such that every combination of values of quasi-identifiers can be indistinctly matched to at least k respondents.*

Since it seems impossible, or highly impractical and limiting, to make assumptions on the datasets available for linking to external attackers or curious data recipients, essentially k-anonymity takes a safe approach requiring that, in the released table itself, the respondents be indistinguishable (within a given set) with respect to the set of attributes. To guarantee the k-anonymity requirement, k-anonymity requires each quasi-identifier value in the released table to have at least k occurrences, as stated by the following definition.

Definition 2 (k-anonymity). *Let $T(A_1, \ldots, A_m)$ be a table, and QI be a quasi-identifier associated with it. T is said to satisfy* k-anonymity *with respect to QI iff each sequence of values in $T[QI]$ appears at least with k occurrences in $T[QI]$.*[1]

This definition is a sufficient condition for the k-anonymity requirement: a table satisfying Definition 2 for a given k clearly satisfies the k-anonymity requirement for such a k. If a set of attributes of external tables appears in the quasi-identifier associated with the private table PT, and the table satisfies Definition 2, the combination of the released data with the external data will never allow the recipient to associate each released tuple with less than k respondents. For instance, with respect to the microdata table in Fig. 1 and the quasi-identifier {`Race, Date of birth, Sex, ZIP, Marital status`}, it easy to see that the table satisfies k-anonymity with $k = 1$ only, since there are single occurrences of values over the considered quasi-identified (e.g., the single occurrence "`asian, 64/04/12, F, 94142, divorced`").

The enforcement of k-anonymity requires the preliminary identification of the *quasi-identifier*. The quasi-identifier depends on the external information available to the recipient, as this determines her linking ability (not all possible external tables are available to every possible data recipient); and different quasi-identifiers can potentially exist for a given table. For the sake of simplicity, the original k-anonymity proposal [26] assumes that private table PT has a single quasi-identifier composed of all attributes in PT that can be externally available and contains at most one tuple for each respondent. Therefore, although the identification of the correct quasi-identifier for a private table can be a difficult task, it is assumed that the quasi-identifier has been properly recognized and defined. For instance, with respect to the microdata table in Fig. 1, a quasi-identifier can be the set of attributes {`Race, Date of birth, Sex, ZIP, Marital status`}.

2.1 Generalization and Suppression

Among the techniques proposed for providing anonymity in the release of microdata, the k-anonymity proposal focuses on two techniques in particular: *generalization* and *suppression*, which, unlike other existing techniques, such as scrambling or swapping, preserve the truthfulness of the information. We have already introduced generalization and suppression in chap. "Microdata Protection". We now illustrate here their specific definition and use in the context of k-anonymity.

Generalization consists in substituting the values of a given attribute with more general values. To this purpose, the notion of *domain* (i.e., the set of values that an attribute can assume) is extended to capture the generalization process by assuming the existence of a set of *generalized domains*. The set of original domains together with their generalizations is referred to as Dom. Each generalized domain contains generalized values and there exists a mapping between each domain and its generalizations. For instance, ZIP codes can be generalized by dropping, at each generalization step, the least significant digit; postal addresses can be generalized to the street

[1] $T[QI]$ denotes the projection, maintaining duplicate tuples, of attributes QI in T.

(dropping the number), then to the city, to the county, to the state, and so on. This mapping is stated by means of a *generalization relationship* $\leq_D$. Given two domains D_i and $D_j \in$ Dom, $D_i \leq_D D_j$ states that values in domain D_j are generalizations of values in D_i. The generalization relationship $\leq_D$ defines a partial order on the set Dom of domains, and is required to satisfy the following conditions:

C1: $\forall D_i, D_j, D_z \in$ Dom:
$D_i \leq_D D_j, D_i \leq_D D_z \Rightarrow D_j \leq_D D_z \vee D_z \leq_D D_j$
C2: all maximal elements of Dom are singleton.

Condition **C1** states that for each domain D_i, the set of domains generalization of D_i is totally ordered and, therefore, each D_i has at most *one* direct generalization domain D_j. It ensures determinism in the generalization process. Condition **C2** ensures that all values in each domain can always be generalized to a single value. The definition of a generalization relationship implies the existence, for each domain $D \in$ Dom, of a totally ordered hierarchy, called *domain generalization hierarchy*, denoted DGH_D.

A value generalization relationship, denoted $\leq_V$, can also be defined, which associates with each value in domain D_i a unique value in domain D_j, direct generalization of D_i. The value generalization relationship implies the existence, for each domain D, of a *value generalization hierarchy*, denoted VGH_D. It is easy to see that the value generalization hierarchy VGH_D is a *tree*, where the leaves are the values in D and the root (i.e., the most general value) is the value in the maximum element in DGH_D. Figure 3 illustrates an example of domain and value generalization hierarchies for domains: races ($\mathtt{R}_0$); sex ($\mathtt{S}_0$); a subset of the ZIP codes of San Francisco, USA ($\mathtt{Z}_0$); marital status ($\mathtt{M}_0$); and dates of birth ($\mathtt{D}_0$). The generalization relationship specified for ZIP codes generalizes a 5-digit ZIP code, first to a 4-digit ZIP code, and then to a 3-digit ZIP code. The other hierarchies are of immediate interpretation.

Since the approach in [26] works on sets of attributes, the generalization relationship and hierarchies are extended to refer to tuples composed of elements of Dom or of their values. Given a domain tuple $DT = \langle D_1, \ldots, D_n \rangle$ such that $D_i \in$ Dom, $i = 1, \ldots, n$, the domain generalization hierarchy of DT is $\mathsf{DGH}_{DT} = \mathsf{DGH}_{D_1} \times \ldots \times \mathsf{DGH}_{D_n}$, where the Cartesian product is ordered by imposing coordinate-wise order. Since each DGH_{D_i} is totally ordered, DGH_{DT} defines a lattice with DT as its minimal element and the tuple composed of the top of each $\mathsf{DGH}_{D_i}, i = 1, \ldots, n$ as its maximal element. Each path from DT to the unique maximal element of DGH_{DT} defines a possible alternative path, called *generalization strategy*, that can be followed when generalizing a quasi-identifier $QI = \{A_1, \ldots, A_n\}$ of attributes on domains $D_1, \ldots, D_n$. For instance, consider domains $\mathtt{R}_0$ (race) and $\mathtt{Z}_0$ (ZIP code) whose generalization hierarchies are illustrated in Fig. 3 (a) and (c). Figure 4 illustrates the domain generalization hierarchy of the domain tuple $\langle \mathtt{R}_0, \mathtt{Z}_0 \rangle$ together with the corresponding domain and value generalization strategies. There are three different generalization strategies, corresponding to the three paths from the bottom to the top element of lattice $\mathsf{DGH}_{\langle \mathtt{R}_0, \mathtt{Z}_0 \rangle}$. Intuitively, each node of the domain generalization hierarchy corresponds to a generalized table where the attributes in the quasi-identifier have been generalized according the

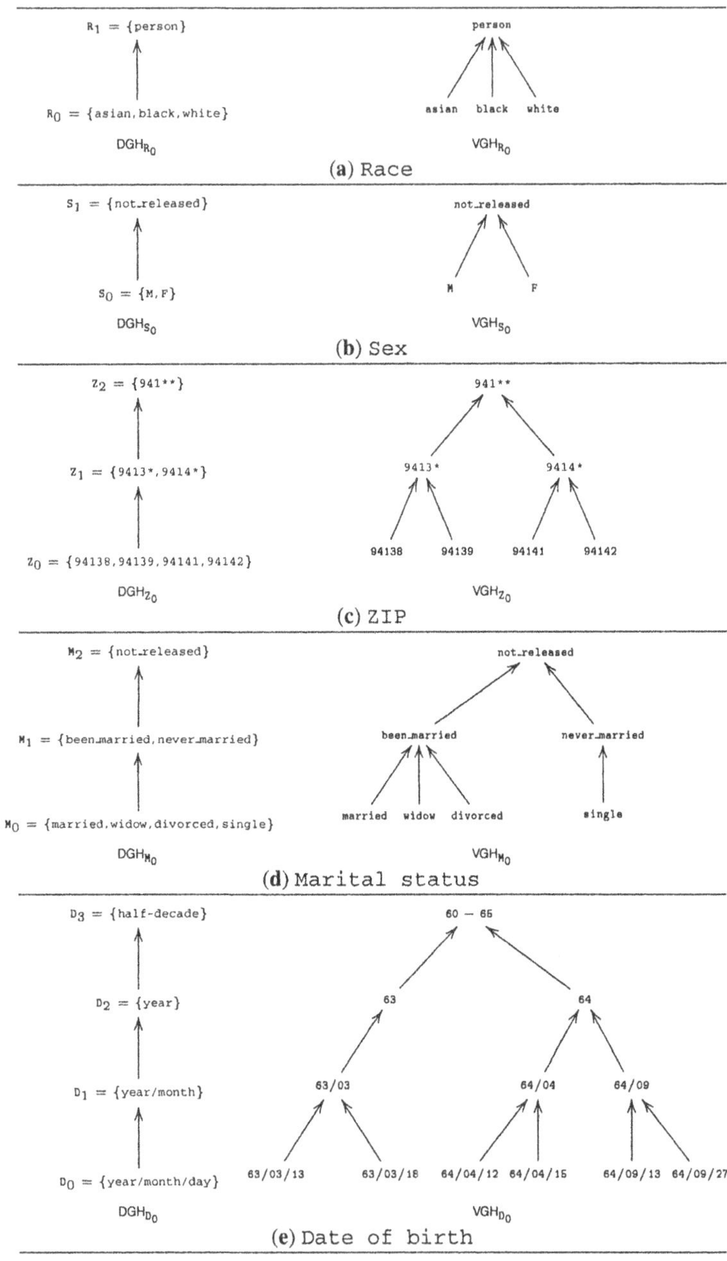

Fig. 3. Examples of generalization hierarchies

corresponding domain tuple. Figure 5 illustrates all the possible generalized tables corresponding to the different nodes of the domain generalization hierarchy in Fig. 4.

Another method adopted in [26] to be applied in conjunction with generalization to obtain k-anonymity is *tuple suppression*. The intuition behind the introduction of suppression is that this additional method can reduce the amount of generalization necessary to satisfy the k-anonymity constraint. Suppression is therefore used to "moderate" the generalization process when a limited number of outliers (i.e., tuples with less than k occurrences) would force a great amount of generalization. For instance, consider the generalized tables in Fig. 5. The tuples in *italic* are those that would need to be suppressed in each generalized table to satisfy 2-anonymity without further generalization.

2.2 k-Minimal Generalization (with Suppression)

The application of generalization and suppression to a private table PT produces more general (less precise) and less complete (if some tuples are suppressed) tables that provide better protection of the respondents' identities. Generalized tables are then defined as follows.

Definition 3 (Generalized table - with suppression). *Let T_i and T_j be two tables defined on the same set of attributes. Table T_j is said to be a* generalization (with tuple suppression) *of table T_i, denoted $T_i \preceq T_j$, if:*

1. $|T_j| \leq |T_i|$;
2. *the domain $dom(A, T_j)$ of each attribute A in T_j is equal to, or a generalization of, the domain $dom(A, T_i)$ of attribute A in T_i;*
3. *it is possible to define an injective function associating each tuple t_j in T_j with a tuple t_i in T_i, such that the value of each attribute in t_j is equal to, or a generalization of, the value of the corresponding attribute in t_i.*

Given a private table PT, many tables obtained generalizing attributes and suppressing tuples in PT satisfy k-anonymity, but some of them are either too general or are obtained suppressing too much tuples. The goal is therefore to compute a table maintaining as much information as possible, under the k-anonymity constraint; in other words minimality of the solution should be guaranteed. The definition of *k-minimal generalization with suppression* is based on the concept of *distance vector*.

Definition 4 (Distance vector). *Let $T_i(A_1, \ldots, A_n)$ and $T_j(A_1, \ldots, A_n)$ be two tables such that $T_i \preceq T_j$. The distance vector of T_j from T_i is the vector $DV_{i,j} = [d_1, \ldots, d_n]$, where each d_z, $z = 1, \ldots, n$, is the length of the* unique *path between $dom(A_z, T_i)$ and $dom(A_z, T_j)$ in the domain generalization hierarchy* DGH_{D_z}.

It is possible to define a partial order relation between distance vectors, that is, $DV = [d_1, \ldots, d_n] \leq DV' = [d'_1, \ldots, d'_n]$ iff $d_i \leq d'_i$, $i = 1 \ldots n$. On the basis of the distance vector order relation, it is possible to build a *hierarchy of distance*

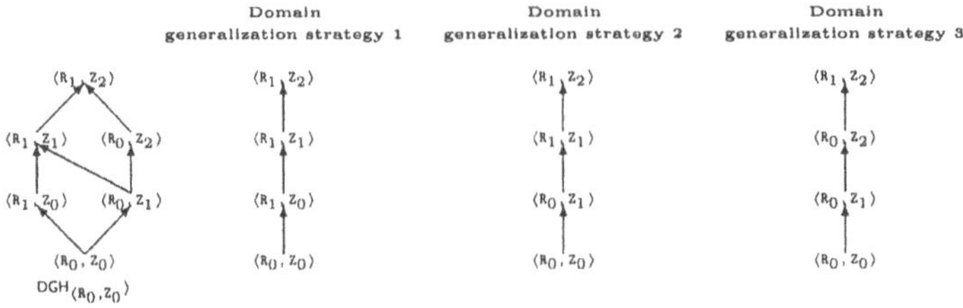

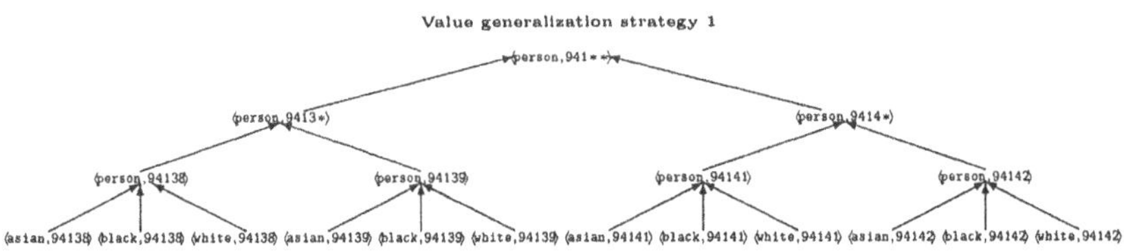

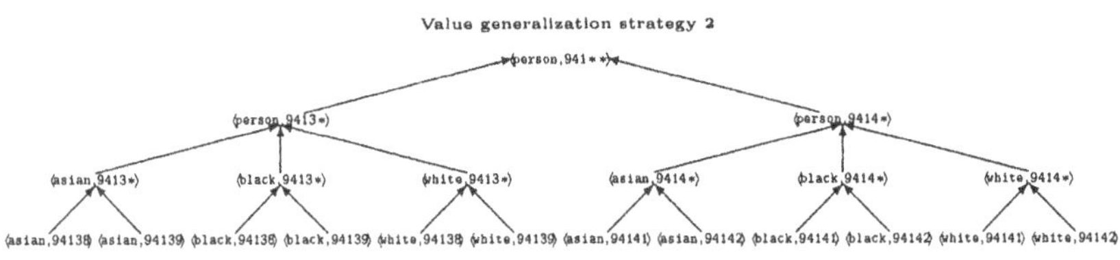

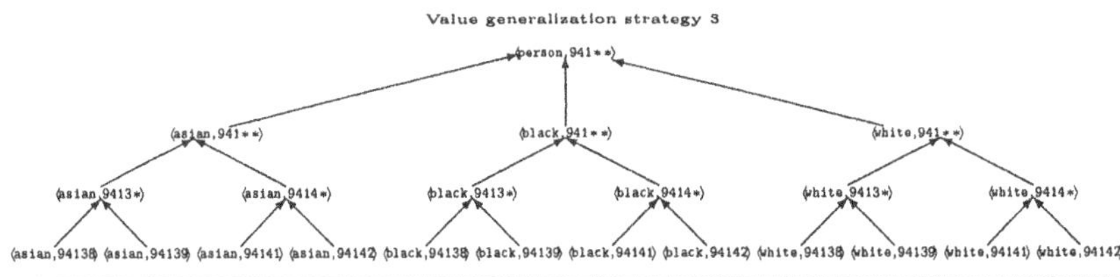

Fig. 4. Hierarchy $\mathsf{DGH}_{\langle R_0, Z_0\rangle}$ and corresponding Domain and Value Generalization Strategies

vectors, which can be graphically represented as a lattice. Figure 6 illustrates the domain generalization hierarchy $\mathsf{DGH}_{\langle R_0, Z_0\rangle}$ together with the corresponding hierarchy of distance vectors.

Note that like for generalization, it is possible to adopt different suppression solutions for guaranteeing k-anonymity without removing more tuples than necessary (i.e., ensuring minimality of the suppression), at a given level of generalization. The joint use of generalization and suppression helps in maintaining as much information as possible in the process of k-anonymization. The question is whether it is better to generalize, loosing data precision, or to suppress, loosing completeness. Samarati in [26] assumes that the data holder establishes a threshold, denoted MaxSup,

Race:R_0	**ZIP:Z_0**
asian	*94142*
asian	*94141*
asian	94139
asian	94139
asian	94139
black	*94138*
black	*94139*
white	*94139*
white	*94141*

(a)

Race:R_1	**ZIP:Z_0**
person	*94142*
person	94141
person	94139
person	94139
person	94139
person	*94138*
person	94139
person	94139
person	94141

(b)

Race:R_0	**ZIP:Z_1**
asian	9414*
asian	9414*
asian	9413*
asian	9413*
asian	9413*
black	9413*
black	9413*
white	*9413**
white	*9414**

(c)

Race:R_1	**ZIP:Z_1**
person	9414*
person	9414*
person	9413*
person	9413*
person	9413*
person	9413*
person	9413*
person	9413*
person	9414*

(d)

Race:R_0	**ZIP:Z_2**
asian	941**
asian	941**
asian	941**
asian	941**
asian	941**
black	941**
black	941**
white	941**
white	941**

(e)

Race:R_1	**ZIP:Z_2**
person	941**
person	941**
person	941**
person	941**
person	941**
person	941**
person	941**
person	941**
person	941**

(f)

Fig. 5. An example of a private table PT (**a**) and its generalizations

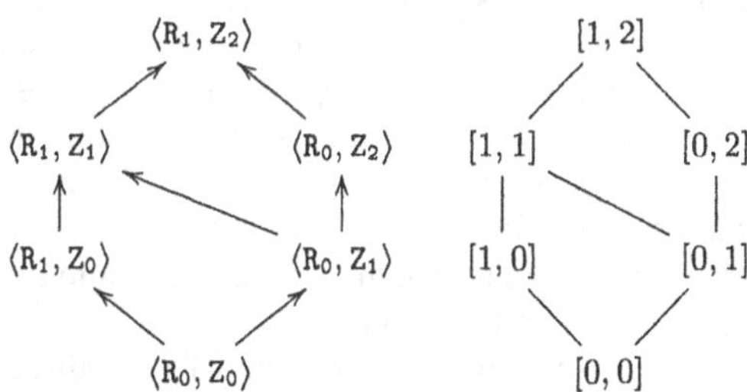

Fig. 6. Hierarchy $\mathsf{DGH}_{\langle R_0, Z_0\rangle}$ and corresponding hierarchy of distance vectors

specifying the maximum number of tuples that can be suppressed. The concept of *k-minimal generalization with suppression* is then formally defined as follows.

Definition 5 (k-minimal generalization - with suppression). *Let T_i and T_j be two tables such that $T_i \preceq T_j$, and let* MaxSup *be the specified threshold of acceptable suppression. T_j is said to be a k-*minimal *generalization of table T_i iff:*

Race:R_0	**ZIP**:Z_0
asian	94142
asian	94141
asian	94139
asian	94139
asian	94139
black	94138
black	94139
white	94139
white	94141

PT

Race:R_1	**ZIP**:Z_0
person	94141
person	94139
person	94139
person	94139
person	94139
person	94139
person	94141

$\mathsf{GT}_{[1,0]}$

Race:R_0	**ZIP**:Z_1
asian	9414*
asian	9414*
asian	9413*
asian	9413*
asian	9413*
black	9413*
black	9413*

$\mathsf{GT}_{[0,1]}$

Fig. 7. A private table PT and its 2-minimal generalizations, assuming MaxSup=2

1. *T_j satisfies k-anonymity enforcing minimal required suppression, that is, T_j satisfies k-anonymity and* $\forall T_z : T_i \preceq T_z, DV_{i,z} = DV_{i,j}, T_z$ *satisfies k-anonymity* $\Rightarrow |T_j| \geq |T_z|$
2. $|T_i| - |T_j| \leq$ MaxSup
3. $\forall T_z : T_i \preceq T_z$ *and* T_z *satisfies conditions 1 and 2* $\Rightarrow \neg(DV_{i,z} < DV_{i,j})$.

Intuitively, this definition states that a generalization T_j is k-minimal iff it satisfies k-anonymity, it does not enforce more suppression than it is allowed ($|T_i| - |T_j| \leq$ MaxSup), and there does not exist another generalization satisfying these conditions with a distance vector smaller than that of T_j.

Consider the private table in Fig. 1 and suppose that MaxSup $= 2$, $QI = \{$`Race`, `Sex`$\}$, and $k = 2$. There are two k-minimal generalizations with suppression for it, namely $\mathsf{GT}_{[0,1]}$ and $\mathsf{GT}_{[1,0]}$ (see Fig. 7). These two tables are obtained from the tables in Figs. 5(b)-(c) by removing the outlier tuples, which are those written in italic. Note that $\mathsf{GT}_{[1,1]}$, $\mathsf{GT}_{[0,2]}$, and $\mathsf{GT}_{[1,2]}$ (corresponding to tables in Figs. 5(d)-(e)-(f), respectively) are not k-minimal, since they do not satisfy condition 3 in Definition 5. $\mathsf{GT}_{[0,0]}$ (corresponding to the table in Fig. 5(a)), which contains the original values with the italic tuples removed is not a k-minimal generalization with suppression as it does not satisfy condition 2 in Definition 5.

A private table may have more than one minimal generalization satisfying a k-anonymity constraint for a suppression threshold (e.g., in the previous example there are two minimal generalizations, $\mathsf{GT}_{[1,0]}$ and $\mathsf{GT}_{[0,1]}$). This is completely legitimate, since the definition of "minimal" only captures the concept that the least amount of generalization and suppression necessary to achieve k-anonymity is enforced. Different *preference criteria* can be applied in choosing a preferred minimal generalization, among which [26]:

- *minimum absolute distance* prefers the generalization(s) with the smallest absolute distance, that is, with the smallest total number of generalization steps (regardless of the hierarchies on which they have been taken);

- *minimum relative distance* prefers the generalization(s) with the smallest relative distance, that is, that minimizes the total number of relative steps (a step is made relative by dividing it over the height of the domain hierarchy to which it refers);
- *maximum distribution* prefers the generalization(s) with the greatest number of distinct tuples;
- *minimum suppression* prefers the generalization(s) that suppresses less tuples, that is, the one with the greatest cardinality.

3 Classification of k-Anonymity Techniques

The original k-anonymity proposal just illustrated [26] considers the application of generalization at the attribute (column) level and suppression at the tuple (row) level. However, both generalization and suppression can also be applied, and have been investigated, at a finer granularity level. Before proceeding illustrating the different approaches to provide k-anonymity, we discuss the different ways in which generalization and suppression can be applied, and introduce the different models for k-anonymity.

	Suppression			
Generalization	*Tuple*	*Attribute*	*Cell*	*None*
Attribute	**AG_TS**	**AG_AS** ≡ AG_	**AG_CS**	**AG_** ≡ AG_AS
Cell	**CG_TS** not applicable	**CG_AS** not applicable	**CG_CS** ≡ CG_	**CG_** ≡ CG_CS
None	**_TS**	**_AS**	**_CS**	**_** not interesting

Fig. 8. Classification of k-anonymity techniques

Generalization can be applied at the level of:

- *Attribute (AG)*: generalization is performed at the level of column; a generalization step generalizes all the values in the column.
- *Cell (CG)*: generalization is performed on single cells; as a result a generalized table may contain, for a specific column, values at different generalization levels. For instance, in the `Date of birth` column some cells can report the specific day (no generalization), others the month (one step of generalization), others the year (two steps of generalization), and so on. Generalizing at the cell level has the advantage of allowing the release of more specific values (as generalization can be confined to specific cells rather than hitting whole columns). However, besides a higher complexity of the problem, a possible drawback in the application of generalization at the cell level is the complication arising from the management of values at different generalization levels within the same column.

Suppression can be applied at the level of:

- *Tuple (TS)*: suppression is performed at the level of row; a suppression operation removes a whole tuple.
- *Attribute (AS)*: suppression is performed at the level of column, a suppression operation obscures all the values of a column.
- *Cell (CS)*: suppression is performed at the level of single cells; as a result a k-anonymized table may wipe out only certain cells of a given tuple/attribute.

The possible combinations of the different choices for generalization and suppression (including also the choice of not applying one of the two techniques) result in different models for k-anonymity, which can represent a taxonomy for classifying the different k-anonymity proposals. Different models bear different complexity and define in different ways the concept of minimality of the solutions.

A first attempt to introduce a taxonomy for classifying k-anonymity approaches has been described in [20], where the authors distinguish between the application of suppression and generalization at the cell or attribute level. Our taxonomy refines and completes this classification. Below we discuss the different models resulting from our classification, characterize them, and classify existing approaches accordingly. We refer to each model with a pair (separated by _), where the first element describes the level of generalization (AG, CG, or none) and the second element describes the level of suppression(TS, AS, CS, or none). Table in Fig. 8 summarizes these models.

AG_TS Generalization is applied at the level of attribute (column) and suppression at the level of tuple (row). This is the assumption considered in the original model [26], as well as in most of the subsequent approaches providing efficient algorithms for solving the k-anonymity problem [5, 18, 20, 29, 33], since it enjoys a tradeoff between the computational complexity and the quality of the anonymized table.

AG_AS Both generalization and suppression are applied at the level of column. No specific approach has investigated this model. It must also be noted that if attribute generalization is applied, attribute suppression is not needed; since suppressing an attribute (i.e., not releasing any of its values) to reach k-anonymity can equivalently be modeled via a generalization of all the attribute values to the maximal element in the value hierarchy. This model is then equivalent to model **AG_** (attribute generalization, no suppression). Note that this observation holds assuming that attribute suppression removes only the values and not the column itself (this assumption seems reasonable since removal of the column is not needed for k-anonymity).

AG_CS Generalization is applied at the level of column, while suppression at the level of cell. It allows to reduce the effect of suppression, at the price however of a higher complexity of the problem. No specific investigation of this model has been performed with reference to k-anonymity. We note, however, that this approach has been investigated in earlier work by the μ-argus [11, 16, 17] and Datafly [28] software, which applied the same principles behind k-anonymity, but without guarantees on the minimality of the solutions (which is instead a basic principle behind k-anonymity).

AG_ Generalization is applied at the level of column, suppression is not considered. As noted above, it is equivalent to model **AG_AS**. Note also that both, **AG_AS** and **AG_**, are subsumed by model **AG_TS**, which reduces to them in the case where the suppression threshold MaxSup is set to zero.

CG_CS Both generalization and suppression are applied at the cell level. Then, for a given attribute we can have values at different levels of generalization. By observations similar to those illustrated for **AG_AS**, this model is equivalent to **CG_** (cell generalization, no suppression). Indeed, suppression of a cell can be equivalently modeled as the generalization of the cell at the maximal element of the value hierarchy.

CG_ Generalization is applied at the level of cell, suppression is not considered [3]. As just noted, it is equivalent to **CG_CS**.

_TS Suppression is applied at the tuple level, generalization is not allowed. No approach has investigated this model, which however can be modeled as a reduction of **AG_TS** to the case where all the generalization hierarchies have height zero (i.e., no hierarchy is defined). It is interesting to note that in this case the computational complexity of the problem of finding a k-anonymous table becomes polynomial (as solving it requires simply to delete from the original table all the outliers), and the minimal solution is unique. The application of tuple suppression alone has however limited applicability.

AS Suppression is applied at the attribute level, generalization is not allowed. No explicit approach has investigated this model. We note, however, that it can be modeled as a reduction of **AG** where all the generalization hierarchies have height of 1.

CS Suppression is applied at the cell level, generalization is not allowed [2, 24]. Again, it can be modeled as a reduction of **AG** where all the generalization hierarchies have height of 1.

In addition to these models, we have the obvious uninteresting combination _ (no generalization, no suppression) and two models, which are not applicable, namely: **CG_TS** (cell generalization, tuple suppression) and **CG_AS** (cell generalization, attribute suppression). The reason for their non applicability is that since generalizing a value at the maximum element in the value hierarchy is equivalent to suppressing it, supporting generalization at the fine grain of cell clearly implies the ability of enforcing suppression at that level too.

Note that, because of the equivalence relationships pointed out in the discussion above, there are essentially seven possible models. For equivalent models, in the following we use **AG_** to indistinguishably refer to **AG_** and **AG_AS**, and **CG_** to indistinguishably refer to **CG_** and **CG_CS**. Fig. 9 illustrates an example of a private table (Fig. 9(a)) and a possible 2-anonymized version of it according to these different models.

Among these seven models: **_TS** is, as noted, straightforward and not that interesting; **AG_CS** has not been formally investigated; while for **_AS** only the complexity has been studied but no solution has been proposed. By contrast, **AG_TS**, **AG_**,

Race	DOB	Sex	ZIP
asian	64/04/12	F	94142
asian	64/09/13	F	94141
asian	64/04/15	F	94139
asian	63/03/13	M	94139
asian	63/03/18	M	94139
black	64/09/27	F	94138
black	64/09/27	F	94139
white	64/09/27	F	94139
white	64/09/27	F	94141

(a) PT

Race	DOB	Sex	ZIP
asian	64/04	F	941**
asian	64/04	F	941**
asian	63/03	M	941**
asian	63/03	M	941**
black	64/09	F	941**
black	64/09	F	941**
white	64/09	F	941**
white	64/09	F	941**

(b) AG_TS

Race	DOB	Sex	ZIP
asian	*	F	*
asian	*	F	*
asian	*	F	*
asian	63/03	M	9413*
asian	63/03	M	9413*
black	64/09	F	9413*
black	64/09	F	9413*
white	64/09	F	*
white	64/09	F	*

(c) AG_CS

Race	DOB	Sex	ZIP
asian	64	F	941**
asian	64	F	941**
asian	64	F	941**
asian	63	M	941**
asian	63	M	941**
black	64	F	941**
black	64	F	941**
white	64	F	941**
white	64	F	941**

(d) AG_≡AG_AS

Race	DOB	Sex	ZIP
asian	64	F	941**
asian	64	F	941**
asian	64	F	941**
asian	63/03	M	94139
asian	63/03	M	94139
black	64/09/27	F	9413*
black	64/09/27	F	9413*
white	64/09/27	F	941**
white	64/09/27	F	941**

(e) CG_≡CG_CS

Race	DOB	Sex	ZIP

(f) _TS

Race	DOB	Sex	ZIP
asian	*	F	*
asian	*	F	*
asian	*	F	*
asian	*	M	*
asian	*	M	*
black	*	F	*
black	*	F	*
white	*	F	*
white	*	F	*

(g) _AS

Race	DOB	Sex	ZIP
asian	*	F	*
asian	*	F	*
asian	*	F	*
asian	*	M	94139
asian	*	M	94139
*	64/09/27	F	*
*	64/09/27	F	94139
*	64/09/27	F	94139
*	64/09/27	F	*

(h) _CS

Fig. 9. A private table (**a**) and some 2-anonymized version of according to different models

CG_, and **_CS** have been extensively studied and algorithms for their enforcement have been proposed; we will then illustrate them in the remainder of the chapter.

Before illustrating the different proposals, it is interesting to note the complexity of the problem. All the models investigated in the literature (**AG_TS**, **AG_**, **CG_**, and **_CS**), as well as **_AS**, are NP-hard. NP-hardness has been proved for **_CS** and **_AS** [2, 3, 24]. Suppose that the private table consists of n m-dimensional vectors (i.e., tuples) $x_1, \ldots, x_n \in \Sigma^m$, where Σ is an alphabet. The NP-hardness of **_AS** has been proved in [24] for $|\Sigma| \geq 2$, by a reduction from the "k-dimensional Perfect Matching" problem. Furthermore, the NP-hardness of the **_CS** problem for $|\Sigma| \geq 3$ has been proved in [3] with a reduction from the NP-hard problem of "Edge Partition into Triangles". The last result is an improvement upon the NP-hardness prove in [24] for the **_CS** problem, which requires an alphabet of size n.

NP-hardness of **_CS** and **_AS** clearly implies NP-hardness of **CG_** and **AG_**, respectively. This implication holds since suppression can be considered as a special case of generalization where all hierarchies have height of 1. Note also that NP-hardness of **AG_** implies NP-hardness of **AG_TS**, where, as in the existing proposals, tuple suppression is regulated with the specification of a maximum number of tuples (MaxSup) that can be suppressed.

It is interesting to note that, instead the decisional versions of **AS_**, **CS_**, **AG_**, **AG_TS**, and **CG_** are in NP [3].

4 Algorithms for AG_TS and AG_

The problem of finding minimal k-anonymous tables, with attribute generalization and tuple suppression, is computationally hard. Consistently with this, the majority of the exact algorithms proposed in literature have computational time exponential in the number of the attributes composing the quasi-identifier. However, when the number $|QI|$ of attributes in the quasi-identifier is small compared with the number n of tuples in the private table PT, these exact algorithms with attribute generalization and tuple suppression are practical. In particular, when $|QI| \in O(\log n)$, these exact algorithms have computational time polynomial in the number of tuples of PT, provided that the threshold on the number of suppressed tuples (MaxSup) is constant in value.

Recently many exact algorithms for producing k-anonymous tables through attribute generalization and tuple suppression have been proposed [5,20,26,29]. Samarati [26] presented an algorithm that exploits a binary search on the domain generalization hierarchy to avoid an exhaustive visit of the whole generalization space. Bayardo and Agrawal [5] presented an optimal algorithm that starts from a fully generalized table (with all tuples equal) and specializes the dataset in a minimal k-anonymous table, exploiting ad-hoc pruning techniques. Finally, LeFevre, DeWitt, and Ramakrishnan [20] described an algorithm that uses a bottom-up technique and a priori computation. Sweeney [29] proposed an algorithm that exhaustively examines all potential generalizations for identifying a minimal one satisfying the k-anonymity

Algorithm	Model	Algorithm's type	Time complexity
Samarati [26]	AG_TS	Exact	exponential in $\|QI\|$
Sweeney [29]	AG_TS	Exact	exponential in $\|QI\|$
Bayardo-Agrawal [5]	AG_TS	Exact	exponential in $\|QI\|$
LeFevre-et-al. [20]	AG_TS	Exact	exponential in $\|QI\|$
Aggarwal-et-al. [2]	_CS	$O(k)$-Approximation	$O(kn^2)$
Meyerson-Williams [24][2]	_CS	$O(k \log k)$-Approximation	$O(n^{2k})$
Aggarwal-et-al. [3]	CG_	$O(k)$-Approximation	$O(kn^2)$
Iyengar [18]	AG_TS	Heuristic	limited number of iterations
Winkler [33]	AG_TS	Heuristic	limited number of iterations
Fung-Wang-Yu [12]	AG_	Heuristic	limited number of iterations

Fig. 10. Some approaches to k-anonymity (n is the number of tuples in PT)

requirement. This latter approach is clearly impractical for large datasets, and we will therefore not discuss it further. We will now describe these approaches in more details.

4.1 Samarati's Algorithm

The first algorithm for guaranteeing k-anonymity was proposed in conjunction with the definition of k-anonymity in [26]. The algorithm exploits both generalization and tuple suppression over quasi-identifier attributes and computes a k-minimal solution according to the minimum absolute distance preference criteria (see Sect. 2). Since the k-anonymity definition is based on a quasi-identifier, the algorithm works only on this set of attributes and on tables with more than k tuples (this last constraint being clearly a necessary condition for a table to satisfy k-anonymity).

As described in Sect. 2, given a domain generalization hierarchy, there are different paths from the bottom element of the hierarchy and the hierarchy's root. Each path corresponds to a different strategy according to which the original private table PT can be generalized (see, for instance, Fig. 4). Along each path there is exactly one *locally minimal* generalization, that is, a table satisfying k-anonymity and maintaining as much information as possible. The locally minimal generalization is the lowest node in the path satisfying k-anonymity. Each k-minimal generalization is locally minimal with respect to a path; the converse is not true, that is, a locally minimal generalization with respect to a given path might not be a k-minimal generalization. A naive approach to compute a k-minimal generalization would then consist in following each generalization strategy (path) in the domain generalization hierarchy stopping the process at the first generalization that satisfies k-anonymity, within the MaxSup constraint. Once all paths have been evaluated, at least one of the locally minimal generalizations is also a k-minimal generalization with suppression and can be chosen according to the preference criteria mentioned in Sect. 2. Given the high number of paths that should be followed, this naive approach is not practically applicable.

2 Meyerson and Williams have also described in [24] a $O(k \log |QI|)$-approximation algorithm with polynomial time complexity ($O(|QI|n^3)$) for the **_CS** model.

The key idea exploited in [26] to cut down the computation is the observation that going up in the hierarchy the number of tuples that must be removed to guarantee k-anonymity decreases. Each node in the domain generalization hierarchy is associated with a number, called *height*, which is equal to the sum of the elements in the corresponding distance vector. The height of a distance vector *DV* in a distance vector lattice VL is denoted by *height*(DV, VL). The observation above ensures that if there is no solution that guarantees k-anonymity suppressing less than MaxSup tuples at height h, there cannot exist a solution, with height lower than h that guarantees it. This property is exploited by using a binary search approach on the lattice of distance vectors corresponding to the domain generalization hierarchy of the domains of the quasi-identifier. Consider lattice VL of height h = *height*(T, VL), where T is the top element of the lattice. First, the vectors at height $\lfloor \frac{h}{2} \rfloor$ are evaluated. If there is a vector that satisfies k-anonymity within the suppression threshold established at height $\lfloor \frac{h}{2} \rfloor$, then the vectors at height $\lfloor \frac{h}{4} \rfloor$ are evaluated, otherwise those at height $\lfloor \frac{3h}{4} \rfloor$, and so on, until the algorithm reaches the lowest height for which there is a distance vector that satisfies k-anonymity by suppressing no more tuples than MaxSup. As an example, consider the microdata table in Fig. 1, and assume $QI = \{$`Race`,`ZIP`$\}$, where the domain generalization hierarchy, of height 3, is as illustrated in Fig. 6. Suppose also that $k = 2$ and MaxSup = 2. The algorithm starts by evaluating the generalizations at height $\lfloor 3/2 \rfloor = 1$, since there is a solution at level 1 (actually both $\mathsf{GT}_{[1,0]}$ and $\mathsf{GT}_{[0,1]}$ are solutions), the algorithm proceeds by evaluating generalizations at level $\lfloor 3/4 \rfloor = 0$. Table $\mathsf{GT}_{[0,0]}$ suppresses more than 2 tuples for 2-anonymity, so it is not a solution. The (local) minimal solutions are then $\mathsf{GT}_{[1,0]}$ and $\mathsf{GT}_{[0,1]}$.

Although this approach is simple, it requires the computation of all the generalized tables. To avoid such a computation, the concept of distance vector between tuples is introduced and exploited. Let T be a table and $x, y \in T$ be two tuples such that $x = \langle v'_1, \ldots, v'_n \rangle$ and $y = \langle v''_1, \ldots, v''_n \rangle$ where v'_i and v''_i are values in domain D_i, for $i = 1 \ldots, n$. The *distance vector* between x and y is the vector $V_{x,y} = [d_1, \ldots, d_n]$ where d_i is the (equal) length of the two paths from v'_i and v''_i to their closest common ancestor in the value generalization hierarchy VGH_{D_i} (or, in other words, the distance from the domain of v'_i and v''_i to the domain at which they generalize to the same value v_i). For instance, with reference to the PT illustrated in Fig. 1 and the hierarchies in Fig. 3, the distance vector between ⟨`asian`, `94139`⟩ and ⟨`black`, `94139`⟩ is [1,0], at which they both generalize to ⟨`person`, `94139`⟩.

Intuitively, the distance vector $V_{x,y}$ between two tuples x and y in table T_i is the distance vector $DV_{i,j}$ between T_i and the table T_j, with $T_i \preceq T_j$ where the domains of the attributes in T_j are the most specific domains for which x and y generalize to the same tuple t. By looking at the distance vectors between the tuples in a table we can determine whether a generalization at a given vector satisfies k-anonymity by suppressing less than MaxSup tuples without computing the generalization. More precisely, we can determine, for each distance vector *DV*, the minimum required suppression for the k-anonymity constraint to be satisfied by the generalization corresponding to *DV*. The approach works as follows. Let T_i = PT[QI] be the table to be considered. For each distinct tuple $x \in T_i$ determine *count*(x, T_i) as the number

	t_1	t_2	$t_3/t_4/t_5$	t_6	t_7	t_8	t_9
t_1	[0, 0]	[0, 1]	[0, 2]	[1, 2]	[1, 2]	[1, 2]	[1, 1]
t_2	[0, 1]	[0, 0]	[0, 2]	[1, 2]	[1, 2]	[1, 2]	[1, 0]
t_6	[1, 2]	[1, 2]	[1, 1]	[0, 0]	[0, 1]	[1, 1]	[1, 2]
t_7	[1, 2]	[1, 2]	[1, 0]	[0, 1]	[0, 0]	[1, 0]	[1, 2]
t_8	[1, 2]	[1, 2]	[1, 0]	[1, 1]	[1, 0]	[0, 0]	[0, 2]
t_9	[1, 1]	[1, 0]	[1, 2]	[1, 2]	[1, 2]	[0, 2]	[0, 0]

Fig. 11. Distance vectors between tuples of table PT in Fig. 7

of occurrences of x in T_i. Build a matrix VT with a row for each of the different outliers (i.e., tuples with less than k occurrences) and a column for each different tuple in the table. Entry VT$[x, y]$ contains the distance vector between tuples x and y, that is, VT$[x, y] = V_{x,y}$. (Note that the table is symmetric so only half on it actually needs to be computed.) Now, let *vec* be the distance vector of a generalization to consider as a potential solution. For each row x, compute C_x as the sum of the occurrences $count(y, T_i)$ of tuples y (column of the matrix) such that VT$[x, y] \leq$ *vec*. These are tuples that at generalization *vec* would generalize to the same tuple as x, and the sum of their occurrences is the size of the resulting cluster. Determine then *req_sup* as the sum of the occurrences of all the outlier tuples x (row of the matrix) such that C_x so computed is smaller than k, that is, *req_sup*= $\sum_{x|C_x<k} count(x, T_i)$. Intuitively, *req_sup* is the number of tuples that would still be outliers in the generalization corresponding to distance vector *vec*, and which would therefore need to be removed for the k-anonymity requirement to be satisfied. Hence, if *req_sup* $\leq$ MaxSup the generalization with distance vector *vec* satisfies k-anonymity by suppressing less tuples than the threshold allowed. Otherwise it does not. Figure 11 illustrates a vector matrix VT for the table of Fig. 7. As an example, consider the generalized table $\mathsf{GT}_{[1,0]}$ and suppose that MaxSup $= 2$ and $k = 2$. It is easy to see that $\mathsf{GT}_{[1,0]}$ satisfies 2-anonymity and that the outlier tuples are t_1 and t_6.

4.2 Bayardo-Agrawal's Algorithm

Bayardo and Agrawal [5] propose an interesting algorithm for **AG_TS**, called *k-Optimize*, which often obtains good solutions with a reduced computational time. According to this approach, an attribute generalization for an attribute A with an ordered domain D consists in a partitioning of the attribute domain into intervals such that each possible value in the domain appears in some interval and each value in a given interval I precedes any value in the intervals following I. As an example, consider attribute `Race` on domain D_1 = {asian, black, white} where the values in D_1 are ordered according to a lexicographic order, and attribute `ZIP` on domain D_2 = {94138, 94139, 94141, 94142} where the values follow a numeric order. For instance, domain D_1 can be partitioned into three intervals, namely [asian], [black], and [white], and domain D_2 can be partitioned into four intervals, namely [94138], [94139], [94141], and [94142]. The approach then assumes an order among quasi-identifier attributes and associates an integer, called *index*, with each each interval in

Race			ZIP			
⟨[asian]	[black]	[white]⟩	⟨[94138]	[94139]	[94141]	[94142]⟩
1	2	3	4	5	6	7

Fig. 12. Index assignment to attributes `Race` and `ZIP`

any domain of the quasi-identifier attributes. The index assignment reflects the total order relationship over intervals in the domains and among quasi-identifier attributes. For instance, consider the quasi-identifier attributes `Race` and `Zip` and suppose that `Race` precedes `ZIP`. Figure 12 illustrates the value ordering and the corresponding index values. As it is visible from this fig., the index values associated with the intervals of domain D_1 of attribute `Race` are lower than the index values associated with the intervals of domain D_2 of attribute `ZIP` since we assume that `Race` precedes `ZIP`. Moreover, within each domain the index assignment reflects the total order among intervals. More formally, the indexes associated with the intervals of domain D_i of attribute A_i are lower than the indexes associated with intervals of domain D_j of attribute A_j, if attribute A_i precedes A_j in the order relationship. Moreover, indexes associated with each interval I of domain D_i follow the same order as intervals in D_i.

A generalization is then represented through the union of the individual index values for each attribute. The least value in an attribute domain can be omitted since it will certainly appear in the generalizations for that domain. For instance, with respect to the total order of the value domains in Fig. 12, notation $\{6\}$ identifies a generalization, where the generalizations are $\{1\}$ for attribute `Race` and $\{4, 6\}$ for attribute `ZIP`. These, in turn, represent the following value intervals: `Race`: ⟨[asian or black or white]⟩; `ZIP`: ⟨[94138 or 94139], [94141 or 94142]⟩. Note that the empty set $\{\ \}$ represents the most general anonymization. For instance, with respect to our example, $\{\ \}$ corresponds to the generalizations $\{1\}$ for attribute `Race` and $\{4\}$ for attribute `ZIP`, which in turn correspond to the generalized values `Race`: ⟨[asian or black or white]⟩; `ZIP`: ⟨[94138 or 94139 or 94141 or 94142]⟩.

k-Optimize builds a *set enumeration tree* over the set I of index values. The root node of the tree is the empty set. The children of a node n will enumerate those sets that can be formed by appending a single element of I to n, with the restriction that this single element must follow every element already in n according to the total order previously defined. Figure 13 illustrates an example of set enumeration tree over $I = \{1, 2, 3\}$. The consideration of a tree guarantees the existence of a unique path between the root and each node. The visit of the set enumeration tree using a standard traversal strategy is equivalent to the evaluation of each possible solution to the k-anonymity problem. At each node n in the tree the cost of the generalization strategy represented by n is computed and compared against the best cost found until that point; if lower it becomes the new best cost. This approach however is not practical because the number of nodes in the tree is $2^{|I|}$; therefore [5] proposes heuristics and pruning strategies. In particular, k-Optimize prunes a node n when it can determine that none of its descendants could be optimal. According to a given cost function, k-Optimize computes a lower bound on the cost that can be obtained by any node in the sub-tree rooted at n. The subtree can be pruned if the computed lower bound is higher than the best cost found by the algorithm until that point. Note that when a subtree is pruned also additional nodes can be removed from the tree. For instance, consider the set enumeration tree in Fig. 13 and suppose that node $\{1, 3\}$ can be pruned. This means that a solution that contains index values 1 and 3 is not optimal and therefore also node $\{1, 2, 3\}$ can be pruned.

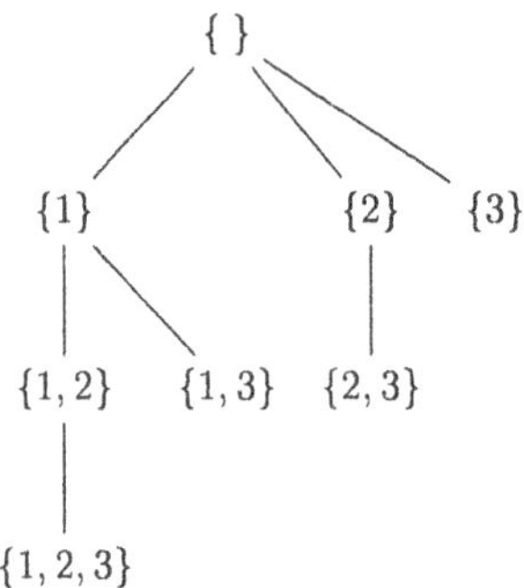

Fig. 13. An example of set enumeration tree over set $I = \{1, 2, 3\}$ of indexes

k-Optimize can always compute the best solution in the space of the generalization strategies. Since the algorithm tries to improve the solution at each visited node evaluating the corresponding generalization strategy, it is possible to fix a maximum computational time, and obtain a good, but not optimal, solution.

4.3 Incognito

LeFevre, DeWitt and Ramakrishnan [20] propose an efficient algorithm for computing k-minimal generalization, called *Incognito*, which takes advantage of a bottom-up aggregation along dimensional hierarchies and a priori aggregate computation.

The key idea of Incognito is that if a table T with quasi-identifier QI of m attributes is k-anonymous, T is k-anonymous with respect to any quasi-identifiers QI', where $QI' \subset QI$. In other words, the k-anonymity with respect to a proper subset of QI is a necessary (not sufficient) condition for the k-anonymity with respect to QI. Exploiting this observation, Incognito excludes in advance some generalizations from the hierarchy in a priori computation.

The strategy followed by Incognito is a bottom-up breadth-first search on the domain generalization hierarchy. The algorithm generates all the possible minimal k-anonymous tables for a given private table PT. First (iteration 1), it checks k-anonymity for each single attribute in QI, discarding those generalizations that do not satisfy k-anonymity for the single attribute. Then, it combines the remaining generalizations in pairs performing the same control on pairs of attributes (iteration

2); then in triples (iteration 3), and so on, until the whole set of attributes in QI is considered (iteration $|QI|$). More precisely, for each combination, Incognito checks the satisfaction of the k-anonymity constraint with a bottom-up approach; when a generalization satisfies k-anonymity, all its direct generalizations also certainly satisfy k-anonymity and therefore they are no more considered. It is important to note that at iteration i, Incognito considers all the combinations of i attributes together, by considering only the generalizations that satisfied the k-anonymity constraint at iteration $i - 1$.

As an example, consider table PT in Fig. 1 and suppose that the quasi-identifier is QI={Race, Sex, Marital status}, and assume $k = 2$. At iteration 1, Incognito checks 2-anonymity on each single attribute, and finds that M_0 does not satisfy 2-anonymity. At iteration 2, Incognito checks 2-anonymity on all the possible pairs of attributes, that is, ⟨Race, Sex⟩, ⟨Race, Marital status⟩, and ⟨Sex, Marital status⟩. In particular, Incognito has to first check the 2-anonymity with respect to the lowest tuples that can be formed with the single attributes generated at iteration 1 (i.e., $\langle R_0, S_0\rangle$, $\langle R_0, M_1\rangle$, and $\langle S_0, M_1\rangle$). It is easy to see that the microdata table in Fig. 1 is 2-anonymous with respect to $\langle R_0, S_0\rangle$ and $\langle S_0, M_1\rangle$ but is not 2-anonymous with respect to $\langle R_0, M_1\rangle$ because, for example, there is only one occurrence of ⟨white, been_married⟩. Incognito therefore proceeds by checking generalizations $\langle R_0, M_2\rangle$ and $\langle R_1, M_1\rangle$. These generalizations satisfy 2-anonymity and then Incognito can start iteration 3. Due to the previous iterations, Incognito has to first check generalizations $\langle R_0, S_0, M_2\rangle$, and $\langle R_1, S_0, M_1\rangle$. Since these two generalizations satisfy the 2-anonymity property, the algorithm terminates. Figure 14 illustrates on the left-hand side the complete domain generalization hierarchies and on the right-hand side the sub-hierarchies computed by Incognito at each iteration (i.e., from which the generalizations, which are a priori known not to satisfy k-anonymity, have been discarded).

4.4 Heuristic Algorithms

The algorithms presented so far find exact solutions for the k-anonymity problem. Since k-anonymity is a NP-hard problem, all these algorithms have complexity exponential in the size of the quasi-identifier. Alternative approaches have proposed the application of heuristic algorithms. The algorithm proposed by Iyengar [18] is based on genetic algorithms and solves the k-anonymity problem using an incomplete stochastic search method. The method does not assure the quality of the solution proposed, but experimental results show the validity of the approach. Winkler [34] proposes a method based on simulated annealing for finding locally minimal solutions, which requires high computational time and does not assure the quality of the solution.

Fung, Wang and Yu [12] present a top-down heuristic to make a table to be released k-anomymous. The approach applies to both continuous and categorical attributes. The top-down algorithm starts from the most general solution, and iteratively specializes some values of the current solution until the k-anonymity requirement is violated. Each step of specialization increases the information and decreases

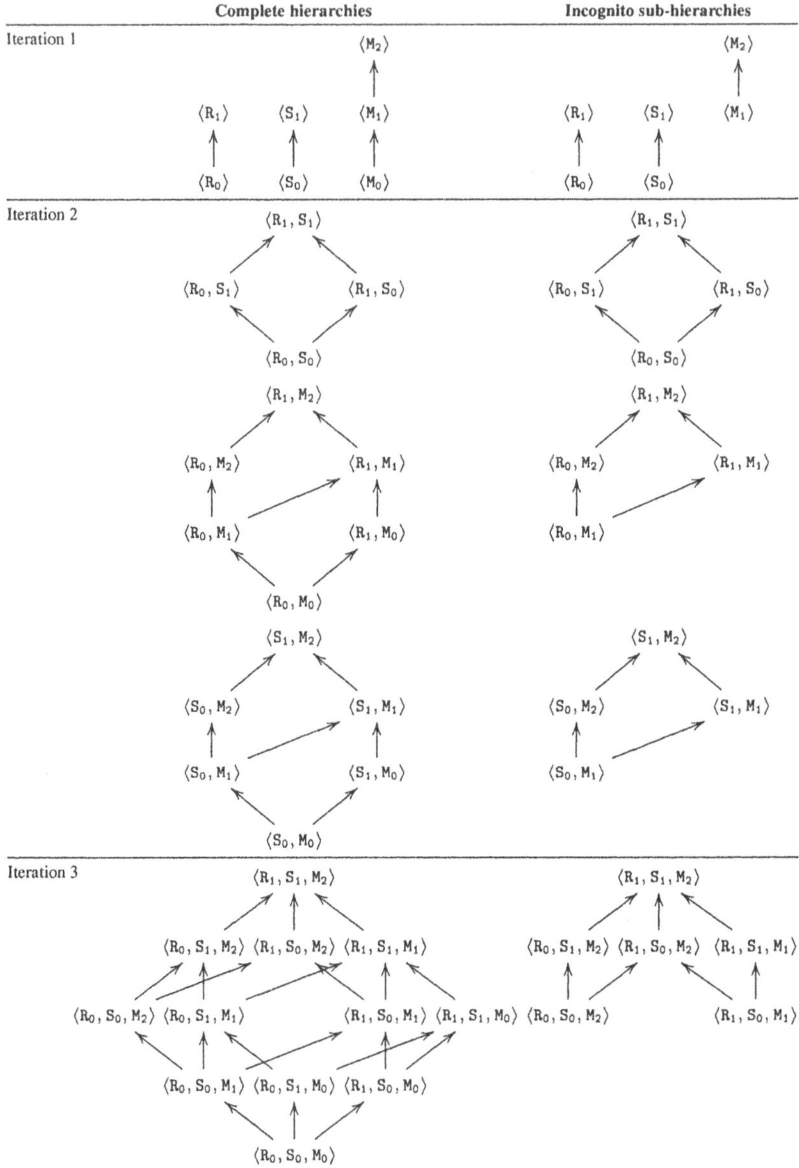

Fig. 14. Sub-hierarchies computed by Incognito for the table in Fig. 1

the anonymity. Therefore, at each iteration, the heuristic selects a "good" specialization guided by a goodness metric. The metric takes into account both the "information gain" and the "anonymity loss".

Due to heuristic nature of these approaches, no bounds on efficiency and goodness of the solutions can be given; however experimental results can be used to assess the quality of the solution retrieved.

5 Algorithms for _CS and CG_ Models

The exact algorithms just illustrated for solving the k-anonymity problem for **AG_TS** and **AG_** are, due to the complexity of the problem, exponential in the size of the quasi-identifier. The exact algorithms for models **_CS** and **CG_** can be much more expensive, since the computational time could be exponential in the number of tuples in the table.

Approximation algorithms for **_CS** and **CG_** have been proposed, both for general and specific values of k (e.g., 1.5-approximation for 2-anonymity, and 2-approximation for 3-anonymity in [3]). In a minimization framework, a p-approximation algorithm guarantees that the cost C of its solution is such that $C/C^* \leq p$, where C^* is the cost of an optimal solution [13]. Both heuristics and approximation algorithms do not guarantee the minimality of their solution, but while we cannot perform any evaluation on the result of a heuristic, an approximation algorithm guarantees near-optimum solutions.

The first approximation algorithm for **_CS** was proposed by Meyerson and Williams [24]. They presented an algorithm for k-anonymity, which guarantees a $O(k\log(k))$-approximation. Two approximation algorithms for **_CS** and **CG_**, with unbounded value of k, are described in [2, 3] and guarantee a $O(k)$-approximation solution.

The best-known approximation algorithm for **_CS** is described in [2] and guarantees a $O(k)$-approximation solution. The algorithm constructs a complete weighted graph from the original private table PT. Each node in the graph corresponds to a tuple in PT, and the arcs are weighted with the number of different attribute values between the two tuples represented by extreme nodes. The algorithm then constructs, starting from the graph, a forest composed of trees containing at least k nodes, which represents the clustering for k-anonymization. All the tuples in the same tree have the same quasi-identifier value. The cost of a vertex is evaluated as the number of cells suppressed, the cost of a tree instead is the sum of the weights of its arcs. The cost of the final solution is equal to the sum of the costs of its trees. On the contrary, the cost of a k-anonymity solution is the cost of the biggest partition in the final forest, since the presence of big clusters implies the unification of many respondents into a single one, which causes information loss. In constructing the forest, the algorithm attempts to limit the maximum number of nodes in a tree to be $3k - 3$. Partitions with more than $3k - 3$ elements are decomposed, without increasing the total solution cost.

An approximation algorithm for **CG_** is described in [3] as a direct generalization of the approximation algorithm for **_CS** presented in [2]. The main difference is that, in this version, the weights of edges depend on the lowest level of generalization, for each attribute, that makes the tuples in the extreme nodes equal.

To find out better results for Boolean attributes, in case $k = 2$ and $k = 3$, a different approach has been provided in [3]. Since **_CS** and **CG_** are equivalent when we use Boolean attributes, we consider here only k-anonymity with **_CS**. The algorithm for $k = 2$ exploits the minimum-weight $[1,2]$-factor built on the graph constructed for the 2-anonymity instance. The $[1,2]$-factor for graph G is the spanning subgraph of G, built using only vertexes of degree 1 or 2 (i.e., with no more than 2 outgoing edges). Such a subgraph is a vertex-disjoint collection of edges and pairs of adjacent nodes and can be computed in polynomial time. Each component in the subgraph is treated as a cluster, and we can obtain a 2-anonymized table by suppressing each cell, for which the vectors in the cluster differ in value. This procedure is a 1.5-approximation algorithm.

The approximation algorithm for $k = 3$ is similar and guarantees a 2-approximation solution.

6 Further Studies on k-Anonymity

We now briefly survey some interesting studies based on the concept of k-anonymity.

Multidimensional k-Anonymity

The generalization procedures in the original k-anonymity proposal [26] assume a value generalization hierarchy, where each value has only a single generalization. For instance, with respect to the hierarchy in Fig. 3, a single step of generalization for ZIP code 94142 produces the unique value 9414∗. However, a generalization step could produce different generalized values. For instance, some possible generalized values corresponding to value 94142 are 9414∗ and 941∗2. If we assume that the generalization hierarchy is a graph instead of a tree, the generalization problem can even be harder. For solving this problem, LeFevre, DeWitt and Ramakrishnan propose a multidimensional model for k-anonymity [21, 22]. The authors show that the problem is still NP-hard and propose a greedy approximation algorithm for both numerical and categorical datasets. The time complexity of the algorithm proposed is $O(n \log n)$, where n is the number of tuples in the original table. The resulting k-anonymous table has a higher quality than the anonymized tables produced by other single-dimensional algorithms.

ℓ-Diversity

Although k-anonymity is a technique adopted to protect microdata respondents' privacy, it is vulnerable to some attacks that may lead to privacy breach. Machanavajjhala, Gehrke, and Kifer describe two possible attacks, namely *homegeneity attack* (already noted in [26]) and *background knowledge attack* [23]. Consider a k-anonymized table, where there is a sensitive attribute and suppose that all tuples with a specific value for the quasi-identifier have the same sensitive attribute value.

Race	DOB	Sex	ZIP	Disease
asian	64	F	941**	hypertension
asian	64	F	941**	obesity
asian	64	F	941**	chest pain
asian	63	M	941**	obesity
asian	63	M	941**	obesity
black	64	F	941**	short breath
black	64	F	941**	short breath
white	64	F	941**	chest pain
white	64	F	941**	short breath

Fig. 15. A 2-anonymous table according to the **AG**$_-$ model

Under these assumptions (homogeneity attack), if an attacker knows both the quasi-identifier value of an entity and knows that this entity is represented in the table, the attacker can infer the sensitive value associated with certainty. For instance, with respect to the 2-anonymous table in Fig. 15, if `Alice` knows that `Carol` is a `black female` and that her data are in the microdata table, she can infer that `Carol` suffers of `short breath`, as both the tuples having these values for the `Race` and `Sex` attributes are associated with the `short breath` value for the `Disease` attribute. The 2-anonymous table is therefore exposed to attribute linkage.

The background knowledge attack is instead based on a prior knowledge of the attacker of some additional external information. For instance, suppose that `Alice` knows that `Hellen` is a `white female`. `Alice` can then infer that `Hellen` suffers of `chest pain` or `short breath`. Suppose now that `Alice` knows that `Hellen` runs for two hours every day. Since a person that suffers of `short breath` cannot run for a long period, `Alice` can infer with probability equal to 1 that `Hellen` suffers of `chest pain`.

To avoid such attacks, Machanavajjhala, Gehrke, and Kifer introduce the notion of *ℓ-diversity* [23]. Given a private table PT and a generalization GT of PT, let q-block be a set of tuples in GT with the same quasi-identifier value. A q-block is said to be *ℓ-diverse* if it contains at least ℓ different values for the sensitive attribute. It is easy to see that with this additional constraint, the homogeneity attack is no more applicable because each q-block set has at least ℓ (≥ 2) distinct sensitive attribute values. Analogously, the background knowledge attack becomes more complicate as ℓ increases because the attacker needs more knowledge to individuate a unique value associable to a predefined entity. The algorithm proposed in [23] therefore generates k-anonymous tables with the ℓ-diversity property. The algorithm checks the ℓ-diversity property, which is a monotonic property with respect to the generalization hierarchies considered for k-anonymity purposes.

It is important to note that the proposed algorithm considers only one sensitive attribute at time. The consequence is that even if each sensitive attribute in GT satifies the ℓ-diversity property, the whole table GT may not respect the ℓ-diversity property because the combination of the background knowledge on two or more sensitive attributes may lead to privacy breaches.

Evaluation of k-Anonymity

Some recent papers evaluate the results of k-anonymization using data mining techniques [1, 12, 32]. In particular, Aggarwal [1] shows that, when the number of attributes in the quasi-identifier increases, the information loss of the resulting k-anonymized table may become very high. The intuition behind this result is that the probability that k tuples in the private table are "similar" (i.e., they correspond to the same tuple in the anonymized table with a reduced loss of information) is very low. The ability to identify minimal quasi-identifiers is therefore important.

Distributed Algorithms

Besides anonymizing data locally maintained by a data holder, it is also important to anonymize data distributed through different interconnected parties. To this purpose, recently some algorithms for distributed k-anonymity have been proposed [19, 31, 38].

Jiang and Clifton [19] suppose a microdata table to be vertically partitioned and stored at two different sites. The whole data can be reconstructed through a join on a common key. The authors propose a communication protocol allowing the two data holders to put together their data, obtaining a k-anonymized table. Basically, the two data holders agree on the tuples that should be generalized to the same quasi-identifier value before release. Once the two data holders agree on the strategy to adopt, they generalize their values following this common strategy. Wang, Fung and Dong [31] propose another approach for vertically partitioned tables, where the parties interact to individuate the best generalization strategy to adopt for k-anonymization.

Zhong, Yang and Wright [38] propose instead a distributed k-anonymity method for a horizontally partitioned table. The table has $m+n$ attributes, where m attributes form a quasi-identifier for the table and the remaining n attributes are the sensitive attributes. Also, there are N customers that own a single tuple in the table. To build a k-anonymous table, the authors propose two different solutions. In the first one, each customer encrypts her sensitive attributes using an encryption key. The decryption of these sensitive attributes can be done only if there are at least k tuples with equal value for the corresponding quasi-identifier. This technique corresponds to the application of tuple suppression because if there are less than k tuples with the same quasi-identifier value, their sensitive attributes cannot be decrypted.

The second solution adopts cell suppression on the original microdata table by applying Meyerson and William's algorithm [24] to the distributed scenario.

k-Anonymity with Multiple Views

The individuals' privacy can be violated by inferring information through multiple views on a private table. This problem is known as *data association*. Data association

Name	Sex	Disease
Sue	F	hypertension
Claire	F	obesity
Ann	F	chest pain
John	M	obesity
David	M	obesity
Mary	F	short breath
Alice	F	short breath
Carol	F	chest pain
Kate	F	short breath

PT

Name	Sex
Sue	F
Claire	F
Ann	F
John	M
David	M
Mary	F
Alice	F
Carol	F
Kate	F

view v_1

Sex	Disease
F	hypertension
F	obesity
F	chest pain
F	short breath
M	obesity

view v_2

Fig. 16. A private table PT and two possible views on PT

refers to the possibility that two or more attributes are considered more sensitive when their values are associated than when either appears separately. For instance, consider the private table PT in Fig. 16, where `Name` is an identifier and `Disease` is a sensitive attribute whose association with `Name` must be protected. Attributes `Name` and `Disease` should therefore be released through different views. Fig. 16 illustrates two possible views, namely v_1 and v_2, of the original private table. By combining the information contained in these two views, it is however possible to reconstruct the associations between `Name` and `Disease` (e.g., `John` and `David` with `obesity`).

Yao, Wang and Jajodia [7] investigate this issue and use k-anonymity as a measure on information disclosure by a set of views with respect to a given data association that has to be protected. The authors first introduce the notion of *association cover* with respect to a set of views as follows. Suppose that the association between attributes `ID` and `P` must be protected, where `ID` is an identifier and `P` is a sensitive attribute. An association cover with respect to a set of views v is a set of pairs $\{\langle \mathtt{id}, \mathtt{p}_1\rangle, \ldots, \langle \mathtt{id}, \mathtt{p}_n\rangle\}$, where `id` is a fixed value of attribute `ID` and $\mathtt{p}_i, i = 1, \ldots, n$, is a value that can be associated with `id` in the set of views v. For instance, $\{\langle$`Sue, hypertension`$\rangle, \langle$`Sue, obesity`$\rangle, \langle$`Sue, chest pain`$\rangle, \langle$`Sue, short breath`$\rangle\}$ is an association cover with respect to views v_1 and v_2 in Fig. 16. Given a set of views v and an integer k, v is said to violate k-anonymity if there exists an association cover w.r.t. v of size less than k. In our example, the association cover $\{\langle$`John, obesity`$\rangle\}$ and the association cover $\{\langle$`David, obesity`$\rangle\}$ violate k-anonymity for any $k > 1$. Intuitively, this means that if a set of views v does not violate k-anonymity for a specific user-defined k value, we can state that the association between attributes `ID` and `P` is protected.

Yao, Wang and Jajodia show that the problem of stating whether a set of views violates k-anonymity is in general computationally hard (NP^{NP}-hard). In the case where no functional dependencies exist among the views, the problem becomes simpler, and a polynomial checking algorithm for its solution is described [7].

k-Anonymity with Micro-Aggregation

Domingo-Ferrer and Mateo-Sanz [9] propose the use of micro-aggregation (instead of generalization and suppression) to achieve k-anonymity.

Micro-aggregation requires to divide a microdata set in a number of clusters of at least k tuples each. For each attribute, the average value over each cluster is computed and used to replace each of the original averaged values. The optimal k-partition solution is a partition that maximizes the homogenity within each cluster; the higher the homogeneity within each cluster, the lower the information loss since the micro-aggregation replaces values in a cluster by the cluster *centroid*. The sum of squares is the traditional criterion to measure homogeneity in clustering. The problem of optimal micro-aggregation is related to the classical minimum sum-of-squares clustering that is a NP-hard problem [25]. Domingo-Ferrer and Mateo-Sanz therefore propose to determine an optimal solution by reducing the solution space. To this purpose, their approach consider only solutions with clusters of size between k and $2k$. The minimum size is fixed to k to achieve k-anonymity, while the maximum is set to $2k$ to minimize information loss.

k-Anonymity for Protecting Location Privacy

The k-anonymity property has been studied also for protecting location privacy [6, 14]. In the context of location-based services, Bettini, Wang and Jajodia [6] present a framework for evaluating the privacy of a user identity when location information is released. In this case, k-anonymity is guaranteed, not among a set of tuples of a database, but in a set of individuals that can send a message in the same spatio-temporal context.

k-Anonymity for Communication Protocols

k-anonymity has also been investigated to preserve privacy in communication protocols [15, 30, 36, 37], with the notion of *sender* (*receiver*, resp.) k-anonymity. A communication protocol is *sender k-anonymous* (*receiver k-anonymous*, resp.) if it guarantees that an attacker, who is trying to discover the sender (receiver, resp.) of a message, can just detect a set of k possible senders (receivers, resp.).

7 Conclusions

k-anonymity has recently been investigated as an interesting approach to protect microdata undergoing public or semi-public release from linking attacks. In this chap., we illustrated the original k-anonymity proposal and its enforcement via generalization and suppression as means to protect respondents' identities while releasing truthful information. We then discussed different ways in which generalization and suppression can be applied, thus defining a possible taxonomy for k-anonymity and discussed the main proposals existing in the literature for solving the k-anonymity problems in the different models. We have also illustrated further studies building on the k-anonymity concept to safeguard privacy.

8 Acknowledgments

This work was supported in part by the European Union within the PRIME Project in the FP6/IST Programme under contract IST-2002-507591 and by the Italian MIUR within the KIWI and MAPS projects.

References

1. Aggarwal C (2005). On k-anonymity and the curse of dimensionality. In Proc. of the 31st International Conference on Very Large Data Bases (VLDB'05), Trondheim, Norway.
2. Aggarwal G, Feder T, Kenthapadi K, Motwani R, Panigrahy R, Thomas D, Zhu A (2005). Anonymizing tables. In Proc. of the 10th International Conference on Database Theory (ICDT'05), pp. 246–258, Edinburgh, Scotland.
3. Aggarwal G, Feder T, Kenthapadi K, Motwani R, Panigrahy R, Thomas D, Zhu A (2005). Approximation algorithms for k-anonymity. Journal of Privacy Technology, paper number 20051120001.
4. Anderson R (1996). A security policy model for clinical information systems. In Proc. of the 1996 IEEE Symposium on Security and Privacy, pp. 30–43, Oakland, CA, USA.
5. Bayardo RJ, Agrawal R (2005). Data privacy through optimal k-anonymization. In Proc. of the 21st International Conference on Data Engineering (ICDE'05), pp. 217–228, Tokyo, Japan.
6. Bettini C, Wang XS, Jajodia S (2005). Protecting privacy against location-based personal identification. In Proc. of the Secure Data Management, Trondheim, Norway.
7. Jajodia S, Yao C, Wang XS (2005). Checking for k-anonymity violation by views. In Proc. of the 31st International Conference on Very Large Data Bases (VLDB'05), Trondheim, Norway.
8. Dobson J, Jajodia S, Olivier M, Samarati P, Thuraisingham B (1998). Privacy issues in www and data mining. In Proc. of the 12th IFIP WG11.3 Working Conference on Database Security, Chalkidiki, Greece. Panel notes.
9. Domingo-Ferrer J, Mateo-Sanz JM (2002). Practical data-oriented microaggregation for statistical disclosure control. IEEE Transactions on Knowledge and Data Engineering, 14(1):189–201.
10. Duncan GT, Jabine TB, de Wolf VA editors (1993). Private Lives and Public Policies. National Academy Press.
11. Franconi L, Polettini S (2004). Individual risk estimation in μ-ARGUS: a review. In Domingo-Ferrer J and Torra V, editors, Privacy in Statistical Databases, vol. 3050 of LNCS, pp. 262–372. Springer, Berlin Heidelberg.
12. Fung B, Wang K, Yu P (2005). Top-down specialization for information and privacy preservation. In Proc. of the 21st International Conference on Data Engineering (ICDE'05), Tokyo, Japan.
13. Garey M, Johnson D (1979). Computers and Intractability. Freeman and Company.
14. Gedik B, Liu L (2005). A customizable k-anonymity model for protecting location privacy. In Proc. of the 25th International Conference on Distributed Computing Systems (IEEE ICDCS), Columbus, Ohio, USA.
15. Hughes D, Shmatikov V (2004). Information hiding, anonymity and privacy: a modular approach. Journal of Computer Security, 12(1):3–36, 2004.

16. Hundepool A, Van deWetering A, Ramaswamy R, Franconi L, Capobianchi A, DeWolf PP, Domingo-Ferrer J, Torra V, Brand R, Giessing S (2003). μ-ARGUS version 3.2 software and user's manual. Statistics Netherlands. http://neon.vb.cbs.nl/casc.
17. Hundepool A, Willenborg L (1996). μ- and τ-ARGUS: software for statistical disclosure control. In Proc. of the 3rd International Seminar on Statistical Confidentiality, Bled.
18. Iyengar V (2002). Transforming data to satisfy privacy constraints. In Proc. of the 8th ACM SIGKDD International Conference on Knowledge Discovery and Data Mining, pp. 279–288, Edmonton, Alberta, Canada.
19. Jiang W, Clifton C (2005). Privacy-preserving distributed k-anonymity. In Proc. of the 19th Annual IFIP WG 11.3 Working Conference on Data and Applications Security, Storrs, CT, USA.
20. LeFevre K, DeWitt DJ, Ramakrishnan R (2005). Incognito: Efficient full-domain k-anonymity. In Proc. of the 24th ACM SIGMOD International Conference on Management of Data, pp. 49–60, Baltimore, Maryland, USA.
21. LeFevre K, DeWitt DJ, Ramakrishnan R (2005). Multidimensional k-anonymity. Technical Report 1521, Department of Computer Sciences, University of Wisconsin, Madison, USA.
22. LeFevre K, DeWitt DJ, Ramakrishnan R (2006). Mondrian multidimensional k-anonymity. In Proc. of the International Conference on Data Engineering (ICDE'06), Atlanta, GA, USA.
23. Machanavajjhala A, Gehrke J, Kifer D (2006). ℓ-diversity: Privacy beyond k-anonymity. In Proc. of the International Conference on Data Engineering (ICDE'06), Atlanta, GA, USA.
24. Meyerson A, Williams R (2004). On the complexity of optimal k-anonymity. In Proc. of the 23rd ACM-SIGMOD-SIGACT-SIGART Symposium on the Principles of Database Systems, pp. 223–228, Paris, France.
25. Oganian A, Domingo-Ferrer J (2001). On the complexity of optimal microaggregation for statistical disclosure control. Statistical Journal of the United Nations Economic Comission for Europe, 18(4):345–354.
26. Samarati P (2001). Protecting respondents' identities in microdata release. IEEE Transactions on Knowledge and Data Engineering, 13(6):1010–1027.
27. Samarati P, Sweeney L (1998). Generalizing data to provide anonymity when disclosing information (Abstract). In Proc. of the 17th ACM-SIGMOD-SIGACT-SIGART Symposium on the Principles of Database Systems, p. 188, Seattle, WA, USA.
28. Sweeney L (1997). Guaranteeing anonymity when sharing medical data, the Datafly system. In Journal of the American Medical Informatics Association, Washington, DC: Hanley & Belfus, Inc.
29. Sweeney L (2002). Achieving k-anonynity privacy protection using generalization and suppression. International Journal on Uncertainty, Fuzziness and Knowledge-based Systems, 10(5):571–588.
30. von Ahn L, Bortz A, Hopper NJ (2003). k-anonymous message transmission. In Proc. of the 10th ACM Conference on Computer and Communications Security, pp. 122–130, Washington, DC, USA.
31. Wang K, Fung B, Dong G (2005). Integrating private databases for data analysis. In Kantor P et al., editor, ISI 2005, vol. 3495 of LNCS, pp. 171–182. Springer-Verlag.
32. Wang K, Yu P, Chakraborty S (2004). Bottom-up generalization: a data mining solution to privacy protection. In Proc. of the 4th International Conference on Data Mining (ICDM'04), Brighton, UK.
33. Winkler WE (2002). Using simulated annealing for k-anonymity. Technical Report 7, U.S. Census Bureau.

34. Winkler WE (2004). Masking and re-identification methods for public-use microdata: Overview and research problems. In Domingo-Ferrer J, editor, Privacy in Statistical Databases 2004. Springer, New York.
35. Woodward B (1995). The computer-based patient record confidentiality. The New England Journal of Medicine, 333(21):1419–1422.
36. Xu S, Yung M (2004). k-anonymous secret handshakes with reusable credentials. In Proc. of the 11th ACM Conference on Computer and Communications Security, pp. 158–167, Washingtion, DC, USA.
37. Yao G, Feng D (2004). A new k-anonymous message transmission protocol. In Proc. of the 5th International Workshop on Information Security Applications,(WISA'04), pp. 388–399, Jeju Island, Korea.
38. Zhong S, Yang Z, and Wright R (2005). Privacy-enhancing k-anonymization of customer data. In Proc. of the 24th ACM SIGMOD-SIGACT-SIGART Symposium on Principles of Database Systems (PODS'05), pp. 139–147, Baltimore, Maryland, USA.

Preserving Privacy in On-line Analytical Processing Data Cubes*

Lingyu Wang, Sushil Jajodia, and Duminda Wijesekera

Center for Secure Information Systems
George Mason University
Fairfax, VA 22030-4444, USA
{lwang3,jajodia,dwijesekera}@gmu.edu

1 Introduction

Privacy in electronic society is drawing more and more attention nowadays. Privacy concerns cause consumers to routinely abandon their shopping carts when too much personal information is being demanded. The estimated loss of internet sales due to such privacy concerns is as much as $18 billion according to analysts [17]. Ongoing efforts such as the platform for privacy preferences (P3P) [9,43] help enterprises make promises about keeping private data secret, but they do not provide mechanisms for them to keep the promises [11]. Unfortunately, keeping one's promises is usually easier said then done. Privacy breaches may occur in various ways after personal data have been collected and stored in the enterprise's data warehouses.

The most challenging threat usually comes from insiders who have legitimate needs to access data. For example, a company may want to study the shopping preferences of each customer to facilitate upsales. The company invites a third party analyst for this purpose. Without sufficient protection of the data, the analyst may obtain and later misuse personal information about individual customers, leading to harmful privacy breaches. On the other hand, in order to extract useful knowledge from data, the analyst needs answers to analytical queries about the data. How to provably keep sensitive data secret while not adversely prohibiting queries is the main topic of this chapter.

OLAP (On-line Analytic Processing) is one of the most popular analysis tools that have been used in real-world applications. OLAP systems allow analysts to gain insights to data from different perspectives. Data are aggregated along dimension hierarchies. Aggregations at different levels are organized into a *data cube* [18]. Rolling up to coarser aggregations, an analyst can obtain global patterns and trends.

* This material is based upon work supported by the National Science Foundation under grants IIS-0242237 and IIS-0430402. Any opinions, findings, and conclusions or recommendations expressed in this material are those of the authors and do not necessarily reflect the views of the National Science Foundation.

Upon observing an exception to established patterns, the analyst may drill down to finer aggregations to catch the outliers. Such an interactive exploration can be repeated in different portions of the data until a satisfactory mental image of the data is constructed.

Like other technologies, OLAP is a double-edged sword. Without sufficient security countermeasures, it becomes a powerful tool in the hands of malicious users in stealing private data about individuals. Unfortunately, most of today's OLAP systems lack effective security countermeasures to protect the private data being analyzed. Traditional security mechanisms can alleviate the threat of privacy breaches but cannot eliminate it. For example, *sanitized data* (that is, data with explicit identifiers such as names deleted) are vulnerable to an attack that aims to re-identify individuals by combining seemingly non-identifying information (such as DOB and zip code) with publicly available data (such as a voter list) [16, 28, 29].

Access control mechanisms can prohibit an unauthorized user from directly accessing private data, but it is unaware of the malicious *inferences* of the data. As a simple example, Bob can infer the amount of Alice's commission from the amount of their total commission, given that Bob has the *external knowledge* of his own commission. Access control mechanisms cannot capture such an inference, because the total salary seems to be an innocent aggregation to access control. OLAP systems are especially vulnerable to such inferences, because they heavily rely on aggregations of data to accentuate global patterns and trends. Small vestiges of sensitive data remaining in aggregations [13] together with external knowledge obtained through outbound channels make inferences of the sensitive data fairly easy.

Although *Inference control* has been studied in statistical databases and census data from 1970's, the complexity results are usually negative in tone [7] for online systems. The detection of sophisticated inferences usually demands complicated computations over entire collection of data or the bookkeeping of every single answered query. Such requirements can rarely be met in real world applications. Even at such a high cost, the proposed method usually applies to only a special case with many unrealistic assumptions. For example, only one type of aggregations is allowed or only exact values can be regarded as sensitive. Those limitations partially explains the fact that most commercial products have no support of inference control at all.

In this chapter we introduce three methods that deal with inferences caused by data cube-style OLAP queries. The *cardinality-based inference control* and the *parity-based inference control* both aim to improve the efficiency of inference control in SUM-only data cubes. We show that by exploiting the special structures of a data cube, the complexity of inference control can be reduced. The *lattice-based inference control* aims to make inference control broadly applicable through supporting generic definition of inferences. The three methods can be implemented on the basis of a three-tier inference control model. This novel model makes inference control more efficient in the sense that most of the computation-intensive tasks can be fulfilled off-line before queries are received.

The rest of the chapter is organized as follows. Section 2 reviews related work. Section 3 introduces the basic model of data cubes and gives motivating examples of inferences. Section 4 introduces the cardinality-based inference control method.

Section 5 introduces the parity-based inference control method. Section 6 introduces the lattice-based inference control method. Finally, Section 7 concludes the chapter.

2 Related Work

The need for security and privacy in data warehouses and OLAP has long been identified [5,32,33]. However, today's commercial OLAP products usually provide only limited support of access control and practically no support of inference control [32].

On the other hand, relational databases have mature techniques for access control. In relational databases, accesses to sensitive data are regulated based on various models. The discretional access control (DAC) uses owner-specified grants and revokes to achieve an owner-centric control of objects [19]. The role-based access control (RBAC) simplifies access control tasks by introducing an intermediate tier of roles that aggregates and bridges users and permissions [30]. The flexible access control framework (FAF) provides a universal solution to handling conflicts in access control policies through authorization derivation and conflict resolution logic rules [22].

Inference control has been extensively studied in statistical databases and census data for more than thirty years, as surveyed in [1,13,40]. The proposed methods can roughly be classified into *restriction-based* techniques and *perturbation-based* techniques. Restriction-based inference control methods prevent malicious inferences by denying some unsafe queries. Those methods determine the safety of queries based on the minimal number of values aggregated by a query [13], the maximal number of common values aggregated by different queries [14], and the maximal rank of a matrix representing answered queries [8]. The perturbation-based techniques prevent inference by inserting random noises to sensitive data [34], to answers of queries [4], or to database structures [31].

Among the restriction-based inference control methods, *Cell suppression* and *partitioning* most closely relate to the methods we shall introduce. To protect census data released in statistical tables, cells that contains small COUNT values are suppressed, and possible inferences of the suppressed cells are then detected and removed using linear (or integer) programming-based techniques. The detection method is effective for two-dimensional cases but becomes intractable for three or more dimensional tables [10, 12]. *Partitioning* defines a partition on sensitive data and restricts queries to aggregate only complete blocks in the partition [7,42]. Similarly, *microaggregation* replaces clusters of sensitive values with their averages [26,40]. Partitioning and microaggregation methods usually assume a specific type of aggregations. Moreover, their partitions are not based on dimension hierarchies inherent to data and hence may contain many blocks that are meaningless to a user.

Perturbation-based methods have been proposed for preserving privacy in data mining [2]. Random noises are added to sensitive values to preserve privacy, while the statistical distribution is approximately reconstructed from the perturbed data to facilitate data mining tasks. Protecting sensitive data in OLAP is different from that in data mining. Unlike most data mining results, such as classifications and association rules, the results of OLAP usually cannot be obtained from distribution models alone. The methods proposed in [3] can approxmiately reconstruct COUNTs from perturbed data with statistically bound errors, so OLAP tasks like classification can be fufiled. However, potential errors in individual values may prevent an OLAP user from gaining trustful insights into small details of the data, such as outliers. The methods we shall introduce do not perturb data so any answer will always be precise and trustful. *Secure multi-party data mining* allows multiple distrusted parties to cooperatively compute aggregations over each other's data [15, 35]. Cryptographic protocols enable each party to obtain the final result with minimal disclosures of their own data. This problem is different from inference control, because the threat of inferences comes from what users know, not from the way they know it.

The *k-anonymity* model enables sensitive values to be released without threatening privacy [29, 41]. Each record is indistinguishable from at least $k-1$ others because they all have exactly the same identifying attribute values. An adversary can link an individual in the physical world to at least (the sensitive values of) k records, which is considered a tolerable privacy threat. Inference control and the k-anonymity model can be considered as dual approaches. Inference control typically hides sensitive values by aggregating them, whereas k-anonymity model makes sensitive values anonymous by generalizing the associated identifying values. The information theoretic approach in [27] formally characterizes insecure queries as those that bring a user with more confidence in guessing possible records [27]. However, such a *perfect-secrecy* metric will not tolerate any partial disclosure, such as those caused by aggregations.

3 Preliminaries

We first review the basic model for data cubes and explains its difference from the original model [18]. Instead of re-inventing terms, we illustrate the concepts through an example. We then give examples of inferences in data cubes to motivate further discussions.

3.1 The Data Cube Model

Roughly speaking, a *data cube* is the collection of all possible aggregations that can be formed with given dimension hierarchies. Figure 1 depicts a fictitious *data cube*. It has two *dimensions*: $time$ and $organization$. The $time$ dimension has three *attributes*: $quarter$, $year$, and all (all is a special attribute having one attribute value ALL that depends on all other values of the same attribute). The $organization$ dimension has four attributes: $employee$, $department$, $branch$, and all. The attributes of each dimension are partially ordered (totally ordered in this special case) by the *dependency relation* $\preceq$ into a *dependency lattice* [20]. That is, $quarter \preceq year \preceq all$ for the $time$ dimension and $employee \preceq department \preceq branch \preceq all$ for the

$organization$ dimension. The product of the two lattices gives the *dependency lattice* of the data cube. Each element of this lattice is a pair $\langle T, O\rangle$, where T is an attribute of the $time$ dimension and O is an attribute of the $organization$ dimension.

The above description is essentially the schema of a data cube, so next we consider populating the data cube with data. Attached to each pair $\langle T, O\rangle$ is an empty two-dimensional array, namely, a *cuboid* (only some of the cuboids are shown due to space limitations). Each *cell* of the cuboid $\langle T, O\rangle$ is also a pair $\langle t, o\rangle$, where t and o are some *attribute values* of the attribute T and O, respectively. The dependency relation between cuboids extend to their cells. For example, the cuboid $\langle year, employee\rangle$ depends on the cuboid $\langle quarter, employee\rangle$, and correspondingly a cell $\langle Y1, Bob\rangle$ in the former depends on the cells $\langle Q1, Bob\rangle$, $\langle Q2, Bob\rangle$, $\langle Q3, Bob\rangle$, and $\langle Q4, Bob\rangle$ in the latter. Similarly, the cell $\langle Q1, Book\rangle$ depends on the cells $\langle Q1, Bob\rangle$, $\langle Q1, Alice\rangle$, $\langle Q1, Jim\rangle$, and $\langle Q1, Mallory\rangle$ (we shall assume the book department only has those four employees). Hence, all the cells in a data cube also form a lattice. When a cell (or cuboid) depends on another, we shall call the former a *descendant* of the latter, and the latter a *ancestor* of the former.

The values in the core cuboid are given by a relational table with schema $(quarter, employee, commission)$, namely, the *fact table*. The attribute $commission$ is called a *measure* attribute. Each record in the fact table (q, e, m) populates a cell $\langle q, e\rangle$ of the *core cuboid* $\langle quarter, employee\rangle$, where q, e, and m are values of the attributes $quarter$, $employee$, and $commission$, respectively. Some cells remain empty (or having the $NULL$ value) if corresponding records are absent in the fact table. The cells in other cuboids are then populated by evaluating the *aggregation function* SUM on their ancestors in any populated cuboid. For example, a cell $\langle Y1, Bob\rangle$ in the cuboid $\langle year, employee\rangle$ has the summation of the values of its four ancestors in the core cuboid, that is $\langle Q1, Bob\rangle$, $\langle Q2, Bob\rangle$,$\langle Q3, Bob\rangle$, and $\langle Q4, Bob\rangle$. An empty cell is deemed as zero in the aggregation process. As another example, the cuboid $\langle all, employee\rangle$ can be computed from either its ancestors in the core cuboid $\langle quarter, employee\rangle$ or those in the cuboid $\langle year, employee\rangle$.

In the above example, a cell in the core cuboid is empty (or having the $NULL$ value), because the fact table does not provide a corresponding value. However, in the following discussion, empty cells will be used to model the values that are previously known by an adversary through outbound channels. Hence, a cell having the $NULL$ value will still be non-empty, if the adversary does not know the fact that the cell has the $NULL$ value. Conversely, any previously known cell is empty regardless of its value. Intuitively, the $NULL$ value is not different from any other values for security purposes; what matters is whether or not the adversary knows the value. We shall consider a sensitive attribute as a measure attribute (such as the commission in Figure 1). The original model in [18] allows any numerical attribute to be a measure attribute. Those differences between the two models reflect our focus on the security perspectives.

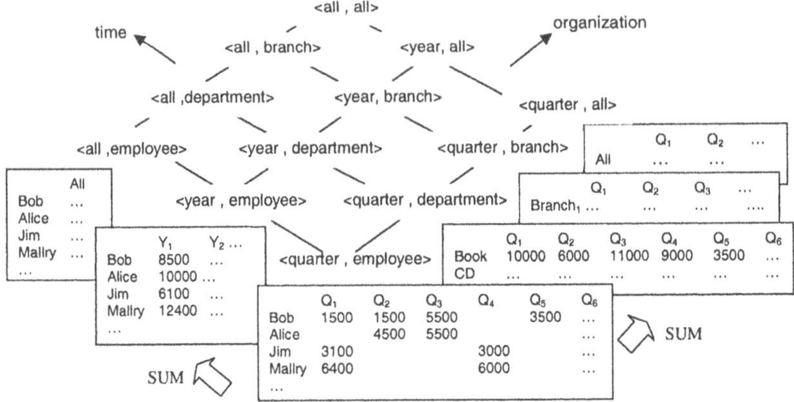

Fig. 1. An Example of Data Cubes

3.2 Motivating Examples of Inferences

When accesses to (the sensitive value in) a cell are prohibited, an adversary may still infer (the sensitive value in) the cell from its descendants to which he/she has accesses. Example 1 illustrates an *one dimensional* (or 1-d for short) inference where the sensitive cell is inferred using exactly one of its descendants (in statistical database, the 1-d inference is usually referred to as a *small query set attack* or a *single query attack* [12]).

Example 1 (1-d Inference). In Figure 1, assume an adversary is prohibited from accessing the cuboid $\langle quarter, employee\rangle$ but allowed to access its descendant $\langle quarter, department\rangle$. Further suppose the empty cells denote the values that the adversary already knows through outbound channels. The adversary can then infer $\langle Q5, Bob\rangle$ as exactly the same value in $\langle Q5, Book\rangle$ (that is, 3500), because Bob is the only person that draws a commission in $Q5$.

A *multi-dimensional* (or m-d) inference refers to the complementary case of 1-d inferences (in statistical databases, m-d inferences are referred to as *linear system attacks* or *multiple query attacks* [14]). That is, a cell is inferred using two or more of its descendants, and each of those descendants does not cause 1-d inference. Example 2 illustrates an m-d inference in a two-dimensional SUM-only data cube. Example 3 and 4 illustrate m-d inferences in MAX-only data cubes and those in a data cube with SUM, MAX, and MIN all allowed.

Example 2 (m-d Inferences with SUM). Suppose now an adversary is prohibited from accessing the core cuboid in Figure 1 but allowed to access its descendants $\langle quarter, department\rangle$ and $\langle year, employee\rangle$. The adversary cannot employ any 1-d inference, as in Example 1, to infer data in the first year because each cell in $\langle quarter, department\rangle$ and $\langle year, employee\rangle$ has at least two ancestors in the core cuboid. However, an m-d inference is possible as follows. the adversary first sums the two cells $\langle Y1, Bob\rangle$ and $\langle Y1, Alice\rangle$ in the cuboid $\langle year, employee\rangle$ and then subtracts from the result (that is, 18500) the two cells $\langle Q2, Book\rangle$ and $\langle Q3, Book\rangle$ (that is, 11000) in the cuboid $\langle quarter, department\rangle$. The final result yields a sensitive cell $\langle Q1, Bob\rangle$ as 1500.

Example 3 (m-d Inferences with MAX). Suppose now an adversary is prevented from knowing the values in the empty cells (that is, we replace each empty cell with a non-empty cell having the $NULL$ value). The core cuboid then seems to the adversary full of unknown values. As we shall show later in Section 4, such a data cube will be free of inferences if the aggregation function is SUM. However, the following m-d inference is possible with MAX as the aggregation function (the data cube would be different from the one in Figure 1). The MAX values in cells $\langle Y1, Mallory\rangle$ and $\langle Q4, Book\rangle$ are 6400 and 6000, respectively. From those two values the adversary can infer that one of the three cells $\langle Q1, Mallory\rangle$, $\langle Q2, Mallory\rangle$, and $\langle Q3, Mallory\rangle$ must be 6400, because $\langle Q4, Mallory\rangle$ must be no greater than 6000. Similarly, an adversary infers that neither $\langle Q2, Mallory\rangle$ and $\langle Q3, Mallory\rangle$ can be 6400. The sensitive cell $\langle Q1, Mallory\rangle$ is then successfully inferred as 6400.

Example 4 (Inferences with SUM, MAX and MIN). Now suppose an adversary can evaluate SUM, MAX, and MIN on the data cube. Following Example 3, $\langle Q1, Mallory\rangle$ is 6400. The MAX, MIN, and SUM values of the cell $\langle Y1, Mallory\rangle$ are 6400,6000, and 12400, respectively. From those three values the adversary can infer the following. That is, $\langle Q2, Mallory\rangle$,$\langle Q3, Mallory\rangle$, and $\langle Q4, Mallory\rangle$ must be 6000 and two zeroes, although he/she does not know exactly which is 6000 and which are zeroes. The MAX,MIN, and SUM values of $\langle Q2, Book\rangle$, $\langle Q3, Book\rangle$ and $\langle Q4, Book\rangle$ then tell the adversary the following facts. In $\langle quarter, employee\rangle$, two cells in $Q2$ are 1500 and 4500; those in $Q3$ are 5500 and 5500; those in $Q4$ are 3000 and 6000; and the rest are all zeroes. The adversary then concludes that $\langle Q4, Mallory\rangle$ must be 6000, because the values in $Q3$ and $Q2$ cannot be. Similarly, the adversary can infer $\langle Q4, Jim\rangle$ as 3000, and consequently infer all cells in the cuboid $\langle quarter, employee\rangle$. Hence, the whole data cube is successfully inferred even without any outbound knowledge.

4 Cardinality-based Inference Control in Sum-only Data Cubes

This section introduces a *cardinality-based* method that determines the existence of inferences based on the number of empty cells in the data cube. Example 1 shows a straightforward connection between 1-d inferences and the number of empty cells in a data cube. That is, an 1-d inference is present when an adversary can access any cell that has exactly one ancestor in the core cuboid. A similar but less straightforward connection also exists between m-d inferences and the number of empty cells, as we shall show in this section.

This section only considers inferences similar to those in Example 1 and Example 2. That is, we assume only SUM is used in aggregation; we assume accesses to the core cuboid are prohibited while accesses to other cuboids are allowed. Moreover, we shall only consider *one-level dimension hierarchy* where a dimension has only two attributes, that is the attribute in core cuboid and *all*. The rest of this section is organized as follows. We first formally model the inference problem in this special case in Section 4.1. Then we give the main results in Section 4.2. Finally in Section 4.3 we describe a three-tier inference control model which will underlie the implementation of all the three methods introduced in this chapter. Proofs of the theorems can be found in [39].

4.1 A Model of Inferences in Sum-only Data Cubes

We describe a model for inferences in sum-only data cubes, as illustrated in Example 1 and Example 2. The model is similar to that given by Chin et. al in statistical databases [8], but our queries are limited to data cube cells. For each attribute of the core cuboid, we assume an arbitrary but fixed order on its domain. Although an attribute may have infinitely many values, we shall only consider the values that appear in at least one non-empty cell in the given data cube instance. The number of such values is thus fixed. From the point of view of an adversary, the value in any non-empty cell is unknown, and hence the cell is denoted by an unknown variable. The central tabulation in Table 1 models part of the core cuboid in Figure 1 that corresponds to the data in the first year and in the Book department.

Table 1. Modeling Part of the Core Cuboid in Figure 1

	Q_1	Q_2	Q_3	Q_4	ALL
Bob	x_1	x_2	x_3		8500
$Alice$		x_4	x_5		10000
Jim	x_6			x_7	6100
$Mallory$	x_8			x_9	12400
ALL	10000	6000	11000	9000	36000

Table 1 also includes cells in descendants of the core cuboid, namely, the *aggregation cuboids*. In this case there are three aggregation cuboids $\langle all, employee\rangle$, $\langle quarter, all\rangle$, and $\langle all, all\rangle$, as we only consider one-level dimension hierarchy. For SUM-only data cubes, the dependency relation can be modeled as linear equations. At the left side of those equations are the unknown variables in the core cuboid, and at the left side the values in the aggregation cuboids. Table 2 shows a system of nine equations corresponding to the nine cells in the aggregation cuboids.

To solve the system of linear equations in Table 2, we obtain the reduced row echelon form (RREF) M_{rref} of the coefficients matrix through a sequence of elementary row operations [21], as shown in Table 3. From M_{rref} it can be observed that the system of linear equations in Table 2 has infinitely many solutions. This means that an adversary cannot infer the *entire* core cuboid from the given aggregation cuboids. However, the first row vector of M_{rref} being a unit vector (that is,

Table 2. Modeling the Dependency Relation As Linear Equations

$$\begin{pmatrix} 1&1&1&0&0&0&0&0&0 \\ 0&0&0&1&1&0&0&0&0 \\ 0&0&0&0&0&1&1&0&0 \\ 0&0&0&0&0&0&0&1&1 \\ 1&0&0&0&0&1&0&1&0 \\ 0&1&0&1&0&0&0&0&0 \\ 0&0&1&0&1&0&0&0&0 \\ 0&0&0&0&0&0&1&0&1 \\ 1&1&1&1&1&1&1&1&1 \end{pmatrix} \times \begin{pmatrix} x_1 \\ x_2 \\ x_3 \\ x_4 \\ x_5 \\ x_6 \\ x_7 \\ x_8 \\ x_9 \end{pmatrix} = \begin{pmatrix} 8500 \\ 10000 \\ 6100 \\ 12400 \\ 10000 \\ 6000 \\ 11000 \\ 9000 \\ 36000 \end{pmatrix}$$

it has a single 1) indicates that the value of x_1 must remain the same among all the solutions to the system of equations. Consequently, the adversary can infer Bob's commission in Q_1.

Table 3. The Reduced Row Echelon Form M_{rref} of the Matrix in Table 2

$$\begin{pmatrix} 1&0&0&0&0&0&0&0&0 \\ 0&1&0&0&-1&0&0&0&0 \\ 0&0&1&0&1&0&0&0&0 \\ 0&0&0&1&1&0&0&0&0 \\ 0&0&0&0&0&1&0&0&-1 \\ 0&0&0&0&0&0&1&0&1 \\ 0&0&0&0&0&0&0&1&1 \\ 0&0&0&0&0&0&0&0&0 \\ 0&0&0&0&0&0&0&0&0 \end{pmatrix}$$

Chin has shown that the existence of unit row vectors in M_{rref} is indeed the necessary and sufficient condition for any unknown variable to have the same value among all the solutions [8]. We shall adopt this notion to model inferences in SUM-only data cubes, as formally stated in Definition 1. Notice that for the special case of 1-d inferences, as shown in Example 1, the coefficients matrix itself would have a unit row vector (which will certainly also appear in M_{rref}). It is well-known that the RREF of a $m \times n$ matrix can be obtained by a Gauss-Jordan elimination with complexity $O(m^2 n)$ [21].

Definition 1. *Given a data cube with one-level dimension hierarchy, suppose the core cuboid C_c has n non-empty cells and the collection of aggregation cuboids C_{all} has totally m cells. By assuming any arbitrary but fixed order among the cells,*

1. *Let* M *stands for an* $m \times n$ *matrix whose* $(i, j)^{th}$ *element is* 1*, if the* j^{th} *cell in* C_{all} *depends on the* i^{th} *cell in* C_c*; the element is* 0*, otherwise.*
2. *Let* M_{rref} *be the RREF of* M.

We say C_{all} *causes* ***inferences*** *to* C_c*, if* M_{rref} *includes at least one unit row vector.*

4.2 Cardinality-based Sufficient Conditions for Preventing Inferences

In this section we prove sufficient conditions that guarantee a data cube to be free of inferences. We first study 1-d inferences and then investigate m-d inferences. The number of empty cells can only determine the existence of 1-d inferences in two extreme cases, as stated in Theorem 1. First, if the core cuboid has no empty cell, then it is free of 1-d inferences as long as all the attributes have more than one value. The second result says that any data cube whose core cuboid has fewer non-empty cells than the given upper bound will always have 1-d inferences. If the number of empty cells falls between the two bounds given in Theorem 1, the existence of 1-d inferences can no longer be determined based on the number of empty cells.

Theorem 1 (1-d Inferences). *In any k-dimensional data cube with one-level dimension hierarchy, let* C_c *be the core cuboid and* C_{all} *be the collection of all aggregation cuboids. Suppose the* i^{th} *attribute of* C_c *has* d_i *values, then*

1. C_{all} *does not cause any 1-d inference to* C_c*, if* C_c *has no empty cells and* $d_i > 1$ *for all* $1 \leq i \leq k$.
2. C_{all} *causes 1-d inferences to* C_c*, if the number of non-empty cells in* C_c *is less than* $2^{k-1} \cdot d_{max}$*, where* d_{max} *is the greatest among* d_i*'s.*

The connection between m-d inferences and the number of empty cells is less straightforward. Similar to the case of 1-d inferences, any data cube with a core cuboid having no empty cells is free of m-d inferences, as stated by the first claim of Theorem 2. To relax this rigid result, the second claim of Theorem 2 gives a tight upper bound on the number of empty cells, if a data cube is to remain free of m-d inferences. The bound is tight in the sense that we can no longer tell whether m-d inferences are present from the number of empty cells, once this number goes beyond the bound. Notice that the bound only guarantees the absence of m-d inferences, while 1-d inferences may still be present as long as the core cuboid has empty cells.

Theorem 2 (m-d Inferences). *In any k-dimensional data cube with one-level dimension hierarchy, let* C_c *be the core cuboid and* C_{all} *be the collection of all aggregation cuboids. Suppose the* i^{th} *attribute of* C_c *has* d_i *values, and let* d_u *and* d_v *be the two smallest among the* d_i*'s,*

1. C_{all} *does not cause any m-d inferences to* C_c*, if* C_c *has no empty cells and* $d_i > 1$ *for all* $1 \leq i \leq k$.

2. *C_{all} does not cause any m-d inferences to C_c, if the number of empty cells in C_c is less than $2(d_u - 4) + 2(d_v - 4) - 1$ and $d_i \geq 4$ for all $1 \leq i \leq k$; for any integer $w \geq 2(d_u - 4) + 2(d_v - 4) - 1$, there always exists a data cube with w empty cells having m-d inferences.*

We have established the following connections between inferences and the number of empty cells in the core cuboid. First, a data cube with no empty cells is always free of inferences. This means that the threat of inferences is absent, if the adversary does not know any cell from outbound channels. Second, a data cube can still be free of m-d inferences, if it has fewer empty cells than a given upper bound; however, the data cube needs to be checked for 1-d inferences. Hence, if an adversary knows about a few cells in the core cuboid, inferences can still be easily controlled. Third, a data cube having more empty cells than a given bound always has inferences. That is, a data cube cannot be protected from an adversary who already knows most of the cells. Finally, if the number of empty cells falls between the given bounds, we can no longer tell whether inferences are possible by only looking at the number of empty cells.

4.3 Three-Tier Inference Control

A typical view of inference control in statistical databases has two tiers, the sensitive *data* and the aggregation *query*. Inference control mechanisms check each aggregation query to decide if answering the query in addition to all other queries answered before will cause any inference of sensitive data.

Applying such a two-tier model to OLAP systems has some inherent drawbacks. Checking queries for inferences at run time may bring unacceptable delay to query processings. The complexity of such checking is usually high, due to the fact that m-d inferences must be checked against *sets* of queries instead of against each individual query. For example, checking inferences by reducing a matrix to its RREF has a complexity of $O(m^2n)$ for m queries over n sensitive values. In OLAP systems, the value of m and n is usually very large while answers to queries are demanded in seconds. Inference control methods cannot take advantage of the special characteristics of OLAP applications under the two-tier model. For example, OLAP queries are usually answered using materialized views such as data cube cells. Inference control methods need to take this fact into consideration to improve its on-line performance.

To address those shortcomings, we add an intermediate *aggregation* tier between the data tier and the query tier, namely, a three-tier inference control model. As formally stated in Definition 2, the model has three tiers and three relations on those tiers, and the aggregation tier must satisfy the three properties. As illustrated in Figure 2, the first property enforces inference control between the aggregation tier and the data tier such that the former is free of inferences. The second property limits the size of the aggregation tier. The third property basically partitions the problem of inference control into blocks such that inferences only need to be checked between each corresponding pair of blocks.

Definition 2. *A* **three-tier inference control model** *is compose of*

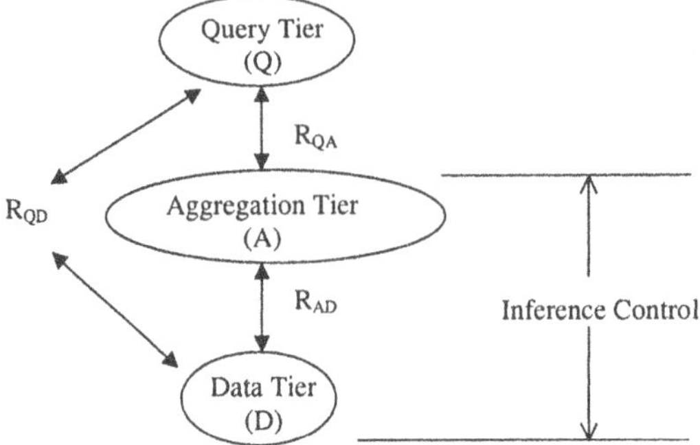

Fig. 2. A Three-Tier Inference Control Model

1. ***Three Tiers:***
   a) *Data D.*
   b) *Aggregation A.*
   c) *Query Q.*
2. ***Relations Between Tiers:***
   a) $R_{AD} \subseteq A \times D$.
   b) $R_{QA} \subseteq Q \times A$.
   c) $R_{QD} = R_{AD} \circ R_{QA}$ *(the symbol $\circ$ denotes the composite relation).*
3. ***Properties:***
   a) $\mid A \mid$ *is polynomial in* $\mid D \mid$.
   b) *Partitions on D and A exist as* $D_1, D_2, \ldots, D_m$ *and* $A_1, A_2, \ldots, A_m$, *satisfying that* $(a, d) \in R_{AD}$ *only if* $d \in D_i$ *and* $a \in A_i$ *for some* $1 \leq i \leq m$.
   c) *A does not cause inferences to D.*

The three-tier model reduces the performance overhead of inference control in several ways. The first property of the model implies that the aggregation tier can be pre-computed so the computation-intensive part of inference control is shifted to off-line processings. The on-line part is to check if a query can be rewritten using the aggregation tier (this function is usually already present for query processing purposes). Second, the last two properties both reduce the size of inputs to inference control algorithms and consequently reduce the complexity. An aggregation tier can be chosen to meet the second property. On the other hand, the size of the query tier is inherently exponential (in the size of the data tier), which contributes to the high complexity of two-tier inference control. The third property *localizes* inference control tasks to blocks of the data tier, whereas in the two-tier model inferences must be checked on the whole data tier.

The cardinality-based method can be implemented on the basis of the three-tier model. The data tier corresponds to the core cuboid, the aggregation tier corresponds to a collection of cells in aggregation cuboids that are free of inferences. The query tier includes any query that can be rewritten using the cells in the aggregation tier. To compute the aggregation tier, we first partition the core cuboid based on the dimension hierarchies. For example, we can partition the data cube in Figure 1, such that each block of the partition contains all the ancestors of a cell in $\langle year, department\rangle$. We then apply the sufficient conditions introduced in Section 4.2 to find the blocks that are free of inferences. The union of those blocks then forms the aggregation tier.

It is straightforward that the aggregation tier then satisfies the three properties stated in Definition 2. The second and the third properties are clear from the above description. The first property holds because any aggregation cuboid must have a size less than that of the core cuboid, and the number of aggregation cuboids is a constant compared to the size of the core cuboid. Computing the aggregation tier has a linear time complexity in nature, because it only requires counting the number of empty cells in each block. This is an improvement over previously known methods, such as transforming a matrix to its RREF.

5 Parity-based Inference Control in Sum-only Data Cubes

The cardinality-based method introduced in Section 4 has the following two limitations. First, the conditions for inference-free data cubes are sufficient but not necessary, and hence one cannot tell whether a data cube has inferences when the conditions fail. Second, only considering one-level dimension hierarchy causes unnecessary restrictions on queries. For example, if we choose to partition the data cube in Figure 1 into years and departments, then any query asking for an employee's half-year commission will be denied even if it causes no inferences. In this section we study a *parity-based* inference control method to remove those limitations.

It is a simple fact that even number is closed under the operation of addition and subtraction. As shown in Example 2, the nature of an m-d inference is to add and to subtract (strictly speaking, set union and set difference) sets of cells in the core cuboid until the result yields a single cell. Suppose now all the sets have even number of cells, then how to add and subtract those sets to obtain *one* cell would be significantly more difficult. That is, restricting queries to only aggregate even number of cells in the core cuboid can alleviate the threat of inferences. The rest of the section is organized as follows. Section 5.1 gives notations and motivating examples. Section 5.2 then describes the main results. Finally, Section 5.3 discusses how those results fit in the three-tier inference control model. Proofs of the theorems can be found in [37].

5.1 Query and The Derivable Relation Between Queries

In this section we consider *query* that can be any non-empty subset of the core cuboid. The answer to a query sums the cells in the query. Specially, for a cell in aggregation cuboids, the collection of its ancestors can be considered as a *multi-dimensional range* (or MDR for short) query that includes all the non-empty cells between two given cells. Here a cell is *between* two others if its value of every attribute falls between those of the others. We use the notation $q^*(u, v)$ to denote an

MDR query, where u and v are any two given cells. Table 4 gives examples of MDR queries and their answers. Notice that the two cells used to denote an MDR query can be empty. For example, the first query in Table 4 is equivalent to another query $q^*(\langle Q_1, Alice\rangle, \langle Q_4, Bob\rangle)$.

Table 4. Examples of Multi-dimensional Range Queries

The Core Cuboid

	Q_1	Q_2	Q_3	Q_4
Bob	x_1	x_2	x_3	
Alice		x_4	x_5	x_6

MDR Queries

MDR Query	Answer
$q^*(\langle Q_1, Bob\rangle, \langle Q_4, Alice\rangle)$	6500
$q^*(\langle Q_1, Bob\rangle, \langle Q_2, Bob\rangle)$	1500
$q^*(\langle Q_2, Alice\rangle, \langle Q_3, Alice\rangle)$	2000
$q^*(\langle Q_3, Alice\rangle, \langle Q_4, Alice\rangle)$	1500
$q^*(\langle Q_3, Bob\rangle, \langle Q_3, Alice\rangle)$	2500

Inference is trivial if all MDR queries are answered. For example, in Table 4 the answer to a valid MDR query $q^*(\langle Q_1, Bob\rangle, \langle Q_1, Bob\rangle)$ is the cell $\langle Q_1, Bob\rangle$ itself. By restricting MDR queries to only include even number of cells, such simple inferences can be prevented. Nonetheless, more sophisticated inferences are still possible with just *even MDR* queries. The first formula in Table 5 models the five queries in Table 4 as a system of five linear equations. The second formula describes an m-d inference. The unit row vector at the left side of the formula is represented as a linear combination of the row vectors in the matrix at the right side. Hence, the unit row vector will also appear in the RREF of the matrix. Informally, if we add up the answers to the last four queries and subtract from it the answer to the first query, then dividing the result by two gives us Bob's commission in Q_2, that is $x_2 = 500$.

Table 5. An Example of Inferences Caused By Even MDR Queries

$$\begin{pmatrix} 1\,1\,1\,1\,1\,1 \\ 1\,1\,0\,0\,0\,0 \\ 0\,0\,0\,1\,1\,0 \\ 0\,0\,0\,0\,1\,1 \\ 0\,0\,1\,0\,1\,0 \end{pmatrix} \times \begin{pmatrix} x_1 \\ x_2 \\ x_3 \\ x_4 \\ x_5 \\ x_6 \end{pmatrix} = \begin{pmatrix} 6500 \\ 1500 \\ 2000 \\ 1500 \\ 2500 \end{pmatrix}$$

$$[0, 0, 0, 0, 1, 0] = [-\tfrac{1}{2}, \tfrac{1}{2}, \tfrac{1}{2}, \tfrac{1}{2}, \tfrac{1}{2}] \cdot \begin{pmatrix} 1\,1\,1\,1\,1\,1 \\ 1\,1\,0\,0\,0\,0 \\ 0\,0\,0\,1\,1\,0 \\ 0\,0\,0\,0\,1\,1 \\ 0\,0\,1\,0\,1\,0 \end{pmatrix}$$

Definition 3 generalizes the previous model of inference in SUM-only data cubes such that queries can be considered. It also introduces the concepts of derivability and equivalence between sets of queries. Intuitively, if a set of queries is derivable from another set, then the answers to the former can be computed using the answers to the latter. For example, consider the second formula in Table 5. If we regard the vector at the left side of the formula as a query, then the formula says that this query is derivable from the five queries at the right side. By definition, if a set of queries S is derivable from another set of queries S', then S is free of inferences if S' is so (the converse is not necessarily true). If two sets of queries are equivalent, then one is free of inferences iff the other is so. In the following section we shall employ this fact to decide whether the collection of even MDR queries causes any inferences.

Definition 3. *Given a data cube with the core cuboid C_c and a set of queries $\mathcal{Q}$, we use $\mathcal{M}(\mathcal{Q})$ for a $\mid \mathcal{Q} \mid \times \mid C_c \mid$ matrix whose $(i,j)^{th}$ element is 1 if the jth cell in C_c is included by the ith query in $\mathcal{Q}$ and the element is 0, otherwise.*

1. *we say $\mathcal{Q}$ causes an* ***inference*** *to C_c, if the RREF of $\mathcal{M}(\mathcal{Q})$ includes at least one unit row vector.*
2. *we say $\mathcal{Q}$ is* ***derivable*** *from another set of queries $\mathcal{Q}'$, denoted as $\mathcal{Q} \preceq_d \mathcal{Q}'$, if the row vectors of $\mathcal{M}(\mathcal{Q})$ can be represented as the linear combination of the row vectors of $\mathcal{M}(\mathcal{Q}')$; $\mathcal{Q}$ is* ***equivalent*** *to $\mathcal{Q}'$, denoted as $\mathcal{Q} \equiv_d \mathcal{Q}'$, if $\mathcal{Q} \preceq_d \mathcal{Q}'$ and $\mathcal{Q}' \preceq_d \mathcal{Q}$ both hold.*

5.2 Detecting Inferences Caused By Even MDR Queries

Given a data cube, we want to determine if the collection of even MDR queries, denoted as $\mathcal{Q}^*$, causes any inferences. We can transform the matrix $\mathcal{M}(\mathcal{Q}^*)$ to its RREF and check if there is any unit row vector. The complexity of this method is $O(m^2n)$, where m is the size of $\mathcal{Q}^*$ and n is the size of the core cuboid. In this section, we introduce a more efficient method with the complexity $O(mn)$. The method reduces the complexity by finding another collection of queries equivalent to $\mathcal{Q}^*$ such that inferences are easier to detect.

Intuitively, the collection of even MDR queries contains redundancy that can be removed by decomposing the queries into the smallest even range queries, that is *pairs* of cells (a pair here refers to a set of size two). For example, in Table 4 the query $q^*(\langle Q_2, Bob\rangle, \langle Q_3, Alice\rangle)$ is derivable from $\{q^*(\langle Q_2, Bob\rangle, \langle Q_3, Bob\rangle), q^*(\langle Q_2, Alice\rangle, \langle Q_3, Alice\rangle)\}$, and hence is redundant in terms of causing inferences. However, it is not straightforward whether we can always find an appropriate collection of pairs equivalent to $\mathcal{Q}^*$. First, the collection of pairs included by $\mathcal{Q}^*$, as shown in Table 6, is *not enough* for this purpose. For example, the query $q^*(\langle Q_1, Bob\rangle, \langle Q_4, Alice\rangle)$ is not derivable from the pairs included by $\mathcal{Q}^*$. Second, the collection of all possible pairs is *too much* for our purpose. For example, the pair $\{\langle Q_1, Bob\rangle, \langle Q_3, Bob\rangle\}$ is not derivable from $\mathcal{Q}^*$.

Fortunately, Theorem 3 shows that there always exists a set of pairs equivalent to the collection of even MDR queries. The proof includes an algorithm that

Table 6. The Collection of Even MDR Queries $\mathcal{Q}^*$ For The Data Cube in Table 4

Pairs		
Pairs	$q^*(\langle Q_1, Bob\rangle, \langle Q_2, Bob\rangle)$	$q^*(\langle Q_2, Bob\rangle, \langle Q_3, Bob\rangle)$
	$q^*(\langle Q_2, Bob\rangle, \langle Q_2, Alice\rangle)$	$q^*(\langle Q_2, Alice\rangle, \langle Q_3, Alice\rangle)$
	$q^*(\langle Q_3, Alice\rangle, \langle Q_4, Alice\rangle)$	$q^*(\langle Q_3, Bob\rangle, \langle Q_3, Alice\rangle)$
Non-pairs	$q^*(\langle Q_1, Bob\rangle, \langle Q_4, Alice\rangle)$	$q^*(\langle Q_2, Bob\rangle, \langle Q_3, Alice\rangle)$

constructs the desired set of pairs $\mathcal{Q}^p$ for any given data cube. We give the intuitions through an example. For each MDR query in Table 6, the algorithm groups cells included by the query into pairs. For example, for $q^*(\langle Q_1, Bob\rangle, \langle Q_4, Alice\rangle)$, it first attempts to group cells along one dimension; it thus have the two pairs $\{\langle Q_1, Bob\rangle, \langle Q_2, Bob\rangle\}$ and $\{\langle Q_2, Alice\rangle, \langle Q_3, Alice\rangle\}$. It then groups the rest two cells $\langle Q_3, Bob\rangle$ and $\langle Q_4, Alice\rangle$ into a third pair. Similarly it processes the other queries in Table 6. The final result $\mathcal{Q}^p$ will include all the pairs given in Table 6 and also $\{\langle Q_3, Bob\rangle, \langle Q_4, Alice\rangle\}$, as shown in Table 7.

Table 7. A Collection of Pairs $\mathcal{Q}^p$ Equivalent To The Even MDR Queries in Table 6

In $\mathcal{Q}^*$	$\{\langle Q_1, Bob\rangle, \langle Q_2, Bob\rangle\}$	$\{\langle Q_2, Bob\rangle, \langle Q_3, Bob\rangle\}$
	$\{\langle Q_2, Bob\rangle, \langle Q_2, Alice\rangle\}$	$\{\langle Q_2, Alice\rangle, \langle Q_3, Alice\rangle\}$
	$\{\langle Q_3, Alice\rangle, \langle Q_4, Alice\rangle\}$	$\{\langle Q_3, Bob\rangle, \langle Q_3, Alice\rangle\}$
Not In $\mathcal{Q}^*$	$\{\langle Q_3, Bob\rangle, \langle Q_4, Alice\rangle\}$	

It can be verified that the $\mathcal{Q}^p$ in Table 7 is indeed equivalent to the $\mathcal{Q}^*$ in Table 6. First, any query in $\mathcal{Q}^*$ can be derived by adding up the corresponding pairs in $\mathcal{Q}^p$, such as $q^*(\langle Q_1, Bob\rangle, \langle Q_4, Alice\rangle)$ by the three pairs $\{\langle Q_1, Bob\rangle, \langle Q_2, Bob\rangle\}$, $\{\langle Q_2, Alice\rangle, \langle Q_3, Alice\rangle\}$, $\{\langle Q_3, Bob\rangle, \langle Q_4, Alice\rangle\}$.
Second, each pair in $\mathcal{Q}^p$ can be derived by subtracting queries in $\mathcal{Q}^*$. For example, $\{\langle Q_3, Bob\rangle, \langle Q_4, Alice\rangle\}$ is derived by subtracting $q^*(\langle Q_1, Bob\rangle, \langle Q_2, Bob\rangle)$ and $q^*(\langle Q_2, Alice\rangle, \langle Q_3, Alice\rangle)$ from $q^*(\langle Q_1, Bob\rangle, \langle Q_4, Alice\rangle)$.

Theorem 3. *Given any data cube, let the core cuboid be C_c and the collection of even MDR queries be $\mathcal{Q}^*$, then a set of pairs $\mathcal{Q}^p = \{\{u, v\} \mid u \in C_c, v \in C_c, u \neq v\}$ can always be found in $O(\mid C_c \mid \cdot \mid \mathcal{Q}^* \mid)$ time, such that $\mathcal{Q}^* \equiv_d \mathcal{Q}^p$ is true.*

Now that the collection of even MDR queries $\mathcal{Q}^*$ is equivalent to the collection of pairs $\mathcal{Q}^p$, we only need to decide if the latter has any inferences. We first denote $\mathcal{Q}^p$ as an undirected simple graph $G(C_c, \mathcal{Q}^p)$. That is, the core cuboid is the vertex set and the collection of pairs $\mathcal{Q}^p$ is the edge set. We then apply Chin's result that a collection of pairs is free of inferences iff the corresponding graph is a bipartite graph (that is, a graph with no cycle composed of odd number of edges) [42]. The existence of odd cycles can easily be decided with a breadth-first search, taking time $O(\mid C_c \mid + \mid \mathcal{Q}^p \mid)$. As an example, Figure 3 shows the graph corresponding to the $\mathcal{Q}^p$ given in Table 7. The graph clearly has an odd cycle of three edges, corresponding to the inference described earlier in this section.

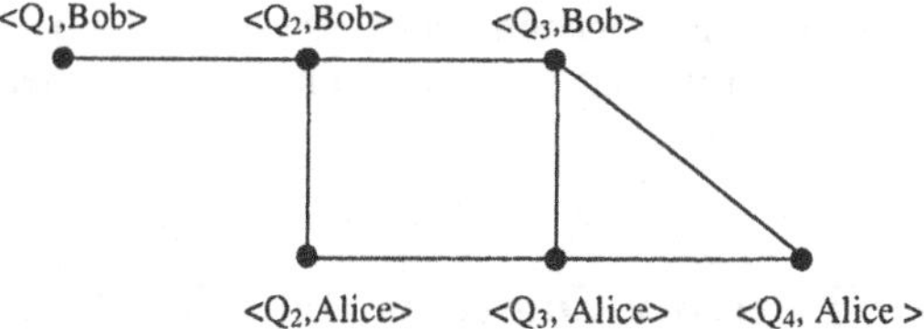

Fig. 3. The Graph Representation of The Q^p in Table 7

In addition to a collection of even MDR queries Q^* free of inferences, we may want to answer other queries. Theorem 4 says that any query can be answered in addition to Q^*, iff it includes equal number of cells in the two color classes of the bipartite graph corresponding to Q^p. One implication is that answering any odd MDR query (that is, an MDR query that includes odd number of cells) in addition to Q^* will cause an inference. However, it is shown that any such odd MDR query can be derived using at most $2k - 1$ even MDR queries in a k-dimensional data cube [38]. Hence, restricting odd MDR queries does not adversely impact the availability.

Theorem 4. *In any data cube with the core cuboid C_c, given that Q^* causes no inferences, any query $q \subseteq C_c$ satisfies $q \preceq_d Q^*$ iff $| q \cap C_1 |=| q \cap C_2 |$, where (C_1, C_2) is the bipartition of $G(C_c, Q^p)$.*

5.3 Integrating The Parity-based Method in The Three-tier Model

The parity-based method can be applied based on the three-tier inference control model given in Section 4.3. A partition of the core cuboid based on dimension hierarchies composes the data tier. We then apply the parity-based method to each block in the partition. If the collection of even MDR queries is free of inferences, we add its equivalent pairs Q^p into the aggregation tier. The query tier includes any query that is derivable from the aggregation tier. The relation R_{AD} and R_{QA} between the three tiers can now be interpreted as the derivable relation $\preceq_d$ given in Definition 3, and the composite relation $R_{QD} = R_{AD} \circ R_{QA}$ is a subset of $\preceq_d$ as $\preceq_d$ is transitive.

The first property of the three-tier model is satisfied because the number of pairs in Q^p must be $O(n^2)$, where n is the size of the core cuboid. Because we partition the core cuboid before applying the parity-based method to each block, the aggregation tier has a natural partition, satisfying the second condition. The last condition is satisfied, because we only use the collection of even MDR queries that does not cause inferences. Alternatively, for those blocks where inferences do exist, large subsets of Q^p that do not cause any inference can be used, although the maximal subsets are difficult to find [37].

In contrast to the cardinality-based method introduced in Section 4, the parity-based method has some advantages. First, the cardinality-based method only considers one-level dimension hierarchy, whereas the parity-based method allows any even MDR queries. The parity-based method thus improves the availability. Second, the cardinality-based method is based on sufficient conditions, whereas the parity-based method on necessary and sufficient conditions. Hence, the former only has limited power over inferences, but the latter can determine whether inferences exist with certainty in all cases.

6 Lattice-based Inference Control in Data Cubes

The two methods introduced in previous sections have the following limitations (which are also shared by many methods proposed for statistical databases). First, all and only the cells in a core cuboid can be regarded as sensitive. Second, only SUM is allowed. Third, the linear algebra-based model of inference can only capture the inference of exact values. For some attributes, a sensitive value can be approximately inferred to be inside a small interval while the exact sensitive value remain secret [24,25]. Removing those limitations has seemed to be difficult. Chin has shown that even allowing MAX in addition to SUM will make detecting inferences intractable [6]. More recently, Kleinberg et. al show that detecting inferences is intractable even for SUM-only queries if an adversary knows the data type of the sensitive attribute to be Boolean [23].

However, this chapter shows that by adopting a novel approach to inference control, the above-mentioned limitations can indeed be removed. The key observation is that 1-d inferences are generally easy to detect, because each query can be examined separately. A set of queries does not cause 1-d inferences iff each query alone does not. In contrast, m-d inferences are hard to detect because a set of queries can cause m-d inferences even when each of them is free of 1-d inferences. We identify this *non-compositional* property of inferences as the root cause to most of the difficulties in inference control. For example, the detecting method for SUM and MAX queries is completely different from the simple mixture of the method for SUM queries and that for MAX queries [6]. This means every combination of aggregation functions may need a unique detecting method.

Instead of detecting m-d inferences, we adopt a more aggressive approach to prevent them by restricting queries. Detecting the rest 1-d inferences then becomes an easier task, because we can now examine each query separately without worrying about their combinations. This approach removes the above limitations. We allow generic definitions of inferences, given that some clearly stated assumptions are satisfied. We also allow any part of the data cube to be specified as sensitive. The rest of the chapter is organized as follows. Section 6.1 devises a framework for specifying authorization objects in data cubes. Section 6.3 proposes a lattice-based solution for controlling inferences in data cubes. Section 6.4 discusses the implementation options. Proofs of the theorems can be found in [36].

6.1 Specifying Authorization Objects in Data Cubes

It is a limitation that all and only the values in the core cuboid may be regarded as sensitive, because values in aggregation cuboids may also carry sensitive information. For example, in Figure 1 a user may need to be prohibited from accessing any employee's yearly or more detailed commissions. This requirement not only makes the values in both the core cuboid $\langle quarter, employee\rangle$ and the aggregation cuboid $\langle year, employee\rangle$ sensitive. The data cube is thus partitioned along the dependency lattice into two parts. As another example, the previous requirement may only need to be applied to the first year data, whereas data in other years can be freely accessed. That is, the data cube should also be partitioned along the time dimension.

To accommodate such security requirements, Definition 4 describes a framework for specifying authorization objects in data cubes. The function $Below()$ partitions the data cube along the dependency lattice, and the function $Slice()$ partitions the data cube along dimensions. An object is simply the intersection of the two. For example, the above security requirements can now be specified as $Object(L, S)$, where $L = \{\langle year, employee\rangle\}$ and S includes all the cells in the first four quarters of the core cuboids. The cells included by $object(L, S)$ must be included by one of the two cuboids in $Below(L)$, that is $\langle year, employee\rangle$ and $\langle quarter, employee\rangle$; the cell must also be in the first year, that is their first attribute must be one of the following values: Q_1 through Q_4, Y_1 , or ALL.

Definition 4. *In a data cube, let C_c be the core cuboid and let $\mathcal{L}$ be the collection of all cuboids,*

1. *For any $L \subseteq \mathcal{L}$, we use $Below(L)$ to denote the collection of ancestors of the cuboids in L.*
2. *For any $S \subseteq C_c$, we use $Slice(S)$ to denote the collection of descendants of the cells in S.*
3. *We use $Object(L, S)$ for the set intersection between $\bigcup_{c \in Below(L)} c$ and $Slice(S)$.*

*We call $Object(L, S)$ an **object** specified by L and S.*

By definition, the object specification satisfies the following desired property. For any cell in an object, the object also includes all the ancestors of that cell. Intuitively, ancestors of a sensitive cell contain more detailed information and should also be regarded as sensitive. For example, if an object includes the cuboid $\langle year, employee\rangle$, then it also includes the core cuboid $\langle quarter, employee\rangle$, because otherwise an adversary may compute the former from the latter.

Definition 4 can be easily extended such that an object can be specified with multiple pairs $O = \{L_i, S_i\}$. This is because of the fact that $Below()$ is distributive over set union, that is $Below(L_1 \cup L_2) = Below(L_1) \cup Below(L_2)$. The union of the objects $Object(L_i, S_i)$ thus composes a new object $Object(O)$. For example, let S be the cells of the core cuboid C_c in the first two quarters, then $Object(S, \phi) \cap Object(C_c - S, \{\langle all, employee\rangle\})$ stands for an object. Accesses to the cell $\langle Y_1, Bob\rangle$ in the cuboid $\langle year, employee\rangle$ will be prohibited, because it is included by $Object(C_c - S, \{\langle all, employee\rangle\})$.

6.2 Reducible Inferences

As examples to the notations introduced in Definition 5, suppose S denotes the union of $\langle all, employee\rangle$ and $\langle year, employee\rangle$, and suppose T includes the cells of $\langle quarter, employee\rangle\rangle\}$ in the first four quarters. Then the cell in $\langle all, employee\rangle$ is *redundant*, because its ancestors in the cuboid $\langle year, employee\rangle$ are all included by S. The cell $\langle Y_2, Bob\rangle$ is *non-comparable*, because it is neither ancestor nor descendant of any cell in T.

Definition 5. *Given any two sets of cells in a data cube, denoted as S and T, we say*

1. *a cell c is **redundant** with respect to T, if S includes both c and all its ancestors in any single cuboid,*
2. *a cell c is **non-comparable** to T, if for every $c' \in T$, c is neither ancestor nor descendant of c'.*

We do not assume specific definitions of inferences. Instead, we consider any *reducible* inferences that satisfy the following assumption. If $c \in S$ is either redundant or non-comparable (or both), then S causes inferences to T iff $S - \{c\}$ does so. That is, reducible inferences can be checked without considering any redundant or non-comparable cells. The inference in SUM-only data cubes, as given by Definition 1, is reducible. We shall only consider reducible inferences from now on.

Intuitively, a redundant cell in S can be ignored, because it can be computed from other cells in S. This assumption implies that we only consider *distributive* aggregation functions [18], because only with such functions can a cell be computed from its ancestors in *any* cuboid. SUM, MAX, MIN, COUNT are all distributive, but AVG and MEDIAN are not. For example, $AVG(S_1 \cup S_2)$ cannot be computed from $AVG(S_1)$ and $AVG(S_2)$. Some non-distributive aggregation functions can be replaced by distributive ones. For example, AVG is not distributive, but it can be considered as a pair $(SUM, COUNT)$.

By ignoring non-comparable cells, we shall only consider the inference caused by descendants. This assumption also implies that if S and T can be partitioned as $S = S_1 \cup S_2$ and $T = T_1 \cup T_2$ such that no cell in S_1 (or S_2) depends on a cell in T_2 (or T_1), then inferences can only exist between S_1 and T_1 or between S_2 and T_2. In another word, inferences are also *partitioned*. This assumption may not hold if outbound knowledge can correlate cells that do not depend on each other. A conservative solution is to consider a cell as empty, if it is correlated to another cell that the adversary has accesses to.

6.3 Lattice-based Inference Control

We first consider a special case where S is a complete cuboid in $Object(L, S)$. The object is thus simply (the union of) the cuboids in $Below(L)$. For example in Figure 4, the lower curve in solid line depicts such an object $Below(\{\langle a^1, b^1, c^2, d^2\rangle, \langle a^1, b^2, c^1, d^2\rangle\})$ in a four-dimensional data cube. Let T be the object and S be its complement to the data cube. Inference control is thus to remove inferences from S to T. Our approach has two steps. First, we find a subset of S that is free of m-d inferences to T and at the same time is maximal for this purpose. We then remove 1-d inferences from this subset.

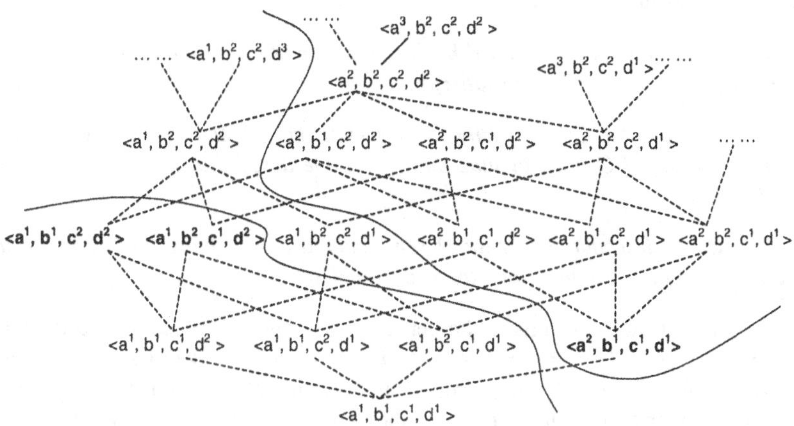

Fig. 4. An Example of Preventing m-d Inferences

We take advantage of our assumptions about reducible inferences to find a maximal subset of S that is free of m-d inferences to T. Informally, with respect to each cuboid in T, we can remove all the redundant and non-comparable cells from S such that only a set of *minimal descendants* need to be considered. For example, in Figure 4 although all the cuboids in S are descendants of the core cuboid $\langle a^1, b^1, c^1, d^1\rangle$, only the two minimal descendants $\langle a^2, b^1, c^1, d^1\rangle$ and $\langle a^1, b^2, c^2, d^1\rangle$ need to be examined for inferences. Any other cuboid in S is a descendant of at least one of the two cuboids, and hence is redundant. However, checking whether the set of minimal descendants cause m-d inferences may still incur high complexity, and we want to avoid such checking.

We take a more aggressive approach by allowing accesses to only one minimal descendant. For example, we can choose to only allow $\langle a^2, b^1, c^1, d^1\rangle$ and remove the other minimal descendant $\langle a^1, b^2, c^2, d^1\rangle$ from S. We also need to remove other cuboids that are no longer redundant, such as $\langle a^1, b^2, c^2, d^2\rangle$ and $\langle a^1, b^2, c^2, d^3\rangle$. The result is a subset of S that includes all the descendants of $\langle a^2, b^1, c^1, d^1\rangle$, namely, a *descendant closure*, as illustrated by the upper curve in Figure 4. This subset has only one minimal descendant of the core cuboid, and hence is free of m-d inferences to the core cuboid. The property actually holds for any other cuboid in T as well. That is, for any $c \in T$, only one minimal descendant of c appears in this subset of S, and hence m-d inferences to c are no longer possible.

On the other hand, it is easy to observe that the upper curve cannot be modified to include any of the cuboids between the current two curves in Figure 4 without inducing possible m-d inferences. More generally, as long as a cuboid c_r satisfies that all its ancestors are included by T, the descendant closure of c_r will be the maximal result for preventing m-d inferences. Moreover, the descendant closure turns out to be the only choice, if any subset of S is to prevent the need for checking m-d inferences and at the same time being maximal for that purpose. The above-described results are summarized in Theorem 5.

Theorem 5. *In any data cube, let $\mathcal{L}$ be the collection of all cuboids. Given any $L \subseteq \mathcal{L}$, any $C \subseteq \mathcal{L} - Below(L)$ can satisfy both that*

1. *each cuboid not in C has exactly one descendant in C that is not redundant, and*
2. *any superset of C must include more than one descendant of some cuboid in $Below(L)$,*

iff C is the descendant closure of some cuboid c_r satisfying that c_r is not in $Below(L)$ but all of its ancestors are in $Below(L)$.

Next we extend the results to the general case where the object is specified by a set of pairs $O = \{(L_i, S_i) : 1 \leq i \leq n\}$. Informally, the key issue in such an extension is that $Slice(S_i)$'s may overlap, and it would be prohibitive if we need to compute a descendant closure for each of their intersections. Fortunately, it turns out that the set intersection of descendant closures is always another descendant closure. This property guarantees that no m-d inferences are possible to the cells included by multiple $Slice(S_i)$'s. However, obtaining the maximal result of Theorem 5 is intractable for the general case, as formally stated in Theorem 6.

Theorem 6. *In any data cube, let $\mathcal{L}$ be the collection of all cuboids. Given an object specified by $O = \{(L_i, S_i) \mid 1 \leq i \leq n\}$, let each $c_i (1 \leq i \leq n)$ be a cuboid not in $Below(L_i)$ but has all of its ancestors in $Below(L_i)$, and use $Answerable(\{c_i\})$ to denote the set intersection between the descendant closures of the c_i's and the $Slice(S_i)$'s, then*

1. *any cell not in $Answerable(\{c_i\})$ has one descendant in $Answerable(\{c_i\})$ that is not redundant, and*
2. *to find a set of c_i's that makes $Answerable(\{c_i\})$ maximal is NP-hard.*

The final step of inference control is to remove 1-d inferences from $Answerable(\{c_i\})$. It may seem to be a viable solution to simply restrict any cell that causes an 1-d inference. However, the restricted cell itself will then be subject to inferences. Hence, we must adopt the following iterative procedure to remove 1-d inferences. First, we check each cell in $Answerable(\{c_i\})$ and add those that cause 1-d inferences to the object. We thus have a larger object. Second, we control m-d inferences to this new object by choosing a new set of c_i's and computing the corresponding $Answerable(\{c_i\})$. By repeating the two steps, we gradually remove all 1-d inferences while preventing m-d inferences. The procedure terminates in at most m steps, where m is the number cuboids. The final result is a set of cells that are guaranteed to be free of inferences to the object.

6.4 Implementation Options

The lattice-based inference control method can be implemented based on the three-tier inference control model given in Section 4.3. The object that includes both the originally specified object and those cells that cause 1-d inferences composes the data tier. The complement of the object includes all the cells that can be disclosed without inferences and thus composes the aggregation tier. The query tier includes any query that is derivable from the aggregation tier. The first property of the three-tier model is satisfied because the number of cuboids is a constant compared to the number of cells, and hence the size of the aggregation tier must be polynomial in the size of the data tier. Because the aggregation tier is a collection of descendant closures of single cuboids, the aggregation tier can be regarded as a partition, satisfying the second property. The aggregation tier apparently satisfies the last property.

In contrast to the previous methods, the lattice-based inference control has the following advantages. First, it allows generic definitions of inferences, which also implies the support of generic aggregation functions and generic criteria for determining what is sensitive. This characteristic makes the lattice-based method broadly applicable. In contrast, the previous two methods (and many other existing methods) can only deal with a specific definition of inferences. Second, the lattice-based method supports flexible specification of objects in data cubes. This capability is important for applications that have different security requirements for different parts of a data cube. In comparison, the previous methods regard all and only the cells in the core cuboid as sensitive.

7 Conclusion

This chapter has discussed three methods that aim to answer data cube style queries about sensitive data while preventing adversaries from gaining unauthorized accesses to the data. The key challenge of the study has been that sensitive data can be inferred using seemingly innocent queries, and detecting such inferences incurs high complexity. The first two methods both cope with inferences in SUM-only data cubes. The cardinality-based method shows that data cubes with few previously known values are not vulnerable to inferences. The parity-based method first prevents simple inferences by restricting queries to aggregate only even number of values, then it detects and removes more sophisticated inferences. The lattice-based method aims to broaden the scope of inference control. It identifies the main drawback of most existing methods as trying to precisely detect sophisticated inferences. It then adopts a novel approach in first aggressively preventing sophisticated inferences and then removing simpler inferences. The support of generic definitions of inferences and flexible object specification makes inference control more practical then before. All the proposed methods can be implemented on the basis of a three-tier inference control model that is especially suitable for decision support systems such as OLAP.

References

1. Adam, N.R. and Wortmann, J.C. (1989). Security-control methods for statistical databases: a comparative study. *ACM Computing Surveys*, 21(4):515–556.
2. Agrawal, R. and Srikant, R. (2000). Privacy-preserving data mining. In *Proceedings of the Nineteenth ACM SIGMOD Conference on Management of Data (SIGMOD'00)*, pages 439–450.
3. Agrawal, R., Srikant, R., and Thomas, D. (2005). Privacy-preserving olap. In *Proceedings of the Twenty-fourth ACM SIGMOD Conference on Management of Data (SIGMOD'05)*, pages 251–262.
4. Beck, L.L. (1980). A security mechanism for statistical databases. *ACM Trans. on Database Systems*, 5(3):316–338.
5. Bhargava, B. (2000). Security in data warehousing (invited talk). In *Proceedings of the 3rd Data Warehousing and Knowledge Discovery (DaWak'00).*
6. Chin, F.Y. (1986). Security problems on inference control for sum, max, and min queries. *Journal of the Association for Computing Machinery*, 33(3):451–464.
7. Chin, F.Y. and Özsoyoglu, G. (1981). Statistical database design. *ACM Trans. on Database Systems*, 6(1):113–139.
8. Chin, F.Y. and Özsoyoglu, G. (1982). Auditing and inference control in statistical databases. *IEEE Trans. on Software Engineering*, 8(6):574–582.
9. Consorortium, WWW. Platform for privacy preferences (p3p) project. http://www.w3.org/P3P/.
10. Cox, L.H. (2003). On properties of multi-dimensional statistical tables. *Journal of Statistical Planning and Inference*, 117(2):251–273.
11. Coyle, K. (1999). P3p: Pretty poor privacy? a social analysis of the platform for privacy preferences (p3p). http: //www.kcoyle.net/ p3p.html. June.
12. Denning, D.E. (1982). *Cryptography and data security*. Addison-Wesley, Reading, Massachusetts.
13. Denning, D.E. and Schlörer, J. (1983). Inference controls for statistical databases. *IEEE Computer*, 16(7):69–82.
14. Dobkin, D., Jones, A.K., and Lipton, R.J. (1979). Secure databases: protection against user influence. *ACM Trans. on Database Systems*, 4(1):97–106.
15. Du, W. and Zhan, Z. (2002). Building decision tree classifier on private data. In *Proceedings of the 2002 IEEE International Conference on Data Mining (ICDM'02).*
16. Fellegi, L.P. and Sunter, A.B. (1969). A theory for record linkage. *Journal of American Statistic Association*, 64(328):1183–1210.
17. Gellman, R. (2002). How the lack of privacy costs consumers and why business studies of privacy costs are biased and incomplete. http://ww w.epic.org/reports/dmfprivacy.html.
18. Gray, J., Bosworth, A., Bosworth, A., Layman, A., Reichart, D., Venkatrao, M., Pellow, F., and Pirahesh, H. (1997). Data cube: A relational aggregation operator generalizing group-by, cross-tab, and sub-totals. *Data Mining and Knowledge Discovery*, 1(1):29–53.
19. Griffiths, P. and Wade, B.W. (1976). An authorization mechanism for a relational database system. *ACM Transactions on Database Systems*, 1(3):242–255.
20. Harinarayan, V., Rajaraman, A., and Ullman, J.D. (1996). Implementing data cubes efficiently. In *Proceedings of the Fifteenth ACM SIGMOD international conference on Management of data (SIGMOD'96)*, pages 205–227.
21. Hoffman, K. (1961). *Linear Algebra*. Prentice-Hall, Englewood Cliffs, New Jersey.
22. Jajodia, S., Samarati, P., Sapino, M.L., and Subrahmanian, V.S. (2001). Flexible support for multiple access control policies. *ACM Transactions on Database Systems*, 26(4):1–57.

23. Kleinberg, J., Papadimitriou, C., and Raghavan, P. (2000). Auditing boolean attributes. In *Proceedings of the Ninth ACM SIGMOD-SIG ACT-SIGART Symposium on Principles of Database System*, pages 86–91.
24. Li, Y., Wang, L., Wang, X.S., and Jajodia, S. (2002). Auditing interval-based inference. In *Proceedings of the Fourteenth Conference on Advanced Information Systems Engineering (CAiSE'02)*, pages 553–568.
25. Malvestuto, F.M. and Mezzini, M. (2003). Auditing sum queries. In *Proceedings of the Ninth International Conference on Database Theory (ICDT'03)*, pages 126–146.
26. Mateo-Sanz, J.M. and Domingo-Ferrer, J. (1998). A method for data-oriented multivariate microaggregation. In *Proceedings of the Conference on Statistical Data Protection'98*, pages 89–99.
27. Miklau, G. and Suciu, D. (2004). A formal analysis of information disclosure in data exchange. In *Proceedings of the 23th ACM SIGMOD Conference on Management of Data (SIGMOD'04)*.
28. Newcombe, H.B., Kennedy, J.M., Axford, S.J., and James, A.P. (1959). Automatic linkage of vital records. *Science*, 130(3381):954–959.
29. Samarati, P. (2001). Protecting respondents' identities in microdata release. *IEEE Transactions on Knowledge and Data Engineering*, 13(6):1 010–1027.
30. Sandhu, R.S., Coyne, E.J., Feinstein, H.L., and Youman, C.E. (1996). Role-based access control models. *IEEE Computer*, 29(2):38–47.
31. Schlörer, J. (1981). Security of statistical databases: multidimensional transformation. *ACM Trans. on Database Systems*, 6(1):95–112.
32. Shoshani, A. (1997). OLAP and statistical databases: Similarities and differences. In *Proceedings of the Sixteenth ACM SIGACT-SIGMOD-SIGART Symposium on Principles of Database Systems (PODS'97)*, pages 185–196.
33. T. Priebe, G. Pernul (2000). Towards olap security design - survey and research issues. In *Proceedings of 3rd ACM International Workshop on Data Warehousing and OLAP (DOLAP'00)*, pages 114–121.
34. Traub, J.F., Yemini, Y., and Woźniakowski, H. (1984). The statistical security of a statistical database. *ACM Trans. on Database Systems*, 9(4):672–679.
35. Vaidya, J. and Clifton, C. (2002). Privacy preserving association rule mining in vertically partitioned data. In *Proceedings of the eighth ACM SIGKDD international conference on Knowledge discovery and data mining (KDD'02)*, pages 639–644.
36. Wang, L., Jajodia, S., and Wijesekera, D. (2004a). Securing OLAP data cubes against privacy breaches. In *Proceedings of the 2004 IEEE Symposium on Security and Privacy (S&P'04)*, pages 161–175.
37. Wang, L., Li, Y.J., Wijesekera, D., and Jajodia, S. (2003a). Precisely answering multi-dimensional range queries without privacy breaches. Technical Report ISE-TR-03-03. Available at http://ise.gmu.edu/tech rep/.
38. Wang, L., Li, Y.J., Wijesekera, D., and Jajodia, S. (2003b). Precisely answering multi-dimensional range queries without privacy breaches. In *Proceedings of the Eighth European Symposium on Research in Computer Security (ESORICS'03)*, pages 100–115.
39. Wang, L., Wijesekera, D., and Jajodia, S. (2004b). Cardinality-based inference control in data cubes. *Journal of Computer Security*, 12(5):655–692.
40. Willenborg, L. and Walal, T. de (1996). *Statistical disclosure control in practice*. Springer Verlag, New York.
41. Yao, C., Wang, X., and Jajodia, S. (2005). Checking for k-anonymity violation by views. In *Proceedings of the Thirty-first Conference on Very Large Data Base (VLDB'05)*.

42. Yu, C.T. and Chin, F.Y. (1977). A study on the protection of statistical data bases. In *Proceedings of the ACM SIGMOD International Conference on Management of Data (SIGMOD'77)*, pages 169–181.
43. Yu, T., Li, N., and Antoń, A. (2004). A formal semantics for P3P. In *Proceedings of the ACM Workshop on Secure Web Services (SWS'04).*

Part V

Security in Emerging Data Services

Search on Encrypted Data

Hakan Hacıgümüş[1], Bijit Hore[2], Bala Iyer[3], and Sharad Mehrotra[4]

[1] IBM Almaden Research Center
hakanh@acm.org
[2] Donald Bren School of Computer Science
University of California, Irvine
bhore@ics.uci.edu
[3] IBM Silicon Valley Lab
balaiyer@us.ibm.com
[4] Donald Bren School of Computer Science
University of California, Irvine
sharad@ics.uci.edu

1 Introduction

The proliferation of a new breed of data management applications that store and process data at remote locations has led to the emergence of search over encrypted data as an important research problem. In a typical setting of the problem, data is stored at the remote location in an encrypted form. A query generated at the client-side is transformed into a representation such that it can be evaluated directly on encrypted data at the remote location. The results might be processed by the client after decryption to determine the final answers.

1.1 Motivation: Database as a Service

The primary interest in search over encrypted data has resulted from the recently proposed *database as a service* (DAS) architecture [7, 10, 12, 26]. DAS architecture is motivated by the *software as a service* initiative of the software industry, also referred to as the application service provider (ASP) model. Today, efficient data processing is a fundamental need not just for academic and business organizations, but also for individuals and end customers. With the advent of new technologies and multimedia devices, the amount of data an average person produces in the form of emails, image and video albums, personal records (e.g., health care, tax documents, financial transactions, etc.) that they need to store and search is rapidly increasing. Effective management of large amounts of diverse types of data requires powerful data management tools. Unfortunately, expecting end-users to develop the ability to install, administer, and manage sophisticated data management systems is both impractical and infeasible. Likewise, in an organizational setting, expecting small or medium size corporations to hire professional staff to manage and run corporation's databases is an expensive and, at times, a cost-prohibitive alternative [12].

The "database as a service" (DAS) model, that offers variety of data management functionalities in the form of a service to clients, is an emerging alternative that overcomes many of the above listed challenges of traditional architectures. A DAS model consists of the following entities:

- **Data Owner**: This is the side that produces data and owns it. It is assumed to have some limited computational resources and storage capabilities but far less than the server.
- **Server**: The remote service provider, or the server stores and manages the data generated by data owners. The service provider supports powerful and intuitive interfaces for data owners/users to create, store, access and manipulate databases. The task of administering the database (e.g., installation, backups, reorganization, migration, software updates, etc.) is entirely taken over by the service provider.
- **Data Clients**: A data client could either be the same as the data owner or if the owner is an organization, it could be its employees and/or its clients (e.g., a bank is the data owner and individuals having accounts with the bank are the data clients). The data clients can only access data according to the access control policies set by the data owner, e.g., a data manager might access all data, a bank-client may only access his personal account data etc.

The DAS architecture offers numerous advantages including lower cost due to the economy of scale, lower operating costs, etc. and enhanced services (e.g., better reliability and availability, access to better hardware and software systems, improved data sharing etc.). Today, DAS model is available in certain vertical market segments – e.g., email service through Yahoo!, MSN, Google, etc., as well as photo albums through companies such as Shutterfly. With the advantages the model offers and the related commercial activities, it is foreseeable that DAS architecture will permeate numerous other consumer as well as business application domains in the near future.

The key technological challenge in DAS is that of *data confidentiality*. In the DAS model, user data resides on the premises of the service provider. Most corporations (and individuals) view their data as a valuable asset. The service provider needs to provide sufficient security measures to guard the data confidentiality. In designing mechanisms to support confidentiality and privacy of user's databases, a key aspect is that of *trust*, i.e., how much trust is placed on the service provider by the data owner.

If servers could be completely trusted, the features are very similar to that of a normal database management system which would have been deployed within the organization of the data owner had the organization chosen to do so. From the security perspective, the service provider has to enable traditional access-control and other network security measures to prevent unauthorized access and in general prevent malicious outsiders from launching any kind of disruptive attacks. Furthermore, service providers may employ additional security mechanisms to ensure safety even if data is stolen from organizations by storing data on disks in an encrypted form [12, 17].

The nature of data processing starts to change when the level of trust in the service-provider itself begins to decrease from complete to partial to (perhaps) none at all! Such a varying trust scenario necessitates the usage of various security enhancing techniques in the context of DAS. The most popular trust model studied is the *passive adversary* or *curious intruder* model. Here, the server-side is considered truthful, in that model, the server implements various data storage and query processing functionalities correctly. The passive adversary is one or more malicious individual(s) on the server-side who has access to the data, e.g., a database administrator. A passive adversary only tries to learn sensitive information about the data without actively modifying it or disrupting any other kind of services [5].

Almost all the proposed solution approaches in literature employ encryption to protect the customers' data. The data is encrypted in a variety of manner, i.e., at different granularity, using different encryption algorithms etc. Since all customer data is encrypted while stored on the server, the key challenge becomes that of implementing the required data modification/querying functionalities on this encrypted data – the topic of this chapter.

1.2 Overview of Problems Studied in Literature

Techniques to support search over the encrypted data depends upon the nature of data as well as on the nature of search queries. The two data management scenarios that have motivated majority of the research in this area are:

- **Keyword-based search on encrypted text documents**: The most common setting is that of a remote (semi-trusted) email server which stores encrypted emails of users and allows them to search and retrieve their emails using keyword-based queries [6, 7, 21, 22].
- **Query Evaluation on encrypted relational databases**: The setting of this problem is that of a remote (semi-trusted) relational database management system, which stores clients' relational data and allows users to search the database using SQL queries [3, 4, 10–12, 14].

In this chapter, we discuss advances in both of the problem settings. We note that the solutions depend upon the particular instantiation of the DAS model being studied. The general model allows for multiple data owners who outsource their database management functionalities to the service provider. Each such owner might have multiple clients who access various functionalities from these services. In cases where the client is a different entity from the owner, different models of data access may be enforced, for instance a session might require the client to connect via the data owner's site onto the service provider. Alternatively it might be a direct session with the service provider, which does not involve the owner. Other models can be

[5] Almost all the approaches we describe in this chapter address data confidentiality and privacy issues for the passive adversarial model. We will refer to this model interchangeably as the *semi-trusted* model.

seen as the simplifications of this general architecture. Different DAS models pose new issues/challenges in ensuring data confidentiality.

For most of this chapter, as is the case with the current literature, we will make a simplifying assumption that the data owner and client are the same entity. We will discuss some of the challenges that arise in generalizing the model towards the end of the chapter. We begin by first discussing approaches to support text search, which is then followed by techniques to support relational/SQL queries.

2 Keyword search on encrypted text data

In this section we discuss approaches proposed in the literature to support keyword based retrieval of text documents. We begin by first setting up the problem. Let Alice be the data owner who has a collection of text documents $D = \{D_1, \ldots, D_n\}$. A document D_i is modelled a set of keywords $D_i = \{W_1^{D_i}, \ldots, W_{n_i}^{D_i}\}$, each word $w \in \mathcal{W}$, and (W) is the set of all possible keywords. Alice stores her document collection at a service provider. Since the service provider is not trusted, documents are stored encrypted. Each document is encrypted at the word level as follows: Each document is divided up into equal length "Words". Typically each such word corresponds to an English language word where extra padding (with '0' and '1' bits) are added to make all words equal in length. Periodically Alice may pose a query to the server to retrieve a subset of documents. The query itself is a set of keywords and the answer corresponds to the set of documents that contain all the keywords in the query. More formally, the answer to a query q is given by:

$$Ans(q) = \{D_i \in D | \forall k_j \in q, k_j \in D_i\}$$

The goal is to design techniques to retrieve answers while not revealing any information beyond the presence (or absence) of the keywords (of the query) in each document.

A few different variations of the basic keyword-search problem have been studied over the past years [1, 2, 6, 7, 21–23]. The authors in [7, 21] study the basic problem where a private-key based encryption scheme is used to design a matching technique on encrypted data that can search for any word in the document. Authors in [1] provide a safe public-key based scheme to carry out "non-interactive" search on data encrypted using user's public-key for a select set of words. [6] proposes a document indexing approach using bloom filters that allows the owner to carry out keyword searches efficiently but could result in some false-positive retrievals. The work in [2, 22] propose secure schemes for conjunctive keyword search where the search term might contain the conjunction of two or more keywords. The goal here again is to avoid any leakage of information over and above the fact that the retrieved set of documents contain all the words specified in the query.

In this section, we describe a private-key based approach which is motivated by [7] and was amongst the first published solutions to the problem of searching over encrypted text data. The approach described incurs significant overhead, requiring

$O(n)$ cryptographic operations per document where n is the number of words in the document. We briefly discuss how such overhead can be prevented using Bloom filters. The technique we discuss is a simplification of [6] though it captures the essence of the idea.

2.1 Private-Key based Search Scheme on Encrypted Text Data

Consider a data owner Alice who wishes to store a collection of documents with Bob (the service provider). Alice encrypts each document D prior to storing it with Bob. In addition, Alice creates a secure index $I(D)$, which is stored at the service provider that will help her perform keyword search. The secure index is such that it reveals no information about its content to the adversary. However, it allows the adversary to test for presence or absence of keywords using a *trapdoor* associated with the keyword where a trapdoor is generated with a secret key that resides with the owner. A user wishing to search for documents containing word w, generates a trapdoor for w which can then be used by the adversary to retrieve relevant documents. We next describe an approach to constructing secure index and the corresponding algorithm to search the index for keywords.

The secure index is created over the keywords in D as follows. Let document D consist of the sequence of words $w_1, \ldots, w_l$. The index is created by computing the bitwise XOR (denoted by the symbol $\oplus$) of the clear-text with a sequence of pseudo-random bits that Alice generates using a stream cipher. Alice first generates a sequence of pseudo-random values $s_1, \ldots, s_l$ using a stream cipher, where each s_i is $n - m$ bit long. For each pseudo-random sequence s_i, Alice computes a pseudo-random function $F_{k_c}(s_i)$ seeded on key k_c which generates a random m-bit sequence[6]. Using the result of $F_k(s_i)$, Alice computes a n-bit sequence $t_i := < s_i, F_k(s_i) >$, where $< a, b >$ denotes concatenation of the string a and b). Now to encrypt the n-bit word w_i, Alice computes the XOR of w_i with t_i, i.e., ciphertext $c_i := w_i \oplus t_i$. Since, only Alice generates the pseudo-random stream $t_1, \ldots, t_l$ so no one else can decrypt c_i.

Given the above representation of text document, the search mechanism works as follows. When Alice needs to search for files that contain a word w, she transmits w and the key k to the server. The server (Bob) searches for w in the index files associated with documents by checking whether $c_i \oplus w$ is of the form $< s, F_k(s) >$. The server returns to Alice documents that contain the keyword w which can then be decrypted by Alice.

The scheme described above provides secrecy if the pseudo-random function F, the stream cipher used to generate s_i, and the encryption of the document D

[6] **Pseudo-random functions:** A pseudo-random function denoted as $F : K_F \times X \rightarrow Y$, where K_F is the set of keys, X denotes the set $\{0,1\}^n$ and Y denotes the set $\{0,1\}^m$. Intuitively, a pseudo-random function is computationally indistinguishable from a random function - given pairs $(x_i, f(x_1, k)), \ldots, (x_m, f(x_m, k))$, an adversary cannot predict $f(x_{m+1}, k)$ for any x_{m+1}. In other words, F takes a key $k \in K_F$ the set of keys, a n bit sequence $x \in X$ where X is the set $\{0,1\}^n$ and returns a m bit sequence $y \in Y$ where Y is the set $\{0,1\}^m$.

are secure(that is, the value t_i are indistinguishable from truly random bits for any computationally bounded adversary). Essentially, the adversary cannot learn content of the documents simply based on ciphertext representation.

While the approach described above is secure, it has a fundamental limitation that the adversary learns the keyword w_i that the client searches for. The search strategy allows the adversary to learn which documents contain which keywords over time using such query logs. Furthermore, the adversary can launch attacks by searching for words on his own without explicit authorization by the user thereby learning document content.

A simple strategy to prevent server from knowing the exact search word is to pre-encrypt each word w of the clear text separately using a deterministic encryption algorithm E_{k_p}, where the key k_p is a private key which is kept hidden from the adversary. After this pre-encryption phase, the user has a sequence of E-encrypted words $x_1, \ldots, x_l$. Now he post-encrypts that sequence using the stream cipher construction as before to obtain $c_i := x_i \oplus t_i$, where $x_i = E_{k_p}(w_i)$ and $t_i =< s_i, F_{k_c}(x_i) >$. During search, the client, instead of revealing the keyword to be searched, Computes $E_{k_p}(w_i)$ with the server.

The proposed scheme is secure and ensures that the adversary does not learn document content from query logs. The scheme is formalized below.

- $\mathbf{k_p}$: Denotes the private-key of the user. $k_p \in \{0,1\}^s$ which is kept a secret by the user.
- $\mathbf{k_c}$: Denotes a key called the *collection key* of the user. $k_c \in \{0,1\}^s$ and is publicly known
- **Pseudo-Random Function:** $F : \{0,1\}^s \times \{0,1\}^{n-m} \rightarrow \{0,1\}^m$, is a pseudo-random function that takes a $n-m$ bit string, a s-bit key and maps it to a random m-bit string. F is publicly known.
- **Trapdoor function**: Let T denote a *trapdoor* function which takes as input, a private-key k_p and a word w and outputs the trapdoor for the word w, i.e., $T(k_p, w) = E_{k_p}(w)$ where E is a deterministic encryption function. For a given document, we denote the trapdoor for the ith word by t_i.
- $\mathbf{BuildIndex(D, k_p, k_c)}$: This function is used to build the index for document D. It uses a pseudo-random generator G which outputs random string of size s. The pseudo-code of the function is given below.
- $\mathbf{SearchIndex(I_D, T(w))}$: Given the document index and the trapdoor for the word w being searched, the $SearchIndex$ functionality returns the document D if the word w is present in it. The pseudo-code is given below.

2.2 Speeding up search on encrypted data

The approach described above to search over encrypted text has a limitation. Essentially, it requires $O(n)$ comparisons (cryptographic operations) at the server to test if the document contains a given keyword, where n is the number of keywords in the document. While such an overhead might be tolerable for small documents and small document collections, the approach is inherently not scalable. Authors

Algorithm 1 : $BuildIndex$

Input: D, k_p, k_c;
Output: I_D /* The index for the document*/
$I_D = \phi$;
for all $w_i \in D$ **do**
  Generate a pseudo-random string s_i using G;
  Compute trapdoor $T(w_i) = E_{k_p}(w_i)$;
  Compute ciphertext $c_i = T(w_i) \oplus \langle s_i, F_{k_c}(s_i) \rangle$;
  $I_D = I_D \cup c_i$;
end for
Return I_D;

Algorithm 2 : $SearchIndex$

Input: $I_D, T(w)$;
Output: D or ϕ
for all $c_i \in I_D$ **do**
  if $c_i \oplus T(w)$ is of the form $\langle s, F_{k_c}(s) \rangle$ **then**
    Return D;
  end if
end for
Return ϕ;

in [6] overcome this limitation by exploiting *bloom filters* for indexing documents. A Bloom filter for a text document is described as follows.

Bloom Filters: A Bloom filter for a document $D = \{w_1, \ldots, w_n\}$ of n words is a m-bit array constructed as follows. All array bits are initially set to 0. The filter uses r independent hash functions $h_1, \ldots, h_r$, where h_i: $\{0,1\}^* \to [1, m]$ for $i \in [1, r]$. For each word $w \in D$, the array bits at the positions $h_1(w), \ldots, h_r(w)$ are set to 1. A location can be set to 1 multiple times. To determine if a word a belongs is contained in the document D, we check the bits at positions $h_1(a), \ldots, h_r(a)$. If all checked bits are 1's, then a is considered contained in the document D. There is however, some probability of a false positive.

A simple Bloom filter can reveal information about the contents of the document since the hash functions are publicly known. A straightforward strategy to create secure index using Bloom filter is to instead index each word w by its encrypted representation $E_{k_p}(w)$. Thus, the Bloom filter will be constructed using the hash values $h_j(E_{k_p}(w))$, $j = 1, \ldots, r$ instead of applying the hash functions on w directly. This strategy has a vulnerability though, the "footprint" of a word (i.e., the bit-positions in the Bloom filter that are set to '1' corresponding to w) is same for all documents containing the word w. This makes the scheme vulnerable to frequency-based attacks. One remedy is to use the document-id while encoding the keywords. For instance, one can compute the hash functions for the Bloom filter as follows:

$h_j(E_{k_c}(\langle id(D), E_{k_p}(w)\rangle))$, $j = 1 \ldots r$ and set the corresponding bits to 1 in the Bloom filter[7]. This way representation of the same word is different across different documents. As a result, unless a trapdoor is provided, the adversary cannot determine if the same word appears across different documents. The pseudo-code for the $BuildIndex_{BF}$ function is given below.

Algorithm 3 : $BuildIndex_{BF}$

Input: $D, k_p, k_c, h_1, \ldots, h_r$
Output: BF_D /* The index for the document*/

$BF_D = \phi$;
for all $w_i \in D$ **do**
    Compute trapdoor $T(w_i) = E_{k_p}(w_i)$;
    Compute string $x_i = E_{k_c}(\langle id(D), T(w_i)\rangle)$
    for $j = 1$ to r **do**
        compute bit-position $b_j = h_j(x_i)$;
        set $BF_D[b_j] = 1$;
    end for
end for
Return BF_D;

In the current scheme, the search needs to be performed in a slightly different manner. If the user wants to search for a word w, he gives the trapdoor $T(w) = E_{k_p}(w)$ to the server. The server executes the function $SearchIndex_{BF}$ (given below) on each document D in the collection and returns the appropriate ones.

Algorithm 4 : $SearchIndex_{BF}$

Input: $BF_D, T(w), k_c, h_1, \ldots, h_r$
Output: D or ϕ

Compute $x = E_{k_c}(\langle id(D), T(w)\rangle)$;
for j=1 to r **do**
    if $BF_D[h_j(x)] \neq 1$ **then**
        Return ϕ;
    end if
end for
Return D;

Above, we sketched an approach on how Bloom filters can be used to do secure indices. The technique of using two levels of security (document-id based encryption) to prevent frequency based attacks is similar to what is proposed in [6]. The au-

[7] The extra level of encryption with k_c is not strictly required if the hash functions h_i's are appropriately chosen to be one-way functions with collision resistance

thor in [6] develops a complete strategy for constructing secure indices using Bloom filters and presents a detailed security analysis.

2.3 Secure Keyword Search using Public-Key Encryption

We now consider a variation to the basic encrypted text search problem where the producer (owner) of the data and the data consumer (client) are different. To motivate the problem, consider an (untrusted) email gateway that stores incoming emails from multiple users. If emails are sensitive they will need to be encrypted. So if Bob needs to send a sensitive email to Alice, he will have to encrypt it using Alice's public key. Now Alice may wish to have the capability to search for such emails using keywords. Alice (or Alice's mail client) could, of course, download such email, decrypt it, create a secure index using a secret key (as in the previous section) and store the index along with the original encrypted email at the gateway. Such a secure index, if integrated appropriately with the email server could provide Alice with the requisite functionality. A more natural approach would be to instead exploit a public-key encryption technique that directly supports keyword search over encrypted representation. Such a public-key system is developed in [1] in the limited context where Alice pre-specifies the set of keywords she might be interested in searching the mail based on. Using the scheme developed in [1], the mail sender (Bob) can send an email to Alice encrypted using her public key. Alice can give the gateway a limited capability to detect some keywords in her emails (encrypted using her public key) and have these mails routed in a different manner, e.g. an email with keyword "lunch" should be routed to her desktop and one with "urgent" should be routed to her pager etc. The scheme prevents the gateway from learning anything beyond the fact that a certain keyword (for which it has the "capability" to test) is present in the set of keywords associated with the mail.

The approach works by requiring the sender of the mail, Bob, to append to the ciphertext (email encrypted using Alice's public key) additional codewords referred to as *Public-key Encryption with Keyword Search* (PEKS), one for each keyword. To send a message M with keywords $W_1, \ldots, W_m$ Bob sends

$$E_{A_{pub}}(M)||PEKS(A_{pub}, W_1)||\ldots||PEKS(A_{pub}, W_m)$$

where A_{pub} is Alice's public key. This allows Alice to give the gateway a certain trapdoor T_W that enables the gateway to test whether one of the keywords associated with the message is equal to the word W of Alice's choice. Given $PEKS(A_{pub}, W')$ and T_W the gateway can test whether $W = W'$. If $W \neq W'$ the gateway learns nothing more about W'.

We next describe the main construction of the approach in [1] which is based on using bilinear maps.

Bilinear maps: Let G_1 and G_2 be two groups of order p for some large prime p. A bilinear map $e : G_1 \times G_1 \rightarrow G_2$ satisfies the following properties:

1. *Computable:* given $g, h \in G_1$ there is a polynomial time algorithm to compute $e(g, h) \in G_2$.

2. *Bilinear:* We say that a map $e : G_1 \times G_1 \rightarrow G_2$ is bilinear if for any integers $s, y \in [1, p]$ we have $e(g^x, g^y) = e(g, g)^{xy}$.
3. *Non-degenerate:* The map does not send all pairs of $G_1 \times G_1$ to the identity in G_2. Since G_1, G_2 are groups of prime order this implies that if g is a generator of G_1 then $e(g, g)$ is a generator of G_2.

[1] builds a searchable encryption scheme using bilinear maps as described below.

- $KeyGen$: The input security parameter, s, determines the size, p of the groups G_1 and G_2. The algorithm picks a random $\alpha \in \mathbb{Z}_p^*$ and a generator g of G_1. It outputs the public/private key pair $A_{pub} = [g, h = g^\alpha]$ and $A_{priv} = \alpha$.
- $PEKS(A_{pub}, W)$: for a public key A_{pub} and a word W, produce a searchable encryption of W. First compute $t = e(H_1(W), h^r) \in G_2$ for a random $r \in \mathbb{Z}_p^*$. Output $PEKS(A_{pub}, W) = [g^r, H_2(t)]$, where $H_1 : \{0,1\}^* \rightarrow G_1$ and $H_2 : G_2 \rightarrow \{0,1\}^{log\ p}$.
- $Trapdoor(A_{priv}, W)$: given a private key and a word W, produce a trapdoor T_W as $T_W = H_1(W)^\alpha \in G_1$.
- $Test(A_{pub}, S, T_W)$: given Alice's public key, a searchable encryption $S = PEKS(A_{pub}, W')$, and a trapdoor $T_W = Trapdoor(A_{priv}, W)$, outputs 'yes' if $W = W'$ and 'no' otherwise. The test is performed as follows: let $S = [C, D]$. Check if $H_2(e(T_W, C)) = D$. If so, output 'yes'; if not, output 'no'.

To illustrate how the $PEKS$ based matching takes place, we can see that for a keyword W in an email sent by Bob to Alice, Bob would create a corresponding codeword $PEKS(A_{pub}, W)$ as follows and attach it to his mail.

$$PEKS(A_{pub}, W) = [g^r, H_2(e(H_1(W), h^r))] = S = [C, D]$$

Now, if Alice wanted to search for the same word W in mails, she would produce the trapdoor $T_W = H_1(W)^\alpha \in G_1$ and give it to the mail server to do encrypted matching. Now we have $C = g^r$ and $D = H_2(e(H_1(W), h^r))$. Using the properties of bilinear maps, and the fact that $h = g^\alpha$, we have $D = H_2(e(H_1(W), g)^{r\alpha})$. In the $Test$ function, the server would compute the following:

$$H_2(e(T_W, C)) = H_2(e(H_1(W)^\alpha, g^r)) = H_2(e(H_1(W), g)^{r\alpha}) = D$$

which results in a match if the the trapdoor and $PEKS$ both correspond to the same word W.

The above scheme allows the email gateway to determine if emails encrypted using Alice's public key contain one of the keywords of interest to Alice without revealing to the gateway any information about the word W unless T_W is available. The scheme provides security against an active attacker who is able to distinguish an encryption of a keyword W_0 from an encryption of a keyword W_1 for which he did not obtain the trapdoor (referred to as *adaptive chosen keyword attack*).

2.4 Other Research

Another variation to the basic keyword search on encrypted data that has recently been studied, is that of "conjunctive keyword search" [2,22]. Most keyword searches contain more than one keyword in general. The straight forward way to support such queries is to carry out the search using single keywords and then return the intersection of the retrieved documents as the result set. The authors in [2,22] claim that such a methodology reveals more information than there is a need for and might make the documents more vulnerable to statistical attacks. They develop special cryptographic protocols that return a document if and only if all the search words are present in it.

There are some shortcomings of all the above cryptographic methods described for keyword search on encrypted data. Once a capability is given to the untrusted server (or once a search for a certain word has been carried out), that capability can be continued to be used forever by the server to check if these words are present in newly arriving (generated) mails (documents) even though the owner might not want to give the server this capability. This can, in turn, make the schemes vulnerable to a variety of statistical attacks.

3 Search over Encrypted Relational Data

In this section, we describe techniques developed in the literature to support queries over encrypted relational data. As in the previous section, we begin by first setting the problem. Consider a user Alice who outsources the database consisting of the following two relations:

```
EMP (eid, ename, salary, addr, did)
DEPARTMENT (did, dname, mgr)
```

The fields in the *EMP* table refer to the employee id, name of the employee, salary, address and the id of the department the employee works for. The fields in the *DEPARTMENT* table correspond to the department id, department name, and name of the manager of the department. In the DAS model, the above tables will be stored at the service provider. Since the service provider is untrusted, the relations must be stored in an encrypted form. Relational data could be encrypted at different granularity – e.g., at the table level, the row level, or the attribute level. As will become clear, the choice of granularity of encryption has significant repercussions on the scheme used to support search and on the system performance. Unless specified otherwise, we will assume that data is encrypted at the row level; that is, each row of each table is encrypted as a single unit. Thus, an encrypted relational representation consists of a set of encrypted records.

The client[8] may wish to execute SQL queries over the database. For instance, Alice may wish to pose following query to evaluate "total salary for employees who work for Bob". Such a query is expressed in SQL as follows:

[8] Alice in this case since we have assumed that the client and the owner is the same entity.

```
SELECT  SUM(E.salary) FROM EMP as E, DEPARTMENT as D
WHERE E.did = D.did AND D.mgr = "Bob"
```

An approach Alice could use to evaluate such a query might be to request the server for the encrypted form of the *EMP* and *DEPARTMENT* tables. The client could then decrypt the tables and execute the query. Such an approach, however, would defeat the purpose of database outsourcing, reducing it to essentially a remote secure storage. Instead, the goal in DAS is to process the queries directly at the server without the need to decrypt the data. Before we discuss techniques proposed in the literature to process relational queries over encrypted data, we note that processing such queries requires mechanisms to support the following basic operators over encrypted data:

- **Comparison operators** such as $=, \neq, <, \leq, =, \geq, >$ These operators may compare attribute values of a given record with constants (e.g., *DEPARTMENT.sal* $>$ 45000 as in selection queries) or with other attributes (e.g., *EMP.did* = *DEPARTMENT.did* as in join conditions).
- **Arithmetic operators** such as addition, multiplication, division that perform simple arithmetic operations on attribute values associated with a set of records in one or more relations. Such operators are part of any SQL query that involves aggregation.

The example query given above illustrates usage of both classes of operators. For instance, to execute the query, the *mgr* field of each record in the *DEPARTMENT* table has to be compared with "Bob". Furthermore, records in the *DEPARTMENT* table whose *mgr* is "Bob" have to be matched with records in *EMP* table based on the *did* attribute. Finally, the *salary* fields of the corresponding record that match the query conditions have to be added to result in the final answer.

The first challenge in supporting SQL queries over encrypted relational representation is to develop mechanisms to support comparison and arithmetic operations on encrypted data. The techniques developed in the literature can be classified into the following two categories.

Approaches based on new encryption techniques: that can support either arithmetic and/or comparison operators directly on encrypted representation. Encryption techniques that support limited computation without decryption have been explored in cryptographic literature in the past. Amongst the first such technique is the *privacy homomorphism* (PH) developed in [24, 32] that supports basic arithmetic operations. While PH can be exploited to support aggregation queries at the remote server (see [25] for details), it does not Support comparison and, as such, cannot be used as basis for designing techniques for relational query processing over encrypted data. In [19], the authors developed a data transformation technique that preserves the order in the original data. Such a transformation serves as an *order-preserving* encryption and can hence support comparison operators. Techniques to implement relational operators such as selection, joins, sorting, grouping can be built on top of the order preserving encryption. The encryption mechanism, however, cannot support aggregation at the server. While new cryptographic approaches are interesting, one of the limitation of such approaches has been that they safe only under limited situations where the adversary's knowledge is limited to the ciphertext representation of data. These techniques have either been shown to break under more general attacks (e.g., PH is not secure under chosen plaintext attack [33, 34]), or the security analysis under diverse types of attacks has not been performed.

Information-hiding based Approaches: Unlike encryption-based approaches, such techniques store additional auxiliary information along with encrypted data to facilitate evaluation of comparison and/or arithmetic operations at the server. Such auxiliary information, stored in the form of indices (which we refer to as *secure indices*) may reveal partial information about the data to the server. Secure indices are designed carefully exploiting information hiding mechanisms (developed in the context of statistical disclosure control) [29–31] to limit the amount of information disclosure.The basic techniques used for disclosure control are the following [30,31]:

1. **Perturbation:** For a numeric attribute of a record, add a random value (chosen from some distribution, like normal with mean 0 and standard deviation σ) to the true value.
2. **Generalization:** Replace a numeric or categorical value by a more general value. For numeric values, it could be a range of that covers the original value and for categorical data, this may be a more generic class, e.g., an ancestor node in a taxonomy tree.
3. **Swapping:** Take two different records in the data set and swap the values of a specific attribute (say, the salary value is swapped between the records corresponding to two individuals).

Of all the disclosure-control methods, the one that has been primarily utilized to realize DAS functionalities is that of generalization. Though this is not to say that DAS functionalities cannot be built using other techniques, e.g., hiding data values by noise-addition and developing techniques for querying on the perturbed data. However, we are not aware of any complete proposal based on such a mechanism.

The nature of disclosure in information hiding based schemes is different from that in cryptographic schemes. In the latter, the disclosure risk is inversely proportional to the difficulty of breaking the encryption scheme and if broken, it means there is complete disclosure of the plaintext values. In contrast, the information disclosure in information hiding approaches could be partial or probabilistic in nature. That is, there could be a non-negligible probability of disclosure of a sensitive value given the transformed data, e.g., the bucket identity might give a clue regarding the actual value of the sensitive attribute.

In this section, we will primarily concentrate on the information hiding based approach and show how it has been utilized to support SQL queries. As will be clear, information hiding approaches can be used to support comparison operators on the server and can hence be the basis for implementing SPJ (select-project-join) queries. They can also support sorting and grouping operators. Such techniques, however, cannot support aggregation at the server. A few papers [25, 39] have combined an information hiding approach with PH to support both server-side aggregation as well as SPJ queries. Of course, with PH being used for aggregation, these techniques

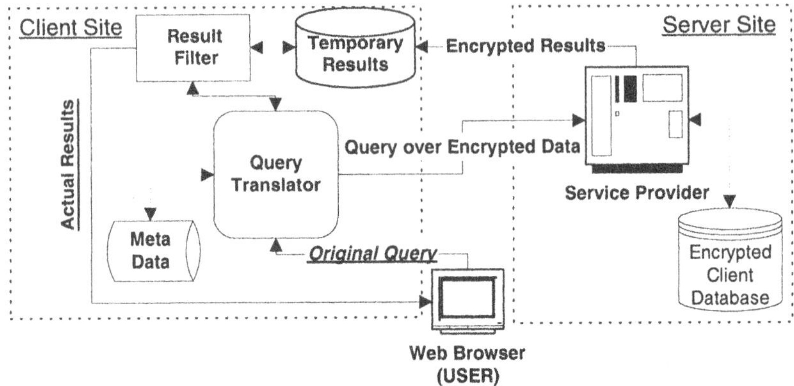

Fig. 1. Query Processing in DAS

become vulnerable to diverse types of attacks. In the remainder of the section, we will concentrate on how information hiding techniques are used to support SPJ queries. We will use the query processing architecture proposed in [12, 26] to explain the approach.

Query Processing Architecture for DAS [26]

Figure 1 illustrates the control flow for queries in DAS where information hiding technique is used to represent data at the server. The figure illustrates the three primary entities of the DAS model: *user*, *client* and *server*. As stated earlier, we will not distinguish between the user and the client and will refer to them together as the *client-side*. The client stores the data at the server which is hosted by the service provider and this is known as the *server-side*. The data is stored in an encrypted format at the server-side at all times for security purposes. The encrypted database is augmented with additional information (which we call the secure index) that allows certain amount of query processing to occur at the server without jeopardizing data privacy. The client also maintains *metadata* for translating user queries to the appropriate representation on the server, and performs post-processing on server-query results. Based on the auxiliary information stored, the original query over un-encrypted relations are broken into (1) a server-query over encrypted relations which run on the server, and (2) a client-query which runs on the client and post-processes the results returned after executing the server-query. We achieve this goal by developing an algebraic framework for query rewriting over encrypted representation.

3.1 Relational Encryption and Storage Model

For each relation

$$R(A_1, A_2, \ldots, A_n)$$

one stores on the server an encrypted relation:

$$R^S(etuple, A_1^S, A_2^S, \ldots, A_n^S)$$

where the attribute *etuple* (*etuple* is defined shortly) stores an encrypted string that corresponds to a tuple in relation R[9]. Each attribute A_i^S corresponds to the index for the attribute A_i and is used for query processing at the server. For example, consider a relation *emp* below that stores information about employees.

eid	ename	salary	addr	did
23	Tom	70K	Maple	40
860	Mary	60K	Main	80
320	John	50K	River	50
875	Jerry	55K	Hopewell	110

The *emp* table is mapped to a corresponding table at the server:

$$emp^S(etuple, eid^S, ename^S, salary^S, addr^S, did^S)$$

It is only necessary to create an index for attributes involved in search and join predicates. In the above example, if one knows that there would be no query that involves attribute *addr* in either a selection or a join, then the index on this attribute need not be created. Without loss of generality, one can assume that an index is created over each attribute of the relation.

Partition Functions: To explain what is stored in attribute A_i^S of R^S for each attribute A_i of R the following notations are useful. The domain of values ($\mathcal{D}_i$) of attribute $R.A_i$ are first mapped into partitions $\{p_1, \ldots, p_k\}$, such that (1) these partitions taken together cover the whole domain; and (2) any two partitions do not overlap. The function *partition* is defined as follows:

$$partition(R.A_i) = \{p_1, p_2, \ldots, p_k\}$$

As an example, consider the attribute *eid* of the *emp* table above. Suppose the values of domain of this attribute lie in the range $[0, 1000]$. Assume that the whole range is divided into 5 partitions

: $[0, 200]$, $(200, 400]$, $(400, 600]$, $(600, 800]$, and $(800, 1000]$. That is:

$$partition(emp.eid) = \{[0, 200], (200, 400], (400, 600], (600, 800], (800, 1000]\}$$

Different attributes may be partitioned using different partition functions. The partition of attribute A_i corresponds to a splitting of its domain into a set of buckets. The strategy used to split the domain into a set of buckets has profound implications

9 Note that one could alternatively choose to encrypt at the attribute level instead of the row-level. Each alternative has its own pros and cons and for greater detail, the interested reader is referred to [10].

on both the efficiency of the resulting query processing as well as on the disclosure risk of sensitive information to the server. For now, to explain the query processing strategy, we will make a simplifying assumption that the bucketization of the domain is based on the equi-width[10] partitioning (though the strategy developed will work for any partitioning of domain). We will revisit the efficiency and disclosure risks in the following subsections.

In the above example, an equi-width histogram was illustrated. Note that when the domain of an attribute corresponds to a field over which ordering is well defined (e.g., the *eid* attribute), we will assume that a partition p_i is a continuous range. We use $p_i.low$ and $p_i.high$ to denote the lower and upper boundary of the partition, respectively.

Identification Functions: An identification function called $ident$ assigns an identifier $ident_{R.A_i}(p_j)$ to each partition p_j of attribute A_i. Figure 2 shows the identifiers assigned to the 5 partitions of the attribute *emp.eid.* For instance, $ident_{emp.eid}([0, 200]) = 2$, and $ident_{emp.eid}((800, 1000]) = 4$.

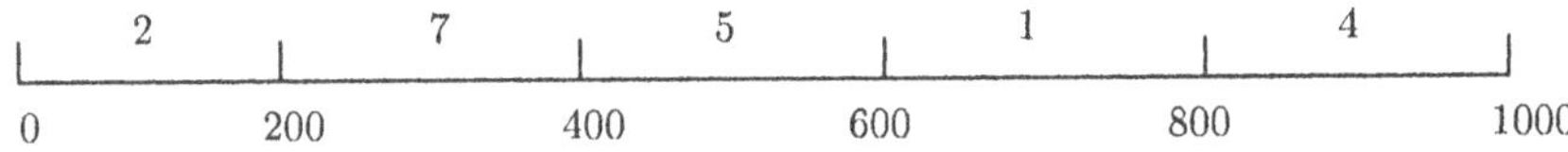

Fig. 2. Partition and identification functions of *emp.eid*

The $ident$ function value for a partition is unique, that is, $ident_{R.A_i}(p_j) \neq ident_{R.A_i}(p_l)$, if $j \neq l$. For this purpose, a collision-free hash function that utilizes properties of the partition may be used as an $ident$ function. For example, in the case where a partition corresponds to a numeric range, the hash function may use the start and/or end values of a range.

Mapping Functions: Given the above partition and identification functions, a mapping function $Map_{R.A_i}$ maps a value v in the domain of attribute A_i to the identifier of the partition to which v belongs: $Map_{R.A_i}(v) = ident_{R.A_i}(p_j)$, where p_j is the partition that contains v.

For the example given above, the following table shows some values of the mapping function for attribute *emp.eid.* For instance, $Map_{emp.eid}(23) = 2$, $Map_{emp.eid}(860) = 4$, and $Map_{emp.eid}(875) = 4$.

eid value v	23	860	320	875
$Map_{emp.eid}(v)$	2	4	7	4

Three generic mapping functions are illustrated below. Let S be a subset of values in the domain of attribute A_i, and v be a value in the domain. We define the following mapping functions on the partitions associated with A_i:

$$Map_{R.A_i}(S) = \{ident_{R.A_i}(p_j) | p_j \cap S \neq \emptyset\}$$

[10] where the domain of each bucket has the same width

$$Map^{\geqslant}_{R.A_i}(v) = \{ident_{R.A_i}(p_j) | p_j.high \geqslant v\}$$
$$Map^{\leqslant}_{R.A_i}(v) = \{ident_{R.A_i}(p_j) | p_j.low \leqslant v\}$$

While the first function defined holds over any attribute, the latter two hold for the attributes whose domain values exhibit total order. Application of the mapping function to a value v, greater than the maximum value in the domain, v_{max}, returns $Map_{R.A_i}(v_{max})$. Similarly, application of the mapping function to a value v, less than the minimum value in the domain, v_{mim}, returns $Map_{R.A_i}(v_{min})$. Essentially, $Map_{R.A_i}(S)$ is the set of identifiers of partitions whose ranges may overlap with the values in S. The result of $Map^{\geqslant}_{R.A_i}(v)$ is the set of identifiers corresponding to partitions whose ranges may contain a value not less than v. Likewise, $Map^{\leqslant}_{R.A_i}(v)$ is the set of identifiers corresponding to partitions whose ranges may contain a value not greater than v.

Storing Encrypted Data: For each tuple $t = \langle a_1, a_2, \ldots, a_n \rangle$ in R, the relation R^S stores a tuple:

$$\langle encrypt(\{a_1, a_2, \ldots, a_n\}), Map_{R.A_1}(a_1), Map_{R.A_2}(a_2), \ldots, Map_{R.A_n}(a_n) \rangle$$

where *encrypt* is the function used to encrypt a tuple of the relation. For instance, the following is the encrypted relation emp^S stored on the server:

etuple	eid^S	$ename^S$	$salary^S$	$addr^S$	did^S
1100110011110010...	2	19	81	18	2
1000000000011101...	4	31	59	41	4
1111101000010001...	7	7	7	22	2
1010101010111110...	4	71	49	22	4

The first column *etuple* contains the string corresponding to the encrypted tuples in *emp*. For instance, the first tuple is encrypted to "1100110011110010..." that is equal to $encrypt(23, Tom, 70K, Maple, 40)$. The second is encrypted to "1000000000011101..." equal to $encrypt(860,$
$Mary, 60K, Main, 80)$. The encryption function is treated as a black box and any block cipher technique such as AES, Blowfish, DES etc., can be used to encrypt the tuples. The second column corresponds to the index on the employee ids. For example, value for attribute *eid* in the first tuple is 23, and its corresponding partition is $[0, 200]$. Since this partition is identified to 2, we store the value "2" as the identifier of the *eid* for this tuple. Similarly, we store the identifier "4" for the second employee id 860. In the table above, we use different mapping functions for different attributes. The mapping functions for the *ename*, *salary*, *addr*, and *did* attributes are not shown, but they are assumed to generate the identifiers listed in the table.

In general the notation "E" ("Encrypt") is used to map a relation R to its encrypted representation. That is, given relation $R(A_1, A_2, \ldots, A_n)$, relation $E(R)$ is $R^S(etuple, A_1^S, A_2^S, \ldots, A_n^S)$. In the above example, $E(emp)$ is the table emp^S.

Decryption Functions: Given the operator E that maps a relation to its encrypted representation, its inverse operator D maps the encrypted representation to its corresponding decrypted representation. That is, $D(R^S) = R$. In the example above, $D(emp^S) = emp$. The D operator may also be applied on query expressions. A query expression consists of multiple tables related by arbitrary relational operators (e.g., joins, selections, etc).

As it will be clear later, the general schema of an encrypted relation or the result of relational operators amongst encrypted relations, R_i^S is:

$$\langle R_1^S.etuple, R_2^S.etuple, \ldots, R_1^S.A_1^S, R_1^S.A_2^S, \ldots, R_2^S.A_1^S, R_2^S.A_2^S, \ldots\rangle$$

When the decryption operator D is applied to R_i^S, it strips off the index values $(R_1^S.A_1^S,\ R_1^S.A_2^S, \ldots, R_2^S.A_1^S, R_2^S.A_2^S, \ldots)$ and decrypts $(R_1^S.etuple,$ $R_2^S.etuple, \ldots)$ to their un-encrypted attribute values.

As an example, assume that another table defined as mgr $(mid,\ did)$ was also stored in the database. The corresponding encrypted representation $E(mgr)$ will be a table mgr^S $(etuple,\ mid^S,\ did^S)$. Suppose we were to compute a join between tables emp^S and mgr^S on their did^S attributes. The resulting relation $temp^S$ will contain the attributes $\langle emp^S.etuple,\ eid^S,\ ename^S,\ salary^S,\ addr^S,\ emp^S.\,did^S,$ $mgr^S.etuple,\ mid^S,\ mgr^S.did^S\rangle$. If we were to decrypt the $temp^S$ relation using the D operator to compute $D(temp^S)$, the corresponding table will contain the attributes

$$\langle eid, ename, salary, addr, emp.did, mid, mgr.did\rangle$$

That is, $D(temp^S)$ will decrypt *all* of the encrypted columns in $temp^S$ and drop the auxiliary columns corresponding to the indices.

Mapping Conditions

To translate specific query conditions in operations (such as selections and joins) to corresponding conditions over the server-side representation, a translation function called Map_{cond} is used. These conditions help translate relational operators for server-side implementation, and how query trees are translated.

For each relation, the server-side stores the encrypted tuples, along with the attribute indices determined by their mapping functions. The client stores the meta data about the specific indices, such as the information about the partitioning of attributes, the mapping functions, etc. The client utilizes this information to translate a given query Q to its server-side representation Q^S, which is then executed by the server. The query conditions are characterized by the following grammar rules:

- Condition ← Attribute *op* Value;
- Condition ← Attribute *op* Attribute;
- Condition ← (Condition ∨ Condition) | (Condition ∧ Condition);.

Allowed operations for *op* include $\{=, <, >, \leqslant, \geqslant\}$. Now consider the following tables to illustrate the translation.

```
emp(eid, ename, salary, addr, did, pid)
mgr(mid, did, mname)
proj(pid, pname, did, budget)
```

Attribute = Value: Such a condition arises in selection operations. The mapping is defined as follows:

$$Map_{cond}(A_i = v) \equiv A_i^S = Map_{A_i}(v)$$

As defined above, function Map_{A_i} maps v to the identifier of A_i's partition that contains the value v. For instance, consider the *emp* table above, we have:

$$Map_{cond}(eid = 860) \equiv eid^S = 4$$

since $eid = 860$ is mapped to 4 by the mapping function of this attribute.

Attribute < Value: Such a condition arises in selection operations. The attribute must have a well-defined ordering over which the "<" operator is defined. The translation is a little complex. One needs to check if the attribute value representation A_i^S lies in any of the partitions that may contain a value v' where $v' < v$. Formally, the translation is:

$$Map_{cond}(A_i < v) \equiv A_i^S \in Map_{A_i}^{<}(v)$$

For instance, the following condition is translated:

$$Map_{cond}(eid < 280) \equiv eid^S \in \{2, 7\}$$

since all employee ids less than 280 have two partitions $[0, 200]$ and $(200, 400]$, whose identifiers are $\{2, 7\}$.

Attribute > Value: This condition is symmetric with the previous one. The translation is as follows:

$$Map_{cond}(A_i > v) \equiv A_i^S \in Map_{A_i}^{>}(v)$$

For instance, the following condition is translated:

$$Map_{cond}(eid > 650) \equiv eid^S \in \{1, 4\}$$

since all employee ids greater than 650 are mapped to identifiers: $\{1, 4\}$.

Attribute1 = Attribute2: Such a condition might arise in a join. The two attributes can be from two different tables, or from two instances of the same table. The condition can also arise in a selection, and the two attributes can be from the same table. The following is the translation:

$$Map_{cond}(A_i = A_j) \equiv \bigvee_{\varphi} (A_i^S = ident_{A_i}(p_k) \wedge A_j^S = ident_{A_j}(p_l))$$

where φ is $p_k \in partition(A_i), p_l \in partition(A_j), p_k \cap p_l \neq \emptyset$. That is, one needs to consider all possible pairs of partitions of A_i and A_j that overlap. For each pair (p_k, p_l), one needs a condition on the identifiers of the two partitions: $A_i^S = ident_{A_i}(p_k) \wedge A_j^S = ident_{A_j}(p_l)$. Finally the disjunction of these conditions need to be taken. The intuition is that each pair of partitions may provide some values of A_i and A_j that can satisfy the condition $A_i = A_j$.

For instance, the table below shows the partition and identification functions of two attributes $emp.did$ and $mgr.did$.

Partitions	$Ident_{emp.did}$	Partitions	$Ident_{mgr.did}$
[0,100]	2	[0,200]	9
(100,200]	4	(200,400]	8
(200,300]	3		
(300,400]	1		

Then condition $emp.did = mgr.did$ is translated to the following condition C_1:

$$\begin{aligned} C_1: \quad & (emp^S.did^S = 2 \wedge mgr^S.did^S = 9) \\ \vee\ & (emp^S.did^S = 4 \wedge mgr^S.did^S = 9) \\ \vee\ & (emp^S.did^S = 3 \wedge mgr^S.did^S = 8) \\ \vee\ & (emp^S.did^S = 1 \wedge mgr^S.did^S = 8). \end{aligned}$$

Attribute1 < Attribute2: Again such a condition might arise in either a join or in a selection. Let the condition be $A_i < A_j$, then the translation is the following:

$$Map_{cond}(A_i < A_j) \equiv \bigvee_{\varphi} (A_i^S = ident_{A_i}(p_k) \wedge A_j^S = ident_{A_j}(p_l))$$

where φ is $p_k \in partition(A_i), p_l \in partition(A_j), p_l.high \geqslant p_k.low$. One needs to consider all pairs of partitions of A_i and A_j that could satisfy the condition. For each pair, there is a condition corresponding to the pair of their identifiers and one needs to take the disjunction of all these conditions.

For example, condition $C_2 : emp.did < mgr.did$ is translated to:

$$\begin{aligned} C_2: \quad & (emp^S.did^S = 2 \wedge mgr^S.did^S = 9) \\ \vee\ & (emp^S.did^S = 2 \wedge mgr^S.did^S = 8) \\ \vee\ & (emp^S.did^S = 4 \wedge mgr^S.did^S = 9) \\ \vee\ & (emp^S.did^S = 4 \wedge mgr^S.did^S = 8) \\ \vee\ & (emp^S.did^S = 3 \wedge mgr^S.did^S = 8) \\ \vee\ & (emp^S.did^S = 1 \wedge mgr^S.did^S = 8). \end{aligned}$$

Condition $emp^S.did^S = 4 \wedge mgr^S.did^S = 9$ is included, since partition $(100, 200]$ for attribute $emp.did$ and partition $(200, 400]$ for attribute $mgr.did$ can provide pairs of values that satisfy $emp.did < mgr.did$.

For condition $Attribute1 > Attribute2$, the Map_{cond} mapping is same as the mapping of $Attribute2 < Attribute1$, as described above with the roles of the attributes reversed.

Condition1 ∨ Condition2, Condition1 ∧ Condition2: The translation of the two composite conditions is given as follows:

$Map_{cond}(Condition1 \vee Condition2) \equiv$
$Map_{cond}(Condition1) \vee Map_{cond}(Condition2)$
$Map_{cond}(Condition1 \wedge Condition2) \equiv$
$Map_{cond}(Condition1) \wedge Map_{cond}(Condition2)$

Operator $\leqslant$ follows the same mapping as $<$ and operator $\geqslant$ follows the same mapping as $>$.

Translating Relational Operators

In this section we describe how relational operators are implemented in [26]. We illustrate the implementation of the selection and join operators in the proposed architecture. The strategy is to partition the computation of the operators across the client and the server such that a superset of answers is generated by the operator using the attribute indices stored at the server. This set is then filtered at the client after decryption to generate the true results. The goal is to minimize the work done at the client as much as possible. We use R and T to denote two relations, and use the operator notations in [8].

The Selection Operator (σ): Consider a selection operation $\sigma_C(R)$ on a relation R, where C is a condition specified on one or more of the attributes $A_1, A_2, \ldots, A_n$ of R. A straightforward implementation of such an operator is to transmit the relation R^S from the server to the client. Then the client decrypts the result using the D operator, and implements the selection. This strategy, however, pushes the entire work of implementing the selection to the client. In addition, the entire encrypted relation needs to be transmitted from the server to the client. An alternative mechanism is to partially compute the selection operator at the server using the indices associated with the attributes in C, and push the results to the client. The client decrypts the results and filters out tuples that do not satisfy C. Specifically, the operator can be rewritten as follows:

$$\sigma_C(R) = \sigma_C\Big(D(\sigma^S_{Map_{cond}(C)}(R^S))\Big)$$

Note that the σ operator that executes at the server with a superscript "S" to highlight the fact that the select operator executes at the server. All non-adorned operators execute at the client. The decryption operator D will only keep the attribute $etuple$ of R^S, and drop all the other A_i^S attributes. We explain the above implementation using an example $\sigma_{eid<395 \wedge did=140}(emp)$. Based on the definition of $Map_{cond}(C)$ discussed in the previous section, the above selection operation will be translated into

$$\sigma_C\Big(D(\sigma^S_{C'}(emp^S))\Big)$$

where the condition C' on the server is:

$$C' = Map_{cond}(C) = \big(eid^S \in [2,7] \wedge did^S = 4\big)$$

The Join Operator ($\bowtie$): Consider a join operation $R \underset{C}{\bowtie} S$. The join condition C could be either an equality condition (in which case the join corresponds to an equi-join), or could be a more general condition (resulting in theta-joins). The above join operation can be implemented as follows:

$$R \underset{C}{\bowtie} T = \sigma_C\Big(D\big(R^S \underset{Map_{cond}(C)}{\bowtie^S} T^S\big)\Big)$$

As before, the S adornment on the join operator denotes the fact that the join is to be executed at the server. For instance, join operation

$$emp \underset{emp.did=mgr.did}{\bowtie} mgr$$

is translated to:

$$\sigma_C\Big(D\big(emp^S \underset{C'}{\bowtie^S} mgr^S\big)\Big)$$

where the condition C' on the server is condition C_1 defined in Section 3.1.

Now we show how the above operators are used to rewrite SQL queries for the purpose of splitting the query computation across the client and the server.

Query Execution

Given a query Q, the goal is to split the computation of Q across the server and the client. The server will use the implementation of the relational operators discussed in the previous subsection to compute "as much of the query as possible", relegating the remainder of the computation to the client. Query processing and optimization have been extensively studied in database research [5,9,20]. The objective is to come up with the "best" query plan for Q that minimizes the amount of work to be done at the client site. In our setting, the cost of a query consists of many components – the I/O and CPU cost of evaluating the query at the server, the network transmission cost, and the I/O and CPU cost at the client. As an example, consider the following query over the *emp* table than retrieves employees whose salary is greater that the average salary of employees in the department identified by $did = 1$.

```
SELECT emp.name FROM emp
WHERE  emp.salary > (SELECT AVG(salary)
FROM emp WHERE did = 1);
```

The corresponding query tree and some of the evaluation strategies are illustrated in Figures 3(a) to (d). The first strategy (Figure 3(b)) is to simply transmit the *emp* table to the client, which evaluates the query. An alternative strategy (Figure 3(c)) is to compute part of the inner query at the server, which selects (as many as possible) tuples corresponding to $Map_{cond}(did = 1)$. The server sends to the client the encrypted version of the *emp* table, i.e., emp^S, along with the encrypted representation of the set of tuples that satisfy the inner query. The client decrypts the tuples to evaluate the remainder of the query. Yet another possibility (Figure 3(d)) is to evaluate the inner query at the server. That is, select the tuples corresponding

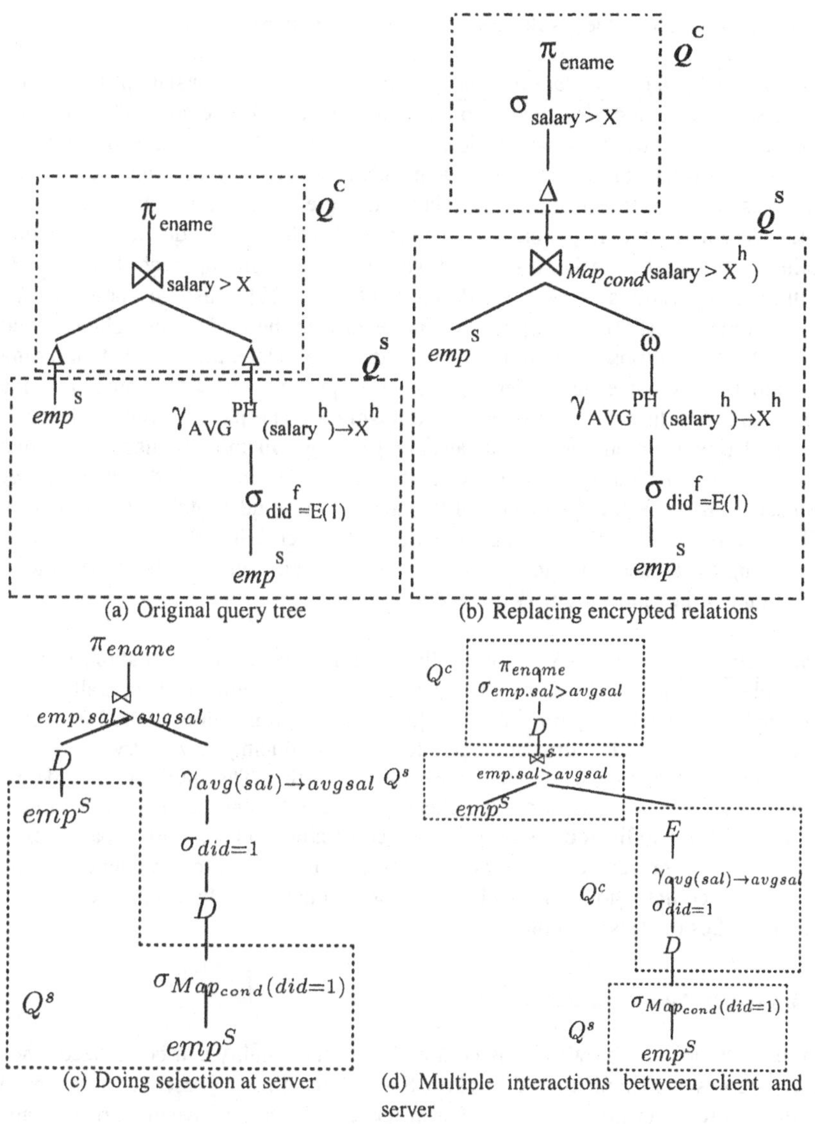

Fig. 3. Query plans for employees who make more than average salary of employees who are in did=1

to the employees that work in department $did = 1$. The results are shipped to the client, which decrypts the tuples and computes average salary. The average salary is encrypted by the client and shipped back to the server, which then computes the join at the server. Finally, the results are decrypted at the client.

Supporting Aggregation Operators in Queries: The query translation techniques discussed above are designed explicitly for relational operators that perform comparisons. While information hiding techniques work for relational operators, they do not work for arithmetic operators such as aggregation. Notice that in the previous query there is an aggregation but that aggregation is done at the client side after decryption. If aggregation is to be performed at the server side, the information hiding approach has to be augmented with an encryption approach that supports arithmetic operations on encrypted representation. [25] illustrates how *privacy homomorphisms* (PH) [24, 32] can be combined with the basic approach described above for this purpose. Additional complexities arise since the information hiding technique does not exactly identify the target group to be aggregated (i.e., the server side results typically contain false positives). The paper develops algebraic manipulation techniques to separate an aggregation group into two subsets, a set that *certainly* qualifies the conditions specified in the query, and a set that *may or may not* satisfy the selection predicates of the query (i.e., could contain false positives). The first set can be directly aggregated at the server using PH while the tuples belonging to the second category will need to be transmitted to the client side to determine if they indeed satisfy the query conditions.

Query Optimization in DAS: As in traditional relational query evaluation, in DAS multiple equivalent realizations for a given query are possible. This naturally raises the challenge of query optimization. In [39], query optimization in DAS is formulated as a cost-based optimization problem by introducing new query processing functions and defining new query transformation rules. The intuition is to define transfer of tuples from server to the client and decryption at the client as operators in the query tree. Given different hardware constraints and software capabilities at the client and the server different cost measures are applied to the client-side and server-side computations. A novel query plan enumeration algorithm is developed that identifies the least cost plan.

3.2 Privacy Aware Bucketization

In the previous section we discussed how DAS functionality can be realized when data is represented in the form of buckets. Such a bucketized representation can result in disclosure of sensitive attributes. For instance, given a sensitive numeric attribute (e.g., salary) which has been bucketized, assume that the adversary somehow comes to know the maximum and minimum values occurring in the bucket B. Now he can be sure that all data elements in this bucket have a value that falls in the range $[min_B, max_B]$, thereby leading to partial disclosure of sensitive values for data elements in B. If, the adversary has knowledge of distribution of values in the bucket, he may also be able to make further inference about the specific records. A natural question is how much information does the generalized representation of data reveal, that is, given the bucket label, how well can the adversary predict/guess the value of the sensitive attribute of a given entity? Intuitively, this depends upon the granularity at which data is generalized. For instance, assigning all values in the domain to a single bucket will make the bucket-label completely non-informative. However, such a strategy will require the client to retrieve every record from the server. On the other extreme, if each possible data value lies has a corresponding bucket, the client will get no confidentiality, though the records returned by the server will contain no false positives. There is a natural trade-off between the performance overhead and the degree of disclosure. Such a tradeoff has been studied in [16] where authors develop a strategy to minimize the disclosure with constraint on the performance degradation[11].

In the rest of this section, we introduce the measures of disclosure-risk arising from bucketization and then tackle the issue of optimal bucketization to support range queries on a numeric data set. Finally, we present the algorithm that allows one to tune the performance-privacy trade-off in this scheme. The discussion is restricted to the case where bucket based generalization is Performed over a single dimensional ordered data set, e.g., a numeric attribute And the query class is that of 1-dimensional range queries.

Measures of Disclosure Risk

The authors in [14] propose *entropy* and *variance* of the value distributions in the bucket as appropriate measure of (the inverse) disclosure risk. Entropy captures the notion of uncertainty associated with a random element chosen with a probability that follows a certain distribution. The higher the value of entropy of a distribution (i.e., larger the number of distinct values and more uniform the frequencies, larger is the value of the entropy), greater is the uncertainty regarding the true value of the element. For example, given a domain having 5 distinct values and the data set having 20 data points, the entropy is maximized if all 5 values appear equal number of time, i.e. each value has a frequency of 4.

Now, the adversary sees only the bucket label B of a data element t. Therefore if the adversary (somehow) knows the complete distribution of values within B, he can guess the true value (say v^*) of t with a probability equal to the fractional proportion of elements with value v^* within the bucket. The notion of uncertainty regarding the true value can be captured in an aggregate manner by the entropy of the value distribution within B. Entropy of a discrete random variable X taking values $x_i = 1, \ldots, n$ with corresponding probabilities $p_i, i = 1, \ldots, n$ is given by:

$$Entropy(X) = H(X) = -\sum_{i=1}^{n} p_i log_2(p_i)$$

If the domain of the attribute has an order defined on it as in the case of a numeric attribute, the above definition of entropy does not capture the notion of distance be-

[11] Notice the dual of the problem – maximize performance with a constraint on information disclosure – would also be addressed once we agree on the metric for information disclosure. However, such an articulation of the problem has not been studied in the literature.

tween two values. In the worst case model, since the value distribution is assumed to be known to the adversary, greater the spread of each bucket distribution, better is the protection against disclosure. Therefore, the authors propose *variance* of the bucket distribution as the second (inverse) measure of disclosure risk associated with each bucket. That is, higher the variance of the value distribution, lower is the disclosure risk.

$$Variance(X) = \sum_{i=1}^{n} p_i(x_i - E(X))^2, \text{ where } E(X) = \frac{1}{n}\sum_{i=1}^{n} p_i x_i$$

For more discussion on the choice of these privacy measures refer to [14]. Next we present the criteria for optimal bucketization.

Optimal Buckets for Range Queries

From the point of view of security, the best case is to put all data into one bucket, but this is obviously very bad from the performance perspective. Assuming the query workload consists of only range queries, intuitively one can see that more the number of buckets, better is the performance on an average. That is, on an average the number of false positives retrieved will be lesser per range query for a partition scheme that uses more number of buckets. In section 3, we assumed that the bucketization was equiwidth, but as we pointed out earlier, that might not be the best case from the point of view of efficiency. Here we present the analysis (from [14]) that tells us how to compute the optimal buckets given a numeric data set and the number of required buckets.

Consider a relational table with single numeric attribute from a discrete domain like **Z** (set of non-negative integers). So given such a data set, what is the optimal criteria for partitioning this set. The problem can be formally posed as follows. (Refer to the table 1 for notations.)

Problem 1 *Given an input relation $R = (V, F)$ (where V is the set of distinct numeric values appearing at least once in the column and F is the set of corresponding frequencies), a query distribution P (defined on the set of all range queries, Q) and the maximum number of buckets M, partition R into at most M buckets such that the total number of* false positives *over all possible range queries (weighted by their respective probabilities) is minimized.*

For an ordered domain with N distinct values, there are $N(N+1)/2$ possible range queries in the query set Q. The problem of histogram construction for summarizing large data, has similarities to the present problem. Optimal histogram algorithms either optimize their buckets i) independent of the workload, by just looking at the data distribution or ii) with respect to a given workload. The authors first address the following two cases:

1) Uniform: All queries are equi-probable. Therefore probability of any query is = $\frac{2}{N(N+1)}$.

V_{min}	minimum possible value for a given attribute
V_{max}	maximum possible value for a given attribute
N	number of possible distinct attribute values; $N = V_{max} - V_{min} + 1$
R	relation (in cleartext), $R = (V, F)$
$\|R\|$	number of tuples in R (i.e. size of table)
V	ordered set (increasing order) of all values from the interval $[V_{min}, V_{max}]$ that occur at least once R; $V = \{v_i \mid 1 \leq i \leq n\}$
F	set of corresponding frequencies (non-zero); $F = \{0 < f_n \leq \|R\| \mid 1 \leq i \leq n\}$ therefore we have $\|R\| = \sum_{i=1}^{n} f_i$
n	$n = \|V\| = \|F\|$ (Note: $n \leq N$)
R^S	encrypted and bucketized relation, on server
M	maximum number of buckets
Q	set of all "legal" range queries over R
q	a random range query drawn from Q; $q = [l, h]$ where $l \leq h$ and $h, l \in [V_{min}, V_{max}]$
Q'	set of all bucket-level queries
q'	random bucket-level query drawn from Q'; basically q' is a sequence of at least one and at most M bucket identifiers.
$T(q)$	translation function (on the client side) which, on input of $q \in Q$, returns $q' \in Q'$
R_q	set of tuples in R satisfying query q
$R^S_{q'}$	set of tuples in R^S satisfying query q'
W	query workload, induces probability dist on Q

Table 1. Notations for Buckets

2) Workload-induced: There is a probability distribution P induced over the set of possible queries Q, where the probability of a query q is given by the fraction of times it occurs in the workload W (W is a bag of queries from Q).

The analysis of the uniform query-distribution is given fist and then a discussion on how the general distribution (workload induced) case can be tackled is presented.

Uniform query distribution: The total number of false positives (TFP), where all queries are equiprobable can be expressed as:

$$\text{TFP} = \sum_{\forall q \in Q} (|R^S_{T(q)}| - |R_q|)$$

The average query precision (AQP) can be expressed as (see notation in table 1):

$$\text{AQP} = \frac{\sum_{q \in Q} |R_q|}{\sum_{q \in Q} |R^S_{T(q)}|} = 1 - \frac{\text{TFP}}{\sum_{q' \in Q'} |R^S_{q'}|}$$

where $q' = T(q)$.

Therefore minimizing the total number of false positives is equivalent to maximizing *average precision* of all queries.

For a bucket B, there are $N_B = (H_B - L_B + 1)$ distinct values (for the discrete numeric domain) where L_B and H_B denote the low and high bucket boundary, respectively. Let V_B denote the set of all values falling in range B and let $F_B = \{f_1^B, \ldots, f_{N_B}^B\}$ denote the set of corresponding value frequencies. Recall that Q is the set of all range queries over the given attribute. One needs to consider all queries that involve at least one value in B and compute the total overhead (false positives) as follows:

Let the set of all queries of size k be denoted by Q_k and $q_k = [l, h]$ denote a random query from Q_k where $h - l + 1 = k$. Then, the total number of queries from Q_k that overlap with one or more points in bucket B can be expressed as: $N_B + k - 1$. Of these, the number of queries that overlap with a single point v_i within the bucket is equal to k. The case for $k = 2$ is illustrated in figure 4. Therefore, for the remaining $N_B - 1$ queries, v_i contributes f_i false positives to the returned set (since the complete bucket needs to be returned). Therefore, for all $N_B + k - 1$ queries of size k that overlap with B, the total number of false positives returned can be written as:

$$\sum_{v_i \in B} (N_B - 1) * f_i = (N_B - 1) * \sum_{v_i \in B} f_i$$

$$= (N_B - 1) * F_B \approx N_B * F_B$$

where F_B is the total number of elements that fall in the bucket (i.e., the sum of the frequencies of the values that fall in B). We make the following important observation here:-

Observation 1 *For the uniform query distribution, the total number of false positives contributed by a bucket B, for set of all queries of size k, is independent of k. In effect the total number of false positives contributed by a bucket (over all query sizes) depends only on the width of the bucket (i.e. minimum and maximum values) and sum of their frequencies.*

From the above observation, it is clear that minimizing the expression $N_B * F_B$ for all buckets would minimize the total number of false-positives for all values of k (over all the $\frac{N(N+1)}{2}$ range queries).

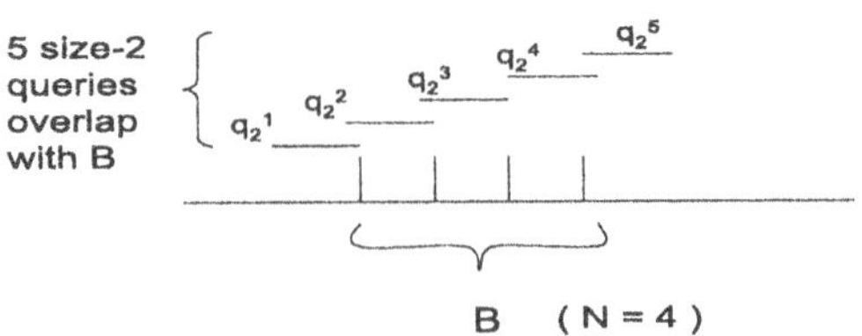

Fig. 4. Queries overlapping with bucket

The Query-Optimal-Bucketization Algorithm (uniform distribution case)

The goal is to minimize the objective function : $\sum_{B_i} N_{B_i} * F_{B_i}$. Let $QOB(1, n, M)$ (*Query Optimal Bucketization*) refer to the problem of optimally bucketizing the set of values $V = \{v_1, \ldots, v_n\}$, using at most M buckets (Note that $v_1 < \ldots < v_n$, each occurring at least once in the table). We make the following two key observations:

1) Optimal substructure property: The problem has the optimal substructure property, therefore allowing one to express the optimum solution of the original problem as the combination of optimum solutions of two smaller sub-problems such that one contains the leftmost $M-1$ buckets covering the $(n-i)$ smallest points from V and the other contains the extreme right single bucket covering the remaining largest i points from V:

$$
\begin{aligned}
QOB(1, n, M) &= Min_i[QOB(1, n-i, M-1) \\
&\quad + BC(n-i+1, n)] \\
\text{where } BC(i, j) &= (v_j - v_i + 1) * \sum_{i \le t \le j} f_t
\end{aligned}
$$

($BC(i, j)$ is cost of a single bucket covering $[v_i, v_j]$)

2) Bucket boundary property: It can be intuitively seen that for an optimal solution, the bucket boundaries will always coincide with some value from the set V (i.e. values with non-zero frequency). Therefore in the solution space, one needs to consider only buckets whose end points coincide with values in V, irrespective of the total size of the domain.

The algorithm solves the problem bottom-up by solving and storing solutions to the smaller sub-problems first and using their optimal solutions to solve the larger problems. All intermediate solutions are stored in the 2-dimensional matrix H. The rows of H are indexed from $1, \ldots, n$ denoting the number of leftmost values from V that are covered by the buckets for the given sub-problem and the columns are indexed by the number of maximum allowed buckets (from $1, \ldots, M$). Also note that the cost of any single bucket covering a consecutive set of values from V can be computed in constant time by storing the cumulative sum of frequencies from the right end of the domain, call them $EndSum$ (i.e. $EndSum_n = f_n, EndSum_{n-1} = f_{n-1} + f_n \ldots$. Storing this information uses $O(n)$ space. The algorithm also stores along with the optimum cost of a bucketization, the lower end point of its last bucket in the $n \times M$ matrix OPP (Optimal Partition Point) for each sub-problem solved. It is easy to see that the matrix OPP can be used to reconstruct the exact bucket boundaries of the optimal partition computed by the algorithm in $O(M)$ time. The

Algorithm: QOB(D, M)
Input: Data set $D = (V, F)$ and max # buckets M
(where $|V| = |F| = n$)
Output: Cost of optimal bucketization & matrix H
Initialize
(i) matrix $H[n][M]$ to 0
(ii) matrix $OPP[n][M]$ to 0
(iii) compute $EndSum(j) = EndSum(j+1) + f_j$
for $j = 1 \dots n$
For $k = 1 \dots n$ // For sub-problems with max 2 buckets
$H[k][2] = Min_{2 \leq i \leq k-1}(BC(1, i) + BC(i+1, K))$
Store *optimal-partition-point* i_{best} in $OPP[k][2]$
For $l = 3 \dots M$ // For the max of 3 up to M buckets
For $k = l \dots n$
$H[k][l] = Min_{l-1 \leq i \leq k-1}(H[i][l-1] + BC(i+1, k))$
Store *optimal-partition-point* i_{best} in $OPP[k][l]$
Output "Min Cost of Bucketization = $H[n][M]$"
end

Fig. 5. Algorithm to compute query optimal buckets

dynamic programming algorithm is shown in figure 5[12] and an illustrative example is given below.

Example: Assume the input to QOB algorithm is the following set of (data-value, frequency) pairs:
$D = \{(1,4), (2,4), (3,4), (4,10), (5,10), (6,4), (7,6), (8,2), (9,4), (10,2)\}$ and say the maximum number of buckets allowed is 4, then (figure 6) displays the optimal histogram that minimizes the cost function. The resulting partition is $\{1,2,3\}, \{4,5\}, \{6,7\}, \{8,9,10\}$. Note that this histogram is not equi-depth (i.e all bucket need not have the same number of elements). The minimum value of the cost function comes out to be = 120. In comparison the approximately equi-depth partition $\{1,2,3\}, \{4\}, \{5,6\}, \{7,8,9,10\}$ has a cost = 130. ◇

Generic Query Workload: The same dynamic programming algorithm of figure 5 can be used for an arbitrary distribution induced by a given query workload W. The workload is represented by $W = \{(q, w_q) | q \in W \cap w_q > 0\}$, where w_q is the probability that a randomly selected query from W is same as q. As in the case of uniform workload, the optimal substructure property holds in this case as well. The only difference is in computation of the bucket costs BC which translates into the computation of the array $Endsum[1, \dots, n]$ in the preprocessing step. The algorithm to compute the entries of the $EndSum$ array for a generic workload W is given in

[12] in the workload-induced case, only the $EndSum$ computation is done differently, the rest of the algorithms remains the same

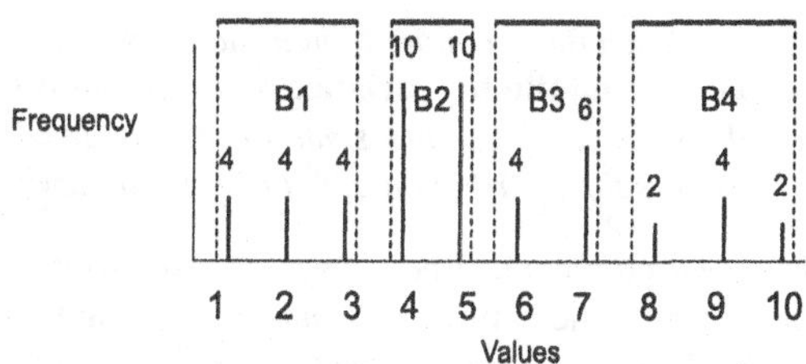

Fig. 6. Optimum buckets for uniform query distribution

figure 7. Any bucket B covering range $[i, j]$ will have the cost given by $BC(i, j) = EndSum[i] - EndSum[j]$.

Algorithm: Compute-EndSum(D, W, $EndSum[1 \ldots n]$)
Input: $D = (V, F)$, workload W & $EndSum[1 \ldots n]$
    (note: $EndSum[1 \ldots n]$ is initialized to $0's$)
Output: Array $EndSum$ with entries filled in
For $i = (n - 1) \ldots 1$
  $EndSum[i] = EndSum[i + 1]$
  For all $q = [l_q, h_q] \in W$ such that $h_q \in [v_i, v_{i+1})$
    $EndSum[i] = EndSum[i] + (\sum_{j=i+1}^{n} f_j) * w_q$
  For all $q = [l_q, h_q] \in W$ such that $l_q \in (v_i, v_n]$
    $EndSum[i] = EndSum[i] + f_i * w_q$
Output $EndSum[1 \ldots n]$
end

Fig. 7. EndSum for generic query workload W

Next we address the issue how the security and performance tradeoff.

The Security-Performance Trade-off

The optimal buckets offer some base level of security due to the indistinguishability of elements within a bucket, but in many cases that might not be good enough, i.e., a bucket's value distributions might not have a large enough variance and/or entropy. To address this problem, the authors in [14] propose a re-bucketization of the data, starting with the optimal buckets and allowing a bounded amount of performance degradation, in order to maximize the two privacy measures (**entropy** and **variance**) simultaneously. The problem is formally presented below:

Problem 2 Trade-off Problem*: Given a dataset $D = (V, F)$ and an optimal set of M buckets on the data $\{B_1, B_2, \ldots, B_M\}$, re-bucketize the data into M new buckets,*

$\{CB_1, CB_2, \ldots, CB_M\}$ *such that no more than a factor* K *of performance degradation is introduced and the* **minimum variance** *and* **minimum entropy** *amongst the* M *random variables* $X_1, \ldots, X_M$ *are simultaneously* **maximized**, *where the random variable* X_i *follows the distribution of values within the* i^{th} *bucket.*

The above mentioned problem can be viewed as a multi-objective constrained optimization problem, where the entities *minimum entropy* and *minimum variance* amongst the set of buckets are the two objective functions and the constraint is the *maximum allowed performance degradation factor* K (called the *Quality of Service*(QoS) constraint). Such problems are combinatorial in nature and the most popular solution techniques seem to revolve around the *Genetic Algorithm* (GA) framework [27], [28]. GA's are iterative algorithms and cannot guarantee termination in polynomial time. Further their efficiency degrades rapidly with the increasing size of the data set. Therefore instead of trying to attain optimality at the cost of efficiency, the authors propose a new algorithm called the *controlled diffusion algorithm* (CDf-algorithm). The CDf-algorithm increases the privacy of buckets substantially while ensuring that the performance constraint is not violated.

Controlled Diffusion: The optimal bucketization for a given data set is computed using the QOB-algorithm presented in figure 5. Let the resulting optimal buckets be denoted by B_i's for $i = 1, \ldots, M$. The controlled diffusion process creates a new set of M approximately equi-depth buckets which are called the *composite buckets* (denoted by $CB_j, j = 1, \ldots, M$) by *diffusing* (i.e. re-distributing) elements from the B_i's into the CB_j's. The diffusion process is carried out in a controlled manner by restricting the number of distinct CB's that the elements from a particular B_i get diffused into. This resulting set of composite buckets, the $\{CB_1, \ldots, CB_M\}$ form the final bucketized representation of the client data. Note that, to retrieve the data elements in response to a range query q, the client needs to first compute the query overlap with the optimal buckets B_i's, say $q(B)$ and then retrieve all the contents of composite buckets CB_j's that overlap with one or more of the buckets in $q(B)$. The retrieved data elements comprise the solution to query q.

The M composite buckets need to be approximately equal in size in order to ensure the QoS constraint, as will become clear below. The equi-depth constraint sets the target size of each CB to be a constant $= f_{CB} = |D|/M$ where $|D|$ is size of the data set (i.e. rows in the table). The QoS constraint is enforced as follows: If the maximum allowed performance degradation $= K$, then for an optimal bucket B_i of size $|B_i|$ its elements are diffused into no more than $d_i = \frac{K*|B_i|}{f_{CB}}$ composite buckets (as mentioned above $f_{CB} = |D|/M$). The diffusion factor d_i is rounded-off to the closest integer. Assume that in response to a range query q, the server using the set of optimal buckets $\{B_1, \ldots, B_M\}$, retrieves a total of t buckets containing T elements in all. Then in response to the same query q this scheme guarantees that the server would extract no more than $K*T$ elements at most, using the set $\{CB_1, \ldots, CB_M\}$ instead of $\{B_1, \ldots, B_M\}$. For example, if the optimal buckets retrieved in response to a query q were B_1 and B_2 (here $t = 2$ and $T = |B_1| + |B_2|$), then to evaluate q using the CB_j's, the server won't retrieve any more than $K * |B_1| + K * |B_2|$

elements, hence ensuring that precision of the retrieved set does not reduce by a factor greater than K.

An added advantage of the diffusion method lies in the fact that it guarantees the QoS lower bound is met not just for the average precision of queries but for each and every individual query. The important point to note is that the domains of the composite buckets overlap where as in the case of the optimal buckets, they do not. Elements with the same value can end up going to multiple CB's as a result of this diffusion procedure. This is the key characteristic that allows one to vary the privacy measure while being able to control the performance degradation. Therefore, this scheme allows one to explore the "privacy-performance trade-off curve". The controlled diffusion algorithm is given in figure 8. The diffusion process is illustrated by an example below.

Algorithm : Controlled-Diffusion(D, M, K)
Input : Data set $D = (V, F)$,
  M = # of $CB's$ (usually same as # opt buckets)
  K = maximum performance-degradation factor
Output : An M-Partition of the dataset (i.e. M buckets)

Compute optimal buckets $\{B_i, \ldots, B_M\}$ using QOB algo
Initialize M empty composite buckets $CB_1 \ldots, CB_M$
For each B_i
  Select $d_i = \frac{K*|B_i|}{f_{CB}}$ distinct CB's randomly, $f_{CB} = \frac{|D|}{M}$
  Assign elements of B_i **equiprobably** to the d_i $CB's$
  (roughly $|B_i|/d_i$ elements of B_i go into each CB)
end For
Return the set buckets $\{CB_j | j = 1, \ldots, M\}$.
end

Fig. 8. Controlled diffusion algorithm

Example: Consider the optimal buckets of the example in figure 6 and say a performance degradation of up to 2 times the optimal ($K = 2$) is allowed. Figure 9 illustrates the procedure. In the figure, the vertical arrows show which of the composite buckets, the elements of an optimal bucket gets assigned to (i.e. diffused to). The final resulting buckets are shown in the bottom right hand-side of the figure and we can see that all the 4 CB's roughly have the same number size (between 11 and 14). The average entropy of a bucket increases from 1.264 to 2.052 and standard deviation increases from 0.628 to 1.875 as one goes from the B's to CB's. In this example the entropy increases since the number of distinct elements in the $CB's$ are more than those in the B's. The variance of the CB's is also higher on an average than that of the B's since the domain (or spread) of each bucket has increased. Note that average precision of the queries (using the composite buckets) remains within a factor of 2 of the optimal. For instance, take the range query $q = [2,4]$, it would have retrieved the buckets B_1 and B_2 had we used the optimal buckets resulting in a precision of $18/32 = 0.5625$. Now evaluating the same query using the composite buckets, we would end up retrieving all the buckets CB_1 through CB_4 with the reduced precision as $18/50 \approx 0.36 > \frac{1}{2} * 0.5625$. (Note: Due to the small error margin allowed in the size of the composite buckets (i.e. they need not be exactly equal in size), the precision of few of the queries might reduce by a factor slightly greater than K). ◊

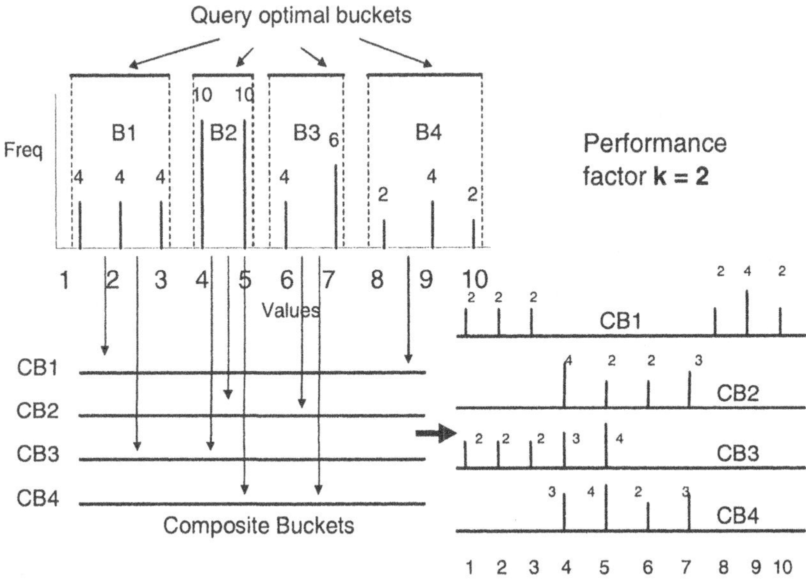

Fig. 9. controlled diffusion (adhoc version)

Discussion

In this section, we considered only single dimensional data. Most real data sets have multiple attributes with various kinds of dependencies and correlations between the attributes. There may be some kinds of functional dependencies (exact or partial) and correlations as in multidimensional relational data or even structural dependencies as in XML data. Therefore, knowledge about one attribute might disclose the value of another via the knowledge of such associations. The security-cost analysis for such data becomes significantly different as shown in [16, 35]. Also, in this section, the analysis that was presented, was carried out for the worst-case scenario where it was assumed that the complete value distribution of the bucket is known to an adversary. In reality it is unrealistic to assume that an adversary has exact knowledge of the complete distribution of a data set. Moreover, to learn the bucket-level joint-distribution of data, the required size of the training set (in order to approximate the distribution to a given level of accuracy) grows exponentially with the number of attributes/dimensions. This makes the assumption of "complete bucket-level" knowledge of distribution even more unrealistic for multidimensional data. [16] proposes a new approach to analyze the disclosure risk for multidimensional data and extends the work in [14] to the this case.

3.3 Two Server Model for DAS

The authors in [4] propose an alternate model for DAS where they propose a distributed approach to ensure data confidentiality. This scheme requires the presence of two or more distinct servers. The individual servers can be untrusted as before, the only constraint being, they should be mutually non-colluding and non-communicating. Also deviating from the previous approach, here the data owner is required to specify the privacy requirement in the form of constraints as we describe below.

Privacy Requirements

Consider a relation R, the privacy requirements are specified as a set of *constraints* $\mathcal{P}$ expressed on the schema of relation R. Each constraint is denoted by a subset, say P, of the attributes of R. The privacy constraints informally mean the following: If R is decomposed into into R_1 and R_2, and let an adversary have access to the entire contents of either R_1 or R_2. The privacy requirement is that for every tuple in R, the value of at least one of the attributes in P should be completely opaque to the adversary, i.e., the adversary should be unable to infer anything about the value of that attribute.

For example, let relation R consist of the attributes *Name, Date of Birth (DoB), Gender, Zipcode, Position, Salary, Email, Telephone*. The company specifies that *Telephone* and *Email* are sensitive even on their own. *Salary, Position* and *DoB* are considered private details of individuals and so cannot be stored together. Similarly {*DoB, Gender, Zipcode*} might also be deemed sensitive since they together can identify an individual. Other things that might be protected are like sensitive rules, e.g., relation between position and salary or between age and salary: {*Position, Salary*}, {*Salary, DoB*}.

The goal is therefore to ensure that each of the the privacy constraints are met. For constraints containing single sensitive attributes, e.g., the "Telephone Number" that needs to be hidden, one can XOR the number with a random number r and store the resulting number in one server and the number r on another. To recover the original telephone number one simply needs to XOR these two pieces of information and each of these by themselves reveal nothing. For the other kind of constraints that contain more than one attribute, say {*Salary, Position*}, the client can vertically partition the attribute sets of R so that the salary information is kept in one column and the position information is kept in another. Since the two servers are assumed to be non-colluding and non-communicating, distributing the attributes across the servers provides an approach to implement such multi-attribute privacy policies. The decomposition criteria is described more formally below.

Relational Decomposition

The two requirements from the decomposition of a relational data set is that it should be *lossless* and *privacy preserving*. Traditional relation decomposition in distributed databases is of two types: *Horizontal Fragmentation* where each tuple of a relation R is either stored in server S_1 or server S_2 and *Vertical Fragmentation* where the attribute set is partitioned across S_1 and S_2 [40]. The vertical fragmentation of data is one that is investigated as a candidate partitioning scheme and is investigated further in this work. Vertical partitioning requires the rows in the two servers to have some unique tuple ID associated with them. They also propose to use *attribute encoding* schemes where can be built by combining the parts stored on the two servers. One-time pad, deterministic encryption and random noise addition are explored as alternative candidates for semantic partitioning of an attribute. The authors propose using partitioning of the attribute set along with attribute encoding to meet the privacy constraints. Remember that $\mathcal{P} \subseteq 2^R$. Consider a decomposition of R as $\mathcal{D}(R) =< R_1, R_2, E >$, where R_1 and R_2 are the sets of attributes in the two fragments, and E refers to the set of attributes that are encoded. $E \subseteq R_1$ and $E \subseteq R_2$ and $R_1 \cup R_2 = R$. Then the privacy constraint need to satisfy the following requirements.

Condition 1 *The decomposition $\mathcal{D}(R)$ is said to obey the privacy constraints $\mathcal{P}$ if, for every $P \in \mathcal{P}$, $P \nsubseteq (R_1 - E)$ and $P \subsetneq (R_2 - E)$*

Each constraint $P \in \mathcal{P}$ can be obeyed in two ways:

1. Ensure that P is not contained in either R_1 or R_2, using vertical fragmentation. For example, the privacy constraint {*Name,Salary*} may be obeyed by placing *Name* in R_1 and *Salary* in R_2
2. Encode at least one of the attributes in P. For example, a different way to obey the privacy constraint {*Name, Salary*} would be to encode *Salary* across R_1 and R_2. For a more detailed discussion, we point the interested reader to [4]

Query Reformulation, Optimization & Execution

The suggested query reformulation is straightforward and identical to that in distributed databases. When a query refers to R, it is replaced by $R_1 \bowtie R_2$, where all the encoded tuples (i.e., those that occur across both R_1 and R_2) are assumed to be suitably decoded in the process. Consider the query with selection condition c. If c

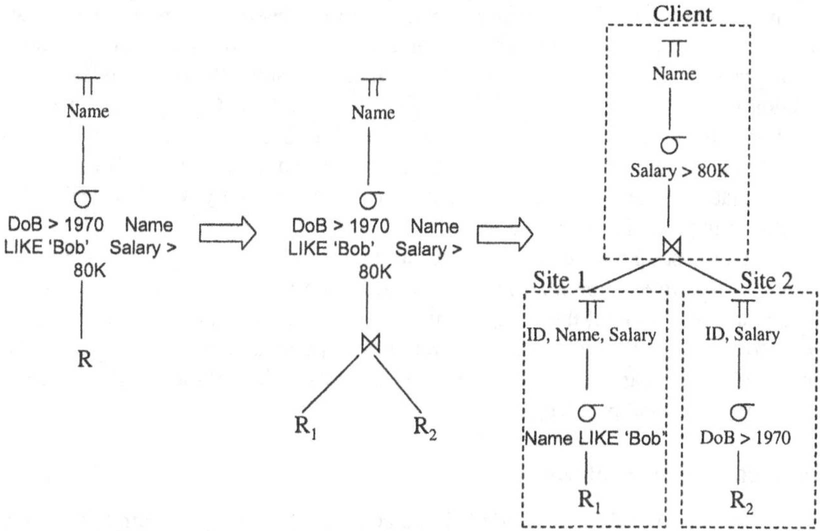

Fig. 10. Example of Query Reformulation and Optimization

is of the form $< Attr >< op >< value >$, and $< Attr >$ has not undergone fragmentation, condition c, may be pushed down to R_1 or R_2, whichever contains $< Attr >$. Similarly if c is of the form $< Attr1 >< op >< Attr2 >$ and both attributes are un-fragmented and present in either R_1 or R_2, the condition may be pushed down to the appropriate relation. Similar "push down" operations can also be applied to projection, Group-by and aggregation clauses. When the computation cannot be done without decoding (or merging from the two servers) then the computation shifts to the client. Notice that unlike in distributed database query processing where semijoin approach (and shipping fields to other servers can be utilized) such techniques cannot be used since that may result in violation of the privacy constraint.

The small example in figure 10 illustrates the process of logical query plan generation and execution in the proposed architecture. For some more examples and discussions, the interested reader can refer to section 4 in the paper [4].

Optimal Decomposition for Minimizing Query Cost

For a given workload W of queries, there is a cost associated with each distinct partitioning of the set of attributes between the two databases. Since there are exponentially many distinct partitioning schemes, a brute force evaluation is not efficient. The authors use an approach from distributed computing based on *affinity matrix* M, where the entry M_{ij} represents the "cost" of placing the unencoded attributes i and j in different segments. The entry M_{ij} represents the "cost" of encoding attribute i across both fragments. The cost of decomposition is assumed to be simply represented by a linear combination of entries in the affinity matrix. Let $R = \{A_1, A_2, \ldots, A_n\}$ represents the original set of n attributes, and consider a decomposition of $\mathcal{D}(R) =< R_1, R_2, E >$. Then we assume the cost of this decomposition $C(\mathcal{D}) = \sum_{i \in (R_1 - E), j \in (R_2 - E)} M_{ij} + \sum_{i \in E} M_{ii}$. Now, the optimization problem is to minimize the above cost while partitioning the data in a way that satisfies all the privacy constraints. The two issues to be addressed are: (i) How can the affinity matrix M be generated from a knowledge of the query workload? (ii) How can the optimization problem be solved?

The simplest scheme to populate the affinity matrix is to set M_{ij} to be the number of queries that refer to both attributes i and j. Similarly M_{ii} is set to the number of queries in the workload that refer to attribute i. Some other heuristics to populate the entries of the affinity matrix are given in the appendix of the paper [4] and the interested reader can refer to it. Now, we summarize the solution outlined in the paper for the second problem.

The Optimization Problem

The optimization problem is modelled as a complete graph $G(R)$, with both vertex and edge weights defined by the affinity matrix M. (Diagonal entries stand for vertex weights). Along with it, the set of privacy constraints are also given, $\mathcal{P} \subseteq 2^R$, representing a hypergraph $H(R, \mathcal{P})$ on the same vertices. The requirement is then, to 2-color the set of vertices in R such that (a) no hypergraph edge in H is monochromatic, and (b) the weight of bichromatic graph edges in G is minimized. The difference is that an additional freedom to delete any vertex in R (and all the hyperedges that contain it) by paying a price equal to the vertex weight. The coloring of a vertex is equivalent to placing the corresponding attribute in one of the two segments and deleting it is equivalent to encoding the attribute; so all privacy constraints associated with the attribute is satisfied by the vertex deletion. Some vertex deletions might always be necessary since it might not be possible to always two color a hypergraph.

The above problem is NP-hard and the authors go on to give three heuristic solutions that use approximation algorithms for "Min-Cut" and "Weighted Set Cover" problems in graphs. The former component is used to determine two-colorings of the graph $G(R)$ (say all cuts of the graph $G(R)$ which are within a small constant factor of the minimum cut) and is used to decide which attributes are assigned to which segment. The weighted set cover algorithm is used for detecting the least costly set of vertices to delete, these correspond to attributes that need to be encoded across both the segments. Good approximation solutions are there for both the algorithms and therefore makes them practical to use. We summarize one of the heuristic approaches mentioned in the paper, and refer the interested reader to the original paper for the remaining ones.

1. Ignore fragmentation, and delete vertices to cover all the constraints using **Approximate Weighted Set Cover**. Call the set of deleted vertices E.
2. Consider the remaining vertices, and use **Approximate Min-Cuts** to find different 2-colorings of the vertices, all of which approximately minimize the weight of the bichromatic edges in G

3. For each of the 2-colorings obtained in step (2): Find all deleted vertices that are present only in bichromatic hyperedges, and consider "rolling back" their deletion, and coloring them instead, to obtain a better solution.
4. Choose the best of (a) the solution from step (3) for each of the 2-colorings, and (b) the decomposition $< R - E, E, E >$.

In the first step, all the privacy constraints are covered by ensuring at least one attribute in each constraint is encoded. This implies a simple solution $\mathcal{D}_1$, where all the unencoded attributes are assigned to one segment. In steps (2) and (3), one tries to improve upon this by avoiding encrypting all the attributes, hoping to use fragmentation to cover some of the constraints. This is done iteratively by computing various other small cuts and trying to roll back some of the encodings. Finally the better solution (computed in step (3) or $\mathcal{D}_1$) is returned.

Discussion

In this paper, the authors have proposed an alternative way of supporting database functionalities in a secure manner in the outsourcing model. The approach deviates from the usual DAS model in that it requires two or more non-communicating service providers to be available to enable privacy. The approach though novel and definitely interesting, does raise many questions which would be interesting to investigate, e.g., what would be the performance of such a system in a real deployment, how would more complicated queries be split between the two servers, what would be the overhead of multiple-rounds in which a query might have to be answered. Also, currently there is no direct communication between the two servers, could some of the distributed query processing overhead be reduced if some kind of secure, "two-party communications" were to be enabled between these two servers. Moreover, the nature of privacy violation due to associations between multiple attributes (that are kept on different servers or are encoded) could lead to privacy violations, how to tackle these is not known. The paper does offer an interesting new approach which could give rise to some new research.

3.4 Summary

In this section, we presented example approaches that have been developed in the literature to support relational queries over encrypted relational data in the DAS setting. Such approaches broadly fall under two categories: (1) cryptographic approaches that attempt to develop encryption algorithms that allow queries to be evaluated directly over encrypted representation, and (2) approaches based on exploiting information hiding techniques developed in the disclosure control literature. While cryptographic approaches prevent leakage of any information (but are applicable only under limited scenarios), approaches based on information hiding may allow limited information disclosure but are more widely applicable. Such approaches explore a natural tradeoff between potential information loss and efficiency that can be achieved. We discussed how data generalization into buckets can be performed such that the information disclosure is minimized while constraining the performance degradation.

We note that information disclosure in bucket-based approach has formally only been studied for single dimensional data, under the worst case assumption that the adversary knows the definition of the buckets and the complete distribution of data within buckets. As we noted earlier, this assumption is too strong in reality and cannot be expected to hold in general for multidimensional data. Some recent work has been done in this area [16] to develop a framework for security analysis for multidimensional bucketization.

There also exist some work in literature [19] that propose data transformation based schemes which allow a richer set of SQL functions to be computed directly on the transformed numeric data like aggregation and sorting. Though, the main shortcoming of this scheme is that it is only secure under the "ciphertext-only attack" model and breaks down when the adversary possesses background knowledge and/or a few plaintext-ciphertext pairs.

Finally, while our focus in this chapter has been on techniques developed in the literature to support relational queries in the DAS model, we note that limited systems that follow the DAS paradigm have also been built [3, 18]. Whereas [3] uses a smart card based safe storage to implement limited SQL functionalities, [18] proposes a system which outsources user profile data (e.g., bookmarks, passwords, query logs, web data, cookies, etc) and supports simple searching capabilities. The rationale is to use DAS approach for supporting mobility across different software and machines. some limited work on schemes such as [19]

4 Conclusions

In this chapter, we summarized research on supporting search over encrypted data representation that has been studied in the context of database as a service model. Much of the existing work has studied the search problem in one of the two contexts: keyword search over encrypted document representations, and SQL search over encrypted relational data. Since the initial work [7, 26] in these areas, many extensions to the problem have been considered. We briefly mention these advances that we have not covered so far to provide interested readers with references.

The problem of query evaluation over encrypted relational databases has been generalized to XML data sources in [35, 36]. XML data, unlike relational databases, is semi-structured which introduces certain additional complications in encrypting as well as translating queries. For instance, authors in [35] propose XML-encryption schemes taking its structure into consideration, develop techniques to evaluate SPJ queries and optimize the search process during query processing.

Besides extending the data model, some researchers have considered relaxing assumptions made by the basic DAS model itself. The basic DAS model, as discussed in this chapter, assumes that the service provider though untrusted, is honest. Such an assumption might not necessarily hold in certain situations. In particular, the service provider may return erroneous data. An error in the result to a query may manifest itself in two ways – the returned answers may be tampered by the service provider, or alternatively, the results returned by the service provider may not be the complete set of matching records. The problem of integrity of the returned results was first studied in [26] which used message authentication codes (MACs) to authenticate the result set. Any such authentication mechanism adds additional processing cost at the client. Authentication mechanisms using Merkle Hash trees and group signatures that attempt to reduce such an overhead have been studied in [37]. The authors have developed techniques for both the situation where the client (i.e., the user who poses the query) is the same as well as different from the data owner.

Another avenue of DAS research has been to exploit secure coprocessor to maintain confidentiality of outsourced database [38]. Unlike the basic DAS model in which the client is trusted and the service provider is entirely untrusted, in the model enhanced with a secure coprocessor, it is assumed that the service provider has a tamper proof hardware – a secure coprocessor – which is attached to the untrusted server and has (limited) amount of storage and processing capabilities. Data while outside the secure processor must be in the encrypted form, it could be in plaintext within the coprocessor without jeopardizing data confidentiality. Exploiting a secure coprocessor significantly simplifies the DAS model since now intermediate query results do not need to be transmitted to the clients if further computation requires data to be in plaintext. Instead, secure coprocessor can perform such a function, therefore significantly reducing network overheads and optimizing performance. Another additional advantage is that such a model can naturally support situations where the owner of the database is different from the user who poses the query.

While much progress in research has been made over the past few years on DAS, we believe that many further challenges remain before the vision outlined in [26] of a secure data management service that simultaneously meets the data confidentiality and efficiency requirements. A few of the many practical challenges that still remain open are the following: (1) techniques to support dynamic updates – some initial approaches to this problem have been studied in [10], (2) mechanisms to support stored procedures and function execution as part of SQL processing, and (3) support for a more complete SQL - e.g., pattern matching queries. Furthermore, given multiple competing models for DAS (e.g., the basic model, the model with secure coprocessor, model with two servers) as well as multiple competing approaches, there is a need for a detailed comparative study that evaluates these approaches from different perspectives: feasibility, applicability under diverse conditions, efficiency, and achievable confidentiality. Finally, a detailed security analysis including the nature of attacks as well as privacy guarantees supported by different schemes needs to be studied.

Acknowledgements

This work has been possible due to the following NSF grants: 0331707 and IIS-0220069.

References

1. D. Boneh, G. di Crescenzo, R. Ostrovsky, and G. Persiano Public Key Encryption with Keyword Search. In *Advances in Cryptology - Eurocrypt 2004* (2004). volume 3027 of *Lecture Notes in Computer Science*, pp. 506-522. Springer-Verlag, 2004.
2. L. Ballard, S. Kamara, F. Monrose Achieving Efficient conjunctive keyword searches over encrypted data. In *Seventh International Conference on Information and Communication Security (ICICS 2005)*, volume 3983 of *Lecture Notes in Computer Science*, pp. 414-426. Springer, 2005.
3. L. Bouganim, and P. Pucheral. Chip-Secured Data Access: Confidential Data on Untrusted Servers In *Proc. of VLDB* 2002.
4. G. Aggarwal, M. Bawa, P. Ganesan, H. Garcia-Molina, K. Kenthapadi, U. Srivastava, D. Thomas, Y. Xu. Two Can Keep a Secret: A Distributed Architecture for Secure Database Services In *Proc. of CIDR* 2005.
5. S. Chaudhuri. An overview of query optimization in relational systems. In *Proc. of ACM Symposium on Principles of Database Systems (PODS)*, 1998.
6. E-J., GOH Secure Indexes. Technical report 2003/216, In IACR ePrint Cryptography Archive, (2003). See http://eprint.iacr.org/2003/216.
7. D. Song and D. Wagner and A. Perrig. Practical Techniques for Search on Encrypted Data. In *Proc. of IEEE SRSP*, 2000.
8. H. Garcia-Molina, J. Ullman, and J. Widom. *Database Systems: The Complete Book*. Prentice Hall, 2002.
9. G. Graefe. Query eveluation techniques for large databases. *ACM Computing Surveys*, 25(2):73–170, 1993.
10. H. Hacıgümüş. Privacy in Database-as-a-Service Model. *Ph.D. Thesis, Department of Information and Computer Science, University of California, Irvine*, 2003.
11. H. Hacıgümüş, B. Iyer, and S. Mehrotra. Encrypted Database Integrity in Database Service Provider Model. In *Proc. of Certification and Security in E-Services (CSES'02), IFIP 17th World Computer Congress*, 2002.
12. H. Hacıgümüş, B. Iyer, and S. Mehrotra. Providing Database as a Service. In *Proc. of ICDE*, 2002.
13. H. Hacıgümüş, B. Iyer, and S. Mehrotra. Ensuring the Integrity of Encrypted Databases in Database as a Service Model. In *Proc. of 17th IFIP WG 11.3 Conference on Data and Applications Security*, 2003.
14. B. Hore, S. Mehrotra, and G. Tsudik. A Privacy-Preserving Index for Range Queries. In *Proc. of VLDB* 2004.
15. B. Hore, S. Mehrotra, and G. Tsudik. A Privacy-Preserving Index for Range Queries. UCI-ICS tech report 2004, http://www.ics.uci.edu/ bhore/papers.
16. B. Hore, and S. Mehrotra. Supporting Multidimensional Range and Join Queries over Remote Encrypted Databases. UCI-ICS tech report 2006.
17. B. Iyer, S. Mehrotra, E. Mykletun, G. Tsudik, and Y. Wu A Framework for Efficient Storage Security in RDBMS In *Proc. of EDBT* 2004.
18. R. C. Jammalamadaka, S. Mehrotra, and N. Venkatasubramanian PVault: A Client-Server System Providing Mobile Access to Personal Data In *International Workshop on Storage Security and Survivability*, 2005.
19. R. Agrawal, J. Kiernan, R. Srikant, Y. Xu Order Preserving Encryption for Numeric Data In *Proc. of SIGMOD* 2004.
20. P. Sellinger, M. Astrahan, D. D. Chamberlin, R. A. Lorie, and T. G. Price. Access Path Selection in Relational Database Management Systems. In *Proc. of ACM SIGMOD*, 1979.

21. Y. Chang and M. Mitzenmacher Privacy preserving keyword searches on remote encrypted data. In *Third International Conference on Applied Cryptography and Network Security (ACNS 2005)*, volume 3531 of *Lecture Notes in Computer Science*, pp. 442-455. Springer-Verlag, 2005.
22. P. Golle, J. Staddon, B. Waters Secure conjunctive keyword search over encrypted data. In *Applied Cryptography and Network Security (ACNS 2004)*, volume 3089 of *Lecture Notes in Computer Science*, pp. 31-45. Springer, 2004.
23. B. Waters, D. Balfanz, G. Durfee, and D. Smetters Building and encrypted and searchable audit log. In *Network and Distributed System Security Symposium (NDSS 2004)* (2004), The Internet Society, 2004.
24. R. Rivest, R.L. Adleman and M. Dertouzos. On Data Banks and Privacy Homomorphisms. In *Foundations of Secure Computations*, 1978.
25. H. Hacıgümüş, B. Iyer, and S. Mehrotra Efficient Execution of Aggregation Queries over Encrypted Relational Databases. In *Proceedings of DASFAA*, 2004.
26. H. Hacıgümüş, B. Iyer, C. Li and S. Mehrotra Executing SQL over encrypted data in the database-service-provider model. In Proc. SIGMOD, 2002.
27. D.E. Goldberg Genetic Algorithms in Search, Optimization and Machine Learning. Published by Addison-Wesley, Reading, Massachusetts.
28. D.R. Jones and M.A. Beltramo Solving Partitioning Problems with Genetic Algorithms. In *Proc. of the 4th International Conference of Genetic Algorithms*, 1991.
29. L. Willenborg, T. De Waal Statistical Disclosure Control in Practice *Springer-Verlag*, 1996.
30. L. Willenborg, T. De Waal Elements of Statistical Disclosure Control *Springer*, 2001.
31. N.R. Adam, J.C. Worthmann Security-control methods for statistical databases: a comparative study In *ACM Computing Surveys, Vol 21, No. 4*, 1989.
32. J. Domingo-Ferrer A New Privacy Homomorphism and Applications In *Information Processing Letters*, 6(5):277-282, 1996.
33. N. Ahituv, Y. Lapid, S. Neumann Processing Encrypted Data In *Communications of the ACM*, 1987 Vol. 30, 9, pp.777-780
34. E. Brickell, Y. Yacobi On Privacy Homomorphisms In *Proc. Adavances in Cryptology-Eurocrypt'87*
35. R. Jammalamadaka, S. Mehrotra Querying Encrypted XML Documents *MS thesis*, 2004.
36. H. Wang, L. Lakshmanan Efficient Secure Query Evaluation over Encrypted XML Databases In *VLDB*, 2006.
37. M. Narasimhan, G. Tsudik DSAC: Integrity of Outsourced Databases with Signature Aggregation and Chaining In *CIKM*, 2005.
38. R. Agrawal, D. Asonov, M. Kantarcioglu, Y. Li Sovereign Joins In *ICDE* 2006.
39. H. Hacıgümüş, B. Iyer, S. Mehrotra Query Optimization in Encrypted Database Systems, In *Proc. of International Conference on Database Systems for Advanced Applications (DASFAA)*, 2005.
40. M. T. Ozsu, and P. Valduirez Principles of Distributed Database Systems, *Prentice Hall*, 2nd Edition, 1999.

Rights Assessment for Relational Data

Radu Sion

Computer Science Department
Stony Brook University
sion@cs.stonybrook.edu

1 Introduction

Mechanisms for privacy assurances (e.g., queries over encrypted data) are essential to a viable and *secure* management solution for outsourced data. On a somewhat orthogonal dimension but equally important, we find the requirement to be able to *assert and protect rights* over such data.

Different avenues are available, each with its advantages and drawbacks. Enforcement by legal means is usually ineffective, unless augmented by a digital counterpart such as Information Hiding. *Digital Watermarking* as a method of Rights Assessment deploys Information Hiding to conceal an indelible "rights witness" ("rights signature", watermark) within the digital Work to be protected (see Figure 1). The soundness of such a method relies on the assumption that altering the Work in the process of hiding the mark does not destroy the value of the Work, while it is difficult for a malicious adversary ("Mallory") to remove or alter the mark beyond detection without doing so. The ability to resist attacks from such an adversary, mostly aimed at removing the watermark, is one of the major concerns in the design of a sound solution.

There exists a multitude of semantic frameworks for discrete information processing and distribution. Each distinct data domain would benefit from the availability of a suitable watermarking solution.

Significant research efforts [2] [3] [8] [11] [14] [15] [22] [24] have been invested in the frameworks of signal processing and multimedia Works (e.g., images, video and audio).

Here we explore Information Hiding as a rights assessment tool for *discrete* data types i.e., in a relational database context. We explore existing watermarking solutions for numeric and categorical data types.

The Chapter is organized as follows. In Section 2 we explore the broader issues and challenges pertaining to steganography for rights protection. Then, in Sections 3 and 4 solutions for numeric respectively categorical data types are introduced. Related work is discussed in Section 5. Section 6 briefly discusses the current state of the art and Section 7 concludes.

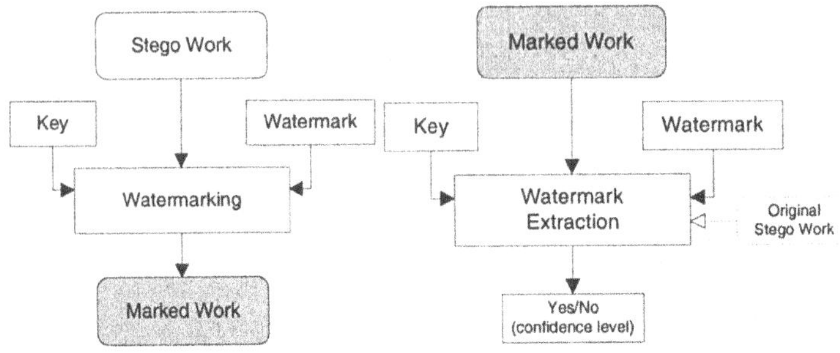

Fig. 1. Introduction: (a) *Digital Watermarking* conceals an indelible "rights witness" ("rights signature", watermark) within the digital Work to be protected. (b) In court, a detection process is deployed to prove the existence of this "witness" beyond reasonable doubt (confidence level) and thus assess ownership.

2 Model

Before we proceed however, let us first understand how the ability to prove rights in court relates to the final desiderata, namely to *protect* those rights. After all, doesn't simply publishing a summary or digest of the Work to be protected – e.g., in a newspaper, just before releasing the Work – do the job? It would seem it enables one to prove later in court that (at least a copy of) the Work was in one's possession at the time of release. In the following we address these and other related issues.

2.1 Rights Protection through Assessment

The ability to prove/assess rights convincingly in court constitutes a deterrent to malicious Mallory. It thus becomes a tool for rights protection if counter-incentives and legal consequences are set high enough. But because Information Hiding does not provide a means of actual access control, the question of rights protection still remains. *How* are rights protected here?

It is intuitive that such a method works only if the rightful rights-holder (Alice) actually knows about Mallory's misbehavior **and** is able to prove to the court that: (i) Mallory possesses a certain Work X and (ii) X contains a "convincing" (e.g., very rare with respect to the space of all considered similar Works) and "relevant" watermark (e.g., the string "(c) by Alice").

What watermarking itself does not offer is a direct deterrent. If Alice does not have knowledge of Mallory's illicit possession of the Work and/or if it is impossible to actually prove this possession in court beyond reasonable doubt, then watermarking cannot be deployed directly to prevent Mallory. If, however, Information Hiding is aided by additional access control levels, it can become very effective.

For example, if in order to derive value from the given Work (e.g., watch a video tape), Mallory has to deploy a known mechanism (e.g., use video player), Information Hiding could be deployed to enable such a proof of possession, as follows:

modify the video player so as to detect the existence of a watermark and match it with a set of purchased credentials and/or "viewing tickets" associated with the player's owner. If no match is found, the tape is simply not played back.

This scenario shows how watermarking can be deployed in conjunction with other technologies to aid in managing and protecting digital rights. Intuitively, a certain cost model is assumed here: the cost of reverse engineering this process is far higher than the potential derived illicit gain.

This illustrates the game theoretic nature at the heart of the watermarking proposition and of information security in general. Watermarking is a game with two adversaries, Mallory and Alice. At stake lies the value inherent in a certain Work X, over which Alice owns certain rights. When Alice releases X, to the public or to a licensed but potentially un-trusted party, she deploys watermarking for the purpose of ensuring that one of the following holds:

- she can always prove rights in court over any copy or valuable derivate of X (e.g., segment thereof)
- any existing derivate Y of X, for which she cannot prove rights, does not preserve any significant value (derived from the value in X)
- the cost to produce such an un-watermarked derivate Y of X that is still valuable (with respect to X) is higher than its value

Newspaper Digests

To achieve the above however, Alice could publish a summary or digest (e.g., cryptographic hash) of X in a newspaper, thus being able to claim later on at least a time-stamp on the possession of X. This could apparently result in a quite effective, albeit costly, alternative to Watermarking the Work X.

There are many simple reasons why it would not work, including (i) scalability issues associated with the need for a trusted third party (newspaper), (ii) the cost of publishing a digest for each released Work, (iii) scenarios when the fact that the Work is watermarked should be kept secret (stealthiness) etc.

Maybe the most important reason however, is that Mallory can now claim that his ownership of the Work precedes X's publication date, and that Alice simply modified it (i.e., a stolen copy) and published a digest thereof herself. It would then be up to the court to decide if Mallory is to be believed or not, hardly an encouraging scenario for Alice. This could work if there existed a mechanism for the mandatory publication of digests for each and every valuable Work, again quite likely impractical due to both costs and lack of scalability to a virtually infinite set of data producers and Works.

Deploying such aids as rights assessment tools makes sense only in the case of the Work being of value only un-modified. In other words if it does not tolerate any changes, without losing its value, and Mallory is caught in possession of an identical copy, Alice can successfully prove in court that she possessed the original at the time of its publication (but she cannot prove more). Considering that, in the case of watermarking, the assumption is that, no matter how small, there are modifications allowed to the Works to be protected, in some sense the two approaches complement each other. If no modifications are allowed, then a third-party "newspaper" service might work for providing a time-stamp type of ownership proof that can be used in court.

Steganography and Watermarking

There exists a fundamental difference between Watermarking and generic Information Hiding (steganography) from an application perspective and associated challenges. Information Hiding in general (and covert communication in particular), aims usually at enabling Alice and Bob to exchange messages in a manner as resilient and stealthy as possible, through a hostile medium where Malory could lurk. On the other hand, Digital Watermarking is deployed by Alice as a court proof of rights over a Work, usually in the case when Mallory benefits from using/selling that very same Work or maliciously modified versions of it.

In Digital Watermarking, the actual value to be protected lies in the Works themselves whereas pure steganography usually makes use of them as simple value "transporters". In Watermarking, Rights Assessment is achieved by demonstrating (with the aid of a "secret" known only to Alice – "watermarking key") that a particular Work exhibits a rare property ("hidden message" or "watermark"). For purposes of convincing the court, this property needs to be so *rare* that if one considers any other random Work "similar enough" to the one in question, this property is "very improbable" to apply (i.e., bound false-positives rate). It also has to be *relevant*, in that it somehow ties to Alice (e.g., by featuring the bit string "(c) by Alice").

There is a threshold determining the ability to convince the court, related to the "very improbable" assessment. This defines a main difference from steganography: from the court's perspective, specifics of the property (e.g., watermark message) are not important as long as they link to Alice (e.g., by saying "(c) by Alice") and, she can prove "convincingly" it is she who induced it to the (non-watermarked) original.

In watermarking the emphasis is on "detection" rather than "extraction". Extraction of a watermark, or bits of it, is usually a part of the detection process but just complements the process up to the extent of increasing the ability to convince in court. If recovering the watermark data in itself becomes more important than detecting the actual existence of it (i.e., "yes/no" answer) then, from an application point of view, this is a drift toward covert communication and pure Information Hiding (steganography).

2.2 Consumer Driven Watermarking

An important point about watermarking should be noted. By its very nature, a watermark modifies the item being watermarked: it inserts an indelible mark in the Work such that (i) the insertion of the mark does not destroy the value of the Work, i.e., it is still useful for the *intended purpose*; and (ii) it is difficult for an adversary to remove or alter the mark beyond detection without destroying this value. If the Work to be watermarked cannot be modified without losing its value then a watermark cannot be inserted. The critical issue is not to avoid alterations, but to limit them to acceptable levels with respect to the intended use of the Work.

Thus, an important first step in inserting a watermark, i.e., by altering it, is to identify changes that are acceptable. Naturally, the nature and level of such change is dependent upon the application for which the data is to be used. Clearly, the notion of value or utility of the data becomes thus central to the watermarking process. For example, in the case of software, the value may be in ensuring equivalent computation, whereas for natural language text it may be in conveying the same meaning – i.e., synonym substitution is acceptable. Similarly, for a collection of numbers, the utility of the data may lie in the actual values, in the relative values of the numbers, or in the distribution (e.g., normal with a certain mean). At the same time, the concept of value of watermarked Works is necessarily relative and largely influenced by each semantic context it appears in. For example, while a statistical analyst would be satisfied with a set of feature summarizations (e.g., average, higher-level moments) of a numeric data set, a data mining application may need a majority of the data items, for example to validate a classification hypothesis.

It is often hard to define the available "bandwidth" for inserting the watermark directly. Instead, allowable distortion bounds for the input data can be defined in terms of consumer metrics. If the watermarked data satisfies the metrics, then the alterations induced by the insertion of the watermark are considered to be acceptable. One such simple yet relevant example for numeric data, is the case of *maximum allowable mean squared error* (MSE), in which the usability metrics are defined in terms of mean squared error tolerances as $(s_i - v_i)^2 < t_i, \forall i = 1, ..., n$ and $\sum (s_i - v_i)^2 < t_{max}$, where $\mathbb{S} = \{s_1, ..., s_n\} \subset \mathbb{R}$, is the data to be watermarked, $\mathbb{V} = \{v_1, ..., v_n\}$ is the result, $\mathbb{T} = \{t_1, ..., t_n\} \subset \mathbb{R}$ and $t_{max} \in \mathbb{R}$ define the guaranteed error bounds at data distribution time. In other words $\mathbb{T}$ defines the allowable distortions for individual elements in terms of MSE and t_{max} its overall permissible value.

Often however, specifying only allowable change limits on individual values, and possibly an overall limit, fails to capture important semantic features associated with the data – especially if the data is structured. Consider for example, age data. While a small change to the age values may be acceptable, it may be critical that individuals that are younger than 21 remain so even after watermarking if the data will be used to determine behavior patterns for under-age drinking. Similarly, if the same data were to be used for identifying legal voters, the cut-off would be 18 years. Further still, for some other application it may be important that the relative ages, in terms of which one is younger, not change. Other examples of constraints include: (i) *uniqueness* – each value must be unique; (ii) *scale* – the ratio between any two number before and after the change must remain the same; and (iii) *classification* – the objects must remain in the same class (defined by a range of values) before and after the watermarking. As is clear from the above examples, simple bounds on the change of numerical values are often not enough.

Structured collections, present further constraints that must be adhered to by the watermarking algorithm. Consider a data warehouse organized using a standard Star schema with a fact table and several dimension tables. It is important that the key relationships be preserved by the watermarking algorithm. This is similar to the "Cascade on update" option for foreign keys in SQL and ensures that tuples that join before watermarking also join after watermarking. This requires that the new value for any attribute should be unique after the watermarking process. In other words, we want to preserve the relationship between the various tables. More generally, the relationship could be expressed in terms of an arbitrary join condition, not just a natural join. In addition to relationships between tuples, relational data may have constraints within tuples. For example, if a relation contains the start and end times of a web interaction, it is important that each tuple satisfies the condition that the end time be later than the start time.

There exists a trade-off between the desired level of marking resilience and resistance to attacks, and the ability to preserve data quality in the result, with respect to the original. Intuitively, at the one extreme, if the encoded watermark is to be very "strong" one can simply modify the *entire* data set aggressively, but at the same time probably also destroy its actual value. As data quality requirements become increasingly restrictive, any applied watermark is necessarily more vulnerable. Often we can express the available bandwidth as an increasing function of allowed alterations. At the other extreme, a disproportionate concern with data quality will hinder most of the watermarking alterations, resulting in a weak, possibly non-existent encoding.

Naturally, one can always identify some use that is affected by even a minor change to any portion of the data. It is therefore important that (i) the main intended purpose and semantics that should be preserved be identified during watermarking and that (ii) *the watermarking process not interfere with the final data consumer requirements*. We call this paradigm *consumer driven watermarking*.

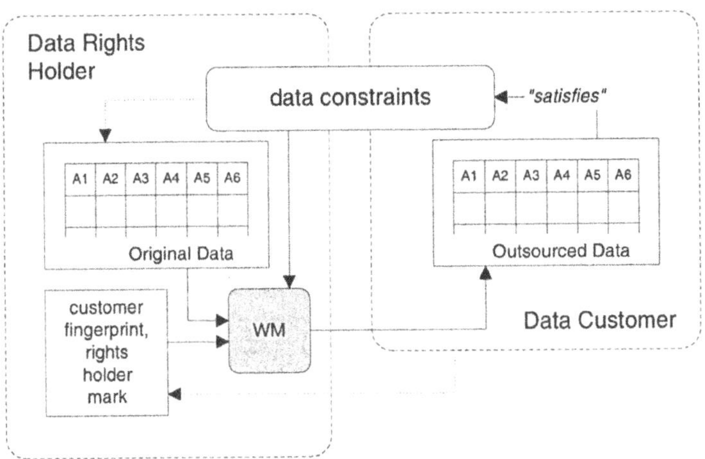

Fig. 2. In *consumer-driven watermarking* a set of data constraints are continuously evaluated in the encoding process to ensure quality of the result.

Some of the solutions discussed here are consumer driven enabled through feedback mechanisms (see Figure 2) that allow the watermarking process to "rollback" modifications that would violate quality constraints in the result on a step by step basis. This ensures the preservation of desired quality metrics with respect to the original un-watermarked input Work.

2.3 Discrete Data vs. Multimedia

An established body of research [2] [3] [8] [11] [14] [15] [22] [24] has resulted from work on Information Hiding and Watermarking in frameworks such as signal processing and multimedia (e.g., images, video and audio). Here we explore Information Hiding as a rights assessment tool for *discrete* data types.

Let us briefly explore the relationship between the challenges and techniques deployed in both frameworks. Because, while the terms might be identical, the associated models, challenges and techniques are different, almost orthogonal. Whereas in the signal processing case there usually exists a large noise bandwidth, due to the fact that the final data consumer is likely human – with associated limitations of the sensory system – in the case of discrete data types this cannot be assumed and data quality assessment needs to be closely tied with the actual watermarking process (see Section 2.2).

Another important differentiating focus is the emphasis on the actual ability to convince in court as a success metric, unlike most approaches in the signal processing realm, centered on bandwidth. While bandwidth is a relevant related metric, it does not consider important additional issues such as malicious transforms and removal attacks. For rights assertion, the concerns lie not as much with packing a large *amount* of information (i.e., watermark bits) in the Works to be protected, as with being able to both *survive* removal attacks and *convince* in court.

Maybe the most important difference between the two domains is that, while in a majority of watermarking solutions in the multimedia framework, the main domain transforms are signal processing primitives (e.g., Works are mainly considered as being compositions of signals rather than strings of bits), in our case data types are mostly discrete and are not naturally handled as continuous signals. Because, while discrete versions of frequency transforms can be deployed as primitives in information encoding for digital images [8], the basis for doing so is the fact that, although digitized, images are at the core defined by a composition of light reflection signals and are consumed as such by the final human consumer. By contrast, arbitrary discrete data is naturally discrete [1] and often to be ingested by a highly sensitive semantic processing component, e.g., a computer rather than a perceptual system tolerant of distortions.

[1] Unless we consider quantum states and uncertainty arising in the spin of the electrons flowing through the silicon.

2.4 Relational Data

For completeness let us briefly overview main components of a relational model [7]. In such a model, relations between information items are explicitly specified: data is organized as "a number of differently sized *tables*" [7] composed of "related" rows/columns. A table is a collection of *rows* or records and each row in a table contains the same *fields*. Certain fields may be designated as data *keys* (not to be confused with "cryptographic keys") when a functional dependency or key constraint, holds for the table. Often, indexing is deployed to speed up searches on values of such primary key fields. Data is structured logically into valued *attributes*. From this perspective, a table is a collection of such attributes (the columns of the table) and models a *relation* among them. The data rows in the tables are also called *tuples*. Data in this model is manipulated using a *relational algebra*. Main operations in this algebra are set operations (e.g., union, intersection, Cartesian product), selection (of some tuples in tables) and projection (of some columns/attributes).

Rights protection for such data is important in scenarios where it is sensitive, valuable and about to be outsourced. A good example is a data mining application, where data is sold in pieces to parties specialized in mining it, e.g., sales patterns database, oil drilling data, financial data. Other scenarios involve for example online B2B interactions, e.g., airline reservation and scheduling portals, in which data is made available for direct, interactive use (see Figure 3). Given the nature of most of the data, it is hard to associate rights of the originator over it. Watermarking can be used to solve this issue.

2.5 The Adversary

Watermarking is a game between the watermarker and malicious Mallory. In this game, the watermarker and Mallory play against each other within subtle trade-off rules aimed at keeping the quality of the result within acceptable bounds. It is as if there exists an impartial referee (the data itself) moderating each and every "move". As discussed above, it is important to make this "referee" an explicit part of the marking process (consumer-driven paradigm). It is also important to understand Mallory and the adversarial setting.

Once outsourced, i.e., out of the control of the watermarker, data might be subjected to a set of attacks or transformations; these may be malicious – e.g., with the explicit intent of removing the watermark – or simply the result of normal use of the data. An effective watermarking technique must be able to survive such use. In a relational data framework important attacks and transformations are:

A1. Sampling. The attacker (Mallory) can randomly select and use a subset of the watermarked data set that might still provide value for its intended purpose ("subset selection"). More specifically, here we are concerned with both (**A1.a**) horizontal and (**A1.b**) vertical data partitioning – in which a valuable subset of the *attributes* are selected by Mallory.

A2. Data Addition. Mallory adds a set of tuples to the watermarked set. This addition is not to significantly alter the useful properties of interest to Mallory.

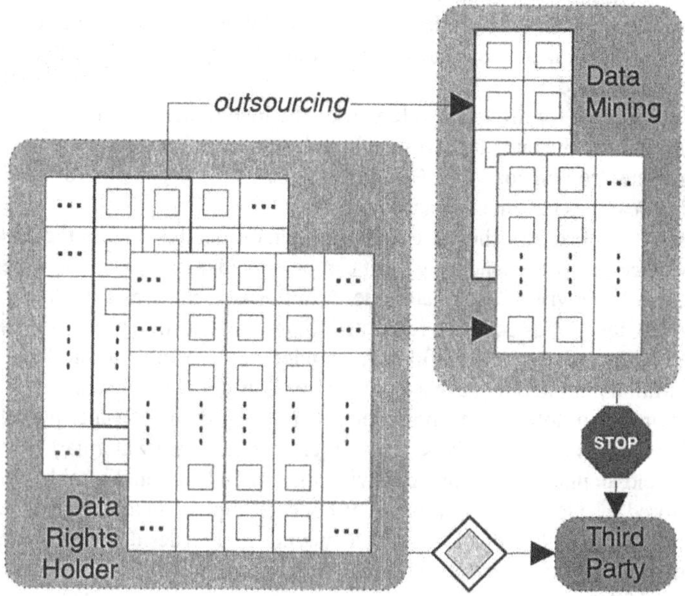

Fig. 3. Rights Assessment is important when valuable data is outsourced to a third party.

A3. Alteration. Altering a subset of the items in the watermarked data set such that there is still value associated with the result. In the case of numeric data types, a special case needs to be outlined here, namely (**A3.a**) a linear transformation performed uniformly to all of the items. This is of particular interest as it can preserve significant valuable data-mining related properties of the data.

A4. Ulterior Claims of Rights. Mallory encodes an additional watermark in the already watermarked data set and claims rights based upon this second watermark.

A5. Invertibility Attack. Mallory attempts to establish a plausible (watermark,key) pair that matches the data set and then claims rights based on this found watermark [8, 9].

Given the attacks above, several properties of a successful solution surface. For immunity against **A1**, the watermark has to be likely encoded in overall data properties that survive sampling, e.g., confidence intervals, statistical bias. With respect to (**A1.b**) special care has to be taken such that the mark survives this partitioning. The encoding method has to feature a certain attribute-level property that could be recovered in such a vertical partition of the data. We believe that while vertical data partitioning attacks are possible and also very likely in certain scenarios, often value is to be found in the association between a set of relation attributes. These attributes are highly likely to survive such an attack, as the final goal of the attacker is to produce a still-valuable result. If the assumption is made that the attack alterations do not destroy the value of the data, then **A3** could be handled by encoding the primitive mark in resilient global data properties. As a special case, **A3.a** can be resisted by a preliminary normalization step in which a common divider to all the items is first identified and applied.

While powerful, for arbitrary watermarks, the invertibility attack **A5** can be defeated by requiring the encoded string to be relevant (e.g. "(c) by Mallory") and the encoding to be "convincing" (see Section 2.1). Then the probability of success of invertibility searches becomes upper bound.

In order to defeat **A4**, the watermarking method has to provide the ability to determine encoding precedence, e.g., if it can be proved in court that one watermark encoding was "overwritten" by a later one. Additionally, in the case of such a (court time) dispute, the parties could be requested to present a portion of the original, un-watermarked data. Only the rightful rights holder would be able to produce such a proof, as Mallory could only have access to already watermarked data.

It is worth also noting that, intuitively, if, in the process of watermarking, the data is altered to its usability limits, any further alteration by a watermarker is likely bound to yield an unusable result. Achieving this might be often desirable [2] and has been explored by Sion et. al. in a proof of concept implementation [34] as well as by Li et. al. in [20]. The challenges of achieving such a desiderata however, lies in the impossibility to define absolute data quality metrics that consider all value dimensions of data.

3 Numeric Types

In this section we explore watermarking solutions in the context of relational data in which one or more of the attributes are of a numeric type. Among existing solutions we distinguish between *single-bit* (the watermark is composed of a single bit) and *multi-bit* (the watermark is a string of bits) types. Orthogonally, the encoding methods can be categorized into two; we chose to call them *direct-domain* and *distribution* encodings. In a direct-domain encoding, each individual bit alteration in the process of watermarking is directly correlated to (a part of) the encoded watermark. In distribution encodings, the encoding channel lies often in higher order moments of the data (e.g., running means, hierarchy of value averages). Each individual bit alteration impacts these moments for the purpose of watermark encoding, but in itself is not directly correlated to any one portion of the encoded watermark.

Single Bit Direct Domain Encoding

In [1, 16] Kiernan, Agrawal et.al. propose a direct domain encoding of a single bit watermark in a numeric relational database.

[2] This is formulated as the "optimality principle" in [26], as well as previous results such as [28] and [31].

Overview. Its main algorithm proceeds as follows. A subset of tuples are selected based on a secret criteria; for each tuple, a secret attribute and corresponding least significant (ξ) bit position are chosen. This bit position is then altered according to yet another secret criteria that is directly correlated to the watermark bit to be encoded. The main assumption is, that changes can be made to any attribute in a tuple at any least significant ξ bit positions. At watermark detection time, the process will re-discover the watermarked tuples and, for each detected accurate encoding, become more "confident" of a true-positive detection.

There are a set of important assumptions underlying this method. Maybe the most important one is that "the relational table being watermarked is such that if all or a large number of the ξ least significant bits of any attribute are dropped or perturbed, then the value of the data is significantly reduced. However, it is possible to change a small number of the bits and not decrease the value of the data significantly" [16].

The authors make an argument for this being a reasonable assumption as such techniques have been used by publishers of books of mathematical tables for a long time – e.g., by introducing small errors in published logarithm tables and astronomical ephemerides to identify pirated copies [15]. Examples of real-world data sets that satisfy such an assumption are given, including tables of parametric specifications (mechanical, electrical, electronic, chemical, etc.), surveys (geological, climatic, etc.), and life sciences data (e.g., gene expression).

Solution Details. For consistency, the original notation is used: a database relation R with the following schema is $R(P, A_0, \ldots, A_{\nu-1})$, is assumed, with P the primary key attribute. All ν attributes $A_0, \ldots, A_{\nu-1}$ are candidates for marking: the values are assumed such that small changes in the ξ least significant bits are imperceptible. γ denotes a control parameter that determines the average number ω of tuples marked ($\omega = \frac{\eta}{\gamma}$), where η is the number of tuples in the database. $r.X$ is used to denote the value of attribute X in tuple r, α denotes a "significance level" and τ a "threshold" for the test of "detecting a watermark". $\mathcal{K}$ is a key known only to the database owner, and there exists $\mathcal{G}$, a pseudo-random sequence number generator [23] (next($\mathcal{G}$) denotes the next generated sequence number).

Note: There are a set of changes between the initial proposed scheme in [16] and its journal version [1]. Here we discuss the (more robust) journal version.

Watermark insertion is illustrated in Figure 4. The main steps of the algorithm are as follows. Initially (step 2) the random sequence generator is initialized such that its output is distinct for any given distinct tuple value. This mechanism is deployed in order to achieve a certain tuple ordering independence of the encoding. The output of $\mathcal{G}$ is then used to determine: (i) if the current tuple is to be watermarked (step 3), (ii) which attribute value to mark (step 4), (iii) which bit within that attribute's value to alter (step 5), and (iv) what new bit-value to assign to that bit-position in the result (step 6, invocation of mark()). This encoding guarantees that, in order to entirely remove a watermark, Mallory is put in the position of guessing correctly the marked tuples, attributes and altered bit positions.

Once R is published, the data owner, Alice, would like to determine whether the (similar) relation S published by Mallory has been pirated from R. The sets of tuples and of attributes in S are assumed to be strict subsets of those in R. Additionally,

1) **foreach** tuple $r \in R$ **do**
2) seed $\mathcal{G}$ with $r.P$ concatenated with $\mathcal{K}$
3) **if** (next($\mathcal{G}$) mod $\gamma = 0$) **then** // mark this tuple
4) attribute_index i = next($\mathcal{G}$) mod ν // mark attribute A_i
5) bit_index j = next($\mathcal{G}$) mod η // mark j^{th} bit
6) $r.A_i$ = mark(next($\mathcal{G}$),$r.A_i$,j)
7) mark(random_number i, value v, bit_index j) **return** value
8) **if** (i is even) **then**
9) set the jth least significant bit of v to 0
10) **else**
11) set the jth least significant bit of v to 1
12) **return** v

Fig. 4. Watermark insertion for the single-bit encoding of [1, 16].

Mallory is assumed not to drop the primary key attribute or change the value of primary keys. Then watermark detection is a direct inverse of insertion. It proceeds as follows (see Figure 5).

1) totalcount = matchcount = 0
2) **foreach** tuple $s \in S$ **do**
3) seed $\mathcal{G}$ with $s.P$ concatenated with $\mathcal{K}$
4) **if** (next($\mathcal{G}$) mod $\gamma = 0$) **then** // tuple was marked
5) attribute_index i = next($\mathcal{G}$) mod ν // A_i was marked
6) bit_index j = next($\mathcal{G}$) mod η // j^{th} bit was marked
7) totalcount = totalcount + 1
8) matchcount = matchcount + match (next($\mathcal{G}$,$s.A_i$,j)
9) τ = threshold(totalcount,α)
10) **if** ((matchcount $< \tau$) **or** (matchcount $>$ totalcount - τ)) **then**
11) *suspect piracy*
12) match(random_number i, value v, bit_index j) **return** integer
13) **if** (i is even) **then**
14) **return** 1 **if** the jth least significant bit of v is 0 **else return** 0
15) **else**
16) **return** 1 **if** the jth least significant bit of v is 1 **else return** 0

Fig. 5. Watermark detection for the single-bit encoding of [1, 16].

Alice starts by identifying the bits that should have been marked by the insertion algorithm. To do so, it executes the operations described in lines 1 through 5 of the insertion algorithm (steps 3 through 6). The assumption is that the original database primary key is preserved in S. Each such identified bit is tested for a match with the value that should have been assigned by the insertion algorithm. Each match is counted. If the resulting count is either too small or too large, piracy is suspected. In the case of too small a number, the method assumes that somehow Mallory has identified the marked bits and systematically flipped each one.

In other words, the insertion algorithm is modulated on a set of successive independent coin tosses. A detection algorithm over ω bits will yield a number of matches with a binomial distribution $(\omega, 1/2)$ for the null hypothesis of non-piracy. Naturally, in the absence of piracy, the expected number of matches is $\frac{\omega}{2}$. The paper proposes to suspect piracy if the observed number of matches m is so large or so small that its probability under the null hypothesis is highly unlikely.

This can be modeled by first fixing an acceptable value for the *significance level* $\alpha \in (0, 1)$ and then computing a threshold $\tau \in (0, \frac{\omega}{2})$ such that the probability of $m < \tau$ or $m > \omega - \tau$ under the null hypothesis is less than or equal to α.

The authors discuss additional extensions and properties of the solution including the following:

- Incremental Updatability: Updates can be handled independently of the existing watermark as the selection and marking criteria are self-sufficient and only depend on the primary key value.
- Blind Watermarking: The method does not require the availability of the un-watermarked data at detection time.
- Varying Parameters: The assumption that any two attributes are marked at the same rate can be removed. Different attributes can be marked at different rates because the attributes may tolerate different error rates and, if the rate parameters are secret, Mallory's task become even more difficult. Additionally, the number of bits available for marking can be varied from one attribute to another.
- Relations Without Primary Keys: The authors also discuss extensions aimed at handling the case of relations without primary keys. This is an important problem as it has the potential to overcome the required assumption of unchanged primary key values in the watermarked data at detection time. In the case of no primary key, the authors propose to designate another attribute, or a number of most significant bit-portions of the currently considered one, as a primary key. This however presents a significant vulnerability due to the very likely existence of duplicates in these values. Mallory could mount a statistical attack by correlating marked bit values among tuples with the same most significant bits. This issue has been also considered in [18] where a similar solution has been adopted. This, however remains an important open problem.

3.1 Multi-Bit Watermarks

While there likely exist applications whose requirements are satisfied by single-bit watermarks, often it is desirable to provide for "relevance", i.e., linking the encoding to the rights holder identity. This is especially important if the watermark aims to defeat against invertibility attacks (**A5**).

In a single-bit encoding this can not be easily achieved. Additionally, while the main proposition of watermarking is not covert communication but rather rights assessment, there could be scenarios where the actual message payload is of importance.

One apparent direct extension from single-bit watermarks to a multi-bit version would be to simply deploy a different encoding, with a separate watermark key, for each bit of the watermark to be embedded. This however, might not be possible, as it will raise significant issues of inter-encoding interference: the encoding of later bits will likely distort previous ones. This will also make it harder to handle ulterior claim of rights attacks (**A4**).

In the following we discuss multi-bit watermark encodings. We start with a direct-domain encoding [19] that extends the work by Kiernan, Agrawal et. al. [1,16] and then explore a distribution-encoding method by Sion et. al. [27,29,30,32,33] and [34].

Multi-Bit Direct Domain Encoding

In [19] Li et. al. extend the work by Kiernan, Agrawal et. al. [1,16] to provide for multi-bit watermarks in a direct domain encoding.
Overview. In summary, given a multi-bit watermark, the scheme functions as follows. The database is parsed and, at each bit-encoding step, one of the watermark bits is randomly chosen for embedding; the solution in [1, 16] is then deployed to encode the selected bit in the data at the "current" point.
Solution Details. The basic encoding method is identical to [1, 16] with the difference that instead of using a generic random sequence generator to determine the altered tuples, attributes and bit value, it uses a cryptographic hash $\mathcal{H}_2(\mathcal{K}, r.P)$ of the concatenation of the secret encoding key $\mathcal{K}$ and the primary database key value for that tuple In other words, the tuple selection criteria (next($\mathcal{G}$) mod $\gamma = 0$) (e.g., in step 3 of Figure 4) becomes now ($\mathcal{H}_2(\mathcal{K}, r.P)$ mod $\gamma = 0$). This is similar to the earlier version of Kiernan et.al.'s work [16].

To support multi-bit watermarking, the scheme proceeds as follows. For each watermark bit string $\Gamma = (f_0, ..., f_{L-1})$ to be embedded, at each embedding step, the "current" watermark bit is selected as one of the L bits. The selected bit is $f_l \oplus mask$, where l is computed as $l = \mathcal{H}_1(\mathcal{K}, r.P) \bmod L$, $mask$ is a bit-sized value, $mask = \mathcal{H}_1(\mathcal{K}, r.P)\&1$, and $\mathcal{H}_1$ is a cryptographic hash. For perfect crypto-hashes, on average, each watermark bit is thus embedded $w = \frac{\eta}{\gamma L}$ times, where η is the number of tuples in the database.

The detection process is also modified accordingly. The scheme scans each tuple, computes the mask bit $mask$ and the marked position in exactly the same way as in watermark insertion. It then extracts the embedded watermark bit by XORing the mask bit with the bit at the marked position in the tuple. Because each watermark bit f_i is inserted multiple times it should be detected the same number of times if the data has not changed.

To handle attacks or benign updates, the scheme uses then majority voting to detect the watermark. This is implemented by keeping two "counters" $count[i][0]$ and $count[i][1]$ corresponding to the numbers of 0's and 1's respectively that have been recovered for watermark bit f_i (similarly to [35]). Watermark bit f_i is set to 0 if the ratio of recovered 0's (the process is similar for 1's) is greater than the threshold τ for detecting a watermark bit:

$$\frac{count[i][0]}{count[i][0] + count[i][1]} > \tau$$

The "strength of the robustness" of the scheme is claimed to be increased with respect to [1,16] due to the fact that the watermark now possesses an additional dimension, namely length. This should guarantee a better upper bound for the probability that a valid watermark is detected from unmarked data, as well as for the probability that a fictitious secret key is discovered from pirated data (i.e., invertibility attacks **A5**). This upper bound is said to be independent of the size of database relations thus yielding robustness against attacks that change the size of database relations.

Multi-Bit Distribution Encoding

Encoding watermarking information in resilient numeric distribution properties of data presents a set of advantages over direct domain encoding, the most important one being its increased resilience to various types of numeric attacks. In [27,29,30, 32,33] and [34], Sion et. al. introduce a multi-bit distribution encoding watermarking scheme for numeric types. The scheme was designed with both an adversary and a data consumer in mind. More specifically the main desiderata were: (i) watermarking should be consumer driven – i.e., desired semantic constraints on the data should be preserved – this is enforced by a feedback-driven rollback mechanism, and (ii) the encoding should survive important numeric attacks, such as linear transformation of the data (**A3.a**), sampling (**A1**) and random alterations (**A3**).
Overview. The solution starts by receiving as user input a reference to the relational data to be protected, a watermark to be encoded as a copyright proof, a secret key used to protect the encoding and a set of data quality constraints to be preserved in the result. It then proceeds to watermark the data while continuously assessing data quality, potentially backtracking and rolling back undesirable alterations that do not preserve data quality.

Watermark *encoding* is composed of two main parts: in the first stage, the input data set is securely partitioned into (secret) subsets of items; the second stage then encodes one bit of the watermark into each subset. If more subsets (than watermark bits) are available, error correction is deployed to result in an increasingly resilient encoding. Each single bit is encoded/represented by introducing a slight skew bias in the tails of the numeric distribution of the corresponding subset. The encoding is proved to be resilient to important classes of attacks, including subset selection, linear data changes and random item(s) alterations.
Solution Details. The algorithm proceeds as follows (see Figure 6): **(a)** User-defined queries and associated guaranteed query usability metrics and bounds are specified with respect to the given database (see below). **(b)** User input determines a set of attributes in the database considered for watermarking, possibly all. **(c)** From the values in each such attribute select a (maximal) number of (e) unique, non-intersecting,

secret subsets. **(d)** For each considered subset, **(d.1)** embed a watermark bit into it using the single-bit encoding convention described below and then **(d.2)** check if data constraints are still satisfied. If data constraints are violated, **(d.3)** retry different encoding parameter variations or, if still no success, **(d.4)** try to mark the subset as invalid (see single-bit encoding convention below), or if still no success **(d.5)** ignore the current set[3]. Repeat step (d) until no more subsets are available.

```
wm(attribute, wm_key, mark_data[], plugin_handler, db_primary_key, subset_size, v_false, v_true, c)
    sorted_attribute ← sort_on_normalized_crypto_hash(wm_key,db_primary_key,wm_key)
    for (i=0; i < length(attribute)/subset_size ;i++)
        subset_bin ← next subset_size elements from sorted_attribute
        compute rollback_data
        encode(mark_data[i % mark_data.length], subset_bin, v_false, v_true, c)
        propagate changes into attribute
        if (not goodness_plugin_handler.isSatisfied(new_data,changes)) then
            rollback rollback_data
            continue
        else
            commit
            map[i] = true
            subset_boundaries[i] = subset_bin[0]
    return map, subset_boundaries
```

Fig. 6. Watermark Embedding (version using subset markers and detection maps shown).

Several methods for subset selection (c) are discussed. In one version, it proceeds as follows. The input data tuples are sorted (lexicographically) on a secret keyed cryptographic hash H of the primary key attribute (K). Based on this value, compose a criteria (e.g., $H(K, key)) \bmod e = 0$) for selecting a set of "special" tuples such that they are uniformly distributed and average a total number of $e = length(attribute)/\ subset\_size$. These special tuples are going to be used as subset "markers". Each subset is defined as the elements between two adjacent markers, having on average $subset\_size$ elements. The detection phase will then rely on this construction criteria to re-discover the subset markers. This process is illustrated in Figure 6.

Encoding the individual mark bits in different subsets increases the ability to defeat different types of transformations including sampling (**A1**) and/or random data addition (**A2**), by "dispersing" their effect throughout the data, as a result of the secret ordering. Thus, if an attack removes 5% of the items, this will result in each subset S_i being roughly 5% smaller. If S_i is small enough and/or if the primitive

[3] This leaves an invalid watermark bit encoded in the data that will be corrected by the deployed error correcting mechanisms (e.g. majority voting) at extraction time.

watermarking method used to encode parts of the watermark (i.e., 1 bit) in S_i is made resilient to these kind of minor transformations then the probability of survival of most of the embedded watermarks is accordingly higher. Additionally, in order to provide resilience to massive "cut" attacks, the subsets are made to be of sizes equal to a given *percent* of the overall data set, i.e., not of fixed absolute sizes.

Note: If enough additional storage is available, these subsets can be in fact constructed differently: given a secretly keyed cryptographic hash function with discrete output values in the interval $[1, e]$, apply it, for each tuple, to the primary key attribute value and let its output determine which subset the tuple belongs to. This would both alleviate the need to deploy subset markers as well as likely offering more resilience to attacks. This simple and nice improvement was suggested to one of the authors during a discussion with a Purdue graduate student (whose identity he cannot remember but whom he invites forward for credit) attending the 2005 Symposium on Security and Privacy.

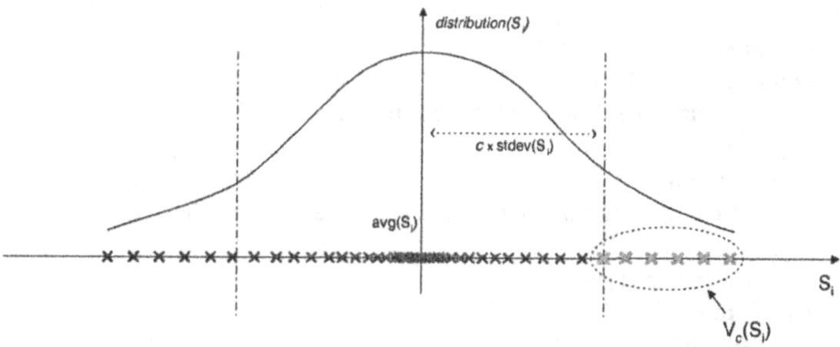

Fig. 7. In the single-bit mark encoding convention, the encoding of the watermark bit relies on altering the size of the "positive violators" set, $v_c(S_i)$.

Once constructed, each separate subset S_i will be marked separately with a single bit, in the order it appears in the actual watermark string. The result will be a e-bit (i.e., $i = 1, \ldots, e$) overall watermark bandwidth in which each bit is "hidden" in each of the marked S_i. If the watermark is of size less than e, error correction can be deployed to make use of the additional bandwidth to increase the encoding resilience.

The single-bit distribution encoding proceeds as follows. Let b be a watermark bit that is to be encoded into S_i and $\mathbb{G}$ represent a set of user specified change tolerance, or usability metrics. The set $\mathbb{G}$ will be used to implement the consumer-driven awareness in the watermark encoding.

Let $v_{false}, v_{true}, c \in (0, 1)$, $v_{false} < v_{true}$ be real numbers (e.g., $c = 90\%$, $v_{true} = 10\%$, $v_{false} = 7\%$). c is called *confidence factor* and the interval (v_{false}, v_{true}) *confidence violators hysteresis*. These are values to be remembered also for watermark detection time. They can be considered as part of the encoding key. Let $avg(S_i)$ and $\delta(S_i)$ be the average and standard deviation, respectively, of S_i. Given S_i and the real number $c \in (0, 1)$ as above, $v_c(S_i)$ is defined as the *number of items of* S_i *that are greater than* $avg(S_i) + c \times \delta(S_i)$. $v_c(S_i)$ is called the number of positive "violators" of the c confidence over S_i, see Figure 7.

The single-bit ***mark encoding convention*** is then formulated: given S_i, c, v_{false} and v_{true} as above, $mark(S_i) \in \{true, false, invalid\}$ is defined to be $true$ if $v_c(S_i) > (v_{true} \times |S_i|)$, $false$ if $v_c(S_i) < v_{false} \times |S_i|$ and $invalid$ if $v_c(S_i) \in (v_{false} \times |S_i|, v_{true} \times |S_i|)$.

In other words, the watermark is modeled by the percentage of positive confidence violators present in S_i for a given confidence factor c and confidence violators hysteresis (v_{false}, v_{true}). Encoding the single bit (see Figure 8), b, into S_i is therefore achieved by minor alterations to some of the data values in S_i such that the number of positive violators ($v_c(S_i)$) is either (a) less than $v_{false} \times |S_i|$ if $b = 0$, or (b) more than $v_{true} \times |S_i|$ if $b = 1$. The alterations are then checked against the change tolerances, $\mathbb{G}$, specified by the user.

---

encode(bit, set, v_{false}, v_{true}, c)
    compute $avg(set)$, $\delta(set)$
    compute $v_c(set)$
    if $v_c(set)$ **satisfies** desired bit value **return** *true*
    if (bit)
        compute $v_* \leftarrow v_{true} - v_c(set)$
        alter v_* items close to the stddev boundary so that they become $> v_{true}$
    else
        (!bit) case is similar
    compute $v_c(set)$
    if $v_c(set)$ **satisfies** desired bit value **return** *true*
    else rollback alterations (distribution shifted too much?)
    return *false*

Fig. 8. Single Bit Encoding Algorithm (illustrative overview).

At detection time the secret subsets are reconstructed and the individual bits are recovered according to the single-bit mark encoding convention. This yields the original e-bit string. If e is larger than the size of the watermark, error correction was deployed to increase the encoding resilience. The watermark string can be then recovered by applying error correction decoding to this string, e.g., majority voting for each watermark bit. This process is illustrated in Figure 9.

In [27, 33] and [34] the authors discuss a proof of concept implementation. It is worth mentioning here due to its consumer-driven design (see Figure 10). In addition to a watermark to be embedded, a secret key to be used for embedding, and a set of relations/attributes to watermark, the software receives as input also a set of external *usability plugin modules*. The role of these plugins is to allow user defined query metrics to be deployed and queried at run-time without recompilation and/or software restart. The software uses those metrics to re-evaluate data usability after each atomic watermarking step.

```
det(attribute, wm_key, db_primary_key, subset_sz, v_false, v_true, c, map[], subset_boundaries[])
    sorted_attribute ← sort_on_normalized_crypto_hash(wm_key,db_primary_key,wm_key)
    read_pipe ← null
    do { tuple ← next_tuple(sorted_attribute) }
    until (exists idx such that (subset_boundaries[idx] == tuple))
    current_subset ← idx
    while (not(sorted_attribute.empty())) do
        do {
            tuple ← next_tuple(sorted_attribute)
            read_pipe = read_pipe.append(tuple)
        } until (exists idx such that (subset_boundaries[idx] == tuple))
        subset_bin ← (at most subset_sz elements from read_pipe, excluding last read)
        read_pipe.remove_all_remaining_elements_but_last_read()
        if (map[current_subset]) then
            mark_data[current_subset] ← decode (subset_bin, v_false, v_true, confidence)
            if (mark_data[current_subset] != DECODING_ERROR)
                    then map[current_subset] ← true
        current_subset ← idx
    return mark_data, map
```

Fig. 9. Watermark Detection (version using subset markers shown).

Constraint metrics can be specified either as SQL queries, stored procedures or simple Java code inside the plug-in modules. Constraints that arise from the schema (e.g., key constraints), can easily be specified in a form similar to (or derived from) SQL *create table* statements. In addition, integrity constraints (e.g., such as *end_time* being greater than *begin_time*) can be expressed. A tolerance is specified for each constraint. The tolerance is the amount of change or violation of the constraint that is acceptable. This is an important parameter since it can be used to tailor the quality of the watermark at the expense of greater change in the data. As mentioned earlier, if the tolerances are too low, it may not be possible to insert a watermark in the data. Various forms of expression are accommodated, e.g., in terms of arbitrary SQL queries over the relations, with associated requirements (usability metric functions). For example, the requirement that the result of the join (natural or otherwise) of two relations does not change by more than 3% can be specified.

Once usability metrics are defined and all other parameters are in place, the watermarking module (see Figure 10) initiates the process of watermarking. An undo/rollback log is kept for each atomic step performed (i.e., 1-bit encoding) until data usability is assessed and confirmed by querying the currently active usability plugins. This allows for rollbacks in the case when data quality is not preserved by the current atomic operation.

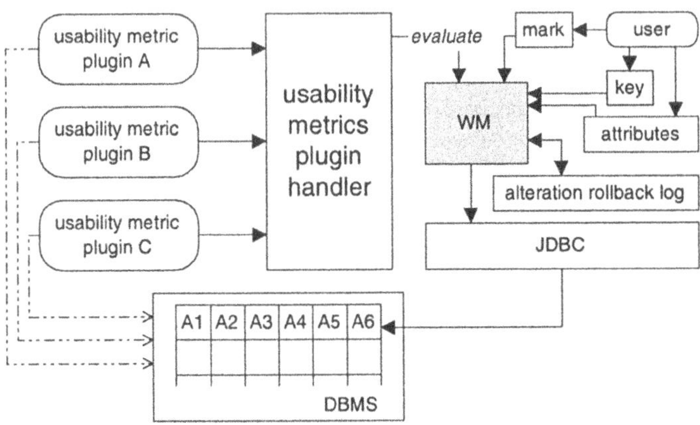

Fig. 10. Overview of the **wmdb.*** package.

To validate this consumer driven design the authors perform a set of experiments showing how, for example, watermarking with classification preservation can be enforced through the usability metric plugin mechanisms. Moreover, the solution is proved experimentally on real data to be extremely resilient to random alterations and uninformed alteration attacks. This is due to its distribution-based encoding which can naturally survive such alterations. For example, altering the *entire* watermarked data set within 1% of its original values only yields a distortion of less than 5% in the detected watermark.

The authors also propose a set of improvements and discuss several properties of the solutions.

- Embedding Optimizations: As the encoding resilience is dependent on a set of parameters (e.g., c, $subset\_size$, v_{false}, v_{true}), an automatic fine-tuning mechanism for searching a near-optimum in this parameter space is proposed. Additionally, the watermarking process could be trained to be resilient to a set of transformations expected from any potential attacker.
- Blind Watermarking: The method does not require the availability of the unwatermarked data at detection time.
- On-the-Fly Updatability: The authors also discuss mechanisms for handling dynamic data updates. Several scenarios of interest are: (i) updates that add fresh tuples to the already watermarked data set, (ii) updates that remove tuples from the already watermarked data and (iii) updates that alter existing tuples.

4 Categorical Types

So far we have explored the issue of watermarking *numeric* relational content. Another important relational data type to be considered is categorical data. Categorical data is data drawn from a discrete distribution, often with a finite domain. By definition, it is either non-ordered (nominal) such as gender or city, or ordered (ordinal) such as high, medium, or low temperatures. There are a multitude of applications that would benefit from a method of rights protection for such data. In this section we propose and analyze watermarking relational data with *categorical* types.

Additional challenges in this domain derive from the fact that one cannot rely on arbitrary small (e.g., numeric) alterations to the data in the embedding process. Any alteration has the potential to be significant, e.g., changing DEPARTURE_CITY from "Chicago" to "Bucharest" is likely to affect the data quality of the result more than a simple change in a numeric domain. There are no "epsilon" changes in this domain. This completely discrete characteristic of the data requires discovery of fundamentally new bandwidth channels and associated encoding algorithms.

4.1 The Adversary Revisited

We outlined above a set of generic attacks in a relational data framework. Here we discuss additional challenges associated with categorical data types.

A3. Alteration. In the categorical data framework, subset alteration is intuitively quite expensive from a data-value preservation perspective. One has also to take into account semantic consistency issues that become immediately visible because of the discrete nature of the data.

A6. Attribute Remapping. If data semantics allow it, re-mapping of relation attributes can amount to a powerful attack that should be carefully considered. In other words, if Mallory can find an even partial value-preserving mapping (the resulting mapped data set is still valuable for illicit purposes) from the original attribute data domain to a new domain, a watermark should hopefully survive such a transformation. The difficulty of this challenge is increased by the fact that there likely are many transformations available for a specific data domain. This is thus a hard task for the generic case. One special case is primary key re-mapping.

4.2 A Solution

In [25], [36] Sion et. al. introduce a novel method of watermarking relational data with categorical types, based on a set of new encoding channels and algorithms. More specifically, two domain-specific watermark embedding channels are used, namely (i) *inter-attribute associations* and (ii) *value occurrence frequency-transforms* of values.

Overview. The solution starts with an initial user-level assessment step in which a set of attributes to be watermarked are selected. In its basic version, watermark encoding in the *inter-attribute association* channel is deployed for each attribute pair (K, A) in the considered attribute set. A subset of "fit" tuples is selected, as determined by the association between A and K. These tuples are then considered for mark encoding. Mark encoding alters the tuple's value according to secret criteria that induces a statistical bias in the distribution for that tuple's altered value. The detection process then relies on discovering this induced statistical bias.

The authors validate the solution both theoretically and experimentally on real data (Wal-Mart sales). They demonstrate resilience to both alteration and data loss attacks, for example being able to recover over 75% of the watermark from under 20% of the data.

Solution Details. For illustration purposes, let there be a set of discrete attributes $\{A, B\}$ and a primary data key K, not necessarily discrete. Any attribute $X \in \{A, B\}$ can yield a value out of n_X possibilities (e.g., city names, airline names). Let the number of tuples in the database be N. Let $b(x)$ be the number of bits required for the accurate representation of value x and $msb(x, b)$ its most significant b bits. If $b(x) < b$, x is left-padded with $(b - b(x))$ zeroes to form a b-bit result. Similarly, $lsb(x, b)$ is used to denote the least significant b bits of x. If by wm denotes a watermark to be embedded, of length $|wm|$, $wm[i]$ will then be the i-th bit of wm. Let $set\_bit(d, a, b)$ be a function that returns value d with the bit position a set to the truth-value of b. In any following mathematical expression let the symbol "&" signify a *bit-AND* operation. Let $T_j(X)$ be the value of attribute X in tuple j. Let $\{a_1, ..., a_{n_A}\}$ be the discrete potential values of attribute A. These are distinct and can be sorted (e.g., by ASCII value). Let $f_A(a_j)$ be the normalized (to 1.0) occurrence frequency of value a_j in attribute A. $f_A(a_j)$ models the de-facto occurrence probability of value a_j in attribute A.

The encoding algorithm (see Figure 11) starts by discovering a set of "fit" tuples determined directly by the association between A and the primary relation key K. These tuples are then considered for mark encoding.

```
wm_embed_alt(K,A,wm,k1,e,ECC)
  wm_data ← ECC.encode(wm, wm.len)
  idx ← 0
  for (j ← 1; j < N; j ← j + 1)
    if (H(T_j(K), k1) mod e = 0) then
      t ← set_bit(H(T_j(K), k1), 0, wm_data[idx])
      T_j(A) ← a_t
      embedding_map[T_j(K)] ← idx
      idx ← idx + 1
  return embedding_map
```

Fig. 11. Encoding Algorithm (alternative using embedding map shown)

Step One. A tuple T_i is said to be "fit" for encoding iff $H(T_i(K), k_1) \bmod e = 0$, where e is an adjustable encoding parameter determining the percentage of considered tuples and k_1 is a secret $max(b(N), b(A))$-bit key. In other words, a tuple is considered "fit" if its primary key value satisfies a certain secret criteria (similar criteria are found in various frameworks, e.g., [16]). The fit tuples set will then contain roughly $\frac{N}{e}$ elements.

The "fitness" selection step provides several advantages. On the one hand this ensures secrecy and resilience and, on the other hand, it effectively "modulates" the watermark encoding process to the actual attribute-primary key association. Additionally, this is the place where the cryptographic safety of the hash one-wayness is leveraged to defeat invertibility attacks (**A5**). If the available embedding bandwidth

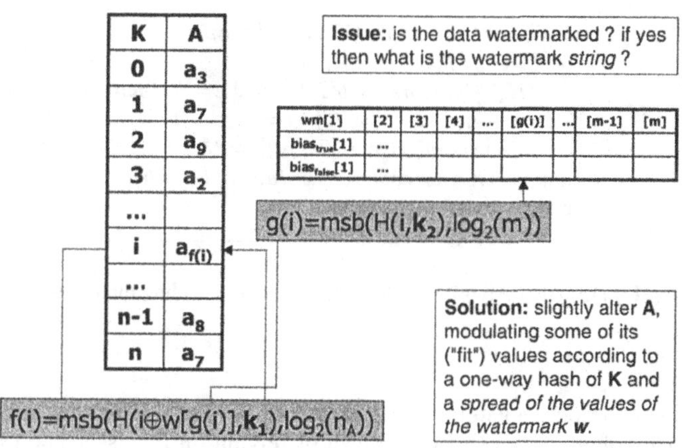

Fig. 12. Overview of multi-bit watermark encoding.

$\frac{N}{e}$ is greater than the watermark bit-size $|wm|$, error correcting codes (ECC) are deployed that take as input a desired watermark wm and produce as output a string of bits wm_data of length $\frac{N}{e}$ containing a redundant encoding of the watermark, tolerating a certain amount of bit-loss, $wm\_data = ECC.encode(wm, \frac{N}{e})$.
Step Two. For each "fit" tuple T_i, we encode one bit by altering $T_i(A)$ to become $T_i(A) = a_t$ where

$$t = set\_bit(msb(H(T_i(K), k_1), b(n_A)), 0, wm\_data[msb(H(T_i(K), k_2), b(\frac{N}{e}))])$$

and k_2 is a secret key $k_2 \neq k_1$. In other words, a secret value of $b(n_A)$ bits is generated – depending on the primary key and k_1 – and then its least significant bit is forced to a value according to a corresponding position in wm_data (random, depending on the primary key and k_2). The new attribute value is thus selected by the secret key k_1, the associated relational primary key value and a corresponding bit from the watermark data wm_data.

In the decoding phase (see Figure 13), the first aim is to discover the embedded wm_data bit string. The same criteria for discovering "fit" tuples is used. For each "fit" tuple T_i, with $T_i(A) = a_t$, its corresponding entry in the result bit string is set to $(t\&1)$

$$wm\_data[msb(H(T_j(K), k_2), b(\frac{N}{e}))] \leftarrow (t\&1)$$

Once wm_data (possibly altered) is available, the error correcting mechanism is invoked to generate the "closest", most likely, corresponding watermark $wm = ECC.decode(wm\_data, |wm|)$.

---

wm_dec_alt(K,A,k_1,e,ECC,$embed\_map$)
  for $(j \leftarrow 1; j < N; j \leftarrow j+1)$
    if $(H(T_j(K), msb(k, b(K)))$ mod $e = 0)$ **then**
    determine t such that $T_j(A) = a_t$
    $wm\_data[embed\_map[T_j(K)]] = t\&1$
  $wm \leftarrow ECC.decode(wm\_data, wm.length)$
  return wm

Fig. 13. Decoding Algorithm (alternative using embedding map shown)

The authors propose a natural extension to the above solution aimed at defeating vertical partitioning attacks (**A1.b**). Instead of relying on the association between the primary key and A, the extended algorithm considers *all* pairs of attributes and embeds a watermark separately in *each* of these associations. Additionally, if data constraints allow, the authors propose watermarking each and every attribute pair by first building a closure for the set of attribute pairs over the entire schema that minimizes the number of encoding interferences while maximizing the number of pairs watermarked. To solve the issue of interference, maintaining a mark "interference graph" is proposed.

The proposed extension features a particular issue of concern in certain cases of multi-attribute embeddings where two non-key attributes are used in the encoding, i.e., mark(A,B). Because of the correlation between the watermarking alteration (the newly selected value $T_i(B) = b_t$) and its actual location (determined by the fitness selection, $H(T_i(A), k_1)$ and e), sometimes Mallory can mount a special attack with the undesirable result of revealing some of the mark bit embedding locations. This occurs if the fitness criteria decides that a particular value of A yields a tuple fit and that value of A appears then in multiple (statistically significant number of) different tuples. This is possible only if A is not a primary key but rather another categorical attribute, with repeating duplicate values.

The authors propose a set of solutions to this issue, including composing the actual watermark encoding out of a combination of several different sub-encodings, each in turn using a different k_1 value. Each such sub-encoding will ignore all tuples with previously seen values of the attribute A (in the fitness criteria). While each of these "low impact" encodings would be weaker than the original solution, their combined "sum" can be made arbitrarily strong, by increasing their number. At the same time correlation attacks would be defeated, as each of the encodings would use a different key thus making such attacks impossible "across" the encodings.

The authors further discuss additional extensions and properties of the solution, including the following.

- Consumer-Driven Design: The solution features a consumer-driven design. Each property of the database that needs to be preserved is written as a constraint on the allowable change to the dataset. The watermarking algorithm is then applied with these constraints as input and re-evaluates them continuously for each alteration. A backtrack log is kept to allow undo operations in case certain constraints are violated by the current watermarking step.
- Incremental Updatability: The solution supports incremental updates naturally. As updates occur to the data, the resulting tuples can be evaluated on the fly for "fitness" and watermarked accordingly.
- Blind Watermarking: The method does not require the availability of the un-watermarked data at detection time.
- Minimizing Alteration Distance: An interesting problem to consider is the case when, for a given "fit" tuple, certain alterations would be preferred to others (e.g., changing "Chicago, O'Hare" into "Chicago" is preferred to "Las Vegas"). The authors propose to handle this scenario by a modified encoding procedure that naturally accommodates and minimizes such an "alteration distance" metric.
- Extreme Vertical Partitioning: To counter extreme vertical partitioning attacks in which only a single attribute A is preserved in the result, the authors propose to encode a watermark in one of the only remaining characteristic properties, namely the value occurrence frequency distribution for each possible value of A. To do so a scheme of watermarking for numeric sets [30] can be applied in this "frequency" domain.
- Multi-Layer Self-Reinforcing Watermarks: To counter the scenario where Mallory gains knowledge, e.g., during a court hearing, of a multiply-used encoding key, the authors propose to embed multiple (i) weak watermarks with different secret keys and reveal in court only a certain subset of these, or (ii) *self-re-enforcing* pairs of watermarks $(w_1, w_2)_i$ with different keys $(k_1^1, k_2^1, k_1^2, k_2^2)_i$ such that, for example, altering w_2 will result in enforcing w_1.
- Multiple Data Sources: The paper also points out that the solution handles recovering watermarks from data derived from multiple data sources. This scenario is of particular interest for example in the case of an equiJOIN performed between two data sets. Because watermarks rely on a bias in the association between attributes, they can be naturally retrieved from such JOIN result under certain reasonable assumptions.
- Categorical and Numerical Data Types: Watermarking at the intersection of categorical and numerical types is also explored. It is of interest to provide a rights

assessment mechanism that could not only prove rights but also that the associated data sets were actually produced "together"; this is relevant for example if the intrinsic value of the data lies in the actual *combination* of the two data types. The authors introduce initial ideas.

- Bijective Attribute Re-mapping: To handle a scenario in which categorical attributes are re-mapped through a bijective function to a new data domain, the authors propose to discover the inverse mapping. This is possible if the initial data domain features distinguishing properties (e.g., value occurrence frequency histogram) that are likely to be preserved in the mapped result.

5 Related Work

So far we have discussed a set of relational data types and associated watermarking methods enabling future rights assessment proofs. We now survey a number of related research efforts that explore Information Hiding and Watermarking for relational data in other security contexts such as privacy enforcement and license violators tracing.

5.1 Privacy and Rights Protection

In [4] Bertino et. al. explore issues at the intersection of two important dimensions in data-centric assurance, namely rights assessment and privacy, in the broader context of medical data. A unified framework is introduced that combines binning and watermarking techniques for the purpose of achieving both data privacy and the ability to assert rights.

The system design borrows components from existing work. More specifically, the binning method (for k-anonymity) is built upon an earlier approach of generalization and suppression by allowing a broader concept of generalization. Similar to the *consumer-driven* paradigm discussed earlier in this chapter, to ensure data usefulness, binning is constrained by usage metrics that define maximal allowable information loss. An initial binning stage is followed then by watermarking. The framework then deploys a version of the encoding for categorical types [36] by Sion et. al. in a hierarchical fashion, for the purpose of defeating a data generalization attack of concern in this framework. The paper then explores whether watermarking can adversely interfere with binning and conclude that the interaction is safe. Experiments were conducted aimed at validating the robustness of the proposed framework.

5.2 Fingerprinting

Another example application of Resilient Information Hiding as a tool aiding rights management, is its deployment to "track" license violators by hiding a specific mark inside the Work, uniquely identifying the party it was sold/outsourced to. This application is commonly referred to as *fingerprinting*. If the Work would then be found in the public domain, that mark could be used to assess the source of the leak.

One significant matter of concern in fingerprinting are collusion attacks. In a collusion attack, multiple attackers "collude" by obtaining multiple copies of the same Work (e.g., by purchasing it separately under different identities) watermarked with different marks, in the hope of "combining" the different copies into a single un-watermarked version. Defending against this attack is not possible in the general case when the number of colluding partners cannot be upper bounded. If this upper bound can be determined however, several results provide appropriate coding techniques that allow tracing even in the case of collusion under minimal assumptions [5] [6] [13].

For relational data, the issue of fingerprinting has been discussed by Li et. al. in [21] where they propose to deploy their multi-bit watermarking method [19] for this very purpose. To handle collusion attacks the authors defer to research in [5] [6] [13].

5.3 Tamper Detection through Fragile Watermarking

In [17] Li et. al. explore the issue of detecting malicious alterations to data by embedding a "fragile" watermark in the data. While in this chapter we presented watermarking as a technique deploying Information Hiding for the purpose of rights assessment, in this context, "watermark" is attached to a different semantics. Whereas in rights assessment, a watermark features resilience to value-preserving data alterations, for the purposes of tamper detection, the "watermark" will be "fragile" so as to become a detector for exactly such alterations. The authors also propose to allow this watermark to point at the locations where alterations have occurred in the data.

At an overview level, the method proceeds as follows. The data is partitioned into secret subsets; a keyed cryptographic hash of each such subset (in effect the traditional message authentication code MAC) is then embedded in the group by re-ordering its items with respect to a canonical ordering, based on a cryptographic hash of their primary key attribute. The encoding is claimed fragile enough to be impacted by even minor alterations to the data with reasonable probabilities. Additionally, the encoding can pinpoint at the exact location of the alteration with the granularity of a subset.

Compared with traditional authentication techniques (e.g., appending signatures of MACs) such a technique can become of relevance, e.g., when the overhead of storing and managing the signatures or MACs for a large number of entities is not negligible. This is why it is important to further explore and understand fragile watermarking scenarios.

5.4 Query Learnability and Consumer-Driven Watermarking

In [12] Gross-Amblard introduce interesting theoretical results investigating alterations to relational data (or associated XML) in a consumer-driven framework in which a set of parametric queries are to be preserved up to an acceptable level of distortion.

The author first shows that the main difficulty preserving such queries "is linked to the informational complexity of sets defined by queries, rather than their computational complexity" [12]. Roughly speaking, if the family of sets defined by the queries is not *learnable* [37], no query-preserving data alteration scheme can be designed.

In a second result, the author shows that under certain assumptions (i.e., query sets defined by first-order logic and monadic second order logic on restricted classes of structures – with a bounded degree for the Gaifman graph or the tree-width of the structure) a query-preserving data alteration scheme exists.

This research is important as it has the potential to enable a better understanding of consumer-driven watermarking designs. For example, as database instances are often having a bounded degree Gaifman graph (or a bounded tree-width), these can now be measured and the information capacity of a query-preserving alteration channel can be computed. This is of interest in the case of extremely restrictive constraints, e.g., when it is not clear if watermarking can yield enough resilience.

6 State of The Art and the Future

Watermarking in relational frameworks is a very young technology that has just begun its maturity cycle towards full deployment in industry-level applications. Many of the solutions discussed above have been prototyped and validated on real data. Patents have been filed for several of them, including Agrawal et.al. [1,16] and Sion et.al. [29,30,32,33] [34] [25,27,36]. In the next few years we expect these solutions to become available commercially, tightly integrated within existing DBMS (e.g., DB2 [10]) or as stand-alone packages that can be deployed simultaneously on top of multiple data types and sources. Ultimately, we believe the process of resilient information hiding will become available as a secure mechanism for not only rights protection but also data tracing and authentication in a multitude of discrete data frameworks.

7 Conclusions

In this chapter we explored how Information Hiding can be successfully deployed as a tool for Rights Assessment for discrete digital Works. We analyzed solutions for resilient Information Hiding for relational data, including numeric and categorical types.

A multitude of associated future research avenues present themselves in a relational framework, including: the design of alternative primary or pseudo-primary key independent encoding methods, a deeper theoretical understanding of limits of watermarking for a broader class of algorithms, the ability to better defeat additive watermark attacks, an exploration of zero-knowledge watermarking etc.

Moreover, while the concept of on-the-fly quality assessment for a consumer-driven design has the potential to function well, another interesting avenue for further research would be to augment the encoding method with direct awareness of semantic consistency (e.g., classification and association rules). This would likely result in an increase in available encoding bandwidth, thus in a higher encoding resilience. One idea would be to define a generic language (possibly subset of SQL) able to naturally express such constraints and their propagation at embedding time.

Additionally, of particular interest for future research exploration, we envision cross-domain applications of Information Hiding in distributed environments such as sensor networks, with applications ranging from resilient content annotation to runtime authentication and data integrity proofs.

References

1. Rakesh Agrawal, Peter J. Haas, and Jerry Kiernan. Watermarking relational data: framework, algorithms and analysis. *The VLDB Journal*, 12(2):157–169, 2003.
2. Michael Arnold, Stephen D. Wolthusen, and Martin Schmucker. *Techniques and Applications of Digital Watermarking and Content Protection*. Artech House Publishers, 2003.
3. Mauro Barni and Franco Bartolini. *Watermarking Systems Engineering: Enabling Digital Assets Security and Other Applications*. Marcel Dekker, 2004.
4. Elisa Bertino, Beng Chin Ooi, Yanjiang Yang, and Robert H. Deng. Privacy and ownership preserving of outsourced medical data. In *Proceedings of the International Conference on Data Engineering*, pages 521–532, 2005.
5. D. Boneh and J. Shaw. Collusion-secure fingerprinting for digital data. *Lecture Notes in Computer Science*, 963:452–464, 1995.
6. D. Boneh and J. Shaw. Collusion-secure fingerprinting for digital data. *IEEE Transactions on Information Theory*, 44(5):1897–1905, 1998.
7. E.F. Codd. A Relational Model of Data for Large Shared Data Banks. *Communications of the ACM*, 13(6):377–387, 1970.
8. I. Cox, J. Bloom, and M. Miller. Digital watermarking. In *Digital Watermarking*. Morgan Kaufmann, 2001.
9. Scott Craver, Nasir Memon, Boon-Lock Yeo, and Minerva M. Yeung. Resolving rightful ownerships with invisible watermarking techniques: Limitations, attacks, and implications. *IEEE Journal of Selected Areas in Communications*, 16(4):573–586, 1998.
10. The IBM DB2 Universal Database. Online at `http://www.ibm.com/software/data/db2`.
11. Joachim Eggers and Bernd Girod. *Informed Watermarking*. Kluwer Academic Publishers, 2002.
12. David Gross-Amblard. Query-preserving watermarking of relational databases and xml documents. In *Proceedings of the Nineteenth ACM SIGMOD-SIGACT-SIGART Symposium on Principles of Database Systems*, pages 191–201, New York, NY, USA, 2003. ACM Press.
13. H. Guth and B. Pfitzman. Error and collusion secure fingerprinting for digital data. In *Proceedings of the Information Hiding Workshop*, 1999.
14. Neil F. Johnson, Zoran Duric, and Sushil Jajodia. *Information Hiding: Steganography and Watermarking - Attacks and Countermeasures*. Kluwer Academic Publishers, 2001.
15. S. Katzenbeisser and F. Petitcolas (editors). *Information Hiding Techniques for Steganography and Digital Watermarking*. Artech House, 2001.

16. J. Kiernan and R. Agrawal. Watermarking relational databases. In *Proceedings of the 28th International Conference on Very Large Databases VLDB*, 2002.
17. Yingjiu Li, Huiping Guo, and Sushil Jajodia. Tamper detection and localization for categorical data using fragile watermarks. In *DRM '04: Proceedings of the 4th ACM workshop on Digital rights management*, pages 73–82, New York, NY, USA, 2004. ACM Press.
18. Yingjiu Li, Vipin Swarup, and Sushil Jajodia. Constructing a virtual primary key for fingerprinting relational data. In *DRM '03: Proceedings of the 2003 ACM workshop on Digital rights management*, pages 133–141, New York, NY, USA, 2003. ACM Press.
19. Yingjiu Li, Vipin Swarup, and Sushil Jajodia. A robust watermarking scheme for relational data. In *Proceedings of the Workshop on Information Technology and Systems (WITS)*, pages 195–200, 2003.
20. Yingjiu Li, Vipin Swarup, and Sushil Jajodia. Defending against additive attacks with maximal errors in watermarking relational databases. In *Proceedings of the IFIP WG 11.3 Working Conference on Data and Application Security*, pages 81–94, 2004.
21. Yingjiu Li, Vipin Swarup, and Sushil Jajodia. Fingerprinting relational databases: Schemes and specialties. *IEEE Transactions on Dependable and Secure Computing*, 2(1):34–45, 2005.
22. Chun-Shien Lu. *Multimedia Security: Steganography and Digital Watermarking Techniques for Protection of Intellectual Property*. Idea Group Publishing, 2004.
23. Bruce Schneier. *Applied Cryptography: Protocols, Algorithms and Source Code in C*. Wiley & Sons, 1996.
24. Husrev T. Sencar, Mahalingam Ramkumar, and Ali N. Akansu. *Data Hiding Fundamentals And Applications: Content Security in Digital Multimedia*. ELSEVIER science and technology books, 2004.
25. Radu Sion. Proving ownership over categorical data. In *Proceedings of the IEEE International Conference on Data Engineering ICDE*, 2004.
26. Radu Sion. *Rights Assessment for Discrete Digital Data, Ph.D. dissertation*. Computer Sciences, Purdue University, 2004.
27. Radu Sion. wmdb.*: A suite for database watermarking (demo). In *Proceedings of the IEEE International Conference on Data Engineering ICDE*, 2004.
28. Radu Sion and Mikhail Atallah. Attacking digital watermarks. In *Proceedings of the Symposium on Electronic Imaging SPIE*, 2004.
29. Radu Sion, Mikhail Atallah, and Sunil Prabhakar. On watermarking numeric sets. Online at `https://www.cerias.purdue.edu/tools_and_resources/bibtex_archive/`, 2001.
30. Radu Sion, Mikhail Atallah, and Sunil Prabhakar. On watermarking numeric sets. In *Proceedings of IWDW 2002, Lecture Notes in Computer Science*. Springer-Verlag, 2002.
31. Radu Sion, Mikhail Atallah, and Sunil Prabhakar. Power: Metrics for evaluating watermarking algorithms. In *Proceedings of IEEE ITCC 2002*. IEEE Computer Society Press, 2002.
32. Radu Sion, Mikhail Atallah, and Sunil Prabhakar. Watermarking databases. Online at `https://www.cerias.purdue.edu/tools_and_resources/bibtex_archive/`, 2002.
33. Radu Sion, Mikhail Atallah, and Sunil Prabhakar. Rights protection for relational data. In *Proceedings of the ACM Special Interest Group on Management of Data Conference SIGMOD*, 2003.
34. Radu Sion, Mikhail Atallah, and Sunil Prabhakar. Relational data rights protection through watermarking. *IEEE Transactions on Knowledge and Data Engineering TKDE*, 16(6), June 2004.

35. Radu Sion, Mikhail Atallah, and Sunil Prabhakar. Resilient rights protection for sensor streams. In *Proceedings of the Very Large Databases Conference VLDB*, 2004.
36. Radu Sion, Mikhail Atallah, and Sunil Prabhakar. Ownership proofs for categorical data. *IEEE Transactions on Knowledge and Data Engineering TKDE*, 2005.
37. L. G. Valiant. A Theory of the Learnable. In *Proceedings of the Symposium on the Theory of Computing*, pages 436–445, 1984.

Index